SANTANA FOSSILS:
An Illustrated Atlas
Edited by JOHN G. MAISEY

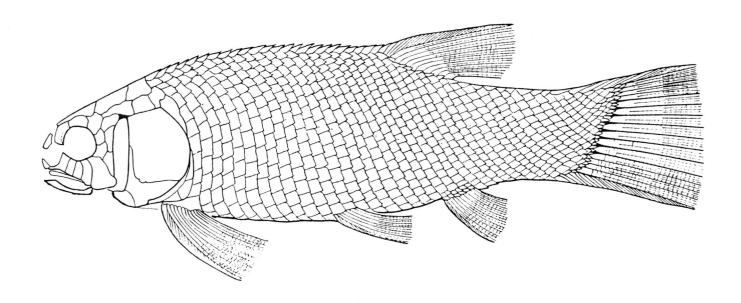

JOHN G. MAISEY
   Curator, Vertebrate Paleontology Department, American Museum of Natural History
   Adjunct Professor, Department of Zoology, College of Biological Science, University of Guelph
   Affiliated Associate Professor, Biology Department, City College of the City University of New York

Contributions to IUGS—IGCP Project No. 242, The Cretaceous of South America.

© **Copyright 1991 by T.F.H. Publications, Inc.**

Distributed in the UNITED STATES by T.F.H. Publications, Inc., One T.F.H. Plaza, Neptune City, NJ 07753; in CANADA to the Pet Trade by H & L Pet Supplies Inc., 27 Kingston Crescent, Kitchener, Ontario N2B 2T6; Rolf C. Hagen Ltd., 3225 Sartelon Street, Montreal 382 Quebec; in CANADA to the Book Trade by Macmillan of Canada (A Division of Canada Publishing Corporation), 164 Commander Boulevard, Agincourt, Ontario M1S 3C7; in ENG-LAND by T.F.H. Publications, PO Box 15, Waterlooville PO7 6BQ; in AUSTRALIA AND THE SOUTH PACIFIC by T.F.H. (Australia) Pty. Ltd., Box 149, Brookvale 2100 N.S.W., Australia; in NEW ZEALAND by Ross Haines & Son, Ltd., 82 D Elizabeth Knox Place, Panmure, Auckland, New Zealand; in the PHILIPPINES by Bio-Research, 5 Lippay Street, San Lorenzo Village, Makati, Rizal; in SOUTH AFRICA by Multipet Pty. Ltd., P.O. Box 35347, Northway, 4065, South Africa. Published by T.F.H. Publications, Inc. Manufactured in the United States of America by T.F.H. Publications, Inc.

Contents

Foreword

This book is, without a doubt, one of the most interesting and complete works ever written about a sedimentary basin in Brazil. Ever since the journeys made during the years 1817 and 1820 by the German naturalists Johann Baptist von Spix and Carl Friedrich Philipp von Martius, the Araripe basin has been studied by many researchers from geological and paleontological institutions not only from Brazil but also from abroad.

These studies demonstrate that the Araripe Basin is one of the most important in Brazil. It should be mentioned that the first Brazilian fossil figured came from this region. This Basin is also known throughout the world because of the great quantity and exceptional preservation, sometimes unique, of the fossils found there in.

This book was produced by Dr. John Maisey and a team of international contributors. It contains all information currently available about the Araripe basin, presenting the state of knowledge of the sedimentology and paleontology of this area.

Beginning with a brief history of the first studies done in the Araripe basin, the following chapters provide a complete description of each group of fossils found, giving all available information about each species, including the diagnostic characteristics, distribution, and type material. The book also discusses the main works on the stratigraphy and paleoenvironments of the Araripe basin and presents some new information.

In order to cover the maximum data possible, the principal researchers who actually are carrying out studies on the Araripe basin were invited to collaborate by writing chapters on their fields of special interest. All of the work was finished within five years by Dr. Maisey's team. It was Dr. Herbert R. Axelrod who sponsored this project and who guaranteed the excellent quality and high standard of this book. It is richly illustrated with photos and reconstructions of the organisms that inhabited this region during the Cretaceous Period, some 100 million years ago. The numerous preparations developed with special chemical methods of the American Museum led to excellent results that can be seen in the photos.

The final result of this project is easy for even the non-specialist to understand. For researchers, it constitutes an important tool for their studies. For fossil enthusiasts and general naturalists, even for those who have never had direct contact with paleontology, this book offers a great opportunity to learn, in a pleasant way, about the secrets of life in the geological past in one of the most interesting parts of the Earth. For Brazilian paleontology, this book is a precious contribution to the studies of one of the country's most important fossil deposits.

Alexander Wilhelm Armin Kellner
Institute of Geosciences
Federal University of Rio de Janeiro

List of Contributors

BLUM, S.D., Axelrod Fellow, Department of Vertebrate Paleontology, American Museum of Natural History, New York

BRITO, P.M., Adjunct Assistant Professor, University Santa Ursula; Bolsista do CNPq, Rio de Janeiro

BUFFETAUT, E., U.A. du CNRS, Laboratoire de Paléontologie des Vertébrés, Université Pierre et Marie Curie, Paris

CAMPOS, D. de A., Seção de Paleontologia, Divisão de Geologia e Mineralogia, DNPM, Rio de Janeiro

CRANE, P., Curator, Paleobotany, Department of Geology, Field Museum, Chicago

ELVERS, W.B., Volunteer, Department of Vertebrate Paleontology, American Museum of Natural History, New York

GAFFNEY, E.S., Curator, Fossil Reptiles, Department of Vertebrate Paleontology, American Museum of Natural History, New York

GRIMALDI, D., Assistant Curator, Entomology Department, American Museum of Natural History, New York

HECHT, M., Professor, Queens College of the City University of New York, Flushing, New York

KELLNER, A.W., Geologist, Bolsista do CNPq, Rio de Janeiro

MAISEY, J.G., Curator, Fossil Fishes, Department of Vertebrate Paleontology, American Museum of Natural History, New York

MARTINS-NETO, R.G., Geologist, Bolsista do CNPq, Universidade São Paulo

MEYLAN, P.A., Thorne Fellow, Department of Vertebrate Paleontology, American Museum of Natural History, New York

NURSALL, J.R., Professor Emeritus, Department of Zoology, University of Alberta, Edmonton

RUTZKY, I.S., Scientific Assistant, Department of Vertebrate Paleontology, American Museum of Natural History, New York

SILVA SANTOS, R. da, Professor, Departamento de Biologia, Universidade do Estado do Rio de Janeiro; Pesquisador 1-A do CNPq

WELLNHOFER, P., Hauptkonservator, Bayerische Staatsammlung für Paläontologie und historische Geologie, München

WENZ, S., Res. du CNRS, Institut de Paléontologie, Muséum national d'Histoire naturelle, Paris

Prefácio

O livro é sem dúvida um dos mais importantes e completos já elaborados sobre uma bacia sedimentar situada no Brasil. Desde as viagens realizadas pelos naturalistas alemães Johann Baptist von Spix e Carl Friedrich Philipp von Martius, durante os anos 1817 a 1820, a Bacia do Araripe vem sendo estudada por pesquisadores dos mais conceituados centros de Geologia e Paleontologia, tanto do Brasil como do exterior. Tais estudos demonstram que esta área de sedimentação é uma das principais existentes no país, valendo salientar que o primeiro fóssil brasileiro a ser figurado é dela proveniente. Também a nível mundial a Bacia do Araripe ocupa uma posição de destaque, em razão da grande quantidade e da preservação excepcional, muitas vezes única, dos seus fósseis.

Esta obra, de autoria do Dr. John Maisey com a ajuda de colaboradores internacionais, reune todas as informações disponíveis sobre esta região, mostrando o estágio mais atualizado do conhecimento nos estudos sedimentológicos e paleontológicos.

Inicialmente, o livro apresenta um breve histórico das primeiras pesquisas realizadas nesta bacia. Em seguida, vêm descrições completas dos grupos fósseis ali encontrados, tendo havido o cuidado de se apresentar o maior número de informações possíveis sobre cada espécie, tais como características diagnósticas, distribuição e material-tipo. Também são discutidos os principais trabalhos publicados sobre a estratigrafia e os paleoambientes durante a formação desta bacia, com a apresentação inclusive de algumas informações novas.

Para que o livro abrangesse o maior número de dados possível, foram convidados os principais pesquisadores que mantêm linhas de estudos com material dessa bacia, cada um contribuindo com capítulos específicos à sua área de conhecimento.

No total, a equipe do Dr. Maisey levou cerca de cinco anos para concluir os trabalhos. O financiamento do projeto foi generosamente concedido pelo Dr. Herbert Axelrod, que não economizou recursos para a apresentação de excepcional qualidade do livro. São apresentadas ilustrações tanto de reconstruções como de fotografias, elaboradas em excelente nível técnico, da maior parte dos organismos que habitavam a Bacia do Araripe durante o período Cretáceo, há 100 milhões de anos atrás. Para um maior detalhamento, foram desenvolvidas numerosas preparações de fósseis, sobretudo com a utilização de métodos químicos, que alcançaram resultados realmente fantásticos, como se verifica nas fotografias.

Como resultado temos um livro completo, de leitura fácil e rara beleza. Para os pesquisadores o livro é uma ferramenta de trabalho preciosa. Para os leigos, mesmo aqueles que nunca tiveram contato direto com a Paleontologia, a obra oferece uma grande oportunidade de penetrar de maneira agradável nos "Segredos da Vida do Passado Geológico" de uma das áreas mais interessantes da Terra. Para a Paleontologia Brasileira, este livro é uma valiosa contribuição para o estudo de uma de suas jazidas fossilíferas mais importantes.

Resumindo, estamos diante de uma daquelas grandes obras, que ficam para sempre em posição de destaque na literatura das Ciências Naturais.

Alexander Wilhelm Armin Kellner
Pos. Grad. Instituto de Geociências
Universidade Federal do Rio de Janeiro.

1: Introduction

Generations of youngsters have been captivated by Sir Arthur Conan Doyle's adventurous Professor Challenger, especially by his supposed discovery of a remote, flat-topped mountain deep in the Brazilian jungle, teeming with animals and plants from the Age of Dinosaurs. Wouldn't it be wonderful to discover such a place?

Well, with a few qualifications, such a place really was discovered, even before Professor Challenger became a twinkle in the eye of his creator. This flat-topped mountain is not in Brazil's jungle, but lies farther to the northeast, within the scrubby Caatinga—a populous, generally poor region of plantations and livestock ranching—on the borders of the states of Ceará, Pernambuco, and Piauí. It is indeed teeming with the remains of animals and plants from the Age of Dinosaurs, but they are all entombed as fossils in rock and therefore live now—like Challenger's discoveries—only within our imagination. Furthermore, these prolific tangible remains of the ancient past are scattered around the flanks and foothills of the great Chapada do Araripe, instead of at its top.

Such a profusion of well-preserved fossils, especially vertebrate fossils, inevitably attracted the attention of scientists. Their occurrence was actually first reported long before many other "classic" sites were described from Europe and North America, in the opening decades of the 19th century. The story of how this site became known is intriguing and tortuous.

As Napoleon Bonaparte's powerful army marched on Portugal in 1807, it triggered a series of momentous political events that heralded the final decline of the Portuguese empire and opened up Brazil, the world's fifth largest country, to methodical scientific exploration and discovery. Crown Prince John and most of the Portuguese court fled for Rio de Janeiro. His second son, Don Pedro, was proclaimed Prince Regent of Brazil and subsequently was to become its first emperor. In 1817 Don Pedro married Caroline, Archduchess of Austria. With her came a retinue of natural historians and philosophers, courtesy of the emperor of Austria. The king of Bavaria, perhaps not wishing to miss out on the politicizing, sent along two members of the Academy of Sciences in Munich, Drs. J. B. von Spix and C. F. P. von Martius.

Under Austrian protection, these two naturalists undertook extensive exploration of southern and northeastern Brazil before navigating the Amazon beyond the mouth of the Rio Negro. In the middle of their three-volume exploits, Spix and Martius were presented with a collection of geological specimens from the northeastern state of Ceará gathered by Major-General Manuel Ignacio de Sapaio. Among the specimens were beautiful fossil fishes of many kinds. Neither Spix (a zoologist) nor Martius (a botanist) were paleontologists, although both had received training in geology. Their report, published in 1828, provided the first hint of what was to prove a major source of exquisitely preserved fossil vertebrates from strata that have become known as the Santana formation.

Even a casual glance at the photographs in this book will reveal why this fossil locality is ranked among the world's greatest. The sheer diversity of fossils—especially fishes, but also pterosaurs and other vertebrates—coupled with their spectacular preservational quality, provides an unparalleled view of a Lower Cretaceous biota some 110 million years old. Rarely are fossils so well preserved as these, and rarely can so much anatomical detail be extracted for so many species. Besides vertebrates, however, these strata have yielded important plant and insect fossils, providing new and sometimes controversial data concerning the local environment all those millions of years ago.

Despite the importance of the Chapada do Araripe as a paleontological site, virtually all that previously has been published about it and its fossils is locked away in scientific papers and monographs. Even within this specialist literature, there have been relatively few attempts at putting together a cohesive overview. It is hoped that the present volume will redress some of those shortcomings, provide access to source materials, and bring a better perspective of this classic locality to both amateur and professional paleontologists.

Scientific investigation of the Chapada do Araripe and its fossils has continued, off and on, for the better part of two centuries. As can be imagined, therefore, a considerable quantity of published information has accumulated in various scientific papers, monographs, and popular articles. During this time, our understanding of the geological and biological processes that have molded our world has undergone some remarkable transformations. The full significance of the "lost world" of the Araripe Plateau can only be appreciated with at least some knowledge of these processes. The non-specialist reader will find some introductory chapters in this book intended to provide a background of current scientific opinion on such topics as global plate tectonics, continental drift, evolution, and phylogeny reconstruction.

As in all other branches of science, different opinions are held by various specialists about some aspects of the subject at hand. There are more than a dozen contributors to this book, and it therefore is not surprising that some remarks contained here may be contradictory or at least controversial. Controversy is a sign of healthy science, however, and provides a focus for continued investigation. Several issues in particular can be readily identified within the following pages, particularly the problems of the phylogenetic relationships of certain fossils (most notably the pterosaurs) and the environments in which these ancient organisms lived, died, and were buried.

A great many people have been directly and indirectly involved with producing this book.

This book is a direct result of the generosity and interest of Dr. Herbert R. Axelrod. He originally donated his large and scientifically important private collection of Santana Formation fossils for study at the American Museum of Natural History; many of these specimens are illustrated here, and include numerous unique and informative pieces. Some measure of the Axelrod Collection's importance is provided by the number of significant scientific papers on this material that have already appeared since the collection was donated a few years ago (e.g., Maisey, 1986; Wellnhofer, 1988; Bennett, 1989; Blum et. al., 1989; Wighton, 1987; Grimaldi, 1990), on subjects as diverse as giant fossil coelacanths, terrestrial locomotion in pterosaurs, preparation techniques and morphological descriptions of hundreds of new fossil insects. Additionally, there are many works in preparation or approaching completion at this time, including studies of new fossil fishes, turtles, crocodiles, pterosaurs, insects and plants in the Axelrod Collection. This material has been made available for research by scientists worldwide, often with financial support from Dr. Axelrod.

The paleontological community owes a debt of gratitude to Dr. Herbert R. Axelrod, President of T.F.H. Publications, Inc., whose financial support of this project was vital. I thank J.

Walls at T.F.H. for all his editorial advice and patience. Chemical preparation of specimens at the American Museum of Natural History was conducted by several personnel, including Walter Sorensen (now retired), Ivy Rutzky, Radford Arrindell, and particularly Dr. Walter Barton Elvers, a volunteer in the Department of Vertebrate Paleontology who has revolutionized the procedures for embedding fossil vertebrates in polyester resin prior to acid preparation. Except where individual authors submitted their own photographs and artwork (see captions for photo credits), most of the color illustrations were taken by Isabel Francais. John Quinn (T.F.H.) produced the maps and environment cartoons. Line drawings of most fossil fishes were rendered by Ellen Garvens; those of the turtles and crocodiles were produced by Lorraine Meeker. Scanning electron microscope photos of fossilized soft tissues were generously provided by David Martill (Open University, UK.) Much of the initial investigation and examination of the fossil fishes described here was conducted by Dr. Stanley D. Blum during a three-year fellowship at the American Museum of Natural History funded by Dr. Axelrod. I also wish to thank all of the contributors, including Professor Rubens da Silva Santos, Drs. Diogenes de Almeida Campos, Rafael Gioia Martins-Neto, Ralph Nursall, Sylvie Wenz, Peter Meylan, Eugene Gaffney, Max Hecht, Eric Buffetaut, Peter Wellnhofer, David Grimaldi, Peter Crane, and Mr. Alexander Kellner and Paulo Brito. Many participants at the June, 1990 Congress on the Araripe basin also provided valuable information and suggestions; where possible these have been incorporated into the text. Parts of the Portuguese text were kindly reviewed and corrected by Maria da Gloria Pires de Carvalho. Numerous others have been consulated about morphological, stratigraphic, preservational, paleoecological, and paleoenvironmental matters. To all, many thanks.

(J.G. Maisey)

2: The Occurrence

The spectacular fossils described and illustrated in this volume are from one of the world's most productive paleontological sites, located in northeastern Brazil. Sedimentary rocks from this region, generally thought to be of Lower Cretaceous age (approximately 110 million years old), are famous for the fossils they contain. These fossils occur in shales, thin limestone layers, and in large, rounded limestone concretions within a series of sedimentary strata that is exposed at the foot of an upland area known as the Araripe Plateau (Chapada do Araripe). This region has yielded magnificent fossils for almost 160 years, and specimens like the ones illustrated here are to be found in museum, university, and other collections throughout the world.

The most prolific sites are found in the state of Ceará, but the plateau and its fossil-producing strata extend into the two neighboring states of Pernambuco and Piauí. The Araripe Plateau is a conspicuous feature of the landscape, reaching altitudes of 600 to 900 meters above sea level and extending some 200 km from east to west. It was uplifted during a geologically active period of faulting and tilting, following the rifting apart of Africa and South America to form the South Atlantic.

The rock strata from which such fossils have long been known represent only a part of the 700 meters thick local sedimentary sequence that was laid down during the Mesozoic era, within the region now known to geologists as the Araripe basin. The full sequence of strata in this basin includes Jurassic as well as Cretaceous sediments, resting upon a much more ancient basement of Precambrian and Paleozoic rocks.

Sedimentary deposition of all these layers was uneven from place to place and was locally intermittent. One result of this is that important unconformities (breaks in sedimentation) are recognized at particular levels. The first of these unconformities occurs at the base of the sequence, where Jurassic strata rest upon the ancient basement rocks. The next important break occurs between the Jurassic rocks (mostly outcropping in the eastern part of the plateau) and overlying sediments of Cretaceous age. In places, the Cretaceous units overlap the Jurassic to rest directly upon the basement rocks. There are also at least two major unconformities within the Cretaceous sequence, one within the Santana formation (only recently detected; Silva, 1986a), and one between the Santana and Exu formations. The top of the Exu formation is marked by yet another unconformity below a patchily distributed younger (Cenozoic) unit, the Barreiras formation.

Nomenclature of the Cretaceous strata within the Araripe basin is controversial. Some earlier proposals were based on paleontological investigations (particularly of fossil fishes and ostracods). Others were based upon field observations and borehole data, but in general there has been no agreed or stable system of nomenclature for the sequence.

The precise age of the Araripe sedimentary sequence also has been problematical. Correlation with strata in other Brazilian sedimentary basins has been impeded by a dearth of stratigraphically informative fossils, even though some of the strata in these other Brazilian basins have been correlated fairly accurately with Cretaceous deposits in other parts of the world. These important technical issues will be reviewed in greater detail elsewhere in this volume, and for the present it will suffice to note that the principal fossiliferous sites in the Cretaceous strata of the Araripe basin appear to occur at two levels. The stratigraphically lowest (and hence oldest) occurrence is within laminated limestones that almost certainly were deposited on an undisturbed lake-bed. These limestones have yielded a profusion of small gonorynchiform fishes, together with a diverse insect fauna and a flora indicative of dry, open terrestrial habitats. Stratigraphically, these limestones have been regarded as the lower part of the Santana formation (Crato member: Beurlen, 1971; Mabesoone and Tinoco, 1973) or else as part of a separate formation (e.g., Crato formation: Beurlen, 1963; Araripina formation: Silva, 1983, 1986b). The better known fossils apparently occur higher in the sequence, within calcareous concretions contained in softer sediments such as oil-shales. These deposits have been termed the Romualdo member of the Santana formation (Beurlen, 1971; Mabesoone and Tinoco, 1973), but H. R. Lima (1979) considered that Beurlen's (1971) subdivision of the Santana formation was artificial and did not represent distinct temporal phases in its deposition. Lima argued that the Romualdo "member" instead may represent a type of depositional environment (facies) that in some areas could have existed contemporaneously with an evaporitic facies (Beurlen's "Ipubi member"). Whatever the case, there is little doubt that the concretion-bearing shales are, in stratigraphic terms, slightly younger than the lacustrine limestones.

One complicating factor is the recent discovery of "Romualdo member" fossil fishes (e.g., *Vinctifer*, *Rhacolepis*) in association with *Dastilbe* (a common "Crato member" fish) at a new locality near Nova Olinda within bituminous shales. According to Viana, et al. (in press), this deposit represents a muddy lacustrine bottom environment. This corroborates the view that at least some "Romualdo member" fishes are freshwater forms, but also suggests that limited faunal mixing took place between adjacent lacustrine (and marine?) environments that were otherwise strongly partitioned. Interestingly, only one fish, the ichthyodectiform *Cladocyclus*, is known occur in all of the assemblages represented by calcareous concretions, Crato member limestone, and the bituminous shales (according to P. Brito, however, some other fishes also occur in the Crato member; pers. comun., June, 1990). *Dastilbe* has been reported from concretions, but all the small gonorynchiforms we have examined from them have turned out to be juvenile *Tharrhias*.

Fossils in the concretions are spectacular and include many different species of fishes, reptiles (crocodilians, turtles, dinosaurs, and pterosaurs), and various plants including conifers. Invertebrates such as small pelecypods and gastropods also occur but are uncommon. The distribution and manner of preservation of fossil species vary among concretions having different lithological composition, which in turn seems to be related to other factors such as stratigraphic level and locality. This variation suggests that important local environmental differences may have existed from place to place and from time to time during the interval that these sediments were accumulating.

The ecological impact of these environmental differences may have been considerable. Not only do certain fossil species seem to be restricted to certain rock types, but differences in the relative abundance and/or size of individuals of particular species are also apparent.

The precise nature of these differences is still under investigation, but it has been established that there are two key factors. The most readily appreciated one is geographic location; there are significant differences in faunal content at the principal collecting sites in various parts of the Araripe Plateau. The other, less obvious factor is stratigraphic age. Because most of the fossils are collected by local people untrained in geology, much valuable stratigraphic information has been lost. Recent attempts by scientists to examine field relations suggest that at each of the principal localities there is more than one layer containing the fossil-bearing concretions. According to Dr. Martill (Open University, England: personal communication), at one locality between Nova Olinda and Santana do Cariri there is "a basal concretion horizon which contains only *Tharrhias*, a higher horizon with only *Vinctifer*, and a higher horizon still which has *Rhacolepis* and others." There are certainly at least two horizon concretions at Brejo Santo. Here, and apparently also at Jardim farther south, the lower level commonly yields *Tharrhias*.

Although the overall picture remains unclear because it has not yet been possible to conduct the field investigations necessary to determine the actual situation, it appears that the Lower Cretaceous fossils of the Araripe basin probably represent several faunal assemblages and at least two floral assemblages. It would be naively misleading to regard the "Santana formation" fossils as a single paleobiota. Recent investigation of the sedimentological and structural history of the Araripe basin by Brazilian geologists indicates at least two major depositional episodes, separated by a period of uplift, erosion, and deformation. In a broad fashion, therefore, paleontological, sedimentological, and structural investigations have helped to produce a unified, but loosely woven, tapestry of the Late Mesozoic geological history of the Araripe basin.

The Early Discoveries (1828-1900)
In 1817, the king of Bavaria arranged for two members of the Academy of Sciences in Munich to accompany an Austrian delegation of philosophers and natural historians to Brazil. These two academicians, Dr. J. B. von Spix and Dr. C. F. P. von Martius, were the first to

record the occurrence of well-preserved fossil fishes in northeastern Brazil (Spix and Martius, 1828, p. 799):

"Fast an der südöstlichen Grenze der Provinz, bei der kleinen Villa do Bom Jardin, in dem Districte von Cayriris Novis, tritt eine ziemlich ausgedehnte Mergelkalk formation auf, in der sich zahlreich Versteinerungen von Fischen befinden. Es sind dieselben sowohl in dem tafelförming geschichteten Gesteine, als in den abgesonderten und gerollten Stücken enthalten. Sie gehören mancherlei Gattungen von Fischen, wie z.B. *Loricaria, Cichla, Mugil* u.s.f., vielleicht auch Schlangen an." ["Almost at the southeastern border of the province, near the little Villa do Bom Jardin, in the district of Cayriris Novis, appeared a fairly extensive marly limestone formation, in which were numerous fish fossils. These are preserved both in platy stratified rocks and in detached, rolled pieces. They belong to several families of fishes, e.g. *Loricaria, Cichla, Mugil* etc., perhaps also to snakes."] Their work was accompanied by a figure (Spix and Martius, 1831, pl. xxii, fig. 5) of a fossil fish, subsequently identified as *Rhacolepis* (Woodward, 1887, Jordan and Branner, 1908), in a limestone concretion.

A decade after Spix and Martius published their findings, Glaswegian botanist George Gardner visited the same region, publishing his preliminary findings with the eminent geologist and paleontologist Louis Agassiz three years later. Traveling to the Villa do Barra do Jardim ("town of the plains of the garden") on the southern side of the plateau, Gardner (1841, p. 80) recorded that:

"I found the ground covered with great abundance of stones of various sizes, and I was informed that almost every one of them, on being broken, presented some part or other of a fish."

He was unable to find any specimens *in situ*, however, and concluded from their rounded appearance and fragmentary condition that they had "apparently been for a long time under the influence of a current of water."

The somewhat mysterious reference to a fossil snake made by Spix and Martius (1828) was reiterated by Gardner (1841, p. 82):

"I was informed by a person in Jardim, that a few years ago he found a small serpent coiled up in a stone which had been split, but this, no doubt, was a species of Ammonites. In the several hundred stones, however, which I broke in search of fish, I met with nothing of this description."

To this day, despite the many concretions that

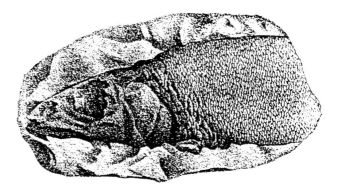

The earliest illustration of a fossil fish from the Santana formation is reproduced here from the work of Spix and Martius (1831, plate xxii, fig. 5). The specimen (now lost) is generally thought to be a *Rhacolepis buccalis*.

have been opened from this locality, there is still no record of an ammonite from them. In fact, the absence of ammonites (marine molluscs related distantly to living squids, octopi, and the nautilus) is a noteworthy feature of the fossil assemblage. One possible explanation of the snake story is that it really was a fossil snake. Fossil turtles, pterosaurs, and crocodilians all have been recovered, so the presence of a snake is not out of the question. Another plausible explanation is that the "snake" was a coiled-up fossil aspidorhynchid fish (Jordan and Branner, 1908), or else perhaps no more than a string of vertebrae from a large fossil fish.

Although the occurrence of fossil-fish-bearing rocks was rather restricted at Jardim, Gardner visited other sites a few kilometers to the east and west. As a result, he ". . . obtained a suite of specimens, embracing upwards of a dozen species of fossil fish. They vary in size from those of a few inches in length, to others which must have been several feet . . . ."

In fact, in a note following Gardner's, Agassiz (1841, p. 83) recognized only seven species, of which two were regarded as "ganoids" (*Aspidorhynchus comptoni, Lepidotes temnurus*), three were assigned to the "ctenoids" (*Phacolepis* [sic] *brama, P. buccalis, P. latus*), and two were referred to the "cycloids" (*Cladocyclus gardneri, Calamopleurus cylindricus*).

The "simultaneous occurrence of Ganoid, Ctenoid and Cycloid fishes" in the Araripe region led Agassiz (ibid., p. 83) to conclude that the Brazilian deposits could be correlated with the "Chalk Formation" (i.e., dating broadly from the Cretaceous period) of Europe. Although Mesozoic strata had been recognized in South America a year or two previously (de Buch, 1839; Lea, 1840), the note by Agassiz (1841) represents the first occasion on which Cretaceous deposits had been identified there.

In what today seems like an attempt to steal some of Agassiz's thunder, Gardner (1849, p. 159) provided more detailed supplementary lithological observations that at first glance seem to corroborate Agassiz's prior claim that the fossils were of Cretaceous age:

". . . the circumstances that first led me to suspect this rock belonged to the Chalk Formation was an immense accumulation of flints and septaria similar to those of the Chalk of England . . . ."

It appears that there are indeed a large number of septarian concretions in the deposits visited by Gardner around Jardim. These concretions largely are ignored by local collectors, who maintain that any contained fossils are badly broken up and obscured by calcite crystal overgrowths and veins. It is said that more than 10% of concretions near Jardim have suffered this fate (usually the smaller ones, although much larger examples are occasionally exhumed). However, it is well known that septarian concretions can occur in sediments of virtually any age and are not particularly diagnostic of Cretaceous strata. Moreover, nobody since Gardner has noted any "immense accumulation of flints" in the collecting areas, and his reference to this material remains an enigma.

Three years after publishing his report on Gardner's fossils, Agassiz (1844b) published a letter to M. Elie de Beaumont in which the relationships of the Brazilian fossil fishes were considered at somewhat greater length in the light of additional specimens sent to M. de Beaumont by M. F. Chabrillac. Agassiz took the opportunity to bemoan that, while the original "mauvais examples" of Spix and Martius had been deposited in the Munich Museum, those of Gardner ". . . se trouvent maintenant dissémines dans les collections de M. Bowman, du marquis de Northampton, de Lord Eniskillen et de Sir Philippe Egerton" ["are now disseminated among the collections of Mr. Bowman, Lord Northampton, Lord Eniskillen and Sir Philip Egerton."] (ibid., p. 1008). Happily, most of these collections eventually found a permanent home in the British Museum (Natural History). In a sentence, Agassiz (ibid., p. 1008) also summarized what has proven a perennial problem concerning the fossils from Araripe:

"Pour fixer définitivement l'âge géologique de cette faune ichthyologique, il serait indispensable d'obtenir . . . de plus amples details sur le gisement de ces poissons et des exemplaires des autres fossiles que l'on trouve associés avec eux." ["In order to fix definitively the geological age of this ichthyological fauna, it would be essential to obtain . . . more details on the occurrence of these fossils and some specimens of other fossils found associated with them."]

For the next 60 years, the rocks of the Araripe Plateau remained little known. Cope (1871) described *Anaedopogon tenuidens*, which turned out to be the head and anterior trunk region of a large specimen of *Cladocyclus* (Woodward, 1895; Jordan and Branner, 1908; Jordan, 1919, 1921; D'Erasmo, 1938; Silva Santos, 1950). The various species of *"Rhacolepis"* were revised by Woodward (1887), who also reinvestigated *Aspidorhynchus comptoni* a few years later, transferring it to *Belonostomus* (Woodward, 1890b, 1895). *Calamopleurus cylindricus* was tentatively included in an extinct group, the Oligopleuridae (Woodward, 1895), and the genus *Notelops* was erected for *Rhacolepis brama* (Woodward, 1901). Thus by the early 20th century the fossil fishes of Araripe, by now authoritatively considered to be of Upper Cretaceous age (Woodward, 1887, 1890, 1895, 1901), still included only Agassiz's original seven species.

20th-Century Investigations

With the publication of Jordan and Branner's (1908) monograph on the fossil fishes from the Araripe Plateau, a first attempt was made to synthesize the various disparate geological observations of earlier investigators with new data obtained from chemical, lithological, and micropaleontological analyses. Diagrammatic geological sections were published by Jordan and Branner (1908), along with brief stratigraphic notes. Jordan and Branner were the first to suggest that lithological variations between concretions might be attributable to their coming from different localities. However, no progress was made concerning the precise geological age of the fossils, although a U.S. Geological Survey paleontologist consulted by Jordan and Branner noted that ostracods obtained from a concretion appeared to be similar to some Late Cretaceous, Eocene, and Miocene cytherids. The fossil fishes were extensively revised and the number of species enlarged by Jordan and Branner (1908), although in hindsight their revision was misguided in some respects. Additional taxonomic revisions were made by Jordan (1919), including the addition of another supposed "elopid," *Ennelichthys derbyi* (later synonymized with *Cladocyclus*; Silva Santos, 1950), and the erection of two new genera for some already-described species (*Brannerion* for an "elopid," *Vinctifer* for the aspidorhynchid). Cope's (1871) old *Anaedopogon tenuidens* was resurrected as yet another "elopid." The culmination of this particular round of taxonomic tinkering appeared just two years later (Jordan, 1921). While the diversity of the "fauna" was expanded to 11 taxa, subsequent investigations have corroborated the validity of only nine.

D'Erasmo (1938) described a collection of fossil fishes from this region belonging to the University of São Paulo. He essentially concurred with Jordan's (1921) summation, adding only a single species, *Rhacolepis de-fiorei*. *Ennelichthys* was retained as an elopid, although *Anaedopogon* was reinterred as a synonym of *Cladocyclus*.

At about the time that Jordan was investigating the fossil fishes, the first detailed stratigraphic account of the Araripe basin was published. Small (1913) recognized two supposedly fluvial (river-lain) sedimentary sequences interbedded with marls and limestones, and named the sequence the Sant'Ana Limestones. He found the greatest thickness of sediments was toward the western flank of the Araripe Plateau, and he recognized four main lithological units. At the top he found red and yellow current-bedded sandstones (today known as the Exu formation). Below this he found concretionary limestones, shales, and calcareous layers (his Sant'Ana formation). Beneath these rocks he recognized a lower red sandstone unit, some 100-150 m thick, also cross-bedded and containing fragments of silicified wood, and a lower unit of conglomeratic sandstone approximately 50 m thick and resting unconformably on the Precambrian basement. Until quite recently, the sandstones below Small's Sant'Ana formation were thought to have formed during the Jurassic period, but some geologists now suspect they also are Lower Cretaceous.

Beurlen (1962, 1963) undertook a more detailed stratigraphic investigation of the Araripe basin, but with mixed results. At first (Beurlen, 1962), the Santana formation was divided informally into three members: a lower member with interbedded shales and laminated limestone; a middle member comprising evaporite deposits; and an upper member with concretionary limestones, shales, marls (calcareous shales), and siltstones. The lower

member subsequently was removed from the Santana formation and named the Crato formation (Beurlen, 1963). Later Beurlen (1971) returned to his original concept and formally recognized three members in the Santana formation (upper Romualdo member, middle Ipubi member, lower Crato member).

This three-fold stratigraphic subdivision was accepted by Mabesoone and Tinoco (1973), but otherwise has proven unpopular. Braun (1966) did not agree with any of Beurlen's (1962, 1963) subdivisions. Moraes, et al. (1963) informally divided the Santana formation into a lower member comprising shales, laminated limestone, and gypsum, and an upper member including concretionary marls, clay, and limestone. Silva Santos and Valença (1968) also adopted this view, arguing that the Crato and Santana "formations" were lithologically and paleontologically very similar, but that the evaporitic sequence (Ipubi member of Beurlen, 1971) was no more than part of a normal carbonate-to-evaporite succession and should not be separated from the lower limestone sequence. Silva Santos and Valença maintained that the evaporite sequence formed a continuous stratigraphic horizon that, they argued, permitted recognition of two members. Beurlen (1971) did not accept their suggestions, however, but instead revived his previous notions of a tripartite stratigraphic succession independent of local facies variations. He also considered that the Santana formation was fully conformable with both the underlying and overlying sandstone sequences.

Intensive geological investigation of and prospecting in the Araripe basin during the 1970's led to further stratigraphic refinement (Moraes, et al., 1975; Moraes, et al., 1976; Scheid, et al., 1978; Oliveira, et al., 1979). H. R. Lima (1979) recognized the importance of facies variation within the Santana formation and considered that Beurlen's (1971) Ipubi and Romualdo members should be abandoned because they represent different contemporaneous facies rather than distinct phases of deposition. However, Lima (1979) retained the Crato member as a distinct unit.

Silva (1983, 1986a, 1986b) concurred with the general conclusions of Moraes, et al. (1963) regarding the presence of two essentially different stratigraphic units, but for the first time identified an important break in sedimentation, marking a period of uplift and erosion between these depositional episodes. This crucial discovery provided the strongest evidence for the existence of two distinct phases of accumulation and led her to distinguish chronologically between certain facies that previously might have been considered contemporaneous.

As knowledge of the sedimentary sequence within the Araripe and other sedimentary basins of Brazil has grown, with it has developed a need for accurate correlations, both local and international. Agassiz (1844b) was moved by the contemporaneity of "ganoids" and "ctenoids" to suggest a broad correlation with the "Chalk Formation" of Europe and North America. Woodward was impressed by similarities between the fish faunas of Ceará and the Cenomanian deposits of Lebanon and Syria, and consequently regarded the Brazilian deposits as Upper Cretaceous. Jordan and Branner (1908) were unable to be more definitive, although their scanty micropaleontological data seemed to corroborate Woodward's assumption of a Late Cretaceous age.

Alex du Toit (arguably the greatest thinker in early 20th century geology) was impressed by lithological similarities between the Cretaceous sedimentary sequences occurring in Ceará, Piauí, and Maranhão with those of Cameroon and Togo in western Africa (du Toit, 1927, 1928). The significance of his profound observations was fully realized only with the emergence of modern theories concerning continental drift and global plate tectonics. In the 1960's, great interest was aroused by publication of several papers demonstrating (by comparisons of microfossils, especially ostracods) the presence of identical Lower Cretaceous deposits in northeastern Brazil (mainly in the Sergipe basin) and western Africa (e.g., Krömmelbein, 1965a, 1965b; Krömmelbein and Wenger, 1966; Viana, 1966; Grekoff and Krömmelbein, 1967). Despite the geological importance of these discoveries, however, their impact upon the Araripe basin has been slight, since most of the correlations were between strata in Brazil and Africa that supposedly are older than the Santana formation. Although ostracods had been recovered from Cretaceous rocks of the Araripe basin, the fossil species seemed either poorly determined, too long-ranging, or else completely endemic (e.g., Braun, 1966; Bate, 1971, 1972). One is reminded of Agassiz's (1844b, p. 1008) plea for . . ." de plus amples details sur le gisement . . . et des exemplaires des autres fossiles" from the Araripe basin.

Faced with a dearth of stratigraphically informative fossils within the Santana formation, Silva Santos and Valença (1968)

conducted a qualitative biostratigraphic comparison of its fossil fishes and other similar fossil assemblages of known geologic age. These included the Kimmeridgian (Upper Jurassic) of Cerin, France; "Wealden" and Purbeckian (Jurassic/Cretaceous boundary) of England; Upper Neocomian (Lower Cretaceous) of the Champagne District, France; Albian-Aptian (later Lower Cretaceous) of Benevento, Italy; Lower Cenomanian (early Upper Cretaceous) of Morocco; Upper Cenomanian, Senonian, and Maestrichtian (Upper Cretaceous) faunas of Lebanon; and the Upper Senonian of Westphalia, Germany. Silva Santos and Valença (1968) espoused the view that the Santana fossil fish assemblage was most probably of Aptian (Lower Cretaceous) age because of broad similarities with the Benevento fauna (sharing eight out of 11 families, the highest proportion among the assemblages sampled). On that basis, however, slightly greater antiquity is also plausible (e.g., seven out of 12 families listed by Silva Santos and Valença (1968) were common to Santana and the English "Wealden," and seven out of 11 were shared by Santana and Cerin, according to the data presented by Silva Santos and Valença, 1968). Younger fossil assemblages displayed markedly less concordance. For example, only five out of 16 Moroccan families, six out of 16 from Hakel, two out of 16 from Sahel Alma, and two out of 12 from Westphalia were also known from Santana.

There is no doubt that the greatest single contributor since Agassiz to the paleoichthyology of the Araripe group is Professor Rubens da Silva Santos, an eminent Brazilian paleontologist who published many descriptions of new fossil fishes and important revisions of old ones from Brazil in the decades following the Second World War. His more important contributions concerning fossils of the Araripe basin include the description of a chanid-like gonorynchiform, *Dastilbe elongatus* (Silva Santos, 1947), and the subsequent recognition (in Silva Santos and Valença, 1968) that *Tharrhias* is a closely related genus; descriptions of a new "leptolepid," *Leptolepis diasii* (Silva Santos, 1958), a pycnodont, *Microdon penalvai* (Silva Santos and Valença, 1968; Silva Santos, 1970), an "elopid" (*Paraelops*; Silva Santos, 1971); and systematic revisions of *Aspidorhynchus, Cladocyclus,* and *Enneles* (Silva Santos, 1945, 1950, 1960).

These studies culminated in publication of a seminal review of the geology and paleontology of the Araripe group (Silva Santos and Valença, 1968) that drew on the combined paleontological

Views of the Araripe Plateau and surrounding areas. Juazeiro do Norte (bottom), located on the northerly side of the plateau, is the principal town and has scheduled air services.

experience of Professor Silva Santos and the ground-breaking efforts of many Brazilian and European geologists and stratigraphers (e.g., Small, 1913; Moraes, 1928; Moraes, et al., 1963; Beurlen, 1962, 1963; Anjos, 1963). According to Silva Santos and Valença (1968), the fish "fauna" of the Santana formation (according to their definition) included 18 species. Several important taxa had yet to be described, although they were named in that publication.

Besides fishes, the Araripe group has also begun to yield fossil tetrapods (terrestrial vertebrates). The first to be described was the skull of a crocodilian, *Araripesuchus* (Price, 1959), but many other fossil tetrapods have now been described including a much larger trematochampsid crocodilian (Kellner, 1987), turtles (*Araripemys*; Price, 1973), and pterosaurs (*Araripesaurus, Araripedactylus, Santanadactylus, Cearadactylus, Anhanguera, Tropeognathus*; Price, 1971; Wellnhofer, 1977, 1985, 1987; De Buisonje, 1980, 1981; Wellnhofer, et al., 1983; Leonardi and Borgomanero, 1983; Campos. et al., 1984; Campos and Kellner, 1985a,b). More recently, dinosaur bones have been recovered; they are described for the first time elsewhere in this book. All of these fossils have been recovered from concretions of the Santana formation. A frog and a bird feather also have been reported, both apparently from the laminated limestone of the Crato member (Kellner and Campos, 1986; Martins-Neto and Kellner, 1988). The fish fauna also has been extended recently to include a new deep-bodied teleost, *Araripichthys* (Silva Santos, 1983, 1985c), an ionoscopid, *Oshunia* (Wenz and Kellner, 1986), two species of coelacanth (Campos and Wenz, 1982), a new genus of pycnodontid, *Iemanja* (Wenz, 1989), and a new hybodont shark, *Tribodus* (Brito and Ferreira, 1989). One of the coelacanths has been placed into a new genus and named after Dr. Herbert Axelrod (*Axelrodichthys*; Maisey, 1986). According to Maisey (1986), the other coelacanth is close to *Mawsonia gigas*. This gigantic coelacanth fossil occurs in the Ilhas group of Bahia (Mawson and Woodward, 1907; Casier, 1961; de Carvalho, 1982) and is considered to be of Neocomian age (lowermost Cretaceous) and therefore slightly older than the Santana formation (Hartt, 1870; Grekoff and Krömmelbein, 1967).

In addition, the invertebrate fossils of the Araripe group have become better documented. The Santana formation has yielded a limited fauna of lamellibranchs (pelecypods), gastropods, conchostracans, ostracods, and parasitic copepods ("the oldest copepods of any sort known"; Cressey and Patterson, 1973), plus rare decapods and echinoids (Mabesoone and Tinoco, 1973; H. R. Lima, 1979). The Crato member, besides yielding abundant specimens of the fish *Dastilbe*, also contains an important assemblage of insects and arachnids. Additionally, fossil plants occur sporadically in concretions within the Romualdo member of the Santana formation (Duarte, 1969) and in the laminated limestones of the Crato member.

The Geological Time Scale

Although the Earth is believed to be at least 4.6 billion years old, the fossil record of life on this planet is restricted to the latter part of this interval, while abundant fossil remains are pretty much confined to the last 600 million or so years of Earth history. This span of time has been subdivided into a series of eras, periods, and stages, largely on the basis of different kinds of fossils found sedimentary rocks.

Three geological eras (Paleozoic, Mesozoic, and Cenozoic) are recognized (representing "ancient life," "middle life," and "recent life," respectively). The Mesozoic era includes three periods, named the Triassic, Jurassic, and Cretaceous. With an estimated duration of about 160 million years, the Mesozoic era comprises a little over 3% of the Earth's history.

Within this era, the Cretaceous period spans the last 70 million years, beginning some 135 million years ago and ending approximately 65 million years ago. Note that the end of the Cretaceous period also marks the close of the Mesozoic era.

All geological time periods are further subdivided into stages. These stages usually represent intervals of tens of millions of years, although some may be shorter or longer. Stages, like periods and eras, are somewhat arbitrary temporal units and are not of equal duration. The names of internationally recognized stages for the Cretaceous period are shown in the accompanying diagram. Note that the terms "Wealden" and "Neocomian" are sometimes used to define broader blocks of Lower Cretaceous time, and consequently are less precise indicators of geologic age.

(J. G. Maisey)

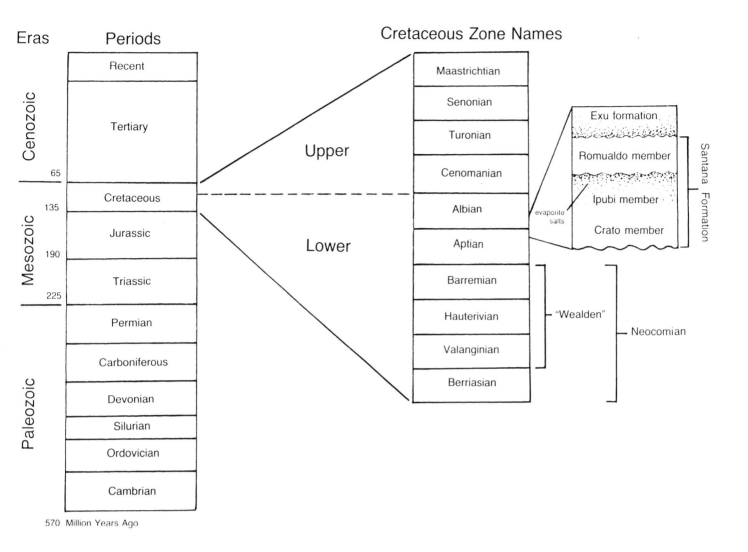

Geological time scale (left), with names applied to Cretaceous time zones throughout this atlas. The approximate temporal position of the Santana formation is shown to the right.

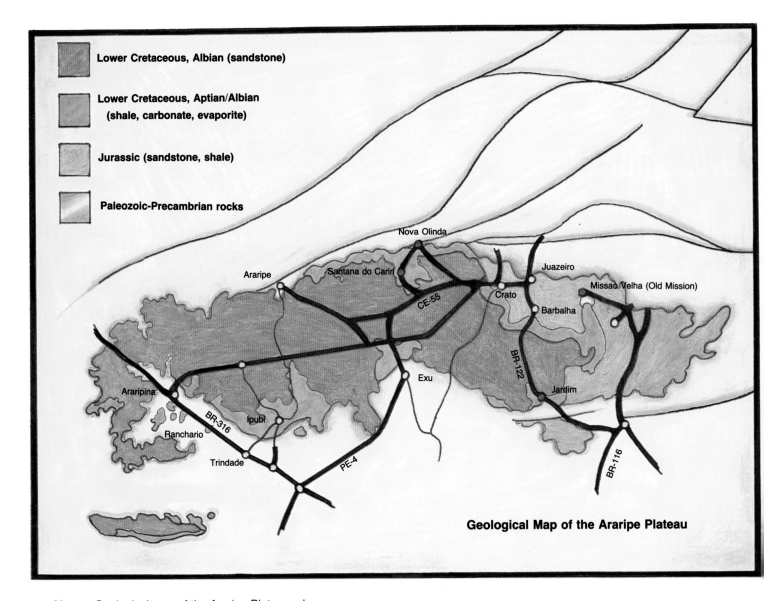

Lower Cretaceous, Albian (sandstone)

Lower Cretaceous, Aptian/Albian
(shale, carbonate, evaporite)

Jurassic (sandstone, shale)

Paleozoic-Precambrian rocks

Nova Olinda

Araripe

Santana do Cariri

Juazeiro

Missão Velha (Old Mission)

CE-55

Crato

Barbalha

Araripina

BR-122

Exu

BR-316

Ipubi

Jardim

Ranchario

Trindade

PE-4

BR-116

Geological Map of the Araripe Plateau

Above: Geological map of the Araripe Plateau, also showing the principal roads and towns including those nearest the classic collecting sites (Santana do Cariri, Jardim, and Missão Velha).

Facing page: Early maps of the Araripe Plateau, published by Small (1913). The plateau is largely defined by the resistant "Arenito superior" (Exu formation). The "Sta. Anna" limestones lie beneath this, and are shown to outcrop at the eastern end of the plateau in a narrow belt extending from "Sant'Anna do Cariry" in the north to Jardim in the south. Photos courtesy of Prof. R. da Silva Santos.

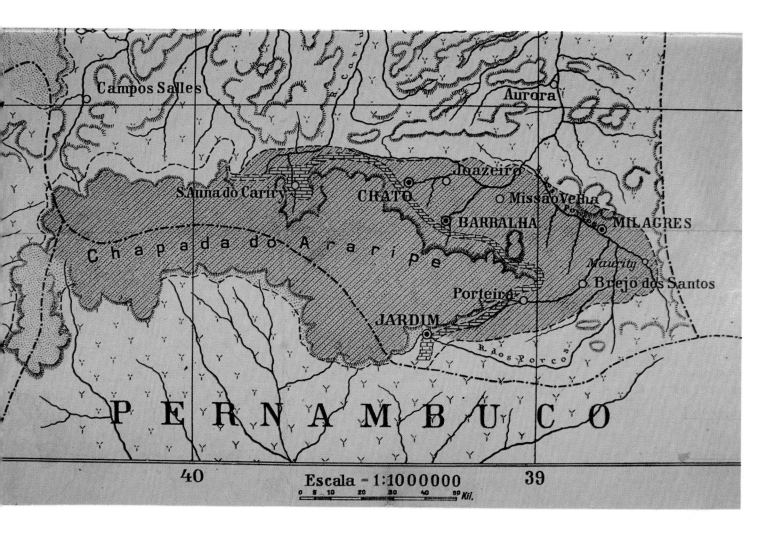

Campos Salles · Aurora · S.Anna do Cariry · Joazeiro · CRATO · Missão Velha · BARBALHA · MILAGRES · Maurity · Brejo dos Santos · Porteira · JARDIM · R. dos Porcos

Chapada do Araripe

P E R N A M B U C O

40   Escala = 1:1000000   39

0 5 10   20   30   40   50 Kil.

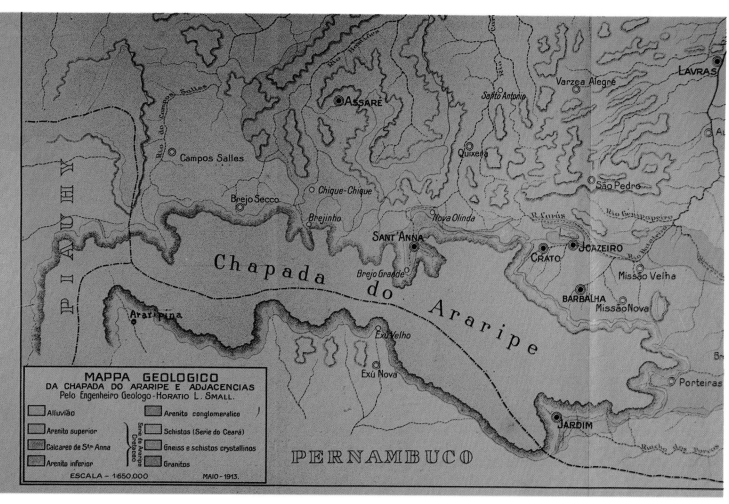

LAVRAS · Varzea Alegre · Santo Antonio · ASSARE · Quixerá · São Pedro · Campos Salles · Chique-Chique · Nova Olinda · R. Carás · Rio Genipapeiro · Brejo Secco · Brejinho · SANT'ANNA · JOAZEIRO · CRATO · Missão Velha · Brejo Grande · BARBALHA · Missão Nova · Araripina · Exú Velho · Exú Nova · Porteiras · JARDIM · Riacho dos Porcos

P I A U H Y

Chapada do Araripe

MAPPA GEOLOGICO
DA CHAPADA DO ARARIPE E ADJACENCIAS
Pelo Engenheiro Geologo - Horatio L. Small.

- Alluvião
- Arenito superior
- Calcareo de Sta Anna
- Arenito inferior

Serie do Araripe Cretaceo

- Arenito conglomeratico
- Schistos (Serie do Ceará)
- Gneiss e schistos crystallinos
- Granitos

ESCALA - 1:650.000   MAIO - 1913.

P E R N A M B U C O

3: The Changing Patterns of Life

The science of paleontology attempts to reconstruct life on Earth as revealed by fossil remains. Although fossils were known to the ancient Greeks, the empirical study of fossilized organisms can be traced back only a few hundred years.

During the late 17th and early 18th centuries it gradually became apparent that certain types of rocks, especially those thought to have formed originally as soft sediments under water, occurred in consistently recognizable sequences across broad areas. With this realization came the birth of stratigraphy, the branch of geological science to do with establishing chronologies of and correlations between past geological events.

As this science developed, increasing reliance came to be placed upon the different kinds of fossils contained within particular stratigraphic sequences. Thus it was accepted early on that fossilized remains reflected widespread changes in the pattern of ancient life and that these changes formed a consistent and, more significantly, irreversible biological sequence. Particular sedimentary strata will produce a characteristic suite of fossils (known as an assemblage), by means of which one can establish the relative position of the strata within a broad geological chronology.

At first this sequential pattern took on only a utilitarian function, for example in drawing up the earliest geological maps by the English surveyor William Smith (1769-1839). Before long, however, many zoologists and botanists began to ponder the significance and meaning of this pattern. Once the old dogma that organic species were immutable had been overcome, a philosophical avenue was to open that encouraged paleontological investigations into the long-range changes of organisms through time.

It is now recognized that most living species have existed for only a few million years, but that closely related organisms once lived and included the presumed ancestors of living animals and plants. The farther back one searches in time, the greater become the differences between living species and their presumed fossil relatives. Sometimes fossils reveal the former existence of entire groups of now-extinct organisms, such as dinosaurs, the coiled-shelled molluscs known as ammonites,

the ancient armored placoderm fishes, and the even more ancient arthropods we call trilobites. It has been pointed out that of all the species that have ever existed on Earth, well over 90% are now extinct.

As paleontological knowledge has increased, our human perception of the pattern of earthly life through time has taken on greater and greater complexity. For example, it is now known that most higher groups of animals (e.g., molluscs, arthropods, annelids, echinoderms, brachiopods, sponges, chordates) and primitive plants such as algae were already present on earth during the Cambrian period (approximately 550-500 million years ago). The earliest reliably identified pieces of vertebrate bone come from Ordovician rocks of Australia and North America, considered to be some 450 million years old. The oldest sea urchins, starfishes, sea lilies (crinoids), pelecypods (clams, etc.), scaphopods (tusk-shells), bryozoans, and corals are also of Ordovician age. The earliest jawed vertebrates, as well as arachnids (spider-like arthropods), bryophytes (mosses, liverworts), and vascular plants occur in Silurian rocks (430-400 million years old). In the Devonian period that followed (ranging between 400 and 360 million years ago), the oldest known tetrapods (terrestrial vertebrates), myriapods (centipedes, millipedes) and insects, ammonoid molluscs, terrestrial clubmosses, lycopsids (scale trees), sphenopsids (horsetails), pterophytes (ferns, etc.), cycadophytes (seed-ferns), and primitive conifers all became established. From our land-bound perspective, therefore, the Devonian period represents a very significant phase in terrestrial colonization of the continents by animals and plants.

Colonization of the world's major land masses evidently proceeded rapidly throughout the Carboniferous and Permian periods, so that by the close of the Paleozoic era (coinciding with the end of the Permian, some 240 million years ago) the terrestrial world was teeming with plants and animals in great abundance and diversity. Among vertebrates, a major adaptational advance was made by a group known as amniotes, which no longer required bodies of water in which to lay eggs, as do fishes and amphibians. Some major groups of plants such as conifers and cycadophytes also acquired a lessened dependence upon water for their fertilization and development and also became abundant. These were destined to become the dominant terrestrial plant groups for much of the following Mesozoic era.

Some late Carboniferous and early Permian plant fossils took on considerable importance in the late 19th and early 20th centuries by providing the first compelling evidence that the Earth's major land masses have not always occupied their present positions and that certain continents may once have been conjoined into one or more supercontinents. The fossils are of net-veined ferns, usually grouped into several species and known as the *Glossopteris* floral assemblage (*Glossopteris* is one of the most prevalent form genera characterizing this floral assemblage, but several other genera have been named).

Glossopteris was first adequately described in 1828 from India and Australia. In 1858, virtually identical fossils were described from South Africa. Professor Edward Suess is credited with being the first to recognize the implications of this distribution, for in the final pages of the first volume of his series *The Face of the Earth*, published in 1885, Suess hypothesized that a mighty supercontinent had once existed that included southern and central Africa, India, and Madagascar (but notably excluded Australia). Following the discovery of the *Glossopteris* flora in southern Brazil, Suess added eastern South America to his "Gondwanaland."

Although Suess's ideas must have seemed outrageous to his contemporary scientific community, in hindsight they have proven to be extremely perceptive. In fact, while his original notion called for a unified supercontinent to explain the distribution of the *Glossopteris* floral assemblage, modern geophysical data indicate that, during the Late Paleozoic, Suess's Gondwanaland was only a part of the even greater supercontinent now known as Pangaea. The *Glossopteris* floral assemblage, although widespread, was nevertheless restricted in its distribution across Pangaea and did not extend into non-Gondwanan regions.

The Mesozoic era was characterized by the success of coniferous plants and amniote vertebrates on land and cephalopod molluscs (ammonites, belemnites) in the oceans. This era saw the entire span of dinosaur evolution and their ultimate extinction, the acme and decline of ammonoid cephalopods and the related belemnites, the rise of two successful groups of warm-blooded tetrapods, the birds and mammals, and also the rise of angiosperms (flowering plants). Primitive mammals and probably birds and angiosperms appeared during the Triassic (approximately 230-200 million years ago) but remained relatively rare and restricted for much of the Mesozoic.

There are indications of a major rise to dominance of dicotyledonous angiosperms in lower-latitude parts of South America and Africa during the Early Cretaceous (around 110-100 million years) and of their spread to higher latitudes a few tens of millions of years later. The earliest mammals, although shrew-like in size, were quickly able to colonize vast tracts of Pangaea; very closely related species have been described from Triassic sediments of Wales and China. Distinctly bird-like bones have been discovered in Triassic rocks of western North America. The oldest undisputed avian fossil is of *Archaeopteryx*, from the late Jurassic of Bavaria in western Germany.

The end of the Mesozoic era is characterized by the extinction of a great many groups of organisms, of which dinosaurs, ammonites, and belemnites are just a few examples.

This was not the first such occurrence, as the end of the Paleozoic era also is marked by a high extinction rate. Nor are these points in time the only ones when previously successful groups were terminated. For example, the armored placoderm fishes achieved worldwide dominance and were very abundant, but practically their entire evolutionary history is squeezed into the Devonian period. The extent of the Late Mesozoic extinction is nevertheless awesome in the range of taxic diversity affected.

In recent years there has been strong advocacy of a catastrophic occurrence, such as asteroid impact, to account for major extinctions. Although this idea has achieved some popularity, the evidence is controversial and has received a great deal of criticism. One major problem encountered by any single model seeking to explain these extinction events is how to account for the survival and continued sucess of other anatomically and physiologically similar organisms that coexisted in the same environments as the defunct groups.

Whatever the reason for these changes, the floras and faunas of the succeeding Cenozoic era evidently differed profoundly from those of the Mesozoic. On land, various groups of flowering plants competed successfully with the gymnosperms and came to dominate low- and mid-latitude floras, although coniferous forests successfully colonized higher latitude and altitude terrains. Birds and mammals quickly established themselves as the dominant groups of larger terrestrial animals. Several lineages of these warm-blooded vertebrates made a successful transition to aquatic habitats, especially in the oceans. Here also important changes occurred in the invertebrate world, with an increasing preponderance of gastropod and pelecypod molluscs in place of their brachiopod competitors, which became relatively restricted.

The history of life on earth is thus broadly conceptualized as a series of long-lived eras, each of which is characterized by floras and faunas dominated by particular groups of organisms and distinguished from the next era by important changes in the relative abundance and diversity of the groups comprising the floras and faunas. Within each era, further temporal subdivisions (periods) are discerned, again on the basis of changes in the relative abundance and diversity of various organisms. Each fossil assemblage represents parts of long-extinct floral and faunal communities, providing clues about past biotas that can be reconstructed only by patiently sifting through their fragmentary paleontological remains.

Many groups can be traced across these conceptual time boundaries, so that the fossil record forms a continuum that is not completely compartmentalized. We are thus given the distinct (if qualitative) impression that the consequences of evolutionary change are variable, both in the rates and extents to which successive biotas were affected though geological time. Currently there is much debate over whether there are corresponding changes in evolutionary rates themselves, and two opposing schools have emerged. The more traditional (Darwinian) gradualist hypothesis has been challenged in recent years by proponents of punctuated equilibrium, an alternative hypothetical model involving rapid ("saltatory") evolutionary change within any given lineage, followed by prolonged stasis during which only relatively minor changes occur. This model is more in accord with a literal interpretation of the fossil record, but advocates of gradualism have objected on the grounds that in most cases the stratigraphic data do not provide means for distinguishing a putative saltatory event from a gap in the fossil record.

In spite of such disagreements over the mechanism of evolution, there is overwhelming evidence that cumulative, irreversible changes have occurred throughout the organic realm with the passage of geological time. Recognizing this fact, a primary role of comparative anatomists and systematists is to define the patterns of change and attempt to resolve the interrelationships of living and fossil organisms.

It is popularly thought that the paleontologist's primary function is to reveal our prehistoric ancestors and that by seeking out these ancestors the paleontologist is bringing an intellectual respectability to this branch of science. Indeed, there still are some paleontologists who believe that "common ancestors" actually can be identified within the fossil record. In recent years, however, it has become increasingly evident that the ancestry-information content of fossils is empirically limited, at least with present levels of technology. Direct ancestry to modern species or to other fossils cannot, in fact, be demonstrated. We cannot tell whether any given fossil species or individual actually gave rise to descendant populations, and even if it did we cannot determine whether these descendants included another given species.

Instead, we may be able to demonstrate that a group of two or more species (whether living or fossil) shares certain attributes, or characters, not found in other similar (and presumably closely related) species or in more distantly related forms. These unique characters thus serve to define taxa (= groups at the species level and above), and the most straightforward explanation of this situation is that they share a common ancestry. Systematic biology has been revolutionized in the last two decades by the realization that relationships between taxa can be expressed on a rational basis only by investigating such shared derived characters (often termed synapomorphies). This concept, which was first expressed cogently by the German entomologist Willi Hennig in the middle 20th century, has formed the basis for a novel approach to systematic biology that has become known as Hennigian or cladistic systematics.

The basis behind this methodology initially was developed for investigating the relationships between living species but soon was extended to the fossil record. Most living species, except for cases where hybridization is common, are regarded as distinct entities, terminal taxa (because each species represents the current end of its ancestral lineage). Investigation of character distributions among groups of terminal taxa reveals sets of characters that may be indicative of relationships at different phylogenetic levels (i.e., earlier or later on an evolutionary lineage). These character distributions can be tested principally by their congruence with other characters, although other tests sometimes are also applied. Where characters do not appear congruent, or where the data are ambiguous, difficulties are met in resolving relationships unless new data are forthcoming. The end product hopefully is a map of shared derived character distributions that is nested, group within higher group. Terminal taxa can be placed within this heirarchy according to which characters are shared.

The fossil record consists of the tangible remains of innumerable long-dead individuals, many of which presumably left viable offspring before meeting their demise. Although we have no way of knowing, any given fossil may have had an unbroken descendant lineage of many, many generations. During the passage of geological time, genetic mutations probably occurred, leading to permanent morphological changes in later generations. Despite the fact that we give taxonomic names (species, genus) to fossils, we actually have no real guarantee that they are terminal taxa in the way that modern species are.

Cladistic systematics allows us to treat fossils as terminal taxa, however, because we are primarily investigating the distribution of morphological characters rather than of ancestor- descendant species. Let us suppose that fossil "A" actually was a direct ancestor of living species "B" (or another fossil), or even of a group of species "BCD." If "B" (or "BCD") is characterized by derived characters not occurring in "A" (and in other organisms considered more distantly related), then "B" (or "BCD") is inferred to be more derived than "A." Note, however, that this has no bearing on the ancestral status of fossil "A." Species "B" (or group "BCD") may be a descendant of "A," but it would be equally plausible (from our present-day viewpoint) for "A" to have lain on another, divergent lineage, or to have been a terminal taxon by becoming extinct. The discovery of additional derived characters shared by "A" and "B" (or "BCD") adds no further resolution, other than admitting that all these organisms are related. Thus cladistic systematics offers a great advantage in allowing fossils to be included with living species in an empirical analysis of character distributions, but by treating fossils as terminal taxa it does not permit recognition of direct ancestor-descendant relationships. Instead, it has allowed us to develop a clearer understanding of the patterns of morphological change within and between different groups of organisms and to formulate scenarios of evolutionary transformations that are empirically based.

(J. G. Maisey)

4: Continents Adrift

The sequence of rocks that contain the various fossils described in this volume originally was deposited as soft sediments that accumulated during an important event, the separation of the South American and African continents, at which time the floor of southern Atlantic Ocean began to form. In this part of the globe, therefore, the Earth's crust was being subjected to enormous stresses that led to great regional instability and crustal movement.

All this may seem rather momentous, even cataclysmic, to anyone without any previous knowledge of global geological processes. Within the context of earth history as it is understood today, however, the rifting of Africa and South America simply is one of the latest of many such events, some involving separations and others great collisions, that have cumulatively shaped the surface of our planet.

As far as we are able to detect, these same awesome mechanisms have been in operation continually ever since the Earth's crust first formed approximately 4.5 billion years ago. In Greenland there are rocks approaching this age, representing some of the oldest rocks exposed anywhere. These rocks are crystalline and display folding and other distortions showing that they have been subjected to great stresses deep within a continental mountain belt. The largest folds have amplitudes that are consistent with those generated in other much younger mountain chains, suggesting to some geologists that the ancient Greenland rocks were part of a continental crustal sequence not appreciably thinner than anything existing today. These earliest traces of the earth's continental crust therefore tell us that it was essentially as thick as today's, that it was mobile, and that it was being subjected to enormous tectonic forces, then as now.

Although the rocks of Greenland and Canada currently hold the record for longevity, every continent across the globe contains a vast area (usually located centrally) comprising crystalline rocks of great antiquity, all displaying evidence that they too were once buried deep within the crust and were subjected to great forces. These central "shield" areas form the continental basement rocks. Upon them successively younger volcanic and sedimentary rocks have

accumulated. Into them younger molten magmas have intruded, and against them younger layers of the ocean floors have been compressed, crushed, wrenched, and obliterated. The continents, we may conclude, are remarkably resilient. The ocean floors located between them are relatively short-lived; in only a few areas have the ocean floors been dated at over 140 million years, which is a mere fraction of the time that the ancient continental shields have existed.

What makes the separation of Africa and South America so interesting to geologists is that it is one of the latest such major crustal fragmentations thought to have occurred. Being relatively new, the event has not been obliterated by subsequent erosion and tectonic activity as much as earlier ones. Even a cursory glance at an atlas or globe will show how closely the facing coasts of these two continents are aligned. In fact, it was this similarity that in large part inspired Professor Alfred Wegener to advance his hypothesis of continental drift in 1929, in defiance of then-conventional belief in the stability of the earth's crust.

For years the scientific establishment was intolerant of Wegener's hypothesis, even after Dr. Alex du Toit published more cogent geological evidence in his now classic work, *The Wandering Continents* (1937). Much of du Toit's evidence came from soundings made in the Atlantic Ocean (from which a mid-oceanic rise and several symmetrically-arranged flanking basins were recognized) and from his own perceptive understanding of geological features he had observed in both Africa and South America.

Significant progress in understanding the global mechanisms behind continental drift was not made for over 20 years. Then, in the mid-1950's, came the revelation that many rocks (especially in volcanic areas) contained a residual magnetic charge representing a small part of the earth's magnetic field when the rocks were formed. By measuring this "paleomagnetism," data were obtained that could be used to determine among other things the latitude at which the rock originally was formed. Very soon there were sufficient data to verify that relative movement between the continents had actually taken place, sometimes by an unexpectedly great amount, but generally after the fashion du Toit had suggested decades earlier.

At the same time these paleomagnetic data were becoming available, new geophysical techniques were developed for investigating the ocean floors. One of the most important again involved paleomagnetism and stems from the fact that the Earth's magnetic field has undergone complete reversal on numerous occasions. These reversals occur spasmodically. Periods ranging from tens of thousands to millions of years between reversals have been measured. The rocks of the ocean floor have trapped this paleomagnetic record as they were formed. Significantly, there are symmetrical reversal patterns on either side of the mid-oceanic rise. Measurements of these patterns, together with the establishment of an absolute time scale for geomagnetic events, have enabled geophysicists to measure the rates of ocean crust formation and thus to determine the relative rates of sea floor spreading and continental movement. Today many other techniques, including the use of ultrasensitive satellite-based equipment, have supplemented the geophysical arsenal and have taken continental drift from the realm of inspired guesswork to one of measurable fact.

During the 1960's arose a revolutionary yet elegantly simple new concept of crustal evolution, that has become known as the theory of plate tectonics. Its basic mechanism is well illustrated by the South Atlantic Ocean floor. This region may be viewed as the product of the drifting apart of the African and South American continents. Actually, "drifted" is a poor descriptor, since the movement is "driven" by geomechanical processes.

Geologically speaking, the southern limit of the South Atlantic Ocean floor is an area known as the Falkland-Agulhas fracture zone, while the northern limit is a series of extremely long fracture zones in the equatorial region. Down the ocean center passes the seismically-active Mid-Atlantic Ridge, and across it runs the aseismic Rio Grande Ridge (separating the Brazil and Argentine basins) in the western South Atlantic and the similarly aseismic Walvis Ridge (separating the Angola and Cape basins) in the east.

The Mid-Atlantic Ridge is part of a globally active zone of crustal tension, where the ocean floor is continually in the process of creation from upwelling molten magmas that are cooled into crystalline basaltic rock and then carried away on either side of the ridge axis. In this way

the ocean floor is gradually widening.

Where the ridge axis turns (parallel to the Atlantic margins of Africa and South America), the simple conveyer-belt mechanism no longer works and adjacent strips of the ocean floor (which do not all expand at once) have slipped laterally past one another, sometimes for hundreds or thousands of kilometers. These slip-zones are known as transform faults. They also occur at intervals across almost the whole ocean floor, but are most plentiful and closely spaced in the equatorial region, where the ridge axis is broken into numerous short north-south segments that are offset by intervening transform faults. These faults are exactly parallel to the direction of ocean floor expansion. In the case of the South Atlantic, because Africa and South America are being carried apart on the margins of the ocean floor, their direction of relative movement also is parallel to the transform faults. The Atlantic margins are seismically inactive and there is little volcanic activity. Because of this, the eastern South Atlantic floor may be considered part of the African plate, while the western floor is part of the South American plate.

A different situation prevails in much of the Pacific, where for example the ocean floor is being over-ridden by South America. There is a deep offshore trench where part of the Pacific Ocean floor (the Nazca Plate) is being subducted beneath South America. The region is seismically active, and volcanic eruptions are common.

The plate tectonic theory thus recognizes relatively few kinds of boundaries between parts of the Earth's crust. There are seismically and volcanically active ones, including extensional margins along mid-ocean ridges, compressional ones where one plate overrides another, and transform faults where plate segments slide past one another. There are also seismically quiet, immobile boundaries, as between South America and the western floor of the South Atlantic.

The transform fault system is clearly an integral part of any ocean floor, and as such is undoubtedly of corresponding age. These fault lines are most easily detected closer to the ridge axis, where the ocean floor is younger and generally shallower and lacks the blanket of sediments that covers the older sea floor nearer to the continents. It is now known that these fault lines continue under the sediments, however, and may even extend into the continents on either side. The Atlantic margins of South America and Africa are fractured by such fault line extensions, known as lineaments. Tectonic movement along these lineaments is usually up or down, however, with relatively little lateral slip.

Downward slipping of the crust on one side of such a lineament results in a fault-bounded basin, like a one-sided rift valley. The surrounding elevated areas are weathered and eroded, while sediments may accumulate in the lower-lying basin.

Two such east-west trending lineaments have played an important role in the formation of the Araripe basin. The Patos lineament is the most important, as its fault line defines the northerly edge of the basin. Farther south is the Pernambuco lineament, truncating the northernmost end of the north-south trending Recôncavo-Tucano-Jatoba basin. The Araripe basin may once have connected with this one, across the Pernambuco lineament, but apparently became isolated by fault activity along both lineaments during the Lower Cretaceous. These fault lines continue to be minor sources of seismic activity, indicating that fault movement is continuing. As these lineaments are essentially continental extensions of oceanic transform fault systems, continuing seismic activity along these lineaments again illustrates the longevity of these important geological features. In fact, since these lineaments have clearly influenced the position, shape, and size of the Araripe basin and many marginal basins, even before the South Atlantic Ocean floor had formed, they may represent the earliest phase in the development of a transform fault system. These major features of the ocean floor thus probably began as relatively small but important gashes across the face of the foundering supercontinent and subsequently were maintained and extended as the continental land-masses were slowly driven apart and new oceanic crust was formed between them in piecemeal fashion.

Many 19th-century biologists were convinced that the distribution of modern animal and plant groups around the world provides compelling evidence for the former existence of connections between now-isolated continents. Indeed, such notions were being seriously invoked long before geologists developed any conception that the continents were capable of moving in relation to each other.

In 1847, the British botanist Sir Joseph Hooker first advocated the prior existence of a large southern continent to explain the distribution of certain flowering plants in Chile, Patagonia, Tasmania, and New Zealand. In 1867, the Swiss paleontologist Rütimeyer theorized that all living animals arose from just a few faunal centers, and he came to the conclusion that all warm-blooded animals (i.e., mammals and birds) of the Southern Hemisphere originated at three centers (Australia, Madagascar, and the islands of the Indian Ocean). Furthermore, he suggested that these three are in reality only one, since their faunas represent remnants of a single original fauna of a large hypothetical Antarctic continent.

In 1870, Sir Thomas Huxley advocated that such a southern continent (including South America, Australia, and New Zealand) existed during the "Age of Reptiles" (i.e., the Mesozoic era), and he suggested that some parts of it became isolated before others—in other words, this southern supercontinent has a decipherable history. A number of other naturalists of the late 19th and early 20th centuries also found corroborating evidence for a single southern landmass from organisms such as worms, molluscs, plants, fishes, and other vertebrates.

In 1900, the American paleontologist Osborn reconstructed the supposed landmass by mapping the present-day 3040-meter sounding line around the southern continents, in an attempt to estimate the extent to which the ancient Antarctic might have foundered. In the absence of any dynamic geophysical model to explain all their observations on the distributions of living plants and animals, however, biologists had little recourse but to invoke the former presence of great land-bridges between now-isolated continents and try to "play down" the fact that the oceans would have to be lowered by about 3 km (almost 2 miles) in order to resurrect the great southern supercontinent.

By combining geophysical data obtained from the continents and ocean floors with other geological and paleontological information discovered in the field or laboratory, scientists have begun to unravel the past complex wanderings of the continents and the effects these have had on the distribution and evolutionary history of plant and animal species. The geophysical revolution of the 1960's thus has spawned a corresponding biological one in the latter part of the 20th century and has opened up entirely new avenues of biogeographical investigations, involving both living and extinct species. Sometimes the geological and biogeographical data are complementary; at other times they are flatly contradictory. In the past few years, however, it

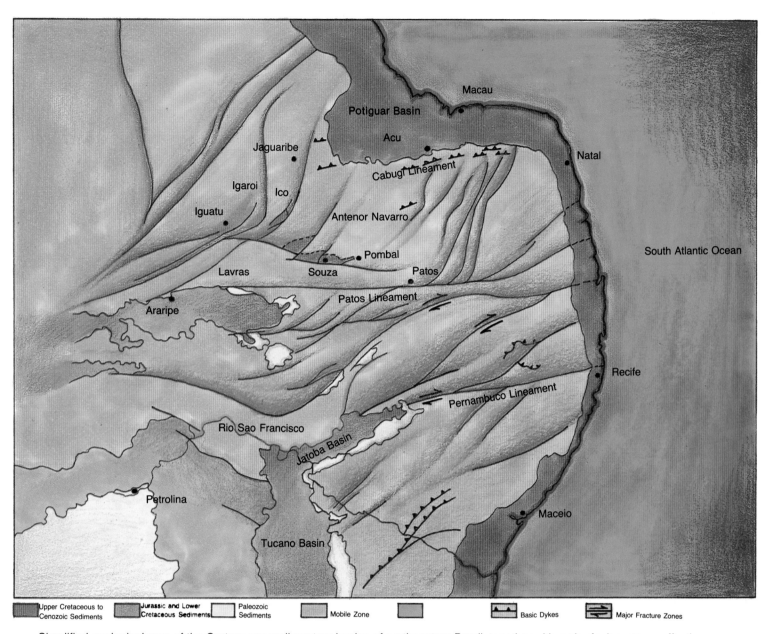

Simplified geological map of the Cretaceous sedimentary basins of northeastern Brazil, together with major fault systems affecting the pan-African mobile zone. The Araripe basin lies immediately to the south of the Patos lineament, forming a half-graben structure like the Jatoba and Tucano basins farther south.

has become evident that global tectonic processes have been an important external influence on the organic realm, affecting not only the distribution and abundance of species, but perhaps also controlling the ultimate destinies of entire biotas.

The general pattern of continental motion has been determined for much of the Earth's last 200 million years. Some time before that, the continents appear to have been coalesced into three major supercontinents. One of these, including all of Africa, South America, Australia, Antarctica, Arabia, India, and Madagascar, has become known as Gondwanaland. The other supercontinents have been named Laurasia (comprising North America, Greenland, Europe, and Asia west of the Urals) and Eurasia (including China,

Siberia, and Kazakhstan, although they may not have been completely united).

No overall pattern for the distribution of these ancient supercontinents can be determined, because none of the presumed ocean floors separating them have survived, except for small slices trapped within remnants of ancient mountain chains (thought to represent now-defunct compressional margins). For example, it is believed that the Ural Mountains in part represent a suture between two originally separate continental plates, and that the Appalachian and Hercynian tectonic belts of North America and Europe represent another such suture. From the Late Paleozoic age of these belts, which were generated by collisions between the continental blocks on either side, it is inferred that ocean floor of unknown extent must have separated these supercontinents up to the Middle Paleozoic (300-350 million years ago).

Fusion of these regions into one gigantic land-mass occurred around 250 million years ago. This single supercontinent, which has become known as Pangaea, survived until around 180 million years ago. Then, in the early part of the Jurassic period, the North American land-mass started to break away and the North Atlantic Ocean floor began to develop. By the Early Cretaceous (about 120 million years ago), further break-up resulted in the separation of Antarctica and Australia from Africa, Madagascar, and India, accompanied by formation of the Indian Ocean floor. Around this time the South Atlantic floor also began to form within a progressively widening gap between the southern ends of Africa and South America.

By the Middle Cretaceous (about 100 million years ago) this separation was essentially complete, although the areas of north-eastern Brazil and western Africa still were in very close proximity. India and Madagascar had by now also separated from Africa. By the end of the Cretaceous period (approximately 80 million years ago) there was a continuous ocean floor extending between Africa and South America. Except for being much narrower than today, the North and South Atlantic Oceans thus took on their present form at the close of the Mesozoic era. The Indian block became increasingly isolated, and by about 60 million years ago lay almost equidistant from Africa and eastern Asia. Then, between 20 and 40 million years ago, India began its collision with Asia that is continuing to thrust up the Himalayan mountain chain. Australia and Antarctica began their separation around this time. Today, Australia occupies a comparable position to India 60 million years ago and appears headed for ultimate collision with Southeast Asia within the next 20 or 30 million years.

Focusing on South America, therefore, we find that its separation from Africa is actually quite modern, relative to the age of the earth's continental crust, and that until about 120 million years ago South America was firmly attached to Africa and the rest of Gondwanaland for as far back in geological time as we can determine. Furthermore, even once this separation had commenced, the great sinuous curve between northeastern Brazil and western Africa resulted in these plates slipping past each other while their margins remained in close proximity. During the Upper Cretaceous and early Tertiary, it is even possible that the continents moved closer together, as a consequence of Africa's rebounding off southern Europe (Szatmari, et al., 1987). Thus it may have been possible for animal and plant species to move across this relatively narrow gap quite freely though the Late Cretaceous, and into the early Tertiary about 50 million years ago, whereas farther south such possibilities had effectively ceased some 70 million years previously.

Recent geological investigations reveal that the Atlantic margin of South America was dissected by faulting during the early phases of separation from Africa, and that small "micro-plates" moved relatively independently of one another, including the slice containing the Araripe basin between the Patos and Pernambuco lineaments and the Recôncavo-Tucano-Jatoba region to its south. Had rifting continued further, it is possible that this part of Brazil would have separated completely from the rest of South America.

The region of northeastern Brazil in which the Santana formation was deposited is today a few hundred kilometers inland from the South Atlantic coast. At the time these deposits were laid down, however, the paleogeography was profoundly different. There may have been a narrow sea somewhat like the Arabian Gulf today, or there may have been nothing but fault-bounded, salt-encrusted valleys into which occasional flash-floods drained and dumped their heavy loads of sediment. The paleontological evidence suggests generally arid conditions on land, which perhaps is not surprising, given that up until a few million years previously and throughout most of its history as part of Gondwanaland, the vicinity of northeastern Brazil had lain close to the center of that great supercontinent.

(J. G. Maisey)

5: Cretaceous Sedimentary Basins in Brazil

The Araripe basin is only one of many such geological structures within Brazil, although its inland location is unusual—the majority of Brazilian sedimentary basins that were active during the Cretaceous period are situated at (or close to) the continental margin. Their distribution and paleogeographic significance recently have been reviewed by Asmus and Campos (1983) and Petri (1987). Stratigraphic data have been derived from subsurface surveys and surface mapping, principally conducted by Petrobras. Earlier studies focused mainly on surface outcrops and were enhanced during the 1960's and 1970's by systematic borehole and seismic surveys (with more than 500 on- and offshore drilling operations). Many sedimentary basins containing important Cretaceous sequences were discovered, particularly in offshore localities. Each of these basins has been named and its stratigraphic sequence described, and it is now possible to begin making interbasinal comparisons and tentative correlations. A number of these sedimentary basins are discussed elsewhere in this book, so it is worthwhile reviewing the location and relative extent of the principal ones.

In very general terms, three different kinds of basinal structures contain Cretaceous sequences in Brazil. These are: (1) ancient inland basins of predominantly Paleozoic age, generally of great extent; (2) inland basins of Jurassic and/or Cretaceous age, of limited extent; and (3) marginal basins, partially or even completely offshore, and sometimes of considerable long-shore extent. Not all the basins fit neatly into one of these categories; an important exception occurs just to the south of the Araripe basin, south of the Pernambuco lineament, where there is a basinal complex trending north-south for several hundred kilometers from its inland northerly extremity to its marginal southern part. The complexities of this particular area have been the focus of some attention in recent years, and an interesting geological picture has emerged that bears upon the history of the nearby Araripe basin (see below).

Three gigantic Paleozoic basins of the Brazilian interior (the Paraná, Parnaiba, and Amazonas basins) evidently were inactive for much of the early Mesozoic era, but sections of them became reactivated as centers of sedimentary accumulation during the Cretaceous. To the south is the enormous Paraná basin, stretching from southern Mato Grosso in the north and across the borders of Paraguay, Argentina, and Uruguay in the southwest. This basin contains a Lower Cretaceous series of basaltic volcanic rocks (Serra Geral) above which is a sedimentary sequence from the Aptian/Albian to the Maestrichtian.

The Parnaiba (or Maranhão) basin to the northeast contains a temporally more restricted Cretaceous sequence, including a small basaltic lava flow associated with Lower Cretaceous sediments whose age probably ranges from the Neocomian to the Cenomanian. The northerly limit of this basin is today close to the coastline, but it probably extended into Africa (in the vicinity of Accra) prior to continental breakup (Popoff, 1988, fig. 5).

Farther west is the east-west trending Amazonas basin, extending from the mouth of the Amazon River toward the interior. Only one Cretaceous formation (of Albian-Cenomanian age) has been noted.

The entire Brazilian coastline is fringed with Cretaceous marginal basins. From south to north the main ones have been named as follows; Pelotas, Florianopolis, Santos, Campos, Espirito Santo, Almada, Camamu, Recôncavo, Sergipe-Alagoas, Cabo, Potiguar, Ceará, Barreirinhas, São Luis, and Amazonas Mouth. There are numerous smaller intervening basins (for further information, see Petri, 1987). Most of these basins first developed during the Cretaceous period or slightly earlier, and some (e.g., Cabo) had a short depositional history.

There are volcanic basalts at the base of the Cretaceous sequence in all the more southerly basins (e.g., Pelotas, Florianopolis, Santos, Campos, Espirito Santo). These volcanics are broadly time-equivalent with each other and with basalts in the Paraná basin, dating from between 130 and 105 million years before present. The volcanic activity responsible for these lavas is related to early rifting between Africa and South America, but in some if not all cases represent terrestrial lava flows upon Precambrian basement rocks and not true oceanic basalts (Asmus and Guazelli, 1981).

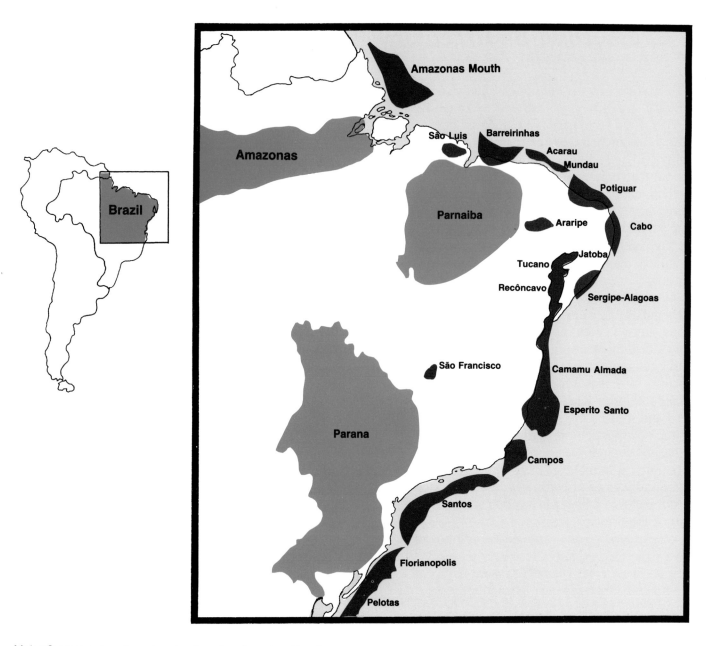

Major Cretaceous sedimentary basins of northeastern Brazil.

Few Brazilian basins have much pre-Aptian sediment. Virtually all of them have sequences of Aptian, Albian, and/or Cenomanian age, although in some cases the sedimentary interval is very restricted. In relatively few cases is it possible to demonstrate time equivalence by paleontological means, and volcanic rocks (from which radiometric dates are readily obtained) are known in very few areas. A broad, tectonically-based lithostratigraphic system of correlation has been attempted (Asmus, 1975; Ponte and Asmus, 1976, 1978), with questionable results (see the chapter "Zonation of the Brazilian Lower Cretaceous").

The number of inland Cretaceous sedimentary basins is low in comparison with marginal ones. Only one (the São Francisco) is located to the south, and its Cretaceous sequence consists mostly of terrestrial sediments, alkaline volcanic rocks, and ashes (dated at some time in the Upper Cretaceous). In the northeast there is a semi-continuous series of small basins extending northward from Salvador (Bahia) and including the Tucano and Jatoba basins. The latter is separated from the Araripe basin to its north by the Pernambuco lineament (i.e., the terminal part of a transform fault). The earlier (Jurassic) history of these basins probably was similar, but differed somewhat during the Lower Cretaceous. Nevertheless, all of them were undoubtedly affected by tectonic activity during the final stages of separation between South America and Africa toward the end of the Lower Cretaceous. It is even possible that the Reĉoncavo-Tucano-Jatoba and Araripe basins are vestiges of a failed rift system that began to develop in response to the separation from Africa.

One additional Brazilian basin deserves mention, although its tectonic and sedimentary histories are unique and only distantly related to events along the eastern seabord. The Acre basin appeared during the Cenomanian and Turonian in western Brazil. It was an open marginal basin with westward connections to the Pastanza basin of Peru and the Oriente basin of Ecuador (Petri, 1987: 145).

It is fairly obvious that global tectonic events responsible for the separation of South America and Africa had a profound impact on the geology of Brazil, not only along its entire coast but also inland, within ancient sedimentary basins and at new sites between. Recent geophysical investigations have demonstrated important links between subsurface features related to crustal movements and the sedimentary history of overlying basins. Perhaps the best documented examples are the Sergipe-Alagoas and Recôncavo-Tucano-Jatoba basins. The latter have recently been reinterpreted as half-graben (rift valley) structures similar to those forming today in eastern Africa (Magnavita and Cupertino, 1988). These asymmetrical graben have a major fault system at their steeper margin, with faults cutting through the sedimentary deposits. Crustal stretching increased the downthrow on the major faults. The basins were infilled initially by coarser sediments, then by swamps and small lakes that locally became very deep. Gradually the basins were filled and the rate of subsidence slowed and was overtaken by the rate of sedimentation. Within the Recôncavo-Tucano-Jatoba basinal complex, several sub-basins now are recognized (e.g., north, central, and south Tucano), each with its own stratigraphic sequence. Precise correlation between each sequence within such tectonic settings may not be possible because of differences in timing and rates of subsidence and in supply of sediments (Rosendahl, et al., 1986).

North of the Patos lineament another series of fault-controlled half-grabens is represented by a series of minor sedimentary basins trending NE-SW and N-S (e.g., Rio de Peixe, Iguatu, Souza, and Pombal; Brito Neves, 1983). These basins again contain basal conglomerates followed by fluviatile and lacustrine sediments of Lower Cretaceous (Neocomian to Aptian) age.

Between the Patos and Pernambuco lineaments lies the Araripe basin. It is regarded as having formed within another half-graben, downthrown to the south of the Patos lineament. Its Mesozoic sedimentary sequence is evocative of that seen in adjacent basins, with a lower conglomeratic sequence (Brejo-Santo Formation, perhaps of Upper Jurassic age), followed by fine-grained sediments including clays, marls, and limestones of lacustrine origin (Silva, 1986a), evaporites, and finally fluviatile sandstones (Exu formation, of Albian age). Although its lower sediments can be correlated well with others in the Recôncavo basin farther south, the Cretaceous history of the Araripe basin is separate from that of the Recôncavo-Tucano-Jatoba basins to the south and the minor sedimentary basins to the north, again creating difficulties in precise correlation.

(J. G. Maisey)

6: Succession Within the Araripe Basin

The Araripe basin today contains approxiately 700 m of a Mesozoic sedimentary sequence thought to be of Upper Jurassic and Lower Cretaceous age. There is controversy in the literature concerning the actual age of the sediments and considerable disagreement over how it should be subdivided stratigraphically (Small, 1913; Beurlen, 1962, 1963, 1971; Moraes, et al., 1963; Braun, 1966; Silva Santos and Valença, 1968; Mabesoone and Tinoco, 1973; Moraes, et al., 1975; Moraes, et al., 1976; Scheid, et al., 1978; Oliveira, et al., 1979; M. R. de Lima, 1979; Silva, 1983, 1986a, 1986b).

The Mesozoic sequence within the Araripe basin can be divided into two parts. The lowest of these (the Brotas group) has an unconformable relationship with the Paleozoic and Precambrian basement and also with overlying younger sediments. Generally accepted as being Jurassic in age (although a Lower Cretaceous age is now being suggested), the rocks of the Brotas group (mostly consisting of interbedded shales and sandstones) are divided into the Alianca formation below and the Sergi formation above.

The Crato member (Araripina formation as defined by Silva, 1986b) lies unconformably on the Brotas group and consists of black shales overlain by laminated limestone and dolostone, algal-laminated shale, and an evaporite sequence (gypsum and anhydrite). Its upper surface is truncated by a regional disconformity, the nature of which varies across the basin. To the north and east there is a calcrete layer, comprising a calcareous and siliceous crust with chert nodules and laminae. In places the surface is slightly brecciated. Silva (1986a) found many lithological similarities with calcrete profiles described by Watts (1978) from the Quaternary of the Kalahari Desert and Permo-Triassic of Scotland, and concluded that the Crato member calcrete is a caliche layer. At Barbalha, it is overlain by a 1-m-thick conglomerate marking the local base of the Romualdo member.

To the south and west the erosional surface at the top of the Crato member has been interpreted by Silva as a paleokarst topography (e.g., in the vicinity of Rancharia-Araripina and Trindade-Ipubi). Solution cavities several meters deep are developed, some of which were connected to subsurface caverns before beng infilled by muds belonging to the Romualdo member of the Santana formation. Some investigators now question Silva's interpretation and have expressed doubt that the "karst" features are of such antiquity.

The Romualdo member forms a conspicuous series of alternating layered concretionary-calcareous shales, limestone, and sandstone. It lies unconformably on the Crato member formation and locally overlaps onto the Paleozoic and Precambrian basement (e.g., near Rancharia, 1.5 km south of Araripina).

THE AGE OF THE ARARIPE GROUP

Earlier investigators (e.g., Agassiz, 1844b; Woodward, 1887, 1890b, 1895, 1901; Jordan and Branner, 1908; Beurlen, 1962) believed that the stratigraphic sequence in question was of Upper Cretaceous age. Silva Santos and Valença (1968) conducted a qualitative comparison of fossil fishes from the Araripe basin and determined that these showed closest similarities with other Lower Cretaceous (Aptian) faunas (see earlier section in this book).

This age determination has been confirmed from fossil ostracods (Braun, 1966) that correlate well with those of Aptian age from the coastal Sergipe-Alagoas basin (Krömmelbein, 1965a; Krömmelbein and Wenger, 1966; Viana, 1966). Palynological data, although incomplete, also confirm the age of at least part of the Araripe sequence. The upper part of the Santana formation and the overlying Exu formation have yielded pollen that suggests an Albian age (Mabesoone and Tinoco, 1973; M. R. de Lima, 1978a, 1978b, 1978c, 1979a, 1979b, 1980). According to Prof. G. Brenner (pers. comm.), of the State University of New York (New Paltz), a Middle Albian age for the Exu formation is suggested by certain polycolpate pollen (e.g., *Galeacornea causea*). Tricolpate pollen (indicative of early angiosperms) has been recovered from both the Santana and Exu formations. Doyle, et al. (1982) provided additional palynological data from a sample of the Santana formation, concluding that it contained a diverse association of angiosperm pollen characteristic of their Zone C-IX of Gabon and with the more northerly (equatorial?) palynofloras of Maranhão, the Ivory Coast, Senegal, and South Atlantic salt basins. The C-IX Zone of Doyle, et al., (1982, fig. 7) falls entirely within the Upper Aptian stage of the Lower Cretaceous. Unfortunately, detailed palynological data for the Crato member formation have not been published, and its age remains enigmatic. It almost certainly pre-dates the Upper Aptian, but by how much is not clear. Polycolpate pollen like those of modern Gnetales were reported by Mabesoone and Tinoco (1973). These are recorded as far back as the Permian, but increase rapidly in abundance and diversity from the Lower Barremian (Lower Cretaceous). Very tentatively, therefore, this suggests a maximum age of Lower Barremian for the Crato member. According to Silva (1983, 1986a), however, the erosional phase leading to karstification and caliche formation may have been transitory, lasting only a few thousand years. In this case, the Crato member also may be of Aptian age.

(J. G. Maisey)

7: Zonation of the Brazilian Lower Cretaceous

Brito (1984) regarded the Romualdo member of the Santana formation as one of several Brazilian sedimentary sequences marking a transition from the local "Alagoan stage" (Brito and Campos, 1982) to the Upper Aptian (an internationally recognized time period). Other Brazilian sequences of comparable age would include the Codo formation (Parnaiba basin), Riachuelo and Muribeca formations (Sergipe-Alagoas basin), and Marizal formation (Recôncavo basin).

The fossil aspidorhynchid fish *Vinctifer* (described later in this volume) has been recorded in all of these sedimentary sequences, and Brito (1984) has proposed a *"Vinctifer* biozone" to mark this "Alagoan"-Aptian transition. Another fish, the small gonorynchiform *Dastilbe* (also described later in this book), occurs in many of these sequences but has not yet been reported from the Riachuelo formation. It apparently is absent from the fish assemblages in concretions from the Romualdo member of the Santana formation, although it is abundant in the underlying lacustrine Crato member. *Cladocyclus* occurs in all but the Codo formation, and various other fishes are common to two or more of these formations (Brito, 1984).

At first glance, therefore, the *"Vinctifer* biozone" appears to be founded upon a reasonable premise that the included formations are broadly time-equivalent. Unfortunately, however, detailed examination of the evidence reveals that critical data are unknown or ambiguous in some of the deposits that have yielded *Vinctifer*. These shortcomings not only render the validity of the *"Vinctifer* biozone" doubtful, but they also cast a shadow on any broad tectonic chronology founded upon the putative biostratigraphic scheme proposed by Brito and Campos (1982).

The overriding difficulty in establishing regional or even local geochronologies for the Cretaceous strata of Brazil is related to rifting between the Brazilian and African plates (Brito and Campos, 1982, 1983; Asmus and Campos, 1983; Brito, 1984). Rapid and often profound regional environmental changes evidently took place in response to tectonic events associated with this rifting. Approximately a dozen tectonically controlled sedimentary basins were active around the margins of what is now Brazil, according to Asmus and Campos (1983), while at least three others (the Parnaiba, Araripe, and São Franciso basins) were located farther inland.

In general, the tectonic and sedimentological history of each of these basins is thought to have been similar, with an initial continental phase, followed by a lacustrine episode, then by evaporites (usually regarded as having formed within a gulf or restricted ocean), ultimately followed by a fully marine phase. Only this last episode has been reliably correlated outside Brazil. By and large, the paleontological record of the earlier (continental, lacustrine, epeiric) lithofacies has not been stratigraphically informative, outside of providing local (i.e., intrabasinal) correlations. In consequence, biostratigraphic data essentially are unavailable for much of this critical period in Brazilian crustal evolution. Furthermore, only in some (especially the more southerly) marginal basins (e.g., Pelotas-Florianopolis, Santos, Campos, Espirito Santos) are any volcanic rocks associated with the sediments. Many of these volcanics date from only about 40-90 million years ago and are associated with linear crustal fractures related to contemporaneous rifting in the South Atlantic (Asmus and Campos, 1983). Other volcanics, for example those within the older sediments of the Santos basin, have been regarded as synchronous with thick basalt lavas of the interior Paraná basin (dated at between 105-130 M.Y.B.P.; Asmus and Campos, 1983). Absolute chronological data are otherwise unavailable, particularly in the northeasterly basins, although there was a short-lived volcanic episode in the vicinity of Recife around Albian and Cenomanian times.

Despite the absence of satisfactory stratigraphic information, some attempts at regional correlation have been made. Asmus and Ponte (1973) recognized three informal lithostratigraphic "units" (i.e., facies) within many Cretaceous basins across Brazil. A lower "continental sequence," a middle "evaporitic sequence," and an upper "marine sequence" supposedly could be recognized in almost all the Brazilian marginal basins. Following the publication of essentially speculative contributions by Dickinson (1974) and Falvey (1974) concerning the development of continental margins, Asmus (1975) and Ponte and Asmus (1976, 1978) elaborated on the possibility that corresponding lithofacies in adjacent Brazilian basins were isochronous and attempted to tie these facies in with pre-rift, proto-oceanic, and oceanic phases of contemporaneous tectonism.

Brito and Campos (1982) went so far as to formalize these putative sequential tectonic episodes by designating them as chronostratigraphic stages. Their earliest (continental) phase, typically represented by the Alianca and Sergi formations of the Recôncavo basin, became known as the "Donjoanian stage." Next they recognized an essentially lacustrine phase (represented by the Recôncavo and Bahia beds and perhaps by the Crato member of the Santana formation), which they termed the "Bahian stage." This supposedly was followed by the "Alagoan stage," supposedly representing a time of restricted marine ingression within an epeiric gulf or inlet, such that poor circulation and relatively high evaporation resulted in the accumulation of gypsiferous salt deposits. Toward the end of this putative episode, environmental conditions were thought to have ameliorated to permit the establishment of rich aquatic and terrestrial vertebrate faunas (e.g., those represented by fossil assemblages in the Muribeca and Riachuelo formations of the Sergipe-Alagoas basin, and in the Romualdo member of the Santana formation of the Araripe basin). The final marine stage is the only one that has been satisfactorily correlated to an international time-scale, mainly on the basis of ammonites. These occur mostly in the northeastern marginal basins and are essentially post-Aptian.

Although Santana-like species of fossil fishes occur in several other Brazilian Cretaceous basins, in only one case has the local succession also yielded a stratigraphically informative ammonite sample. This is from the upper part of the Riachuelo formation, in the Sergipe-Alagoas basin (Hartt, 1870; Hyatt, 1875; White, 1887; Maury, 1934, 1936; Beurlen, 1961, 1970;

Bengtson, 1979; Brito, 1984). Four Lower Cretaceous ammonite biozones have been distinguished in this basin (Beurlen, 1961). The Upper, Middle, and Lower Albian are convincingly represented by three biozones (*Mortoniceras-Alobiceras, Oxytropidoceras,* and *Douvilleiceras,* respectively), below which is a doubtful record of *Cheloniceras* (an Upper Aptian indicator, corroborated by foraminiferan and calcareous nannoplankton data; Brito, 1984). Below this level, unfortunately, no further ammonite data are available (Brito and Campos, 1983). Silva Santos (1981) recorded the presence of *Vinctifer, Rhacolepis, Tharrhias, Cladocyclus,* and probably *Notelops, Letolepis,* and *"Microdon"* from calcareous sediments considered to be an integral part of the Riachuelo formation. Furthermore, he advocated that these taxa were conspecific with those from the Santana formation, although he gave no further details. According to Brito (1984), these fishes occur below the ammonite and foraminiferal levels within the Riachuelo formation, although Silva Santos (1981) stated that: "Estão associados com ammonoides, principalmente, ocorrendo, também, alguns gastrópodes e pelecípodes." ["They are associated with ammonoids, mainly, together with some gastropods and pelecypods."] Whatever the case, the Riachuelo formation fossil assemblage probably predates the Upper Aptian stage, albeit by an unknown interval.

Above the Aptian strata, ammonite and foraminiferal biozones have been identified in various Brazilian marginal basins (especially the more northerly ones) for the Lower, Middle, and Upper Albian; Cenomanian; Lower, Middle, and Upper Turonian; Coniacian; Santonian; Campanian; and Maestrichtian stages (Bengtson, 1983; Brito and Campos, 1983). By Aptian and Albian times, boreal and tethyan ammonoid realms no longer were distinct (Rawson, 1980). Moreover, the West African/Brazilian area was a center of endemism for some Albian ammonoid taxa (e.g., *Elobiceras, Neokentroceras, Angolaites;* Kennedy and Cobban, 1976). These two factors have hampered attempts to determine whether the earliest influx of ammonites was the consequence of a boreal or tethyan connection, although subsequent (Cenomanian-Coniacian) ammonites suggest tethyan affinity (Bengtson, 1983).

According to the ostracod data (Grekoff and Krömmelbein, 1967), the Bahia series (and therefore by definition part of the "middle evaporitic sequence" of Asmus and Ponte, 1973, and "Bahian stage" of Brito and Campos, 1982) is of Neocomian age. This determination appears to contradict the admittedly poor palynological data for the supposedly contemporaneous Crato member of the Santana formation (thought to be Aptian, and certainly not older than the Lower Barremian; see above). Otherwise (assuming for the moment that the "Bahian stage" represents a true chronostratigraphic interval), early Cretaceous gnetale radiation must be assumed to have occurred sooner in the Gondwanan equatorial region than is otherwise accepted.

The Bahian beds (essentially freshwater or brackish) of the Bahia and Sergipe-Alagoas basins contain a "Wealden"-like molluscan and ostracod assemblage (Hartt, 1870; Schaller, 1969), but this helps very little since the "Wealden" may extend from the Berriasian to the Aptian stage, spanning some 30 million years. It nevertheless ties in with available ammonite data suggesting that the Sergipe-Alagoas fossil fish assemblage, with its supposed similarities to that of the Santana formation, loosely occupies some time in the Cretaceous period prior to the Upper Aptian stage. But it is far from settled whether similar fossil fish assemblages in the different marginal basins of Brazil (or West Africa) are contemporaneous, or even if the same species are present.

For fossils to serve effectively as a means to define a range zone (acrozone) or even more broadly as an assemblage (faunal) zone, they must necessarily meet certain requirements, including:

1) the fossils should be widely distributed geographically;
2) the temporal duration (and thus stratigraphic distribution) of the zone fossil species should be defined by both an upper and a lower limit and preferably should be short;
3) status as an acrozone or faunal zone should be firmly established (e.g., by stratigraphic congruence with other zones).

In the case of the "Vinctifer biozone," only the first of these criteria is met, but then only with some qualifications. Vinctifer comptoni so far has been discovered in only some northeastern marginal basins, limiting its value as a correlative tool. Another aspidorhynchid species, Belonostomus (?) carinatus (dubiously founded upon some rhombic ganoid scales: Mawson and Woodward, 1907, pl. vi, figs. 4, 5), is recorded from strata of Neocomian age near Bahia (Hartt, 1870; Grekoff and Krömmelbein, 1967). At the generic level, Vinctifer is an unsatisfactory zone fossil, since it can be distinguished from Belonostomus and Aspidorhynchus by only a few morphological characters. Using Vinctifer comptoni itself as a marker seems to offer little advantage; its lower range limit has not been determined, it has yet to be distinguished from B. carinatus, and it is endemic to only some of the Brazilian basins. These criticisms may not preclude using V. comptoni as a local stratigraphic indicator, within its region of endemism, but its value as a datum line for international correlation or even within Brazil itself is doubtful. Brito's (1984) claim that the "Vinctifer biozone" represents a passage from a local stage (Alagoan) to an international one (Upper Aptian) therefore must be treated with caution.

As far as the other criteria for zone fossils are concerned, there is little to inspire confidence in this case. As already discussed, an upper limit (pre-Upper Aptian) to the Vinctifer acrozone has been established in only the Sergipe-Alagoas and Araripe basins, and a lower limit has not been determined at all. Thus the temporal duration of Vinctifer is unknown, and congruence between the "Vinctifer biozone" and other (international) zones has not been properly demonstrated. Even if it eventually should be shown that the distribution of Vinctifer is isochronous with established international zones (e.g., those based on Aptian and Albian ammonites determined in the Sergipe-Alagoas basin), all that would have been determined is its pre-Upper Albian age.

Turning next to the validity of the regional chronostratigraphic zonation presented by Brito and Campos (1982), the occurrence of Vinctifer is again of critical importance. As a zone fossil it ought to be confined to the latter part of their "Alagoan stage" throughout the Brazilian Cretaceous, within aquatic facies transitional to the fully marine Upper Aptian. Nevertheless, Vinctifer occurs below an evaporite sequence in the Codo formation of the Parnaiba basin (Brito, 1984), which logically ought to place Vinctifer low in the "Alagoan" or even within the "Bahian" stage of Brito and Campos (1982). Within the Sergipe-Alagoas basin, Vinctifer occurs in both the Riachuelo and underlying Muribeca formations. Brito (1984, p. 90) has suggested that the Muribeca ichthyofauna "could probably be correlated with the Dastilbe level of the Santana formation." However, this level (the Araripina formation of Silva, 1983, 1986a, 1986b; = Crato member of others) occurs below the Vinctifer-bearing Santana formation, an unconformity, and a 30 m evaporite sequence, again implying that Vinctifer extends below the "Alagoan" and into the "Bahian" stage of Brito and Campos (1982).

To conclude, it is difficult to reconcile the concept of a *"Vinctifer* biozone" with the lithostratigraphic divisions proposed by Brito and Campos (1982) from the limited data available at present. It of course is possible that their "stages" are local reflections of a regional tectonic trend associated with rifting of the South Atlantic, developed diachronously within individual marginal basins. This would explain the seemingly disjunct temporal distribution of similar Late Mesozoic fossil fish assemblages in different parts of Brazil. Given the choice of biostratigraphic or lithostratigraphic data in order to formulate a chronological sequence, most stratigraphers probably would opt for the former. In this particular case, however, there may be little to choose between these alternatives, because the *"Vinctifer* biozone" has poorly defined limits and the alternative lithostratigraphic divisions are tectonically controlled. At present, these data seem contradictory and incompatible. The tectonic histories of individual sedimentary basins during this critical phase in the final dismemberment of Gondwanaland undoubtedly are complex and varied. Correlations of Late Mesozoic continental, lacustrine, and epeiric facies as broader isochronous "stages" may result in only an oversimplified picture of events. The separation of South America from Africa was a heterochronous event occupying much of the Lower Cretaceous, and it is reasonable to expect heterochroneity between similar lithofacies occurring in different parts of the region within that broad time-period.

(J. G. Maisey)

8: Paleogeography of the Araripe Basin

The present knowledge of the paleoichthyofauna of the Santana formation as well as other Lower Cretaceous geological formations in Brazil (mainly in the northeastern region) allows a reconstruction of the paleogeography of the Ariripe basin relative to other sedimentary basins of that region.

The Araripe plateau, situated in the region along the border between the states of Ceará and Pernambuco, has been the subject of geological investigations since the last century. In the beginning of the second decade of the 20th century, in 1913, Horatio L. Small, in a detailed geological study of that region, defined a series of almost horizontal layers of conglomerates and sandstone in that region, below which predominately calcareous rocks are found, including shales with calcareous concretions, siltstones, evaporites (gypsite), laminated limestones, and bituminous shales, all overlying the crystalline basement.

This sedimentary sequence, known today as the Araripe series, later was studied by various other geologists who confirmed Small's observations and recognized four geological formations: the upper sandstones of Small—Exu formation; the calcareous sequence—Santana formation; the sandstones just below calcareous rocks—Missao Velha formation; and the basal conglomeratic arenites—Cariri formation.

The Santana formation is the most fossiliferous, and in its sediments (especially in the calcareous concretions) are found many fossil fishes. The evaporites represent a stratigraphic horizon of great importance for paleoecological interpretations of the Araripe basin.

The Araripe basin does not represent, as previously thought, a unique occurrence in the geological Brazilian panorama. The wider distribution of the fossil fishes of the Santana formation refutes the hypothesis that the Araripe region was an isolated intracontinental basin. Some ichthyological components found in this formation are present in other Brazilian sedimentary basins of the same geological age, which makes us conclude that there has been some communication between the Araripe basin and these other basins. A paleogeographic relationship therefore can be proposed from Araripe to the west with the Parnaiba (= Maranhão) basin, in the state of Maranhão, at the time of deposition of the Codo formation; to the south with the Recôncavo and Tucano basins, in the state of Bahia, at the time of deposition respectively of the Marfim formation (Ilhas group) and Marizal formation; and to the Atlantic coast with the Sergipe-Alagoas basin respectively related to the Riachuelo formation (Mearim member), in the state of Sergipe, and in the Muribeca formation, in the state of Alagoas.

A communication of the Araripe basin northwards with the Chapada do Apodi in the Potiguar basin, in Rio Grande do Norte, is no longer plausible given that the Apodi Cretaceous sequence began its deposition much after the Aptian.

The communication of the Araripe basin with the Parnaiba basin is impressive both paleontologically and lithologically. The stratigraphic profile of the Codo formation, which also includes evaporites (gypsite), agrees with the profile of the Santana formation. The fish assemblage includes several species found in that formation and, what is more noteworthy, the fishes are preserved in calcareous concretions similar to those found in the Santana formation. The fishes identified in the Codo formation are: *Araripelepidotes temnurus* (Agassiz); *Leptolepis diasii* Silva Santos; *Cladocyclus gardneri* Agassiz; *Dastilbe elongatus* Silva Santos; *Tharrhias araripis* Jordan and Branner; *Brannerion vestitum* Jordan and Branner; *Rhacolepis buccalis* Agassiz; and *Knightia carnavali* Silva Santos. This last species is a clupeid not yet identified among Araripe ichthyolites (Silva Santos, 1985a).

The occurrence of coelacanthid remains identified as *Mawsonia* cf. *gigas* Woodward in the Chapada do Araripe (Maisey, 1986) strenghthens the idea of a southward link with the Marfim formation (Ilhas group) of the Recôncavo basin, where remains of *Cladocyclus* are also found (Silva Santos, 1949). Remains of an ophiopsid (*Ophiopsis longipectoralis* Silva

Santos), an amiid (*Amiidarum* sp.), an aspidorhynchid (*Vinctifer longirostris* Silva Santos), an ichthyodectid (*Cladocyclus* sp.), a clupeid (*Clupavus braziliensis* Silva Santos), and a gonorynchiform (*Dastilbe elongatus* Silva Santos) were found in Aptian sediments of the Marizal formation of the Tucano basin (Silva Santos, 1972).

A paleogeographic relationship between the Araripe basin eastwards and the Sergipe-Alagoas basin recently was shown with the discovery of several Araripian fish genera and species in the sedimentary rocks of the Riachuelo formation (Mearim member), in Sergipe State. *Vinctifer comptoni* (Agassiz), *Rhacolepis buccalis* Agassiz, *Notelops brama* (Agassiz), *Tharrhias araripis* Jordan and Branner, *Cladocyclus gardneri* Agassiz, and *Neoproscinetes penalvai* (Silva Santos, 1985e) were identified in the rocks of this formation in sediments and calcareous concretions associated with small ammonoids (Silva Santos, 1985e). The presence of *Vinctifer*, *Cladocyclus*, *Dastilbe*, and *Knightia* (Schaeffer, 1947; Silva Santos, 1976, 1985a) from the Sergipe-Alagoas basin in bituminous sediments confirms the possibility that this basin has been connected with not only the Araripe basin but also with the Recôncavo-Tucano and Parnaiba basins.

Dastilbe Jordan was a gonorynchiform of wide distribution in Brazil during the Aptian. This genus, sometimes represented by the same species, is present in almost all the basins mentioned. In the Araripe basin its remains are said to be found both in concretions and laminated limestones that supposedly were deposited in fresh or brackish water facies of the Santana formation. This fish, possibly of euryhaline habits, was perfectly adaptable to freshwater environments, in view of its presence in bituminous shales and arenites of the Areado formation in the small inland São Francisco basin in the western part of Minas Gerais State in southeastern Brazil (Silva Santos, 1985f).

The Aptian age attributed to the Araripe fossils (Silva Santos and Valença, 1968) is corroborated mainly by paleobotanical discoveries. Among the plant remains found among sediments (concretions, laminar limestone, and shales) of the Santana formation, gymnosperm remains of the genus *Brachyphylum* Brongniart, an Aptian age species, deserve notice. These gymnosperms are present not only in the sediments of the Araripe basin, but also in other Brazilian sedimentary basins. *Brachyphylum obesum* Heer, originally described from the Aptian of Portugal, also was identified

in the Araripe (Duarte, 1985a). This species of *Brachyphylum* also occurs in Aptian sediments of the Marizal formation (Tucano basin) and Areado formation (São Francisco basin) (Duarte, 1985b). In the Riachuelo formation, *Brachyphylum corallinum* Heer (also from the Aptian of Portugal), was identified together with fish remains (Duarte, 1989).

The great resemblance between *Mawsonia* fossils from the Santana formation of Araripe and the Marfim (Ilhas group, Recôncavo basin, Bahia State) suggests, according to Maisey (1986: 28), that part of the sediments of that formation could have been deposited during the Neocomian. The ichthyofauna of the Marfim formation includes coelacanthids (*Mawsonia gigas = M. minor*), semionotids (*Lepidotes roxoi* Silva Santos and *Lepidotes mawsoni* Woodward), an amiid (*Amiidarum mawsoni* [Woodward]), ichthyodectids (*Cladocyclus mawsoni* [Cope] and *Itaparica woodwardi* [Silva Santos]), and clupeids (*Diplomystus longicaustatus* Cope and *Scutatuspinosus itapagipensis* Silva Santos and Correa) (Schaeffer, 1947; Silva Santos, 1949, 1953, 1986; Silva Santos and Correa, 1985).

The clupeids of the Marfim formation (Ilhas group) are not completely studied but are similar to species that occur in the Aptian of the Muribeca formation in the Sergipe-Alagoas basin. *Cladocyclus alagoensis* (also from the Muribeca formation) seems to be a synonym of *Cladocyclus mawsoni* of the Marfim formation, Recôncavo basin (Silva Santos, 1949).

Geologic and paleontologic structural particularities, consequently, make us admit that the links among the basins discussed above have been the result of marine transgression begun in the Neocomian and extending through the Aptian, from the eastern coast of the South Atlantic toward the region of the Tucano basin, extending through the Araripe up to the Parnaiba basin. The Potiguar basin, in spite of lithological similarities with the Araripe basin in terms of its evaporite sedimentary sequence (gypsite) and (muddy) limestone, is independent in its paleontological characters. The marine ingression in the Potiguar basin occurred during the Turonian, that is, in a later geological period than the other basins of the northeastern region.

(R. da Silva Santos, translated by M. de Pinna)

GEOLOGICAL SECTION SHOWING ARARIPE PLATEAU'S STRUCTURE (cf. Small, 1913)

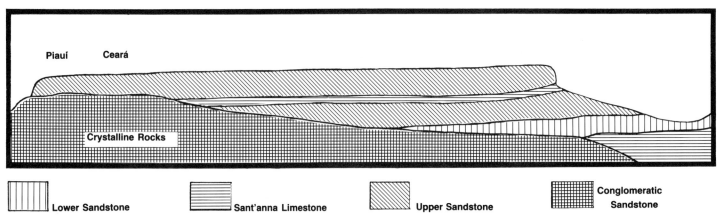

Piauí   Ceará

Crystalline Rocks

Lower Sandstone   Sant'anna Limestone   Upper Sandstone   Conglomeratic Sandstone

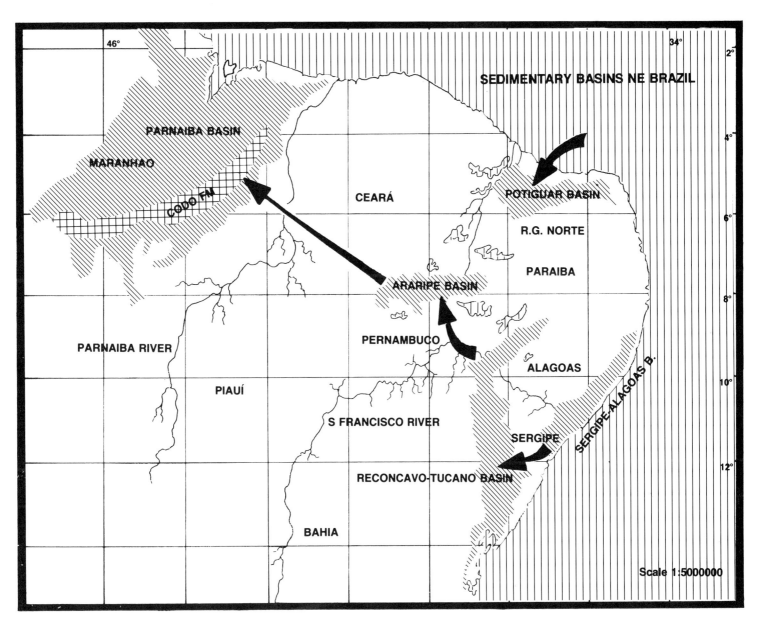

Possible Lower Cretaceous communications (arrowed)
between the Parnaiba, Santana, Recôncavo, and
Sergipe-Alagoas basins discussed in the text.

9: An Ocean is Formed

The Emerging Picture

The final stages in the disintegration of Gondwanaland, involving the separation of South America from Africa, have been studied intensively by geologists over the past two decades. Much remains to be learned, but we now are able to at least formulate appropriate questions to ask concerning this major event in Earth history. To what extent can local sedimentary sequences be accurately correlated, both within and between sedimentary basins? How do these lithological sequences relate to geological events responsible for the separation of the continents? Can these events and their impact upon the stratigraphic column be combined in such a way as to create a "big picture" overview of the geological history in this region of the globe?

A geological history of the South Atlantic was presented by Simpson (1977) as part of a series of Alex du Toit Memorial Lectures. Many aspects of Simpson's synthesis have not been surpassed, and it represents a seminal effort to condense a vast quantity of geological data into a few lucid pages. Subsequent research has permitted certain hypotheses presented in that work to be tested and refined, and an updated paleogeographic history of the South Atlantic has been presented by Reyment and Dingle (1987).

In Brazil a great deal of geophysical and geological research has been conducted within the marginal basins of Cretaceous age. Using these data, Petri (1987) has produced a synoptic sketch of the Cretaceous paleogeographic history of Brazil. Drawing upon these and other reports, the following section is an attempt to place the Araripe fossil occurrences within a simplified paleogeographic scenario for the final break-up of the ancient Gondwana supercontinent.

Early Events: The North Atlantic

Separation of Africa from eastern North America had already commenced some 40 or 50 million years previously, probably during what is known as the Callovian stage of the Jurassic period (around 160 million years ago). This event has important consequences upon aspects of the scenario presented below, and it is worthwhile for the reader to become familiarized with the broad outlines of North Atlantic history during the Cretaceous period with which we are primarily concerned.

The southeasterly margins of the North Atlantic were effectively defined from Gibraltar to the equatorial Atlantic by Upper Jurassic times, and the North Atlantic has continued to widen ever since. By the time South America began to separate from Africa, the North Atlantic already was well developed. Its late Jurassic southeasterly margin extended essentially from western Venezuela to near the present-day mouth of the Amazon, then turned northward, taking in the western coast of Africa north of Sierra Leone.

Throughout the early Cretaceous, the margins of present-day equatorial Africa and northern Brazil remained in close proximity but behaved as two separate masses rotating and moving laterally past each other. As this relative plate motion continued, a southeasterly embayment of the North Atlantic appears to have extended farther between them as a narrow inlet. By late Aptian times its easternmost limit lay to the north of Fortaleza or Natal, although during the succeeding Albian stage there is evidence that this seaway was temporarily closed farther west as Surinam and French Guiana collided with Liberia and the Ivory Coast.

The earliest evidence of an open seaway to the South Atlantic dates from the late Albian stage of the Cretaceous period, with periodic exchange of surface waters in what has now become the Niger Delta region. These exchanges were almost certainly intermittent at first, to judge from the sporadic occurrence of critical northerly zone fossils in marginal basins of the South Atlantic. By the Cenomanian stage, however, a permanent oceanic connection seems to have developed, helped in part by an important eustatic rise in sea level that caused repeated flooding by ocean waters across most of the Saharan region.

This transgressive episode reached an extreme by the close of the Cenomanian stage, when a narrow epicontinental seaway also extended from the eastern Mediterranean right across Africa to the Niger Delta region, where it met the narrow arms of the North and South Atlantic. The succeeding Turonian stage generally was marked by regression, so that the epicontinental seaway across Africa no longer was open at this northern end. By then, however, Africa and South America had become irreversibly separated by the equatorial Atlantic Ocean. It is important to realize the relative extent of the North Atlantic through the Lower Cretaceous. Up until the Cenomanian stage, the paleogeographic history of the more northerly Brazilian marginal basins (e.g., Ceará, Barreirinhas, São Luis, Amazonas Mouth) was inextricably bound to that of the North Atlantic. Those basins situated around Brazil's westerly and southerly margins (e.g., Sergipe-Alagoas, Recôncavo, Almada, Espirito Santo, Campos, Santos, Florianopolis, Pelotas) essentially reflect the early history of the western South Atlantic margin. Although the broad tectonic history of all the Brazilian basins is similar throughout the Cretaceous, their regional settings therefore may have been very different. A few basins (including the inland Araripe basin and the marginal Cabo and Potiguar basins) occupy a critical position midway between the maturing North and embryonic South Atlantic Oceans. The paleogeographic histories of these basins are among the most enigmatic, possibly as a consequence of their intermediate position.

The Afro-Brazilian Lake

During the late Jurassic and into the earliest Cretaceous, an inland lake system was developed within the rupture zone between Africa and South America, analogous to the modern Great Rift Valley of eastern Africa. Tensional stresses existed in the southern half of the region, although compressional stresses existed to the north, in what today would be the Gulf of Guinea. Popoff (1988) envisioned a series of austral, tropical, and equatorial tectonic domains with axial rifting propagated from south to north by successive reproduction of continental rifting-drifting processes in adjoining domains about every 20 million years during the Lower Cretaceous.

The areas surrounding the rift valley lakes evidently were well vegetated, and the lacustrine sediments are rich in pollen. Thick deposits of terrestrial sediments and lagoonal deposits accumulated in rift valleys from Liberia to Ghana and in the Recôncavo, Jatobá, and some northerly Brazilian basins. Farther southward there were extensive outpourings of basaltic lavas and minor alkaline volcanoes, particularly in the interior Paraná basin but also in the marginal Campos and Santos basins.

An extensive lake (termed the "Afro-Brazilian Lake" by Petri, 1987), shallow at first but becoming gradually deeper, extended during the earliest Cretaceous through the Recôncavo and Sergipe-Alagoas basins. Correlations outside the region are inexact but suggest that the lake existed from the Hauterivian stage of the Lower Cretaceous and deepened during the Barremian stage that followed. Scattered occurrences of gypsiferous salt deposits suggest that the lake periodically became hypersaline.

The earliest occurrence in Brazil of Cretaceous fishes similar to those from the Santana formation is from the state of Bahia, immediately north and west of Salvador (Carvalho, 1982). These fossils occur in the Ilhas group of the Bahia supergroup, at the southern end of the Recôncavo basin, and have been dated somewhat broadly as Neocomian.

The occurrence is interesting for at least two reasons. Firstly, the fossils include fishes closely related to those that occur in the much younger (Aptian-Albian) Santana formation, including *Cladocyclus*, "*Lepidotes*," *Mawsonia*, "*Belonostomus*," and "*Amiidarum*". There also are clupeoids (*Diplomystus*, *Scombroclupeoides*) and a hybodont shark ("*Acrodus*").

Secondly, the sedimentary sequence containing these fossils is essentially lacustrine, apparently originating within the southerly part of the Afro-Brazilian Lake. Dark, organic-rich mudstones were laid down in the deepest parts of the lake within a rift valley (graben) that was being deepened by activity along the Salvador fault system (Petri, 1987).

Stratigraphic evidence suggests that the Recôncavo limb of the Afro-Brazilian Lake ultimately was filled by the late Barremian or early Aptian stage. The lake probably persisted within the Sergipe-Alagoas basin until the end of the Aptian stage, although there was uplift and erosion here locally, as well as in the Recôncavo basin. It is possible that a drainage system persisted within the Recôncavo basin at this time, but there is no evidence. Fluvial deposits continued to form in the Parnaiba basin to the northwest of Araripe.

At this time there is no evidence of sedimentary deposition in the Araripe basin, which appears to have lain in an upland area to the north of the Recôncavo limb of the great Afro-Brazilian Lake and southeast of another lowland area of rivers and small lakes within the ancient interior Parnaiba basin. This more northerly basin apparently drained to the north (i.e., into an embayment of the North Atlantic), while the Afro-Brazilian lake evidently was controlled by southerly, rift-related tectonic events.

Paleogeographically, the Araripe region probably occupied a watershed during the earliest part of the Cretaceous period, and it may not be too much of an exaggeration to regard the area as part of a continental divide. Szatmari, et al. (1987) have presented a compelling argument that the principal axis of rotation between Africa and South America during the Neocomian stage was located almost exactly in the vicinity of the Araripe basin. To the west of this point the two continents were essentially in collision, which generated great compressional stresses along the northerly margins of Brazil, but to the southeast the continents were separating along a zone of tensional stresses. Popoff (1988) also argued for delayed continental rifting and drifting in the more northerly (equatorial) domain of the incipient South Atlantic.

The Great Drying

By the end of the Neocomian stage, the South Atlantic was represented by a narrow triangular ocean floor tapering northward approximately to the level of Recife and Cameroon, which at that time were probably less than 100 kilometers apart. To the extreme south lay a shallow-water barrier, the Falkland-Agulhas Rise, which had not yet become divided into separate platforms as occurs today. The Falkland-Agulhas barrier permitted surface water exchange but prevented the establishment of deep ocean circulation, which in turn led to the formation of a confined, anoxic deep-water basin extending northward from the Falkland Plateau to the Walvis Ridge and Rio Grande Rise. This second barrier traversed the developing southern ocean roughly at its center. To the south lay the deep anoxic ocean floor. North of the barrier was a fairly shallow sea, which for at least part of its existence seems to have been cut off from other oceanic waters by subaerial exposure of the Walvis and Rio Grande barriers. Extensive deposits of evaporitic salts were formed along the Brazilian margin from the Sergipe- Alagoas basins in the northeast to the Santos basin in the south.

An inevitable parallel has been drawn with the Messinian salinity event of the Mediterranean (Reyment and Dingle, 1987). There, in the early 1970's, scientists from the Lamont Geological Observatory of Columbia University encountered unmistakable evidence of desert conditions in core samples of Late Miocene age (between seven and ten million years old) taken from the floor of the Mediterranean. These sediments (including wind-blown sand dunes and salt deposits) were found over much of the Mediterranean floor, beneath younger marine sediments. According to current hypotheses, the Straits of Gibraltar became blocked, denying replenishment of oceanic water within the arid Mediterranean basin. River systems entering the Mediterranean Sea were simply unable to keep pace with evaporation rates, and the sea essentially dried up during what has become known as the Messinian event.

Could a similar catastrophic event have occurred in the northerly part of the South Atlantic during the Lower Cretaceous, about 100 million years before the Messinian event? Some scientists think not and have regarded the evaporite deposits of the marginal South Atlantic as being of localized origins, perhaps in lagoons, while others have suggested that the salts were deposited without high evaporation rates. Reyment and Dingle (1987) pointed out that the evaporite deposits are far too extensive for the lagoonal hypothesis and that the salts include tachyhydrite, which only forms on exposure to air. Furthermore, there is other evidence for extreme aridity during this time, such as gnetale pollen and sabkha-like caliche terrains. The Messinian event certainly offers compelling parallels, and to date much of the sedimentological and paleontological evidence from Aptian deposits within the meridional South Atlantic is consistent with a similar paleogeographic model to that proposed for the Mediterranean during the Miocene period.

Evaporites are the predominant sedimentary deposits of the southern basins from Sergipe-Alagoas to Santos, but they also formed in the Ceará basin to the north, as well as in the Araripe and Parnaiba basins farther inland. Petri (1987) supposed that a restricted sea extended locally into the Ceará and northern Parnaiba basins and that the surrounding lands were desert. The Araripe basin does not seem to have been inundated by the sea at that time, but may instead have been occupied by a saline lake, according to Silva's (1983, 1986a, 1986b) findings.

The Significance of *Dastilbe*

Possibly because of its isolated position as suggested in this paleogeographic model, the lacustrine and evaporite deposits of the Crato member that formed in this lake have yet to be correlated precisely with other Lower Cretaceous occurrences in Brazil. Nevertheless, the primitive gonorynchiform fish *Dastilbe*, which is so abundant in the Crato member of the Araripe basin, also occurs in the Marizal formation of the Recôncavo basin, in the Muribeca formation of Alagoas, in the Codo formation of the Parnaiba basin (Brito, 1984), and elsewhere (Silva Santos; this volume).

The distribution of *Dastilbe* strongly supports the existence of aquatic connections between at least some adjacent basins. Past theories invoked to explain this distribution pattern include a marine incursion either from the north, possibly via the Parnaiba (= Maranhão) basin, or from the south via the Sergipe-Alagoas basins. These models have been rejected by some paleogeographers and sedimentologists in favor of a non-marine (essentially lacustrine) environment for the Araripe, Recôncavo, Parnaiba, and Sergipe-Alagoas fish-bearing horizons.

There seems little reason to doubt that the Crato member of the Araripe basin is of lacustrine origin (Silva, 1983). Quite possibly the distribution of *Dastilbe* in the adjacent Parnaiba basin to the west and Recôncavo basin to the south reflects different populations in separate drainage systems, one (within the Parnaiba basin) flowing ultimately into the North Atlantic, the other (in the Recôncavo basin) with links to the south. The centrally located Araripe basin may have maintained links periodically with each of these catchment areas, permitting faunal exchanges to occur.

Dastilbe itself has a wider distribution, with species described from the inland São Francisco basin of Minas Gerais and others from Gabon and Equatorial Guinea in Africa. Patterson (1984) has suggested that these all may be referable to a single species (see discussion of *Dastilbe* systematics elsewhere in this volume). The pre-drift distribution of *Dastilbe* certainly is evocative of a highly endemic group. Its African occurrences would have been extremely near the Alagoas and Recôncavo ones and may very well have occupied the same Lower Cretaceous catchment area.

The principal localities at which *Dastilbe* occurs tend to be southerly, once the continents are replaced in their supposed Aptian position.

Dastilbe therefore may have arisen within a non-marine (lacustrine?) habitat along the Afro-Brazilian zone of tensional rifting. Its distribution farther north may have been prevented by uplift across the compressional zone along the margins of what is now the equatorial Atlantic.

As the two continents continued their pirouette, it is likely that the pivotal Araripe region was tilted and uplifted. Its lakes became clogged with sediments and then dried up completely, producing a sequence of evaporites showing evidence of subaerial exposure and erosion (Silva, 1983, 1986a, 1986b). The surrounding lands were dry and arid. According to the correlation charts published by Petri (1987, figs. 1-3), this stratigraphic level is marked by an unconformity (indicating a break in deposition, possibly followed by uplift and erosion) in virtually every Cretaceous sedimentary basin within Brazil.

To the south, most of these basins subsequently became filled with a thick sequence of younger Cretaceous sediments. Farther north, however, only some basins appear to have accumulated a sequence of strata immediately after this erosional episode. These include the Potiguar, Cabo, Araripe, and Sergipe-Alagoas basins. Other northerly sedimentary basins apparently were active only sporadically, although some (e.g., Ceará, Recife basins) eventually contained significant Upper Cretaceous sequences.

Break-up and Collision

According to the paleogeographic reconstruction offered by Szatmari, et al. (1987), the axis about which South America was rotating during the Neocomian stage shifted dramatically from its former position near the Araripe Basin, to lie instead some 1900 kilometers (1200 miles) farther to the northwest at a new collision point that was located approximately between Cabo Orange, in the extreme north of Brazil, and Liberia on the equatorial margin of Africa. Popoff (1988) has suggested that continental rifting and drifting were initiated in this northerly "equatorial domain" of the South Atlantic during this time.

This presumed shift in the rotation of South America during the Aptian-Albian stages would have had enormous geological and paleogeographical impact upon the northeastern part of Brazil, which in a relatively short interval went from being a collision point, under enormous compressional stress, to an essentially tensional region of rifting along a reactivated ancient Precambrian fault system.

In the areas surrounding Recife, reactivation of this fault system was accompanied by formation of a volcanic hot-spot in the Cabo basin. Extension of this fault system along the Pernambuco lineament also led to separation of several minor interior sedimentary basins and undoubtedly influenced deposition within the Araripe basin (see below).

The Cabo volcanic episode is unusual in being so far removed from other Brazilian Cretaceous volcanic events in time and space, but it seems to correlate well with a belt of volcanoes in Cameroon that also may be related to extension of a fault zone. The N'Gaoundere lineament lines up very well with the Pernambuco lineament, according to Szatmari, et al. (1987), and the two may be directly related, for example as the opposite ends of a major transform fault. Between the Patos and Pernambuco lineaments (and other related faults) lie the Cabo and Cameroon volcanics, and it is tempting to regard these as marking the time and place of final continental separation. Possibly the section of South America lying between the Pernambuco and Patos lineaments acted as an independent microplate, with delayed separation from Africa relative to adjacent areas.

In the Araripe basin, this period of tumultuous activity may have been marked by tilting and slight deformation of the Crato member and by erosion of its surface (Silva, 1983, 1986a, 1986b). For a brief interval, this region therefore seems to have been re-elevated into an upland divide, separating an essentially saline province to the south from an apparently less arid northerly coastal region.

Szatmari, et al. (1987) have summarized the tectonic situation as follows: In response to the rotational movement, compression of northeastern Brazil against Africa reactivated an ancient Precambrian shear zone aligned roughly east-west. Rifting consequently propagated to the west, along the equatorial margin of Africa and Brazil, and also eastward along the Benue trough in Nigeria. Both of these areas became open seaways during the Aptian stage.

This series of events is significant, as it was to herald the final conjoining of the North and South Atlantic in the latter part of the Cretaceous period. Flooding of the Benue trough effectively extended the slender arm of the North Atlantic well to the east of northeastern Brazil. Intermittent exchange of surface waters evidently occurred during the Albian (or even perhaps the late Aptian) stage,

effectively by detouring around the volcanic Cabo basin via the Benue trough. At first such periodic exchanges probably involved minor epicontinental transgressions until such time as a basaltic equatorial sea floor had developed. Moreover, any links with the main body of the North Atlantic undoubtedly were limited by the new collision zone between Brazil and Africa farther west. This new (and geologically short-lived) barrier may help explain the apparent dearth of certain northeasterly marginal basins in Brazil, as suggested by correlation charts published by Petri (1987).

The Great Inundation

The entire complexion of the South Atlantic underwent clear and dramatic transformations at about the same time these equatorial events were occurring. During the early Albian stage, the southerly barrier to deep oceanic circulation generated by the Falkland-Agulhas Platform was increasingly breached as the ocean floor became widened, dispelling the earlier anoxic bottom environment. The Walvis-Rio Grande Rise continued to act as a barrier to deep circulation in the northerly part of the South Atlantic, but apparently it was no longer a subaerial barrier to surface water exchange. The arid, epeiric conditions of the Aptian were ended as the northerly South Atlantic became transformed into a deep, anoxic-bottomed ocean during the Albian.

Since the Aptian history of the northern South Atlantic has been compared with the Messinian event in the Mediterranean by some investigators, the obvious question is whether it also ended in such an abrupt and spectacular fashion. On the western Mediterranean floor there is evidence of a sudden re-opening of the Straits of Gibraltar in the Late Miocene, followed by cataclysmic inundation of the Mediterranean basin by oceanic waters spilling in from the Atlantic. It has been estimated that the deafening surge of waters must have resembled a hundred or more Niagaras, falling for centuries until the intense evaporation was beaten and the basin finally filled to its present level. Terrestrial life-forms within the basin would have been obliterated by the inundation.

Marginal environments also would have been transformed, particularly in the vicinity of the few river systems draining into the Mediterranean. The Nile River had cut a deep canyon, greater than the Grand Canyon, into its bedrock during the Messinian event. Suddenly this canyon was flooded by rising ocean waters, sending an arm of the new Late Miocene sea

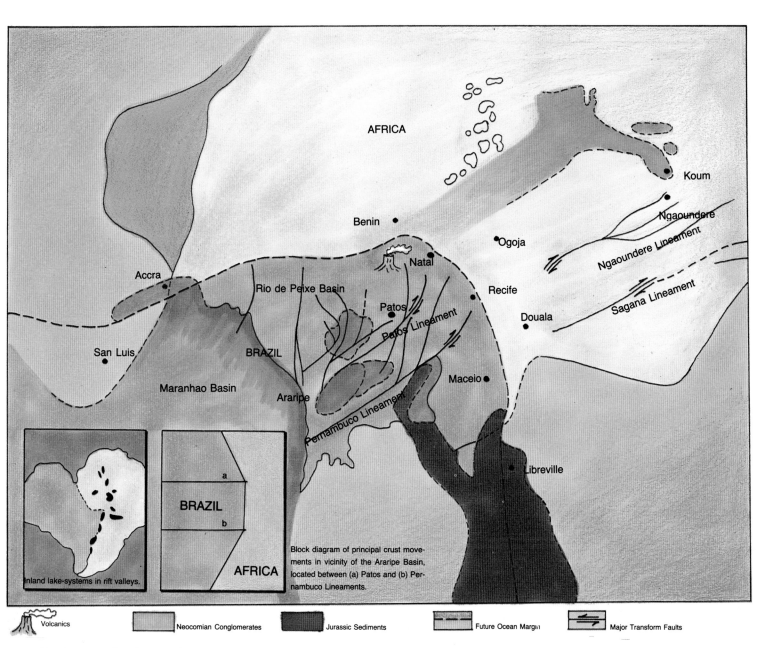

AFRICA

Koum

Ngaoundere

Ngaoundere Lineament

Benin

Ogoja

Sagana Lineament

Accra

Natal

Rio de Peixe Basin

Recife

Patos

Patos Lineament

Douala

San Luis

BRAZIL

Maranhao Basin

Araripe

Maceio

Pernambuco Lineament

Libreville

Inland lake-systems in rift valleys.

BRAZIL

a

b

AFRICA

Block diagram of principal crust movements in vicinity of the Araripe Basin,
located between (a) Patos and (b) Pernambuco Lineaments.

Volcanics   Neocomian Conglomerates   Jurassic Sediments   Future Ocean Margin   Major Transform Faults

Northeastern Brazil and adjacent parts of Africa in Upper
Jurassic to early Lower Cretaceous (Neocomian) times,
showing major structural features related to the Araripe
basin.

more than a thousand kilometers inland to a point near the modern border of Egypt and Sudan. During the next few million years this inlet was filled rapidly with estuarine and fluviatile sediments, until by the Late Pliocene period (approximately two million years ago) the canyon was filled and the Nile delta began to push its way into the ocean basin.

Did such a cataclysmic event ever occur during the Cretaceous history of the South Atlantic? At the moment it has not been determined whether certain Late Aptian or Early Albian sediments were formed as a result of such an event. Nevertheless, there certainly are accumulations of coarse, water-borne sediments of about the right age in a number of marginal Brazilian basins, mostly resting unconformably on older Cretaceous sediments. In most cases the coarse overlying sediments have been attributed to non-marine alluvial fans built by rapidly flowing streams or floods running off highland areas to the west. Such heterogeneous conglomerates, with pebbles and cobbles of quartz, granites, and basalts, occur at the base of the Albian sequence in the southerly Santos basin, passing laterally into a shelf-sea environment with a carbonate platform where calcareous sediments accumulated. Farther south, however, the Florianopolis basin contains a sequence of Albian high-energy marine carbonates, while the most southerly Pelotas basin has a more open oceanic aspect, with shelf, slope, and bathyal sub- environments.

Thus only from the Santos basin northward is there evidence of high-energy aquatic environments leading to dumping of poorly sorted, heterogeneous sediments within marginal basins. In the Campos basin there is a narrow landward sandstone-shale sequence adjacent to a thick carbonate platform. In the margins of the Espirito Santo basin there are poorly sorted and bedded sands and conglomerates containing arkosic feldspar fragments (usually an indication of rapid terrestrial burial, since subaerial weathering and high moisture levels lead to their decomposition). More centrally within this basin are extensive carbonate banks, some of which accumulated in shallow troughs between upwelling salt domes within the underlying sediments, while others formed within tidal channels and intertidal zones.

The Sergipe-Alagoas basins contain a sequence of fan-delta, carbonate shelf, and continental slope sediments of Albian age. These sediments include ammonite fossils in their upper part, indicating at least a temporary link with the ocean far to the north, perhaps via the Benue trough.

The area of the Cabo basin evidently still was subjected to great tectonic stresses as this part of South America continued to be torn away from Africa. Volcanic activity that had commenced here during the Aptian continued until t⌐ ⌐ate Albian. There is little doubt that basaltic ocean crust was by now beginning to be emplaced between the "nose" of Brazil and the region of Cameroon, Equatorial Guinea, and Gabon. As the Cabo basin was carried farther west, away from the newly created mid-oceanic rift, it appears to have lost its heat source and its volcanoes were ultimately extinguished by the close of the Albian stage.

At the present time, we may conclude that there is no compelling evidence to support the notion of a particularly sudden inundation of the southerly marginal basins. Nevertheless, the "Messinian" phase in the South Atlantic may not have ended altogether quietly, as there is plenty of evidence for local high-energy depositional environments around its westerly margins.

The Araripe Fossils

The Romualdo member of the Santana formation probably was deposited within the Araripe basin during these Late Aptian to Albian times. As in several other basins, there is evidence of an early high-energy depositional phase. In places the Romualdo member lies directly upon Paleozoic basement rocks, but mostly it overlies the Crato member and may develop a conglomeratic base (Silva, 1986b). Otherwise, the Romualdo member accumulated mainly in a low-energy aquatic environment permitting deposition of laminated shales, limestones, and sandstones. Episodic higher energy regimes are indicated by local banks of gastropod shells, often broken, within coarser detrital sediments that become finer upward (Mabesoone and Tinoco, 1973). The presence of pyrite and cellulose remains (pollen, dinoflagellates), plus certain preservational features of the fossil fishes, all point toward generally anoxic bottom environments.

This environment at times was occupied by one or more large and taxonomically diverse fish faunas, augmented by terrestrial and semi-aquatic vertebrates such as crocodilians and turtles. As will be discussed below, there is strong evidence for at least three fossil assemblages in the concretionary limestones of the Romualdo member of the Santana formation, together with an earlier and profoundly different assemblage in the Crato member.

Environmental fluctuations periodically may have decimated or even annihilated the Lower Cretaceous vertebrate population in the Araripe basin. Although it still is not clear whether there was a single mass mortality (suggested by Mabesoone and Tinoco, 1973) or several such events, evidence for the latter now is growing. It even is possible that the vertebrates were not permanent denizens of the Araripe basin but became trapped there following one or perhaps more inundations from outside sources. Such a model has been suggested for the marine Jurassic Solnhofen occurrence in West Germany (Keupp, 1977; Barthel, 1978), and parallels have been drawn in the case of the Santana concretions (Martill, 1988, 1989).

There are strong similarities between the fossil fish assemblages of the Santana formation and those of adjacent sedimentary basins in the south, particularly the Riachuelo formation in Sergipe that shares *Vinctifer, Rhacolepis, Notelops, Tharrhias,* "*Leptolepis,*" *Cladocyclus,* and *Neoproscinetes*. Less profound similarities are noted elsewhere. For example, the Muribeca formation of Alagoas has yielded *Vinctifer, Cladocyclus,* and *Dastilbe*. A mixed bag of fossil fishes has been recorded from the Lower Cretaceous of the Recôncavo basin, although published faunal lists are somewhat vague and some lists may have confused records from the Neocomian Ilhas group and younger occurrences.

One of the most frequently-asked questions is whether the Santana fishes are marine or non-marine. In truth, there is no simple answer. Perhaps significantly, many of these other fossil fishes occur in sedimentary sequences that have been interpreted as lacustrine and non-marine. Basinal sequences with a strong marine aspect in the south of Brazil have not produced comparable fossil fish faunal assemblages. Only in the Riachuelo formation of Sergipe is there compelling evidence (from ammonites) of a marine episode (Brito, 1984), and then only later in the sequence. In the Santana formation a few late echinoids occur toward the top of the sequence (Beurlen, 1962), again hinting at a later marine phase. This also appears to be true in the contemporaneous African basins, although many of these remain poorly investigated. As in the case of *Dastilbe* discussed earlier, many of the other fossil fishes from the Santana formation are highly endemic, with genera occurring in a relatively few closely clustered sedimentary basins within northeastern Brazil and adjacent parts of Africa. Assuming for the moment that most of these occurrences are closely linked in time as well as space, their distribution is evocative of an originally discrete region of endemism in the process of becoming subdivided by a vicariant event, namely the final separation of the African and South American continents. Sedimentological, paleogeographic, tectonic, and biogeographical data seem in unison to support the view that the Cretaceous fossil fishes from the Araripe basin were trapped within an essentially non-marine habitat; if there is a marine aspect to this occurrence, it is a very peculiar one.

This conclusion corroborates Silva's (1983) opinion concerning the depositional environment of the Santana formation and contrasts with the views of Silva Santos and Valença (1968), Mabesoone and Tinoco (1973), Martill (1988), and others who postulated an essentially marine environment. The relative merits of these competing hypotheses will not be discussed here, but it is of interest that quite different conclusions have been reached concerning the putative marine connection with the Araripe basin at this time.

Beurlen and Mabesoone (1969) contended that there was a marine link to the northern ocean via the Parnaiba basin. That view was countered by the discovery that this area showed no evidence of a marine connection during the critical period and was separated from the ocean by an upland barrier, the Ferer-Urbano Santos Ridge.

In an alternative model, Beurlen (1971a, 1971b) proposed a "Codo-Santana transgression" from the southeast, which he believed was related to the opening of the South Atlantic and formation of the extensive evaporite deposits during the Aptian stage. According to this model, a broad epicontinental sea may have spread over much of the northeastern interior of Brazil. Although several objections to the model were raised (reviewed by Silva, 1983), no alternatives were offered and Beurlen's hypothesis became widely accepted (e.g., Mabesoone and Tinoco, 1973). The hypothesis eventually foundered, however, once it became clear that no evidence for a former connection between the Parnaiba and Araripe basins could be found (Moraes, et al., 1976).

Petri (1987) maintained that the sea somehow must have entered the Araripe basin, perhaps via the Potiguar basin to the northeast, reflecting an earlier but long-rejected suggestion by Beurlen (1962) and based on the presence of

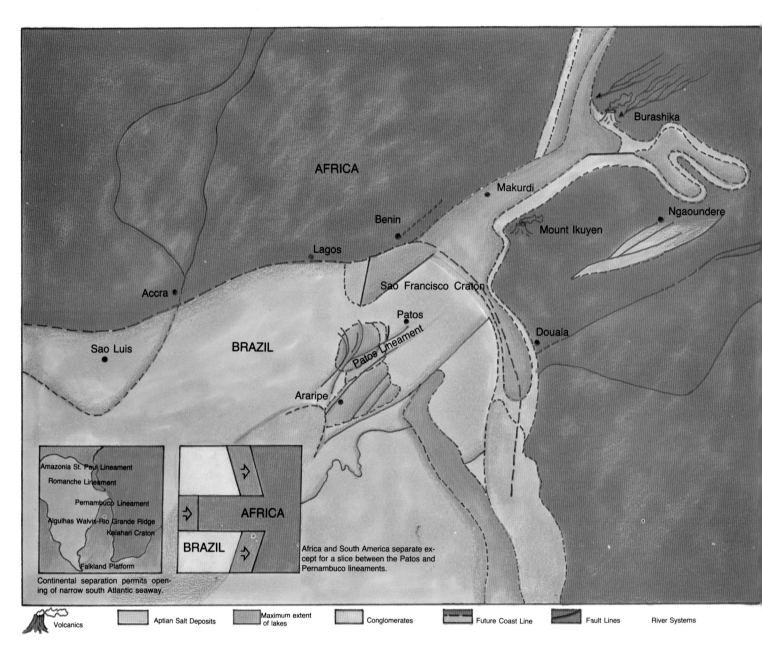

Early rift movements and inland lake systems of north-eastern Brazil during the Aptian (Lower Cretaceous).

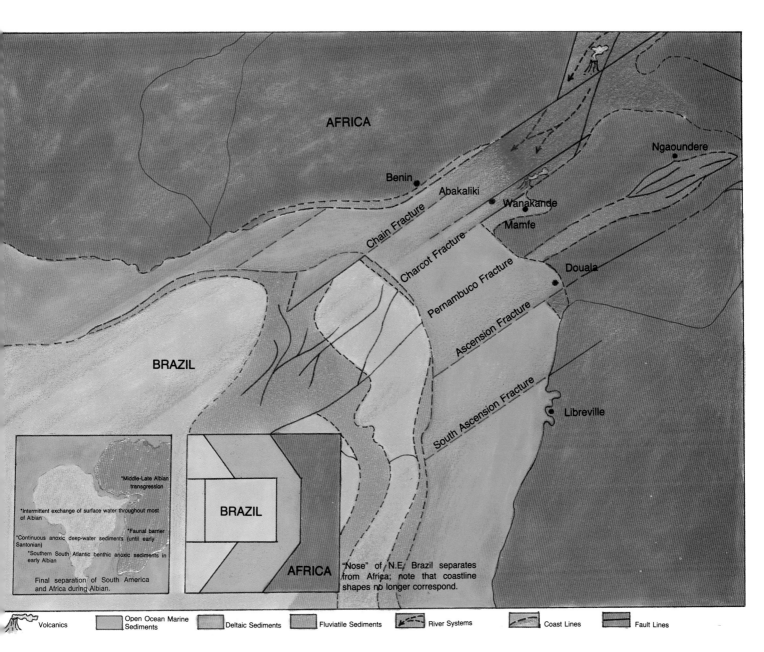

AFRICA

Benin

Abakaliki

Wanakande

Mamfe

Ngaoundere

Douala

BRAZIL

Chain Fracture

Charcot Fracture

Pernambuco Fracture

Ascension Fracture

South Ascension Fracture

Libreville

*Middle-Late Albian
transgression

*Intermittent exchange of surface water throughout most
of Albian

*Continuous anoxic deep-water sediments (until early
Santonian)

*Faunal barrier

*Southern South Atlantic benthic anoxic sediments in
early Albian

Final separation of South America
and Africa during Albian.

BRAZIL

AFRICA

"Nose" of N.E. Brazil separates
from Africa; note that coastline
shapes no longer correspond.

Volcanics	Open Ocean Marine Sediments	Deltaic Sediments
Fluviatile Sediments	River Systems	Coast Lines
Fault Lines		

Marine seaway extends between Brazil and Africa during
Albian, uniting North and South Atlantic Oceans.

echinoids locally in the upper limestones of the Santana formation. The occurrence of these rare echinoids remains the strongest piece of paleontological evidence for marine conditions at some time in this episode (there is now some suggestion that some ostracods from the Romualdo member are marine). This would certainly be the shortest and most plausible route for an epicontinental seaway, given what is now known of Aptian/Albian paleogeography in Brazil, although the echinoid occurrences (toward the southwesterly end of the Araripe basin, near Araripina) remain paradoxical and enigmatic.

Mabesoone and Tinoco (1973) suggested that the Araripe basin probably was connected to the southern Atlantic ocean via the Sergipe-Alagoas basins, principally because they regarded the Riachuelo formation as marine and because the only alternative was via the Recôncavo basin, which has only a non-marine sedimentary sequence. Only the uppermost, ammonite-bearing part of the Riachuelo formation is demonstrably marine, however, whereas the fossil fishes are said to occur at some unspecified depth below this level. Despite the alleged similarities between the fossil fishes of the Santana and Riachuelo formations, they do not provide direct evidence for a marine connection, and a non-marine aquatic link between the Recôncavo and Araripe basins during the Aptian/Albian stages cannot be dismissed as summarily as Mabesoone and Tinoco (1973) supposed.

If we are to cut through all the conflicts of these arguments, it seems that the occurrence of marine fossils in the upper part of the Santana formation should be regarded at best as evidence of at least a relatively minor marine incursion, and it should not be permitted to color interpretations of the underlying concretionary sediments with their important vertebrate fossils.

The extent and nature of marine incursions (if any) earlier in Romualdo member times need to be carefully appraised in the light of continued studies. Important recent developments include the recognition of pulsative marine ingressions in the Romualdo member (Arai and Coimbra, in press). These are indicated in borehole samples by microfossil assemblages including ostracods and dinoflagellates (represented mostly by the marine genus *Subtilisphaera*). Where the dinoflagellate content is higher, there are "ostracodes typical of the Alagoas stage"; where there is a more moderate frequency of dinoflagellates, the ostracods (when present) are represented only by *Pattersoncypris micropapillosa*. Arai and Coimbra postulate that a mixihaline environment prevented development of high-diversity ostracod faunas. Whether incursions came from the north or the south may be less important than establishing the provenance of the fossil assemblages dominating the lower part of the Romualdo member.

The Open Seaway

By the close of the Albian stage, a continuous equatorial seaway existed between the North and South Atlantic, floored continuously by basaltic ocean crust. Volcanic activity gradually ceased in the Cabo basin, and a narrow marine carbonate platform was developed (Petri, 1987). Similar carbonate platforms already had begun to form within many of the other Brazilian marginal basins, which generally are characterized by low depositional rates and shallow marine environments. All of the marginal basins from Sergipe-Alagoas southward accumulated a sequence of marine sediments from the Cenomanian into the Late Cretaceous (Maestrichtian stage) or even the Early Tertiary, and in many cases this protracted deposition began even earlier.

Some of the northerly marginal basins also accumulated marine sediments throughout the Upper Cretaceous, including the Potiguar, Ceará, and Barreirinhas basins. However, these northerly areas of deposition are separated from the southerly ones by a belt trending east-west and including the ancient interior Amazonas and Parnaiba basins, the younger interior Araripe basin, and the even younger marginal Cabo basin. None of these basins contains any Cretaceous sediments younger than the Cenomanian or early Turonian. Other minor northerly basins similarly lack any later Cretaceous sediments, except for some late developers such as the Recife and Amazonas Mouth basins (Petri, 1987). However, in the Araripe basin there is a thick sequence of cross-bedded fluviatile sandstones (the Exu formation) capping the Santana formation and today forming the upstanding mass of the Araripe Plateau. Palynological data suggest an Albian age for the Exu sandstones.

In complete contrast, farther southward the interior Paraná and younger São Francisco basins contain non-marine Upper Cretaceous sequences. In the huge Paraná basin the climate seems to have been warm, but alternately dry and humid. Eolian, fluvial, deltaic, and lacustrine sediments are present, dominated by braided fluvial sandstones. Volcanoes were active in the São Francisco basin and adjoining areas, and volcanic activity here continued through later Cretaceous times.

As Africa became farther removed from South America, its lower-lying coastal and interior regions became inundated by a shallow sea, beginning in the Benue trough and eventually extending across central Africa and on to the eastern Mediterranean. This epicontinental transgression reached its maximum extent in the Cenomanian and Turonian stages of the Upper Cretaceous. The short-lived seaway between the Mediterranean and equatorial Atlantic expanded at its northerly end to include much of Libya and also sent a westerly arm into central Chad.

A similar transgression over large tracts of land also occurred in Europe, North America, and other continents during the Upper Cretaceous, during which time there is evidence of widespread eustatic rises in sea level. It is therefore curious that the major interior basins of Brazil apparently were not inundated in this manner, adding further support to the notion that much of South America was uplifted geologically at the time. It is clear from the preponderance of Upper Cretaceous calcareous algal barriers and carbonate platforms within the marginal basins of Brazil that the South Atlantic coastline was nowhere far from its present position.

The river system responsible for depositing the Exu sandstone of the Araripe basin during Albian times probably lay within a northerly-draining catchment area, ending up in the Potiguar basin (Petri, 1987). By Cenomanian times, however, this river system seems to have disappeared. After this there is no further evidence of Cretaceous sedimentation in the Araripe basin. Late Turonian uplift occurred along both sides of the Pernambuco lineament. This uplift obliterated the small Cabo basin to the east and also may have affected the Araripe basin.

The earliest evidence of subsidence in the Amazonas Mouth basin dates from the Campanian stage of the Upper Cretaceous. A great thickness of conglomeratic sandstones, siltstones, and mudstones accumulated continuously through the later Cretaceous and into the Tertiary period. The lower part of this succession is intruded by basaltic igneous rocks, suggesting that the onset of subsidence in this basin was accompanied by local crustal instability.

During the Campanian stage a widespread change in marginal sedimentation patterns occurred from the Barreirhinhas basin in the north to the Campos basin in the south. Continued uplift of the interior of Brazil effectively rejuvenated the source of detrital sediments flowing into the marginal basins, allowing the continental shelf to become widened as the sediments built up in a seaward progradation. This process was accelerated during the Tertiary period, producing impressive thicknesses of shelf sediments over a wide area. Deep submarine canyons were cut into these widening shelf deposits, with turbidite deposits suggesting sudden earthquake-triggered flows of sediment-charged waters across the continental shelf and slope. As the continental shelf was built out, it also gradually extended into deeper waters. In the Potiguar basin, for example, it is estimated that the continental slope only extended to a depth of about 400 m during the Coniacian and Santonian stages of the Upper Cretaceous, but it had reached approximately 1500 m during the Campanian and Maestrichtian stages. For comparison, the continental slope today bottoms out on the Ceará abyssal plain at around 4800 m.

In very general terms, the Cretaceous paleogeographic history of Brazil evidently is tied closely to development of the South Atlantic and its eventual equatorial connection to the North Atlantic. This history can be summarized as follows:
1) Continental, Gondwanan pre-rift phase (Jurassic);
2) Afro-Brazilian rifting, development of rift valleys containing lakes; intense volcanic activity to the south (Jurassic to Neocomian);
3) Rotational separation of southern Africa and South America, tensional tectonic events to the south, compressional events to the north; axial rifting of South Atlantic propagates from south to north within successive domains (microplates?), with continental rifting-drifting processes reproduced in each domain at approximately 20-million-year intervals; narrow southern ocean developed, deep and anoxic to the south, shallow and epeiric to the north;
4) Rotational axis shifts westward, redefining northeastern Brazilian tectonism as tensional rather than compressional; intense localized vulcanicity (Cabo basin) as northeastern Brazil finally tears away from Cameroon; uplift of northern interior (late Aptian-Albian);
5) Equatorial link with North Atlantic established; north-eastern hot-spot

extinguished; slow sediment accumulation; narrow carbonate platforms develop around Brazilian coast; interior uplifted to west, producing volumes of detrital sands, silts; late volcanic hot-spot in São Francisco basin (Albian-Cenomanian);

6) Continued continental uplift denies epicontinental marine transgression and leads to increased coastal sedimentation and progradation of continental shelf into deeper waters; establishment of modern drainage systems including Amazon, following late tectonic subsidence of Amazonas Mouth basin (Turonian-Maestrichtian, continuing into Tertiary).

Szatmari, et al. (1987) have suggested that, during later Cretaceous and Early Tertiary times, Africa may have rebounded from its collision with southern Europe, creating a compressional zone across the narrow straits between West Africa and northeastern Brazil. This event would have increased the potential for faunal and floral interchanges at a much later geological time than is generally supposed. It is even possible that a temporary terrestrial connection could have existed (either a land bridge or island system?) between these continents well into the early Tertiary.

(J. G. Maisey)

10: Fossil Forensics

Taphonomy: An Introduction

Fossils may be viewed simply as the petrified remains of once living organisms. Usually, but not invariably, fossils occur in rocks that formed originally as soft sediments at approximately the same time that these organisms died.

Paleontology is a multidisciplinary science investigating not only morphological and phylogenetic aspects of these organic remains but also their ecology, their distribution through space (paleobiogeography) and through time (biostratigraphy), and their different modes of preservation. This last discipline has been termed taphonomy and can be considered a forensic analysis of the factors originally responsible for the preservation of a particular fossil. In certain cases, taphonomic investigations even may reveal the probable cause of death.

Many paleontologists have realized the importance of taphonomy in order to evaluate the extent of bias in the fossil record and also to determine the extent to which any original ecological factors have become masked or overprinted by later preservational ones. Take, for example, a lowly fossil clamshell enclosed within a mudstone. It could have arrived there by any one of several combinations of ecological and taphonomic factors. The clam could have burrowed into an existing muddy bottom before death and been preserved essentially as it had once lived. Alternatively, it could have lived on top of the muddy substrate and been buried after death. Or it could have preferred clearer waters, but may have been catastrophically inundated by a mud-slide or by a sudden deadly influx of mud-laden water. It could even have lived and died elsewhere, and its shell subsequently could have been carried along by currents and dumped in a new locality far from its original habitat. Furthermore, such transport may even have occurred after the shell was fossilized in its original locale.

This simple example serves to illustrate the importance of separating taphonomic from ecological factors within the preservational environment. Few people ever actually lived or died in graveyards, but just as grave-goods provide important glimpses into the lifestyles and cultures of our human ancestors, so do taphonomic clues provide insights into the life and postmortem history of fossilized remains.

Preservation of a tangible fossil record therefore is dependent upon several factors, of which the most important are: (a) the presence of suitably robust body parts (e.g., carbonate or phosphate shells, tests, cuticles, or bones) or woody cellulose; (b) an in-life environment that is "sympathetic" to the preservation of organic remains; (c) the presence of favorable preservational (taphonomic) factors after death. The last category may be further subdivided into essentially mechanical preservational processes occurring between death of the organism and its burial within sediment and essentially chemical processes occurring after burial. The mechanical processes may be equated crudely with those involved with the accumulation of sediments. Later chemical changes, combined with certain mechanical processes such as compaction and the removal of water, lead to hardening of sediments and formation of new minerals. The blanket term diagenesis is applied to these later changes, which effectively are responsible for turning soft sediments into harder, lithified strata.

Because the study of taphonomy involves investigating both the physical aspects of burial and sedimentary compaction (in what has been termed biostratinomy) and the chemical aspects of diagenesis, it is as much an aspect of sedimentology as it is of paleontology. During the life-span of an organism, it forms a small part of the dynamic, living continuum we know as the biosphere. The organism both influences and is influenced by the physical and biological world around it. After death this interaction briefly continues during the natural processes of decomposition and decay, but ultimately only the more resilient and relatively indigestible skeletal parts are left. From this point on the organic remains behave essentially as any other sedimentary detritus.

Accident Investigation

Through the 1970's and 80's, a team of

research scientists at Tübingen University, West Germany, developed a special program to investigate various aspects of paleoecology (the study of ancient environments). Their efforts were concentrated on some important German fossil localities of world reknown, including Sölnhofen, Holzmaden, and Gmund, and their findings were presented at a special symposium on extraordinary fossil biotas held in 1985 at the University of Cambridge, England (Seilacher, et al., 1985).

These scientists concluded that exceptionally rich fossil occurrences differed from "normal" ones only in the quality and/or quantity of preserved remains within the assemblage. From a sedimentological point of view, they argued, these occurrences (which they termed "Fossil Lagerstätten") are accidental and represent the end-members of ordinary sedimentary environments (facies). We can extend their philosophical viewpoint to suggest that all fossil occurrences represent accidental, or at the very least incidental, sedimentological events. The unusual numbers and quality of fossils deposited under the circumstances investigated by the Tübingen team provided a better than usual opportunity to identify the taphonomic factors responsible for their preservation. At this level, paleontology effectively becomes a forensic investigation of the circumstances surrounding the accidental preservation of fossils and may provide valuable insights into the processes of fossilization in general.

The most informative Lagerstätten investigated by the Tübingen team was the Upper Jurassic Sölnhofen Limestone of Bavaria. A succession of taphonomic events was recognized in relation to several aspects of preservation that may be summarized as follows, with reference to one of their localities (Sölnhofen).

(a) *Stratigraphic and environmental setting*, e.g., permanently submerged shallow hypersaline coastal basin with a stratified water column (occasionally affected by storm wave action), in which salinity levels rose and oxygen levels probably declined with increasing depth.

(b) *Ecological spectrum*, e.g., dominance of pelagic (open- ocean) organisms (sometimes barnacle- or oyster-encrusted) within the assemblage, rarity of benthic (bottom-dwelling) or burrowing organisms except where accidentally washed in.

(c) *Necrolytic features*, e.g., postmortem curvature of vertebral columns resulting from dehydration of muscle and tendinous tissues (can occur through either desiccation or high salinity).

(d) *Biostratinomic features*, e.g., movement or disarticulation by current action, indicated by preferred orientation of fossil remains and by marks left by remains being dragged across the soft sediment substrate.

(e) *Diagenetic features*, e.g., solution of aragonite and replacement by calcite or other minerals, rapid phosphatization of soft tissues (muscle fibers, etc.) and coprolitic material prior to compaction.

(f) *Microbiological activity*, e.g., biochemical processes thought to involve cyanobacterial mineralization of organic remains, with a bacterial scum either on or just below the substrate surface (a common occurrence in modern hypersaline environments).

The importance of prokaryotic bacterial action as a preservational factor has been neglected until recently. One important consequence of the Cambridge symposium was the somewhat paradoxical-sounding revelation that some kinds of bacterial decomposition probably are essential to certain fossilization processes. In these cases, without decay there might be no fossils! Several contributors to the conference suggested that bacterial action was at least partially responsible for particular modes of preservation investigated by them, from silica crystallization of Precambrian microfossils to formation of siderite (iron hydroxide) within the soft tissues of Oligocene vertebrates from Messel, near Hesse (West Germany). Bacterial remains actually have been recognized in these fossils and in Jurassic vertebrates from England (Knoll, 1985; Franzen, 1985; Martill, 1985; Conway Morris, 1985). More recently, Martill (1988, 1989) has presented a case for rapid bacterially induced phosphate permineralization of muscle tissue in fossil fishes from the Santana formation (what Martill has termed "the Medusa Effect"). Meanwhile, other paleontologists are finding further examples of possible bacterial participation in fossilization, for example at Mazon Creek, Illinois (Baird, et al., 1986).

Concretions: Fossils in the Round

Given the variable nature of all the potential mechanical and chemical factors that may affect fossilization, it is no wonder that modern taphonomic investigations are complex and intricate. This is particularly true when we examine concretions, hard rounded lumps of rock generally found in softer strata. Such concretions (or nodules) may occur in great profusion; the Santana formation probably contains millions. Concretions are common in sedimentary strata of all ages from the Cambrian period onward and are important sources of vertebrate fossils from rocks as old as the Devonian period.

There are many different kinds of concretions, but the most abundant are calcareous and ferruginous types. Several lines of evidence point to the geologically rapid formation of many concretions.

Firstly, they often contain fossils that are not flattened or crushed, indicating that sediments surrounding the fossil were quickly indurated by the deposition of new interstitial minerals before the sediment became compacted by the tremendous weight of overburden.

Secondly, fine details of the "soft" anatomy sometimes are preserved, such as muscle fibers (seen in some Araripe fossil fishes), gut contents, and kidney tissue (known from some Upper Devonian sharks from large concretions in the Cleveland Shale of Ohio). Delicate leaves and soft-bodied worms are preserved in small ferruginous Pennsylvanian concretions from Mazon Creek, Illinois. Such preservation only could occur if the organic remains were removed quickly from potential scavengers to become buried within a substrate in which only limited decomposition could occur.

Thirdly, concretions can occur in relatively young sediments, for example in Pleistocene sequences of Green's Creek, Ontario, and Greenland. Here ironstone concretions have produced numerous fossilized skeletons of a still-living fish species, the capelin (*Mallotus villosus*). This places an approximate uppper limit on the age of these concretions of about one million years, but in all probability they were formed in considerably less time than this. In the tidal marshes of Norfolk, England, sideritic concretions are forming today within the upper few feet of muddy sediments over a very short span of time, perhaps in as little as 30 years (Pye, 1984).

Fourthly, at least some aspects of the chemistry of concretion formation are now understood, particularly in the case of calcareous concretions. Laboratory experiments have replicated successfully conditions known to occur in nature that seem to lead to concretion formation. Although the experimental time frame necessarily is limited, these experiments nevertheless support the contention that certain kinds of fossilization processes can occur extremely rapidly.

For the paleontologist interested in fossil vertebrates, calcareous concretions are particularly valuable because modern chemical peparation techniques often permit complete extraction of the fossilized remains without

significant damage. This certainly is true of the concretions from the Santana formation, although the results of preparation seemingly depend upon the nature and composition of the concretion, which apparently can vary among different collecting sites across the Araripe Plateau. Perhaps the differences among concretions from the Santana formation may be accounted for by localized environmental variation back in Lower Cretaceous times. Support for this view comes from the fact that the fossils recovered from different concretion lithologies seem to represent slightly different assemblages. It also is possible that minor differences in the modern environment across the plateau may be affecting the rates at which leaching and erosion of the concretions occur today, although this also could be affected by original lithological differences.

In the following pages, the nature of the calcareous concretions from the Romualdo member of the Santana formation will be examined in detail, and subtle but significant lithological and paleontological differences among them will be documented. Drawing upon these observations, an attempt then will be made to determine their depositional and diagenetic history.

Description of the Concretions

The Santana formation concretions can be categorized broadly into three lithological types, although there seems to be a certain amount of variation within each of these categories. Jordan and Branner (1908) were the first to appreciate these differences, suggesting that they might reflect different collecting sites. Indeed, from the sparse information obtainable from Brazilians living in the region, each category of concretion seems to characterize one of the three most productive localities, but again this must be taken as a qualitative remark in the absence of any detailed field evidence; it is possible that different kinds of concretions occur at each locality, perhaps at different horizons. Nevertheless, we may conveniently discuss the different kinds of concretions by reference to general collecting areas that are said to be characterized by a particular kind of concretion lithology.

1) *"Santana" concretions*: These concretions usually are ovoid in outline, often elongated parallel to the long axis of the fossil and not reflecting the fossil outline. Fossils usually are complete, but partial skeletons (especially fish skeletons stripped of scales) occasionally are

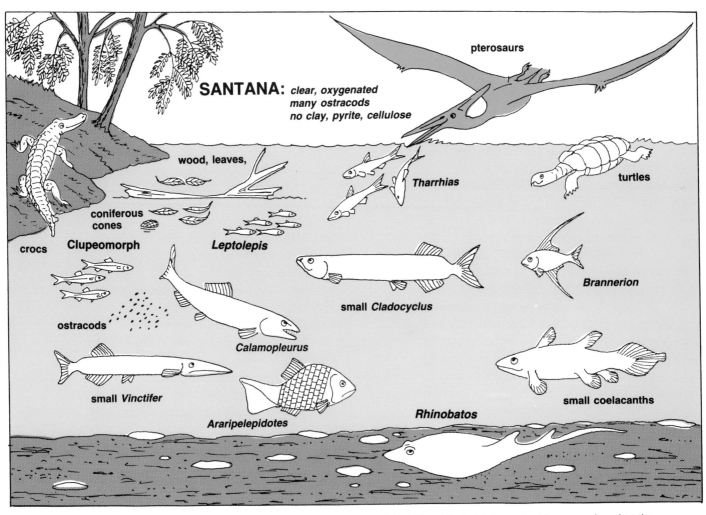

SANTANA: *clear, oxygenated*
many ostracods
no clay, pyrite, cellulose

pterosaurs

wood, leaves,

Tharrhias

turtles

coniferous cones

crocs   Clupeomorph   *Leptolepis*

Brannerion

small *Cladocyclus*

ostracods

Calamopleurus

small *Vinctifer*

Araripelepidotes   *Rhinobatos*   small coelacanths

"Santana" assemblage (diagram, top) and typical concretion (below, containing *Tharrhias*). It is important to remember that the fishes and other organisms shown are from one particular lithology, not necessarily from one locality or horizon, and may not have actually lived together. This also applies to the next two illustrations.

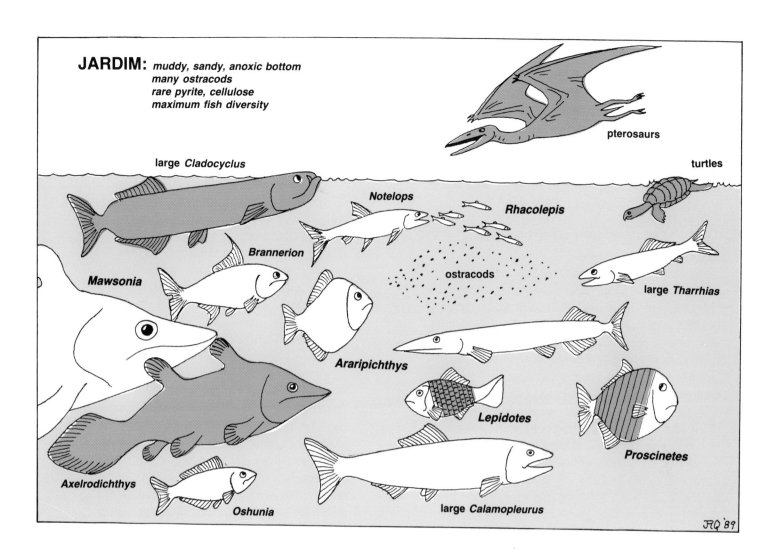

JARDIM: *muddy, sandy, anoxic bottom*
many ostracods
rare pyrite, cellulose
maximum fish diversity

pterosaurs

turtles

large *Cladocyclus*

Notelops

Rhacolepis

Brannerion

Mawsonia

ostracods

large *Tharrhias*

Araripichthys

Lepidotes

Axelrodichthys

Proscinetes

Oshunia

large *Calamopleurus*

"Jardim" assemblage (diagram, top) and typical concretion (below, containing *Brannerion*). See note in caption to "Santana" assemblage.

found. The limestone matrix is poorly laminated and has a granular, sugary, or peppery appearance when fresh. It is a pale cream or beige color and consists mostly of fossilized ostracod tests infilled by calcite, with very little argillaceous (clay) material or dark organic detritus. Pyrite generally is absent, as are pollen grains and dinoflagellates (in contrast with some other concretions). These lithological features collectively suggest that the bottom environment may have been at least partially oxygenated.

"Santana" concretions rarely exceed 40-46 cm (16-18 in) total length and are mostly 25-30 cm (10-12 in) or less. Fossil fishes are similarly limited in size and do not attain the dimensions seen elsewhere. *Tharrhias* is the most abundant fossil fish in this lithology, followed by small *Brannerion* and rare examples of small *Vinctifer*, *Calamopleurus*, and *Cladocyclus*. Tetrapods (crocodilians, turtles, pterosaurs) and terrestrial plant remains (mostly fronds of coniferous trees) also occur in this type of concretion. Fossils usually occur singly, although *Tharrhias* rarely occurs in two's and three's, and even more rarely occurs with a *Brannerion* or *Vinctifer* in the same concretion.

Phosphatic pellets (coprolites) are rare, although small ones sometimes occur loose within the matrix. Many of the fossil fishes have a white chalky residue among their bones and scales, apparently representing the badly leached remains of once-calcified muscle fibers and other soft tissues. Parts of a small crustacean, tentatively identified as a branchiopod ("fairy shrimp") were recovered from the residue of an acid-prepared "Santana" concretion containing *Brannerion*.

This kind of concretion lithology contains exceptionally well preserved fossil bones and generally is recognized by paleontologists as producing the best results after acid preparation. Cavities within many bones (including the endocranial cavity) apparently never were filled with matrix or secondary calcite in many instances, revealing internal osteological structures even without preparation.

Many specimens of *Tharrhias* inside "Santana" concretions have a dark band running diagonally from the vertebral column below the dorsal fin toward the cloaca. This dark band is interpreted as an iron-rich residue that remained following decomposition of kidney tissue.

Concretions of this kind are said to be prevalent around Santana do Cariri, which is fairly centrally located near the northern edge of the Araripe Plateau.

2) *"Jardim"* concretions: These can attain a large size and may be irregular and platy in shape, but sometimes their outline accurately refects the shape of a contained fossil. Fossils often are complete, but may be so large that their extremities projected beyond the concretion and either were not preserved or else have been destroyed by weathering and erosion. Partial skeletons (heads, tails) are not unusual, and smaller concretions may form around isolated bones and other elements. Unweathered matrix is a buff color but may weather to a bright rusty red or orange externally. Once weathered, the limestone matrix becomes soft and porous. The matrix usually is well-laminated by thin light and dark laminae, perhaps reflecting differences in organic content. There is a high clay content that is left as a residue following acid preparation. Iron minerals also are present, but there is little evidence for primary (authigenic) pyrite, and the iron is predominantly in the form of ferrous oxides and hydroxides. Dinoflagellates and pollen have not yet been reported from these concretions. Ostracods may be locally abundant in the matrix adjacent to fossil fishes but generally are uncommon. Small grains of carbonized organic matter sometimes are recovered in acid bath residues, but larger plant remains have not been noted.

Some very large fossil fishes have been recovered from concretions with "Jardim" lithology, including *Cladocyclus*, *Calamopleurus*, *Vinctifer*, *Brannerion*, and coelacanths, besides smaller fishes (*Rhacolepis*, *Rhinobatos*), parts of pterosaurs, and some turtles.

Fossilized bone is well preserved in "Jardim" concretions, and excellent acid preparations are obtainable despite generally deep weathering. Some calcite overgrowth of specimens commonly occurs, and concretions are often septarian (as noted by Gardner, 1849), with cracks infilled by dark brown sparry calcite. This calcite growth is secondary and frequently has resulted in damage to bones that may act as zones of weakness during diagenetic alteration. In some cases secondary calcite has developed between fish scales and the underlying endoskeleton, forcing them apart.

Most of the fossils inside "Jardim" concretions lie parallel to the bedding laminations. Sometimes the bodies are flattened, although bones are not compressed, appearing instead to have remained bloated throughout burial. This mode of preservation is particularly characteristic of the genus *Rhacolepis*, although some *Notelops* and *Brannerion* specimens also are preserved in this manner.

Curiously, a fairly high proportion (perhaps as high as 50%) of *Rhacolepis* preserved "in the round" do not lie parallel to the laminations but instead lie at various angles through considerable thicknesses of original sediment. Angles of 30-40° to the bedding planes are not unusual, and in some examples the body of the fish is almost perpendicular. Fin-rays often are splayed out within the laminations, and the dorsal, anal, and caudal fins often are perpendicular to the bedding.

Such specimens are of great interest because of what they reveal about sedimentation and the preservational environment of these fossils (discussed further below). Accumulation of well-laminated, fine-grained sediments of this type would not occur rapidly, suggesting that the "up-ended" corpses were partially exposed on the bottom environment for a considerable time before they became buried completely. Very little compaction of the sediments could have occurred, although there is some evidence of post-depositional collapse before the matrix became hardened into a concretion. Originally hollow body cavities usually are infilled by brown calcite, occasionally with a thin crust of authigenic pyrite (Martill, 1988).

In many three-dimensional *Rhacolepis*, the intestinal tract in the ventral part of the body is infilled by phosphatic material like that making up isolated coprolites that occur scattered through the concretions. In a few cases the body of the fossil is completely filled with white chalky calcareous matter instead of crystalline calcite. This may have replaced original soft tissue, although it generally lacks any fiber orientation or evidence of organic structure. Nevertheless, this chalky material occupies the muscle space filled by crystalline calcite in the majority of three-dimensional *Rhacolepis* and may have been present in all these specimens prior to secondary calcite formation. In general, three-dimensional fossil *Rhacolepis* and other fishes lack fossilized body musculature, although it may be well-developed in specimens where the body is flattened. Martill (1988) believed that all this muscle fiber had been phosphatized, perhaps as a consequence of bacterial decay. In many cases the fossilized muscle is only partially phosphatized, however, and the fossilized soft tissues in most specimens are easily disintegrated in dilute formic or acetic acid, suggesting that they are preserved as (or held together by) calcium carbonate instead of phosphate. X-ray diffraction analysis of fossilized muscle tissue of *Notelops* and

Neoproscinetes specimens in these concretions has been conducted by Dr. H.-P. Schultze (University of Kansas); his tests suggested that the mineralizing agent, in much of the soft tissue, is calcium carbonate (Schultze, 1989).

Concretions having the "Jardim" lithology are said to be most abundant from localities near Jardim, on the southeasterly side of the Araripe Plateau. These concretions sometimes are deeply weathered, with a thick crust of iron minerals and gypsum.

3) *"Old Mission" concretions:* These also attain large size, but unlike "Jardim" concretions are rarely platy. Instead they form chunky, heavy concretions with several inches of dense limestone matrix on either side of the specimen. The matrix generally is dark gray to dark olive, variably laminated, and usually hard. In some specimens, however, the clay content is so high that the concretion may be flaky or fissile, splitting into muddy layers. Sometimes the outer muddy component contains many small calcified or pyritized pelecypods, and coarse authigenic (grown *in situ*) crystals of iron pyrite also may be abundant. Some secondary calcite also occurs, but more rarely than in the "Jardim" lithology. Concretions rarely are shaped like the fossils they contain, apart from being elongated parallel to the longest dimension. The outermost 12 mm or so of matrix may be leached a pale gray or beige but is not appreciably softened by weathering. The high clay content leaves a sticky residue after acid preparation, making it harder to prepare fossil bone. Authigenic iron pyrite frequently encrusts the bones, which commonly are riddled with hairline fractures. All these properties tend to make "Old Mission" specimens less favorable candidates for acid preparation.

Dinoflagellates have been recovered from this matrix. At the time of writing these had not been identified. According to Arai and Coimbra (in press), dinoflagellates obtained from borehole samples in the Romualdo member belong to the marine genus *Subtilisphaera*. Ostracods occur in many concretions, usually scattered but sometimes in great profusion within fish skeletons. Small pieces of crustacean (shrimp?) carapaces and one or two small pyritized gastropods and pelecypods have been recovered from "Old Mission" acid residues. Rarely, small clusters of pelecypods may crowd a particular bedding plane.

Bone is least satisfactorily preserved in these concretions. Contributing factors seem to include pyritization and microscopic fracturing of the bone, which causes it to disintegrate

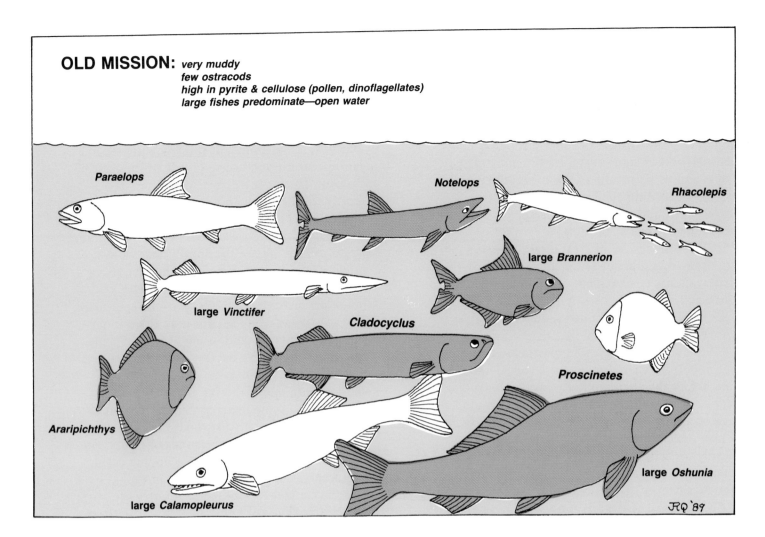

"Old Mission" assemblage (diagram, top) and typical concretion (below, containing *Rhacolepis*). See note in caption to "Santana" assemblage.

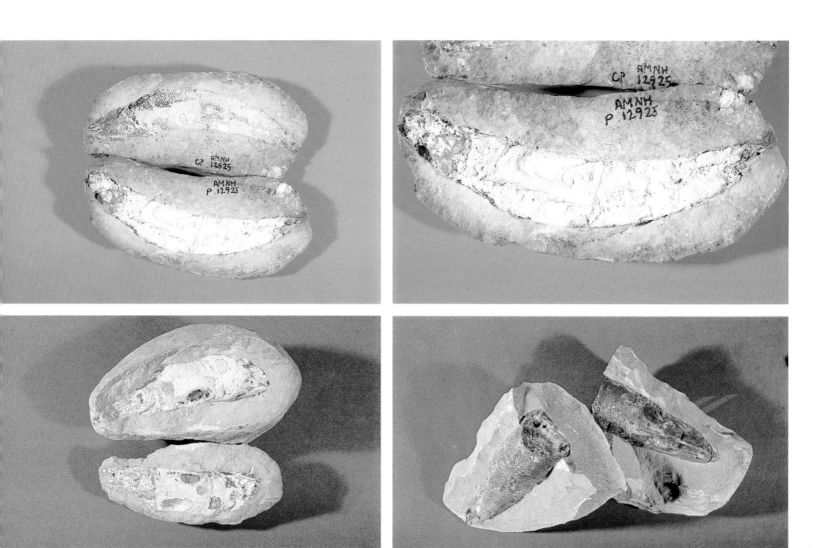

Preservation and taphonomy. **Top:** Two *Rhacolepis* with body wall replaced by chalky, amorphous carbonate. **Upper center:** Another chalky *Rhacolepis* (left) and a broken example with completely recrystallized calcite. **Lower center:** Small *Rhacolepis* lying oblique to bedding laminations (left); large *Vinctifer* with head passing through laminations and flattened body parallel to bedding (presumably collapsed after partial burial). **Bottom:** Example of flattened fish (a small *Notelops*) with fossilized muscle tissue preserving original myotomal arrangement.

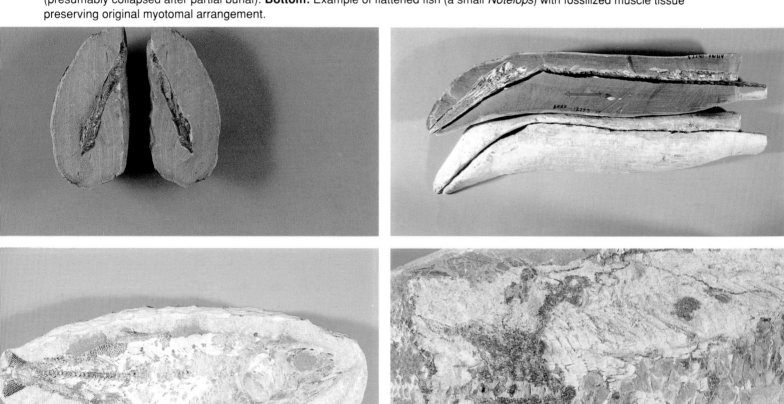

during acid preparation. Certain fossils are affected worse than others. For example, large *Notelops* and some *Vinctifer* have been problematical, whereas far better results have been obtained preparing *Neoproscinetes*. This variation may reflect a general tendency for the more primitive fossil taxa to be more robustly ossified or for their bone to be less susceptible to diagenetically related damage.

Most fossils in the "Old Mission" lithology tend to be preserved parallel to the bedding of the concretions. Bloated *Rhacolepis* sometimes occur, and as in the "Jardim" concretions may be angled through the bedding planes.

Specimens of "bloated" *Rhacolepis* in "Jardim" and "Old Mission" matrix can be sliced longitudinally using a rock-saw, perpendicular to the bedding, in order to investigate this unusual mode of preservation. Although *Rhacolepis* in both lithologies appeared superficially alike, when sectioned it was found that those in "Old Mission" matrix invariably had suffered far greater collapse than those in "Jardim" matrix. Following their burial by sediment, the degree of internal disorganization and disarticulation evidently was much greater in the "Old Mission" matrix.

The body musculature usually is well-preserved in "Jardim" or "Old Mission" matrix only where the body is flattened. Some specimens recently were illustrated by Martill (1988). Its fibrous structure and segmented arrangement are preserved, and at higher magnifications (using a scanning electron microscope) the muscle fibers reveal their original structure and features such as nuclear membranes. Fossil muscle and many other soft tissues are now known, most often in specimens of *Notelops* but also in examples of *Brannerion* and *Rhacolepis*. In one "Old Mission" *Notelops* a dark diagonal streak was observed, like those seen in "Santana" *Tharrhias*, and again presumably representing kidney tissue residue.

"Old Mission" concretions are said to be abundant at Missão Velha, on the northern margin of the Araripe Plateau, toward its eastern end. Geographically, the principal sites yielding concretions with "Old Mission" and "Jardim" lithologies are farther east than the "Santana" ones, suggesting that the depositional environment may have been somewhat different between the easterly and westerly parts of the Araripe basin, with less marked differences from north to south across its eastern end. The presence of authigenic pyrite, pollen, and dinoflagellate tests in "Old Mission" matrix suggests that sedimentation occurred in a reducing, anoxic bottom environment. This also may be true in the case of "Jardim" concretions, but perhaps not for "Santana" ones.

Shapes and Sizes

Concretions from the Santana formation can be categorized according to variation in their lithology, as described above. However, they also can be characterized by shape, size, and the ways in which they enclose fossil remains. This variation provides some additional clues as to how the concretions were formed.

Martill (1988) recognized five shape categories of concretions from the Santana formation, but many additional ones are distinguished here:

(a) concretions containing no recognizable organic remains, usually 15 cm (6 in) or under, often spherical (common in the field, but usually not represented in collections);

(b) similar to (a), but containing isolated scraps (vertebrae, dermal bones) or coprolites, not necessarily in center of concretion (uncommon);

(c) small concretions enclosing extremity of skeleton (head or tail), but with vertebral column extending to end of concretion suggesting that the skeletal remains were originally more extensive (common);

(d) concretions with body of fossil but lacking extremities (common in "Jardim" and "Old Mission" concretions, especially in more elongate species such as *Vinctifer*; rare in "Santana" concretions);

(e) concretions with outline closely following shape of fossil, including fins and extremities (uncommon except for "Jardim" concretions);

(f) ovoid concretions completely enclosing fossil specimen but not following its shape (common in all matrix types, including plant fossils);

(g) rounded concretions containing isolated heads and tails that clearly are detached from rest of skeleton (common, especially in "Jardim" concretions);

(h) rounded slabs containing two or more (sometimes several) individuals, usually of one species (e.g., "Jardim" *Rhacolepis*, "Santana" *Tharrhias*, "Old Mission" *Vinctifer*) or rarely different species (e.g., "Santana" *Tharrhias* with *Vinctifer* or *Brannerion*); individuals toward margin of concretion usually incomplete (uncommon); may indicate schooling behavior;

(i) curved concretions around curved skeletons (e.g., *Vinctifer*) (common in "Jardim" concretions, otherwise uncommon);

(j) composites where two adjacent concretions apparently grew together and coalesced;

concretions not necessarily originating on the same bedding plane (uncommon; noted in "Jardim" concretions);

(k) "transgressive" concretions formed around fossils lying oblique to bedding planes (common, particularly in "Jardim" and "Old Mission" concretions containing *Rhacolepis*), with body of fossil passing through several centimeters of accumulated thickness of sediment;

(l) partly "transgressive" concretions, with part of fossil (usually the head) angled through successive layers of laminated sediment, but with remainder of body flattened and parallel to bedding (rare in both "Jardim" and "Old Mission" concretions, and affecting only larger fossils such as *Vinctifer* and *Brannerion*).

In (k), the concretion's external shape is rounded and does not reflect the form of the fossil it contains. In (l), however, the concretion may vaguely resemble the shape of the fossil, as in (e).

Several conclusions may be drawn from these observations:

1) Concretions often form in the absence of any obvious organic nucleus.

2) Somewhat paradoxically, where such a nucleus is present it frequently influences the final shape of the concretion, even to the extent that it may cut across several centimeters of accumulated sediment, as in the case of examples (k) and (l).

3) The concretions were formed diagenetically, after the deposition of sediments had buried the organic remains.

4) The majority of fossils occur singly within concretions, except for rare examples where small groups of apparently schooling fish died and were preserved together.

5) Fishes whose remains were deposited in the same location but at different times (separated by 2-4 cm of sediment) may each form a concretion that can coalesce without apparent discontinuity.

6) The nucleation center is not necessarily a vertebrate fossil (although this is the most common situation), and concretions can form readily around scraps of plant remains (leaves, cones, carbonized wood), whose organic chemistry is very different from that of vertebrates, and around coprolitic material.

7) Non-skeletal (plant, coprolite, shell) fossils generally do not influence concretion shape.

8) The majority of complete fossil vertebrates show no evidence of scavenging, and only occasionally is any postmortem disarticulation evident. Incomplete remains are common and may be attributed to postmortem drifting of decomposing body parts. This seems more plausible than disturbance by scavengers, for which there is little evidence apart from the presence of ostracods and rare shrimp remains around some of the fish carcasses.

9) It is evident from the fine preservation of soft tissues and from the three-dimensional shapes of presumably very soft coprolitic matter and intestinal content that diagenetic formation of the concretion commenced soon after burial, before any appreciable sediment compaction had occurred.

Faunal and Floral Distributions

The Sanatana formation concretions are variable not only in their lithology and composition, but also in their fossil content, suggesting that some environmental compartmentalization existed locally at the time these fossils were living organisms. The local sedimentary environment (termed "facies" by geologists) varied from one area to the next, perhaps because of factors such as closeness to shore, depth and/or stratification of the water column, proximity to sediment sources like streams and rivers, adjacent upland topography and vegetation, and perhaps even exposure to prevailing winds.

Such environmental factors conceivably may have also influenced the plant and animal communities both within and around the water body in which the Santana formation sediments accumulated. Lithologically, "Jardim" and "Old Mission" concretions resemble each other quite closely except for the higher clay content and prevalence of authigenic pyrite in the darker "Old Mission" matrix. "Santana" concretions differ from both these other kinds in several lithological respects. Interestingly, the fossil content of the concretions also is variable, and again the greatest contrast is between "Santana" and other concretions. This observation offers compelling evidence that perhaps three or more fossil assemblages are recognizable in concretions from the Santana formation.

The following semi-quantitative list is based mainly on observations of Araripe fossils in several museum collections in Europe, North America, and Brazil. The sample undoubtedly is biased toward more unusual or exotic specimens, but it at least provides insight into the relative abundance of the different taxa. In the list, several categories are used. "Abundant" means more than 20-30% of the fossils observed from a particular type of concretion are represented by the genera listed (in some cases the percentage actually may be higher, as in *Tharrhias, Rhacolepis,* and *Vinctifer*).

"Common" means simply that the taxon is well-represented; "uncommon" means that only a few specimens have been observed; and "rare" means that only one or two are known. "Exotic" means that the fossils represent organisms that probably fell into the environment (e.g., terrestrial plants and animals).

The "other" category is for occurrences of small additional fossils (mainly invertebrates) within the concretion surrounding the principal fossil. These other fossils rarely had any effect on the shape of the concretion, and may be regarded as serendipitous occurrences resulting from diagenetic growth of the concretions around the principal fossils.

For completeness, data for the Crato member limestones and a new site in bituminous shales at Pedra Blanca are appended.

1. *"Santana" concretion assemblage*

Abundant	*Tharrhias*
Common	*Brannerion, Araripelepidotes, Calamopleurus* (= *Enneles*)
Uncommon	*Cladocyclus, Axelrodichthys*
Rare	*Vinctifer, Rhinobatos, Notelops,* "*Leptolepis,*" clupeoid
Exotic	crocodilians, turtles, pterosaurs, terrestrial plant remains (leaves, wood, cones, etc.)
Other	ostracods (abundant), "fairy shrimp" (rare)

2. *"Jardim" concretion assemblage*

Abundant	*Rhacolepis, Vinctifer*
Common	*Notelops, Brannerion, Araripelepidotes, Cladocyclus, Calamopleurus, Axelrodichthys, Rhinobatos*
Uncommon	*Neoproscinetes, Araripichthys, Paraelops, Mawsonia*
Rare	*Tharrhias* (large), *Oshunia*
Exotic	turtles, pterosaurs, ?crocodilians
Other	ostracods (common)

3. *"Old Mission" concretion assemblage*

Abundant	*Rhacolepis, Vinctifer, Notelops*
Common	*Brannerion, Neoproscinetes*
Uncommon	*Araripichthys, Calamopleurus, Cladocyclus, Paraelops*
Rare	*Oshunia*
Other	ostracods (common to rare), parasitic copepods (exotic), "shrimp" (rare), *Corbula*-like pelecypods (occasionally common), small gastropods (rare)

4. *Crato member (laminated limestones)*

Abundant	*Dastilbe*
Rare	*Cladocyclus* (small), ?*Araripelepidotes*
Exotic	insects (uncommon), other arthropods (rare), plants (uncommon), bird feather (rare), frog (rare)

5. *Bituminous shales at Pedra Blanca, near Nova Olinda*
(data from Viana, Brito & Silva-Telles, MS).

Fishes	*Vinctifer, Cladocyclus, Rhacolepis*
Ostracods	*Hourquia angulata angulata*

Four examples of "transgressive" *Rhacolepis* specimens cutting across bedding planes (indicated by red arrows).

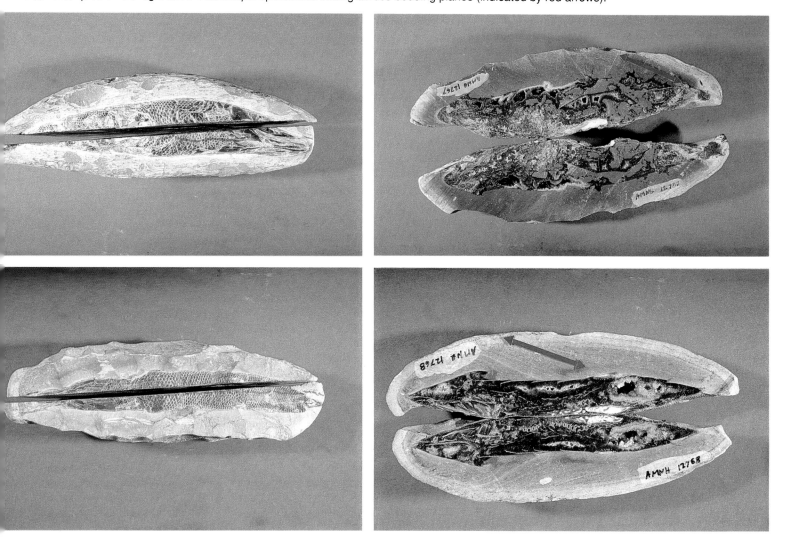

From a qualitative viewpoint, the fossil content of the concretions is still more variable, particularly with regard to the sizes of individual specimens. The "Santana" concretions contain many specimens of the gonorynchiform fish *Tharrhias*, plus small *Brannerion* and much rarer *Vinctifer*, *Calamopleurus*, *Notelops*, and *Cladocyclus*, all of them much smaller than those from "Jardim" and "Old Mission" concretions. *Tharrhias* has not been found in "Old Mission" concretions, and only three have been observed in "Jardim" concretions, but these three represent unusually large individuals. *Rhinobatos*, a small specimen of the coelacanth *Axelrodichthys*, and a clupeomorph also have been observed in "Santana" concretions. Crocodiles, turtles, pterosaurs, and terrestrial plants occur here, but they have not been found in "Old Mission" concretions, and only rarely have pterosaurs and turtles been found in "Jardim" concretions.

The largest fishes to have been described from the Santana formation are the coelacanths (*Mawsonia*, *Axelrodichthys*), elopomorphs (*Paraelops*, *Notelops*), and the ichthyodectiform *Cladocyclus*. Of these, the largest elopomorphs and *Cladocyclus* occur in "Old Mission" concretions. Extremely large coelacanths occur in "Jardim" concretions, but the largest skeletons observed are incomplete.

Preservationally, fossil fishes in the "Santana" matrix usually are complete, but it is not uncommon to find specimens lacking scales. The fossils rarely show signs of postmortem necrolytic curvature, unlike in "Jardim" concretions where many of the corpses are arched or curled (usually in longer-bodied fishes such as *Vinctifer* and *Cladocyclus*). Necrolytic curvature is unusual in "Old Mission" concretions. Specimens in which the head is angled down through successive layers of matrix, but with the body lying parallel to the lamination, probably got into this condition during burial (i.e., the curvature is biostratinomic rather than necrolytic, using the terminology developed by Seilacher, et al., 1985).

The qualitative remarks above undoubtedly are biased by the availability of material and by limited field observations. Nevertheless, there is an apparent link between the lithology and fossil content of different concretions. These differences may reflect actual paleoenvironmental variation that existed within the Araripe basin during the Lower Cretaceous and apparently had an impact upon not only the biota represented by these fossil assemblages but also upon their diagenetic mode of preservation and ultimately upon the quality of preparation and information content.

If it is accepted that particular concretion lithologies are characteristic of particular localities or stratigraphic horizons (scenarios that need to be tested by intensive collecting under rigorously controlled conditions), it appears that "Santana" concretions may have been formed in a near-shore sedimentary environment into which terrestrial plants and vertebrates occasionally fell. The fish fauna of the "Santana" environment was restricted both in size and taxic diversity compared with areas (farther to the east?). The bottom environment probably was better oxygenated, explaining the absence of pollen and pyrite from the "Santana" matrix (cellulose structures such as pollen and spore cuticles would decompose readily in an oxygenated subsrate, and pyrite is a sulphide of iron that apparently forms in anoxic environments, particularly in the presence of certain sulphide-loving bacteria). The absence of clay particles and abundance of ostracods in "Santana" concretions suggest that the water column was relatively clear, allowing sunlight to penetrate to a reasonable depth.

Extending this scenario to the "Jardim" and "Old Mission" lithologies, these may have formed in waters that probably were deeper and perhaps stratified, with an anoxic bottom environment and a higher influx of fine clay sediments. Nevertheless, the presence of ostracods even in these concretions suggests a clearer upper part to the water column. It is possible that inflowing waters were heavily charged with a suspension of clay particles, imparting a greater density than the clearer surface waters. This would be likely, for example, if there had been a marine ingression into a fluviatile or lacustrine environment. Lamination of the accumulated sediments may have resulted from pulsatory causal agencies, ranging from diurnal temperature changes and wind-shifts to seasonal adjustments of flow rates, current strengths, and sediment loading. According to this scenario, the muddier bottom environments may have been more prevalent at some time or in part of the Araripe basin, where the waters apparently were dominated by a wide variety of large predaceous fishes. Terrestrial vertebrates such as pterosaurs and turtles occasionally drifted into the fringes of the area.

Previous Taphonomic Investigations

How did these concretions form, and under what physical, chemical, and biological conditions were these exquisite fossils preserved? Somewhat surprisingly, very little has been published on the subject.

Sir Arthur Smith Woodward noted in 1887 that some of the fossil fishes showed signs of having been crushed or telescoped lengthwise, with their scales thrust over each other more than they should be.

This observation was confirmed by Jordan and Branner (1908), who suggested that this telescoping may be due to shrinking of the original limestone, caused by replacement of calcium carbonate by magnesium carbonate (a diagenetic process known as dolomitization). Shrinkage by dolomitization theoretically also might result in the development of radial cracks and fissures inside the concretions, with subsequent deposition of new calcite within the fissures, resulting in a septarian structure (first reported at Jardim by Gardner, 1849).

Several Santana formation concretions were analyzed chemically for Jordan and Branner. According to the results they published, the matrix contained between 89.98% and 93.26% $CaCO_3$ (calcium carbonate). All the samples they investigated had between 1.16 and 1.38% $MgCO_3$ (magnesium carbonate), with higher $MgCO_3$ levels where $CaCO_3$ is correspondingly lower. This is hardly sufficient $MgCO_3$ to produce much dolomite, which is a complex carbonate of calcium and magnesium comprising approximately 54.35% calcium carbonate and 45.65% magnesium carbonate. According to these figures, only some 3% of the carbonate matrix could be in the form of dolomite. Jordan and Branner's dolomitization hypothesis is consequently unconvincing.

Mabesoone and Tinoco (1973, p. 106) concluded that the concretions were formed at the margins of major water bodies, where fish and tetrapod corpses were exposed to strong solar and subaerial desiccation. This, they postulated, might explain how various external and internal structures (bones, muscle fibers, intervertebral discs) came to be so well-preserved. It was suggested that plasmolysis of internal organs possibly created a different environment within the carcass, and exudation of lipids probably caused surrounding sediments to adhere to the organic remains.

Although this hypothesis could explain a few preservational aspects seen in the Santana formation concretions, it does not provide a convincing model. Firstly, only the longer-bodied fishes show signs of necrolytic curvature from dehydration, and this could have occurred equally in a saline or hypersaline aquatic environment. Secondly, a subaerial, well-oxygenated environment is contraindicated, at least in "Old Mission" concretions, by the presence of cellulose from dinoflagellates and pollen and also by high levels of finely disseminated, authigenic iron pyrite. Oxygen may have been more freely available within both "Santana" and "Jardim" depositional environments, but there is no evidence to suggest that subaerial exposure occurred here but not in the "Old Mission" depositional environment.

Many years earlier, the probable origin of calcareous concretions within shales had been investigated by a research geologist with the Standard Oil Company, Dr. L. G. Weeks. While conducting field surveys along the Magdalena River in northern Colombia, Mr. D. J. Podesta, a geologist working for International Petroleum (Colombia, Ltd.), discovered well-preserved fossil fishes inside calcareous concretions of Cretaceous (probably Albian) age. These fossils were brought to the attention of Dr. Weeks, who in turn showed them to Dr. Bobb Schaeffer, a paleoichthyologist at the American Museum of Natural History. The fossils subsequently were studied by Dr. Rubens da Silva Santos, who has determined that they are specimens of *Rhacolepis* (pers. comm., 1989).

Dr. Weeks published his findings in two papers (Weeks, 1953, 1957). He drew several astute paleoenvironmental conclusions concerning the occurrence of calcareous concretions. Widespread concretion development occurs principally, he noted, in sedimentary facies where limestones are not present or else occur in very impure form. In other words, he contended, concretions characterize only parts of a sedimentary basin with a stagnant bottom environment, where any free oxygen rapidly is depleted and carbon dioxide removal is inhibited, enabling lime to remain in solution as bicarbonate. This environment is in sharp contrast to the carbon dioxide-free, aerated bottom environment of many marginal sedimentary basins and shallow interbasinal "highs," where calcium carbonate most readily is removed from the waters and deposited as calcareous sediment.

Dr. Weeks then posed an important question. Why is it that in an environment so unsuitable for limestone formation, calcareous concretions can develop locally around some organic nucleus such as a fish skeleton? He realized that a highly localized microenvironment must have been established in which the conditions were favorable for calcium carbonate precipitation. Since the solubility of calcium carbonate is controlled mainly by the hydrogen-ion concentration (pH), any condition that causes the removal of carbon dioxide increases the pH and so induces deposition of lime. Examples of factors that would affect pH by removing carbon dioxide include increased water temperature, agitation and aeration, and decreased carbon dioxide levels in the atmosphere.

Ocean waters generally are alkaline, with a pH ranging from about 7.5 to 8.5 (a neutral solution has a pH of 7). On stagnant, anaerobic sea bottoms, the pH often is below 7, within the acid range. Carbonate deposition normally requires a pH of at least 7.8. Dr. Weeks suggested that decomposition of organic remains by anaerobic bacteria within a stagnant bottom environment could in fact raise pH values locally by the release of ammonia or amines to the level where bicarbonate ions could come out of solution as carbonate.

The decomposition of nitrogen-rich proteinaceous tissues is known to occur more rapidly than the breakdown of fatty tissues (Hecht, 1933; Trask, 1937), thereby liberating large amounts of ammonia and amines. Nitrogen usually escapes rapidly as ammonia, accounting for the higher ratio of carbon to nitrogen in sedimentary organic matter than in living organisms. More resistant fatty substances may permeate into surrounding sediments as a brownish waxy substance known as adipocere (usually generated in dead and long-immersed bodies, especially in sea water). The adipocere even may cement the surrounding sediment into a concretion-like mass.

Weeks was perhaps the first scientist to appreciate the importance of bacterial decomposition to localized carbonate deposition and concretion formation. Unfortunately, his work largely was ignored. Furthermore, later investigations of sedimentary environments of lake bottoms seemed to contradict his concept of local alkaline microenvironments. According to Wetzel (1975), for example, there is considerable mixing of hypolimnic layers, which would allow the escape of nitrogenous matter and prevent the pH from rising to levels suitable for carbonate precipitation.

Only in exceptional circumstances, for example in lakes heavily laden with the products of industrial pollution, were alkaline conditions found to predominate for much of the time (e.g., Lake Onondaga in upper New York state; Berner 1968; Wilcox and Effler, 1981). Interestingly, in these conditions it is possible for calcareous concretions to form around the bodies of recently dead, lipid-rich alewife fish. The chemical processes leading to the production of these alewife concretions have been investigated thoroughly by Wilcox and Effler (1981). Although modern pollution evidently is responsible for creating a highly unusual and unpleasant environment within Lake Onondaga, it at least shows that calcium carbonate can be rapidly deposited within a corpse if the surrounding environment is suitably alkaline and supersaturated with carbonate.

Berner (1968) investigated this peculiar environment and proposed a mechanism for production of calcium-fatty acid concretions from organic matter anaerobically, concluding that it probably involved bacterial decay, precipitation of calcium carbonate, and subsequent reaction between lipids and calcium carbonate to form calcium salts of fatty acids. Such reactions require an alkaline microenvironment, whereas most decay processes occur in strongly acidic conditions.

Some unusual preservational features. **Top row** and **upper center left:** Two *Vinctifer* specimens on different bedding planes in one concretion. **Upper center right:** *Vinctifer* with postmortem damage to vertebral column, reflected by concretion shape. **Lower center:** Heavy secondary calcite growth extending from three-dimensional *Rhacolepis* (left) and flattened *Brannerion* (right). **Bottom left:** Large calcite crystals in body of *Rhacolepis*. **Bottom right:** Concretion with natural fracture and partial dissolution, resulting in shortened caudal peduncle of fossil *Brannerion*.

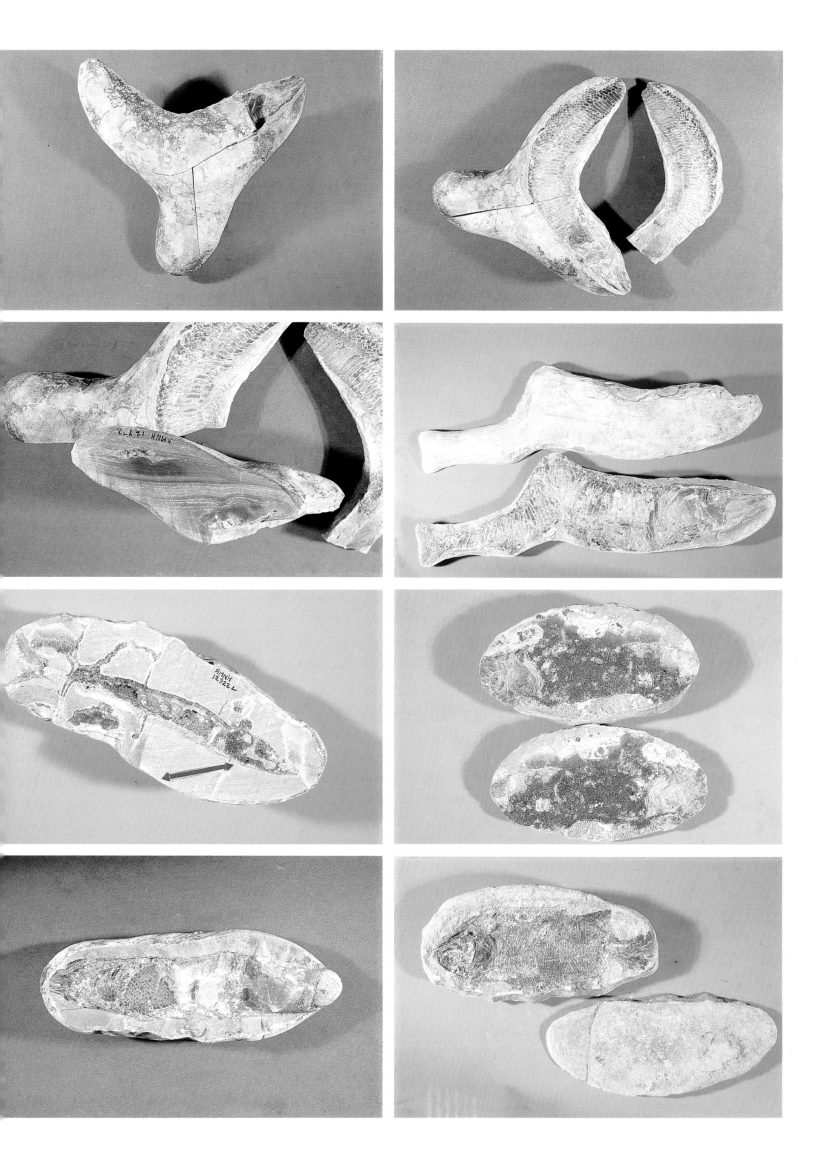

Lake Onondaga is heavily loaded with chlor-alkaline salts and has particularly high levels of chlorine, sodium, calcium, and bicarbonate ions. Its waters also are stratified, with an anaerobic bottom environment (hypolimnion). Extremely high sedimentation rates (5-9 cm/year) are experienced, mainly as a consequence of industrial loading of calcium. This calcium loading is virtually continuous, and during the summer period the lower rate of water flushing into the lake can result in continuous supersaturation of calcium, particularly in its upper waters.

The alewife, *Alosa pseudoharengus*, is a primarily marine clupeomorph (herring group) fish that has become established in Lake Onondaga. Large numbers of dead, lipid-rich individuals are sometimes washed ashore as combustible chalky concretions. Wilcox and Effler (1981) were able to replicate the conditions necessary to produce alewife concretions in the laboratory. These investigators concluded that high calcium carbonate concentrations are necessary to permit formation of calcium-lipid salts within body tissues, and that the process also required anaerobic conditions within the lake hypolimnion.

Although this last condition commonly occurs in many lacustrine and other aquatic environments, it is unusual for any of these systems to be supersaturated with calcium or carbonate. Nevertheless, in the case of the Romualdo member it is very possible that such conditions prevailed at certain times. The presence of an evaporite sequence at the top of the underlying lacustrine sequence (Crato member) support the contention that salinity levels were high toward the end of its depositional episode, and it is not unreasonable to suppose that calcium carbonate levels occasionally approached supersaturation in certain parts of the bottom environment. Influx of high numbers of lipid-rich fishes into such an environment, followed by mass mortality, could tip the balance and trigger the production of lipid salts.

The chemistry behind carbonate concretion formation was resolved only partially by Wilcox and Effler (1981). For example, vertebrates are not the only fossils around which these concretions may form. In the Romualdo member of the Santana formation they have nucleated around plant remains (e.g., carbonized wood fragments, cones, leaf fronds), in which any original lipid content would be low. Other concretions have formed around phosphatic coprolites, and there also are numerous small (10-15 cm) rounded concretions that lack an obvious organic nucleus. Some other mechanism may have triggered calcium carbonate nucleation in these cases, resulting in essentially the same matrix as occurs in the fish concretions.

We can be reasonably certain that there was no industrial pollution 110 million years ago in the Lower Cretaceous. It is possible, however, that the bottom environment where the Santana formation concretions formed had unusually elevated carbonate and pH levels, if for example there was a continuous influx of volcanic gases (including carbon dioxide) or heavily mineralized ground waters percolating up through the bottom sediments. The Araripe basin is but a short distance from the alkaline volcanic center in the Cabo basin, which was active at this time (see geological history earlier). The Cabo and Cameroon volcanics developed during the final stages of separation of Brazil and Africa.

If unusually widespread alkaline conditions were not created by some mechanism such as this, the only reasonable alternative seems to be that proposed by Weeks of a very localized microenvironment. The major drawback to his suggestion was admixture of bottom layers, supposedly preventing the accumulation of ammonia and an increase in alkalinity.

This difficulty was overcome once the importance of bacterial scum over the substrate was fully realized by Seilacher, et al. (1985) and others. This scum (consisting mainly of cyanobacteria) protects sediments and delicate fossils from erosion and from decay processes involving free oxygen. The scum also may have fueled certain diagenetic chemical processes such as carbonate and phosphate deposition locally, initially only within the corpses but ultimately extending into the surrounding matrix.

Martill (1988) suggested that mass mortality events were responsible for the large numbers of fossil fishes preserved in Santana formation concretions. One plausible mechanism is fluctuating salinities. Martill contended that the fishes were essentially marine and that their deaths were perhaps the result of a migrating halocine, although other causes (e.g., sudden changes in water temperature or an algal bloom) could not be ruled out.

Accumulation of corpses on the bottom was followed, according to Martill, by their becoming encased rapidly by a prokaryotic scum that extended across the entire substrate much as Seilacher, et al. (1985) suggested was the case at Sölnhofen. Martill's hypothesis required an initial stage of lowered pH, during which phosphates were precipitated, followed rapidly by much higher pH levels leading to carbonate precipitation. Furthermore, he contended that such changes may have occurred within a few hours of death.

Martill's (1988) model is certainly more in accordance with present observations than either of the scenarios presented earlier by Jordan and Branner (1908) or Mabesoone and Tinoco (1973). Nevertheless, there is some disagreement over the extent to which phosphate is involved in soft tissue preservation. Phosphatization may occur only sporadically and be very localized even within a concretion. In consequence of this, Martill's conclusions about pH fluctuation in the bottom environment are questionable (Maisey, 1988; Schultze, 1989).

Taphonomic Pattern of the Santana Formation Concretions

Stratigraphic Setting As will by now be apparent, there is some uncertainty surrounding the stratigraphic situation. The Romualdo member of the Santana formation is regarded here as unconformably overlying the Crato member.

The stratigraphic sequence consists of calcareous-concretionary, keragen-rich shales, plus clayey limestones and sandstones. The average thickness of the unit is around 50 meters (Silva, 1986b), although a maximum thickness of 150 meters has been reported (Mabesoone and Tinoco, 1973). Near the top of the sequence is a fairly thick-bedded limestone. The top of the Romualdo member is truncated by an erosion surface and is uncomformably overlain by cross-bedded sandstones of the Exu formation.

The age of the Romualdo member still is not known with precision, but it appears to date in part from the Middle to Upper Aptian and Early Albian. The overlying Exu formation has yielded pollen suggestive of a Middle Albian age.

Ecological Spectrum The fossil assemblages are dominated by pelagic organisms, especially fishes, but are perhaps even more remarkable for the absence of any large pelagic invertebrates such as cephalopods and crustaceans. Land-

going reptiles also occur, but not marine-adapted ones such as ichthyosaurs. Pelagic sharks are absent, the only chondrichthyans being the apparently benthic *Rhinobatos* and *Tribodus* (Brito and Ferreira, 1989). Epibenthic molluscs (pelecypods, gastropods) are locally abundant in the formation as a whole but are rarer in the concretions. Other epibenthic marine invertebrates that reasonably might be expected, such as brachiopods, limulids, corals, and crinoids, have not been recorded, and echinoids have been found but rarely. There is no trace of any encrusting epiplanktonic fauna such as oysters or barnacles, nor of any burrowing endobenthos. It is conceivable that the depauperate benthic invertebrate fauna was washed in accidentally, although *Corbula*-like pelecypods found in some calcareous concretions usually have both valves closed, suggesting that they were not transported appreciably after death. Terrestrial plants are invariably fragmentary and of localized occurrence, and include cheirolepidiaceous leafy fronds, fragments of carbonized twigs and branches, and entire cones. The latter contain calcified seeds and presumably were not fully ripened, suggesting premature removal from the parent plant. It is possible that the exceptionally rare plant material was washed in following storms or some other catastrophic event.

The consensus (but not necessarily correct) view is that the paleoenvironment was a shallow embayment passing into a coastal region with beaches, estuaries, and tidal flats (Silva Santos and Valença, 1968; Mabesoone and Tinoco, 1973; Santos, 1982). Periodic pulsatory marine incusions are indicated by microfossils such as ostracods and dinoflagellates. The extent to which marine and non-marine waters became mixed seems to have varied, which resulted in different assemblages of microfossils and which may also have influenced the distribution and relative abundance of fishes and other organisms. If this is true, then it must have been a remarkable setting to have permitted the ingress of such a wide variety of fishes while it simultaneously lacked an established marine endobenthos or diverse invertebrate epibenthos.

It has been suggested that "normal" benthonic life (including bivalves, worms, snails, crustaceans, and echinoderms) will not occur in deep, stagnant waters that are devoid of currents (Schäffer, 1972). Oxygen-free conditions may develop by decomposition of planktonic or other organisms. There is a gradual downward drift of decomposition products, and the level of hydrogen sulfide becomes elevated. A temporary or permanent anoxic zone may even develop in the water above the benthic zone. According to Schäffer, in the absence of oxygen the body cavity of a fish carcass does not become inflated with gas, and the skeleton therefore is more likely to be preserved intact, even with some soft parts preserved.

Ostracods are abundant, and it has been suggested that these were benthic scavengers feeding upon the fish carcasses and algae (Bate, 1972). The low diversity of ostracods here suggests a non-marine habitat. The presence of an extensive cyanobacterial scum (Martill, 1988) may indicate high salinity levels, since these scums are thought to be restricted largely to hypersaline environments (Seilacher, et al., 1985). Higher than normal salinity levels are quite feasible, since water exchange may well have been restricted (suggested by the strongly biased content of the fossil assemblage), the ambient air temperatures may have been high (permitting high evaporation rates, particularly at low humidity levels), and the ground water may have contained high levels of dissolved salts derived from underlying evaporites at the top of the Araripina formation. These salt deposits would have had only a thin sedimentary cover at the time.

Necrolytic Features The vertebral column commonly is arched in specimens of the elongate fishes *Vinctifer* and *Cladocyclus*, suggesting some dehydration of body tissues. Similar necrolytic curvature in Sölnhofen fossil fishes has been attributed to dehydration within hypersaline water, instead of subaerial desiccation (Seilacher, et al., 1985).

Schäffer (1972) noted that a dead pipefish (*Syngnathus*), with a body form not unlike that of *Vinctifer*, will sink belly-down onto the substrate. After a few days the body becomes arched upward, with the head and tail remaining in contact with the bottom as gases accumulate in the pectoral area. Then the head rises from the substrate, leaving the tail on the bottom. Although the epidermis begins to decompose, its bony armor holds the body together in its original form. Eventually the head sinks back to the bottom. The body armor remains intact for about 18 days before individual pieces become detached.

Many specimens of *Rhacolepis* are preserved with the body apparently bloated, especially those occurring at angles to the bedding lamination. From this it may be inferred that many of the fish carcasses became bloated during the early stages of decay, although in most cases the gases escaped either just prior to

burial or else shortly afterward. It is unlikely that any fishes remained bloated by gases for an extended period, however, and an alternative explanation for three-dimensional preservation of the body must be sought.

Some significance can be attached to the observation that in most *Rhacolepis* specimens, even where the body has a bloated appearance, the head and body are more or less intact and do not show characteristic signs of violent separation by escaping gas. This is frequently a feature of modern fish carcasses and is a very common occurrence among the *Dastilbe* from the Crato member. Schäffer (1972) found that the head did not separate from the body in certain kinds of fishes, such as the plaice (*Pleuronectes*), a dragonet (*Callionymus*), sea robin (*Trigla*), and lesser sand-eel (*Ammodytes*). In these cases, the carcasses remained on the bottom. In cases where the carcass was buoyant (usually after a few days of lying on the bottom), varying amounts of decomposition and skeletal dismemberment were commonly observed. Schäffer also noted that by artificially introducing oxygen into stagnant water, skeletal remains may become buoyant even after they have lain on the bottom for some months. When this occurs, individual skeletal parts become widely scattered.

Since bloating is confined largely to *Rhacolepis*, we may postulate that, like the modern alewife, *Alosa*, the fish was particularly rich in lipids. Interestingly, the ossified swim-bladder of fossil coelacanths from this formation (and from other localities) also is preserved in three-dimensions. In the living coelacanth *Latimeria* the swim-bladder largely is filled with fatty tissue. It therefore may be no coincidence that *Rhacolepis* and coelacanth swim-bladders are preserved in this manner.

Apparently the proteinaceous tissues forming the body musculature of *Rhacolepis* became calcified at a very early stage in decomposition, leading to replacement of muscle fibers by chalky, microcrystalline calcium carbonate. If the bloated carcass burst, it rapidly would have been buried horizontally within the muddy

Top: Secondary calcite overgrowth shown diagrammatically (left) and in an actual specimen (right). **Center:** Phosphatic coprolites within small concretions. **Bottom:** Nearly vertical *Rhacolepis* in concretion (red arrow indicates bedding plane orientation).

SECONDARY CALCITE OVERGROWTH WITHIN FISH SCALES

sediment, sometimes with the myotomal muscle pattern still intact. Where bursting did not occur, however, decomposition of body musculature may have continued until its original segmented arrangement became obliterated and replaced by a disordered chalky white mass like that described from decomposed *Alosa* in Lake Onondaga (Berner, 1968; Wilcox and Effler, 1981). Burial of these still somewhat buoyant corpses evidently took longer than for those already flattened, because of their end-up orientation.

Quite probably the gut contents also were undergoing biochemical changes at this time, with phosphate enrichment possibly caused by continued bacterial action, perhaps within the closed, highly acidic microenvironment of the intact gut. The alimentary canal thus forms a continuous cololite (= intestinal contents, as distinct from a coprolite, which is fossilized excrement). Schäffer (1972) found that the anus commonly protrudes during the early stages of decay. In this regard it is of interest that in some specimens of *Rhacolepis* the phosphatic cololite extends beyond the body, suggesting that here also the anus became distended.

Martill (1989, fig. 9) illustrated phosphatized fragments of *Notelops* gill filaments with secondary lamellae. He pointed out that such features would not survive bacterial infestation for more than a few days, and argued that phosphatization probably occurred within a few hours of death because the secondary lamellae (which would normally collapse from loss of blood pressure) are almost intact in the fossil he examined.

These initial stages in corpse mineralization are included here as necrolytic factors rather than diagenetic ones (see below), because they are early postmortem changes that probably began even before the corpse had become buried by sediments, perhaps even before it had settled on the substrate. It is unlikely that a gas-filled corpse would be able to withstand the compaction of burial beneath even a few centimeters of mud, and many of these fossils seem to have behaved as semi-rigid objects even as the sediment accumulated around them.

Mabesoone and Tinoco (1973) noted that the tail frequently is missing from fishes preserved in these concretions. It may have been lost, they argued, because it is largely bony or cartilaginous and lacks fatty tissue that would decompose to adipocere and become cemented to the surrounding sediment. It is clear from Schäffer's (1972) experiments that this may have resulted from the effects of buoyancy during decomposition.

Moreover, the tail and other fins frequently are preserved in their in-life positions in bloated *Rhacolepis*, projecting out into the surrounding matrix. The extremities are preserved in many concretions containing other kinds of fossil fishes, particularly where the concretion outline does not follow that of the fossil.

Within the bloated body cavity, some individual vertebrae became detached and jumbled as the connective tissues holding them together rotted away. These loose bones evidently fell to the lowest part of the body cavity where they became piled up, providing a useful "way-up" indicator.

It seems that decomposition of proteinaceous tissues within the unburied fish corpses raised local amine and pH levels to the point where bacterially-related deposition of microcrystalline calcium carbonate could occur. High adipocere levels within the corpse initially may have helped retain the microcrystallites in their original arrangement around muscle fibers, but as decomposition became more advanced this pattern was lost.

Some fish skeletons are preserved without their scaly covering. Since the scales are missing from both sides of the skeleton (making these ideal specimens for acid preparation), they probably were lost prior to burial rather than by subsequent removal by current action. Decomposition probably was far advanced, and it is therefore remarkable that so much of the endoskeleton usually is preserved intact in such cases. Nevertheless, Schäffer (1972) found cases among modern fishes where the scales were lost even though the internal skeleton remained intact.

Scattered, isolated fish bones commonly are recovered in acid preparation residues and many times do not belong to the specimen being prepared. Usually it cannot be determined whether these bones have been carried by currents or represent the most advanced stages of pre-burial decomposition. However, they rarely show signs of wear or attrition and thus are unlikely to have been transported very far.

Biostratinomic Features There has been no attempt to determine whether the fossil fishes of the Romualdo member have a preferred azimuth orientation, and such data would be difficult to obtain given the temporary nature of many exposures and the haphazard collecting methods generally employed. Strong currents are unlikely, however, given the fine sediment size and quality of fossil preservation.

Rarely, fish skeletons are broken into sections, all of which remain together but not in their original orientation. Each section of the skeleton remains intact, suggesting that scavenging was not responsible. Instead, the remains may have been disturbed by the light current action prior to burial and while most of the bones were still connected by soft tissues.

Some *Vinctifer* and *Brannerion* corpses seem to have been partially buoyant, like many of the *Rhacolepis*, and were buried with the head angled downward through the sediments. Behind the head, however, the bodies are flattened and lie parallel to bedding. These specimens are interpreted as follows: The partially decomposed (and mineralized?) corpse sank head-down into the substrate, and the head became buried. Unlike smaller *Rhacolepis* corpses, the still-projecting bodies of these larger *Brannerion* and *Vinctifer* specimens lacked sufficient internal strength to support themselves prior to becoming entirely buried, perhaps having lost their initial buoyancy. The body apparently snapped behind the head and collapsed onto the flat substrate, where it became rapidly buried.

This interpretation is preferred over the alternative one suggested by Schäffer's (1972) experiments, in which he often observed fish corpses settling belly-down and head-up. It would, of course, be possible to imagine dead *Rhacolepis* in that orientation, but it is contraindicated by the sedimentological criteria already alluded to.

Schäffer (1972) recognized two categories of decomposition among the fishes he studies: (1) where the body refloats following the accumulation of gases, sinking only after the gas escapes when the body wall is ruptured; and (2) where the body cavity and/or volume of gases is too small to permit refloating. He concluded that the mode of decay in fishes is determined by the ratio of body cavity size to body mass. As he pointed out, however, gas production is influenced by factors such as water temperature, oxygen availability, and salinity, which probably affect rates of bacterial activity. At lower water temperatures, higher salinities, or in anoxic environments, he argued, some "re-floaters" may not become buoyant. Most fishes possess quite delicate skeletons that readily become disarticulated, and the preservation of so many articulated skeletons in Santana formation concretions, including many forms that might be considered "re-floaters," is compelling evidence for low rates of bacterial action on the substrate. Under these circumstances, how may we explain the presence of so many bloated *Rhacolepis* among these fossils? One possibility is that they represent "re-floaters" that became

bloated higher in the water column but for some reason were able to retain their shape as they subsequently sank back into the gloomy depths. These fossils therefore seem to represent a different pattern of decomposition that does not fit conveniently into either of Schäffer's categories. We must seek an alternative pathway of events involving early diagenetic or even necrolytic processes that would help preserve the body form intact. Such processes, including early (even pre-burial) mineralization of the body tissues, are examined in the following section.

Diagenetic Features In the following section, reference will be made to calcification and phosphatization. It is important to note that, although phosphatization involves calcium phosphate, it is not included by the term "calcification" in the present context. Calcification is used in preference to "carbonatization" as a descriptor of calcium carbonate precipitation. Correspondingly, "calcified" and "phosphatized" are used as terms denoting tissues mineralized predominantly by calcium carbonate and calcium phosphate respectively.

Martill (1988) proposed that initial calcification and phosphatization of soft tissues in Santana formation concretions is essentially a diagenetic phenomenon involving decomposition within or below a benthic cyanobacterial scum. Although the importance of bacterial action cannot be denied, there is reasonable evidence to support the view that the initial stages of corpse mineralization occurred prior to burial and are essentially necrolytic rather than diagenetic phenomena, and in a later paper Martill (1989) seems to adopt this position. It well may be that the corpses continued to accrete additional carbonate and phosphate as decomposition continued after burial. In the case of bloated corpses buried across the stratification, however, decompositionally-related mineralization of body tissues probably was completed before final burial. This is supported by the absence of obvious scavenging, despite the fact that the corpse probably was exposed for some time, and by the way in which the bloated corpses behaved after burial.

As was long ago noted by Woodward (1887) and by Jordan and Branner (1908), some of the fish corpses show signs of telescoping. Actually, their scaly covering often appears to have behaved more like a brittle sheath than a flexible skin, suggesting that it formed a thin but rigid exterior. As this sheath became compacted by additional sediment, it sometimes cracked and collapsed so that adjacent sections were imbricated and overlapped each other. If the corpse had been filled with liquefied contents, it seems more likely that the body would flex gradually as compaction increased. Sometimes this appears to have occurred, with small amounts of fluid being ejected into the surrounding muds and locally disrupting the lamination pattern. Where this occurred, some sediment made its way locally into the corpse. More frequently, however, the skin behaved as a brittle sheet, suggesting abrupt failure. Although surrounding sediments were disturbed, evidently they were unable to penetrate inside the corpse, probably because it already was filled with microcrystalline calcium carbonate and phosphate.

Whether initial fossilization of soft tissues occurred before burial (as suggested here) or subsequently (as Martill, 1988, believed), it evidently was a crucial early step in the preservation of these remains. The investigations of Berner (1968) and others suggest that calcification could occur only under alkaline conditions and with particularly high levels of dissolved calcium and carbonate ions. In Martill's (1988) preservational hypothesis, these conditions would be attained only within the substrate, and then perhaps only within the internal microenvironment of the corpse. According to our own observations, however, initial mineralization actually could have occurred within the water column (i.e., as a necrolytic phenomenon) as well as on or in the substrate (i.e., during early diagenesis). In all likelihood, early phosphatization and calcification of soft tissues occurred deep within the water column, perhaps just above substrate level. From the data available, it cannot be determined whether such processes could occur generally, throughout the bottom waters (i.e., following the mechanism proposed by Wilcox and Effler, 1981), or only locally, within the cadaverous microenvironment of semi-buoyant carcasses.

As Martill (1988) noted, the presence of numerous decomposing bodies within the aquatic environment would rapidly deplete the level of dissolved oxygen, thereby creating anaerobic conditions. Not only would this inhibit continued growth of the prokaryote mat, but it also might have overwhelmed the depauperate benthic fauna of ostracods, shrimp, pelecypods, and gastropods (assuming that they had not already been annihilated by the same event responsible for the fish-kills, for example by a dinoflagellate bloom). It also would inhibit certain kinds of bacterial decomposition, thereby depleting gas production within the body cavity of fishes and denying further buoyancy.

At this point it seems appropriate to consider several aspects of the preservational *schema* offered by Martill (1988). Firstly, as he admitted, anaerobic conditions in the vicinity of the substrate probably would inhibit further growth of a prokaryotic scum. Thus only those corpses already caught up by this mat would be situated favorably for subsequent diagenetic changes of the kinds Martill postulated. Yet there is clear evidence of prolonged exposure of many well-preserved fish corpses whose ultimate burial well could have been delayed until after any free oxygen had been depleted and prokaryote growth halted. Perhaps significantly, in these "floaters" (or "re-floaters"?) there is little evidence of soft tissue being preserved.

There also is less evidence of phosphatization of soft tissues than Martill suggested. Much of the fossilized muscle is dissolved readily in formic or acetic acid, and according to mineralogical X-ray analyses conducted at the University of Kansas (Schultze, 1989, fig. 21) most of it actually is composed of calcium carbonate. Where phosphatized soft tissues occur, their component parts are held together by calcium carbonate. While it is possible that Schultze's analyses picked up only this carbonate, it is also possible that phosphate is absent from certain areas and may be quite localized in its development. As Martill noted, phosphate is relatively rare in sea water (his postulated environment). Martill nevertheless claimed that a short-term elevation of carbon dioxide levels and lowered pH would not only inhibit precipitation of calcium carbonate, but would also enhance the precipitation of francolite (a form of calcium phosphate).

Top left: Variation in the form and fossil content of concretions from the Santana formation (diagrammatic). **Top right:** Necrolytic influences on preservation. **Bottom left:** Mass mortality of modern alewives (*Alosa*) in the Great Lakes. **Bottom right:** Fossil mass mortality from the Eocene Green River formation of Wyoming.

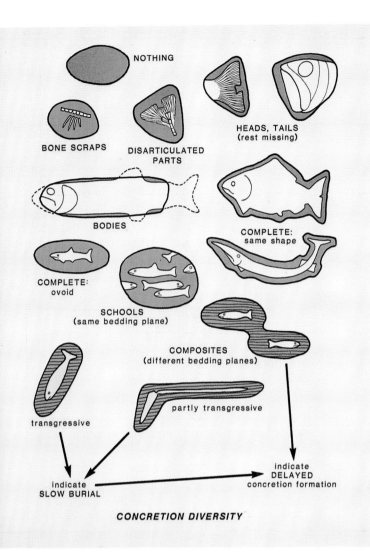

NOTHING

BONE SCRAPS

DISARTICULATED PARTS

HEADS, TAILS (rest missing)

BODIES

COMPLETE: same shape

COMPLETE: ovoid

SCHOOLS (same bedding plane)

COMPOSITES (different bedding planes)

transgressive

partly transgressive

indicate SLOW BURIAL

indicate DELAYED concretion formation

CONCRETION DIVERSITY

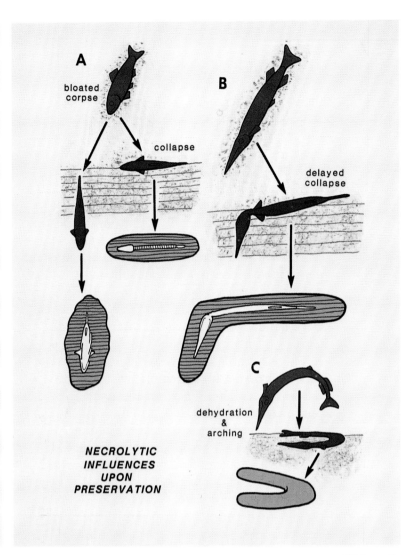

A

bloated corpse

collapse

B

delayed collapse

C

dehydration & arching

NECROLYTIC INFLUENCES UPON PRESERVATION

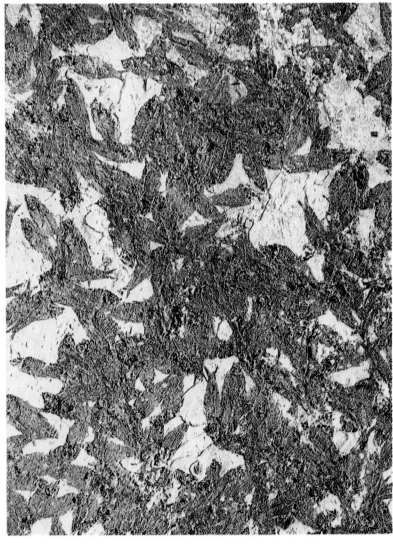

It is possible that carbon dioxide levels actually were lower and pH levels much higher than Martill suggested, in consequence of elevated ammonia and amine production within the decaying corpses. Martill admitted that such elevated pH levels would be attained rapidly by such decomposition of nitrogenous tissues, perhaps within hours of death. As discussed above, these conditions of high pH and carbonate precipitation already may have begun before burial. There may be no need to postulate capricious external fluctuations in pH, nor is there a need for vast amounts of phosphate-enriched pore-water to be flushed through the system. Furthermore, experimental work has shown that lowered carbon dioxide levels, under warm, strongly alkaline conditions, can lead to greatly increased rates of apatite formation, for example by flushing a solution of sodium phosphate through precipitated calcium carbonate (Ames, 1959).

Martill (1988) suggested that the bottom environment was initially oxygenated; indeed, this is a prerequisite for his model of phosphatization. Since there may not have been all that much phosphate, however, an aerobic bottom environment seems less plausible, particularly in the case of the "Old Mission" concretion lithology in which cellulose (pollen, dinoflagellates) and pyrite are abundant. It is clear from examination of many sectioned concretions that authigenic pyrite (iron sulphide) was able to grow around bones and within cavities inside the corpses, prior to calcification of the external matrix. Martill postulated that such precipitation of iron sulphides would not occur until after the corpses had been removed from an oxidizing to a reducing zone following burial, but again the need for this switch is redundant if the bottom environment already was anoxic. According to his hypothesis, pyrite precipitation occurred only after carbonate concretion formation had begun, whereas many sectioned concretions show the reverse situation.

It also is difficult to reconcile Martill's postulated aerobic bottom environment with Schäffer's (1972) experimental studies of fish decomposition, unless one accepts that gas production within all the carcasses was inhibited by other factors such as high salinity or low water temperature. Although Martill has indeed postulated a high salinity for the Romualdo member environments, it is not clear what the required theoretical levels would be in order to compensate for the presence of oxygen. In the normal course of decompositional events, Schäffer's work predicts that most of the

Santana formation fossil fishes would be disarticulated in an environment like that postulated by Martill. What is needed is an anaerobic bottom environment in which certain kinds of bacterial processes can take place without causing disruption of the skeletal remains.

In this context, it is of interest that pyrite and cellulose material do not occur in the "Santana" concretion lithology, which consists of a rather clean carbonate matrix rich in ostracods and very low in clay content. Some "Santana" concretions display evidence that muscle fibers and other soft tissues once were mineralized, but in most examples these tissues have been leached away, leaving only scattered traces. There is no evidence to suggest secondary loss (by oxidation) of cellulose matter or pyrite within the concretion, and it must be presumed that the present composition of "Santana" concretions is a reflection of some original depositional or diagenetic peculiarities. Possibly the bottom environment was better aerated, or perhaps it lay below a higher energy current regime that prevented local accumulation of finer muddy sediments. There rarely is evidence that any bottom or current action has affected the fossils themselves, and most were undisturbed after deposition. Under these circumstances, it is likely that particulate iron minerals were also flushed away and that there simply was insufficient ferruginous bottom matter to lead to formation of iron sulphides. Such an aerated bottom environment probably had low levels of dissolved carbon dioxide, in which case carbonate precipitation could occur readily around a variety of organic nuclei (including plants and coprolites as well as vertebrates).

Phosphatization apparently played only a minor (albeit paleontologically important) role in the preservation of these concretionary fossils. The vertebrate skeletons contain high levels of originally biogenic apatite but do not seem to have become further phosphatized diagenetically. Phosphatization of soft tissues is relatively unusual and is highly variable in extent even within these specimens.

Martill (1988, 1989) believed that phosphatization occurred prior to burial because it involves soft tissues that usually decay rapidly and that sometimes are in direct contact with surrounding sediment (e.g., the gills, and body muscle where scales have been lost). There is little doubt that necrolytic mineralization of these tissues began prior to burial. Although limited primary phosphatization may have taken place locally within the corpse, by far the most pervasive mineralization of soft tissues (especially of muscle fibers) seems to have been by carbonate.

Indirect evidence for diagenetic (i.e., later) rather than necrolytic phosphatization comes from the presence of phosphatized ostracods. Ostracod fossils are extremely abundant in the concretions, but nearly always are preserved in calcium carbonate. Phosphatized specimens of the kind described by Bate (1971, 1972) have been observed by us very rarely in acid-prepared specimens, usually less than 1 or 2 cm from a fish fossil, and only in the vicinity of soft tissues that are now phosphatized. Farther from the corpse, one usually finds only calcified ostracods. This suggests that phosphate enrichment occurred in this case only locally, after burial by sediments but probably before calcification of the surrounding matrix, and not prior to burial as Martill (1989) suggested.

Other phosphatized remains found in close proximity to a phosphatized fish corpse include copepods (Cressey and Patterson, 1973) and indeterminate shrimp-like crustaceans. A wide variety of phosphatized soft tissues from fossil fishes were illustrated by Martill (1988, 1989, 1990), including body muscle, secondary gill lamellae, stomach wall fragments, and possibly nerve fibers.

Whatever its preservational history may be, there is no escaping the fact that the "Medusa Effect" represents a dramatic and spectacular paleontological phenomenon. We may justifiably claim that the fossils of the Romualdo member concretions may be the best preserved in the world. Dr. Martill has generously given permission for us to reproduce some of his remarkable scanning electron microscope images of fossilized soft tissues. The wide range of tissue types, coupled with their remarkably detailed preservation, makes the "Medusa Effect" a truly awesome discovery.

SEM photographs of fossilized soft tissues from Santana formation fishes. **Top:** Single striated muscle fiber from *Notelops*, with nuclei. **Bottom:** Single nucleus in close-up detail (same specimen as above). Photos courtesy D. Martill.

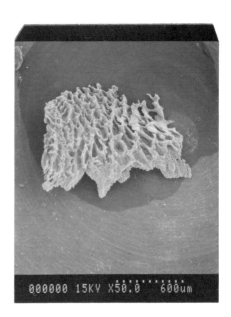

Left: SEM photo of sheath (sarcolemma) of striated muscle fibers from *Rhacolepis* (muscle fibers absent).

Above and below: SEM photos of fragments of stomach wall from *Notelops* or *Rhacolepis*.

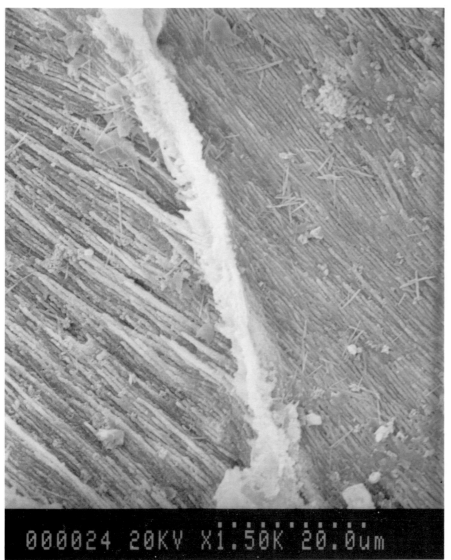

Left: SEM photo of surface of myoseptum between muscle blocks, showing replaced collagen from *Rhacolepis*. All SEM photos courtesy D. Martill.

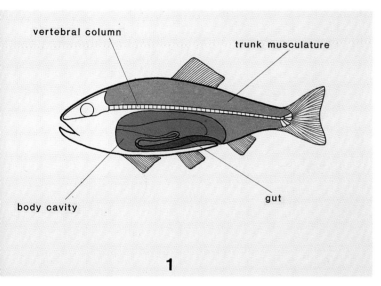

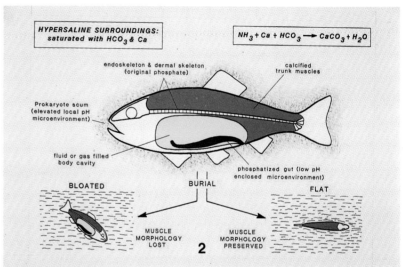

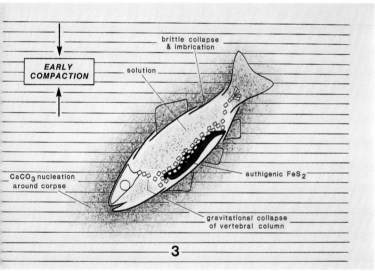

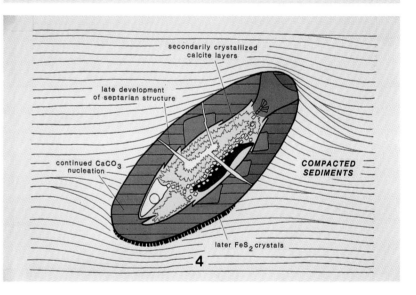

Scenario for preservation of Romualdo member fossil fishes. **1:** Diagrammatic representation of fish showing chief elements in scenario. **2:** Local microenvironments within and surrounding fish corpse shortly after death. **3:** Burial and early fossilization of gut (phosphatized), solution of calcified body wall, and collapse of vertebral column. **4:** Later diagenesis, concretion formation, and secondary mineralization phenomena. Phosphatization may occur early in stage 2, possibly following rupture of gut as body becomes compressed.

Subsequent diagenetic processes include calcification of matrix surrounding the fossils, thus defining the concretionary shapes, accompanied and followed by calcite crystallization within voids. These changes undoubtedly occurred some time after burial was complete. Concretions that were formed around corpses lying at angles to the bedding may cut through several centimeters of finely laminated sediment. More rarely, a single concretion may form around two bodies lying at different horizons, again demonstrating a lag-time of unknown duration in calcification of the concretionary matrix.

Although the timing of this phase in concretion formation is uncertain, it evidently commenced after the soft sediments began to get compacted, because some skeletal remains display evidence of bone breakage and carcass flattening. Shearing of the semi-rigid scaly exterior of three-dimensional specimens (especially *Rhacolepis*) probably also occurred as a consequence of compaction. Nevertheless, the degree of compaction generally is slight and in many cases has had a negligible effect on preservation. Where the matrix is calcified around three-dimensional fish bodies, it probably approximates the original thickness of sediment fairly closely, particularly in the case of specimens oriented obliquely through many layers of sediment. If the cause and duration of sedimentary lamination could be determined, sedimentation rates probably could be calculated with reasonable accuracy.

Sometimes some of the microcrystalline calcium carbonate and phosphate filling the corpse seem to have been retained in a virtually unaltered condition within the concretion. This is most evident where certain features of the soft anatomy are preserved, particularly where the body has suffered compaction after burial. More rarely the uncrushed void of the body may be completely filled with an unstructured chalky mass of carbonate. A few specimens of *Rhacolepis* have been preserved in this fashion. In most three-dimensionally preserved *Rhacolepis*, however, this presumably earlier chalky material appears to have gone into solution and recrystallized as (or been replaced by) sparry crystalline calcite.

This sparry calcite crystallized around the interior of the corpse toward its center, around the inside of the scaly covering, around articulated and disarticulated bones, and around the phosphatized gut contents. Similarly, sparry calcite grew around the insides of voids such as the braincase and hollow bones in virtually every concretion. In "Old Mission" and "Jardim" concretions this sparry calcite is tinged brown by iron minerals and entirely lines any voids or cavities in geode-like fashion. In "Santana" concretions, however, there may be large voids without any infilling whatsoever. Single, well-formed calcite crystals sometimes occur within voids inside the braincase in some of these specimens. In "Santana" concretions this calcite is colorless and usually transparent. Although the causes of these diagenetic peculiarities in "Santana" concretions are obscure, they may relate to the relatively "clean" nature of the original matrix, low in clay and ferruginous matter.

Within sectioned concretions the sedimentary laminations become more closely bunched together toward the periphery. This phenomenon is well known in calcareous concretions from many other deposits throughout the world and probably is best interpreted as evidence of concretion growth during sediment compaction (Clifton, 1957; Criss, et al., 1988). In this way the sediments located more centrally (in which fossils are preserved with little or no evidence of flattening) probably were incorporated into the concretion before any appreciable compaction had occurred. Those areas of surrounding sediment that subsequently were incorporated into the concretion suffered progressively more compaction with increasing distance from its nucleus. Finally, after concretion growth had ceased, surrounding sediments continued to suffer compaction and became arched around the harder, more resistant concretions.

This compelling scenario was advocated more than a century ago by the eminent American paleontologist Professor J. S. Newberry (1873), who was the first to describe archaic and monstrous armored fishes known as arthrodires from gigantic calcareous concretions in muddy Upper Devonian sediments of Ohio. Alternative explanations of concretion formation, such as that advocated by Doly (1900) and Westgate (1926) involving secondary internal expansion of sedimentary layers toward the center of the concretion, are less satisfactory. That mechanism would surely result in extensive damage or even obliteration of any contained fossil structures. Although concretion formation through secondary expansion may occur under certain peculiar conditions, it does not offer a favorable model for the origin of carbonate concretions containing well-preserved fossil remains.

We may conclude that the formation of such

concretions commenced soon after burial, in initially soft and unconsolidated sediments. According to a hypothesis presented recently by Criss, et al. (1988: 1), the high ratio of authigenic (i.e., formed *in situ*) to detrital components in calcareous concretions (from the Cleveland Shale) suggests "...that they underwent rapid early diagenetic growth as soft, low-density bodies that cemented the void space of extremely porous... sediment near the sediment-water interface." Their analyses revealed that possibly less than 6% of the sediment volume originally consisted of actual sedimentary detritus, the remainder being fluid-filled pore spaces (much like muddy sediments forming today).

As Criss, et al. (1988: 14) pointed out, however, the density of these extremely diffuse, porous sediments would have been far too low to support a great mass of carbonate hydrostatically. If dense calcareous concretions were to form at such an early post-depositional phase, they would simply sink within the soft ooze. Therefore, Criss and his colleagues postulated, the concretions initially were composed of a much lighter, diffuse matter such as the organically-produced adipocere associated with decaying organisms (Hecht, 1933; Trask, 1937; Berner, 1968; Wilcox and Effler, 1981). This organic matter could have been secondarily replaced by calcium carbonate during early diagenesis, by which time the muddy sediments presumably were more consolidated and better able to support the dense concretions hydrostatically.

Some support for a delayed onset of calcification is provided by oxygen and carbon isotope data. Criss, et al. (1988) reported ^{18}O ratios of dolomitic matrix consistent with early growth and replacement at low but progressively increasing temperatures in pore fluid. They also found ^{13}C values consistently higher in various calcareous concretions than in what they considered "normal" marine limestones, but similar to those obtained from organic carbon and diagenetic carbonates.

Although the evidence presented by Criss, et al. (1988) in support of their hypothesis of delayed (i.e., diagenetic) calcification of the concretion matrix is impressive, the onset of mineralization within decaying corpses may commence much sooner, as discussed already. How might such relatively dense organic remains be supported instead of sinking within these extremely fluid and unconsolidated bottom sediments?

One possibility is that an extensive prokaryote mat, like that postulated by Seilacher, et al. (1985) and Martill (1988), may have covered and pervaded these sediments, providing a supporting organic substrate for the sedimentary particles and even for much larger organic remains. The importance of a prokaryote mat in helping to bind these otherwise diffuse components together was given scant attention by Criss, et al. (1988), yet may provide the answer to the problem of relative densities that they considered so paradoxical. Within this mat, locally high adipocere levels may have existed adjacent to any ensnared corpses, creating a heterogenous and highly variable microenvironment with respect to amine and pH levels.

In the case of plants and other remains that presumably were low in proteinaceous matter initially, the situation is less clear. Possibly these waterlogged and by now entrapped remains were able to "borrow" adipocere-like matter from nearby vertebrate corpses, or else perhaps absorbed dissolved amines and were able to raise the pH locally by releasing humic acid into the surrounding sediments to levels appropriate for subsequent carbonate diagenesis.

To summarize, although the evidence is incomplete and somewhat equivocal, we may postulate that initial calcification and phosphatization of soft organic tissues occurred rapidly in the dank bottom environments of the Araripe basin, so soon in fact that it may be regarded in part as a necrolytic phenomenon. High adipocere levels surrounding these remains trapped within a prokaryote mat led to local elevation of amine and pH levels, while the mat itself may have prevented the partially mineralized remains from sinking farther into the substrate. As the sediments become compacted, secondary calcium carbonate was progressively deposited diagenetically within pore spaces of the matrix surrounding the fossil remains. The extent of calcification may be a function of the initial extent of adipocere surrounding each corpse and in many cases reflects closely the shape and orientation of skeletal elements.

As these organic remains became buried deeper by progressive accumulation of sediments, further diagenetic changes apparently occurred involving some shrinkage of the limestone matrix. Probably some of the shrinkage is due to gradual dewatering, caused by compressive forces generated by the overburden. This dewatering perhaps was accompanied by slight dolomitization (magnesium enrichment) as suggested by Jordan and Branner in 1908. A number of later diagenetic features can be tied to this shrinkage.

Firstly, many concretions have developed internal fractures radiating from the center to form a complex three-dimensional reticulate system that commonly extends to the exterior. These fractures are infilled, usually by impure calcite but also quite frequently by oxides and hydroxides of iron. These deposits produce a compartmentalized appearance with intervening walls or "septa." Geologists use the term "septarian concretion" to define this structure. It is prevalent in "Jardim" concretions (Gardner, 1849), particularly large and flat ones. By contrast, no examples of septarian "Santana" concretions have been observed. Less shrinkage in this case may perhaps be attributed to low clay mineral content. In the case of extremely muddy "Old Mission" concretions, in which septarian structures also are unusual, it may be that the matrix was more plastic and thus better able to withstand brittle failure during shrinkage.

A second feature related to shrinkage sometimes is seen within the fossils themselves, especially in broken or sawn sections across the body. Bones and scales sometimes act as planes of weakness within the concretion and split apart as shrinkage occurred, creating a new space between their inner and outer surfaces. This space subsequently became infilled by sparry calcite, creating the illusion that the skeletal remains are less compressed than they actually are. This feature is common among the bodies of fossil fishes from "Jardim" concretions, with a centimeter or more of calcite between inner and outer surfaces of the scales in some larger *Cladocyclus* and *Vinctifer* specimens.

This secondary calcite growth can be extensive, frustrating attempts at acid preparation unless the greatest care is taken to conserve the diagenetically damaged bone as it emerges from the matrix. Sometimes only the bones or scales of one side are affected. By judicious inspection, the better side (with less calcite within the skeletal remains) may be selected. Even following plastic embedment, acid preparation can yield disappointing results if the bone is badly fractured and separated from the plastic by a layer of calcite, because the bone becomes detached as the calcite is dissolved.

It often is possible to distinguish between earlier and later generations of sparry calcite. Early calcite crystallization usually is confined to the body of the fossil, forming a thin but continuous crystalline drusy (layer of small crystals) over various surfaces. This drusy layer may be overlain by subsequent generations of sparry calcite. The subsequent layers may partially or completely fill remaining vacuities within the fossil and sometimes are laterally continuous with the calcite linings of the septarian cracks extending into the matrix surrounding the fossil. Crystalline calcite typically is not found around the exterior of the concretions, possibly because this region lay outside the pH threshold for carbonate precipitation (Martill, 1988). Later weathering, including chemical processes leading to production of a gypsum crust, may also have led to removal of some carbonate from around the outside of the concretion.

(J. G. Maisey)

Top: Northerly aerial views of Jardim, looking toward Araripe Plateau. **Bottom:** General views of plateau above Jardim.

11: Local Collecting and Preparation Methods

Very different preparation techniques have been utilized by local collectors and scientific investigators of the Araripe fossils. To some extent these techniques are complementary, although specimens have been spoiled all too frequently and damaged by zealous local handiwork. In many cases this artistry is clearly evident even to the untrained eye, although the unwitting tourist or rockhound may be duped into obtaining very poor specimens that have been beguilingly "improved" by carving, painting, or fabrication from incomplete fragments. Occasionally such handiwork is very hard to detect, however. Whenever a critical specimen is to be prepared for scientific study, technicians usually start by removing all traces of local craftsmanship and dismantling any broken pieces, to see whether they really belong together. Many "tricks of the trade" have been revealed by this means. In the following section, some of these are described in order to acquaint the reader with the subtle and not-so-subtle handiwork that untrained local collectors may inflict upon Araripe fossils.

It should be made quite clear that many examples of local handiwork are acceptable from both the scientific and esthetic point of view, provided that the integrity of the specimen is not lost. It may be that even a heavily worked specimen still is pleasing to the beholder. All the available evidence suggests that many of the repairs, improvisations, and fabrications one sees on fossil specimens from the Santana formation were made locally shortly after they were collected. It seems that these fossils almost invariably get broken during collection, so some repairs therefore are to be expected.

Perhaps the simplest collecting and preparation techniques practiced by Brazilians living close by the Araripe Plateau involve the small fishes and insects preserved in the finely bedded limestones of the Crato member. This limestone is worked locally by being split into thin sheets as crude slabs that sometimes are used for paving stones in sidewalks, as roofing "slate," and even for building decorative walls. Little attempt is made to trim the pieces uniformly, unless they are to be used as floor tiles. A small but thriving cottage industry apparently now exists whereby specimens of the small fossil gonorynchiform fish *Dastilbe* are mounted as pendants or key-rings for sale in larger cities such as Rio de Janeiro. At the present time, the most productive fossil localities in these limestones are said to be near Nova Olinda, some 40 km to the west of Juazeiro do Norte, on the mid-northern margin of the Chapada do Araripe. The limestone crops out on a low rise as a small, deeply weathered escarpment only 4 or 5 meters high. The fossils supposedly are not well preserved in the layers near the surface, making it necessary to excavate more deeply.

Quarrying appears to be basically simple. A rectangular pit several meters across is dug adjacent to an old disused dig. The rock is split apart, apparently with nothing more sophisticated than hammers and cold chisels, layer by layer, and discarded pieces are thrown into a disused adjacent area. Some of the more affluent local collectors possess small rock-cutting circular saws with which the matrix may be further trimmed at home. Eventually the pit is worked out and a new one is started nearby. Layer by layer, the fissile limestone apparently is removed and broken up, but a lot of the rock also is excavated without being thoroughly inspected. Fossil collecting here therefore gives every impression of being somewhat inefficient and erratic, because the local collectors seem to work quickly through parts of the sequence in order to reach layers supposedly yielding greater numbers of fossils.

Virtually no additional preparation of these small fossils is attempted, except unfortunately on some fossil insects that may be attacked with a knife or scraper in order to expose legs or antennae. Fossil insects are rare; one inhabitant of Nova Olinda estimated that he collected approximately 200 *Dastilbe* for every scrap of insect, and perhaps only one insect in ten is tolerably complete. Fake fossil insects from this area are now manufactured, according to reports from some Brazilian paleontologists.

The best-known fossils from the Araripe Plateau are undoubtedly those found in large, elongated limestone concretions or nodules from the Romualdo member. These display tremendous variation in size, shape, lithology, and kinds of fossils. The majority of Romualdo member concretions that one sees in collections have no locality data. Sometimes the general locale is given by reference to some nearby town. The most widely used reference towns are Santana (or Santana do Cariri), Missão Velha (or Barra Missão Velha), and Jardim (or Barra do Jardim). One also sees mention of Crato and Nova Olinda, but apparently these localities rarely produce good concretions and are better known for outcrops of the thin-bedded limestone of the Crato member. Locality data simply stating "Araripe" should be treated with caution. The town of Araripe lies on the northern margin of the Plateau, about 85 km west of Juazeiro do Norte, and it is a collecting area (although less important today than Santana do Cariri). However, the designation "Araripe" may refer only to the Araripe Plateau, and fossils having this locality information could have come from virtually anywhere in the region.

The following information was provided by local inhabitants and may not be completely reliable. It must be stressed that while some of this information is consistent with observations made when touring the area, it has been verified at only a few sites. Concretions said to be from Barra do Jardim ("Plains of the Garden") usually have a porous, chalky exterior that spalls off in concentric layers. These concretions show signs of deep weathering and can be very crumbly. Iron minerals within the sandy limestone matrix are strongly oxidized, with red and brown ochers that can rub off easily onto hands and clothes. When split open, these concretions show that weathering may extend deeply, with a leached outer rim surrounding the paler cream or gray sandy limestone. Many of these concretions are very large and irregular in shape, and some are weathered into several pieces. The largest fossil fishes are said to occur in these concretions, as well as articulated pterosaurs and turtles.

By contrast, concretions said to be from Barra Missão Velha ("Plains of the Old Mission") generally consist of very much harder, massive, and chippy limestone that has only a thinly weathered crust. The limestones are dark in color and contain moderately high amounts of clay minerals (this can generate a troublesome residue during acid preparation). Very large fossil fishes also occur in these concretions, but tetrapod remains usually are not found.

Santana do Cariri has yielded perhaps the most interesting fossils, both in terms of taxic diversity and preservational quality. The most abundant concretions usually are not as large as those from the other localities, but contain a wide assortment of fossil fishes, turtles, pterosaur bones, crocodilian remains, plants, and invertebrates. The limestone matrix contains hardly any clay minerals or coarser sediment and consists largely of minute calcareous ostracods (easily recognized by their ovoid shape) that can be discerned easily with a loupe.

Collecting methods adopted by the local inhabitants are again basic. Instead of quarrying (as at Nova Olinda), the limestone concretions apparently are excavated more or less intact by simply digging pits or trenches in areas of proven productivity. The concretions are entombed in softer shales and marls that often have a high keragen content ("oil-shales") and may be greasy to the touch. Collecting supposedly is restricted to drier seasons, although the "rainy" season actually can be quite arid in the scrubby Caatinga of northeastern Brazil. During the wetter intervals, however, the weathered shales become muddy and outcrops are covered quickly by a thick layer of vegetation. Access by motor vehicle becomes impossible, and even transportation by mule or on foot is difficult.

The local collecting and preparation techniques were observed at Jardim, and this site therefore is used as an example. Similar practices are said to be followed at other sites. The subtle differences in concretion types from site to site do not seem to affect their collection in any profound manner.

At Jardim, the rock succession is divided informally by the local inhabitants as follows. There is an overburden of 1.5 m or more of heavy clay, called *masape* ("foot-clay," i.e., what one walks on), below which is a thin chalky layer (*gesso*). This is followed by an oil-shale, *barro seco* ("dry clay"), the main concretion-bearing unit. The concretions are said to occur at various levels throughout the shale. This also is the case at localities between Nova Olinda and Santana do Cariri.

Undoubtedly some of these concretions have been disturbed or dislodged by solifluction (soil creep) and erosion, but the majority apparently are still *in situ*. The evidence for this is indirect but can be inferred from the fact that when a concretion is recovered at Jardim, it is customary for the collector to scratch a crude cross into its weathered lower surface. These markings often are still discernible in museum specimens. Since marking the lower surface of

Top three views: Exu formation, current-bedded sandstones forming steep cliffs of plateau above Jardim. **Bottom three views:** Santana formation with concretions .

Top row: An old spoil-heap in the Romualdo member made by fossil collectors near Jardim from discarded broken specimens. **Upper center:** An odd concretion-within-concretion, containing no fossils. **Lower center:** Skull of a *Vinctifer* projecting from concretion (left), and head of a *Cladocyclus* (right). A thriving cottage industry exists here "repairing" small *Vinctifer* specimens, drying in front of an open fire (**bottom left**). Even discarded fragments may have ornamental use, such as protecting a young plant (**bottom right**).

the concretion apparently is not practiced at sites other than Jardim, it may offer a supplemental guide to the origin of a specimen whose provenance is uncertain. However, the intended function of this mark is simply to remind the finder of the original orientation. The marked ("down") side usually yields the better "half" of the fossil, and some care is therefore taken in preparing this half. Logically, this suggests that most concretions are *in situ* when collected and that some paleoenvironmental factors are responsible for these preservational differences (for example, the more complete "down" side may have been held together better by soft sediments and also would be less vulnerable to scavenging or disruption by escape of gas bubbles from the decaying corpses).

The concretions occur in various shapes and sizes. Often the shape of the concretion reflects that of the fossil contained inside. Most of the fish fossils occur in elongate concretions, and the concretion even may have projecting lumps around the fins, giving the stone a distinctly fish-like shape. Smaller fishes sometimes occur in nearly spherical concretions ranging from grapefruit-size upward. Some elongate fishes (especially the aspidorhynchid, *Vinctifer*) are preserved curled up (giving a flattened, rounded shape to the concretion) or else bent into a curve (producing a boomerang-shaped concretion). The experienced eye of the local collector seldom is deceived by these shapes, and some collectors apparently are proud of their ability to predict with confidence what kind of fossil a particular concretion will yield. One collector even allowed a test of his skills of identification. Not only was he able to distinguish the kinds of fossil fishes correctly before splitting open the concretions, but he also was able to discern which concretions contained nothing but rock or only scraps of bone or fossilized wood. Very rarely one hears muttered curses and *"Pedra mintiu"* ("The stone is pretending," meaning it looked as though it should have had a fossil, but didn't). The collectors cannot avoid picking up the *"Pedra mintirosa"* ("pretending stone"), and their annoyance is understandable when it is realized that these weighty rocks sometimes have been carried, on foot, for considerable distances to reach the preparation site.

A typical concretion containing a large fossil fish would be prepared in the following manner. The preparator either sits or kneels in the open, with the concretion held between his feet or knees. After the ritual lighting of a cigarette, the outer weathered crust is chipped away using a hammer and cold chisel. Then a notch is chiselled the length of the concretion, just to one side of the midline, so that the "down" side is slightly thicker. The concretion then is split by a sharp chisel blow in the center of the notch. With luck, the specimen consists of two intact halves, but some additional breakage is common. The entire process can be quite rapid, with three or four specimens opened within a cigarette-span. Larger concretions invariably demand greater attention, however, and the preparator may expend 20 minutes or longer in splitting one open.

Specimens sometimes are incomplete or else are badly damaged during preparation. Unless the damage is severe, however, the pieces are not discarded. Instead, they are stockpiled for future repairs or for reconstitution with other fragments as composite specimens. This aspect of local preparation is highly developed, sometimes involving whole community groups and families. The techniques adopted are for the most part simple but effective (frustratingly so in some cases). Whether the specimen simply is undergoing repair or actually is a composite created from carefully matched pieces, the reconstruction process is the same. Pieces are joined using a plaster/rock-dust mix, a strong glue, or even automobile epoxy filler. The latter is expensive for the local inhabitants and is reserved for larger pieces requiring greater bonding strength, and especially for rarer discoveries that presumably may fetch greater financial returns. Such specimens seem to offer the greatest temptation for artistic "improvements" and composite reconstructions. One of the great advantages to the preparator (and disadvantages to the scientist or serious collector) is that the epoxy bond is stronger than the rock itself. If a bonded specimen subsequently is broken, it usually snaps adjacent to the epoxied join, rather than through it, tearing matrix and fossilized bone from one piece and leaving it attached to the epoxy. This effectively disguises the original break and creates the impression that the pieces fit together closely. Whenever an epoxied joint is suspected, it should be carefully cleaned by mechanical preparation in order to inspect the true nature of the contact between pieces. There frequently is no other way to determine whether the specimen is a composite or has simply been repaired.

A glued-up specimen (whether real or created) is quite obvious at this stage, since the plaster/glue/epoxy usually is a different color or tone from the rock. Local artisans therefore mix together a thin mixture of plaster, rock-dust, and ocher (obtained from the concretion's weathered crust). This mixture then is liberally painted over the back of the concretion and across breaks in the fossil, usually by younger family members. Two or more coats may be applied, and after each application the specimens are dried in front of a small open fire. Parts of the fossil that are obscured by the plaster mix now require some artistic handiwork. A skilled older family member makes scale impressions in a final coat of plaster and rock-dust by using a stick or metal strip shaped to imitate the scales. An optional final step is a swift wipe with some brown boot polish, rubbed well into the surface, to tone down the coloration.

Smaller specimens may not be treated so elaborately. Instead, a false outline may be sculpted around the major part of the fossil. New "fins" and "tail" may be added or a "head" built up in plaster. In some cases one sees the vertebral column of a fossil fish trailing behind the new "tail." In other instances quite fanciful fossils are carved. The Paleontological Institute in Munich has two splendid examples of "frogs" carved from fossil *Rhacolepis* fishes from the Araripe Plateau. On occasion, even the "*Pedra mintirosa*" is carved. A Brazilian visitor to the American Museum once brought in a supposed fossil "turtle" completely carved into a concretion containing no bone whatsoever. The only way this visitor could be convinced of the deception was by showing that the "turtle" could be dissolved in acetic acid, whereas real fossil bones could not! Such deceptions fortunately are rare, but many otherwise excellent examples of the smaller fossil fishes are ruined by enthusiastic "outlining." It is common to see this in *Tharrhias* and *Rhacolepis* specimens.

Sometimes it is easy to spot a composite specimen. There is a magnificent monster *Calamopleurus* (=*Enneles*) in the American Museum collection with three sets of dorsal and pelvic fins instead of the usual one; presumably the specimen was manufactured entirely from spare parts. In the past, one particular preparator from Jardim seems to have had an unfortunate tendency to put the tails on his composite specimens upside-down. Since his preparation was otherwise excellent, this provided a useful means to spot his handiwork.

(J. G. Maisey)

In June 1990, the first Symposium on the Geology of the Araripe Basin was convened in Crato. The meeting, attended by many Brazilian and visiting scientists, was wide-ranging in scope. Here some of the participants are seen visiting exposures in the Exu Formation.

Facing page: Aerial views along the northern margin of the Araripe Plateau from Santana do Cariri (top left) to Nova Olinda (upper center right), showing cliffs of Exu formation (top right) and exposures of Crato member limestones (upper center left). Other views are from vicinity of Santana do Cariri (lower center and bottom rows).

12: Laboratory Preparation Techniques

The majority of fossils from the Araripe region evidently never undergo further preparation once they leave the hands of local collectors. Most amateur paleontologists and rockhounds are content to leave their specimens the way they are, and much of the material deposited in museum collections also remains in this state. This is certainly the safest way to conserve these fossils, because the hard limestone matrix protects the delicate fossilized matter from all but the roughest handling.

In this condition, however, the amount of retrievable scientific data is limited. The rocks cannot be X-rayed satisfactorily because of the high calcium content of the rock. The plane of fracture often passes through fossilized structures, rather than separating them cleanly, exposing only broken surfaces. Small, delicate features may be obscured or entirely obliterated. It can be difficult to obtain accurate measurements and other important numerical data (e.g., vertebral counts, scale counts, fin-ray numbers). Attempts at writing technical descriptions of these fossils using specimens in their "natural" state therefore are limited in scope and information content.

The rules of scientific nomenclature require every valid species (living and fossil) to have a type specimen. In the case of the Araripe fossils, many of the type specimens are incomplete, and virtually all of them are unprepared. The literature dealing with them consequently is somewhat limited in technical content. There are cases of the same species apparently being described under different names (synonyms) and many examples where the anatomy of species has been misinterpreted, leading to erroneous conclusions about their relationships. More accurate technical descriptions are made possible only by carefully preparing new material using modern laboratory techniques. Institutions holding critical types naturally are reticent about further preparation of these specimens in case of inadvertent damage. Unfortunately, this can leave the investigator in a quandary, since it may be necessary to reveal important features of a type specimen by preparation in order to test whether species are valid and to determine whether more completely prepared material actually belongs to an already-named species.

The techniques described here are not beyond the scope of many amateurs but involve the use of laboratory equipment and chemicals that may not be readily available. The enthusiast may be able to adopt these techniques on a limited scale but should be warned of the many potential pitfalls that can result in irreversible damage to a specimen. Also, all chemicals must be handled with care and only after rigidly following the manufacturer's instructions and warnings. Modern paleontological laboratories usually are equipped for both mechanical and chemical preparation techniques. Traditionally, preparation was a slow, laborious process involving mechanical methods only (mounted needles, fine chisels, etc.) and usually conducted under a binocular microscope. These relatively simple techniques still are used widely and in some circumstances still provide superior results. Mechanized preparation (e.g., using miniature pneumatic drills and air-abrasive machines) has speeded up the process considerably but has met only limited success with the concretions from Brazil.

Chemical preparation methods have greater utility than mechanical ones for the Araripe fossils. Excellent results are obtained quite quickly, and much more delicate structures may be revealed than by mechanical means. Basically, two kinds of chemical techniques have been successfully employed. The best-known of these is acid preparation, using dilute organic (formic, acetic) acids to dissolve limestone (calcium carbonate) but leaving bones (mostly calcium phosphate) intact. Although the technique has become widely utilized, we have made a few refinements that will be described below.

The other kind of chemical preparation is a reducing technique, whereby oxides and hydroxides of iron are reduced chemically to a water-soluble state. This reduction technique, originally developed by mineralogists as a way to clean crystal specimens (Waller, 1980; King, 1983), has facilitated the removal of ferruginous crusts and crystalline deposits from around the bone. Spectacular results were obtained by cleaning small fossil fishes embedded in the laminated limestone of the Crato member (Blum, et al., 1989). Instead of a fuzzy brown outline on a dirty beige-colored matrix, it is now possible to produce crisp, ginger-colored fossils against a uniform creamy white background, with far greater resolution of detail than was previously possible. An advantage of this technique is that it is essentially non-corrosive and uses no acids, unlike an alternative reducing process developed by Howie (1974) using thioglycollic acid. Another advantage is that the chemicals needed are somewhat less expensive than the acid and have a considerably longer shelf-life. Both techniques require a well-ventilated area, since hydrogen sulphide is released.

Removal of Hydrated Iron Dioxides: The Waller Method

This technique takes advantage of the fact that ferrous hydroxide is more soluble than ferric hydroxide and over a wider pH range. Ferric hydroxide is dissolved by a neutral solution containing sequestering ions. This solution contains three sodium salts. A stock solution comprises 71 g of sodium citrate, $Na_3C_6H_5O_7 \cdot 2H_2O$ (which sequestrates ferrous ions) and 8.5 g of sodium bicarbonate, $NaHCO_3$ (which acts as a buffer to maintain a neutral pH) per liter of distilled water. This stock solution may be stored indefinitely. A third salt, sodium dithionite ($Na_2S_2O_4$), is added when the solution is required, in the ratio of 1 g per 50 ml of solution. Sodium dithionite oxidizes readily and therefore must be added only when needed.

A suitable plastic or glass container is taken, the activated solution is poured in, and the specimens to be cleaned are immersed. A batch of 12-18 small specimens or 2-4 larger ones can be treated in a single bath of 2-3 liters. The container should be covered and placed in a fume-hood or well-ventilated area, preferably using a magnetic stirrer to enhance the sequestering action. The solution remains active for about 12 hours at room temperature, after which time the specimens are removed, the used solution discarded, and the specimens washed in distilled water for another 12-24 hours before air-drying. If a crust of iron remains, the specimens can be transferred to a fresh sequestering solution prior to washing. It is important to keep the container covered during this process, as sodium dithionite readily oxidizes on exposure to the atmosphere.

There is a tendency for the sodium citrate to sequestrate calcium as well as ferrous ions, so the limestone matrix becomes porous and chalky. King (1982) thus recommended that the Waller method should not be used on calcite or aragonite mineral specimens, but in the case of vertebrate fossils embedded in limestone the sequestration of calcium can be advantageous.

Best results are obtained by cleaning fossil fishes left embedded in their limestone matrix. Attempts at combining sequestration and acid preparation generally are unsatisfactory, primarily because the presence of complex iron phosphates in the matrix surrounding the bone prevents its complete removal.

Removal of Carbonate Matrix Using Organic Acid

This technique is well-established and involves dissolving away the calcareous limestone matrix in order to expose the phosphatic skeleton (which essentially is unaffected by dilute organic acids), usually after embedding the fossil in a frame of transparent polyester resin. This technique has become known as the "Transfer Method," because the fossilized remains are effectively transferred from the limestone matrix to the polyester, so that the previously entombed skeleton becomes visible. It may not be necessary or even desirable to embed a specimen prior to acid preparation. Free-standing specimens may also be obtained, especially of individual bones.

Because polyester resins are expensive, the basic embedding technique developed by preparators at the British Museum (Natural History) has been refined so as to minimize the amounts of materials used. Dr. W. B. Elvers, a volunteer in the Department of Vertebrate Paleontology at the American Museum of Natural History, has devised a method that produces a strong but light-weight support for the fossil without the need to trim away excess resin after embedding. Details of this technique are given here as it may be of general interest.

EMBEDDING: The initial (and optional) step involves trimming away as much excess matrix as possible, using a diamond saw. The trimmed block then is placed on a board or other flat base, fossil-side up. Modeling clay wedges are inserted under the block to level the fossil surface (checked with a spirit-level).

A dam to contain the embedding resin then is constructed using a silver-foil and polyethylene-faced heavy stock paper (we used 40-lb paper stock supplied by the Hampton Paper Co., Holyoke, MA). A strip of this paper, pretreated with a mold-releasing agent, is affixed to the base and to the perimeter of the specimen with a water-based contact cement, forming a wall surrounding the matrix. This wall protects the

Above: Abandoned quarry in laminated limestones of Crato member, and local use of stone in wall and street (lower right).

Facing page: Fake fossils. Large composite *Calamopleurus* with three dorsal fins and inverted tail (top left); heavily carved *Notelops* with fake fins and body outline (top right); tail of *Oshunia* and head of *Calamopleurus* combined (center left); front part of *Notelops*, with heavily carved outline and fake tail (note vertebrae continuing behind "tail" (center right); the "bagel fish," actually a *Cladocyclus* tail, *Araripichthys* body, and plaster head (bottom left); "frog" in Paleontological Institute, Munich, carved from a *Rhacolepis* head (bottom right).

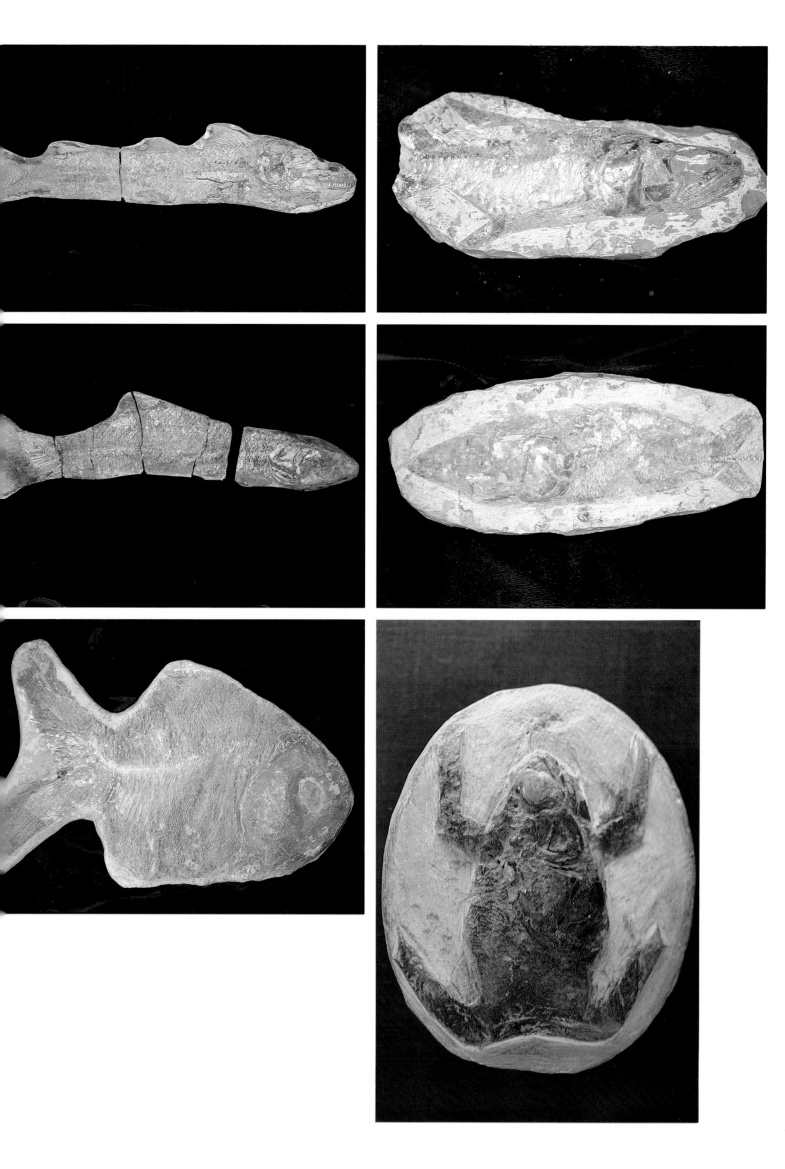

matrix from any resin contact that might block its subsequent removal by acid.

A second wall, about 2.5 cm higher than the highest point of the specimen, is fixed to the base approximately 6 mm outside of the first, paralleling its contours. The upper 12 mm edge is slotted and bent outward at right-angles to provide flanges that are reinforced with masking tape to increase the outer wall's rigidity.

The specimen is next embedded in a water-clear, cold-setting polyester resin that achieves an initial set in one or two hours and exhibits acceptable dimensional stability when properly employed. The embedding liquid ("Alplex") is prepared by adding hardener to the resin at a concentration of 0.5% (three drops per fluid ounce) and is poured onto the specimen, filling the moat between the paper walls and covering the specimen to depth of approximately 6 mm.

Prolonged exposure to acid tends to etch the resin overlaying the fossil. To overcome this problem, a "window" of acid-resistant transparent acrylic, cut to the specimen outline, is bonded to the cured surface with a thin layer of freshly prepared polyester resin.

When completely set (e.g., overnight), the paper walls are peeled away, any sharp edges are trimmed and smoothed, and the embedded fossils are committed to acid development.

ACID PREPARATION: When the technique was first developed in the British Museum (Natural History), acetic acid was used with success, but formic acid can be substituted. Although this is more expensive, formic acid's reactivity rate is considerably greater than that of acetic acid, and formic acid probably removes more matrix per dollar than acetic. There are times when a less vigorous reaction is required, in which case a very dilute solution of formic acid is preferable, rather than changing to acetic acid. In fact, changing from one acid to the other is not advisable, since the pH can be adversely affected and cause the fossilized bone to dissolve. This will also occur if acetic and formic acids are mixed.

Formic acid generally is used at much lower concentrations than acetic. Following the advice of Daniel Goujet, Museum National d'Historie Naturelle, normally a 5% solution is made, but 4% or less may be used for delicate specimens or in the final stages of preparation. The weaker the solution, the less matrix is removed, and the number of sessions in acid thus may be increased. The preparator must judge which is the preferable alternative in a given case; usually, slower is better.

Although carbonates react best with the acid, there is always a risk that some phosphate also will be lost. To avoid this, approximately 1 g of finely powdered calcium phosphate is added per liter of diluted acid. This has the effect of saturating the solution with phosphate ions and prevents further dissolution of bones. The phosphate should be stirred into the acid to assist its dissolving.

The acid is mixed in a suitably-sized rubber or durable plastic container and the embedded specimen then is immersed. If possible, the specimen should be leaning on one side, otherwise sediment tends to collect on the specimen. There is always the chance that isolated bones will drift away, but these generally can be retrieved from the acid bath later. More than one specimen can be treated in a single tub of acid, although care should be taken in later stages that isolated skeletal elements from different specimens do not get mixed up. It is a good idea to treat both halves of a single concretion in the same tub.

A single immersion can vary in duration, depending on solution strength, specimen size, matrix content, and relative volumes of the specimen(s) and acid bath. A 24-hour immersion is reasonable, especially in the initial stages and where larger specimens are being treated. Reaction rates also will vary; generally between 3 mm and 6 mm of matrix will be dissolved, although local dissolution may be much faster or slower.

Specimens are removed from the acid bath with a "scooping" motion. This tends to contain any loose pieces within the rim of the embedded specimen. The specimen then is given a thorough but gentle preliminary wash in running water. We like to tip the specimens, propping them up with a small wooden wedge or sandbag, so that fine matrix will be skimmed over the lip but loose bones will not be lost. By using a gentle rocking motion and brushing the matrix, much of the debris can be removed successfully. As a precaution, however, this may be done over a large strainer.

The washed specimens then are soaked in water for at least 24 hours to remove any residual acid and soluble by-products. The specimens are gently removed from the water and drained, then left to dry for several hours. A specimen should not be permitted to dry out completely, but should look damp (not slippery-wet). It is then ready for conservation treatment before being returned to a fresh acid bath. Many acid immersions may be required in order to prepare a specimen completely. Quite often we prefer not to remove the last vestiges of matrix if this means some already-exposed parts may be jeopardized.

The above remarks apply equally to specimens embedded in resin and to "free-standing" preparations. Even greater care is required when handling the latter, however, because exposed, wet, and untreated bone is easily destroyed. One useful tip is to fabricate some kind of support, for example a piece of plastic grid from a fluorescent light cover. Wire handles can be attached to each end of the grid to aid in lifting it in and out of the acid or water. We have prepared "free-standing" skulls of some fossil fishes in this way, and Alexander Kellner (Federal University, Rio de Janeiro) has even prepared delicate, hollow pterosaur bones by carefully dissolving matrix in formic acid.

CONSERVATION OF ETCHED BONE:

This treatment is necessary each time a specimen is treated in acid, in order to harden and strengthen the exposed bones. Failure to do so inevitably will lead to destruction of these parts during subsequent immersions.

Various conservation materials are used by preparators in different institutions. We use a standard solution of "Glyptal," diluted to a very weak strength in acetone and applied liberally with an eyedropper. There is less damage to the bone than if applied with a brush.

The "Glyptal" will turn white on contact with a damp specimen, but this color will disappear with the next application. This is a cursory application; no attempt is made to clean exposed bones until the next application, when they will be stronger. Specimens may be stored this way indefinitely. Very thin bones would tend to curl up and break at this stage without this treatment. An alternative strategy is to apply a thin solution of water-soluble gum arabic. This is a stopgap measure, however, and cannot be regarded as permanent conservation since it will be dissolved by subsequent immersions in acid.

Very thin "Glyptal" hardener tends to soak into the bone, which is preferable. Thicker "Glyptal" covers the surface but leaves the interior unprotected.

Cyanoacrylate ("Super-Glue") also may be employed with success, particularly when thinned in acetone. It is not as easily reversible as "Glyptal," however, and can become gummy and difficult to remove. Its advantage over the conventional range of acetone-based hardeners is its hygroscopic nature—it actually bonds better in damp conditions. Certain widely used hardeners such as "Butvar" should be avoided,

as they tend to dissolve in formic acid. Thinned cyanoacrylate can be dropped onto exposed bone using a glass pipette while the bone is still damp after washing (not when soaking wet, however). This is advantageous where the bone is liable to curl, peel apart, or split as it dries (a common problem with thin dermal bones and scales of fish fossils). Some whitening of the cyanoacrylate usually occurs, but this usually disappears with subsequent applications of "Glyptal" or other acetone-based hardeners.

The second application of "Glyptal" is more involved, since the exposed bone is to be cleaned. With a brush in one hand, and an eyedropper full of acetone or dilute "Glyptal" in the other, the bones are carefully cleaned of silt and bone fragments. Heavier "Glyptal" or cyanoacrylate is used to repair broken bones. A high-quality sable-hair watercolor brush, size 1 or 0, is recommended. Artificial-fiber brushes may be damaged by acetone and are best avoided.

Additional applications of "Glyptal" may be necessary, particularly once the acid treatment is finished. At this stage it is as well to protect the exposed bones from damage. If available, an acrylic plastic top can be cut to the shape of the embedded piece and fixed temporarily in place. Failing this, a piece of transparent plastic food-wrap will at least keep out any dust.

As with any delicate and valuable object, great care is needed when storing, moving, or studying acid-prepared fossils, as they are easily damaged. It is not a good idea to commit specimens to acid preparation without first ensuring that they can be curated in safety for the foreseeable future.

(J. G. Maisey, I. Rutzky, S. Blum, W. Elvers)

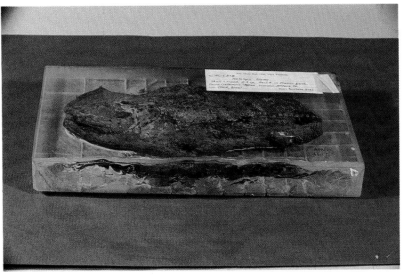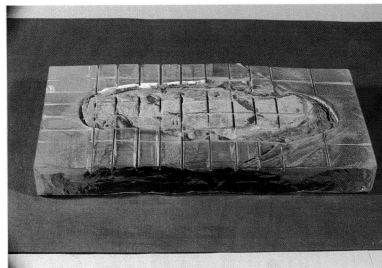

Transfer preparation. Early embedding techniques were generally crude and wasted material (top row); improved embedment technique provides several advantages. Specimen to be embedded (in this case *Brannerion*) is first levelled on foil-coated board (upper center left); an inner wall of foil-coated card is constructed (upper center right) and sealed to specimen and board (lower center left); an outer facing wall is installed (lower center right) and sealed (bottom left); resin is poured over specimen and into space between walls (bottom right). Photos courtesy Dr. W. B. Elvers.

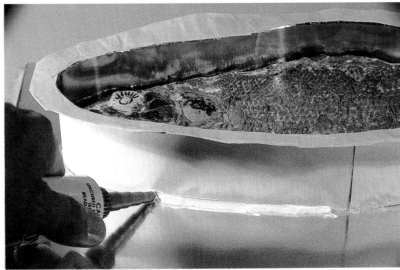

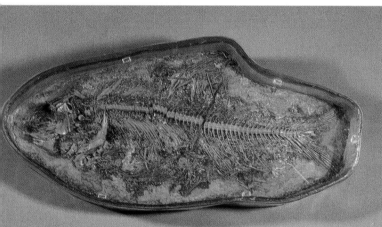

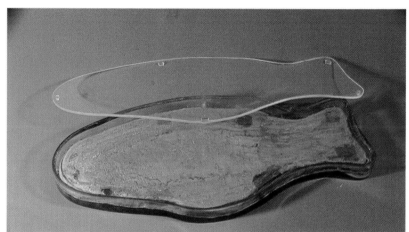

Transfer preparation (continued). Two views of embedded *Brannerion* specimen after resin has set and card has been removed (top row); a similar specimen after acid preparation (upper center left); a plexiglass lid is custom-made before acid treatment (upper center right). Two stages in acid preparation of a *Tharrhias* specimen are seen in the other pictures. Photos courtesy Dr. W. B. Elvers.

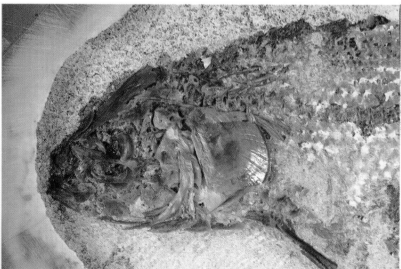

The following abbreviations are used on the illustrations in the systematic section.

FISH

adf:	anterior dorsal fontanelle
Ames:	"anterior mesethmoid"
An:	angular
An-art:	angular-articular
antpr:	antotic process
Ao:	antorbital
Aoc:	antorbital cartilage
apal:	articular facet for palatine
Art:	articular
Asp:	autosphenotic
Au:	autopalatine
Boc:	basioccipital
bpt:	basipterygoid process
Bsp:	basisphenoid
Cha:	anterior ceratohyal
Chp:	posterior ceratohyal
Cl:	cleithrum
Cla:	clavicle
Cor:	coracoid
D:	dentary
De:	dermethmoid
df:	dilatator fossa
Dpt:	dermopterotic
Dpt dl:	dermopterotic descending lamina
Dpto:	dermopterotic
Dsoc:	dermosupraoccipital
Dsp:	dermosphenotic
Ecl:	extracleithrum
Ecpt:	ectopterygoid
Ect:	ectethmoid
end f:	endolymphatic fossa
Ep:	epurals
Epo:	epioccipital
Exo:	exoccipital
fb:	fossa bridgei
fepsa:	foramen for efferent pseudobranchial artery
fica:	foramen for internal carotid artery
foa:	foramen for orbital artery
foc:	otic canal foramen
fp:	pre-epiotic fossa
Fr:	frontal
frde:	frontal descending lamina
G:	gular
H:	hypural (numbered sequentially)
Hh:	hypohyal
Hm:	hyomandibula
hmf:	hyomandibular facet
hm VII:	hyomandibular nerve foramen
Hsp:	hemal spine
Ic:	intercalar
Ih:	interhyal
In:	internasal
Io:	infraorbital (numbered sequentially)
Iop:	interopercular
jc:	jugular canal
jg:	jugular groove
Lac:	lachrymal
lcom:	lateral commissure
Le:	lateral ethmoid
Lj:	lachrymojugal
Lr:	lateral rostral
Mes:	mesethmoid
Mpt:	metapterygoid
Msp:	mesopterygoid
Mx:	maxilla
Na:	nasal
Npu:	preural neural arch
Nsp:	neural spine
oc:	occipital condyle
occ:	occipital centrum
Op:	opercular
Opo:	opisthotic
Orsp:	orbitosphenoid
Pa:	parietal
Padpt:	parietal-dermopterotic
Pal:	palatine
Part:	prearticular
Pb:	pelvic bone (= basipterygium)
Pd:	predentary
Pe:	pre-ethmoid
perf:	perilymphatic fenestra
pf:	posterior fontanelle
Ph:	parhypural
pitf:	pituitary fossa
Pmes:	"posterior mesethmoid"
Pmx:	premaxilla
Pop:	preopercular
pp:	parietal peniculus
Ppl:	lateral postparietal (lateral extrascapular)
Ppm:	median postparietal (median extrascapular)
prc:	preorbital canal
prcon:	processus connectens
prf:	precerbral fontanelle
Pro:	prootic
prob:	prootic bridge
Psp:	parasphenoid
Pt:	pterygoid
ptf:	posttemporal fossa
ptfc:	posterior opening of pars jugularis
Pto:	pterotic
Ptsp:	pterosphenoid
Ptt:	posttemporal
Pu:	preural centrum
Q:	quadrate
Qj:	quadratojugal
R:	rostral
Rart:	retroarticular
Ro:	rostral ossicles
Rode:	rostrodermethmoid
Sca:	scapular
Scl:	supracleithrum
Smx:	supramaxilla
Smxa:	anterior supramaxilla
Smxp:	posterior supramaxilla
So:	suborbital
Sop:	subopercular
spic:	spiracular canal
Spl:	splenial
Spop:	suprapreopercular
Sq:	squamosal
Stt:	supratemporal [= lateral extrascapular, see Ppl]
suf:	subtemporal fossa
Suo:	supraorbital
Sy:	symplectic
Tec:	tectal
tf:	temporal foramen
U:	ural centrum
Ud:	uroneural (numbered sequentially)
Vo:	vomer
II:	foramen for optic nerve
III:	foramen for oculomotor nerve
VI:	foramen for abducens nerve
VII:	foramen for facial nerve
IX:	foramen for glossopharyngeal nerve
X:	foramen for vagus nerve

REPTILES

a:	angular
ar:	articular
cor dex:	right coracoid
cr:	crest
cw:	last cervical vertebra
D:	dentary
den:	dentary
ec:	ectopterygoid
f:	frontal
hum dex:	right humerus
j:	jugal
l:	lacrimal
m:	maxillary
mcr:	mandibular crest
n:	nasal
op:	opisthotic
p:	parietal
pa:	parietal
pl:	palatine
pm:	premaxillary
pmcr:	premaxillary crest
po:	postorbital
prf:	prefrontal
PT:	pterygoid
pt:	pterygoid
q:	quadrate
qj:	quadratojugal
r:	dorsal ribs (ordered sequentially)
R:	radius
RA:	radius
S:	supraoccipital
Sc dex:	right scapula
Scf:	articular facet for scapula
Scl:	left scapula
Sc sin:	left scapula
So:	supraoccipital
soa:	superorbital anterior
sop:	superorbital posterior
sq:	squamosal
U:	ulna
UL:	ulna
1-9:	first to ninth dorsal vertebra

INSECTS

Cul:	Cubital vein
M:	Medial vein (ordered sequentially)
R:	Radial vein (ordered sequentially)
Sc:	Subcostal vein

13: Systematic Atlas

The remainder of this book consists largely of systematic descriptions of various fossils from the Santana formation of the Chapada do Araripe. A heirarchical arrangement has been adopted for the vertebrates, which still are the best-known components of these assemblages. Contributors to this section were left to their own devices regarding their arrangement, as the nature of the material to be covered is so variable. Fishes, turtles, and crocodiles have separate sections at generic level. There are two contributions for pterosaurs, within which all described taxa are reviewed systematically. In the cases of plants and insects and other invertebrates, the contributions also differ in content depending on how much published data are available. The insects, pterosaurs, and plant fossils are still the subjects of intensive research by various specialists, and only an outline of the taxic diversity is given in these instances. The dinosaurs and certain fishes are also still under investigation; the descriptions given in such cases are to be regarded as preliminary. Although some new taxa are discussed, there are no formal descriptions of new genera or species in this book. These will be published in appropriate scientific journals. As far as possible, all pertinent technical literature is cited, and the reader should be able to identify the whereabouts of type specimens in most cases. Authors' names appear at the end of each contribution, for the convenience of future workers who may wish to cite only part of this volume.

TRIBODUS Brito and Ferreira, 1989

Class CHONDRICHTHYES
Subclass ELASMOBRANCHII
Cohort EUSELACHII
Order HYBODONTIFORMES
    Suborder HYBODONTOIDEI Maisey, 1989
    Family HYBODONTIDAE Owen, 1846
    Subfamily ACRODONTINAE Maisey, 1989
Genus *Tribodus* Brito and Ferreira, 1989
    1989 *Tribodus* Brito and Ferreira: 53

Emended diagnosis: Hybodont shark of approximately 700 mm total length; teeth weakly heterodont, higher than broad, not exceeding 5 mm in lenght; tooth crown with striae, deeper than broad in postero-lateral teeth and shallower than broad in anterior and antero-lateral teeth; root much more developed than the crown, showing in labial view a central foramen; fin spines slender, reaching about 125 mm in length, lateral faces with 8 to 10 sharp, continuous ridges, single anterior ridge forming a keel on the anterior border, posterior denticles in two series; large dermal denticles with thorn-like shape, measuring approximately 2.5 to 3.0 mm.

Type species: *Tribodus limae* Brito and Ferreira, 1989.
Tribodus limae Brito and Ferreira
    1989 *Tribodus limae* Brito and Ferreira: 53
    Diagnosis: As for genus.
    Holotype: Almost complete individual, lacking caudal fin; Sanatana formation, lower unit of Romualdo member, Ceara; GP/2T-2 IG-USP.

This shark is an interesting addition to the ichthyofauna of the Santana formation. The dermal denticles occur over the entire body and are non-growing, like those of *Egertonodus basanus* and *E. fraasi*, and unlike the growing scales of many earlier hybdontiform sharks. The large size and thorn-like shape of the scales in *Tribodus* and *Egertonodus* are typical of many modern demersal sharks, skates, and rays.

Tribodus is the first hybodont shark to be recorded from the Santana formation and is only the second one from the Brazilian Cretaceous (the first was *Acrodus nitidus* Woodward, 1888, from the Bahia Group).

(P. M. Brito)

Reconstruction of a typical hybodontid shark of the Mesozoic era. *Tribodus* probably looked something like this, although its jaws are arranged more transversely and do not extend to the snout as in the reconstruction below.

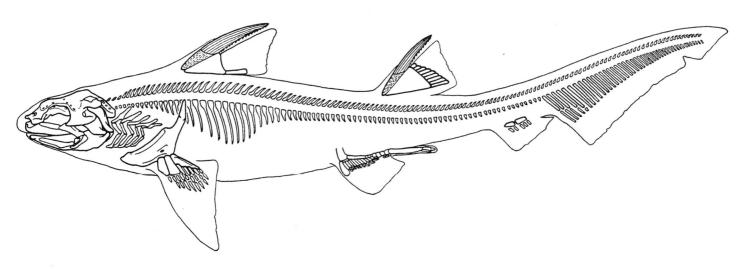

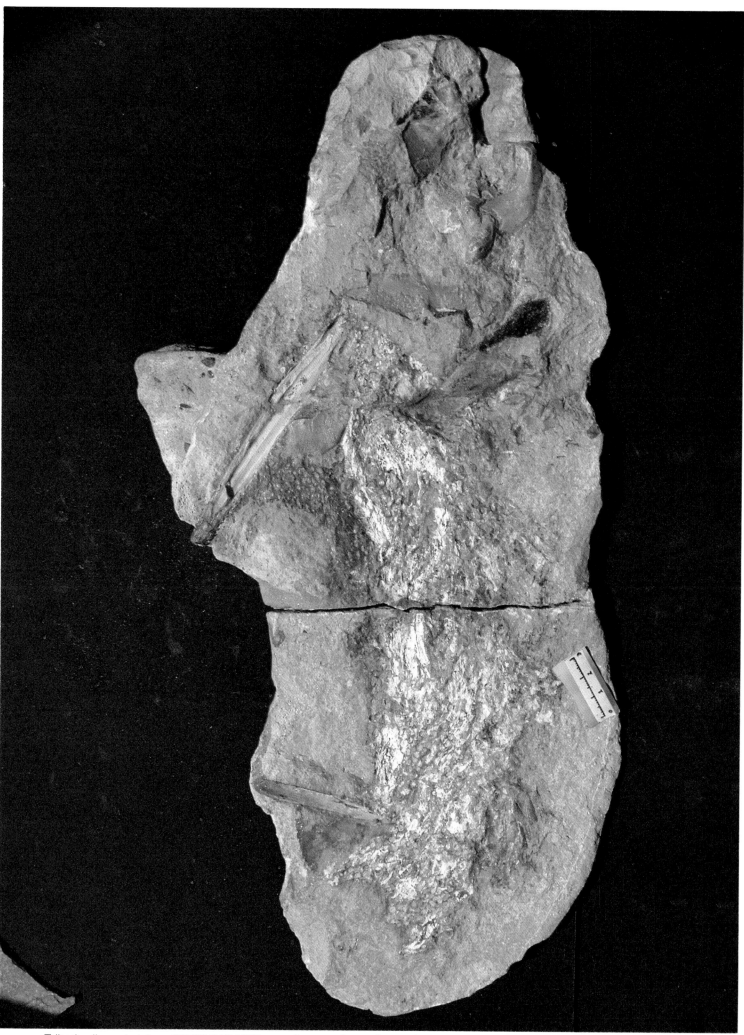

Tribodus limae, holotype GP/2T-2 IG-USP, complete specimen of a newly described hybodontid shark from the Santana formation. Photo courtesy P. M. Brito.

RHINOBATOS Link, 1790

Class CHONDRICHTHYES
Subclass ELASMOBRANCHII
Cohort EUSELACHII
Subcohort NEOSELACHII
Superorder BATOMORPHII
Order RAJIFORMES Berg, 1940
Suborder RHINOBATOIDEI Fowler, 1941
Family RHINOBATIDAE Müller and Henle, 1838

Genus *Rhinobatos* Link, 1790

Emended diagnosis: Rhinobatid with subtriangular disc, wider and rounded posteriorly; pectorals narrow, most developed behind shoulder girdle, narrowing to acute anteriorly, not incorporated into snout; elongate snout pointed, formed by long rostral cartilage and "vascular" (electrosensory) areas on each side; nostrils oblique, anterior valve not jointed across the space between them, not reaching mouth; spiracles large, mostly with two folds on the hind margin, rarely with one or none; pelvic (ventral) fins close to pectorals; dorsals behind ventrals; tail depressed, robust anteriorly; caudal small, subcaudal region weak, without lobe; tooth with massive, high crown, often sharp; oral face with distinct transverse ridge; crown base with median and paired lingual torus (uvula); root massive, displaced lingually, not larger than crown; dentition homodont, lacking expanded or constricted areas.

Type species: *Raja rhinobatos* Linnaeus, 1758

"Rhinobatos" beurleni Silva Santos

1968 *Rhinobatos beurleni* Silva Santos; Silva Santos and Valença: 349 (name only)

1968 *Rhinobatos beurleni* Silva Santos; Silva Santos: 492

1986 *Rhinobatos beurleni* Silva Santos; Mones: 28

Diagnosis: Rhinobatid of small size, rarely attaining length in excess of 0.5 m; rostrum short, with narrow but blunt end and flanked by small triangular "vascular" areas; nostrils oblique, apparently not reaching mouth; teeth homodont, very small, crowns with lateral uvulae almost as strong as median one, slightly convex transverse (occlusal) crest, lingual surface of crown concave; pectoral fin with large metapterygium and 16-18 propterygial radials, 9 or 10 mesopterygial radials, 20-23 metapterygial radials, primary pectoral radials with few joints; pelvic fin with 7-8 radials; approx. 15 vertebral centra incorporated into synarcual, with 12 centra visibly developed ventrally; approx. 17 monospondylous centra; remainder of tail with at least 81 diplospondylous centra (probably 90 +).

Holotype: Escola de Geologia de Pernambuco, EGP 2510; partial disc lacking tail; Santana formation, Lagoa de Dentro, Municipality of Araripe, Pernambuco.

Paratype: Divisão de Geologia e Mineralogia, Rio de Janeiro, DGM-DNPM 917; partial disc; Santana formation, north side of Chapada do Araripe, Ceará.

The chondrichthyan fishes (sharks, skates, and rays) are poorly represented in the Santana formation. For many years only one species, *"Rhinobatos" beurleni*, was known. This is a species of rhinobatid; rhinobatids are primitive rays that lack many of the morphological peculiarities of their more advanced relatives such as eagle rays, butterfly rays, skates, etc.

Unfortunately, the interrelationships of modern rhinobatids are poorly resolved, and thus the phylogenetic status of many fossil species has not been determined. *"Rhinobatos" beurleni* shares many characters with modern *Rhinobatos* spp. and usually is included within this genus (indeed, it has been claimed to be the oldest representative of the genus; Silva Santos, 1968). As with all other fossil species that are referred to living genera, many characters (particularly those involving soft anatomy and external appearance, coloration, etc.) are unavailable for comparison in the fossils, and in general only skeletal characters can be accurately compared. In the case of *"Rhinobatos" beurleni*, there are some features in the skeleton that do not, on the face of it, seem to agree with the generic diagnosis. Until the Rhinobatoidei are thoroughly revised, however, it would be premature to separate *"R." beurleni* formally from other *Rhinobatos* spp.

The Rhinobatoidei are relatively primitive Rajiformes and outwardly display little evidence (in the form of shared derived characters) that they form a natural (i.e., monophyletic) group. Internally, however, living rhinobatoids possess a unique arrangement of ventral gill-arch elements (hypobranchials). The arrangement of these elements in *"R." beurleni* has never been determined. Unfortunately, in all the material studied these elements apparently were uncalcified and thus have left no fossil record. It is of interest that some older (Upper Jurassic)

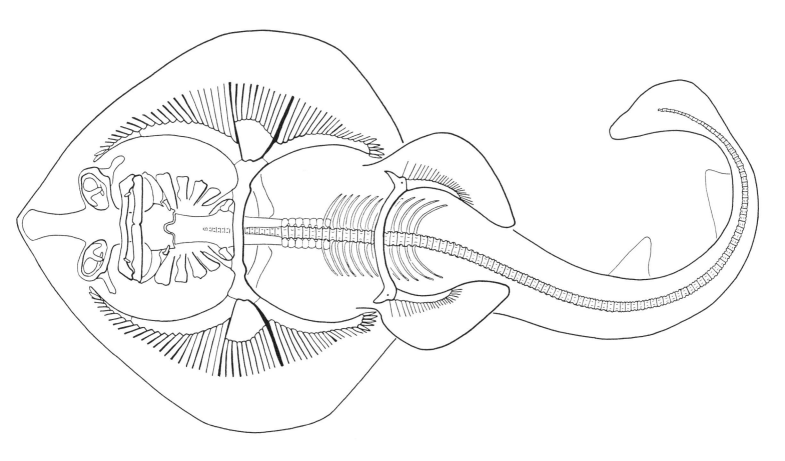

"Rhinobatos" beurleni. Skeletal reconstruction, ventral view.

supposed rhinobatoids (e.g., *Belemnobatis sismondae* and *Spathobatis bugesiacus*) lack the typical rhinobatoid hypobranchial pattern (see Saint-Seine, 1949, figs. 13, 28). Instead, their hypobranchials are arranged as in *Torpedo*, pristiophoroids (saw-sharks), and some squaloids (e.g., *Deania*, larval *Etmopterus*). On this basis, *Belemnobatis* and *Spathobatis* perhaps should be excluded from the Rhinobatoidei (Maisey, 1984b: 38) and should not be grouped within the family Rhinobatidae (cf. Cappetta, 1987: 134 et seq.).

Authors differ over how many Recent rhinobatoid families there are, but for comparative purposes it is convenient to follow Compagno (1973) in recognizing four (the Rhinobatidae, Rhinidae, Rhynchobatidae, and Platyrhinidae). *"Rhinobatos" beurleni* differs from modern platyrhinids in disc morphology, the extent to which the pectorals are confluent with the snout, in tail morphology, and in some features of tooth shape. The Rhynchobatidae and Rhinidae are united by an unusual dentition in which the lower tooth-rows are expanded at the mandibular symphysis, then alternately constricted, expanded, and gradually reduced in

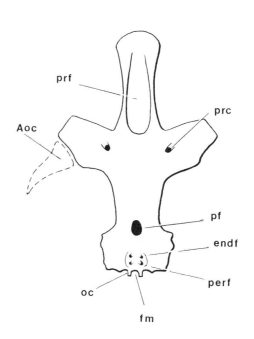

"Rhinobatos" beurleni. Braincase reconstruction, dorsal view.

111

Some Recent rhinobatoids.
Top: *Rhinobatos productus*; K. Lucas photo, Steinhart. **Center:** *Platyrhina sinensis*; Dr. S. Shen. **Bottom:** *Rhinobatos hynnicephalus*; Dr. S. Shen.

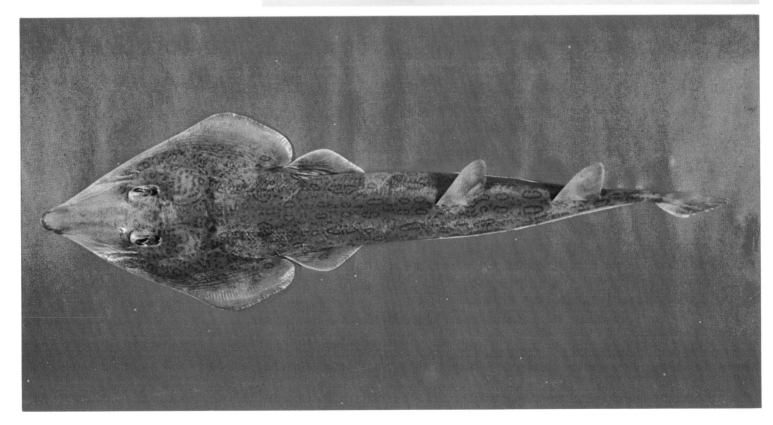

Magnificent example of "*Rhinobatos*" *beurleni* lacking only the caudal extremity, pectoral fin margins, and tip of the snout.

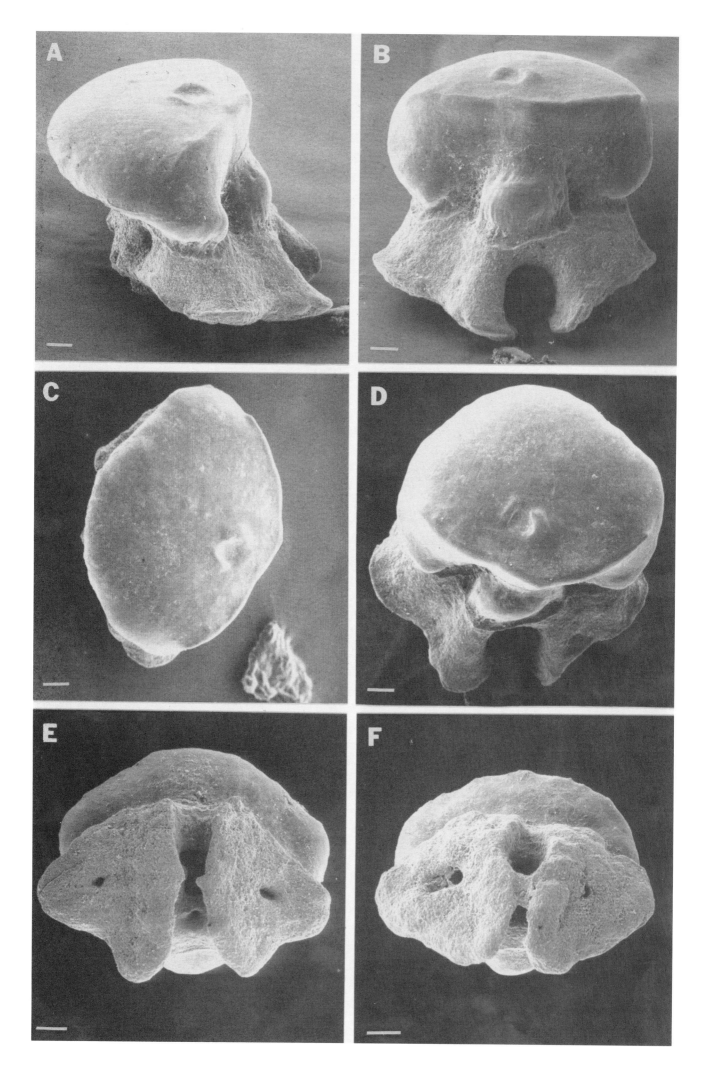

size laterally. The upper dentition is modified correspondingly, with a symphyseal constriction followed by expansion, constriction, and slight re-expansion before diminishing in size laterally. There is no evidence of similar dentitional modifications in "R." beurleni. This leaves the Rhinobatidae, with which "R." beurleni has most similarity. Unfortunately, no shared derived characters for the Rhinobatidae have been determined, and it is therefore unclear whether the group is monophyletic. "Rhinobatos" beurleni displays a number of primitive rhinobatid or rhinobatoid characters. Does it possess any features suggesting closer relationship to any of the more derived rhinobatoid taxa?

The snout of "R." beurleni is unusually short for a rhinobatid. In living Rhinobatos the rostral cartilage is very prominent, producing an elongate snout with rather long "vascular" areas laterally. The snout is much shorter in Rhina and platyrhinids and also in some other fossil species referred to Rhinobatos (e.g., R. hakelensis, R. primartus; Cappetta, 1980, pls. 10, 12), and therefore may be an unreliable taxonomic character. Alternatively, these Upper Cretaceous species may be united with "R." beurleni and together perhaps represent a monophyletic group within the Rhinobatidae. Tooth crown topography is quite similar in "R." beurleni and R. primartus, with a low-pointed occlusal crest and well developed lateral uvulae (very weakly developed in R. hakelensis). Lateral uvulae are also prominent in Platyrhina, but are lacking in Rhina and Rhynchobatus. An abbreviated snout and the presence of lateral uvulae in "R." beurleni, R. hakelensis, R. primartus, and Platyrhina suggest that these taxa are related.

The internal skeleton of "R." beurleni is prismatically calcified, with thousands of individual prisms of calcium phosphate. This is the characteristic calcification pattern of all chondrichthyan fishes. Prismatic calcification presents many problems to a paleontologist seeking to prepare fossil chondrichthyans. The use of acids in the transfer preparation technique (widely applied to the bony fishes from the Santana formation) has met with limited success in the case of "R." beurleni, because the prisms usually disintegrate and became separated once they become freed from the matrix. Only mechanical preparation has proven effective, but the results are inevitably not as informative as acid preparations.

Living rhinobatoids prefer to occupy shallow coral cays and sandy marine or brackish habitats. They are all live-bearers, probably being ovoviviparous. Some individuals may exceed 2.75 meters in total length, and weights of 180 kg are not unusual. "Rhinobatos" beurleni was therefore a comparatively small rhinobatoid, as it is not known to exceed 64 cm in length. Its presence in the fish assemblages of the Romualdo member of the Santana formation is of considerable paleoenvironmental interest.

Assemblage: Santana, Jardim.

(J. G. Maisey)

"Rhinobatos" beurleni. Teeth, removed from matrix by acid and viewed under scanning electron microscope. American Museum photographs. Scale bar = 50 microns.

Representative specimens of "*Rhinobatos*" *beurleni* showing characteristically poor preservation of prismatic calcified cartilage. Examples such as those at top of page are sometimes mistakenly identified as fossil birds by collectors.

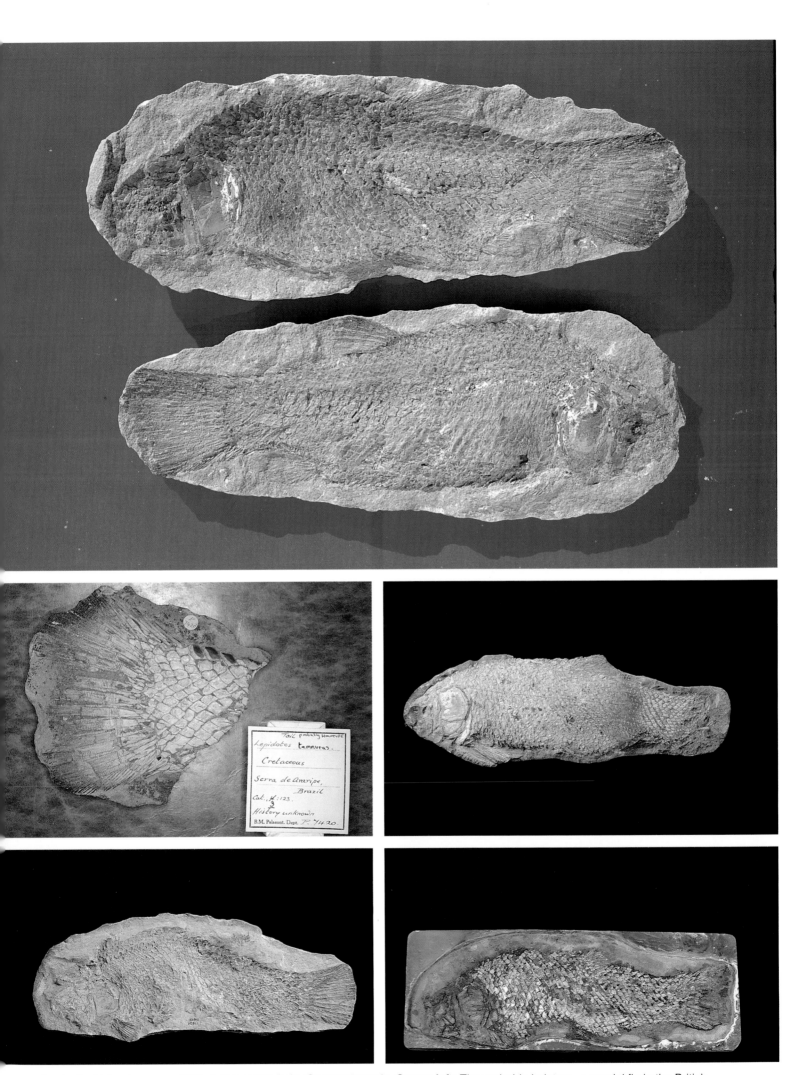

Araripelepidotes temnurus. **Top:** A fine example in "Santana" matrix. **Center left:** The probable holotype, a caudal fin in the British Museum (Natural History) collection. Other representative specimens are seen in remaining views. See description starting on page 118.

ARARIPELEPIDOTES Silva Santos, 1985

Class OSTEICHTHYES
Subclass ACTINOPTERYGII
Infraclass NEOPTERYGII
incertae sedis
Order SEMIONOTIFORMES
Family SEMIONOTIDAE Woodward, 1890a
Genus *Araripelepidotes* Silva Santos, 1985
1985 *Araripelepidotes* Silva Santos: 16

Diagnosis: Semionotid fishes with anterior-most infraorbitals subdivided, fifth infraorbital large, extending to meet preoperculum; three suborbital bones between dermopterotic and fifth infraorbital; dermopterotic separated from frontal by dermosphenotic; preoperculum nearly vertical; mandibular joint located behind level of orbit; lower jaw splint-like, lacking coronoid process; dentary, maxilla, and pterygoids apparently edentulous; dorsal ridge scales conspicuous and acuminate; fringing fulcral scales well developed in all fins.

Type species: *Lepidotes temnurus* Agassiz, 1841.

Araripelepidotes temnurus (Agassiz)
1841 *Lepidotes temnurus* Agassiz: 84
1844 *Lepidotes lemnurus* Ag.; Agassiz: 1010 (sic.)
1895 *Lepidotes* (?) *pustulatus* Woodward: 123
1908 *Lepidotes temnurus* Ag.; Jordan and Branner: 12

1908 *Lepidotes mawsoni* Woodward; Jordan and Branner: 12
1923 *Lepidotes temnurus* Ag.; Jordan: 3, 15
1938 *Lepidotes temnurus* Ag.; D'Erasmo: 13
1966 *Lepidotes temnurus* Ag.; Silva Santos: card (holotype designated)
1968 *Lepidotes temnurus* Ag.; Silva Santos and Valença: 349
1985 *Araripelepidotes temnurus* (Ag.); Silva Santos: 16
1986 *Lepidotes temnurus* Ag; Mones: 32

Diagnosis: *Araripelepidotes* ranging from 17-45 cm overall length; approx. 50-52 scale rows (measured along lateral line series); 21 rows to insertion of dorsal and anal fins; 8 rows to insertion of pelvics; deepest part of body with 18-20 scales per row; D9-10; A4-6; P10-11; V5-6; C15-16; fin margins with complete fringing series, dorsal with 15-16, anal with 11-12, pectoral with 10-13, ventral with 12-13, dorsal margin of caudal with 15-16, ventral margin with 18-20; seven infraorbitals and three suborbitals; interoperculum short and triangular, contact with preoperculum shorter than that of suboperculum; two pairs of supratemporals; scalloped lower margin of operculum.

Holotype: British Museum (Natural History), BM(NH) P7420; tail region lacking

Araripelepidotes temnurus. Skeletal reconstruction, complete apart from parts of snout and jaws.

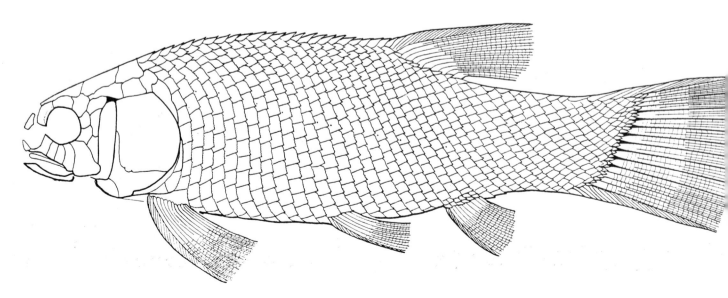

rest of body; Santana formation, locality uncertain, from Chapada do Araripe (matrix suggests Jardim).

The type specimen (illustrated in this volume) is somewhat unsatisfactory as it is represented by only a tail and lacks essentially all diagnostic characters for the genus and species. This also is true of the specimens described by Jordan and Branner (1908) and Jordan (1923). The example that was referred to *Lepidotes temnurus* and figured by d'Erasmo (1938: 13, pl. 2, fig. 3) is more complete and illustrates the skull roof and parts of the opercular and circumorbital series. From his figure three important features in the head may be discerned, all of which occur in specimens examined here and are regarded as taxonomic characters. These are discussed below. They include the dermosphenotic-dermopterotic arrangement, extent of the fifth infraorbital, and the supratemporal arrangement.

Because the type specimen of *Lepidotes temnurus* is so fragmentary, there is a real possibility that the specimens investigated by Jordan, d'Erasmo, and in the present work belong to some other, as yet undiagnosed taxon. At the moment, however, there is no evidence for more than one species of semionotid in the Santana formation, and all material may be referred provisionally to *Araripelepidotes temnurus.*

Semionotids are primitive, heavily armored halecostome fishes that were very abundant throughout the Mesozoic era, during which time they successfully colonized various marine, brackish, and freshwater habitats throughout most of the world. Unfortunately for paleontologists wishing to study them, these fishes had a conservative anatomy that apparently changed little throughout their period of dominance. In many respects, semionotids represent little more than generalized halecostomes that have retained a large number of primitive actinopterygian features characteristic of the "holostean level of organization" (Schaeffer, 1968; Schaeffer and Dunkle, 1950). Indeed, it has yet to be demonstrated that semionotids can be defined in terms of shared derived characters. According to one recent investigator (McCune, 1986: 218), "The Semionotidae may include as many as thirteen to twenty-two genera…, and as such is most certainly a grade, there being no good synapomorphies to demonstrate monophyly of the family." McCune (ibid.) went on to suggest that the Semionotidae perhaps should be restricted to include only the genera *Lepidotes* and *Semionotus.*

The genus *Lepidotes* is known from many nominal species; Woodward (1895) listed over 50, but the validity of most is doubtful. The situation remains confused to the present day, and is in fact worsened by the loss of critical type specimens during the two World Wars. There is some controversy as to how *Lepidotes* should be distinguished from *Semionotus,* although the taxonomic status of the latter has at least been critically investigated recently (McCune, 1986). There is little doubt that *Semionotus* and *Lepidotes* are closely related.

The most convincing single character separating *Lepidotes* from *Semionotus* is the presence of only a single suborbital in the latter (McCune, 1986). In *Lepidotes* there is a series of two or more suborbitals separating the infraorbitals from the preoperculum. A single suborbital bone apparently is a derived condition among actinopterygians (Schaeffer and Dunkle, 1950; Patterson, 1973; Wiley, 1976). There is a series of several suborbitals in the Permian semionotiform *Acentrophorus,* which adds biostratigraphic support to the view that *Lepidotes* has retained the primitive condition. Several other supposed differences between *Semionotus* and *Lepidotes,* given by Woodward (1916) and Jain (1983), have not withstood critical appraisal (see McCune, 1986: 219).

Araripelepidotes temnurus had until recently been considered simply one more species of *Lepidotes* (Agassiz, 1841, 1844; Woodward, 1895; Jordan and Branner, 1908; Jordan, 1923; d'Erasmo, 1938; Silva Santos and Valença, 1968). It shares with other *Lepidotes* spp. a series of suborbital bones, but this probably is a primitive similarity without phylogenetic significance at this level. *Araripelepidotes temnurus* differs from *Lepidotes* and *Semionotus* in several features of its dermal skeleton, in view of which it should perhaps be treated as a separate and distinct genus as proposed by Silva Santos (1984).

In the skull roof of *Lepidotes* and *Semionotus* the frontal and dermopterotic generally meet at a sutural margin, separating the dermosphenotic and parietal. This condition is widespread among neopterygian fishes generally (e.g., *Amia, Lepisosteus,* primitive teleosts, *Ophiopsis, Macrosemius, Watsonulus, Pteronisculus;* Olsen, 1984, fig. 18). In *Lepidotes lennieri* the frontal, dermosphenotic, dermopterotic, and parietal were figured by Wenz (1968, fig. 40) as meeting at a single point, although in another view (ibid., fig. 39) they are shown arranged as in other *Lepidotes* spp. In *Araripelepidotes* an unusual "reversed" configuration of these bones exists, in which the frontal and dermopterotic

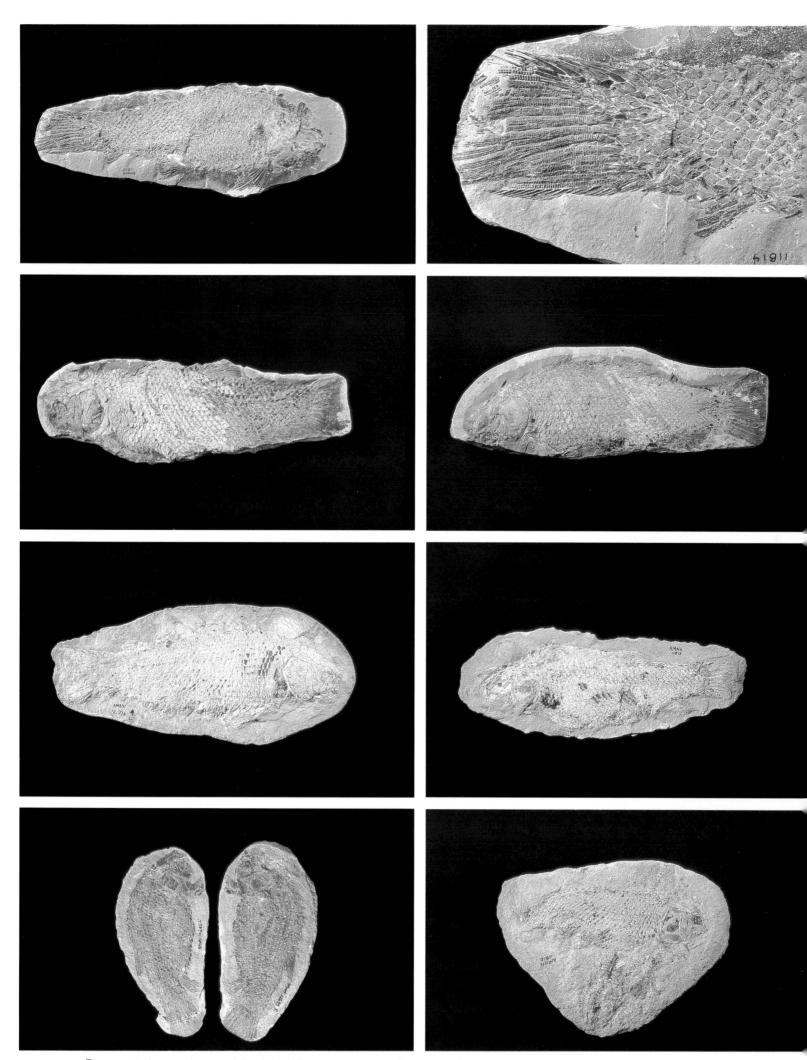

Representative specimens of *Araripelepidotes temnurus*; top four are in "Old Mission" matrix; others are in "Santana" matrix. Example at bottom right lies across a specimen of *Tharrhias*.

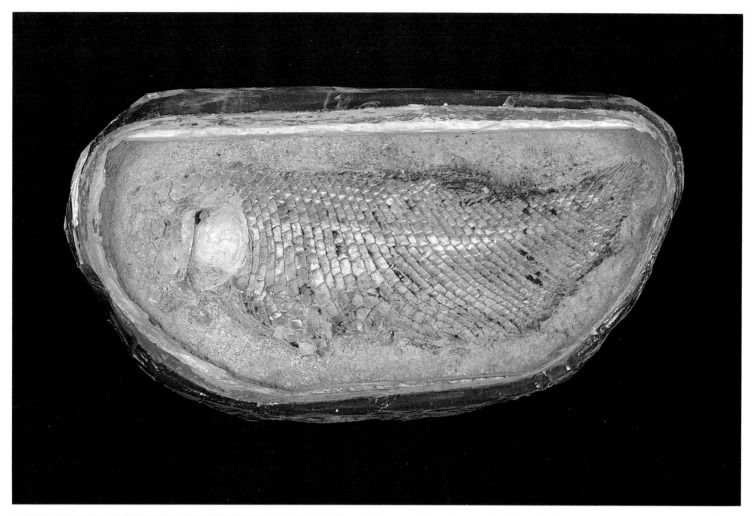

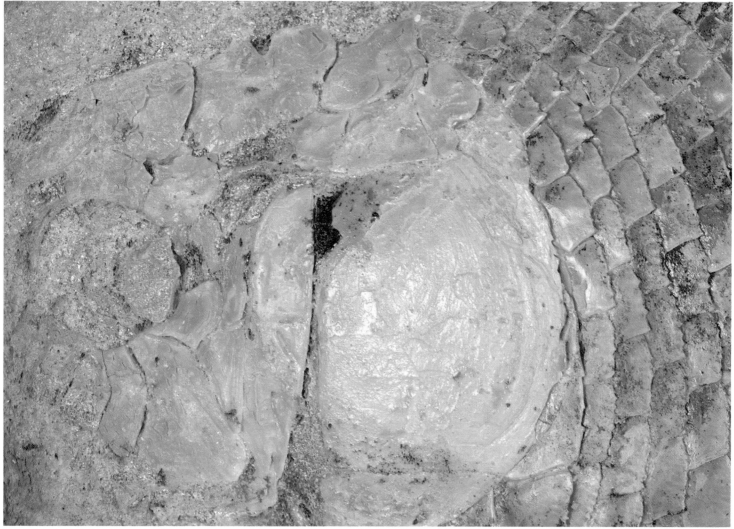

Small *Araripelepidotes temnurus* after acid preparation (top), with details of head (below) including characteristic arrangement of infraorbitals and skull roofing bones.

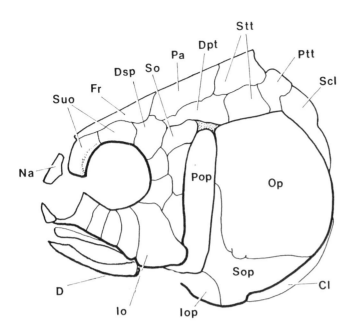

Araripelepidotes temnurus. Outline reconstruction of head in lateral view.

are separated by the dermosphenotic and parietal, which meet at a sutured margin. This arrangement apparently represents a derived condition among neopterygian fishes, although it also occurs in some extremely primitive "paleoniscoid" actinopterygians (e.g., *Moythomasia, Cheirolepis*; Moy-Thomas and Miles, 1971).

In *Araripelepidotes temnurus* there are two pairs of supratemporal (extrascapular) bones incorporated into the skull roof. The uppermost pair is large and is located essentially behind the parietals. The lower pair is smaller and lies behind the dermopterotic (e.g., AMNH 12716, 11833).

At least seven infraorbitals surround the eye, rather as in *Lepidotes* and *Semionotus*. The fifth infraorbital is much enlarged in *Araripelepidotes*, however, and extends from the orbit to the preoperculum. There are three suborbitals aligned in a vertical series that is limited in extent ventrally by the large fifth infraorbital.

There are two supraorbitals in front of the dermosphenotic. Traces of a separate nasal bone have been seen in only a few specimens. The ethmoid ossifications are not preserved in any material examined.

The jaw arrangement in *Araripelepidotes* differs from that in *Semionotus, Lepidotes, Acentrophorus,* and *Macrosemius*. In those taxa the mandibular joint is located below the orbit or even slightly ahead of it. The dentary and maxilla are abbreviated, although the maxilla reaches the snout and may (in *Lepidotes* and

Semionotus) have an anterior process that projects medial to the premaxilla. The ventral lobe of the preoperculum extends obliquely forward below the level of the orbit. In *Araripelepidotes* the mandibular joint is located behind this level and the ventral lobe of the preoperculum is short. The lower jaw is slender, lacks a coronoid process, and apparently is toothless. The maxilla apparently is separated from the cheek. Preservation of the jaws and snout is poor in the majority of specimens observed, and few details are discernible.

Semionotid fishes appear to have been a highly successful group of ecological generalists, retaining an evolutionarily conservative morphology for a considerable period of geological time (for much of the Mesozoic era, or some 150 million years). Semionotids first occur in Triassic rocks of Europe and North America.

Some species attained considerable size. The largest known complete fossil semionotid is *Lepidotes maximus*, from the Sölnhofen Limestone (Upper Jurassic) of Bavaria. One particular specimen, displayed in the Senckenberg Museum, Frankfurt-am-Main, is 2050 cm in length (Barthel, 1978, pl. 25).

Many semionotids lived in freshwater habitats, particularly during the Triassic. Their fossils also occur in marine deposits, however, and it is possible that some species were partially or completely euryhaline. The presence of *Araripelepidotes temnurus* in the Santana formation is not particularly informative concerning the aquatic habitat in which the concretions were formed. Nevertheless, this species seems to be more abundant in the creamy, ostracod-rich concretions from the vicinity of Crato and Santana do Cariri. These concretions have tended to produce more terrestrial plant and vertebrate fossils than elsewhere, so a fresh to brackish environment for *Araripelepidotes temnurus* is distinctly plausible.

Although Woodward (1895) placed *A. temnurus* into synonymy with a then newly-erected species (*Lepidotes pustulatus*), it seems futile to maintain that opinion since *L. pustulatus* is founded upon fragmentary, non-diagnostic material. The scales of *A. temnurus* lack the "irregularly-arranged, large, round shallow pits" said to be diagnostic of *L. pustulatus* (Woodward, ibid., p. 121). In an earlier work, Woodward (1888) founded the species *L. mawsoni* upon detached scales, teeth, and fragments from the Lower Cretaceous of Bahia. It is possible that *A. temnurus* and *L.*

mawsoni are closely related, but *L. mawsoni* is still too poorly diagnosed. The absence of teeth in *A. temnurus* suggests that it is not synonymous with *L. mawsoni*. Jordan and Branner (1908, p. 13) considered that the scales of *A. temnurus* were not ornamented like those of *L. mawsoni*.

Jordan and Branner's (1908, fig. 6) illustration of *A. temnurus* inaccurately depicts the dorsal margin of the body with a series of projecting ray-like ridge scales. Although *A. temnurus* does possess a series of dorsal ridge-scales, they do not project in the manner indicated by Jordan and Branner. Body scales from behind the shoulder girdle to the level of the dorsal fin have a fluted or spiny posterior margin, as in many (perhaps all) other semionotids. There are only three or four projections per scale, however, whereas more may be present in other species (e.g., *L. mantelli, L. maximus*).

According to Jordan (1923, p. 17), there is "no trace of a lateral line" in *A. temnurus*. This is undoubtedly because he was examining specimens that were split open through the thickness of the scales. Where scale surfaces are revealed following acid preparation, some are seen to be perforated by a lateral line pore, as illustrated in other semionotids (e.g., Woodward, 1895, fig. 22; 1916, fig. 14; 1919, fig. 41). Apparently not every scale in the lateral line series is perforated in this way.

There is no direct evidence to show what *A. temnurus* fed upon, and its jaws are weak and probably edentulous. The rounded, button-like teeth of most *Lepidotes* spp. seem admirably suited for a durophagous habitat, crunching up molluscs, crustaceans, or small fishes. Neither is there direct evidence of predation on *L. temnurus*, although it perhaps could have been eaten by larger crocodilians. In England, remains of a carnivorous Lower Cretaceous dinosaur were recently discovered with a large number of *Lepidotes* scales inside the body cavity. It has been suggested that the dinosaur fed largely or exclusively on these fishes.

Assemblages: Santana (small); Jardim (rare).

(J. G. Maisey)

Neoproscinetes penalvai. Representative examples in "Old Mission" matrix.

NEOPROSCINETES Figueiredo and Silva Santos, 1987

Division HALECOSTOMI
incertae sedis
Order PYCNODONTIFORMES
Family MACROMESODONTIDAE
Genus *Neoproscinetes* Figueiredo and Silva
Santos, 1987
  1986 *Neomicrodon* Figueiredo and Silva
Santos: 15 (name unavailable)
  1987 *Neoproscinetes* Figueiredo and Silva
Santos: 29

Diagnosis: Pycnodontiform fish, laterally compressed and deep-bodied, usually nearly circular in lateral outline, maximum depth in notochordal length usually between 0.8-0.9; scales reduced to bars in front of median fins, except heavy scales protecting the abdomen antero-ventrally; head and caudal part of body naked; dorsal ridge and ventral keel scutes denticulate, posterior denticles of each being larger; 2-4 postanal scutes; caudal fin high,

Other examples of *Neoproscinetes penalvai.*

hardly forked, sometimes reversed to low convex at middle of trailing edge; 18-24 segmented rays, 2-5 unsegmented rays dorsally, 2-6 ventrally, the first of which is a basal scute, both above and below; dorsal fin long, 40-55 rays, acuminate, much lower posteriorly; anal fin similar, 30-45 rays; small gape terminal, antero-ventral to large orbit; two incisiform teeth in each premaxilla; 2 or 3 in each dentary; 3 or 4 longitudinal rows of vomerine teeth, with central row alternating antero-posteriorly between a single, broad tooth and a laterally disposed small pair; 4 rows of prearticular teeth; maxilla reniform; 28 or more neural spines in front of caudal fin; up to 8 neural spines separated from their basidorsals anteriorly; 12 or more hemal spines in front of caudal fin; 2-5 hypurals; 1-3 urodermals; parietal peniculus present.

Type species: *Microdon penalvai* Silva Santos, 1970

Neoproscinites penalvai (Silva Santos)

1968 *Microdon penalvai* Silva Santos and Valença: 349 (name only)

1970 *Microdon penalvai* Silva Santos: 446

1986 *Microdon penalvai* Silva Santos; Mones: 33

1986 *Neomicrodon penalvai* (Silva Santos); Figueiredo and Silva Santos: 15 (generic name unavailable)

1987 *Neoproscinetes penalvai* (Silva Santos); Figueiredo and Silva Santos: 29

Diagnosis: *Neoproscinetes* ca. 350 mm total length (ca. 310 SL); 32-34 neural spines in front of caudal fin; 7 anterior-most neural spines separated from their arcualia; caudal fin rays borne on 6 unmodified neural spines; 15-16 pairs of ribs; 14-16 hemal spines in front of caudal fin; caudal fin rays borne on 11 hemal spines, at least 5 of which form hypurals (i.e., do not possess a hemal arch); caudal fin high and shallowly forked; ca. 30 caudal rays; ca. 42 dorsal fin rays; ca. 33 anal fin rays; three incisiform teeth on dentary. Prominent condyle on head of hyomandibula for articulation with round hyomandibular fossa of endocranium; dermalization apparent on the ventral, external surface of the hyomandibula; snout slightly concave above premaxilla.

Holotype: Divisão de Geologia e Mineralogia, Departamento Nacional da Produção Mineral,

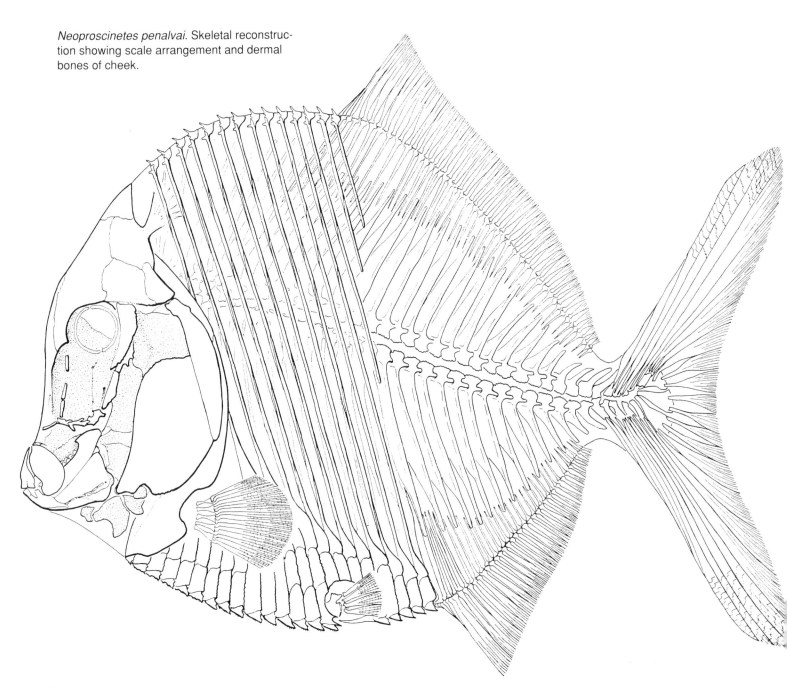

Neoproscinetes penalvai. Skeletal reconstruction showing scale arrangement and dermal bones of cheek.

Rio de Janeiro, DGM-DNPM 918-P; complete individual; Santana formation, north side of Chapada do Araripe (?Missão Velha), Ceará.

Systematic Note: Following a detailed comparison, it is concluded that many morphometric characteristics of the Santana species fall outside of the ranges established for European *Proscinetes*, and that some character states (e.g., numbers and arrangement of teeth, the form of the hyomandibular condyle) are sufficiently distinct to merit distinction at generic level. The name *Neoproscinetes* Figueiredo and Silva Santos (1987) is available and is adopted here. These authors had previously used another name, *Neomicrodon* (apparently in error; Figueiredo and Silva

Santos, 1986), but this name cannot be regarded as available because it appears only in a typed and photocopied abstract of a communication, which does not constitute a a publication under the Code of Zoological Nomenclature.

Pycnodonts are highly specialized, deep-bodied, extinct fishes that evidently were adapted to capture armored prey such as molluscs (snails and clams), echinoderms (sea urchins), and probably arthropods (such as crabs and shrimp). Almost all pycnodonts were laterally compressed and deep-bodied. Most of them were small (less than about 200 mm in total length), although the largest reached about 1000 mm. Superficially, many pycnodonts resemble Recent fishes found among coral reefs,

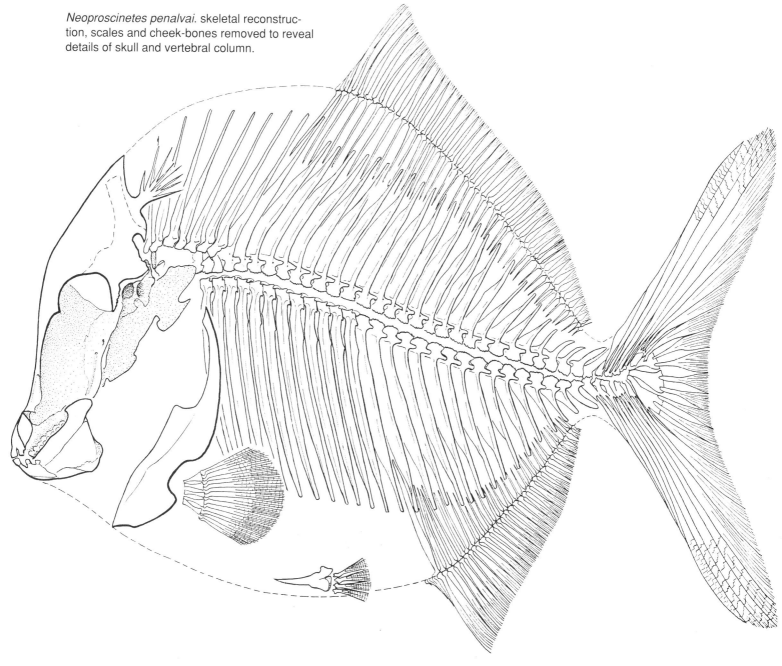

Neoproscinetes penalvai. skeletal reconstruction, scales and cheek-bones removed to reveal details of skull and vertebral column.

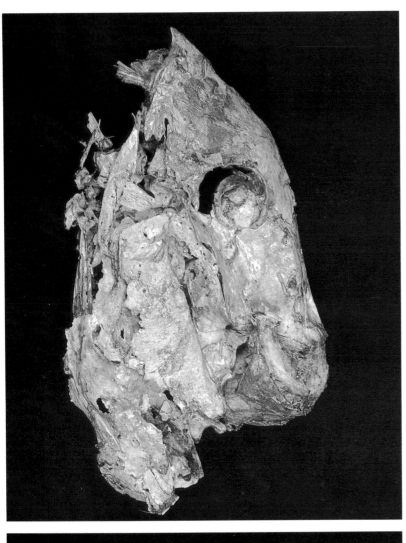

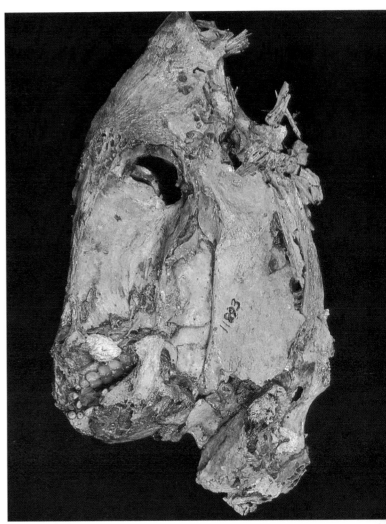

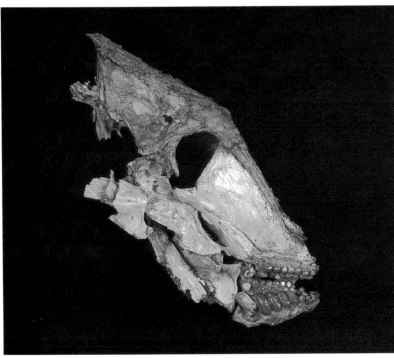

Acid-prepared skulls of *Neoproscinetes penalvai*,
including three free-standing specimens and one
transfer-prepared example (bottom right).

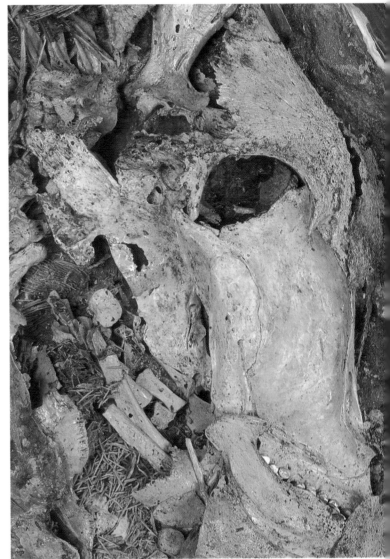

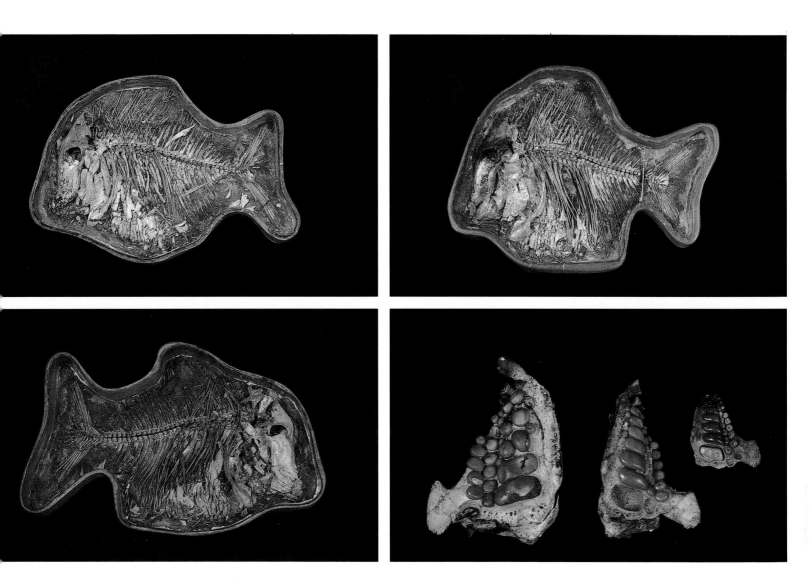

Above: Three complete skeletons of *Neoproscinetes penalvai* after acid preparation, together with isolated lower jaws of three acid-prepared specimens (largest jaw belongs to specimen shown at top left; middle example goes with skull in previous color plate, lower left; smallest example is from another specimen not illustrated).

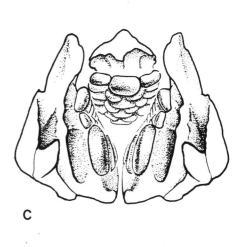

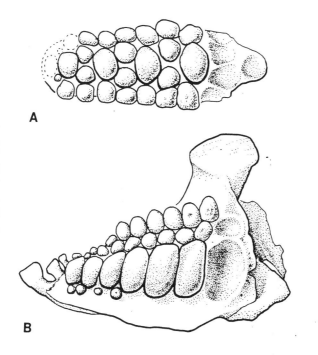

Neoproscinetes penalvai. Dentition. A: Vomerine teeth, oral view. B: Mandibular teeth, oblique oral view. C: Vomerine and mandibular teeth restored together, posterior view, from AMNH 11852.

129

such as surgeonfishes (Acanthuridae), triggerfishes (Balistidae), damselfishes (Pomacentridae), and parrotfishes (Scaridae). However, such similarities are convergent and do not represent phylogenetic relationships. They do suggest similarity in behavior and habits, and perhaps habitat. Evidence from the deposits in which they are found indicates that most pycnodonts were marine, generally associated with coral reefs and warm lagoons. They may have penetrated into bodies of brackish water near the sea coasts along which they lived. It is often very difficult to determine with certainty the conditions within which fossil specimens lived, and conditions in coastal deposits may be especially confused owing to the mixture of influence from sea and land.

There is no doubt that the order is monophyletic. Some early investigators placed pycnodonts among the chondrosteans (i.e., allied to the fishes that gave rise to sturgeons and paddlefishes), but modern studies suggest that they are phylogenetically more advanced and perhaps closely related to teleosts, the modern bony fishes with which we are all familiar. Among the characters shared by pycnodonts and teleosts are the following: a median vomer with longitudinal rows of teeth; several caudal fin rays for every endoskeletal support; a compound ethmoid region with an intricate mesethmoid-vomer-parasphenoid connection; a post-coelomic bone supporting the rear wall of the abdominal cavity; a supraoccipital crest; and two sclerotic bones, placed antero-posteriorly, supporting each eyeball. A peculiar jaw articulation between the symplectic and articular nevertheless suggests a radical alternative, that pycnodonts may be halecomorphs (i.e., related to *Amia calva*), which, in the opinion of many, form the sister group of teleosts.

The order Pycnodontiformes may be divided into several families, perhaps as many as nine or ten, based on characters of teeth, scales, dermal roofing bones, and vertebral units, as well as the position of the anus, the presence of the parietal peniculus (a small, brush-like posterior extension of the parietal into the epaxial muscle, analogous to epiotic processes found in some Recent teleosts such as barracudas and mullets), the temporal fenestra, a notch in the maxilla, pharyngeal teeth, and the form of the hyomandibula. *Neoproscinetes* has been included here in the Macromesodontidae, a large and possibly paraphyletic family that existed from Jurassic into Cretaceous times. Macromesodontids are distinguished by having a

foramen in the keel of the parasphenoid and by having only four or fewer scutes between the anus and the anal fin. The family includes the earliest pycnodonts in which the premaxillary and dentary teeth become incisive instead of peg-like in form and the parietal peniculus appears. Neither a temporal fenestra nor a notched maxilla nor pharyngeal teeth are found. Some dermalization of the hyomandibula is seen, but only in *Stemmatodus rhombus* had it proceeded very far. Macromesodontids represent a median grade in the phylogeny of pycnodonts; they display the chief characters of the order, but lack several primitive characters as well as more highly derived characters of other representatives of the order.

The specimens of *Neoproscinetes penalvai* have a special place in the study of pycnodonts because of their superb three-dimensional, almost complete skeletons. From a few specimens, investigators have been able to confirm details of structure laboriously reconstructed over many years from dozens of less well-preserved pycnodonts. The following paragraphs describe pycnodont characteristics that can be seen clearly in acid-prepared *Neoproscinetes penalvai*.

The teeth of *N. penalvai* are typical of pycnodonts. The name "pycnodont" means "dense tooth" and refers to the tritoral teeth. Premaxillae and dentaries each bear incisor-like teeth, two pairs above and three below, that probably were used to pluck prey from the substrate. The median vomer in the roof of the mouth and the paired prearticular bones in the floor each bore rows of heavy, round to ovoid teeth that formed a crushing mill in occlusion to break up the shells or skeletal structures of the prey so that the soft tissues would be exposed for digestion. There are specimens of other species of pycnodont in which gut contents, such as comminuted mollusc shells and echinoderm spines, have been preserved. In *N. penalvai*, however, no trace of food remains have been found, and its exact diet remains unknown.

The mandible of a pycnodont is massive, with a long symphysis involving the prearticular bones, and a high, strongly developed coronoid process of the prearticular for attachment of the mandibular musculature. Each side of the mandible always comprises a dermal dentary, prearticular and angular, and an endochondral articular.

The articulation of the mandible is double, that is, involving two pairs of bones, which relates pycnodonts to halecomorphs, but the jaw

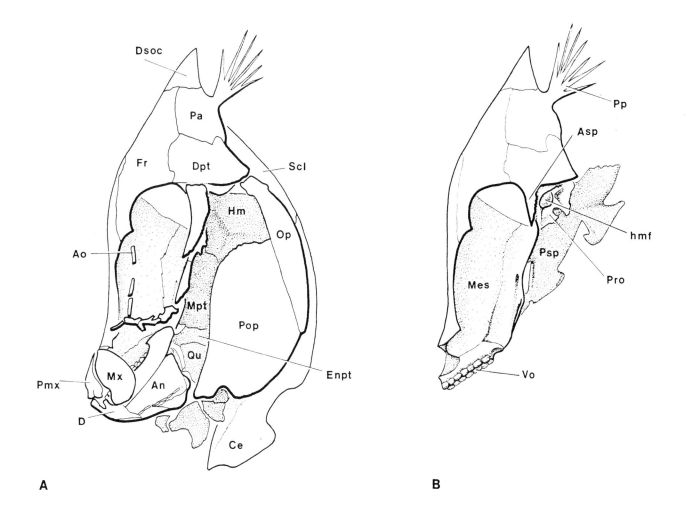

Neoproscinetes penalvai. Outline
reconstruction of head (A) and skull only
(B).

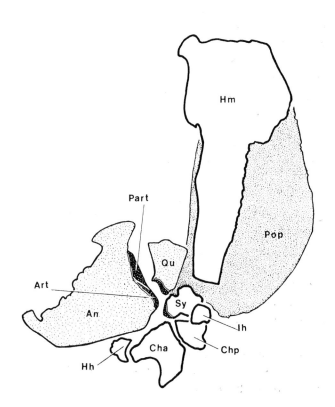

Neoproscinetes penalvai. Mesial view of hyoid arch and
associated elements, based on AMNH 11893.

joint of the pycnodonts has its own unique characteristics. Patterson (1973) defined Halecomorphi in part by the presence of a double mandibular joint, with both quadrate and symplectic articulating with Bridge's ossicles, which represent derivatives of the articular and retroarticular bones (Nelson, 1973). The symplectic involvement is the unique feature. The pycnodont symplectic bone moved against the articular at the antero-ventral corner of the preoperculum, which resembles the condition in *Amia*. Immediately dorsal to the symplectic articulation, the quadrate articulated with a largely cartilaginous part of the mandible supported externally by the angular. The involvement of the angular in the mandibular joint may be a parallelism with some teleosts. The pycnodont quadrate is reinforced by a crest that may represent a fused quadratojugal, a character shared with halecomorphs and teleosts. There is also an articular surface between the quadrate and symplectic, which suggests a complex jaw movement that could adjust to a wide range of bite pressures.

It seems as if the gape of pycnodonts could not have been very wide although great pressure could have been applied during occlusion. To resist the force generated by the closure of the powerful mandible, the vomer is strongly buttressed by the mesethmoid, parasphenoid, and palatine process of the quadrate. With the mouth located terminally and ventrally, the snout was supported by a single mesethmoid bone of complicated shape. In cross-section, the mesethmoid is T-shaped. The cross-piece is narrow and forms the anterior margin of the snout; dorsally, it emerges from beneath the frontal (a teleost characteristic); ventrally, it expands to bear lateral fossae for the olfactory sacs. The upright portion of the T is long and bilaminar, to envelop the median dorsal crest of the parasphenoid posteriorly and the median dorsal crest of the vomer anteriorly.

The edentulous parasphenoid, typical of pycnodonts, is very long and is inflected downward at about its mid-point (an unusual condition in fishes). Posteriorly, it forms two wings that extend back beyond the skull. The anterior section of the parasphenoid has a dorsal crest (lying between the laminae of the mesethmoid) and a ventral keel, as well as narrow lateral wings that flare out below the mesethmoid laminae to form the roof of the branchial chamber. The mesethmoid and parasphenoid held the vomer firmly in place against the pressures of the closing mandible. An additional buttress, in the form of an

anterior palatine process of the quadrate making contact in a posterior fossa of the vomer, must have braced the vomer when the mandible closed against it.

The ventral keel of the parasphenoid in *N. penalvai* bears a long, oval fenestra that appears to be a character of the Macromesodontidae. Openings for the efferent pseudobranchial and internal carotid arteries lie at the posterior end of the parasphenoid fenestra.

Pycnodont fishes are characterized *inter alia* by a much-reduced opercular series of bones, shown well by *N. penalvai*. There is a small, dagger-shaped operculum located behind and extending above a large, roughly triangular preoperculum. The junction between the operculum and preoperculum forms nearly a straight line passing obliquely down and backward. Below the preoperculum of each side lie two branchiostegal rays.

The hyomandibula is prominent above the preoperculum and in front of the operculum. The hyomandibular head is round and carries a lateral ridge that presumably separated mandibular and opercular muscles. There is no opercular process, but the posterior margin of the hyomandibular head instead articulates with a groove and ridge on the medial surface of the operculum. This arrangement is typical of pycnodonts generally.

The head of the hyomandibula in *N. penalvai* is different from that in *Macromesodon* spp. in having a distinct condylar portion to fit the circular hyomandibular fossa of the skull. Primitively, pycnodonts possessed an elongated hyomandibular fossa within which the edge of the flat, round hyomandibular head articulated (e.g., *Mesturus, Macromesodon*). The more derived pycnodonts (Family Pycnodontidae) have reduced the head of the hyomandibula entirely to a condylar process. *N. penalvai* also shows well a step in the presumed dermalization of the hyomandibula that is found in advanced pycnodonts. The most derived pycnodonts (e.g., *Pycnodus* spp.) lack an operculum; the preoperculum is reduced to a somewhat square bone occupying the space that corresponds approximately to the lower half of the preoperculum in more generalized neopterygians. The upper half is formed by an apparent dermal bone, recognized as such by its surface decoration. It often has been called the operculum (e.g., Blot, 1987) but is interpreted here as an expanded hyomandibula, the surface of which may have formed under the influence of ectodermal epithelium, and is decorated like a dermal bone. The process whereby an

Fine details of fin rays and internal bony supports of a *Neoproscinetes penalvai* caudal fin are very evident following acid preparation. Specimen from which this is taken appears at top right of previous color plate; note that tail is upside-down in that specimen, which may be a composite.

endochondral bone takes on surface characteristics of a dermal bone owing to its contiguity to ectodermal epithelium is called dermalization. A dermalized hyomandibula bone may be termed a dermohyomandibula (as distinct from a dermohyal, which is a dermal cheek bone). The dermohyomandibula bears a strong condylar articulation with the skull. In *Pycnodus* the condyle is produced beyond the dermohyomandibula in the same position as the condylar process of the head of the hyomandibula in *Neoproscinetes*. Among other macromesodontids, faint traces of dermalization are seen on the head of the hyomandibula in *Macromesodon* just above the preopercular margin, somewhat less than in *N. penalvai*, but more extensive dermalization has taken place in *Stemmatodus*. The process apparently has been taken still further in *Coelodus* and *Pycnodus*.

The shaft of the hyomandibula lies behind the leading edge of the preoperculum. It becomes attenuated at its ventral end, below which lies the symplectic. There is a kind of a preopercular shield for the symplectic, which forms an antero-ventral process to the preoperculum. The ceratohyal is located ventral to the preoperculum, supporting the two branchiostegal rays on its postero-ventral margin. The interhyal and hypohyal are present and usually well-ossified.

Many pycnodont specimens show traces of gill filaments and sometimes other branchial structures in confused array. The acid-prepared specimens of *N. penalvai*, (e.g., AMNH 11990) are unusual in that parts of the branchial skeleton are preserved. In AMNH 11990 the operculum and preoperculum of the right side are missing and the cleithrum has been displaced backward. Five ceratobranchials are present; the first is the longest. They are U-shaped in cross-section, with gill filaments arising from the hollow of the U, which opens posteriorly. Parts of other elements are present, but are so disarticulated and scattered that relationships cannot be made out. One or two putative epibranchials are seen, but they are reversed in relation to each other, so their connections with the ceratobranchials are not clear. Remains of two to four flat, rounded structures are present that somewhat resemble the pharyngobranchials of *Amia*.

A prominent ridge lies along the side of the parasphenoid keel, from where the parasphenoid articulates with the prootic to below the parasphenoid fenestra anteriorly. The ridge probably marks the dorsal limit of the area in which the pharyngobranchials lay. It seems likely that further Santana specimens, when acid-treated, will give rise to a much fuller understanding of the branchial apparatus. There is no sign of pharyngeal teeth, and these have not been found in macromesodontids.

A large, palaform (spade-shaped) cleithrum supports a smaller supracleithrum. The connection, if any, between supracleithrum and skull is not clear. In the acid-prepared specimens of *N. penalvai* there is consistently a gap in the angle between parietal and dermopterotic from which a bone (post-temporal?) may be missing. Unprepared specimens from the Field Museum of Natural History, Chicago, show what appears to be a complete posterior margin to the dermal roofing bones of the skull, formed ventrally by the parietal and dermopterotic. Generally in pycnodonts the supracleithrum articulates directly with the dermopterotic without intervention of a post-temporal bone. The gap in the posterior skull margin of acid-prepared specimens thus seems to be either a loss through breakage of the parietal and dermopterotic or the development of a postero-ventral process of the parietal (preserved in the New York specimens but lost from those in Chicago). A structure that resembles a small left scapulo-coracoid can be seen in *N. penalvai* AMNH 11893. That is the only sign of a scapulocoracoid recognized to date in a pycnodont.

The dermal roof of phylogenetically derived pycnodonts comprises a pair of frontals, a pair of parietals, a pair of dermopterotics, and a median element interpreted here as a dermosupraoccipital. Additional dermal bones, often numerous, are found in more primitive families (e.g., Brembodontidae, Eomesodontidae, Mesturidae, Gyrodontidae). Examination of the acid-prepared specimens of *N. penalvai* revealed a most interesting relationship of the bone identified as a dermosupraoccipital. It is separate and distinct from the endochondral supraoccipital, a condition found throughout the Macromesodontidae and Pycnodontidae as far as can be determined. That probably also is the case in other families, but preservation is not so clear and underlying structures are not so well-defined. In *N. penalvai* a spectacularly well-developed endochondral supraoccipital crest is present. The supraoccipital apparently is supported by the pterotic bones of the endocranium, a condition noted by Patterson (1975) in Upper Jurassic pholidophorids. The crest rises sharply from the roof of the endocranium, dividing the cranial vault into two

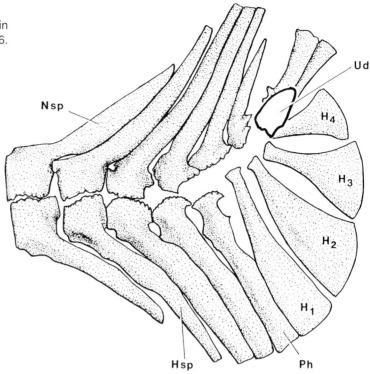

Neoproscinetes penalvai. Caudal fin endoskeleton, from AMNH 11846.

large, lateral post-temporal fossae to receive anterior epaxial somatic musculature. The supraoccipital crest is buried completely beneath the dermal skull roof and does not make osseous connection with it. The crest is longest at its dorsal margin, shortest at its base. Its greatest length antero-posteriorly is only about two-thirds of its height. The dorsal edge evidently was cartilaginous, and cartilaginous or fibrous connection probably was made with overlying dermal bones, especially the dermosupraoccipital. This seems to have been a unique pycnodont specialization. The dermal bones of the skull roof are largely separate from those of the endocranium. Endocranial ossification is very much reduced, except at sites of muscle attachment (e.g., the supraoccipital crest and basicranium).

The anterior-most two or three paired dorsal arcualia are sutured (in smaller individuals) or fused together with the paired exoccipitals to form a backward-projecting block of bone ("synarcual") that encloses the spinal canal. The canal sends off dorsal segmental nerve foramina, while the ventral nerves lie in grooves that traverse the ventral surface of the "synarcual." The vagal canal forms a notch on either side of the exoccipital part of the "synarcual" anteriorly. There is a sutural connection between the exoccipital part of the "synarcual" and a pair of processes at the posterior extremity

of the parasphenoid. The basisphenoid may be represented by a small ossification between the posterior parasphenoid processes (e.g., AMNH 11990). This ossification cannot be seen in specimens where the exoccipitals are *in situ;* the presumed basisphenoid is completely surrounded by these and the parasphenoid.

Other endocranial bones include the paired orbitosphenoids and prootics, which together form much of the posterior orbital wall. The prootic and sphenotic each bear about half of the hyomandibular facet, which is deep and round, but the ascending process of the parasphenoid just reaches the lower margin of the facet. There is a well developed posterior myodome, roofed by the prootics and floored by the parasphenoid.

Another pycnodont characteristic beautifully shown in *N. penalvai* is the separation of anterior neural spines from their arcualia (seven in this species). These spines are anterior to the dorsal pterygiophores and reach the lappets of the dorsal scutes. Farther posteriorly the neural dorsal spines are attached to their arcualia, are much shorter, and have their free ends interdigitating with the dorsal fin pterygiophores, deep in the median vertical septum.

Other pycnodont characters that are clearly displayed in the acid-prepared specimens of *Neoproscinetes penalvai* include the anterior medial flanges on neural and hemal spines, the ribs, which are flanged fore and aft, and the unmodified ray-bearing neural spines of the caudal fin. Although the caudal fin of pycnodonts is classically homocercal (except for that of the early and primitive *Gibbodon*; Tintori, 1981), the neural spines that support the epaxial fin rays remain attached to their arcualia, and separate epurals and uroneurals are not formed. Ray-bearing hemal spines grade almost imperceptibly into hypurals. At least one urodermal is present on each side. Urodermals are common among pycnodonts with reduced squamation (e.g., macromesodontids, pycnodontids).

The nature of the pycnodont endocranium has long puzzled investigators. It is poorly ossified in derived pycnodonts and rarely is well preserved. Some detail of the endocranium is known from a *Mesturus* specimen in which very generalized similarities can be seen with that of *Amia*, teleosts, and the semionotiform *Dapedium*. Perhaps the closest similarities in the endocrania of *Mesturus* and *Neoproscinetes* are seen in the relationships of the optic fenestra, the trigemino-facialis chamber, other nerve foramina, and the posterior myodome.

The pycnodonts first appeared in latest Triassic (Norian) times in locations now in northern Italy. As the Tethyan Sea expanded, they colonized lagoonal waters around and ultimately beyond its margins, eventually extending from Tibet to Bolivia. As the Tethyan Sea contracted during the Cretaceous, so did the range of pycnodonts. The latest specimens come from Monte Bolca, an Eocene (Ypresian) formation again in northern Italy. The success of pycnodonts paralleled the rise and diversification of the scleractinian corals, and the last survivors (e.g., *Pycnodus platessus*, *Palaeobalistum orbiculatum*, *Nursallia veronae*) mingled with a near-modern Indo-Pacific fauna of warm-water, reef-dwelling teleosts. *Neoproscinetes penalvai* is somewhat unusual in its Gondwanan occurrence many hundreds of kilometers from known marginal Cretaceous reef or lagoonal deposits. These are conspicuously absent in the Santana formation. This species may have become an obligate predator of shrimp and other small crustaceans, whose fragmentary remains are not uncommon in the concretions.

The phylogenetic position of pycnodonts among neopterygians is controversial, and several alternative hypotheses of relationship can be proposed, depending on how various characters are interpreted.

Assemblages: Jardim, Old Mission.

(J. R. Nursall, J. G. Maisey)

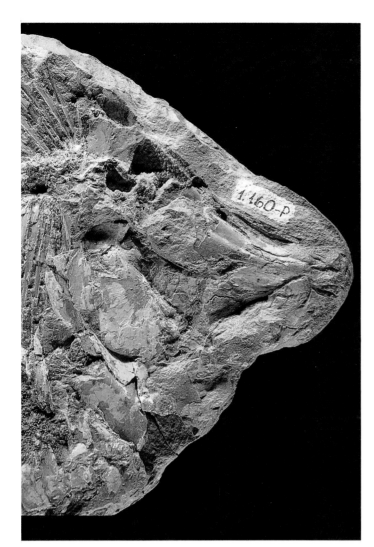

Above and below and facing page: *lemanja palma*, the holotype in part and counterpart. Photos by D. Serrete, courtesy S. Wenz. See description on page 138.

IEMANJA Wenz, 1989

Division HALECOSTOMI
incertae sedis
Order PYCNODONTIFORMES
Family GYRODONTIDAE Berg, 1940
Genus *Iemanja* Wenz, 1989
1989 *Iemanja* Wenz: 976
Emended and simplified diagnosis:
Subdiscoidal gyrodontid of average dimensions; standard length (SL) 280 mm; length of head more than one-third of SL; maximum body depth four-fifths of SL; gape horizontal, situated entirely beneath preorbital region; prognathous jaws; concave frontal profile; infraorbital bones regressive; lateral ethmoids and separate mesethmoid present; single preoperculum, quadrangular, vertical, as wide as high; large gap between dorsal edge of preoperculum and lateral margin of skull roof; narrow crescent-shaped operculum; lengthy vomer and mandible; vomer long, straight, and narrow, with strongly convex oral margin; teeth smooth; mandibular teeth small, numerous, subcircular, and irregularly arranged; vomerine posteromedian tooth-rows in three principal rows (one median, two lateral) with seven or eight teeth each, flanked by two additional smaller rows of four or five teeth, only a few teeth in medial row enlarged and paved; approximately 36-38 dorsal and ventral arcualia; four or five neural spines attached at head, 12 abdominal and 12-13 post-abdominal elements, six epichordal and nine hypochordal elements supporting caudal exoskeleton; indented bases of neural and hemal arches partially enclose notochord in abdominal and post-abdominal region, and wrap around it completely in caudal region; each hemal and neural spine with well-developed anterior and posterior lamellar expansions; neural arches connected by anterior and posterior processes, claviform in anterior and mid-trunk regions, each articulating with the one in front and behind; caudal endoskeleton formed from six complete neural spines and nine hemal spines plus hypurals; three enlarged last hypurals form enlarged triangular plate; two urodermals present; strong hypurostegy of caudal fin-rays; D42, A40-42, Cv,21,vi; 19 of principal caudal rays branched; squamation restricted to anteroventral part of body anterior to unpaired fins; 12-13 scale rows antero-ventrally, antero-dorsal scales reduced at points of articulation.

Type species: *Iemanja palma* Wenz, 1989.
Iemanja palma Wenz
1989 *Iemanja palma* Wenz: 976

Diagnosis: As for genus.
Holotype: Muséum National d'Histoire Naturelle, Paris, MNHN BCE 166a and b; entire fish in part and counterpart; Santana formation, locality not known, from Chapada do Araripe. See photos on pages 136, 137, and 140.

As are nearly all pycnodontids, *Iemanja palma* (an approximately 280 mm standard length fish) is flattened from side to side and has a deep, almost circular, body. The long median dorsal and anal fins occupy the whole second half of the body, the anal fin being slightly shorter than the dorsal. The mouth is small in spite of the antero-posterior elongation of the vomer and mandibles (which is characteristic of *I. palma*). The dentition is highly specialized, with incisiform teeth in the front of the jaws and crushing teeth that are arranged more or less in pavement fashion at the back of the jaws.

I. palma has been identified as a gyrodontid on the basis of a complete dermal cover of the skull (without fenestra between the supraoccipital, parietal, and frontal bones) and the lack of cephalic spine (Wenz, 1989: 977). *I. palma* is distinguished from the other genera in the family essentially by various details of the dermal skull pattern, the body shape, the vertebral and fin formulae, characteristics of the dentition, expansion of the neural and hemal arches, and the type of articulation between adjacent neural or hemal arches. Teeth are numerous, subcircular, and smooth. They are arranged irregularly except those in the posterior region of the vomer, which are transversely elongated and arranged in three longitudinal series. The bases of the neural and hemal arches are expanded along the notochord and adjacent neural or hemal arches are linked by anterior and posterior claviform processes.

Pycnodontids are neither numerous nor diversified in the Chapada do Araripe: there are only a few individuals belonging to two species. The shape of the body is indicative of probably slow-swimming sedentary fishes. The dentition indicates that they were able to seize their prey with the incisiform teeth and break shells of molluscs and crustaceans with crushing teeth.

Only three specimens of this species are known. Besides the holotype (in Paris), one other specimen was figured by Wenz (1989: fig. 2), belonging to the Departamento nacional da Produção Mineral, DGM-DNPM 160P. The third specimen has not been figured; it is in the Desirée collection of Mr. R. A. von Blittersdorf, Rio de Janeiro (cat. no. 88-CD-P-44, half nodule).

(S. Wenz)

CALAMOPLEURUS Agassiz, 1841

Division HALECOSTOMI
Subdivision HALECOMORPHI
Family AMIIDAE Bonaparte, 1837
Subfamily AMIINAE Patterson, 1973
Genus *Calamopleurus* Agassiz, 1841
1841 *Calamopleurus* Agassiz: 84
1908 *Enneles* Jordan and Branner: 23

Emended diagnosis: Large amiid, with ample mouth bearing large fang-like conical teeth; vomers with outer tooth row and inner patch of teeth; mandibular suspensorium inclined slightly forward; premaxilla with strong dorsal process containing large olfactory foramen; maxilla large and strongly tapered anteriorly, extending back behind infraorbitals and with pronounced embayment in posterior margin; supramaxilla low and triangular; premaxillary dentition of six teeth; approximately 24 maxillary and dentary teeth; supraorbitals numerous; infraorbital canal contained by small dermosphenotic (apparently not incorporated into skull roof) plus five infraorbitals, of which the fourth is much the largest; dermopterotic fused to elongate series of "ossified ligaments" extending beneath supratemporal and posttemporal; extra dermopalatine present as in *Amia*; pterotic and basisphenoid strongly ossified; pterosphenoid pedicle absent; spiracular canal enclosed by sphenotic; D19-21; C16-18; A10-12; P17; V8; approx. 55 scales along lateral line; 15 scales deep just ahead of dorsal, 7 above and 7 below the lateral line; 16 or 17 ural and at least 40 abdominal centra (approx. 88 centra in total).

Type species: *Calamopleurus cylindricus* Agassiz, 1841.

Calamopleurus cylindricus Agassiz
1841 *Calamopleurus cylindricus* Agassiz: 84 (name only)
1844b *Calamopleurus cylindricus* Agassiz: 1012 (name only)
1895 *Calamopleurus cylindricus* Ag.; Woodward: 499 (name only)
Non 1907 *Calamopleurus cylindricus* Ag.: Jordan: 139 (elopomorph)
Non 1908 *Calamopleurus cylindricus* Ag.; Jordan and Branner: 16 (elopomorph)
Non 1923 *Calamopleurus brama* (Ag.); Jordan: 46 (elopomorph)
1908 *Enneles audax* Jordan and Branner: 23
1923 *Enneles audax* J&B; Jordan: 75
1960 *Enneles audax* J&B; Silva Santos: 5
1968 *Enneles audax* J&B; Silva Santos and Valença: 348
1974a *Enneles audax* J&B; Taverne: 61

1977 *Enneles audax* J&B; Wenz: 342
Diagnosis: As for genus.

Cotypes of *Calamopleurus cylindricus*: British Museum (Natural History), BM(NH) P7584; fragment of trunk and fin labelled by L. Agassiz; BM(NH) 15499, part of body showing vertebrae and lateral line scales. Both from unknown localities in the Chapada do Araripe (matrix suggests Jardim); P7584 said to be from "Province of Ceará" (Woodward, 1895).

Holotype of *Enneles audax*: Museu Rocha, Ceará, no. 22, large head in part and counterpart, Santana formation, locality uncertain, near Jardim, Ceará.

Calamopleurus cylindricus was one of the seven original species of fossil fishes from the Santana formation to be named by Agassiz (1841, 1844b). It was erected by him on the basis of fragments of some large fossil fishes collected by Dr. Gardner. Agassiz (1841) regarded *Calamopleurus* as a "cycloid" fish, distinct from his "*Phacolepis*" (*sic*), which possess "ctenoid" scales. This distinction was maintained in a second, slightly more comprehensive report (Agassiz, 1844b), but *Calamopleurus cylindricus* was there listed as "Famille douteuse." Unfortunately Agassiz never published figures of his *Calamopleurus* material, and its subsequent history is unknown until Woodward (1895: 499) noted that the fragments intended by Agassiz to represent *C. cylindricus* were by then in the British Museum (Natural History). He remarked that they "probably represent a member of the family Oligopleuridae," which at that time included the fossil genera *Oligopleurus*, *Spathiurus*, and *Oenoscopus*.

Jordan's (1907) work on the Santana fossil fishes was to prove disastrous for the taxonomic stability of *Calamopleurus*. He obtained a complete specimen of *Notelops brama* of some 48 cm total length, but erroneously identified it as *Calamopleurus cylindricus*, without having examined the type material of either *Notelops* or *Calamopleurus* in London. Had he done so, Jordan might have realized that these genera are profoundly different. Jordan's subsequent remarks on *Calamopleurus* (Jordan and Branner, 1908; Jordan, 1923) continued to be influenced by the complete *Notelops* specimen (deposited originally at Stanford University, now in the California Academy of Sciences, catalog no. 58319).

Even though Jordan had by 1923 obtained photographs of the British Museum *Calamopleurus* specimens, he was evidently so

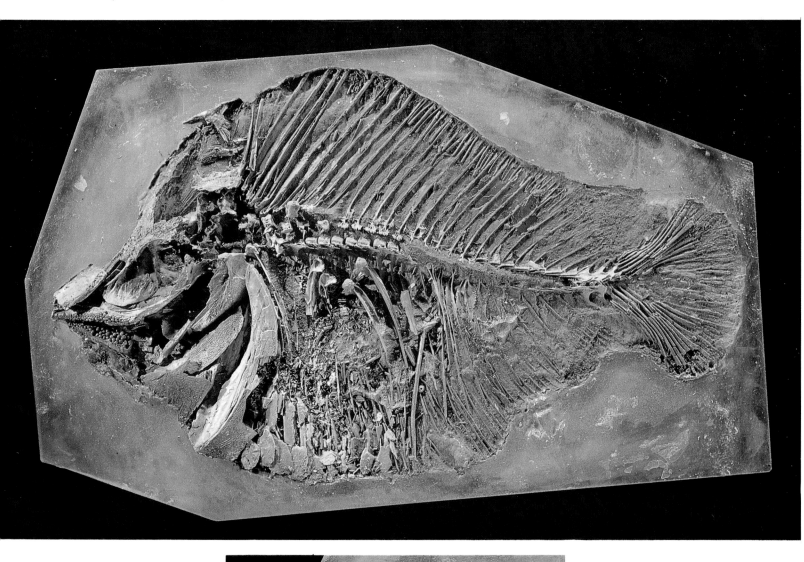

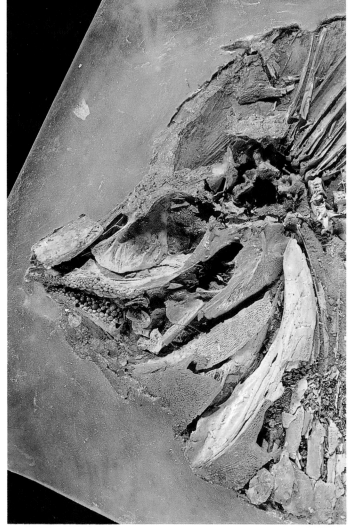

lemanja palma, one half of the holotype following acid preparation. Photos by D. Serrete, courtesy S. Wenz.

Calamopleurus cylindricus. **Top:** Complete specimen in matrix. **Bottom:** Another specimen after acid preparation.

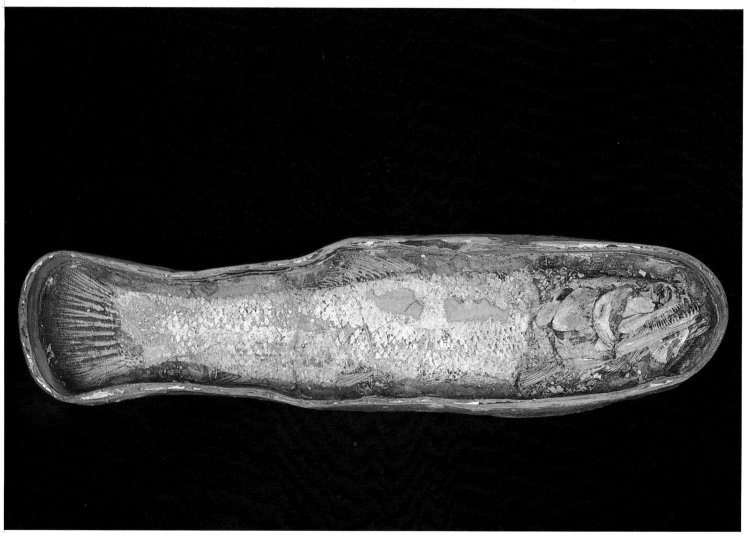

confused that he was unable to decide whether to retain *Calamopleurus* as a separate genus or to combine it with *Notelops* (e.g., Jordan, 1923, pp. 41, 44, 46, 48). In this unfortunate situation the central issue was shifted away from whether *Calamopleurus* represented a distinct fish (as realized by Agassiz and Woodward) to whether *Calamopleurus* or *Notelops* should have priority. Jordan (1923) wrote of *Calamopleurus brama*; other authors subsequently relegated *C. cylindricus* to synonymy with *Notelops brama* (e.g., d'Erasmo, 1938; Dunkle, 1940; Silva Santos and Valença, 1968; Forey, 1977).

Further compounding these difficulties, Jordan and Branner (1908) erected a new genus and species of supposed elopid, *Enneles audax*, founded on a large head in part and counterpart (holotype: No. 22, Museu Rocha, Ceará). Additional specimens were described by Jordan (1923), but the true identity of this fish as an amioid was first realized by Silva Santos (1960). Subsequent investigators have unquestioningly accepted the name *Enneles audax* for this amioid (e.g., Patterson, 1973; Taverne, 1974a; Wenz, 1977).

In hindsight, and with the availability of more complete material, it is evident that the fragments named *Calamopleurus cylindricus* in the British Museum (Natural History) are from the same kind of fish as *Enneles audax*. One of the cotypes of *C. cylindricus* (a fragment from the trunk region with fin-rays intact; P7584) is very similar to a specimen referred to *E. audax* by Silva Santos (1960, pl. 5, fig. 1). The cycloid scale morphology in the British Museum (Natural History) *Calamopleurus* material is identical to that found in specimens of *Enneles audax* (see Silva Santos, 1960, p. 23 for a description). Furthermore, the lateral line scales are traversed by a continuous tube in *E. audax*, as in *C. cylindricus*.

Under the *International Code of Zoological Nomenclature*, both *Calamopleurus cylindricus* and *Enneles audax* are available names for the Santana formation amiid. As *Enneles audax* is the name by which this amiid has customarily been known, its retention could be pleaded on the grounds of nomenclatural stability. On the other hand, *Calamopleurus cylindricus* had been taxonomically stable for over 60 years prior to

Calamopleurus cylindricus. Skeletal reconstruction.

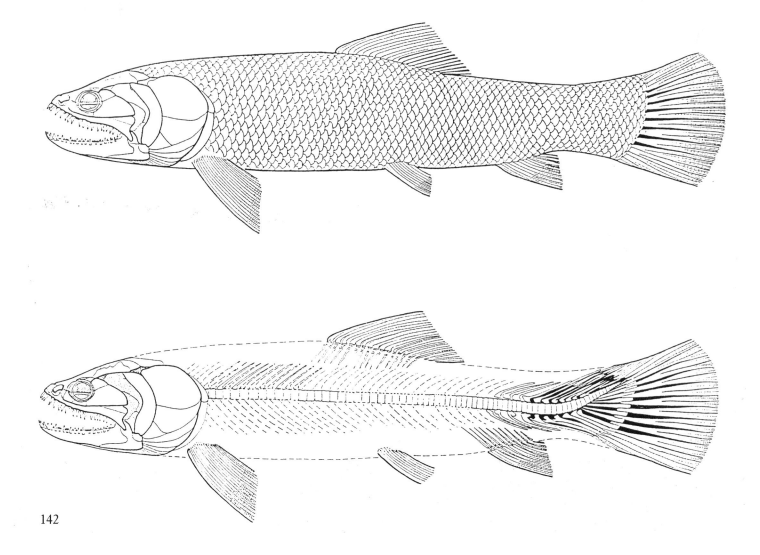

142

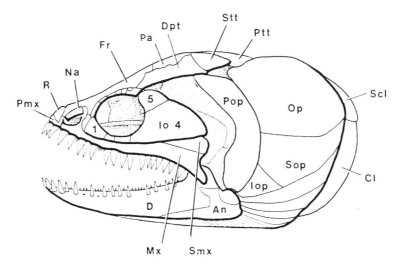

Calamopleurus cylindricus. Outline reconstruction of head.

Lateral views of the skull in (A) Recent *Amia calva* and (B) *Calamopleurus cylindricus*. Important differences include basisphenoid and pterotic ossifications and relatively larger pre-ethmoid in *C. cylindricus*.

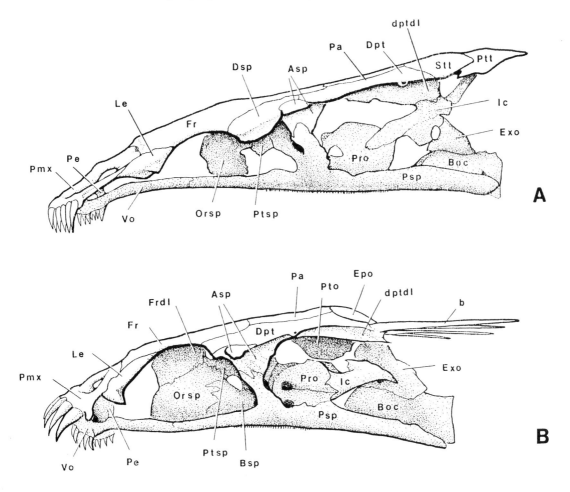

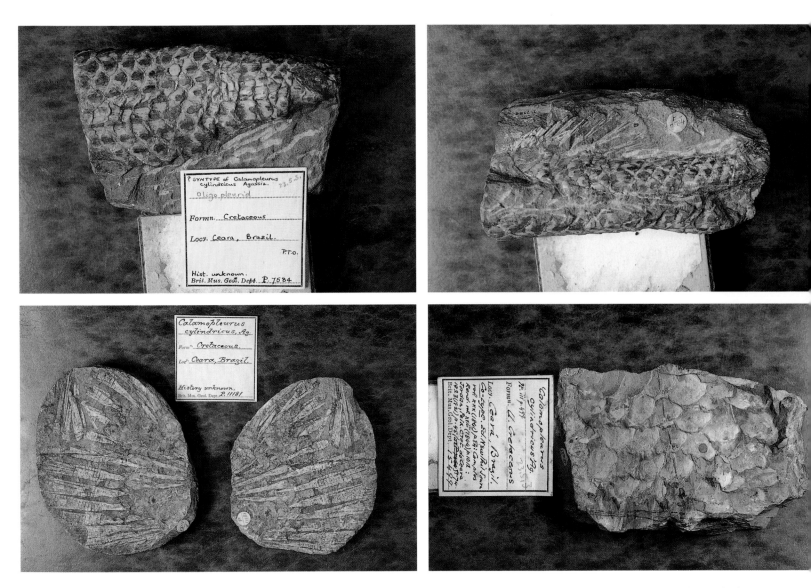

Important specimens of *Calamopleurus cylindricus* in the British Museum (Natural History) collection, including two pieces designated as types.

Jordan's handiwork. Despite the fact that the holotype of *C. cylindricus* was formally designated and figured by Jordan (1923, p. 45, pl. 9, fig. 3) some years after *Enneles audax* was erected (Jordan and Branner, 1908), the descriptions of *C. cylindricus* by Agassiz (1841, 1844b) and Woodward (1895) nevertheless provide an indication for the species and genus that appears to meet the criteria of the *International Code of Zoological Nomenclature*. On this basis, therefore, *Calamopleurus cylindricus* is the earliest available name for this amiid and is here given priority over *Enneles audax*. *Calamopleurus cylindricus* is not a synonym of *Notelops brama*, and all previous citations of it as such are erroneous.

Jordan and Branner (1908) erected a second *Calamopleurus* species, *C. vestitus*, but following the unfortunate relegation of that genus to synonymy with *Notelops*, Jordan (1923) created a new genus for the second species (*Brannerion vestitum*). This species is certainly not an amioid; its relationships are discussed elsewhere in this work.

The group of fishes to which *Calamopleurus* belongs is represented today by a solitary species, *Amia calva* (the bowfin). This species is restricted to freshwater habitats in the eastern and mid-eastern regions of the United States and Canada, ranging southward from the Great Lakes (except Lake Superior) to the Gulf of Mexico. The fossil record of *Amia* shows that its present restricted distribution was acquired before the Pleistocene, although 35-40 million years ago it was widespread throughout the Northern Hemisphere (also in fresh water). Other fossils referred to *Amia* or the closely allied *Kindleia* are recorded from as far back as the Upper Cretaceous (Maestrichtian and Campanian) of Canada and North America and the Late Paleocene of Europe. Other amiid fossils are known from Cretaceous and Late Jurassic rocks in many parts of the world, including China and South America, and in some cases are probably not freshwater occurrences. Amiids probably first evolved in a marine environment and subsequently became restricted to brackish and then freshwater habitats.

Amia and its fossil allies occupy an important position in the history of fishes because of their supposed primitive relationship to the vast group known as teleosts. *Amia* has a peculiar type of jaw articulation in which the symplectic bone (formed as an outgrowth of the hyomandibula, in front of the interhyal, and found in all neopterygian fishes; Patterson, 1973, 1982) is attached to the quadrate and lower jaw (in gars and teleosts the symplectic is attached only to the quadrate). This peculiar arrangement effectively produces a double jaw articulation. Besides *Amia* and its immediate fossil relatives, this arrangement occurs in a few other fossil neopterygians (e.g., ionoscopids, "parasemionotids"). Patterson (1973, 1982, and elsewhere) regarded this *Amia*-like suspensorial pattern as a shared derived character of an apparently monophyletic group known as halecomorphs.

This hypothesis has received wide acceptance, although it was questioned by Olsen (1984), who instead regarded symplectic involvement in the jaw-joint as a primitive feature of all neopterygian fishes that has been secondarily modified in gars and teleosts (by reduction) and which has become divergently specialized in amiids (by tightly combining the symplectic and preopercular). According to Olsen (1984), this latter condition would define Patterson's (1973) halecomorphs, rather than the mere presence of the suspensory symplectic (discussed in further detail below).

Phylogenetic relationships among fossil and Recent amiids are poorly resolved, and considerable disagreement exists between the different schemes that have been put forward. Three alternative hypotheses have been proposed in recent years, each defended by a

Magnificent specimen of a *Calamopleurus* head seen from below, revealing the jaws, teeth, large triangular gular plate, and rows of branchiostegal rays.

different suite of characters (Chalifa and Tchernov, 1982; Schultze and Wiley, 1984; Bryant, 1987). The position of *Calamopleurus* (= *Enneles* of these authors) varies considerably within these competing phylogenies.

Chalifa and Tchernov (1982, fig. 14) recognized three amiid groups, one containing *Amia* and the extinct genera *Urocles* and *Vidalamia;* another containing *Calamopleurus, Amiopsis,* and *Pachymia;* and a third including *Ikechaoamia* and *Sinamia.* Bryant (1987, fig. 17) considered fewer taxa, but agreed (albeit on the basis of different evidence) that *Calamopleurus* and *Pachyamia* (together with a new genus, *Melvius*) formed a monophyletic group that excludes *Amia* (regarded by Bryant as the most plesiomorph amiid in her scheme). Schultze and Wiley (1984) regarded *Calamopleurus* as the most primitive member of a monophyletic group that also includes *Pachymia, Kindleia,* and *Amia.* These genera collectively form the sister group to another supposedly monophyletic taxon comprising *Vidalamia, Urocles,* and *Amiopsis.* Like Chalifa and Tchernov (1982), Schultze and Wiley (1984) placed *Sinamia* outside a group containing other amiid taxa, but their hypotheses differ in their treatment of *Sinamia* and another primitive fossil halecomorph, *Liodesmus.* According to Chalifa and Tchernov (1982), *Liodesmus* is a primitive sister group of all amiids including *Sinamia.* In Schultze and Wiley's (1984) scheme, however, *Sinamia* is placed outside their Amiidae while *Liodesmus* is included as a primitive amiid.

As far as *Calamopleurus* is concerned, therefore, published phylogenetic hypotheses differ profoundly. There is little agreement over how various genera are related, and none whatsoever as to which characters are phylogenetically informative. Our knowledge of morphological data among fossil amiids is very uneven, which undoubtedly has contributed toward this unsatisfactory state of affairs.

Calamopleurus was described originally from scrappy material, but its cranial morphology has been described in some detail (Silva Santos, 1960). Its caudal fin was investigated by Wenz (1977). The information provided in those works can now be supplemented following acid preparation of complete specimens.

In the skull roof, the paired frontals are more than three times as long as wide. Bryant (1987) used a 3:1 frontal length:width ratio as a character uniting *Pachyamia* and *Melvius.* However the frontal length:width ratio is also approximately 3:1 in *Sinamia* and *Ikechaoamia* (Stensiö, 1935; Liu, et al., 1963; Liu and Su,

1983). The frontals are even longer than wide in *Urocles* (Lange, 1968, fig. 4) and *Vidalamia* (Wenz, 1971, fig. 1). On this basis the 3:1 frontal length:width ratio cannot be credited with much phylogenetic significance, except perhaps as a character of amiids in general. In *Amia* the frontals are relatively shorter (length:width ratio approximately 2:1), which may be an autapomorphy of the genus.

Unlike in *Amia,* the frontal in *Calamopleurus* has an ossified descending lamina that is sutured to the orbitosphenoid and pterosphenoid (= "alisphenoid"; Silva Santos, 1960, fig. 2). Anteriorly the frontal also is sutured to the lateral ethmoid, much as in *Amia.*

In *Calamopleurus* the parietals are paired (a primitive condition). In *Sinamia* and *Ikechaoamia* there is a median, unpaired parietal, a feature that may be a synapomorphy of these two genera. The parietals apparently are paired in all other amiids, although a single median parietal has been noted in one aberrant specimen of *Amia calva* (Jain, 1985).

In *Amia* (including *Kindleia*), *Pachyamia, Vidalamia, Sinamia,* and *Ikechaoamia* the dermosphenotic is incorporated into the skull roof (a character uniting amiids, *Caturus,* ophiopsids, *Heterolepidotes,* and *Macrepistius,* according to Olsen, 1984: fig. 19). In *Calamopleurus* the dermosphenotic is small and free from the skull roof, but overlies the sphenotic and the postero-lateral corner of the frontal. In *Urocles* the dermosphenotic, although small, apparently is incorporated into the skull roof (Lange, 1968). The condition of the dermosphenotic in *Calamopleurus* may represent homoplasy (= "reversal"), perhaps representing an autapomorphy of the genus.

Numerous supraorbital bones are present in *Calamopleurus.* Their high number may represent an autapomorphy of the genus (Bryant, 1987), although a similar arrangement occurs in *Caturus* (Rayner, 1941). Moreover, in *Sinamia* there may be at least five small supraorbitals. Chalifa and Tchernov (1986) used the presence of supraorbitals to unite *Calamopleurus* with *Pachymia* and *Amiopsis.* In view of their widespread occurence among other halecostomes, however, supraorbitals undoubtedly represent a plesiomorphic character in these amiids. Supraorbitals also occur in *Amia* (*Kindleia*) *fragosa* (Janot, 1967). The absence of supraorbitals in *Vidalamia, Urocles,* and *Amia* probably is secondary, but may have arisen independently at least twice. The utility of this feature as a synapomorphy is undermined by some aspects of caudal fin morphology (see below).

Paired nasal bones overlie the large nasal opening of the premaxilla but are free from the rest of the skull roof and usually are seen only in well-preserved specimens. The nasals are relatively smaller than those of *Amia*, *Pachyamia*, *Sinamia*, *Ikechaoamia*, *Urocles*, *Caturus*, and *Ophiopsis*. A transverse, canal-bearing median rostral bone is present in *Calamopleurus*, although usually it too is seen only in well-preserved specimens.

In the back of the skull roof of *Calamopleurus* there is a pair of supratemporals that meet at the midline. A similar arrangement occurs in *Amia* and many fossil amiids, but in *Sinamia* and *Ikechaoamia* there is more than one pair (two in *Ikechaoamia*, three plus a median element in *Sinamia*). A single pair probably is the primitive condition, and multiple pairs of supratemporals may therefore represent a synapomorphy of *Sinamia* and *Ikechaoamia*.

In the cheek region of *Calamopleurus* there are five infraorbitals, of which the fourth is by far the largest. This pattern also occurs in *Sinamia* and *Ikechaoamia* (Stensiö, 1935; Liu and Su, 1983), and in *Urocles* (Lange, 1968). In *Caturus*, *Allothrissops*, and *Watsonulus* there are four infraorbitals, but the penultimate one is larger than the others. Possibly the presence of five infraorbitals is an amiid synapomorphy retained today by *Amia*. In *Pachyamia* there are only four infraorbitals, apparently the result of fusion between the fourth and fifth bones in the series. Bryant (1987) suggested that similar fusion had occurred in *Melvius*, but the evidence (from isolated bones only) is somewhat tenuous.

A more compelling case can be made for divergent specialization of the last (fifth) infraorbital in *Calamopleurus* (where this element is extremely small; Bryant, 1987), and in *Amia*, *Pachyamia*, and *Urocles* (where the last infraorbital equals or exceeds the size of the preceding one). In the living *Amia calva* the fourth and fifth infraorbitals extend back almost to the preopercular margin, but in other amiids (including some fossil *Amia* spp.) there is a gap between the last infraorbitals and preoperculum. Rarely, in *Amia calva* only a single large infraorbital (representing infraorbitals 4 + 5 in normal specimens) may be present.

The braincase in *Calamopleurus* was partly cartilaginous and poorly ossified, as in living *Amia*. One important point concerns the pterotic, a perichondral bone that never ossifies in *Amia* (Allis, 1897). According to Silva Santos (1960, fig. 8), the pterotic was also unossified in *Calamopleurus*. Patterson (1973) suggested that

this may represent a characteristic of halecomorphs in general, but Schultze and Wiley (1984) thought the feature was of restricted distribution within amiids. Taverne (1974a, fig. 1) interpreted a specimen of *Calamopleurus* at his disposal as having an ossified pterotic.

In AMNH 11837 the braincase is entirely visible in lateral view. The left pterotic is missing, but the right one is well ossified, filling much of the space between the prootic, exoccipital, intercalar, and dermopterotic. There are two openings within the pterotic ossification, interpreted as anterior and posterior semicircular canals, plus another opening situated ventrally and probably housing the external semicircular canal.

The dermopterotic is long and slender, with a broad descending lamina that presumably passes lateral to the upper part of the pterotic. In *Amia* there is a similar descending lamina on the dermopterotic, meeting the intercalar posteroventrally. This also may have been the case in *Calamopleurus*, although in AMNH 11837 the intercalar no longer reaches the dermopterotic descending lamina. *Calamopleurus* differs from *Amia* in the presence of elongate, posteriorly-directed ray-like processes arising from the mesial surface of the dermopterotic descending lamina. These processes form a radiating bundle covering the epioccipital dorsolaterally and extending below the supratemporal, and posttemporal, reaching the supercleithrum. According to Silva Santos (1960: 8) and Taverne (1974a: 63), these rays are ossified ligaments. In most specimens these rays are obscured by dermal bones. A single and somewhat shorter splint is attached to the dermopterotic in *Oshunia*.

The prootic is more extensively ossified in *Calamopleurus* than in *Amia*. The main part of the cavity for the otic capsule is exposed in medial view in *Amia*. The inner surface of the prootic thus reflects the shape of the membranous labyrinth. In *Calamopleurus*, however, the labyrinth is more completely enclosed by the prootic and there are two foramina for the anterior and posterior semicircular canals in its upper unfinished margin.

The intercalar, exoccipitals, basioccipital, and epioccipitals are similar in *Calamopleurus* and *Amia*. According to Silva Santos (1960: 6), the intercalar of *Calamopleurus* does not meet the basioccipital as in *Amia* and *Sinamia*, but in AMNH 1837 these two bones are in virtual contact. In *Calamopleurus* the epioccipitals nearly meet at the midline. They are covered dorso-laterally by the curious ossified ligaments radiating posteriorly from the dermopterotics.

The sphenotic is well ossified and is partially exposed between the dermosphenotic (a separate bone; see above), the dermopterotic, and the last infraorbital. The exposed part bears dermal ornamentation like that covering the rest of the skull roof. This feature once was thought to be restricted to some caturids but has now been identified in living gars and in the primitive neopterygian *Watsonulus* (Olsen, 1984).

by *Calamopleurus*. In "pholidophorids" the spiracular canal is located medial to the sphenotic, but in "leptolepids" the sphenotic is more extensive and may enclose the lower opening of the spiracular canal; in all living teleosts the canal is obliterated (Patterson, 1975a: 381, 398).

An opisthotic is absent in *Calamopleurus*, as in *Amia* and *Sinamia*. This bone is present in *Watsonulus* and other parasemionotids, as well as in caturids, *Macrepistius*, and ionoscopids, and its absence in amiids may be regarded as a

The Eocene fossil *Amia kehreri* from Messel, Germany. L. A. Fuchs photo.

In *Calamopleurus* there is a spiracular canal (Silva Santos, 1960) that appears to be entirely contained within the sphenotic. In *Amia* and *Sinamia* this canal penetrates the postorbital process between the sphenotic and prootic. In *Lepidotes* and large *Lepisosteus* the canal is enclosed by the prootic (Patterson, 1975a: 399), an apparently specialized condition. In some primitive actinopterygians (e.g., *Pteronisculus, Kentuckia, Kansasiella*) the spiracular canal is thought to be contained within the sphenotic (Gardiner, 1984: 244), and in the "parasemionotid" *Watsonulus* this canal enters the sphenotic from the parasphenoid without passing through a canal in the prootic (Olsen, 1984: 485). This pattern therefore may represent a primitive actinopterygian one that is retained

derived condition. An opisthotic is, nevertheless, absent in some other halecostomes including *Lepidotes*, semionotids, "leptolepids," and more advanced teleosts (Gardiner, 1984: 212).

In *Calamopleurus* the pterosphenoid is sutured laterally to the sphenotic as in *Amia*, thus roofing over the trigemino-facialis chamber. In *Amia* the pterosphenoid also sends off a process (termed the pterosphenoid pedicle by Patterson, 1975a: 409) that is sutured to the ascending process of the parasphenoid ventrally. According to Patterson (1975a) this is also the case in *Calamopleurus* and *Sinamia*. In *Calamopleurus*, however, there is no connection between the pterosphenoid and parasphenoid. The pterosphenoid pedicle in AMNH 11837 is

148

Amia calva, the bowfin, the only Recent amiid. K. Lucas photo, Steinhart.

represented by a short protuberance, mesial to which is a pterosphenoid lamina that meets the basisphenoid. In *Amia* the pterosphenoid pedicle thus separates the trigemino-facialis chamber from the posterior myodome, but in *Calamopleurus* these spaces are essentially confluent. In *Sinamia* the pterosphenoid pedicle meets the parasphenoid as in *Amia*, but there is also a "sagittal lamina" (Stensiö, 1935: 11) that may be fused to the pars basisphenoidea, although there is some doubt as to whether a basisphenoid ossification is present (ibid.: 12).

The presence of a pterosphenoid pedicle probably is a primitive actinopterygian feature (Patterson, 1975a; Gardiner, 1984). Its reduction in *Calamopleurus* may represent a derived condition. The dorsal part of the orbital wall in *Calamopleurus* is formed by the descending lamina of the frontal (discussed above), to which the pterosphenoid and orbitosphenoid are sutured (Silva Santos, 1960, fig. 2). The orbital wall thus is more extensively ossified than in *Amia*, where a frontal descending lamina is absent. Furthermore, in *Calamopleurus* there is a large, well-ossified basisphenoid (not ossified in *Amia*). *Calamopleurus* thus exhibits the full complement of cranial bones (except for a suproccipital) found in primitive teleosts.

The parasphenoid has a well developed posterior moiety as in *Amia* and is somewhat narrower than in *Sinamia*, extending completely underneath the basioccipital. There is a deep notch posteriorly, on either side of paired foramina for the intermetameric arteries piercing the basioccipital. There is no basipterygoid process. The oral surface bears a much less extensive tooth patch than in *Amia*. There is no opening for a buccohypophyseal canal. As in *Amia* and *Sinamia*, the efferent pseudobranchial and internal carotid arteries pass through notches in the base of the parasphenoid ascending process, instead of via foramina as in many teleots. The ascending process bears a spiracular groove distally. In *Amia* (and *Sinamia*) this groove runs off the posterior margin of the ascending process, but in *Calamopleurus* it is located more centrally along the ascending process, becoming progressively deeper until it becomes enclosed to form a spiracular canal that enters the sphenotic (discussed above).

The vomers in *Calamopleurus* are paired, as in *Amia* and many primitive actinopterygians. A median vomer occurs in "leptolepids," "pholidophorids," and virtually all living teleosts, as well as in *Lepidotes*, *Dapedium*,

Bobastrania, and pycnodontids (Patterson, 1975a: 513). The outer margin of each vomer in *Calamopleurus* bears a row of several large teeth, mesial to which is a patch of several smaller fused teeth. In *Amia* only the inner tooth patch is present. The vomerine dentition in *Sinamia* is unknown (Stensiö, 1935), but there are no indications of any alveoli for an outer tooth row.

There are large, paired lateral ethmoids, as in *Amia*, meeting the frontals dorsally and the ascending (nasal) process of the premaxillae antero-dorsally. Immediately in front of each lateral ethmoid is a smaller "pre-ethmoid." As in *Amia*, this paired bone is sandwiched between the vomer and ascending process of the premaxilla and forms the posterior surface of a deep socket for the anterior process of the maxilla. Unlike in *Amia*, where the snout is somewhat elongated and the lateral and pre-ethmoids are separated, in *Calamopleurus* these ethmoid ossifications are close together and may even meet. Large paired pre-ethmoids are known in a pachycormid (*Hypsocormus*: Stensiö, 1935; Rayner, 1948; Patterson, 1975a), but other supposed occurrences (e.g., *Pachycormus*, *Lepidotes*) have been questioned (Patterson, 1975a: 499). Paired pre-ethmoids also are present in ionoscopids (see below), and may be primitively present in halecomorphs generally. Patterson (1975a: 502) regarded the presence of paired pre-ethmoids as a primitive feature probably related to the development of paired vomers. In teleosts the vomer is unpaired and there is primitively a median mesethmoid.

There are large, well-ossified premaxillae with a massive ascending nasal process meeting the frontals as in *Amia*. The premaxillae each bear six large teeth (Silva Santos, 1960) and are immovably sutured to the vomers and mesially to each other.

The maxilla is large and dentigerous and bears between 26 and 28 teeth. Above the first tooth socket there is a pit forming an articulation with the premaxilla, as in *Melvius* and large *Amia robusta* (Bryant, 1987; Janot, 1967). Posteriorly there is a deep notch in the maxilla, more pronounced than is evident from the illustrations given by Silva Santos (1960). Bryant (1987) suggested that the posteriorly notched maxilla is a synapomorphy of *Calamopleurus*, *Melvius*, and *Pachyamia*. This feature is much more widespread among amiids, however, occurring in *Urocles* and *Amiopsis* and even in some specimens of *Amia* (see references in Chalifa and Tchernov, 1982). Moreover, a notch occurs in *Caturus* (Rayner, 1941), *Furo* (Wenz, 1968), some pholidophorids (Nybelin, 1966),

and perhaps *Eugnathus* (Gregory, 1959, fig. 27).

A single supramaxilla is present in *Calamopleurus*, as in *Amia*, *Kindleia*, and *Urocles*. According to Chalifa and Tchernov (1982) there is no supramaxilla in *Pachyamia*; they suggested that it may have become secondarily fused to the maxilla. Bryant (1987) argued that *Melvius* similarly lacks a separate supramaxilla, regarding this as a synapomorphy shared with *Pachyamia*, but the condition in *Melvius* cannot be convincingly demonstrated on the basis of the available disarticulated material.

The mandible in *Calamopleurus* is extremely long, and the dentary bears approximately 20-23 teeth. The gape extends far behind the level of the orbit, unlike in *Amia*, *Kindleia*, *Pachyamia*, *Ikechaoamia*, and *Sinamia*, where the gape ends approximately level with the posterior margin of the orbit, or in *Urocles*, where it is even shorter. The elongate gape of *Calamopleurus* is reminiscent of many Paleozoic actinopterygians yet is quite unusual among halecostomes and may represent a derived condition among amiids. Interestingly, Wenz (1971) reported a similar condition in *Vidalamia*, although it was not illustrated.

The jaw teeth of *Calamopleurus* possess enamelled crowns with a carinate (keeled) cutting edge, a feature said by Bryant (1987) to unite this genus with *Melvius*. A further feature said to unite these two genera is the crenulated form of the alveoli, but according to Patterson and Longbottom (in press) none of these dental characters is restricted to the taxa in question.

The ectopterygoid and dermopalatines bear a row of large teeth along their outer margin. The teeth are enamelled and their crowns are carinate, like those of the outer jaw arcade. The ectopterygoid has about 24 teeth, the posterior dermopalatine about five or six, and the anterior dermopalatine about seven. The entopterygoid margin also is toothed, but the teeth are smaller than those of the ectopterygoid and dermopalatines. A row of carinate, enamelled prearticular and coronoid teeth opposes the upper inner dental arcade.

The symplectic of *Calamopleurus* is *Amia*-like in that it is bound by membranous outgrowths to the preopercular and articulates with the mandible along with the quadrate. A similar symplectic-articular relationship has been identified in caturids, ophiopsids, ionoscopids, and some "parasemionotids" such as *Watsonulus*. The symplectic also supports the mandibular joint in pycnodonts.

Patterson (1973, 1975a) and Bartram (1977) have advocated that the *Amia*-style jaw joint is a derived condition and that the pattern found in gars (with the symplectic ending on the quadratojugal before reaching the quadrate, and with the quadrate condyle supported against the preoperculum by the quadratojugal) is the primitive one for all neopterygians. Olsen (1984) has questioned that interpretation, arguing instead that symplectic involvement in the jaw joint is the primitive state for neopterygians, although having symplectic bound to the preopercular was still regarded as a synapomorphy of amiids and caturids. One consequence of Olsen's hypothesis is that gars and teleosts would be united by removal of the symplectic from the jaw joint to end blindly on the medial face of the quadrate. Interestingly, although pycnodonts customarily have been considered allies of semionotids or forms such as *Dapedium*, the *Amia*-like symplectic (e.g., in *Neoproscinetes*; see elsewhere) is an intriguing similarity with halecomorphs demanding further investigation.

In the postcranial skeleton, only the caudal fin has been described in detail (Wenz, 1977; see below). The vertebral column consists of approximately 88 amphicoelous vertebrae, of which at least 40 are abdominal, and some 16-17 pterygiophores, the first of which lies above the neural spine of abdominal centrum 20 or 21. There are two fringing and 19 or 20 principal dorsal fin-rays. In the anal fin there are two fringing and 11 principal fin-rays supported by nine pterygiophores. There are approximately 17 pectoral and eight pelvic fin-rays.

According to Wenz (1977) there are approximately eight hypurals in the caudal skeleton, although there is so little difference between the first hypurals and hemal arches that she experienced difficulty in distinguishing them. However, acid-prepared specimens such as AMNH 11837 verify that the first hypural is the element she identified as such. The hypurals and hemal arches are distinguishable proximally; all of the latter have expanded bases where they meet the vertebral centra, whereas the hypurals are gently tapered. In AMNH 11837 there are nine hypurals.Only four hypurals are known in *Pachyamia*, although there are seven ural centra; only the first hypural is not fused to its ural centrum (Chalifa and Tchervov, 1982), as in some *Amia* (Schultze and Arratia, 1986). There are 10 or 11 hypurals in *Amia, Vidalamia, Ikechaoamia. Urocles*, and *Amiopsis*. The hypurals are not fused to the ural centra as in *Amia* and *Pachyamia*, suggesting that fusion between hypurals and ural centra has arisen within the Amiidae independently of teleosts

(Patterson, 1973). Occasional fusions also may occur between adjacent neural centra and their hypurals in *Amia* (Schultze and Arratia, 1986, fig. 10A).

According to AMNH 11837, in *Calamopleurus* there are approximately 16 or 17 ural centra that form an elongate, tapering string (i.e., more than found by Wenz). Thus only about half the ural centra are supporting a hypural (in AMNH 11837 ural 1 supports hypurals 1 and 2; succeeding hypurals appear to be individually supported by ural centra 2, 3, 4, 6, 8, 11, and 15 or 16.

Wenz (1977) identified only three "epurals" in *Calamopleurus*, but in AMNH 11837 there are five. Only three occur in *Amia* and *Amiopsis*, but some fossil amiids have a higher number (e.g., *Urocles* with six or eight, *Ikechaoamia* with seven, *Pachyamia* with nine, *Vidalamia* with ten; Lange, 1968; Wenz, 1971, 1979; Chalifa and Tchernov, 1982; Liu and Su, 1983). According to a recent study by Schultze and Arratia (1986), the "epurals" of amiids are not homologous with neural spines and should not therefore be regarded as epurals (e.g., as in *Lepisosteus*, where the epurals are fused to the ural centra like the neural arches). Instead, the "epurals" of *Amia* and fossil amiids apparently represent fin radials.

Urocles and *Amiopsis* lack ossified neural arches behind the first ural centrum, which Patterson (1973, p. 277) considered decisive evidence of relationship with *Amia*. Ossified ural neural arches nevertheless are present in *Amia*, associated with the first two ural centra; occasionally the third centrum also has a neural arch, and a pair of incompletely segmented cartilaginous bodies may overlie ural centra 3-9 (Schultze and Arratia, 1986). Among fossils, *Calamopleurus* has at least one neural arch with a spine, located behind the first ural centrum, and there are vestiges of a second ossified neural arch (Wenz, 1977, fig. 1). All the ural centra nevertheless bear paired pits dorsally, reminiscent of the articular pits for neural arches on pre-ural centra. In *Vidalamia* and *Pachyamia* there are no ossified neural arches behind the first ural centrum (Wenz, 1971, fig. 3; Chalifa and Tchernov, 1982, fig. 11).

There is a one-to-one hypural/fin-ray relationship over ten or more hypurals in *Amia, Vidalamia*, and *Urocles*, 12 in *Amiopsis*, eight or nine in *Calamopleurus*, and apparently seven in *Pachyamia*. In addition there is a one-to-one hemal arch/fin-ray relationship in the pre-ural region of *Amia* and (apparently) *Pachyamia* (parhypural plus five or six pre-ural hemal

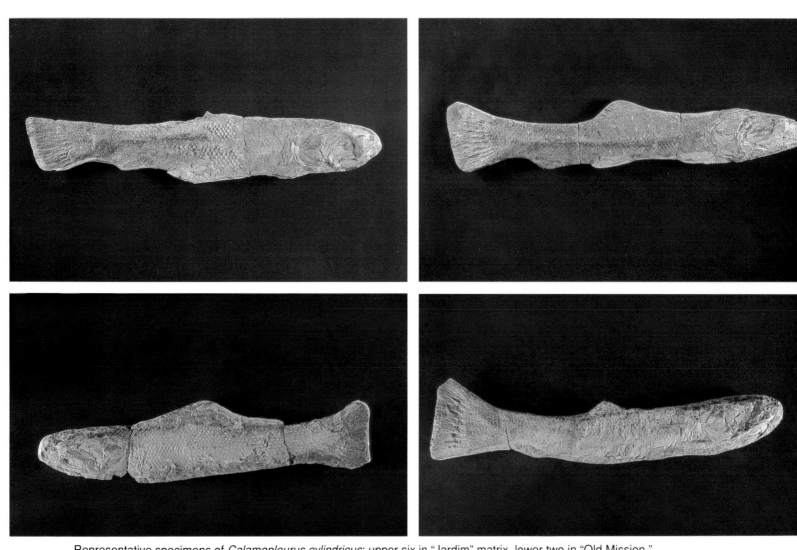

Representative specimens of *Calamopleurus cylindricus*; upper six in "Jardim" matrix, lower two in "Old Mission."

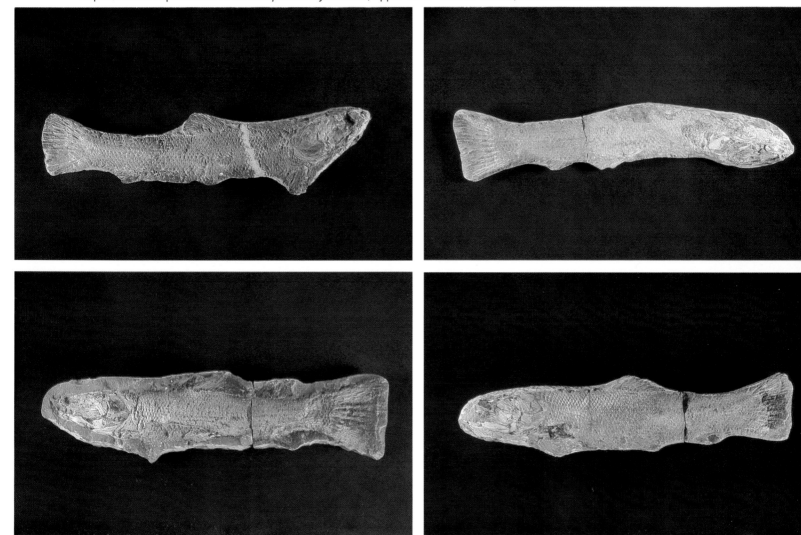

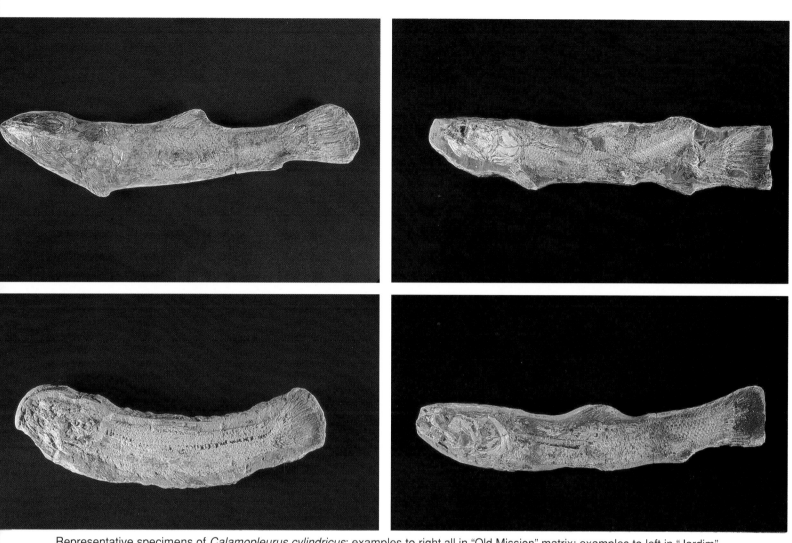

Representative specimens of *Calamopleurus cylindricus*; examples to right all in "Old Mission" matrix; examples to left in "Jardim" matrix except upper center, which is in "Santana" matrix.

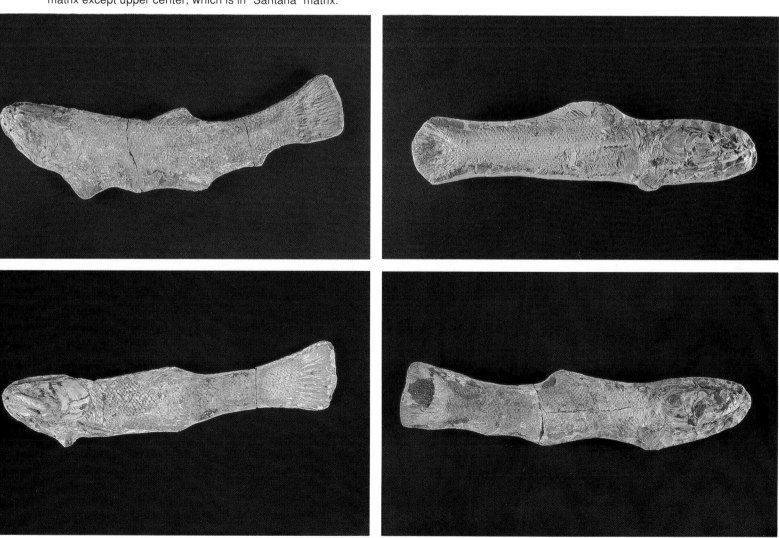

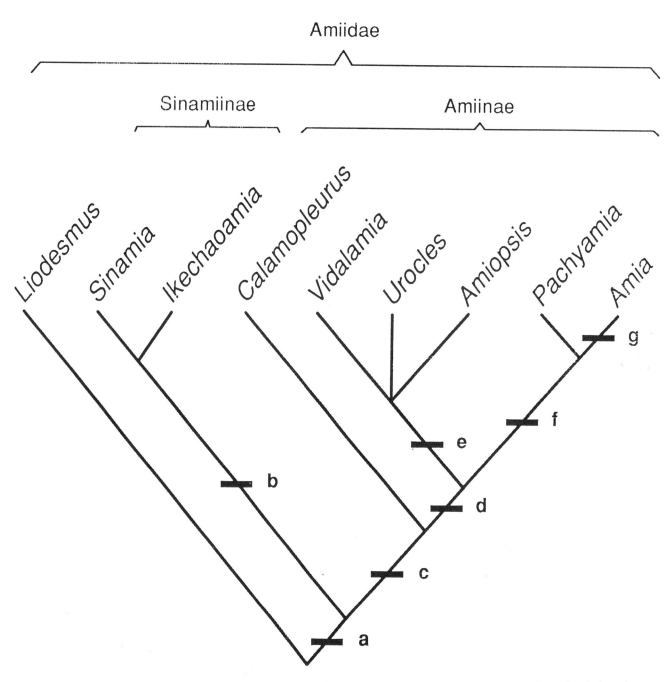

Hypothesis of relationships among amiid fishes, based on the following characters: (**a**) amiid vertebrae; (**b**) parietals fused, supratemporals subdivided; (**c**) amiid scales; (**d**) enlarged first infraorbital, preural hemal spines with 1-to-1 relationship with fin-rays; (**e**) supraorbitals absent, alternating diplospondyly; (**f**) all but the first hypural fused to ural centra, first infraorbital the largest; (**g**) supraorbitals absent (convergent with **e**).

arches). In *Calamopleurus*, however, there is no such relationship in the pre-ural region (Wenz, 1977). In *Vidalamia* there seem to be three or four pre-ural hemal arches with a one-to-one relationship with fin-rays, and in *Urocles* there may be four or five (Wenz, 1971, 1979). In *Liodesmus*, a primitive halecomorph retained by Patterson (1973) in the Amiidae, there is no one-to-one hypural/fin-ray relationship. The one-to-one pattern occurs in sinamiines, according to Schultze and Wiley (1984).

Patterson (1973) and Chalifa and Tchernov (1982) regarded the Late Jurassic fish *Liodesmus* to be the primitive sister group of all other amiids, which generally are divided into two groups (the Amiinae and Sinamiinae of Patterson, 1973). Schultze and Wiley (1984) have presented an alternative phylogeny in which their Sinamiidae are the sister group of the Amiidae, including *Liodesmus*.

Schultze and Wiley's (1984) phylogeny is founded on the proposition that enlargement and truncation of the upper branchiostegal ray and ossification of only the first one to three ural neural arches represent derived characters not shared by *Sinamia* or *Ikechaoamia*. That hypothesis requires secondary loss of ossified vertebrae in *Liodesmus*, and independent acquisition of the one-to-one hypural/fin-ray pattern in sinamiids and "higher" amiids. This is less parsimonious than the phylogeny advanced by Patterson (1973) and elaborated by Chalifa and Tchernov (1982). In that model, sinamiines and amiines are separated from *Liodesmus* by possession of "amiid" vertebrae and the hypural/fin-ray relationship. Amiines and sinamiines primitively retain a high number of supraorbitals (*Sinamia, Ikechaoamia, Calamopleurus*), as in caturids. Sinamiines are united by fusion of the parietals and subdivided supratemporals.

Within the amiine subgroup, Chalifa and Tchernov (1982, fig. 14) recognized two groups, one characterized by suborbitals present (*Calamopleurus, Amiopsis, Pachyamia*) and the other characterized by their absence (*Urocles, Vidalamia, Amia*). This arrangement is somewhat unsatisfactory since it *inter alia* involves plesiomorphic characters and requires independent reduction of ural neural arches, fusion of hypurals to ural centra, and enlargement of the first infraorbital in both groups. Instead, I agree with Schultze and Wiley (1984), who suggested that *Pachyamia* is closely related to *Amia*, but placed *Calamopleurus* (as *Enneles*) high in their cladogram on the basis of a character now known to be spurious (absence of pterotic ossification).

An alternative phylogenetic hypothesis proposed here is that *Calamopleurus* may be the most primitive known amiine, since it possesses "amiid" scales but otherwise retains a primitive (high) number of supraorbitals and a primitive infraorbital arrangement. Furthermore, none of its pre-ural hemal arches appears to have a one-to-one relationship with the fin-rays. Remaining amiines have this hemal arch/fin-ray relationship and retain only four or fewer supraorbitals.

The "normal" diplospondyly of *Amia* (with an anterior hemicentrum devoid of arches, followed by a posterior hemicentrum bearing the neural and hemal arch) also occurs in *Pachyamia* and *Calamopleurus*. "Alternating" diplospondyly (in which hemicentra alternately bear a neural or hemal arch) occurs only in some fossil taxa (e.g., *Urocles, Vidalamia, Amiopsis*), and may define a monophyletic group (Schultze and Wiley, 1984). *Ikechaoamia* seems to lack any form of diplospondyly (Liu and Su, 1983, fig. 8). *Amia* is united with *Pachyamia* (and *Kindleia*) by fusion of all but the first hypural with ural centra. *Amia* may be homoplaseous in having one or two ossified neural arches behind the first ural centrum, since these are absent in *Pachyamia, Amiopsis, Urocles,* and *Vidalamia*. *Pachyamia* and some fossils considered very close to *Amia* (e.g., *Kindleia*) retain some small supraorbitals, although these are lacking in Recent *Amia*. Absence of supraorbitals thus occurs twice in amiid phylogeny, once in the forms characterized by alternating diplospondyly and also in *Amia*.

In conclusion, it is worth pointing out that while many fossil taxa (e.g., *Kindleia, Pachyamia, Calamopleurus, Urocles, Vidalamia, Amiopsis*) apparently are closely related to *Amia*, there really is very little evidence to suggest affinity between sinamiines (*Sinamia, Ikechaoamia*) and amiids other than primitive halecomorph characters. The relationships of all these taxa to other halecomorphs such as caturids and ionoscopids are largely unresolved, undermining attempts at phylogenetic reconstruction. A thorough revision of halecomorph relationships is sorely needed.

Calamopleurus was an effetive predator capable of handling large prey; a specimen in the American Museum has in its pharynx a sizable *Vinctifer* that was swallowed head-first.

Assemblages: Santana, Jardim, Old Mission (generally larger from Jardim and Old Mission concretions than from Santana).

(J. G. Maisey)

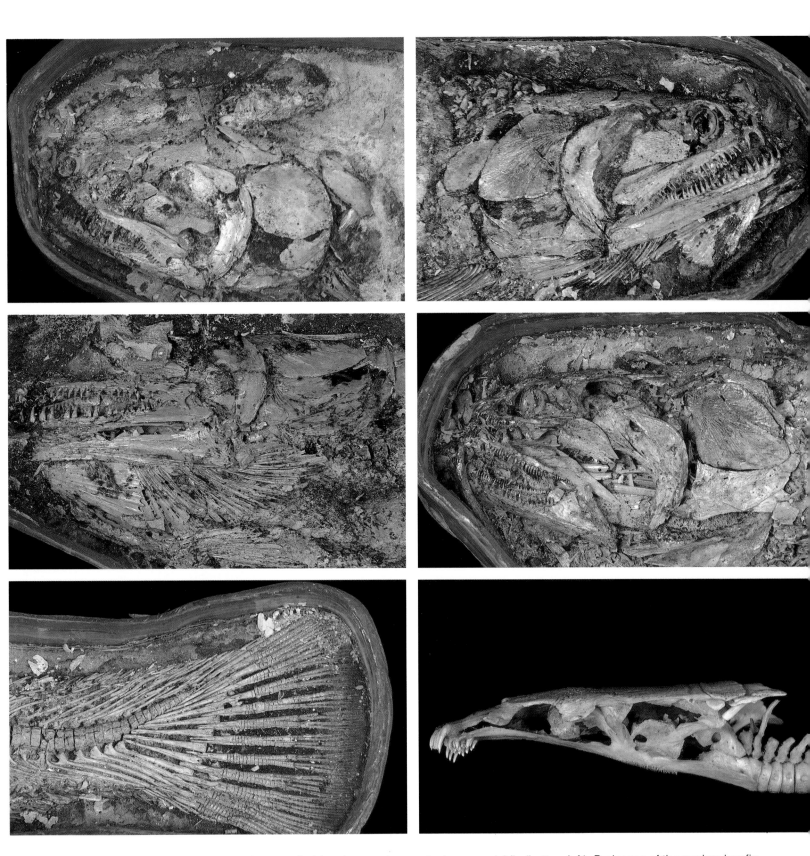

Acid-prepared heads of *Calamopleurus cylindricus* (top, center rows), plus a caudal fin (bottom left). Braincase of the modern bowfin *Amia*, a relative of *Calamopleurus*, shown at bottom right for comparison.

156

OSHUNIA Wenz and Kellner, 1986

Division HALECOSTOMI
Subdivision HALECOMORPHI
Family IONOSCOPIDAE Lehman, 1966
Genus **Oshunia** Wenz and Kellner, 1986
1986 *Oshunia* Wenz and Kellner: 78

Emended diagnosis: Ionoscopids attaining lengths of at least 40 cm; large gape; mandibular joint situated level with posterior margin of orbit; supraorbitals absent; dermal bones of head smooth but pitted; gular plate forming a broad triangle; supramaxilla apparently absent; *Amia*-like articulation present between symplectic and lower jaw; three infraorbitals present, with a single suborbital meeting the dermopterotic above; antorbital extending anteriorly below nostrils and posteriorly as far as orbital margin; infraorbital canal of dermosphenotic wrapped around autosphenotic deep within orbit; elongate dorsal fin extending from in front of pelvics to the caudal peduncle; caudal fin lacking caudal scutes; vertebral centra fully ossified, monospondylous, with laminar longitudinal reinforcement; dentition comprising single series of larger, close-set marginal teeth on dentary and maxilla, plus numerous smaller teeth on coronoids, dermopalatines, and vomers, as in *Spathiurus*; scales of "amiid" type.

Type species: *Oshunia brevis* Wenz and Kellner, 1986.

Oshunia brevis Wenz and Kellner, 1986
    1986. *Oshunia brevis* Wenz and Kellner: 78

Oshunia brevis. Skeletal reconstruction.

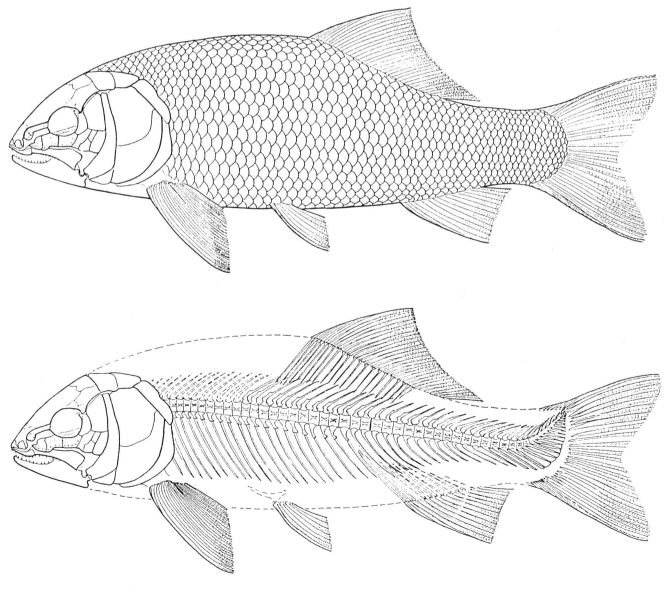

Diagnosis: Small *Oshunia* attaining approximately 280 mm standard length; proportions as percentage of standard length: head length 30%, greatest body depth 25%, distance to dorsal from snout almost 50%, to pelvics 45%, to anal approx. 70%; vertebral counts (mainly from AMNH 12793): abdominal 21 or 22, caudal 25, ural 7-10; 11-12 hypurals; Pii, 22; V5-7?; Dii, 22+; Aiii, 12; 15 or 16 scales in vertical series between pelvics and dorsal, and around 50 scales along lateral line (AMNH 12793); dorsal fin supported by 15 pterygiophores, between neural arches of preural centra 23 to 33.

Holotype: Désirée Collection CD-P-3l; nearly entire fish lacking dorsal region of head and extremity of tail; Lower Cretaceous (Aptian), Santana formation, locality uncertain in the Chapada do Araripe.

Referred material: AMNH 12793, acid-prepared specimen in part and counterpart.

Oshunia sp. form A

Diagnosis: *Oshunia* with estimated standard length of 380-400 mm; deep body (approx. 38% of estimated standard length); head length approx. 28% of ESL; distance from snout to dorsal insertion approx. 50%; to pelvics approx. 43%; to anal approx. 68%; P9-11; Viii, 5-6; Dv, 28+, Ai+, 12; 19 to 20 scales in vertical series at deepest part of body, estimated 55+ scales along lateral line.

Referred material: AMNH 12000, specimen lacking caudal extremity.

Oshunia sp. form B

Diagnosis: Large *Oshunia* known only from trunk and tail; 21 caudal centra, 12 + ural centra, 16-17 hypurals; dorsal fin supported by 25 pterygiophores between neural arches of preural centra 17-34.

Referred material: AMNH 11895.

The Ionoscopidae are extinct fishes that are known with certainty only from Late Mesozoic (Upper Jurassic-Cretaceous) sediments. They are quite rare, and very few taxa have been described. In his *Catalogue*, Woodward (1895) grouped together the fossil genera *Oligopleurus*, *Ionoscopus*, *Spathiurus*, and *Opsigonus*. According to d'Erasmo (1915), however, *Opsigonus* is a junior synonym of *Ionoscopus*. Probably the most informative work on ionoscopids is that by Saint-Seine (1949), at least as far as general aspects of cranial morphology

in *Ionoscopus* are concerned. In that work Saint-Seine removed *Oligopleurus* from any close relationship to ionoscopids, and instead placed it closer to teleosts. That view was reinforced by Patterson (1973), who suggested that the presence of two supramaxillae in *Oligopleurus* united it with teleosts. Nevertheless, he also was impressed by similarities in the caudal fins of *Oligopleurus*, *Ionoscopus*, *Spathiurus*, and the "caturid" *Callopterus*, in which there are several elongate, slender ural neural arches.

The relationships of *Ionoscopus* and its allies have not been adequately resolved. Superficial features shared with modern *Amia*, the bowfin, suggested amiid affinity to Woodward (1895). Such a relationship was maintained by Saint-Seine (1949) and Lehman (1966) for *Ionoscopus* but not for *Oligopleurus*. Patterson (1973, p. 290) left these issues open, commenting only that there is "slight evidence from the skull that *Ionoscopus* is related to *Amia*."

The first report of an ionoscopid from the Santana formation of Brazil appeared only recently (Wenz and Kellner, 1986). Although only a single small specimen was available, it was sufficiently well preserved to determine that its jaw suspension resembles that of *Amia*. In particular, the symplectic has an articulation with the quadrate bone of the mandible. This critical halecomorph character also was confirmed by Wenz and Kellner in *Ionoscopus*, thus placing ionoscopids firmly within Patterson's (1973) Halecomorphi.

Unfortunately, the skull morphology in *Oshunia* could not be described from Wenz and Kellner's specimen. However, additional specimens of *Oshunia* in the American Museum (AMNH) have been acid-prepared, providing a wealth of new morphological data particularly in the head region, and making *Oshunia* the best-known example of an ionoscopid.

The following description of *Oshunia* is based mainly on AMNH 12793, supplemented by data from AMNH 12000. In general, the degree of ossification and the skull proportions in *Oshunia* are similar to those in *Watsonulus* (Olsen, 1984), *Heterolepidotus* (Patterson, 1975a), *Macrepistius* (Schaeffer, 1971), *Caturus*, and "*Aspidorhynchus*" (Rayner, 1948; the latter specimen is actually caturid, according to Patterson, 1975a) and various Triassic "parasemionotids" from eastern Greenland (Patterson, 1975a). In *Oshunia* the sutures between skull bones are visible, and the extent of most bones therefore can be determined, as in some of the taxa listed above (in *Heterolepidotus*, *Watsonulus*, and most other parasemionotids many of the sutures have become obliterated).

The skull roof includes large, elongate paired frontals, somewhat less elongate paired parietals, plus paired dermopterotics and dermosphenotics. The dermosphenotic is an integral part of the skull roof as in *Amia*, *Macrepistius* (Schaeffer, 1971), *Ophiopsis* (Bartram, 1975), *Heterolepidotus* and most caturids (Patterson, 1973), and probably *Ionoscopus* (Saint-Seine, 1949, but see below). In *Watsonulus* (Olsen, 1984) the dermosphenotic overlies the autosphenotic but apparently is not sutured into the skull roof (a presumed primitive character state).

Patterson (1973: 244) noted that in *Amia* the dermosphenotic lies mainly anterior to the autosphenotic, with a ventral flange wrapping around this cartilage bone and binding the two bones together. This feature also occurs in *Oshunia* and also is known in *Heterolepidotus*, *Macrepistius*, *Ophiopsis*, and various caturids.

In *Oshunia* the dermosphenotic is very elaborate, with a well-developed ventral flange forming part of the orbital wall antero-medial to the autosphenotic. This flange carries with it the infraorbital sensory canal, which is plastered against the anterior face of the autosphenotic within the orbit. The postorbital process in *Oshunia* thus has two projections, one posteriorly (formed by the autosphenotic) and one anteriorly (formed by the canal-bearing flange of the dermosphenotic).

Interestingly, a comparable situation exists in *Ophiopsis procera* (Bartram, 1975: 188, fig. 2A, 5) and probably in "*Aspidorhynchus*" (Patterson, 1975a, figs. 99, 101), suggesting that these taxa may be closely related. Examination of the braincase in the holotype of *Macrepistius arenatus* (AMNH 2435) reveals that here, too, the infraorbital canal of the dermosphenotic is plastered against the anterior surface of the

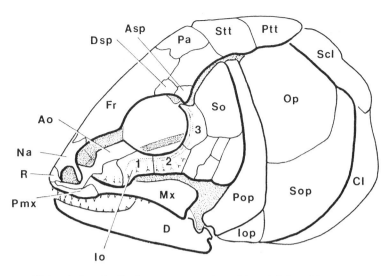

Oshunia brevis. Outline reconstruction of head. Infraorbital and suborbital arrangement is somewhat speculative.

autosphenotic. The condition in *Ionoscopus* has yet to be determined. Possibly the bone identified as the dermosphenotic by Saint-Seine (1949, fig. 78) is actually an exposed part of the autosphenotic (as in *Oshunia*, *Ophiopsis*, *Macrepistius*, *Watsonulus*, and perhaps *Furo* and *Heterolepidotus*; Bartram, 1975; Olsen, 1984).

The frontals are constricted above the orbits, then widen again over the ethmoid region, as in *Ionoscopus*, *Ophiopsis*, *Heterolepidotus*, *Watsonulus*, and *Macrepistius*. In some if not all these taxa the outer surface of the frontals is divided into two regions. Posteriorly, the surface is ornamented by fine pits and minute ganoine tubercles extending anteriorly above the orbits. Farther anteriorly the frontals are

Oshunia brevis. Lateral view of skull, from AMNH 12793.

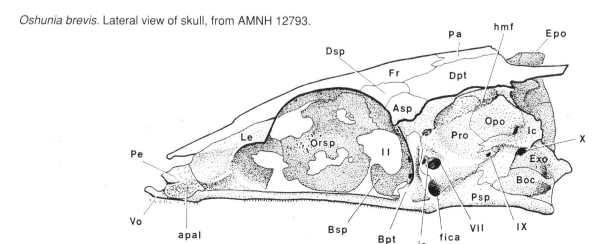

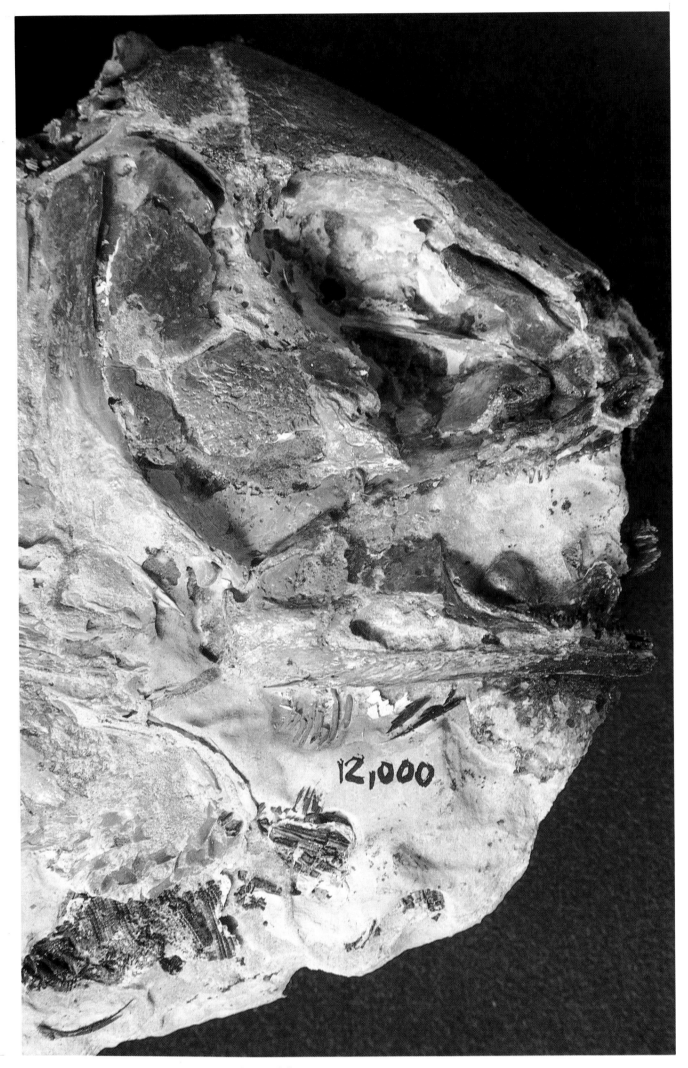

A partially prepared head of *Oshunia* gapes from soft limestone.

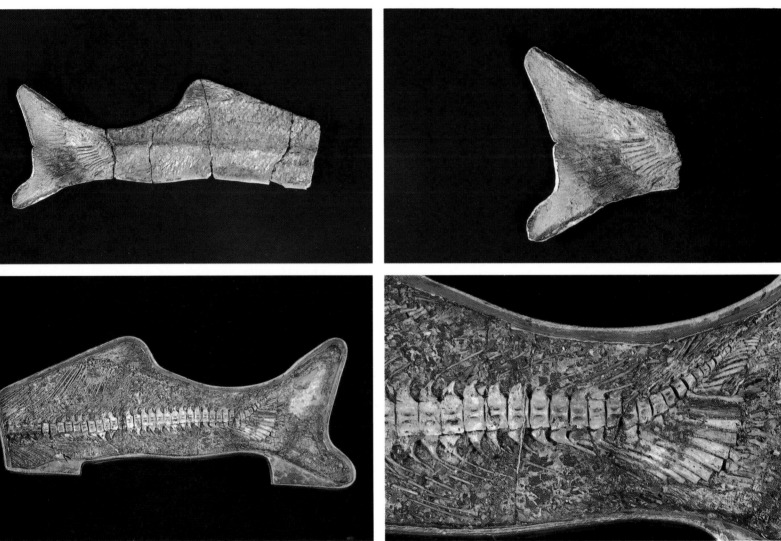

Top: Almost complete *Oshunia* specimen, lacking only part of the tail (see close-up of head in preceding color plate). Other views are of a large *Oshunia* tail before (**center**) and after (**bottom**) acid preparation.

161

unornamented but may bear elongate suture-like ridges and grooves oriented antero-posteriorly; there may be a marked change in profile where the two regions meet (e.g., *Macrepistius*; Schaeffer, 1971, fig. 3).

The nasals in *Oshunia* are complex and bifurcate anteriorly above the olfactory area. The supraorbital canal lies close to the lateral margin of the nasal and gives off several extremely fine pores. Lateral to the canal there is a down-turned extension of the nasal passing beneath and following the curved shape of the antorbital. This lateral extension of the nasal appears to separate the anterior and posterior narial openings.

The antorbital also has a complex shape. There is a narrow anterior canal-bearing arm extending beneath the anterior nostril to meet the rostral, a medially-directed flange that partly overlies the lateral extension of the nasal, and a wing-like posterior flange that extends into the orbit, overlying part of the lateral ethmoid and meeting the lachrymal and first infraorbital.

The rostral consits of two elongate ventro-laterally directed arms with a thickened median region enclosing the rostral commissural sensory canal. The overall arrangement of the nasals, antorbitals, and rostral in *Oshunia* is reminiscent of that in *Ophiopsis* as described by Bartram (1975).

The parietals are slightly longer than wide and are sutured to the frontals, dermopterotics, and epioccipitals. The posterior part of each parietal dips downward, with a distinct unornamented region extending beneath the supratemporals to meet the epioccipitals, which form a hump-like posterior region extending behind the dermal skull roof.

The dermopterotic meets the parietal, frontal, dermosphenotic, and autosphenotic. The descending lamina of the dermopterotic defines the lateral wall of the post-temporal fossa. A separate pterotic cannot be discerned, and this bone may be fused with the dermopterotic.

The ossification pattern of the otico-occipital region in *Oshunia* is very similar to that described in "*Aspidorhynchus*" and *Macrepistius* (Rayner, 1948; Schaeffer, 1971; Patterson, 1975a). There is a median basioccipital, basisphenoid, and orbitosphenoid, plus paired exoccipitals, intercalars, epioccipitals, pterotics (not discrete, however), opisthotics, prootics, sphenotics, and pterosphenoids. Additionally there is a well-developed median dorsal ossification that (following Patterson, 1975a: 437) is interpreted as a supraotic. According to Patterson (ibid.), such an ossification occurs in

the "*Aspidorhynchus*" braincase described by Rayner (1948) and in some *Lepidotes*.

The morphology of the basioccipital, prootics, and intercalar is virtually identical in *Oshunia* and "*Aspidorhynchus*" (see Patterson, 1975a: 437 and figs. 99, 100). The intercalar apparently has an endochondral component as in "*Aspidorhynchus*" and *Heterolepidotus*, as well as extensive membranous outgrowths overlying the junctions of the opisthotic/exoccipital and basioccipital/prootic.

According to Patterson (1973: 280), the caturid intercalar is "of amiid rather than teleostean type, extending over the lateral surface of the saccular chamber, below the jugular vein." Precisely the same arrangement occurs in *Oshunia*, further strengthening the view that ionoscopids are halecomorphs. Moreover, the membranous part of the intercalar meets a flange from the posterior process of the parasphenoid. This peculiar arrangement occurs in the caturid "*Aspidorhynchus*" as well as in *Macrepistius* and *Neorhombolepis*. In *Heterolepidotus*, *Watsonulus*, *Amia*, and *Calamopleurus* the intercalar does not meet the parasphenoid. The intercalar in *Ophiopsis* is unknown. In *Sinamia* the intercalar has an elongate ventral arm that may reach the parasphenoid (Stensiö, 1935).

The opisthotic is located entirely behind the prootic, as in "*Aspidorhynchus*," unlike *Macrepistius*, where the opisthotic extends farther anterodorsally. The glossopharyngeal foramen is enclosed by the prootic, close to its posterior margin, and lies below the membranous outgrowth of the intercalar that in "*Aspidorhynchus*" surrounds the foramen.

The pterosphenoid and orbitosphenoid are large, and there is a well-developed interorbital septum in *Oshunia*.

There are large paired lateral ethmoids and pre-ethmoids. A narrow unossified gap separates the pre-ethmoid and lateral ethmoid. Together, these ossifications share the articular facet for the palatine and closely resemble the "lateral" ethmoid of *Macrepistius* and *Heterolepidotus* (Schaeffer, 1971, fig. 3; Patterson, 1975a, fig. 102). In those taxa the pre-ethmoid and lateral ethmoid may have formed a continuous ossification. Separate pre-ethmoid ossifications occur in *Calamopleurus* (this volume) and *Amia* (usually in large individuals), but they are more widely spaced than in *Oshunia*.

Elongate, paired vomers extend beneath the lateral ethmoids and pre-ethmoids. Each vomer bears a patch of small, pointed teeth, but none of the teeth is enlarged as in *Calamopleurus*.

The parasphenoid is quite broad, with a more extensive toothed area than in *Heterolepidotus*. Posteriorly the parasphenoid extends the full length of the basioccipital on either side of a depression for the aortic ligament. A short basipterygoid process is present just lateral to the notch in the ascending process for the efferent pseudobranchial artery. The hypophyseal duct is closed. The internal carotid foramen lies at the junction of the parasphenoid and prootic. Above the notch for the efferent pseudobranchial artery is a delicate pterosphenoid process connecting the ascending process of the parasphenoid with the basisphenoid. A well-developed spiracular groove is present on the ventrolateral surface of the ascending process. Farther dorsally a spiracular canal is present between the autosphenotic and prootic. A small median pit in the parasphenoid, located approximately one-third of the distance between the ascending process and occipital condyle, may have contained the origin of a subcephalic muscle.

The dermal bones of the cheek region are incompletely preserved in AMNH 12000 and 12793, and those elements that are present are somewhat damaged. There probably are three infraorbitals plus a lachrymal. A small third infraorbital extends to just below the autosphenotic and also has a canal-bearing process antero-dorsally. This process evidently extended to meet the infraorbital canal of the dermosphenotic, situated within the orbit. There apparently is a single anamestic suborbital between the last infraorbital and the preoperculum.

There is a short, mobile toothed maxilla that extends only to the level of the middle of the orbit. A vestige of what may be a supramaxilla is present in AMNH 12793. Anteriorly the maxilla bears a stout articular process fitting into a deep depression between the premaxilla and pre-ethmoid. The pterygoids are covered mesially by numerous small teeth resembling those on the parasphenoid.

The symplectic apparently contributed to the mandibular joint (Wenz, 1986, fig. 3), although in both AMNH 12000 and 12793 it is separated from the upper part of the articular by a gap, and their union cannot have been as intimate as in *Amia*. The symplectic nevertheless bears a pronounced lower articular surface, suggesting that there was an extensive joint in life.

The preoperculum is elongate and narrow, as in *Ophiopsis* and *Macrepistius*, and the symplectic seems to be firmly attached to its mesial surface. The quadrate is also tightly bound to the anterior margin of the preoperculum, as in *Amia*. There is no sign of a quadratojugal.

The operculum is relatively small and the suboperculum comparatively large. The area of the interopercular is damaged in the American Museum specimens, but one is present in the holotype according to Wenz (1986, fig. 2). The number of gulars, although high, cannot be determined. There is a large, triangular median gular.

The posterior ceratohyal is far smaller than the anterior one, and the hypohyals are single on each side. The anterior ceratohyal is proportionately deeper than in *Amia*.

The supratemporals meet at the dorsal midline much as in *Amia*. The posttemporals also meet at the midline beneath the supratemporals (again as in *Amia*). Each posttemporal bears two processes. One of these descends antero-ventrally to meet the intercalar. The other, apparently canal-bearing, extends anteriorly beneath the supratemporal. In *Amia* there is a descending posttemporal process that meets the intercalar, but only a short rounded forward extension beneath the supratemporal. A single ray-like bone extends posteriorly beneath the supratemporal from just below the point where the lateral line canal exits from the dermopterotic, but does not reach the supercleithrum like the "ossified ligaments" in *Calamopleurus*.

Although the supratemporal in *Oshunia* carries the commisural canal and its surface is covered by minute sensory pores connected by an anastomosing network of tubules, the lateral line canal itself apparently passed directly from the dermopterotic to the posttemporal, apparently sandwiched between the supratemporal and the anterior process of the posttemporal.

The supercleithrum is a large, elongate bone with a strong articulation with the posttemporal. The cleithrum is slender and gently recurved anteroventrally, with a relatively longer upright dorsal region than in *Amia*.

The vertebral column is strongly ossified. The vertebrae are monospondylous, about as deep as long, and each is strengthened by a longitudinal lamina separating two very deep depressions. In AMNH 12793 a few of the anterior vertebrae are displaced, but the arcualia are all intact, permitting a fairly accurate vertebral count. The first abdominal centrum is modified, with separate articular facets for the basioccipital and exoccipitals. In *Amia* the first free centrum does not meet the exoccipitals, and it seems likely

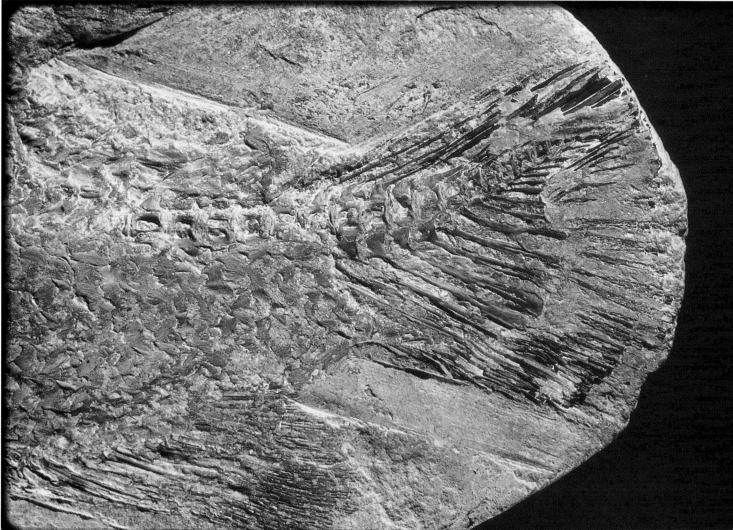

The holotype of *Oshunia brevis* (photos courtesy S. Wenz, Paris).

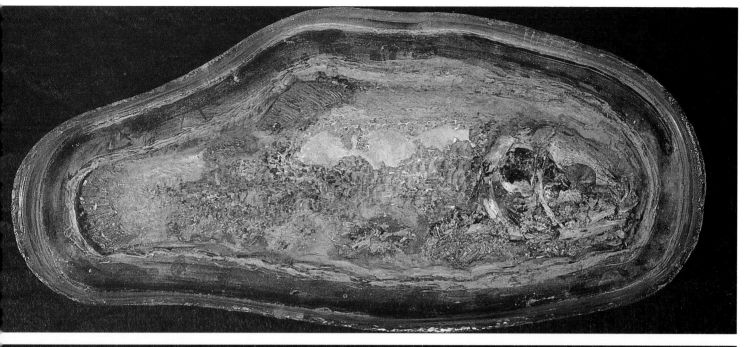

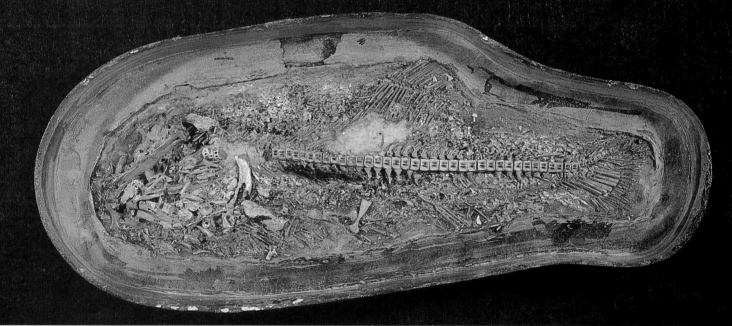

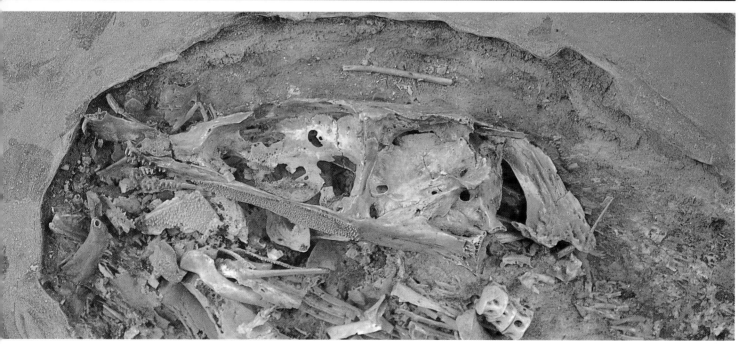

Acid-prepared specimen of *Oshunia* in part and counterpart, with detail of braincase (bottom). Photos by E. Garvens.

165

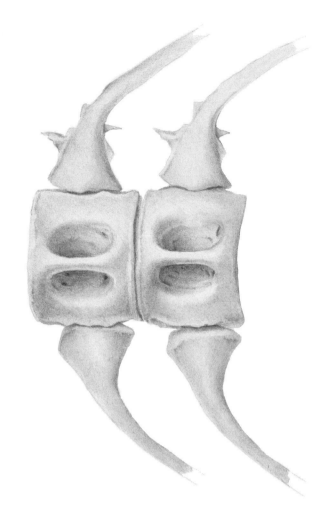

Oshunia brevis. Caudal vertebrae, from AMNH 12793.

that the first free centrum in *Oshunia* corresponds to a segment that in *Amia* is incorporated into the cranium.

There are 21 or 22 rib-bearing abdominal centra and 25 caudal centra, plus at least seven ural centra in AMNH 12793 (the last few ural centra apparently are missing, so the total number was probably higher). In this specimen all the dorsal and ventral arcualia are autogenous. In the much larger tail region represented by AMNH 11895 there are 21 caudal centra followed by at least 12 ural centra. In this specimen the arches and hypurals are all autogenous, but many of the neural arches and the more anteriorly situated rib attachments are fused to their respective centra. Since the specimen is from a very large individual, however, this fusion may be a secondary age-related phenomenon. The number of post-abdominal vertebrae is very close in AMNH 12793 and 11895, with the main difference being

the relative position of the last hemal arch and first hypural. Wenz (1986, fig. 4) found ten ural centra in the holotype of *Oshunia brevis*.

In AMNH 12793 all the hypurals have unfinished, spongy distal extremities. In AMNH 11895 a second series of short ossifications is present distal to the last three or four hemal spines and first one or two hypurals. These additional ossifications may represent further evidence of longevity in the largest individual.

The caudal fin is supported by approximately five pre-ural hemal arches plus the hypurals. These ventral arcualia are spine-like and relatively unspecialized. The first ural centrum supports both the last hemal arch and first hypural. As noted by Wenz (1986: 82), there is no correspondence between the number of ural centra and hypurals. In the holotype of *Oshunia brevis*, Wenz (1986, fig. 4) identified 12 hypurals but only ten ural centra. In AMNH 11895 there are 16 or 17 hypurals. In AMNH 12793 an exact count is not possible, but at least 11 or 12 hypurals were probably present.

Neural arches are present on all pre-ural centra plus ural centra 1-6 in the holotype (Wenz, 1986) and U1 to 11 in AMNH 11895. These neural arches gradually diminish in height caudally, retaining a 1:1 relationship with the ural centra. Wenz (1986: 82) noted the presence of six doubled "epurals" along the distal extremity of the neural spines between Pu4 to U5. At least seven such "epurals" are present in the large specimen AMNH 11895, but only three or four now remain in AMNH 12793 (the original number probably was higher).

Three urodermals were identified in the holotype of *Oshunia brevis* by Wenz (1986). Traces of presumed urodermals are present in AMNH 12793 and 11895, but their number and arrangement are uncertain.

The form of the caudal fin cannot be determined in the holotype of *Oshunia brevis* or in AMNH 12000 and 12793, but in AMNH 11895 the caudal fin is nearly complete. In outline it resembles that of *Ionoscopus* in being strongly forked, with an indented posterior margin. Fringing fulcral scales are well developed along the dorsal and ventral margins. Wenz (1986) found only a few ventral fulcral scales in her specimen, but this may be because its tail is less complete than in AMNH 11895.

The number and arrangement of caudal fin-rays can be determined approximately from AMNH 12793 and 11895. Their number certainly exceeds that of the hypurals and there is not a 1:1 relationship of the kind seen in

Amia. In AMNH 11895 there are approximately 27 fin-rays and at least 24 in AMNH 12793 and the holotype of *Oshunia brevis.* The more dorsal fin-rays are strongly recurved proximally across the upper hypurals.

The dorsal fin is elongate, extending from above the level of the pelvics to a point slightly anterior to the caudal peduncle. Only the anterior part of the fin is supported by ossified pterygiophores. In AMNH 12793, 15 pterygiophores are present above the neural spines of pre-ural centra 23-33 (i.e., the last eight abdominal and first three caudal vertebrae). In AMNH 11895 there are 25 dorsal pterygiophores extending between the neural spines of pre-ural centra 17-34 (the last 12 abdominal and first five caudal vertebrae). Wenz (1986) reported 25 dorsal fin-rays in the holotype of *Oshunia brevis,* but in AMNH 12000 the number may exceed 35.

The anal fin is well-preserved in the holotype of *Oshunia brevis,* with three marginal and 12 principal fin-rays (Wenz, 1986: 79). By contrast, in all three AMNH specimens referred to *Oshunia* the anal fin is incomplete. In AMNH 11895 the posteriormost anal pterygiophore lies between the hemal arches of the 15th and 16th pre-ural centrum.

The pectoral fins also are better preserved in the holotype than in other specimens. According to Wenz (1986:84) there are approximately 22 pectoral radials, preceded by two short, unsegmented marginal fin-rays. The first principal fin-ray is the longest. Posteriorly the fin-rays extend almost to the origin of the pelvics. The pelvics arise just a little in front of the dorsal fin. There are six or seven principal fin-rays in AMNH 12000, preceded by three short marginal rays. The pelvic girdles are elongate, with a narrow central constriction and expanded, plate-like proximal and distal extremities (seen in the holotype and AMNH 12793).

The scales are short, cycloid, elongated antero-posteriorly, finely striated horizontally, have a pronounced median keel, are strongly imbricated, and are said by Wenz (1986) to be of amioid type. The number of scale rows in the holotype of *Oshunia brevis* is uncertain. In AMNH 12000 there are approximately 19 or 20 scales in a vertical series from the origin of the pelvics to the dorsal fin. In AMNH 12793, however, fewer scales seem to be present (15 to 16 in the corresponding vertical series). There are around 50 + scales along the lateral line in AMNH 12793. There are apparently more than this in AMNH 12000, but because the caudal region is incomplete an accurate count cannot be made.

It is clear from the above descriptions that significant differences exist between various specimens referred here to *Oshunia.* AMNH 12793 seems to be closest to the holotype of *Oshunia brevis* in its general proportions and hypural number. AMNH 11895 differs from AMNH 12793 in its number of caudal and ural centra, hypurals, and the number and arrangement of dorsal pterygiophores. AMNH 12000 differs from AMNH 12793 and the holotype of *Oshunia brevis* in its deeper body. It is suggested that AMNH 11895 and 12000 may represent different species of *Oshunia.* Unfortunately, no numerical data are available for AMNH 12000 that can be compared in AMNH 11895, and it cannot be determined whether they are conspecific. Consequently, these specimens are left as indeterminate and separate forms of *Oshunia,* pending further investigation of the holotype of *O. brevis.* In the absence of contrary data, AMNH 12793 is referred to that species (see taxonomic section above).

The halecomorph symplectic arrangement seen in ionoscopids also has been found in a number of other Mesozoic fishes including the caturids *Neorhombolepis, Heterolepidotus, Furo,* and *Caturus* (Patterson, 1973); some Triassic "parasemionotids" (Patterson, 1973; Olsen, 1984); and pycnodonts (e.g., *Neoproscinetes*). The symplectic is unknown in ophiopsids (*Ophiopsis, Macrepistius*), although these fishes have been included within the Halecomorphi on the basis of other similarities with caturids and *Amia* (Bartram, 1975). *Macrosemius* and other macrosemiids (*sensu* Bartram, 1977) do not possess a halecomorph-like symplectic and are no longer considered close relatives of *Ophiopsis.* They also lack the characters used by Patterson (1973) to unite teleosts, and Bartram (1977) consequenty left macrosemiids as an *incertae sedis* group of halecostomes (a larger group including halecomorphs plus teleosts).

Additional support for a halecomorph relationship comes from the intercalar arrangement, with a membranous ventral extension below the jugular vein and meeting the parasphenoid as in "*Aspidorhynchus,*" *Macrepistius,* and *Sinamia.*

There are similarities in the antorbital and nasal arrangement in *Oshunia* and *Ophiopsis* (Bartram, 1975, figs. 3-5), particularly in the way that the nasal extends laterally and the curvature of the antorbital below the olfactory region. An additional similarity is seen in the morphology of the dermosphenotic infraorbital canal within the orbit. This last feature also is seen in *Macrepistius* and perhaps offers the most compelling evidence for a close phylogenetic relationship between ionoscopids and ophiopsids.

Returning to the relationships of *Oshunia*, there are similarities with *Spathiurus* in the length of the dorsal and anal fins and in tooth arrangement, according to descriptions given by Davis (1887) and Patterson (1973). The dorsal fin of *Oshunia* probably is longer and contains more fin-rays than reported by Wenz and Kellner (1986). The dorsal fin is short in *Ionoscopus*, as in *Oligopleurus, Callopterus, Caturus,* and cladistically primitive amiids (it is very long in *Amia*). The dorsal fin is of moderate length in *Ophiopsis* (Bartram, 1975) but does not attain the extreme lengths seen in some macrosemiids (Bartram, 1977), *Spathiurus, Oshunia,* and *Amia*. It is concluded that an elongate dorsal fin has appeared at least twice in halecomorphs, once in cladistically derived amiids (*Amia, Pachyamia*) and once in derived ionoscopids (*Oshunia, Spathiurus*). *Ionoscopus* may be allied to these two genera on the basis of having ossified ural centra (Patterson, 1973). These generally are absent in *Callopterus* (except in very large individuals). *Ionoscopus* may be united with *Oshunia, Spathiurus,* and *Callopterus insignis* by the presence of "amiid" cycloid scales (actually more elongated antero-posteriorly than in amiids). *Callopterus agassizi* has almost no scales apart from small, granular "ganoid" scales along the caudal peduncle margins (Saint-Seine, 1949). All these taxa also may be united by similarities in the caudal fin skeleton discussed by Patterson (1973).

In Woodward's (1895) original work on ionoscopid fishes, these were rather unsatisfactorily defined by such characters as ossified monospondylous vertebrae and the absence of a surangular (=supra-angular) and coronoids on the lower jaw.

Woodward's analysis was flawed by data obtained from fossils that, in hindsight, are unrelated to *Ionoscopus* (Patterson, 1973, p. 288). Ossification of vertebral centra apparently occurs independently in several neopterygian groups. There are tooth-bearing coronoids in *Oshunia* and apparently in *Spathiurus* (Patterson, 1973, p. 289), and there is a surangular in *Oshunia*; probably the mandible of *Ionoscopus* simply is not known sufficiently.

Perhaps the most convincing evidence for ionoscopid monophyly is found in the postcranial skeleton, with fully ossified vertebrae having transverse ridges separated by pits, plus a very high number of ural centra (up to 13), hypurals (up to 20), and slender ural neural arches and spines (up to six).

The ural neurals differ from those of teleosts, *Amia, Caturus,* and parasemionotids (Patterson, 1973) but are nevertheless similar to those of *Oligopleurus*. Additionally, there are similarities between *Oshunia* and Saint-Seine's (1949, figs. 78, 79) reconstructions of *Ionoscopus* in the convex and somewhat domed shape of the cranial roofing bones.

Oshunia is a moderately deep-bodied, laterally compressed fish. Aside from its long-based dorsal, the fins are arranged conservatively. With its relatively unspecialized but nevertheless well-developed dentition, *Oshunia* was perhaps an opportunistic generalist that preyed on various small fishes or invertebrates.

Assemblages: Jardim, ?Old Mission.

(J. G. Maisey)

Hypothesis of relationships among ionoscopid fishes, based on the following characters: (**a**) elongate, slender neural spines; (**b**) amiid scales; (**c**) ossified ural centra; (**d**) tooth arrangement, long dorsal and anal fins.

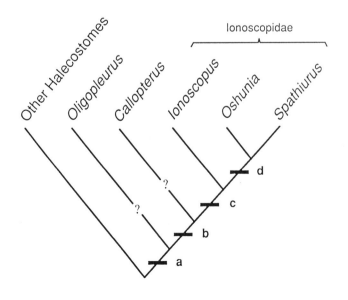

OPHIOPSIS Agassiz, 1834

Division HALECOSTOMI
Subdivision HALECOMORPHI
Family OPHIOPSIDAE Bartram, 1975
Genus *Ophiopsis* Agassiz, 1834

Diagnosis: The most informative modern diagnosis is that given by Bartram (1975).

Type species: *Ophiopsis procera* Agassiz, 1834.

Ophiopsis cretaceus Silva Santos and Valença

1968 *Ophiopsis cretaceus* Silva Santos and Valença: 349 (name only)

1975 *Ophiopsis cretaceus* Silva Santos and Valença; Bartram: 20 (name only)

1986 *Ophiopsis cretaceus* Silva Santos and Valença; Mones: 34 (declared *nomen nudum*)

Diagnosis: None.

The species has never been described, nor was any specimen designated as a type. It was declared a *nomen nudum* by Mones (1986). Professor R. da Silva Santos has generously furnished a photograph of the specimen evidently intended for the holotype of *Ophiopsis cretaceus*.

(J. G. Maisey)

Photo of specimen apparently intended as the type of *Ophiopsis cretaceus*. Courtesy Prof. R. da Silva Santos.

VINCTIFER Jordan, 1919

Division HALECOSTOMI
Subdivision TELEOSTEI
incertae sedis
Family ASPIDORHYNCHIDAE Nicholson and Lydekker, 1889
Genus *Vinctifer* Jordan, 1919

1919 *Vinctifer* Jordan: 210

Emended diagnosis: Aspidorhynchid attaining lengths of 60 cm or more; distinguished from *Belonostomus* and resembling *Aspidorhynchus* in having short predentary, anterior part of snout lacking teeth, and dermosphenotic not reaching preoperculum; differing from *Aspidorhynchus* in possessing scales with ganoine and deep lateral line scales, as in *Belonostomus*; differing from all other aspidorhynchids in lack of supramaxilla and in having a cleaver-shaped maxilla with strongly inclined postero-dorsal margin, deep triangular lower jaw; resembles *Belonostomus helgolandicus* in dentition of numerous very fine teeth and posterior extent of parietal-dermopterotic; approx. 67-70 scale rows, with regular flank scales back to rows 61 or 62; 25 scale rows to V; 41 to A; 48 to D; P8-9; V7-8; D14; A16; C30-33.

1919 *Vinctifer* Jordan:210
1923 *Vinctifer comptoni* (Ag.); Jordan: 10
1938 *Belonostomus comptoni* (Ag.); d'Erasmo: 5
1945 *Aspidorhynchus comptoni* Ag.; Silva Santos: 1
1968 *Aspidorhynchus comptoni* Ag.; Silva Santos & Valenca:349
1985b *Vinctifer comptoni* (Ag.); Silva Santos: 151
1988 *Vinctifer comptoni* (Ag.); Brito:819

Diagnosis: As for genus.

Lectotype: British Museum (Natural History), BM(NH) 47892; distorted head and most of body; Santana formation, Jardim, Chapada do Araripe, Ceará.

Aspidorhynchids are a highly specialized, extinct, monophyletic group of Late Mesozoic neopterygians with a known range from the Middle Jurassic (Bathonian, approximately 160 million years) to the Upper Cretaceous (Maestrichtian, approx. 65 million years). The Santana formation genus *Vinctifer* thus lived some time in the middle of aspidorhynchid history.

Despite the evident specializations of the group (e.g., the elongate pike-like shape, long

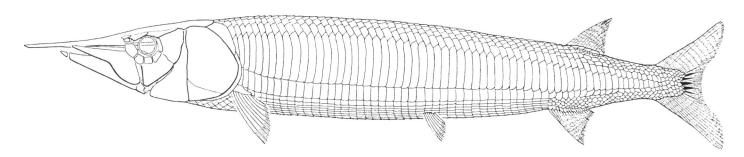

Vinctifer comptoni. Skeletal reconstruction.

Type species: *Aspidorhynchus comptoni* Agassiz.

Vinctifer comptoni (Agassiz)

1841 *Aspidorhynchus comptoni* Agassiz: 83 (name only)

1844b *Aspidorhynchus comptoni* Ag.; Agassiz: 1009 (name only)

1890 *Belonostomus comptoni* (Ag.); Woodward: 629

1895 *Belonostomus comptoni* (Ag.); Woodward: 435

1908 *Belonostomus comptoni* (Ag.); Jordan and Branner: 10

snout, and caudal location of the unpaired fins), little is known concerning the origins and relationships of aspidorhynchids. Woodward (1890: 636) remarked that these fishes may be related to older "ganoid" fishes from the Triassic such as *Pholidopleurus*, whose scales and fins were said to resemble those of aspidorhynchids. This notion has not proven popular, however, and the pholidopleurids are usually regarded as a distinct order of primitive neopterygians. Selezneva (1985: 108) maintained that aspidorhynchids are "nothing but derivatives of Paleonisci," because . . . "their respiratory mechanism is not teleostoid but just one of the modifications of the paleoniscoid mechanism." Since the similarities are in primitive characters, however, and his "Paleonisci" is undefinable except in primitive terms, Selezneva's remarks are uninformative.

Berg (1940) regarded aspidorhynchids as a distinct order at the "holostean" grade of organization. Obruchev (1967) also treated aspidorhynchids as a separate order within the superorder Holostei, along with pycnodontids, pachycormids, lepisosteids, and pholidophorids, but this grouping was again founded on primitive characters (the group comprises "bony ganoids"). Arambourg and Bertin (1958) united aspidorhynchids with pholidophoriforms and leptolepiforms as a "grade" group characterized by a suite of primitive (= "ganoid" or "chondrostean") and derived (= "teleostean") characters. The latter were said to include the form of the preoperculum and mandible, thinly enamelled scales, and presence of a supraoccipital bone (in *Aspidorhynchus*). This last character is particularly interesting, since a supraoccipital is characteristically present in Recent teleosts, plus fossil "leptolepids" and "pholidophorids" (generalized fossil teleost fishes; Patterson, 1975a; Patterson and Rosen, 1977). Outside of these groups, a supraoccipital has been reported in *Dapedium* (Gardiner, 1960), although Patterson (1975a: 455) considered this speculative. He went on to suggest (ibid. :457) that there may have been a supraoccipital in *Perleidus*, but again there is no direct evidence.

Perhaps the most implicit statement of aspidorhynchid relationships is that given by Andrews, et al. (1967: 654). The Aspidorhynchidae were placed within the "holostean" order Leptolepiformes, along with leptolepids, oligopleurids, and protelopids. Elsewhere (e.g., Patterson, 1975a; Patterson and Rosen, 1977), "leptolepids" (and "pholidophorids") are treated as stem teleosts within the halecostomes. "Leptolepiformes" probably comprise an artificial assemblage. Nevertheless, by suggesting "leptolepid" rather than "pholidophorid" affinities, Andrews, et al. (1967) placed aspidorhynchids at a higher organizational level among neopterygians than anyone else has suggested. Silva Santos (1985b) concluded that aspidorhynchids are primitive halecostomes.

Morphological comparisons can be made between *Vinctifer comptoni*, "pholidophorids," "leptolepids," and modern teleosts, plus *Amia*, *Lepisosteus*, and various fossil "holosteans."

Most of the following comparative data have been taken from Patterson (1973, 1975a) and Patterson and Rosen (1977), and the following discussion primarily concerns characters that seemed phylogenetically informative to those investigators.

The surfaces of the bony scales, fin-rays, and dermal bones in the head of *Vinctifer* have a thin, enamelled surface (ganoine, according to Woodward, 1890) that is quite thick locally (e.g., over the caudal scales and along rugosities over the head and operculum). It has not been determined whether the ganoine possesses lepisosteoid tubules. The ganoine is much thicker in large specimens than in smaller ones (Woodward, 1890), suggesting periodic thickening throughout life. All of the scales are articulated by means of a feeble peg-and-socket arrangement (Silva Santos, 1945, 1985b). There is a row of dorsal ridge-scales, but apparently not a ventral series.

Another aspidorhynchid, *Belonostomus*, also has ganoine- covered scales (Saint-Seine, 1949), but in *Aspidorhynchus* ganoine is said to be absent (Schultze, 1966). In this respect *Aspidorhynchus* may be more derived than other aspidorhynchids, although ganoine appears to be present on dermal bones of the head in all aspidorhynchids.

Living teleosts and *Amia* possess thin scales that lack an enamelled outer layer, although this condition apparently arose independently, as ganoid scales occur primitively in fossil teleosts and halecomorphs. In living teleosts and *Amia* the scales also lack peg-and-socket articulations, there is no enamel on the fin-rays or skull bones, and fulcral scales at the bases of the fins are absent. Fulcral scales are present in some "pholidophorids," and one or two small fulcra seem to be present in the caudal fin of some *Vinctifer* specimens.

The vertebral column of *Vinctifer* is composed mainly of monospondylous vertebrae, but in the caudal region the first pre- urals and all ural segments comprise only hemichordacentra. There are median neural spines, as in *Amia* and teleosts, rather than paired ones as in *Lepisosteus* and chondrosteans. Intermuscular bones have yet to be found in *Vinctifer*; even "pholidophorid" teleosts have long intermuscular epineurals developed throughout the abdominal region.

In the caudal fin of *Vinctifer* there is a distinctly teleost-like ural region. There are autogenous, unpaired neural spines present above the dorsal hemichordacentra as far back as the first pre-ural and ural. Only two or three

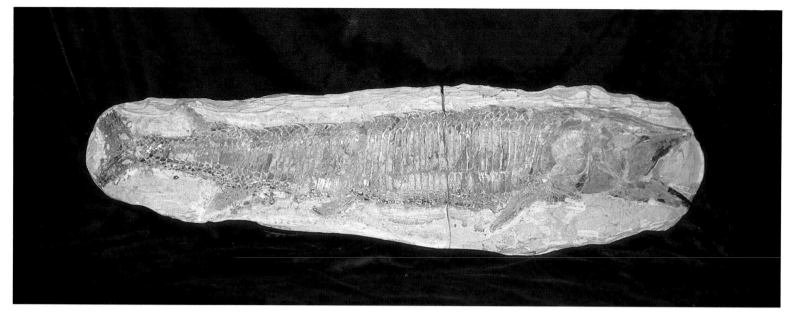

Above: *Vinctifer comptoni*. A large complete specimen in "Old Mission" matrix (top), and the British Museum (Natural History) specimen (47892) designated as the neotype by Woodward (1890) (bottom).

Lepisosteus platostomus, a Recent gar. Dr. H. R. Axelrod photo. Although gars are unrelated to aspidorhynchids, they offer an interesting parallel in body shape and perhaps behavior.

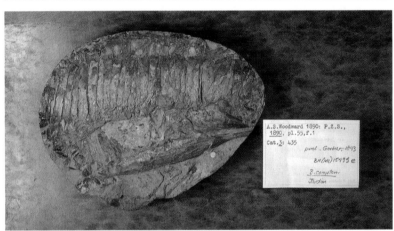

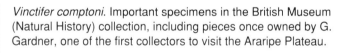

Vinctifer comptoni. Important specimens in the British Museum (Natural History) collection, including pieces once owned by G. Gardner, one of the first collectors to visit the Araripe Plateau.

ural hemichordacentra are ossified. First and second hypurals are fused together proximally, as in a number of primitive teleosts, but are associated with a single hemichordacentrum instead of a complete vertebral centrum. A similar pattern occurs in some specimens of *Caturus* (Patterson, 1973, fig. 21). In *Anaethalion*, *Tharsis*, *Leptolepis* spp., *Thrissops*, *Allothrissops*, and many other fossil teleosts, hypurals 1 and 2 are attached to the first ural centrum (Patterson and Rosen, 1977). In *Pholidophorus bechei* only ural hemichordacentra are present, as in *Vinctifer*, but hypurals 1 and 2 do not converge or fuse together. In *Pleuropholis*, hypurals 1 and 2 are also separate, and each meets its own ural centrum (Patterson, 1973, fig. 17). In its hypural arrangement, therefore, *Vinctifer* more closely aproaches modern teleosts than does *Pholidophorus*.

There are no ossified radials at the tips of the hemal spines in *Vinctifer*. These sometimes are present in *Pholidophorus* but are generally absent in more derived teleosts. There is no one-to-one correspondence in *Vinctifer* between fin-rays and endoskeletal supports like that of *Amia*. Epaxial fin-rays are present, as in *Amia* and teleosts (where they may have arisen independently; Patterson, 1973). These fin-rays are absent in *Lepisosteus* and "pholidophorids," again suggesting that *Vinctifer* is more derived than *Pholidophorus*, but epaxial fin-rays also occur in pholidopleurids, pachycormids, pycnodontids, and saurichthyids, suggesting that their presence is cladistically primitive at the teleost level and that their absence in "pholidophorids" may be secondary.

In *Vinctifer*, hypural 1 is broad and triangular; hypural 2 is more gently tapered and contains a fenestra (as in *Tharsis*; Patterson and Rosen, 1977, fig. 35); hypural 3 is slender, meets ural hemichordacentrum 2, and apparently articulates with the base of hypural 2. A similar relationship between hypurals 2 and 3 is seen in "*Leptolepis*" *talbragarensis*, *Pachythrissops*, *Ascalabos*, *Crossognathus*, *Diplomystus*, and *Albula* (Patterson and Rosen, 1977). There is a small fourth hypural in *Vinctifer*, apparently not associated with any ural ossification. Three uroneurals are present, none extending beyond the base of NPU_1.

The head of *Vinctifer* (and of aspidorhynchids in general) is greatly elongated, which has resulted in considerable departures from what might be considered a generalized skeletal morphology. In certain respects (e.g., presence of large suborbitals), aspidorhynchids are nevertheless remarkably primitive.

Contrary to the reconstruction given by Silva Santos (1945), in none of the specimens examined here was there evidence for a supramaxilla in *Vinctifer*. The bone Silva Santos (1945) identified as a supramaxilla is regarded here as the hind margin of the ectopterygoid. No supramaxilla was shown in the revised restoration of *Vinctifer* published by Silva Santos (1985b, pl. 1, fig. 2). American Museum specimens confirm the presence of a supramaxilla in *Aspidorhynchus* and *Belonostomus*, and there is one in *B. helgolandicus* according to Taverne (1981). A supramaxilla is primitively absent in actinopterygians, where the maxilla is immobile. There is no supramaxilla in *Lepisosteus*, but there is one in *Amia* and two in generalized teleosts, including fossil "leptolepids" and "pholidophoroids." These comparisons collectively suggest that *Vinctifer* has secondarily lost the supramaxilla.

The maxilla of *Vinctifer* probably was mobile; it is not attached to other cheek bones dorsally and posteriorly, nor apparently to the ectopterygoid and dermopalatine. This also is true of *Aspidorhynchus* and *Belonostomus*, where the maxilla is more splint-like than in *Vinctifer*. The maxilla has an elongated anterior ramus running parallel to the ventral margin of the snout. Its posterior margin slopes obliquely down from the olfactory area to the base of the preoperculum. The deep, triangular shape of the maxilla is an important distinguishing feature of *Vinctifer* (Silva Santos, 1985b).

The aspidorhynchid maxilla seems to lack a peg-like articulation with the vomer and ethmoid bones of the kind found in *Amia* and primitive teleosts. A small ventro-laterally directed flange is present on either side of the snout, however, level with the anterior extremity of the maxilla. Between these small flanges is a narrow, elongated patch of small vomerine teeth.

The snout of all aspidorhynchids is greatly elongated rostro-caudally. As might be expected, its morphology represents a radical departure from that seen in primitive teleosts generally. One result of this is considerable confusion in the naming of bones that go to make up the snout. For example, in *Belonostomus* spp. most of this region is toothed, suggesting that it consists largely of fixed premaxillae (e.g., Saint-Seine, 1949, fig. 114; Taverne, 1981, fig. 4). In *Aspidorhynchus euodus* this same region has been termed the premaxilla (Woodward, 1895, pl. 17, fig. 6), but in *A. acutirostris* some reconstructions show a short,

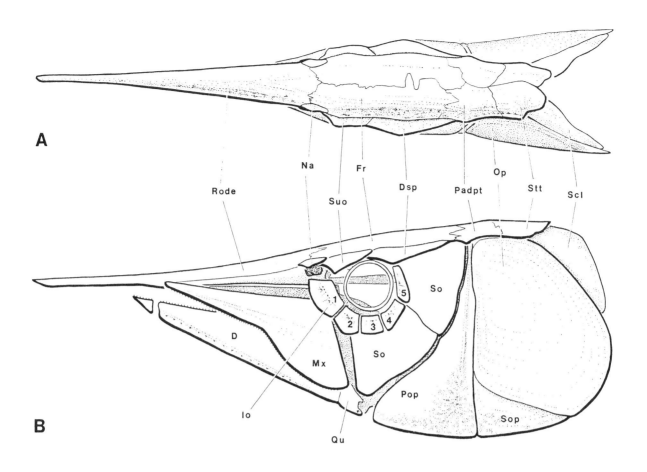

A

Na
Fr
Rode
Suo
Dsp
Padpt
Op
Stt
Scl

B

D
Mx
Io
Qu
1
2 3 4
5
So
So
Pop
Sop

Vinctifer comptoni. (A) Dorsal and (B) lateral views of head; (C) lateral view with superficial dermal bones removed; (D) skull in lateral view.

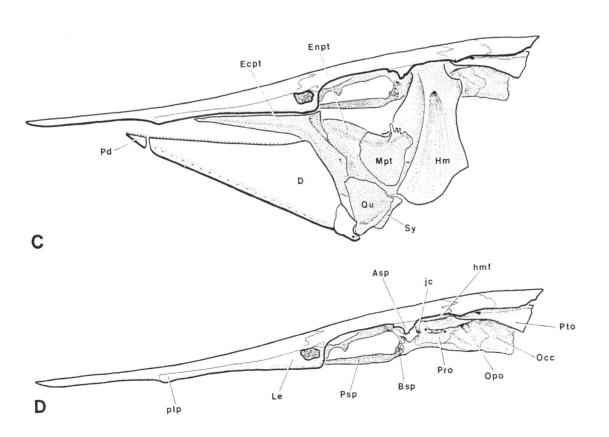

C

Enpt
Ecpt
Pd
D
Mpt
Hm
Qu
Sy

D

Asp
jc
hmf
Pto
Occ
Opo
Pro
Bsp
Psp
Le
plp

175

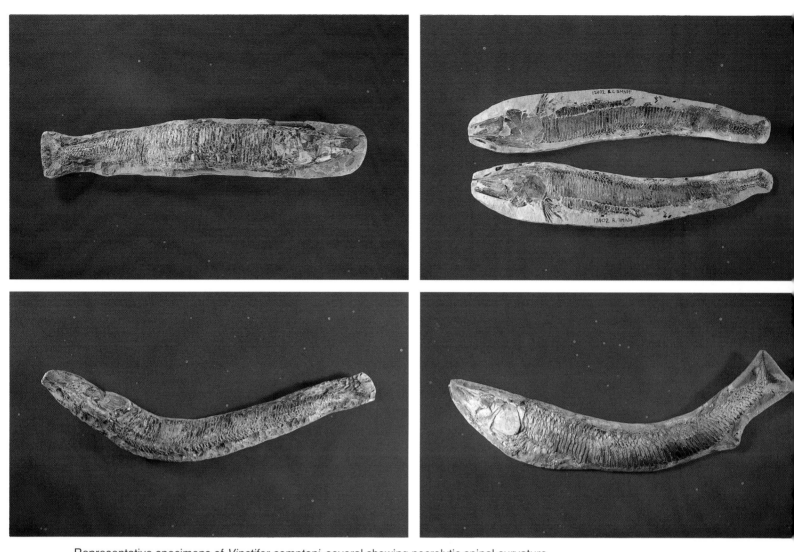

Representative specimens of *Vinctifer comptoni*, several showing necrolytic spinal curvature.

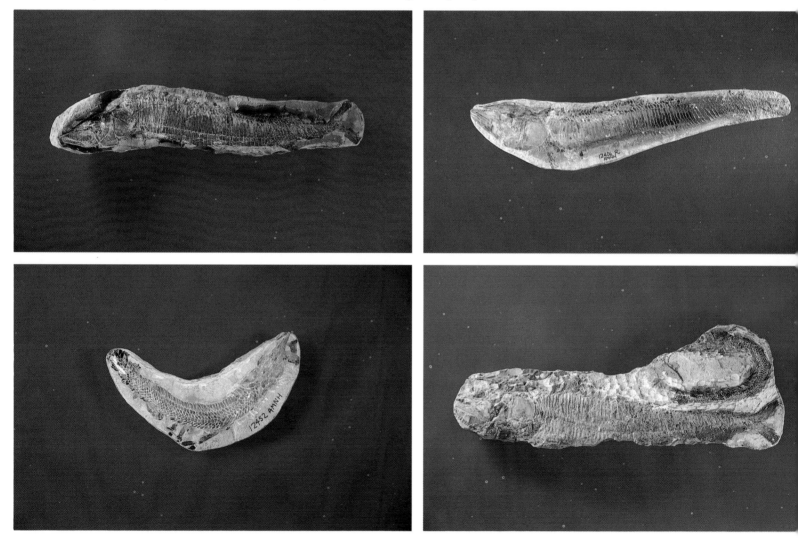

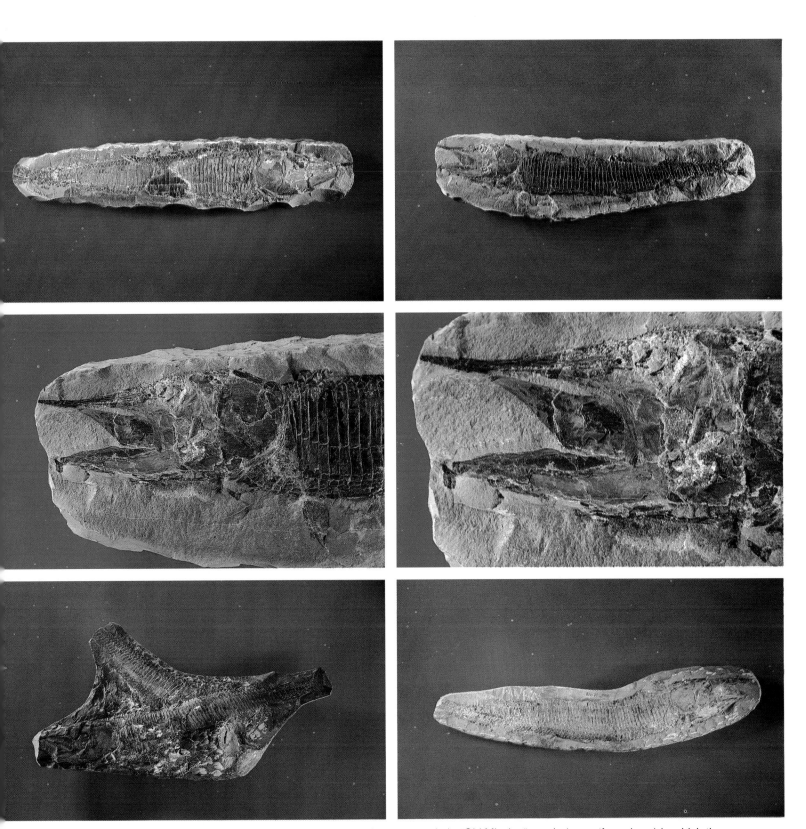

Representative specimens of *Vinctifer comptoni*, including a large example in "Old Mission" matrix (upper four views) in which the small predentary is visible.

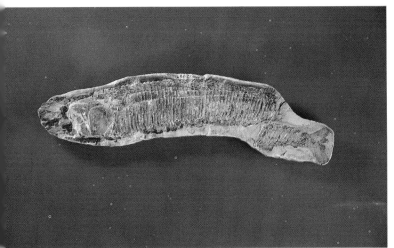

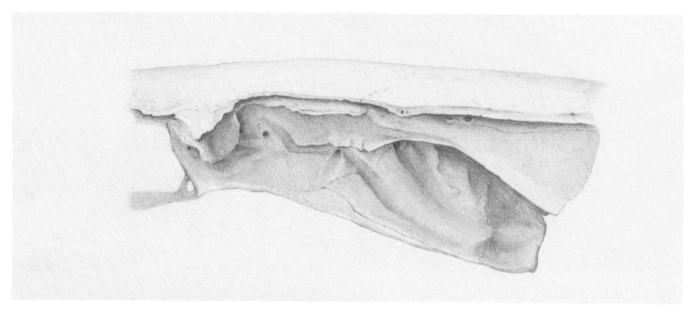

Vinctifer comptoni. Otico-occipital region in lateral view, based on AMNH 13109 and 13110.

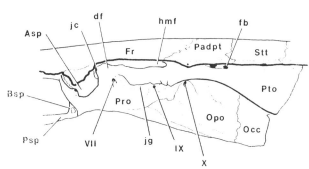

toothed premaxilla and a separate, edentulous "rostrum" (Assmann, 1906; Berg. 1940, fig. 100). The earlier reconstruction of *Vinctifer comptoni* by Silva Santos (1945, figs. 1, 3, 4) showed no premaxilla, and he identified all of the snout as a "rostrum." In his later version, however, Silva Santos (1985b, pl. 1, fig. 1) identified a small separate premaxilla, somewhat like the one said to be present in *Aspidorhynchus acutirostris*.

The snout has been examined in numerous acid-prepared specimens of *V. comptoni*, and comparisons were made with two acid-prepared heads of *Aspidorhynchus acutirostris* and one of *Belonostomus tenuirostris*. In none of these is there any evidence of a free premaxilla. The presence of well-developed teeth along much (*Belonostomus*) or part (*Aspidorhynchus*) of the snout certainly suggests premaxillary involvement, although these teeth could also belong to vomers or to lateral dermethmoids.

It would clearly be advantageous to resolve the morphological arrangement of the snout in aspidorhynchids, because premaxillary structure is a critical character in early teleost phylogeny. According to Patterson (1975a), the teleost lateral dermethmoid is topographically homologous with the medial part of the premaxilla in generalized halecostomes (e.g., *Amia*). Patterson advanced the scenario that the actinopterygian premaxilla became subdivided phylogenetically into a fixed inner component (lateral dermethmoid) and mobile outer part (the teleost premaxilla). This derived condition would unite pachycormids and all teleosts above the "pholidophorid" level.

There is a deep olfactory pit located immmediately in front of the orbit in *Vinctifer*. The entire posterior wall, floor, and roof of each pit usually is formed by a single perichondral ethmoid bone, with a median septum separating the capsules on each side. In a few instances (perhaps representing incompletely ossified individuals) there is a suggestion of a separate mesethmoid and paired lateral ethmoids. Taverne (1981b, fig. 4) reported a large nasal bone in *B. helgolandicus*, but this is probably the outer wall of the lateral ethmoid, as had previously been supposed (Taverne and Ross, 1973, pl. 2). The posterior surface of the ethmoid bone extends mesially to meet the interorbital septum, thereby defining a dorsal and ventral myodome (depression for the insertion of oblique eye muscles). The dorsal myodome was evidently traversed by the olfactory nerve. The ventral myodome is pierced by a pair of small foramina for the orbitonasal vein. A similar arrangement has been described in *Belonostomus helgolandicus* (Taverne, 1981b).

The parasphenoid meets the ethmoid bone ventrally, extending anteriorly between the ectopterygoids. Dorsally, the frontals are sutured to the mesethmoid and continue

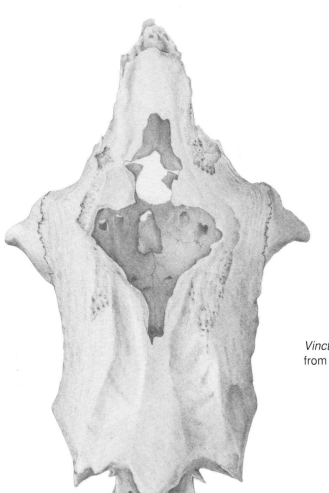

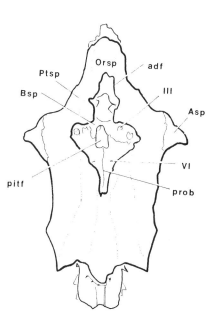

Vinctifer comptoni. Otico-occipital region in dorsal view, from AMNH 13110.

anteriorly beneath the posterior margin of the elongate rostral bone. According to Silva Santos (1985b, pl. 1, fig. 3), in *Vinctifer* the supraorbital sensory canals terminate at a short ethmoid commissure approximately one-third of the distance to the tip of the rostral bone, but this arrangement has not been confirmed in *Aspidorhynchus* or *Belonostomus.*

The nasal pits in *Vinctifer* are extended anteriorly by a pair of elongate, gently tapering tubular dermal or membrane bones that are in sutural contact posteriorly with the ethmoid bone (which they overlie). Ventrally these bones contact the parasphenoid and farther anteriorly are covered ventrally by a small (vomerine?) tooth patch, about level with the tips of the jaws. Dorsally they are overlain by the rostral bone. They are hollow only for about half the distance from the nasal pit to the anterior limit of the maxilla, and their inner surface is smooth.

Topographically the paired tubes correspond to part of the lateral dermethmoids of generalized teleosts (e.g., *Pholidophorus macrocephalus*; Patterson, 1975a, fig. 145), although their extreme length and unusual shape in aspidorhynchids are undoubtedly derived character states. In *Belonostomus* the ventro-lateral margins of these bones bear numerous teeth, but in *Aspidorhynchus* the toothed area is somewhat shorter, and in *Vinctifer* there are only small rugosities rising to form small teeth at the point of maxillary attachment anteriorly.

This point is expanded into a low triangular flange or process on either side of the snout. It marks the beginning of the "rostral" dentition and in both *Aspidorhynchus* and *Belonostomus* bears some of the largest teeth. The tips of the maxilla and palatine bones extend this far, with the tip of the maxilla passing lateral to the toothed process. Topographically the latter is homologous with the lateral process of the teleostean dermethmoid. Interestingly, where a free premaxilla has been reported in aspidorhynchids (Assmann, 1906; Silva Santos, 1985b), it is adjacent to this process (i.e., where it would be, relative to the dermethmoid lateral process, in teleosts). In *Belonostomus helgolandicus* the dentition consists mostly of minute, undifferentiated teeth as in *Vinctifer* and differs from both *Aspidorhynchus* and *Belonostomus tenuirostris* in lacking large teeth (although a few predentary teeth are slightly enlarged; Taverne and Ross, 1973, pl. 2).

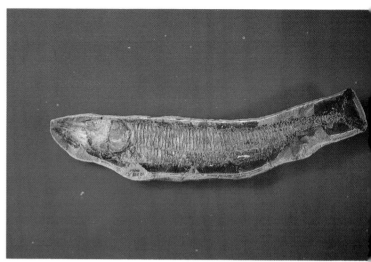

Representative specimens of *Vinctifer comptoni*.

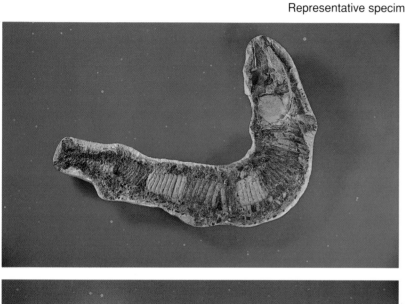
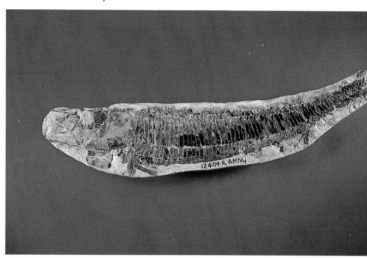

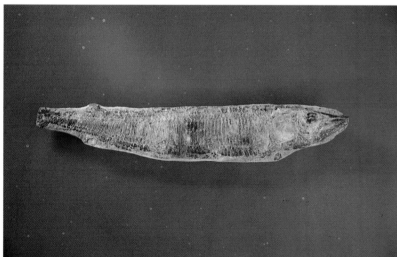
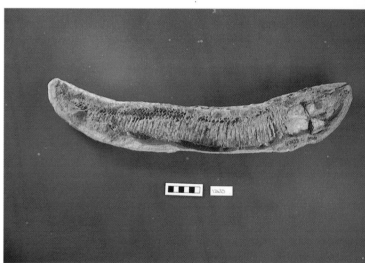

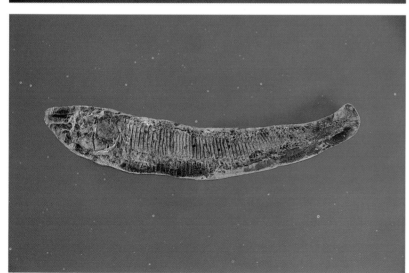

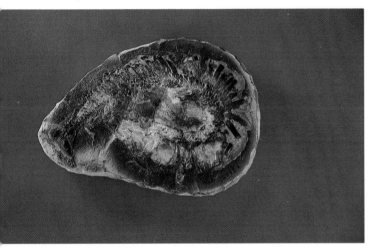

Representative specimens of *Vinctifer comptoni*, several with extreme necrolytic curvature, and one (bottom left) disarticulated example.

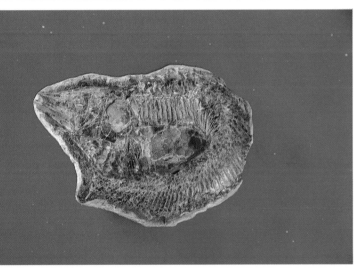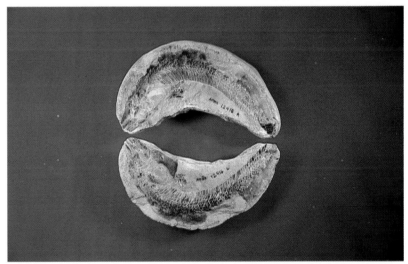

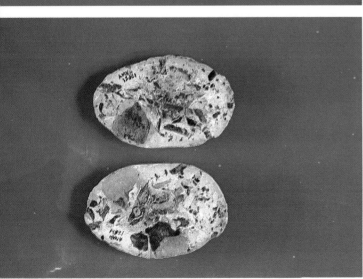

It is concluded that most of the aspidorhynchid snout consists of highly modified lateral dermethmoids, primitively toothed, with an elongate tubular part possibly homologous with the halecostome ascending "nasal" process, and a small flange representing the lateral process of the teleost lateral dermethmoid. If this interpretation is correct, the snout region includes a rostral bone and paired lateral dermethmoids as in teleosts. Furthermore, there appears to be at least partial fusion between these elements, especially toward the end of the snout, a condition known otherwise in teleosts above the "leptolepid" level and in pachycormids (Patterson, 1975; Lambers, 1988). Other morphological features of aspidorhynchids rule out higher (e.g., elopocephalan) relationship. Pachycormid affinity is suggested by certain characteristics of the aspidorhynchid snout.

According to Patterson (1975a: 510), the pachycormid snout is capped by a large rostral bone, which he interpreted as a rostro-dermethmoid. That interpretation has been accepted in subsequent investigations of pachycormids (e.g., Mainwaring, 1978; Lambers, 1988). This bone bears teeth, contains the ethmoid sensory canal commissure, meets the frontals posteriorly, separates the nasals, borders the anterior nostril, and meets the antorbital and premaxilla antero-ventrally. The bones comprising the snout in aspidorhynchids agree in every respect save perhaps the last (depending on whether one accepts or denies the presence of a premaxilla). Support for a pachycormid-aspidorhynchid relationship is found also in: (a) the fact that the pachycormid premaxilla is not always well-developed (it has sometimes been reported that pachycormids lack a premaxilla); (b) the presence of paired pits for the nasal capsule on the posterior surface of the rostro-dermethmoid of *Pachycormus* (Patterson, 1975a, fig. 139); (c) the tendency for the snout to become elongated in certain pachycormids (e.g., *Protosphyraena*; Felix, 1890); and (d) the possibility (never properly confirmed) of a separate "predentary" in *Protosphyraena* (Felix, 1890; Woodward, 1895).

The orbit in *Vinctifer* is surrounded by a supraorbital and an infraorbital series. The single supraorbital bone has an anterior embayment where it abuts the olfactory chamber. Behind this is an elongate dermosphenotic. This is loosely attached to the autosphenotic and is not incorporated into the skull roof. A similar arrangement is found in

other aspidorhynchids. There is a very small canal-bearing nasal bone (rarely preserved) recessed above the olfactory opening between the frontal and rostro-dermethmoid. The supratemporal canal passed through this bone and over the nasal pit (where it may have lain in a flap of skin between the incurrent and excurrent nares). It then presumably swung anteriorly along the sides of the snout, entering the rostral bone farther anteriorly. As was noted above, the "nasal" of *B. helgolandicus* may be the lateral ethmoid; in other aspidorhynchids the nasal is more like that in *Vinctifer*.

In some *Vinctifer* individuals, ganoine has developed across sutures, especially along the lateral margins of the skull roof, thereby obscuring certain osteological features. In other specimens where the sutures are still open, however, the arrangement of the dermal skull roof can be determined with some confidence.

The skull roofing bones of aspidorhynchids are poorly known and their terminology is confused. There is general agreement over the presence of large paired frontals. These extend from the rostral bone, back above the orbits, terminating posteriorly either level with the preopercular ascending ramus (*Vinctifer*, *Belonostomus helgolandicus*) or else slightly ahead of it (*Aspidorhynchus*, *Belonostomus acutirostris*). Behind the frontals of *Vinctifer* there is a pair of "parietals" and a posterior pair of supratemporals (Silva Santos, 1945, 1985b). The presence of the supratemporal commissure within these bones and their relationship to underlying cranial bones support their identification as supratemporals (see below).

Silva Santos (1985b, pl. 1, figs. 2, 3) added to these characters separate dermopterotics flanking the parietals in *Vinctifer*, in much the same way that Saint-Seine (1949, fig. 114) illustrated the "supratemporals" in *Belonostomus* (reinterpreted as dermopterotics by Andrews, et al., 1967). Despite looking at numerous specimens of *Vinctifer* in the AMNH collection, however, not a single example with separate parietals and dermopterotics has been found. Instead, these bones may be fused together in *Vinctifer* to form a parietal-dermopterotic. Support for this is found in the sensory canal arrangement (including a branch for the preopercular canal) and in the relationship of this bone to the underlying pterotic region, in which a descending lamina from the dermopterotic moiety helps to separate the post-temporal fossa from the fossa bridgei (see below). It seems that parietal-dermopterotic fusion also may have occurred in

Aspidorhynchus. Separate parietals and dermopterotics were illustrated in *Belonostomus helgolandicus* by Taverne (1981b, fig. 4).

According to Silva Santos (1985b), the supratemporal canal in *Vinctifer* extends from his "dermopterotic" into the frontal, where it is confluent with the supraorbital canal as described in *Aspidorhynchus* by Assmann (1906). Examination of other material suggests a somewhat different arrangement, however, more as in *Belonostomus* (Saint-Seine, 1949), with the supratemporal canal passing out of the parietal-dermopterotic into the dermosphenotic to form the infraorbital canal. The supraorbital canal terminates close to the posterior margin of the frontal and does not join the supratemporal canal. Farther anteriorly the supraorbital canal leaves the frontal and passes through the nasal, rather than continuing straight onto the rostral bone as suggested by Silva Santos (1985b). As in *Aspidorhynchus*, the supraorbital canal sends off numerous radiating branches, especially at the posterior end of the frontals.

There is a series of five small infraorbitals in *Vinctifer*, but these are weakly ossified in smaller individuals and usually are poorly preserved. The infraorbitals overlie the margins of two large, anamestic suborbitals. The same arrangement occurs in *Belonostomus helgolandicus* (Taverne, 1981b). In "pholidophorids" there also are two or three suborbitals, and there is one in some "leptolepids" and ichthyodectoids, but suborbitals are absent in modern teleosts and *Amia*. The upper suborbital in *Vinctifer* overlies the antero-dorsal part of the hyomandibula but is not attached to it. The bone could be regarded as a dermohyal, but alternatively may be a suprapreopercular (found in *Chanos* and some other primitive teleosts).

An interoperculum (derived from the opercular-gular series) usually occurs only in those actinopterygians where the maxilla is free (the "chondrostean" *Platysiagum* is an exception; Patterson, 1973). There is no interoperculum in *Vinctifer* (nor in other aspidorhynchids), however, even though the maxilla apparently is free. In this important respect, aspidorhynchids are more primitive than pachycormids and modern teleosts.

The jaws are much modified anteriorly. In *Vinctifer* there is an elongate, angled ectopterygoid with a long, tapered anterior splint. The autopalatine is also attenuated anteriorly. In *Belonostomus helgolandicus* the ectopterygoid is broadened anteriorly (Taverne, 1981b), and a similar expansion occurs in Sölnhofen aspidorhynchids. The metapterygoid

bears a lateral process, located more centrally than Taverne (1981) showed in *B. helgolandicus*. In the specimen figured by Brito (1988, fig. 2) the metapterygoid almost certainly is rotated out of its original position.

On the mesial side of the lower jaw the articular-retroarticular is a single bone, as in "pholidophorids" and some "leptolepids" (separate bones were reported by Brito, 1988: 820). A possible surangular is discernible in some *Vinctifer* specimens, partially fused to the articular, but a separate surangular (as in "leptolepids" and modern teleosts) has not been found. The angular is separate in *Vinctifer*, *Belonostomus*, and *Aspidorhynchus*, as in "pholidophorids" and some "leptolepid" teleosts. The mandibular canal is contained within the angular and dentary, emerging from the angular just below the glenoid fossa. The prearticular and dentary together form a low coronoid process in all aspidorhynchids, but it is never pronounced. It is better developed in *Belonostomus* and *Aspidorhynchus* than in *Vinctifer*. Both the maxilla and lower jaw of *Vinctifer* are triangular, with a deep posterior margin. In *Aspidorhynchus*, *Belonostomus helgolandicus*, and especially *B. tenuirostris* the maxilla and entire lower jaw are slender.

The symplectic of *Vinctifer* and *Aspidorhynchus* is splint-like, as in *Lepisosteus* and generalized teleosts. It lies partly on the inner face of the quadrate as in teleosts rather than being remote from it as in *Lepisosteus*. The quadrate lacks a distinct spine-like postero-dorsal process (quadratojugal; Patterson, 1973: 250) as found in teleosts (including "pholidophorids"), but it may be represented in both *Vinctifer* and *Aspidorhynchus* by a small shelf or flange like that at the base of the process in *Pholidophorus germanicus* (Patterson, 1973, fig. 7). A pronounced postero-dorsal process was identified in *Belonostomus helgolandicus* by Taverne (1981b, fig. 5, "p. qj"). In *Vinctifer* the symplectic is overlain by the preopercular, and these bones are in contact. According to Brito (1988: 822) the symplectic contributes to the jaw-joint in halecomorph fashion. However, its distal end is rounded and fails to reach the lower jaw. The symplectic is not attached to the preopercular, unlike in *Amia*. It is concluded that the symplectic and quadrate arrangement in aspidorhynchids is essentially primitive and not halecomorph-like.

In the parasphenoid of *Vinctifer*, *Aspidorhynchus*, and *B. helgolandicus* there is a delicate dermal basipterygoid process lacking any endoskeletal contribution from the prootic.

A similar dermal basipterygoid process occurs in "pholidophorids," "leptolepids," and some primitive teleosts. This condition is considered to be derived (primitively there is also an endoskeletal component), although in *Amia* and most teleosts there is no basipterygoid process at all (Patterson, 1973, 1975a).

There is no buccohypophyseal canal in the parasphenoid of *Vinctifer* or *Aspidorhynchus*. In teleosts this canal is usually absent, but it occurs in "leptolepids," "pholidophorids," *Elops*, some clupeomorphs, and a few other teleosts (Patterson, 1975a). There are no parasphenoid teeth in *Vinctifer*, but a small patch is present in *Aspidorhynchus* and possibly in *B. tenuirostris*. Parasphenoid teeth also are absent in most teleosts, but various primitive neopterygians also lack them (Patterson, 1975a, p. 529). Paired foramina have been found for the internal carotid in *Vinctifer* and *Aspidorhynchus* and also for efferent pseudobranchial arteries in *Vinctifer*. There is no spiracular groove (found in some "pholidophorids"), but in *Vinctifer* there is a groove for the orbital artery (occurs in "pholidophorids," "leptolepids," and primitive living teleosts). Among teleosts, the absence of both grooves is considered a derived condition (Patterson, 1975a, p. 534).

The hind wall of the orbit in bony fishes contains a median embayment, known as the posterior myodome, for housing the rectus muscles that move the eye. This myodome is primitively quite shallow and is confined to the prootics in *Lepisosteus* and *Amia*. In teleosts, "leptolepids," and "pholidophorids," however, the myodome extends farther posteriorly, between the paired saccular recesses in the base of the otic region and into the occipital segment. In *Vinctifer* the myodome is confined to the prootics and does not extend between the saccular recesses. Either the posterior myodome has become secondarily reduced in *Vinctifer* or else is more primitive than in generalized "leptolepid" and "pholidophorid" teleosts. Its postero-lateral wall contains foramina, probably for the abducens nerve (VI) and palatine branch of the facial nerve (VII). A very extensive myodome was reported in *Belonostomus helgolandicus* (Taverne, 1981), suggesting it is more like generalized teleosts than *Vinctifer*. Nevertheless, the "cavite assez grande" considered to be the myodome by Taverne apparently is restricted anteriorly. In *Vinctifer*, which is known from much better-preserved material, two large cavities occur in this region of the braincase: the saccular recesses, and the large notochordal pit located between the occiput and first vertebral centrum (fused to the occiput; see below). The "myodome" found by Taverne in *B. helgolandicus* therefore could be reinterpreted as either the saccular recess or a notochordal pit.

Ossification centers and individual bones of the braincase are indistinct in most specimens of *Vinctifer* because original sutures are largely obliterated. Taverne (1981b) reported the same condition in *Belonostomus helgolandicus*. The entire lateral wall of the braincase is ossified, including the region surrounding the vagus nerve foramen (X). This typically lies between the intercalar and exoccipital bones (e.g., *Amia*, *Pholidophorus*, "leptolepids," teleosts). The intercalar is unossified in *Lepisosteus* (perhaps a primitive condition). *Vinctifer* is interpreted here as possessing an ossified intercalar, even though its exact limits have not been determined. In one specimen of *Aspidorhynchus acutirostris* (AMNH 12482) there are separate prootics and a separate orbitosphenoid. In other specimens sutures still persist between the orbitosphenoid, pterosphenoid, sphenotic, and basisphenoid, even though ossification centers farther posteriorly have become indistinguishably fused.

The pterosphenoid sends off a pronounced lamina (the pedicel), which meets the parasphenoid ascending process ventrally. This lamina sharply defines the lateral wall of the myodome and the inner surface of the spiracular groove, which passes antero-dorsally and then apparently swings laterally to end in a blind-ending spiracular canal at the pterosphenoid-sphenotic suture. According to this interpretation the spiracular canal is situated on the anterior face of the postorbital process, some distance from the hyomandibular facet.

In some *Vinctifer* specimens a narrow unossified gap is present ventro-laterally between the otic and occipital segments, extending almost to the vagus foramen. This gap is interpreted as part of the ventral otic fissure. As in many teleosts, the extent to which this fissure is closed evidently varies, although in the majority of *Vinctifer* specimens it is obliterated. The presence or absence of the open fissure is therefore phylogenetically uninformative (Patterson, 1975a: 466). Its position in *Vinctifer* is noteworthy, however, since in primitive neopterygians it usually marks the position of the hind end of the myodome, but in this case it lies some distance behind the myodome (in "pholidophorids," "leptolepids," and teleosts the myodome secondarily extends past the ventral otic fissure).

184

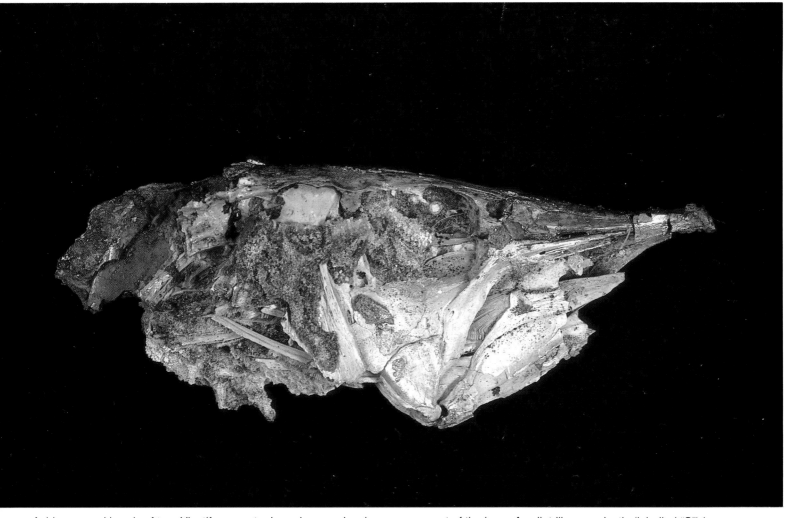

Acid-prepared heads of two *Vinctifer comptoni* specimens, showing arrangement of the jaws. A splint-like symplectic (labelled "S") is visible in the lower example behind the quadrate ("qu"); it is clearly separated by the quadrate from the preopercular (removed here) and does not reach the mandibular joint.

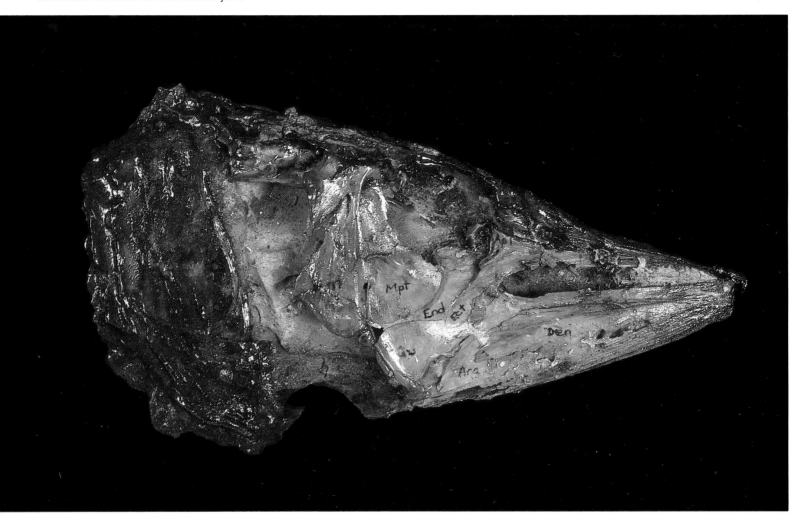

In teleosts generally, the back of the skull is formed into depressions for the insertion of the anteriormost trunk muscles. There usually are paired post-temporal fossae on the hind margin, plus (in many forms) extensions on the top of the skull (known as the fossa bridgei) for anterior slips of the trunk musculature. The post-temporal fossa is very large in some primitive teleosts (e.g., *Elops*) but is absent in chondrosteans, *Lepisosteus*, and fossil paleoniscoid fishes (although the fossa bridgei may be present). In *Vinctifer* the pterotic and dermopterotic bones (forming the upper postero-lateral part of the braincase) are produced posteriorly as a pair of laterally compressed blades. Instead of becoming fused together, these two bones remain separated by a longitudinal suture. Toward the anterior end of the suture is a small fenestra opening into a short, narrow groove on the lateral surface of the pterotic. The blade-like posterior extension of the pterotic and dermopterotic defines the lateral extent of an extremely deep post-temporal fossa, which has become greatly extended in this long-skulled fish. The fenestra and the short groove antero-lateral to it are interpreted as vestiges of the fossa bridgei, and it is possible that a slip of the trunk musculature extended through the fenestra on to the side of the pterotic, terminating just behind the hyomandibular facet. If this interpretation is correct, the post-temporal fossa and fossa bridgei are still partly separated by the pterotic and dermopterotic, as in some Lower Jurassic "pholidophorids," and are not totally confluent as in "leptolepids," Upper Jurassic "pholidophorids," and more advanced teleosts. In living teleosts the medial wall of the post-temporal fossa is formed by the epioccipital bone, but in *Vinctifer* all the bones forming the hind end of the braincase are indistinguishably fused, making recognition of epioccipitals or a teleost-like supraoccipital uncertain. Arambourg and Bertin (1958) alluded to a supraoccipital in *Aspidorhynchus*.

The first vertebral centrum in *Vinctifer* is invariably fused to the occiput, and there are ossified neural arches both for this vertebra and the occipital segment. The notochordal pit can only be observed by grinding away or cutting into the occiput and first vertebra. When this is done, the notochordal pit is found to be lined with a smooth notochordal calcification, as in "pholidophorids." Similar vertebral fusion occurs in *Belonostomus* (e.g., AMNH 12483) and may be a characteristic of all aspidorhynchids.

To summarize, *Vinctifer* displays a mosaic of primitive and derived characters when compared with teleosts. Derived characters shared with pachycormids, "pholidophorids," "leptolepids," and living teleosts include median neural spines (also in *Amia*), lateral dermethmoids, and a free maxilla (the latter also occurs in *Amia*). A free premaxilla may have been secondarily lost in some aspidorhynchids. Shared derived characters of aspidorhynchids and teleosts, but not known in pachycormids, include a possible supraoccipital, monospondylous autocentra (also in *Amia*), dermal basipterygoid process, ossified intercalar, and post-temporal fossa (also in *Amia*). Aspidorhynchids, "leptolepids," and living teleosts also share hypurals 1 and 2 fused and associated with the first ural centrum, epaxial fin-rays, absence of ossified radials on hemal spines, absence of any endoskeletal contribution to the basipterygoid process, and absence of a spiracular groove. The absence of a buccohypohyseal canal and of parasphenoid teeth in *Vinctifer* suggests it is more derived than "pholidophorid" and "leptolepid" teleosts, but the presence of pharyngeal teeth in other aspidorhynchids shows that their absence is convergent.

Aspidorhynchids are more primitive than living teleosts in numerous character states, including the presence of ganoine, fulcral scales, peg-and-socket scale articulations, caudal hemichordacentra, suborbital bones, compound articular- retroarticular, basipterygoid process, groove for orbital artery, short myodome, separation of the fossa bridgei and post-temporal fossa by pterotic and dermopterotic, and absence of an interoperculum.

From the above list it is fairly clear that aspidorhynchids are primitive teleostean halecostomes. It is difficult to formulate a more specific hypothesis concerning aspidorhynchid relationships. Some possibilities (in descending order of probability) are: 1) aspidorhynchids are the sister-group of all other teleosteans, including pachycormids, "pholidophorids," "leptolepids," and living taxa; or 2) they are the sister-group of pachycormids (suggested by rostral morphology), with which they collectively form the sister-group of all other teleosts; or 3) aspidorhynchids occupy a more derived phylogenetic position than pachycormids and "pholidophorids" (suggested by caudal fin morphology, but inconsistent with many other cladistically primitive features of aspidorhynchids). As far as the myodome is concerned, the skull of *Vinctifer* is greatly elongated, and its otic and occipital regions display many unusual features related to this elongation. The myodome may have become secondarily reduced as part of this modification.

Lambers (1988, based in part on data from Mainwaring, 1978) defined pachycormids on the basis of six characters that were considered to be derived (compound rostro-dermethmoid meeting frontals and separating premaxillae and nasals; no supraorbitals, dorsal margin of orbit formed by dermosphenotic; at least nine infraorbitals; no extrascapulars, supratemporal commissural canal contained by dermopterotics; pectoral fins scythe-like, fin-rays branching only at their extreme ends; distinctive uroneural morphology). Aspidorhynchids share only the first of these attributes with pachycormids, apparently retaining the primitive state of the other five.

Vinctifer, Aspidorhynchus, and *Belonostomus* share several derived characters regarded here as aspidorhynchid synapomorphies. These characters include the fusiform body with caudally-located median fins, elongate flank scales, elongate snout (including a rostral bone, lateral dermethmoids, and vomer), a toothed predentary, large triangular preoperculum with posteriorly located sensory canal, absence of a free premaxilla, an elongate dermopterotic flanking a deep post-temporal fossa, and perhaps fusion between the occiput and first centrum.

Within the Aspidorhynchidae, *Vinctifer* and *Belonostomus helgolandicus* possess small, undifferentiated teeth, as in generalized teleosts. Larger teeth (as in *B. tenuirostris* and *Aspidorhynchus*) may be a derived feature (analogous to the situation among pachycormids and ichthyodectids). *Vinctifer* is also primitive in having the dermosphenotic separated from the preoperculum by the suborbital series (e.g., as in *Lepisosteus, Amia, Pachycormus, Hulettia*). A similar arrangement is seen in *Aspidorhynchus* (Assmann, 1906), but in *Belonostomus tenuirostris* (and to a lesser extent in *B. helgolandicus*) the dermosphenotic extends back to the vertical tip of the preopercular, separating the suborbitals from the skull roof (Saint-Seine, 1949; Taverne, 1981).

Although the flank scales of all aspidorhynchids are elongate, those of *Aspidorhynchus* are less so than in the other taxa. *Aspidorhynchus* scales also lack ganoine, unlike in other aspidorhynchids. There is a small, ill-defined coronoid process on the lower jaw in *Aspidorhynchus* and *Belonostomus,* but in *Vinctifer* it is absent. Fusion between

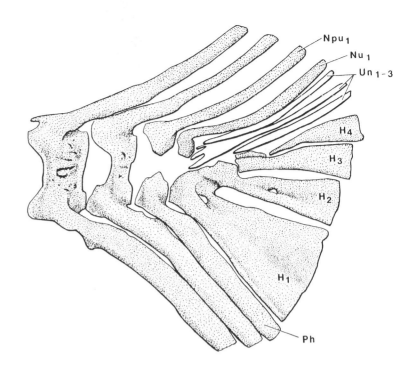

Vinctifer comptoni. Caudal endoskeleton, from AMNH 13107.

endocranial bones occurs in *Vinctifer* and *Belonostomus* but may not occur in *Aspidorhynchus*. The predentary is short in *Aspidorhynchus* and *Vinctifer* but is much longer in *Belonostomus* where the "rostral" dentition also is more extensive. A supramaxilla is primitively present in *Aspidorhynchus* and *Belonostomus,* but is absent in *Vinctifer,* which also has a deeper maxilla and mandible, more triangular ectopterygoid, and ventrally broader preopercular than in other aspidorhynchids.

In most of these characters, *Aspidorhynchus* possesses the primitive state when comparisons are made with other generalized halecostome taxa. One exception is its differentiated dentition, which is like that of *Belonostomus tenuistriatus,* but this feature is not ubiquitous even within *Belonostomus,* and its presence here and in *Aspidorhynchus* may be convergent.

A toothed predentary is fairly unusual among teleosts; one is present in *Saurodon* (an icthyodectoid) and perhaps in the pachycormid *Protosphyraena.* If one considers a short predentary to be primitive, then *Belonostomus* is derived. On the other hand, if one considers the presence of teeth along the entire lateral dermethmoid and premaxillary margin to be primitive, then *Vinctifer* and *Aspidorhynchus* are derived. This interpretation seems less congruent with other character distributions than the first, however, and it is concluded that *Aspidorhynchus* is a cladistically primitive genus

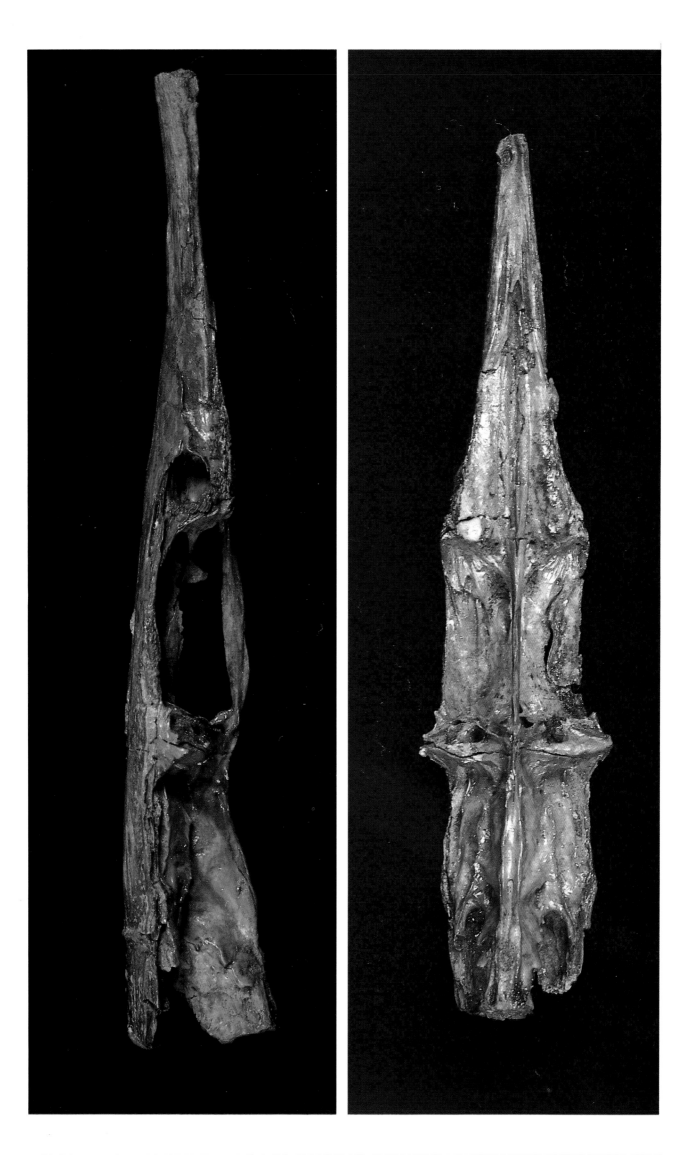

of aspidorhynchid displaying one autapomorphy (loss of scale ganoine) and a convergent character (enlarged teeth). *Vinctifer* and *Belonostomus* share elongate lateral line scales and endocranial fusion. *Vinctifer* uniquely possesses a deep, triangular maxilla, mandible, and pterygoid, plus a broad preopercular, and lacks a coronoid process. *Belonostomus* has a long predentary and completely toothed snout, and some species (e.g., *B. tenuirostris*) acquired large teeth independently of *Aspidorhynchus*. *Belonostomus* also is peculiar in its dermosphenotic arrangement.

Vinctifer is one of the most common fossil fishes from the Santana formation, surpassed in numbers only by *Rhacolepis* and perhaps *Tharrhias*. *Vinctifer comptoni* is known primarily from the Araripe basin, but it has also been recorded from the Riachuelo formation of the Sergipe-Alagoas basin (Silva Santos, 1981; also see earlier in this volume). Another species, *V. punctatus*, was described from the Muribeca formation of the Sergipe-Alagoas basin (Silva Santos, 1985a). Yet another species (*V. longirostris*) has been recognized in the Marizal formation of Bahia (Silva Santos, 1972) and is supposedly different from "*Belonostomus*" *carinatus*, founded upon some rhombic ganoid scales that also were collected from Bahia (Mawson and Woodward, 1907).

Vinctifer has yet to be unequivocally demonstrated from African Cretaceous deposits, but Taverne (1969) described the caudal region of a supposed *Belonostomus* from the Lower Cretaceous of Equatorial Guinea. The specimen lacks the head and could just as readily represent *Vinctifer* as *Belonostomus*. Some Brazilian stratigraphers have suggested that *Vinctifer* is a useful "zone-fossil" (i.e., can be used to establish the same relative age of strata in different regions containing the same fossils). Brito and Campos (1982) and Brito (1984) have recognized a "*Vinctifer* Biozone," supposedly marking the transition from a local stage (the Alagoan) to an internationally recognized one (Upper Aptian). However, the utility of this "*Vinctifer* Biozone" is questionable (discussed elsewhere in this volume).

Assemblages: Santana, Jardim, Old Mission; rare and small in Santana concretions, generally largest in Old Mission concretions. *Vinctifer* also is reported from a new locality in bituminous shales at Pedra Blanca, near Nova Olinda (Viana, Brito & Silva-Telles, MS).

(J. G. Maisey)

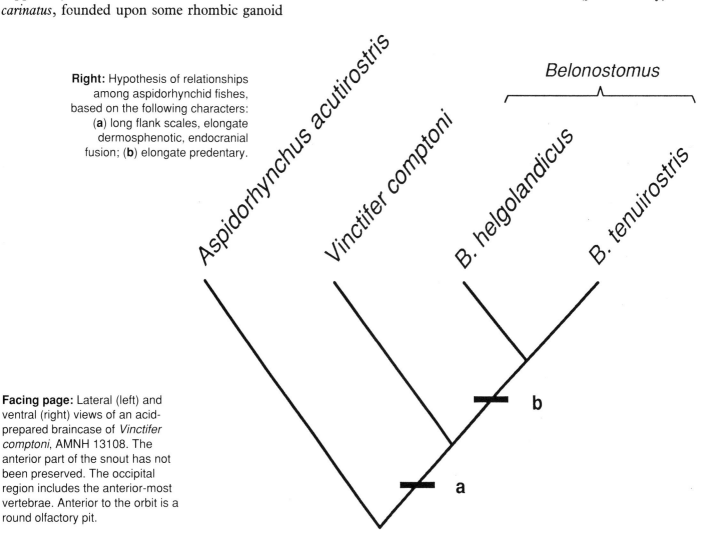

Right: Hypothesis of relationships among aspidorhynchid fishes, based on the following characters: (**a**) long flank scales, elongate dermosphenotic, endocranial fusion; (**b**) elongate predentary.

Facing page: Lateral (left) and ventral (right) views of an acid-prepared braincase of *Vinctifer comptoni*, AMNH 13108. The anterior part of the snout has not been preserved. The occipital region includes the anterior-most vertebrae. Anterior to the orbit is a round olfactory pit.

CLADOCYCLUS Agassiz, 1841

Division HALECOSTOMI
Subdivision TELEOSTEI
incertae sedis
Order ICHTHYODECTIFORMES (Bardack and Sprinkle, 1969)
Suborder ICHTHYODECTOIDEI (Romer, 1966)
Family CLADOCYCLIDAE, **new family**
Diagnosis: Ichthyodectoids with the supraoccipital crest extending posteriorly to overhang the occiput; vertebral count as low as 40, never exceeding 64, with greatest variation in number of abdominal centra.
Genus *Cladocyclus* Agassiz, 1841
   1841 *Cladocyclus* Agassiz: 83
   1871 *Anaedopogon* Cope: 53
   1909 *Proportheus* Jaekel: 396
   1919 *Ennelichthys* Jordan: 208
Diagnosis: Cladocyclids with maxillary and premaxillary teeth of comparable size, but mandibular teeth slightly larger and enlarged to form fangs anteriorly; approximately 64 vertebrae.
Type species: *Cladocyclus gardneri* Agassiz.

Cladocyclus gardneri Agassiz
   1841 *Cladocyclus gardneri* Agassiz: 83
   1844a *Cladocyclus gardneri* Ag.; Agassiz: 8, 103
   1844b *Cladocyclus gardneri* Agassiz: 1013
   1871 *Anaedopogon tenuidens* Cope: 53
   1888 *Cladocyclus gardneri* Ag.; Woodward: 326
   1890 *Anaedopogon tenuidens* Cope; Woodward: 394
   1901 *Cladocyclus gardneri* Ag.; Woodward: 108
   1908 *Cladocyclus gardneri* Ag.; Jordan & Branner: 26
   1919 *Ennelichthys derbyi* Jordan: 208
   1923 *Anaedopogon tenuidens* Cope; Jordan: 68
   1923 *Ennelichthys derbyi* Jordan; Jordan: 80
   1923 *Cladocyclus gardneri* Ag.; Jordan: 87
   1938 *Cladocyclus gardneri* Ag.; D'Erasmo: 38
   1950 *Cladocyclus gardneri* Ag; Silva Santos: 128
   1965 *Cladocyclus gardneri* Ag.; Bardack: 36
   1977 *Cladocyclus* sp. (in part); Patterson & Rosen: 91
   1986 *Cladocyclus gardneri* Ag; Mones: 36
Emended diagnosis: Large *Cladocyclus*, sometimes exceeding 1 meter standard length; orbit diameter ⅕ of head length; circumorbital

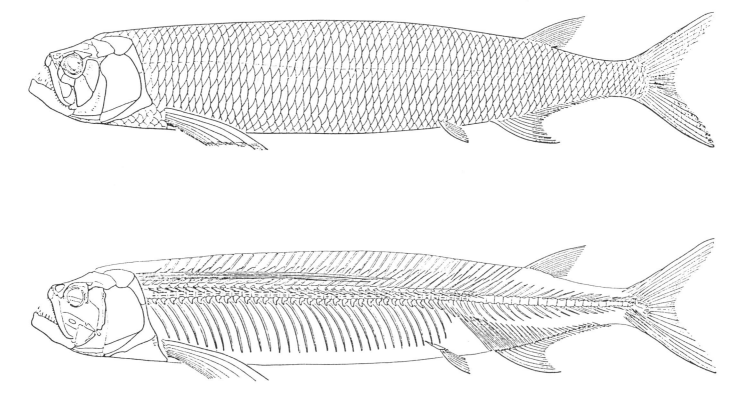

Cladocyclus gardneri. Skeletal reconstruction.

bones strongly pitted; margins of opercular, subopercular, and preopercular entire, not fringed; preopercular canal with many (30-35) branches; infraorbital canal also with numerous branches; premaxillary teeth twice as long as maxillary teeth; first and second pectoral fin-rays of approximately equal width.

Cotypes of *Cladocyclus gardneri*: British Museum (Natural History), BM(NH) 28901A; two fragments labeled by L. Agassiz, one a much fractured head, anterior abdominal scales and part of the pectoral fin, the other a portion of the abdominal region showing vertebrae; Santana formation, perhaps from Jardim.

Holotype of *Anaedopogon tenuidens*: National Museum of Natural History, Washington D. C., USNM 4231.

Holotype of *Ennelichthys derbyi*: Divisão de Geologia e Mineralogia, Departamento Nacional da Produção Mineral, Rio de Janeiro, DGM-DNPM 215-P; counterpart California Academy of Sciences (*ex* Stanford University Department of Geology), CAS 58200.

Cladocyclus ferus Silva Santos

1950 *Cladocyclus ferus* Silva Santos: 130

1965 *Cladocyclus ferus* Silva Santos; Bardack: 36

1977 *Cladocyclus* sp. (in part); Patterson & Rosen: 91

1986 *Cladocyclus ferus* Silva Santos; Mones: 36

Emended diagnosis: Smaller *Cladocyclus*, usually below 50 cm standard length; orbit diameter slightly under one-fourth of head length; circumorbital bones smooth; margins of opercular, subopercular, and preopercular fringed; preopercular canal with about 15 branches; infraorbital canal also with few branches; premaxillary and maxillary teeth of comparable size; first pectoral fin-ray twice width of second.

Holotype: Divisão de Geologia e Mineralogia, Departamento Nacional da Produção Mineral, Rio de Janeiro DGM-DNPM 527-P; head, anterior part of abdominal region, and pectoral fin; Santana formation, Romualdo, near Crato, Ceará.

Cladocyclus gardneri is one of the seven original species of fossil fishes from the Santana formation to be named by Agassiz (1841, 1844a). As the synonymy list given above indicates, some other species erected subsequently are now regarded as synonyms of *Cladocyclus gardneri* (Silva Santos, 1950). In passing it should be noted that Mones (1986: 36) erroneously gave an 1839 date for Agassiz (1844a: 8, 103) and declared that to be the earliest mention of *C. gardneri*. It appears that Mones misread the publication dates of *Poissons Fossiles* vol. V (for these, see Brown, 1900).

While placing *Anaedopogon tenuidens* and *Ennelichthys derbyi* into synonymy with *Cladocyclus gardneri*, Silva Santos (1950) also erected another species, distinguishing it from *C. gardneri* by several features that are given in the species diagnoses presented here. As pointed out by Patterson and Rosen (1977), however, distinction at the species level is not always straight-forward, and some specimens seem to exhibit a mixture of features. The two species recognized by Silva Santos (1950) are retained here because *Cladocyclus* specimens from the Santana formation appear to fall broadly into two groups, more or less along the lines indicated. A more detailed investigation of the Santana formation ichthyodectids would be desirable in view of this taxonomic uncertainty.

Cladocyclus is a member of an important group of large, predaceous extinct teleost fishes known as ichthyodectoids. The largest and most spectacular of these appeared during the Upper Cretaceous, including *Gillicus* at 1.5 meters and *Xiphactinus* (= "*Portheus*") at over 4 meters. All were elongate, slender, and laterally compressed, with strongly forked mackerel-like tails, narrow caudal peduncle, stiffened hydrofoil-like pectorals, and a huge gape that was angled obliquely and armed with many needle-sharp, fang-like teeth. There is plenty of evidence that some ichthyodectoids were ferocious predators. From the Niobrara Chalk of Kansas, huge specimens of *Xiphactinus* have been collected with large *Gillicus* skeletons inside, evidently swallowed head-first. From the Santana formation, at least one *Cladocyclus* in the American Museum collection (AMNH 2983) managed to hunt down and swallow an entire *Rhacolepis* tail-first. This supports the morphological evidence that *Cladocyclus* was capable of high swimming speeds.

It is possible that the Ichthyodectidae of Patterson and Rosen (1977) do not form a natural (i.e., monophyletic) group. They share at least two features that Patterson and Rosen (1977) considered derived (parietals of the skull roof fused into a single median bone; a basal sclerotic bone with serrated margins present behind the eye). According to as-yet unpublished data, however, both these features have been found in saurodontids (J. F. Stewart, pers. comm.), contrary to earlier opinion (Bardack and Sprinkle, 1969; Patterson and Rosen, 1977).

The following genera were provisionally included by Patterson and Rosen (1977) in the

Chriocentrus sp., a Recent wolfherring. Art by Tomita. Although it is no longer considered a close relative of ichthyodectiform fishes, there is a strong overall similarity of body shape, suggesting a similar pattern of behavior.

Ichthyodectidae; *Ichthyodectes, Xiphactinus, Gillicus, Cladocyclus, Eubiodectes, Proportheus, Chirocentrites, Thrissops,* and *Spathodactylus.* Of these, it was suggested that *Eubiodectes* and some Cretaceous species of *"Thrissops"* may be synonymous with *Ichthyodectes,* while some other *Thrissops* species may be *Gillicus,* and that *Chirocentrites* may be synonymous with *Xiphactinus* and *Proportheus* synonymous with *Cladocyclus.* On the basis of Taverne's (1986) redescription of *Chirocentrites vexillifer,* however, the genus is probably distinct. Taverne (ibid.) nevertheless regarded *Spathodactylus* as a junior synonym of *Chirocentrites.* He also maintained that *Eubiodectes* and *Ichthyodectes* are distinct. Minimizing the genera this way would leave only *Ichthyodectes, Xiphactinus, Gillicus, Cladocyclus, Chirocentrites,* and perhaps some species of *Thrissops.* Silva Santos (1950) and Bardack (1965) treated *Chiromystus* Cope (1885) as a synonym of *Cladocyclus,* but there are grounds for resurrecting Cope's genus (discussed below).

Woodward (1901: 198) was of the opinion that *Cladocyclus* differed from *Ichthyodectes* only in the position of its dorsal fin, which he believed to be above the pelvics in *Cladocyclus* instead of opposite the anal fin as in *Icthyodectes.* In fact, the dorsal fin of *C. gardneri* and *C. ferus* is opposite the anal, even slightly posterior to it. The specimen on which Woodward's (1901) opinion was based is almost certainly a composite "reconstruction." The correct position of the dorsal fin was determined by Silva Santos (1950: 128) and is confirmed by many other specimens. *Cladocyclus* was nevertheless retained as a distinct genus by Bardack (1965) and by Patterson and Rosen (1977), a view which is maintained here. *Proportheus* is included here as a synonym of *Cladocyclus* for reasons that will be outlined below (see also Taverne, 1986).

Patterson and Rosen (1977) placed ichthyodectids within a higher group (suborder Ichthyodectoidei), along with *Saurodon* and *Saurocephalus,* which were placed in a separate family (Saurodontidae). The latter differ from other ichthyodectoids in possessing a median, toothless predentary bone and a notch or foramen at the base of each tooth in the maxilla, premaxilla, and dentary.

Ichthyodectoids have been characterized by six complex morphological characters in the head and tail (Patterson and Rosen, 1977: 115). These characters are: (1) high, triangular supraoccipital crest, with the parietals displaced forward; (2) intercalar enlarged, forming part of the hyomandibular facet and enclosing a canal for the jugular vein; (3) ethmo-palatine bone with membranous outgrowths separating and suturing with the rostro-dermethmoid and lateral ethmoid; (4) palatine head modified into disc-like malleolus (articular surface for the ethmoid region of the braincase); (5) angular bone contributes to the articular facet for the quadrate; (6) first hypural set into ural centrum by a ball-and-socket joint. Taverne (1986) found saurodontids and ichthyodectids (excluding *Thrissops*) similar in additional features: (7) premaxilla articulates posteriorly with maxilla; (8) deep dentary symphysis.

The order Ichthyodectiformes contains the ichthyodectoids, as well as the Upper Jurassic genus *Allothrissops,* which was placed in its own suborder Allothrissopoidei by Patterson and Rosen (1977). These taxa share five characters, including: (1) floor of nasal capsule has an ethmo-palatine ossification; (2) uroneurals in the caudal fin, with the first three or four extending antero-ventrally to cover the sides of the first, second, and third pre-ural centra; (3) teeth in a single series on the jaws; (4) coracoids enlarged and meeting each other in a midventral symphysis; (5) anal fin long, falcate, and

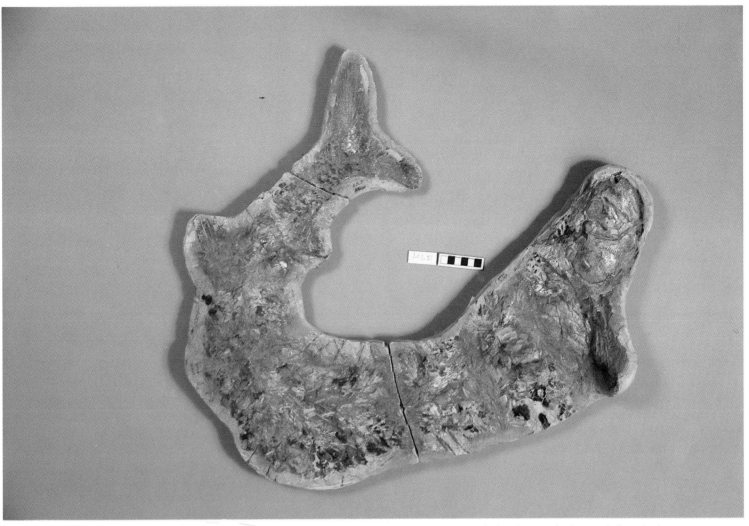

Cladocyclus gardneri. Two examples, one extremely large in "Jardim" matrix (top) and showing marked necrolytic spinal curvature, the other (below) much smaller, from the Crato member limestones. Lower photo courtesy Dr. H. Frickinger (Munich).

opposed by a short, remote dorsal fin.

According to Patterson and Rosen (1977), *Allothrissops* differs from ichthyodectoids in lacking a suborbital bone, having the infraorbital sensory canal ending blindly in the lacrymal bone, and having caudal hemal arches fused with the centra. However, this distinction is lessened by the presence of the last character in large specimens of *Thrissops formosus* and *T. subovatus* (Schaeffer and Patterson, 1984: 50) and by the absence of a suborbital in some specimens of *Cladocyclus*.

Until fairly recently it was commonly supposed that all these fishes were related to the living wolf herring, *Chirocentrus dorab*, a small, elongate fish today confined to the Indian Ocean and China Seas (Woodward, 1901; Silva Santos, 1950; Bardack, 1965). That view was questioned by Cavender (1966) and by Greenwood, et al. (1966), who suggested that ichthyodectids are much more primitive teleost fishes than *Chirocentrus*, which is generally considered to be a clupeomorph (herring-like group). Patterson and Rosen (1977, fig. 54) expanded this concept cladistically and concluded that the ichthyodectiforms are an extinct sister-group to all living teleosts. This hypothesis leaves the ichthyodectiform fishes with no living descendents.

Patterson and Rosen (1977) attempted firstly to establish whether ichthyodectiform fishes are monophyletic, and secondly to determine their phylogenetic position among teleosts. Although morphological data supporting monophyly of the ichthyodectoids and saurodontids were presented, phylogenetic relationships among the various genera were not investigated. This question had earlier been studied by Bardack (1965), although his approach was essentially phenetic and did not involve searching for shared derived characters as evidence of relationship. Taverne (1986) presented an explicit hypothesis of relationship among various ichthyodectids based on some thirty characters.

Bardack (1965) and Taverne (1986) considered the phylogenetic position of *Cladocyclus*. Now that more is known concerning *Cladocyclus* it seems worthwhile to review the relationships of the better known ichthyodectid genera (*Ichthyodectes, Xiphactinus, Gillicus, Cladocyclus, Chirocentrites, Chiromystus*) from a more rigorous phylogenetic viewpoint.

These taxa were grouped by Bardack (1965) into a "*Xiphactinus* group." He believed that the supposedly earliest (Neocomian) genus *Spathodactylus* is also the most primitive one

phylogenetically (a view shared by Taverne, 1986), resembling certain species of *Thrissops* in the straightness of its maxillary border, low coronoid process, enlarged mandibular dentition, vertebral number, anal fin-ray count, and scale morphology. Characters thought to unite *Spathodactylus* with other members of the "*Xiphactinus* group" by Bardack (1965) included body length over 1 m, teeth in deep alveoli, maxillary with straight dental border and dentition of uniform size, mandible with straight alveolar border, mandibular teeth larger than those of the maxilla, enlarged lateral ridge on vertebral centra, and broad pectoral fin.

Bardack (1965) separated *Gillicus* from all remaining members of his "*Xiphactinus* group" apart from the poorly known genus *Prymnetes*. *Gillicus* was differentiated on the basis of its sharp parasphenoid flexure, falcate maxilla, deep and short mandible, and dentition of minute teeth. Although *Gillicus* was effectively treated as the sister-group of *Ichthyodectes, Xiphactinus*, and *Chirocentrites* (Bardack, 1965, fig. 3), it is not clear whether the characters used to differentiate *Gillicus* are autapomorphies or plesiomorphic characters; in either case, they are phylogenetically uninformative about higher level relationships.

According to Bardack (1965: 20), *Cladocyclus* is closely allied to *Xiphactinus, Ichthyodectes* and *Chirocentrites*. He implied that *Xiphactinus, Ichthyodectes*, and *Chirocentrites* are collectively more derived than *Cladocyclus*, and that *Xiphactinus* and *Ichthyodectes* are together the most advanced members of the group. There is clearly a problem with all of this if *Chirocentrites* and *Spathodactylus* are synonymous as Taverne (1986) contended.

The two characters used by Patterson and Rosen (1977: 116) to unite ichthyodectids (single median parietal bone, basal sclerotic bone) are not known in material originally referred to *Spathodactylus* (Pictet, 1858; Bardack, 1965), but both are present in *Chirocentrites vexillifer* (Taverne, 1986). The characters said by Bardack (1965) to unite *Spathodactylus* and other ichthyodectids are difficult to evaluate (Nelson, 1973), although among ichthyodectiforms the presence of deep alveoli, the straight alveolar borders of the maxilla and mandible, the enlarged maxillary teeth, and the enlarged lateral ridge on the vertebral centra all may represent derived characters. Taverne's (1986) view that *Spathodactylus* and *Chirocentrites* are synonymous is compelling, and there is no longer any reason to regard *Spathodactylus* as an *incertae sedis* member of the Ichthyodectoidei.

sprattiformis and presumably represents the primitive teleost condition.

The otic region of the parasphenoid is angled at approximately 160° in *Xiphactinus* and 150° in *Ichthyodectes*, but in *Gillicus* the angle is sharper (around 130°). Bardack (1965) used the difference in parasphenoid angle to emphasize the distinctiveness of *Gillicus*, but a comparable angle occurs in *Cladocyclus*, *Saurodon*, and probably *Allothrissops*, as well as in pachyrhizodontids, pholidophorids, and leptolepids (Bardack and Sprinkle, 1967; Patterson, 1975a; Forey, 1977). While the utility of such a character is questionable, it does appear that the parasphenoid profile is consistently straighter in *Ichthyodectes* and *Xiphactinus* among ichthyodectiform fishes, perhaps in relation to some specialization in the suspensorial arrangement. In this regard it also may be significant that in *Xiphactinus* and *Ichthyodectes* the long axis of the hyomandibular facet is oriented almost parallel to the orbital part of the parasphenoid in lateral view, whereas in *Gillicus*, *Cladocyclus*, *Saurodon*, *Allothrissops*, and many primitive teleosts the same axis is tilted toward the ethmoid region in the snout. As restored by Taverne (1986, fig. 3), the parasphenoid angle in *Chirocentrites* is around 150°, but the shape of the occipital region is conjectural and the angle could be less. From Taverne's fig. 2, the long axis of the hyomandibular facet passes through the ethmoid region as in *Cladocyclus*.

A large dermal basipterygoid process is primitively present in teleosts but is absent in most living forms (Patterson, 1975: 529). It is well-developed in ichthyodectoids (Bardack, 1965; Bardack and Sprinkle, 1967; Patterson and Rosen, 1977; Taverne, 1986). This process usually is angled slightly downward, forward, and outward, but in *Gillicus* and *Cladocyclus* it is angled upward and outward.

Ichthyodectoid dentitions appear to be divergently specialized. This variation may provide some generically diagnostic features. The dentition of *Gillicus* consists entirely of small, uniform teeth as in *Allothrissops* and primitive teleosts. Slightly larger and stouter uniform teeth characterize *Ichthyodectes* as well as *Thrissops*, *Occithrissops*, and saurodontids (Bardack, 1965; Bardack and Sprinkle, 1967; Patterson and Rosen, 1977; Schaeffer and Patterson, 1984). Some anterior premaxillary teeth of *Ichthyodectes* are slightly enlarged, but not to the extent seen in *Xiphactinus*. Two premaxillary teeth supposedly are enlarged in *Chirocentrites* (Heckel, 1849, 1850), perhaps

In ichthyodectoids there is a well-developed triangular supraoccipital crest extending forward onto the skull roof, where it contacts a median parietal. In *Saurodon* the supraoccipital crest is said to meet paired parietals (Bardack and Sprinkle, 1969) although this is contested by J. D. Stewart (pers. comm.), who claims that an unpaired parietal is present in both *Saurodon* and *Saurocephalus* (which would elevate this character to an ichthyodectoid synapomorphy). In *Chirocentrites*, *Chiromystus*, *Gillicus*, *Cladocyclus*, and *Saurodon* the crest is formed only by the supraoccipital, and its leading edge is angled outward only slightly from the profile of the orbitotemporal region (albeit more so in *Cladocyclus* and *Gillicus* than in *Saurodon*). In *Xiphactinus* and *Ichthyodectes*, however, the median parietal forms an anterior extension of the supraoccipital crest (Bardack, 1965, figs. 6, 14), and the crest projects abruptly from the orbitotemporal profile. The posterior margin of the crest generally does not extend behind the level of the occiput, except in *Cladocyclus*, *Chiromystus*, and *Chirocentrites*, where it curves posteriorly so that over half its length is behind the occiput. In *Saurodon*, *Cladocyclus*, and *Chirocentrites* the paired epioccipitals extend anteriorly approximately half as far as the supraoccipital before meeting the parietal (Bardack and Sprinkle, 1967, fig. 2; Patterson and Rosen, 1977, fig. 4; Taverne, 1986, fig. 3). In *Gillicus* and *Xiphactinus* the epioccipitals extend farther anteriorly, although the supraoccipital is still longer (Bardack, 1965, figs. 5, 18). The most extreme condition occurs in *Ichthyodectes*, where the epioccipitals and supraoccipital are almost of the same length (Bardack, 1965, fig. 15).

In *Allothrissops*, leptolepids, and other primitive teleosts the supraoccipital is small, the parietals are paired, and the epioccipitals are confined largely to the posterior face of the braincase (Patterson, 1975; Patterson and Rosen, 1977).

In *Cladocyclus* there are no foramina piercing the supraoccipital to form a communication with the subtemporal fossa. The latter is small but extremely deep. No distinction can be made between the post-temporal and subepiotic fossae, which are essentially confluent.

The nasal bone of *Ichthyodectes*, *Xiphactinus*, and *Gillicus* is subdivided into two elements (Bardack, 1965). In *Cladocyclus*, however, the nasal bone is single (Patterson and Rosen, 1977). The condition in *Saurodon* and *Chirocentrites* is unknown. A single nasal is present in *Allothrissops*, *Tharsis dubius*, and *Leptolepides* allying this Albian-Cenomanian genus with the stratigraphically younger *Xiphactinus*. However, in *C. vexillifer* the premaxilla, maxilla, and dentary are edentulous (Taverne, 1986). *Cladocyclus gardneri* has greatly enlarged, fang-like anterior teeth on the dentary (Silva Santos, 1950). Other South American species formerly referred to *Chiromystus* (e.g., *C. mawsoni* Cope, 1885; *C. alagoensis* Jordan, 1910) possess similarly enlarged mandibular teeth and have been referred to *Cladocyclus* (Silva Santos, 1950; Bardack, 1965), but see later in this section. In *C. woodwardi* the mandibular teeth display less size differentiation (Silva Santos, 1949) and this species has been placed in a separate genus (*Itaparica*), partly for this reason (Silva Santos, 1986), although there seems little to distinguish this species from other members of *Cladocyclus* in the broad sense (see below).

Jaekel (1909) described an incomplete specimen of Cretaceous ichthyodectid from Cameroon as a new genus and species, *Proportheus kameruni*. Weiler (1922) subsequently described *Chirocentrites? guinensis* from strata in Spanish (now Equatorial) Guinea. These species were synonymized by Bardack (1965). Examination of two specimens of "*C. guinensis*" (AMNH 6302, head and trunk; AMNH 8394, complete individual) reveals the presence of enlarged anterior mandibular teeth, suggesting that this form (and *Proportheus kameruni*) should be referred to *Cladocyclus*, as suggested by Patterson and Rosen (1977).

On the lower jaw, Nelson (1973a) found that the mandibular joint was developed only on two bones (the angular and articular) in *Ichthyodectes*, *Xiphactinus*, *Gillicus*, and *Saurodon*, an apparently derived condition (according to Bardack, 1965, the joint is confined to the angular in *Gillicus*, but this is shown to be incorrect from AMNH 8563; Nelson, 1973a, fig. 6A). In *Cladocyclus*, Patterson and Rosen (1977) identified a presumably more primitive arrangement in which the articular surface is shared by three bones (angular, articular, and retroarticular, seen in AMNH 9980 and 9981). Unfortunately the condition of the mandibular joint is unknown in other ichthyodectoids, although Taverne (1986: 38) presumed it included all three elements in *Chirocentrites*.

According to a hypothesis developed by Nelson (1973b), the primitive teleostean condition (seen in "leptolepids" and *Allothrissops*, for example) is for the mandibular joint to be formed only by the articular and retroarticular. In modern elopomorphs, the angular becomes fused with the retroarticular and secondarily may become involved with the joint surface. In clupeomorphs and higher euteleosteans the angular becomes fused with the articular and again may become involved secondarily in forming part of the joint. Both the elopomorph and clupeomorph-higher euteleostean conditions can be considered derived. According to Forey (1977), the clupeomorph-euteleostean condition is found in *Rhacolepis* and North American species of *Pachyrhizodus*, separating these fossils from modern elopomorphs. In *Notelops* a separate angular, articular, and retroarticular are present, as in *Cladocyclus*. This may represent a primitive teleost condition (Nelson, 1973a; Forey, 1977) retained plesiomorphically by *Notelops* and *Cladocyclus*. In *Notelops* only the articular and retroarticular contribute to the mandibular joint, which again may be primitive. In *Cladocyclus*, however, there seems to be an additional angular contribution to the joint. According to the phylogenetic hypothesis presented by Patterson and Rosen (1977), the retroarticular failed to contribute to the mandibular joint in two separate ichthyodectoid lineages (saurodontids and derived members of the Ichthyodectidae). According to more recent investigation this character could be a synapomorphy of these taxa (J.D. Stewart, pers. comm.).

Facing page: Various *Cladocyclus* specimens, including the two "syntypes" of *C. gardneri* (top left, bottom left) in the British Museum (Natural History) collection; the two "paratypes" of *Ennelichthys derbyi* (center) in the California Academy of Sciences; head of a complete *Cladocyclus* (top right) and a partially disarticulated *Cladocyclus* skeleton (bottom right), both in "Santana" matrix.

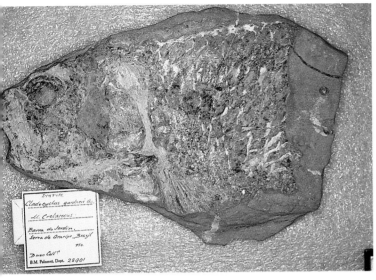

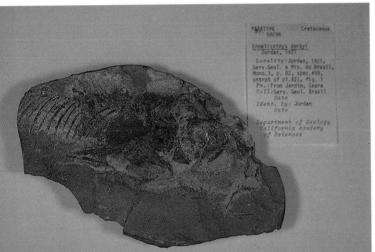

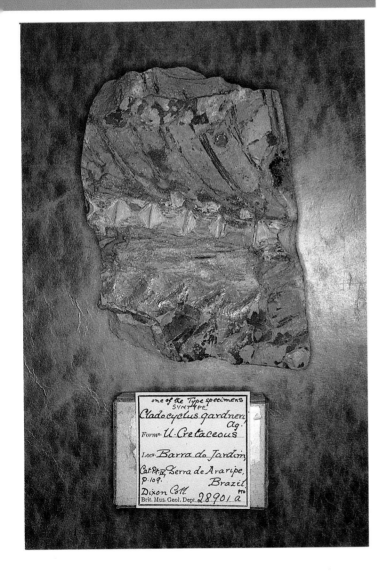

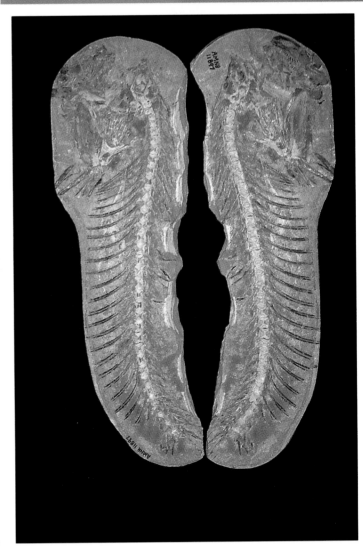

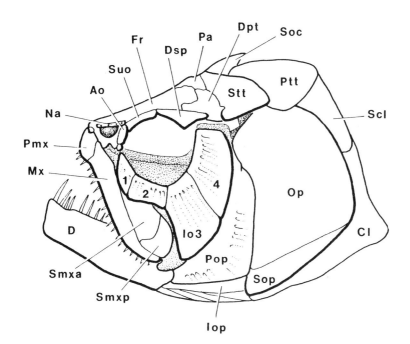

Cladocyclus gardneri. Outline reconstruction of head in lateral view.

The hyomandibula of *Cladocyclus* lacks a preopercular process like the one found in *Allothrissops* by Patterson and Rosen (1977, fig. 9). It also is lacking in *Chirocentrites*, *Xiphactinus*, and *Saurodon*; instead, the preoperculum fits against a prominent vertical ridge extending down the lateral surface of the hyomandibula from just below the braincase to just above the symplectic (Bardack, 1965; Bardack and Sprinkle, 1967; Taverne, 1986). A preopercular process occurs in primitive "leptolepid" euteleosteans, and its absence probably is a derived condition.

There is a large fenestra within the distal ceratohyal of *Cladocyclus*, *Ichthyodectes*, and *Allothrissops* (Bardack, 1965; Patterson and Rosen, 1977). Although this feature is unusual, a fenestrated ceratohyal also occurs in *Pachyrhizodus marathonesis*, *Rhacolepis buccalis*, and *Notelops brama* (Forey, 1977), as well as in living acanthopterygians (McAllister, 1968). It has been suggested that fenestration of the ceratohyal is a primitive feature of all major groups of teleosts, living and fossil (Rosen, 1984). The anterior ceratohyal is fenestrated in *Tharsis dubius* and apparently also in *Leptolepis coryphaenoides* (Nybelin, 1974), which supports Rosen's contention.

Patterson and Rosen (1977) found firm evidence of only six branchiostegals in *Cladocyclus*, all inserting on the posterior part of the hyoid bar, although they suggested that a few hair-like branchiostegals also may be present farther anteriorly in AMNH 2982. In fact, there

are considerably more than this; as now shown by AMNH 11897, there are some 12-14 fine and recurved branchiostegals attached to the anterior ceratohyal, one attached at the suture of the two ceratohyal ossifications, and at least seven or eight associated with the posterior ceratohyal. The posteriormost three branchiostegals are spathiform (long, broad, and thin), whereas the remainder are more hair-like. In branchiostegal number and arrangement, therefore, *Cladocyclus* resembles *Tharsis dubius* and *Allothrissops* (Nybelin, 1974; Patterson and Rosen, 1977), again hinting at a primitive condition. There is no indication of a gular plate in *Cladocyclus* or any other ichthyodectiform.

The gill arch skeleton was accurately described in *Cladocyclus* by Patterson and Rosen (1977) and little can be added here. There are numerous elongate gill-rakers covered with many small, pointed denticles (particularly on the lateral face of each raker), as in *Elops*.

The preopercular bone shows some variability in its sensory canal tubule arrangement (particularly in the ventral area) among specimens of *Cladocyclus* from the Santana formation. According to Silva Santos (1950), the preoperculum of *C. ferus* is characterized by small radiating grooves ("poucos sulcos radiantes"), whereas that of *C. gardneri* is covered by numerous radial striations ("numerosas etrias radiantes"), corresponding to branches of the preopercular sensory canal. The preopercular margin (together with that of the operculum) was said to be fringed in *C. ferus*

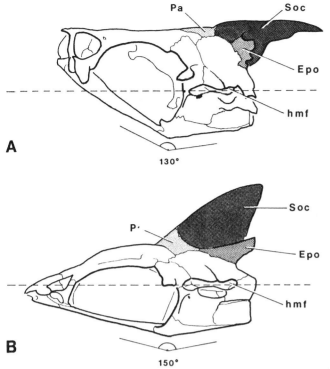

A

130°

B

150°

Lateral views of the skull in (A) *Cladocyclus* and (B) *Ichthyodectes* (after Bardack) to illustrate differences in suspensorial geometry and supraoccipital crest. Dashed axis through hyomandibular facet passes through ethmoid region in (B), but lies below it in (A).

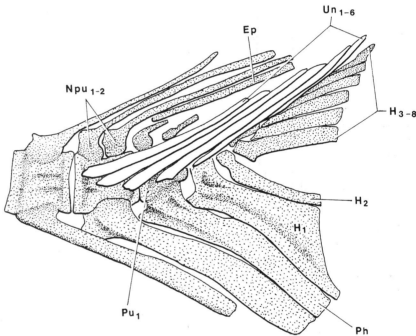

Cladocyclus gardneri caudal endoskeleton, redrawn after Patterson and Rosen from AMNH 9982A.

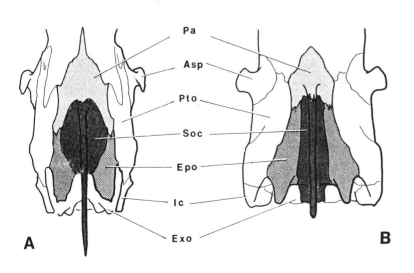

A

B

Dorsal views of back of skull in (A) *Cladocyclus* and (B) *Ichthyodectes* (after Bardack) to show differences in epioccipital, supraoccipital, and parietal morphology.

but not in *C. gardneri*. These differences were to some extent corroborated by Patterson and Rosen (1977), although they exercised caution in identifying their *Cladocyclus* material to species. The majority of *Cladocyclus* specimens from the Araripe Basin seem to have the finer preopercular canal pattern (25 or more in the lower part, with 30-35 in all), supposedly characteristic of *C. gardneri*; the coarser *"ferus"* pattern (with ten or fewer branches ventrally and only 15 or so in all) is rather rare. The infraorbital canal of the largest circumorbital bones is correspondingly much more branched in specimens with a great number of preopercular branches (e.g., 12 or more on the fourth infraorbital of AMNH 9980, with a finely striated preoperculum, but only five or six in AMNH 9981, with a more coarsely grooved preoperculum).

The preoperculum of *Cladocyclus alagoensis* from Riacho Doce (Alagoas, Brazil) has the coarser *"ferus"* pattern of sensory canal tubes (seen in AMNH 10015 and 10016). This also is the case in specimens from Equatorial Guinea that have been referred to *Proportheus kameruni* (= *Chirocentrites guinensis*), e.g., AMNH 6302 and 8394. Only in one of these specimens (AMNH 6302, referred here to *Cladocyclus kameruni*) is there any trace of canal- bearing infraorbitals, and here too the pattern is distinctly *"ferus"*-like. A low number of preopercular canal tubules also is seen in *Chiromystus mawsoni* (Silva Santos, 1949).

Among other ichthyodectoids it is more usual for the preoperculum to be pierced by a relatively low number of openings for branches of the preopercular sensory canal (12-14 in *Gillicus*, 15 in *Ichthyodectes*, 10-13 in *Xiphactinus*; Bardack, 1965). This apparently also is the case in *Saurodon* (Bardack and Sprinkle, 1969, fig. 5). In *Chirocentrites vexillifer* there are numerous branches of the sensory canal on the ventral part of the preoperculum. In *Allothrissops* there are only 13-14 openings for the sensory canal in the lower plate-like part of the preoperculum, although there may be more in the ascending part (Patterson and Rosen, 1977, fig. 5). The number is somewhat variable in various "leptolepids" (Nybelin, 1974), but there are usually fewer than 14-15 in the lower part of the preoperculum and rarely more than 25 in the entire bone.

Although somewhat speculative, it is inferred that the finely striated appearance of the preoperculum in specimens referred to *Cladocyclus gardneri* is derived and provides a useful means to distinguish that species. The coarser preopercular pattern characterizes more than one *Cladocyclus* species, suggesting either that those species are synonymous or else that the character is widespread and cannot be used to define *C. ferus*.

Taverne (1986) separated *Chirocentrites/Spathodactylus* from other ichthyodectids in part on preoperculum morphology. The dorsal part of the preoperculum is reduced and lacks a posterior indentation dorsally in *C. vexillifer*, which probably is a derived condition in this form. The posterior margin of the preoperculum is indented in other ichthyodectoids, but apparently not in *Allothrissops* or *Occithrissops*. Nevertheless, the interpretation of the condition in *C. vexillifer* given by Taverne is arbitrary since it could be derived from the notched ichthyodectoid pattern.

The pectoral girdle of *Cladocyclus* was described but not figured by Patterson and Rosen (1977). As in all ichthyodectiforms, the coracoid is large and plate-like. They reported finding three postcleithra in *Cladocyclus* and *Allothrissops*, although only one has been reported in other ichthyodectoids (Bardack, 1965). The number in *Cladocyclus* cannot be confirmed from available material, and only one scale-like postcleithrum seems to be present between the supracleithrum and cleithrum in a specimen figured by Silva Santos (1950, pl. 3).

The pectoral fin of many *Cladocyclus* specimens from the Santana formation often is folded back against the body, with the smaller posterior fin-rays obscured by the much larger anterior ones. In AMNH 12712 the pectoral fin is splayed out, revealing six or seven fin-rays, but even here the smaller posterior rays probably are obscured. Silva Santos (1950) found ten fin-rays in *C. gardneri* and about nine in *C. ferus*. In specimens of *C. alagoensis* there are ten or 12 pectoral fin-rays in AMNH 10015 and 10016. In *C. kameruni* seven or eight fin-rays can be seen in AMNH 8394 and ten in AMNH 6302. In all cases, the first five or six rays are the most prominent, especially the anteriormost

Facing page: Representative specimens of *Cladocyclus*: "Santana" (top left, lower center); "Jardim" (top right, upper center); and "Old Mission" (bottom) matrix.

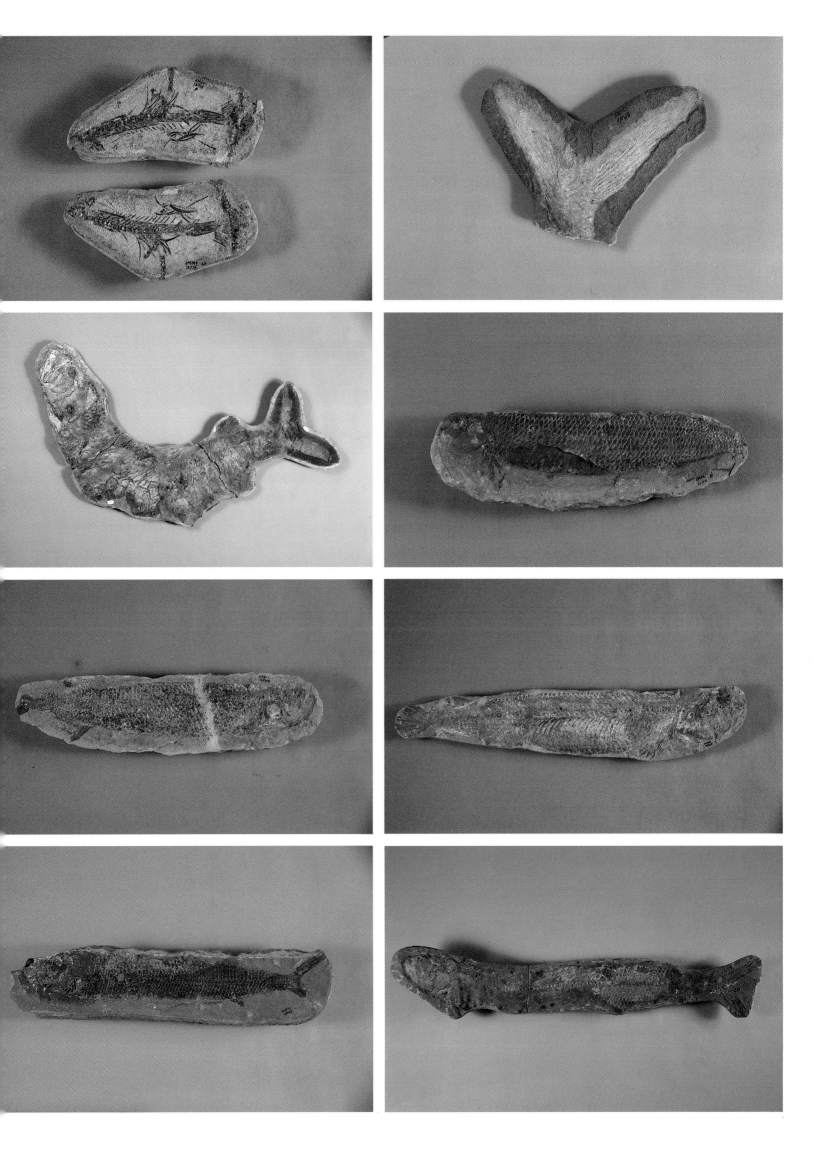

ones. Even where the fin-ray count is observable, however, the number is appreciably less than the 16 reported in *Allothrissops* (Patterson and Rosen, 1977). Bardack (1965) reported a maximum of 11 pectoral fin-rays in *Ichthyodectes* and eight or nine in *Xiphactinus* and *Gillicus*. Bardack and Sprinkle (1969) found about eight rays in a specimen of *Saurodon*. The pectoral fin of *Occithrissops willsoni* includes at least 14 rays (Schaeffer and Patterson, 1984). It may be that fin-ray number is reduced in phylogenetically advanced ichthyodectiforms, but more accurate data are required in order to be sure.

The pelvic fins are small in all ichthyodectiforms where they are known. There are nine pelvic fin-rays in *Xiphactinus*, *Allothrissops*, and *Occithrissops* (Bardack, 1965; Patterson and Rosen, 1977; Schaeffer and Patterson, 1984). An accurate count has not been possible in *Cladocyclus* from the Santana formation or in *C. kameruni* from Equatorial Guinea. Seven rays are exposed in *C. alagoensis* (AMNH 10015).

The anal fin of *C. gardneri* and *C. ferus* originates beneath vertebra 44-45, with the first pterygiophore inserted in front of the hemal spine of vertebra 38-39. The fin comprises only two or three short supernumerary and 30+ branched principal rays. The fin is falcate, and its main area is made up from the first eight or nine rays; the remaining rays all are relatively short. Similar fin-ray counts were obtained for *C. alagoensis* (AMNH 10015) and *C. kameruni* (AMNH 8394). According to data provided by Schaeffer and Patterson (1984), this compares well with the number in *Thrissops formosus* (four or five unbranched, about 30 branched) and *Allothrissops mesogaster* (four or five unbranched, about 25 branched) and is slightly higher than in *Occithrissops willsoni* (four or five unbranched, 18-20 branched). Taverne (1986) reported two supernumerary rays plus 35 principal rays in *Chirocentrites vexillifer*. It is possible that a low number of unbranched rays in the anal fin is a characteristic of more derived ichthyodectids, but an accurate count is available in few cases. There are approximately 29-30 pterygiophores in *Cladocyclus*, again comparing closely with *Allothrissops* (24-30) and *Thrissops formosus* (29-32); in *Occithrissops* there are only 18-20 (Schaeffer and Patterson, 1984). The longest anal ray of *Cladocyclus* is equal in length to about seven or eight caudal vertebrae, as in *Chirocentrites vexillifer*, *Occithrissops*, and *Thrissops formosus*. In *Allothrissops* the longest rays apparently are equal in length to only four

caudal vertebrae. The anal fin is long-based in many ichthyodectiforms, a feature that Patterson and Rosen (1977) considered derived. In *Xiphactinus* and *Gillicus* the anal fin apparently is short and remote. Within ichthyodectiforms, the short anal fin may represent a derived condition (see below and Taverne, 1986, character 25).

The caudal fin skeleton of *Cladocyclus* was described by Patterson and Rosen (1977, fig. 19) and compared with various primitive euteleostean caudal fins. One peculiarity noted by them is the tendency for uroneurals to extend over the sides of the ural centra of the tail. This they found in *Cladocyclus*, *Allothrissops*, *Eubiodectes*, and *Thrissops formosus*; it also has been found in *Saurodon* (Bardack and Sprinkle, 1969, fig. 7) and *Chirocentrites vexillifer* (Taverne, 1986: 41), but not in *Occithrissops* (Schaeffer and Patterson, 1984). Although the uroneural arrangement was considered an ichthyodectiform synapomorphy by Patterson and Rosen (1977), they noted a similar pattern in another extinct teleost group, the crossognathids. Schaeffer and Patterson (1984) effectively suspended judgement on the phylogenetic value of this character in ichthyodectiforms.

Another tantalizing ichthyodectoid character is the presence of a ball-like process at the base of the first hypural, set into a socket within the ural centrum (the second hypural also may develop a ball-and-socket articulation with the ural centrum). This feature is well-developed in specialized ichthyodectids (e.g., *Gillicus*, *Icthyodectes*, *Xiphactinus*; Cavender, 1966) but is less prominent in *Thrissops* and *Allothrissops* (Patterson and Rosen, 1977) and apparently is lacking in *Occithrissops* (Schaeffer and Patterson, 1984). The first two hypurals of *Cladocyclus* (and *Chirocentrites vexillifer*; Taverne, 1986) are set into sockets in the first ural centrum, but the hypural process is not as well- developed in AMNH 9982 (an isolated tail from a small individual) as in some Upper Cretaceous ichthyodectids (e.g., those figured by Patterson and Rosen, 1977, figs. 15, 16). Taverne (1986: 48) proposed that elongation of the articular head so it forms an angle with the rest of the hypural is a shared derived character of *Gillicus*, *Ichthyodectus*, and *Xiphactinus*. There apparently is a well-developed ball-and-socket articulation in *Saurodon* (Bardack and Sprinkle, 1969, fig. 7), but its detailed structure has yet to be determined.

It is concluded that *Cladocyclus* from the Santana formation may be represented by two species, as proposed by Silva Santos (1950). One of these (the type species, *C. gardneri*) may be distinguished by the high number of branches extending from the infraorbital and preopercular sensory canals. The other form is less distinct, primitively resembling *Chiromystus alagoensis*, *C. mawsoni*, *C. woodwardi*, and *Cladocyclus kameruni* in its infraorbital and preopercular canal arrangement.

Silva Santos (1986) separated *Chiromystus woodwardi*, making it the type species of a new genus, *Itaparica*. From his diagnosis, *Itaparica* resembles species of *Cladocyclus* in most respects except as follows: 1) its mandibular teeth are slightly larger than the uppers, but are not differentiated in size (i.e., it supposedly lacks mandibular fangs); 2) the vertical ramus of the preoperculum does not extend as far as the dorsal margin of the operculum; and 3) the lower ramus of the preoperculum is elongate.

In all these features, *I. woodwardi* resembles *Allothrissops* and *Saurodon*, and it also is like *Thrissops* and *Occithrissops* in its tooth morphology and relatively short preopercular vertical ramus. Silva Santos (1986) placed *Itaparica* in the Icthyodectidae of Patterson and Rosen (1977). However, its low vertebral count (40) places it closest to *Chiromystus mawsoni* and *C. alagoensis* (see below). *Itaparica* is consequently regarded here as a junior synonym of *Chiromystus* Cope (1885).

Cladocyclus kameruni is provisionally retained as a separate species because its enlarged mandibular teeth are stouter and more strongly developed than in the other species.

Cladocyclus gardneri has 64 vertebrae (37 abdominal, 25 caudal, and 2 ural centra; e.g., AMNH 11992). The number in *C. ferus* has not yet been determined. In *C. kameruni* there are 63 centra (32 abdominal, 29 caudal, and 2 ural; AMNH 8394). In *Chirocentrites vexillifer* there are 64 centra (36 abdominal, 26 caudal, 2 ural; Taverne, 1986:40). For *Chiromystus*, excluding the ural centra, which have not been documented properly, the following much lower vertebral counts have been reported (data in part from Schaeffer, 1947; Silva Santos; 1949, 1950, 1986; Patterson and Rosen, 1977): *Chiromystus mawsoni*, 50 (28 abdominal, 22 caudal); *C. alagoensis*, 49 (24 abdominal, 25 caudal; 2 ural centra also present in AMNH 10015); *C. woodwardi*, 40 (19 abdominal, 21 caudal). *Chiromystus alagoensis, mawsoni*, and *woodwardi* are distinguished here on the basis of their relatively low vertebral number.

Vertebral counts in the species referred here to *Chiromystus* are low, not only in comparison with *Cladocyclus gardneri* but with other ichthyodectiforms generally (e.g., *Allothrissops*, *Spathodactylus*, and *Thrissops* spp. with 56 to 63; *Occithrissops* with 58; *Eubiodectes* with about 65; *Ichthyodectes* with 68-72; *Xiphactinus* with 85-89; *Gillicus* with about 70; *Saurodon* with almost 100). The major differences are found in the abdominal count; caudal centra numbers usually remain more constant.

From the data available the following scenario is plausible: assuming that the primitive ichthyodectiform vertebral column included some 33-35 abdominal and 22-26 caudal centra (as in *Allothrissops*, *Occithrissops* and *Thrissops* spp.), the condition in *Cladocyclus gardneri* and *Chirocentrites vexillifer* is primitive. The lower abdominal vertebral count in *Chiromystus* probably represents a derived character state. An unresolved polychotomy is formed between *C. kameruni* (with a primitive vertebral count and sensory canal pattern), *C. gardneri* and *Chirocentrites vexillifer* (primitive vertebral count, derived sensory canal pattern), *Chiromystus* (primitive sensory canal pattern, derived vertebral count), and "*Cladocyclus*" *ferus* (primitive sensory canal pattern, unknown vertebral count).

An opposite tendency, toward increased vertebral number, is noted in other ichthyodectoids such as *Eubiodectes*, *Gillicus*, *Ichthyodectes*, *Xiphactinus*, and *Saurodon*. According to the hypothesis of relationships presented by Patterson and Rosen (1977), this increase would have occurred separately in saurodontids and ichthyodectids.

To conclude, three presumably monophyletic groups of ichthyodectoids are distinguishable. One of these (family Cladocyclidae) includes *Cladocyclus* and several probably synonymous genera (e.g., *Anaedopogon*, *Proportheus*, and *Ennelichthys*), as well as *Chirocentrites vexillifer* and *Chiromystus*. Cladocyclids are characterized by having the supraoccipital crest extending posteriorly so as to overhang the occiput. Within the group divergent trends are noted, e.g., toward increased sensory canal complexity in the cheek (represented by *C. gardneri*), toward lower vertebral number particularly in the abdominal region (*Chiromystus*), and toward toothlessness and shorter gape (*Chirocentrites*).

The second ichthyodectoid group (family Ichthyodectidae in a new, restricted sense) includes *Gillicus*, *Xiphactinus*, and *Ichthyodectes* (see also Taverne, 1986). The group is characterized by anterior extension of the epioccipitals and a subdivided nasal bone. Additionally, in *Xiphactinus* and *Gillicus* the anal fin is short and remote (not yet determined in *Ichthyodectes*). Quite possibly this feature unites all ichthyodectids, but the anal fin is unknown in saurodontids. Within ichthyodectids, *Ichthyodectes* and *Xiphactinus* are united by incorporation of the parietal into the supraoccipital crest, enlarged premaxillary fangs, straightened parasphenoid profile, reduced ventral branch of the preoperculum, and orientation of the hyomandibular facet.

The third ichthyodectoid group includes *Saurodon* and *Saurocephalus* and is characterized by a notch or foramen at the base of every tooth and the presence of a predentary. Other ichthyodectiforms (e.g., *Allothrissops*, *Eubiodectes*, *Thrissops*, *Occithrissops*) cannot be placed within any of these groups, and are left as *incertae sedis* taxa. Uroneurals overlapping the ural centra may unite *Allothrissops*, *Thrissops*, and *Eubiodectes* to ichthyodectoids more closely than to *Occithrissops*.

Patterson and Rosen (1977) recognized only two ichthyodectoid groups. One of these (their Ichthyodectidae) is here separated into two smaller groups (a more restricted Ichthyodectidae and the new Cladocyclidae). According to the present analysis, these families only share synapomorphies that also occur in saurodontids, while certain other characters (e.g., mandibular joint confined to angular and articular, shape of "coronoid process," ball-and-socket hypural articulation, high vertebral number) shared by saurodontids and ichthyodectids do not occur in cladocyclids. On this basis, Patterson and Rosen's Ichthyodectidae is paraphyletic, and saurodontids are a specialized sister-group to some but not all other ichthyodectoids.

Assemblages: All; smaller individuals in Santana concretions, largest from Jardim. The type specimens of *C. gardneri* are in "Jardim" matrix. The holotype of *C. ferus* is from near Crato, in the area noted for its "Santana" lithology concretions. *Cladocyclus* sp. also occurs in laminated limestones of the Crato member, where, however, it is extremely rare. *Cladocyclus* also is reported from a new locality in bituminous shales at Pedra Blanca, near Nova Olinda (Viana, Brito & Silva-Telles, MS).

(J. G. Maisey)

Facing page: Representative specimens of *Cladocyclus*, mostly acid-prepared.

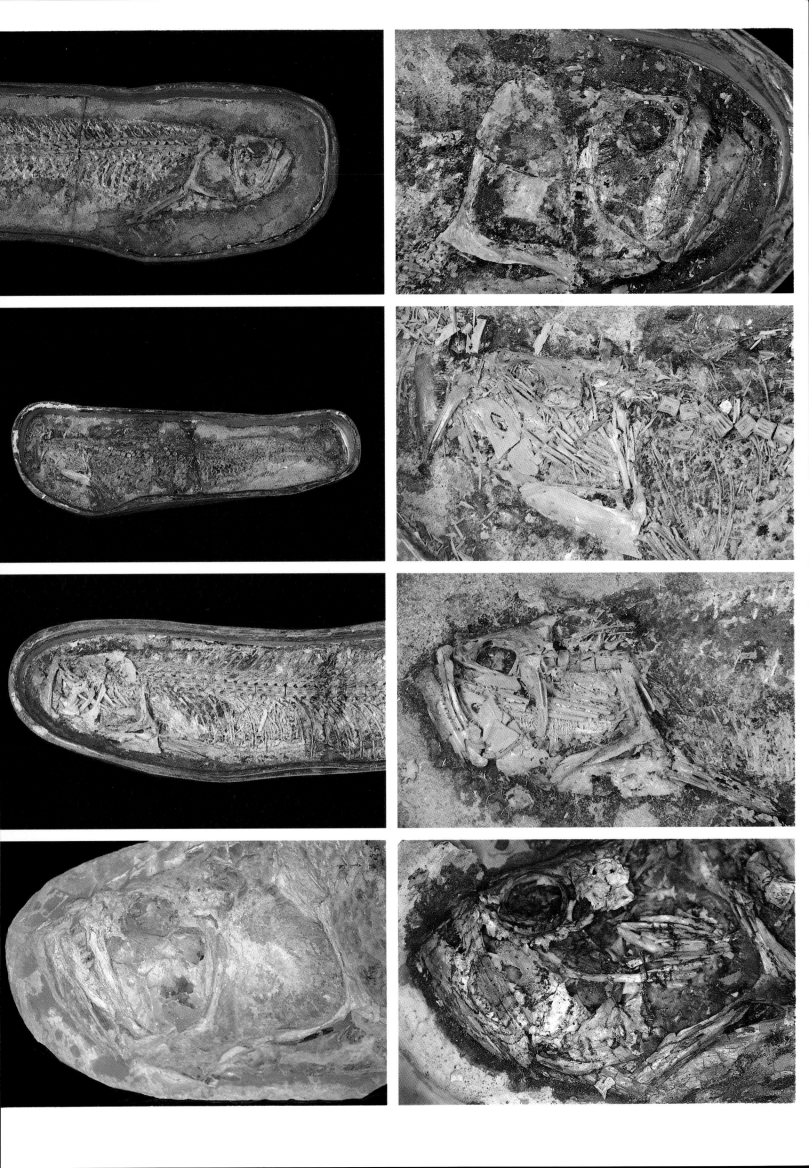

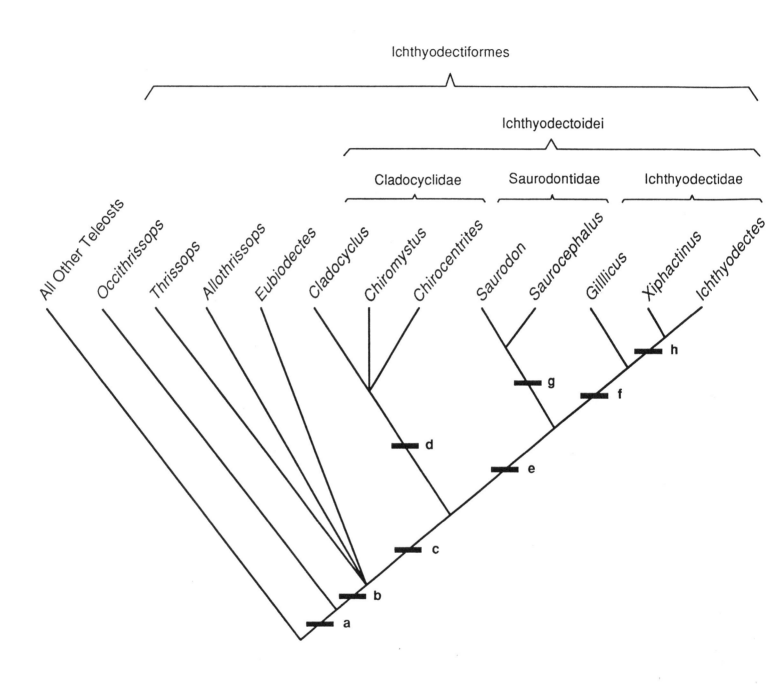

Hypothesis of relationships among ichthyodectiform fishes, based on characters listed on the facing page and numbered as follows: (a) characters 1-3; (b) character 4; (c) characters 5-16; (d) character 17; (e) characters 18-22; (f) characters 25-27; (g) characters 23-24; (h) characters 28-32.

Synapomorphy scheme for ichthyodectiform fishes

1. Teeth in a single series in jaws.
2. Coracoid enlarged, meeting its fellow in a long midventral symphysis.
3. Long, falcate anal fin opposed by short, remote dorsal fin.
4. First 3 or 4 uroneurals extending antero-ventrally over sides of pre-ural centra 1-3.
5. First ural centrum with sockets for hypurals 1 and 2.
6. High, triangular supraoccipital crest.
7. Unpaired parietal, displaced anteriorly.
8. Sclerotic bone.
9. Intercalar enlarged, foming part of hyomandibular facet and enclosing a canal for jugular vein.
10. Ethmopalatine bone with membranous outgrowths separating and suturing with rostro-dermethmoid and lateral ethmoid.
11. Palatine head modified into malleolus.
12. Premaxilla firmly attached posteriorly to maxilla.
13. Dentary with deep symphysis.
14. Angular contributes to mandibular facet for quadrate.
15. ?Single elongate epural asssociated with NPU_1 (Taverne, 1986, character 8).
16. Upper posterior margin of preoperculum indented.
17. Supraoccipital crest overhangs occiput.
18. ?Uroneural number reduced to five (Taverne, 1986, character 5b).
19. Mandibular joint confined to angular and articular.
20. ?Angled "coronoid process" on dentary (Taverne, 1986, character 16).
21. Ball-and-socket hypural attachment.
22. High (approx. 70-100) vertebral number.
23. Predentary.
24. Notch or foramen at base of each tooth.
25. Anteriorly extended epioccipitals.
26. Subdivided nasal bone.
27. ?Short, remote anal fin.
28. Parietal involved in supraoccipital crest.
29. Epioccipitals and supraoccipital of equal forward extent.
30. Broad parasphenoid angle.
31. Hyomandibular facet parallel to orbital part of parasphenoid.
32. Enlarged premaxillary fangs.

ARARIPICHTHYS Silva Santos, 1985

Subdivision TELEOSTEI
Supercohort ELOPOCEPHALA
incertae sedis
Family ARARIPICHTHYIDAE Silva Santos
Genus ***Araripichthys*** Silva Santos 1985
  1983 *Araripichthys* Silva Santos: 27 (nomen nudum)
  1985c *Araripichthys* Silva Santos: 135
  Emended diagnosis: Deep-bodied euteleost with long and deep dorsal and anal fin, narrow forked caudal fin; body, fins, and posterior part of head covered by numerous circular, deeply overlapping cycloid scales; head short, high; jaws edentulous, premaxilla protrusible, maxilla with large condylar articulation against vomer; prominent supraoccipital crest with lateral ridges dividing deep sub-epiotic fossa into upper and lower parts, but lacking a spina occipitalis; large opening between pterosphenoid and autosphenotic unites orbit with dilatator fossa; supraorbitals absent; supramaxillae present; anterior ceratohyal fenestrated; pelvic girdle and fins absent; neural and hemal arches fused to

respective centra, but ribs and hypurals separate; D53; A32; P:12 + ; V absent; about 86 scales along lateral line, 33 scales in vertical series at deepest point above lateral line, 18-20 below.

  Type species: *Araripichthys castilhoi* Silva Santos 1985.

Araripichthys castilhoi Silva Santos
  1983 *Araripichthys castilhoi* Silva Santos: 27 (nomen nudum)
  1985c *Araripichthys castilhoi* Silva Santos: 135
  Diagnosis: As for genus.
  Holotype: No. 21-P³, Departamento de Biologia Animal e Vegetal, Instituto de Biologia, University of Rio de Janeiro; almost complete individual; Lower Cretaceous, Aptian, Santana formation, Chapada do Araripe (exact location unknown).

This spectacular deep-bodied fish is a rare component of the Santana Formation fossil fish assemblages. It was first described only in 1985 on the basis of five reasonably complete specimens, although its name had been

Below and facing page: *Araripichthys castilhoi*. Skeletal reconstruction.

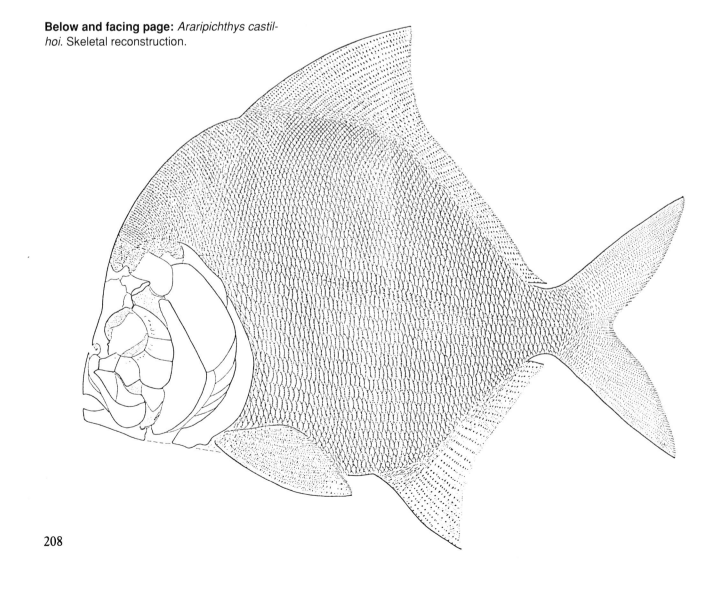

published previously (Silva Santos, 1983). In earlier times it apparently had been confused with pycnodont specimens, although there are many significant morphological features separating these fishes and they are phylogenetically remote from each other.

Silva Santos (1983) isolated this distinctive fish in its own family, the Araripichthyidae, which he placed at an undetermined level within the Acanthopterygii (spiny-finned teleosts). He subsequently (Silva Santos, 1985c) proposed that *Araripichthys* belongs to a new beryciform suborder (Araripichthyoidei). Supposed acanthopterygian characters said to be present in *Araripichthys* include spiny rays in the dorsal and anal fins, an elevated supraoccipital crest, morphology of the maxilla (which is excluded from the superior border of the mouth), premaxilla with a long ascending process and with an articular process for the maxilla, and absence of supraorbitals. An elevated supraoccipital crest is present in various non-acanthopterygian teleosts (e.g., ichthyodectids, *Chanos*, mormyroids, *Hydrocyon*, many catfishes) and cannot be regarded as an exclusively acanthopterygian character.

Although free supraorbitals are absent in Recent acanthopterygians, their presence in other teleosts is not universal, and their absence in *Araripichthys* is at best an ambiguous character.

Although Silva Santos (1985c) was emphatic about the presence of spiny fin-rays in *Araripichthys*, these are not evident in any of the specimens we have examined. In one small individual (AMNH 11949) the anteriormost dorsal fin-rays, although unsegmented, still consist of separate left and right components; they are not median spines as in the majority of acanthopterygians. Furthermore, in one particularly well preserved larger specimen (AMNH 12576) all the dorsal and anal fin-rays are covered by scales and are an integral part of these fins; there are no separate rays. Paradoxically, the absence of spiny rays does not totally preclude *Araripichthys* from the Acanthopterygii, as they rarely are present in Recent lampridiforms (opahs, moonfish). In this regard, *Araripichthys* and lampridiforms are both primitive, but the mandibular apparatus of *Araripichthys* resembles the lampridiform arrangement (Silva Santos, 1985c: 137), strengthening the possibility of a phylogenetic

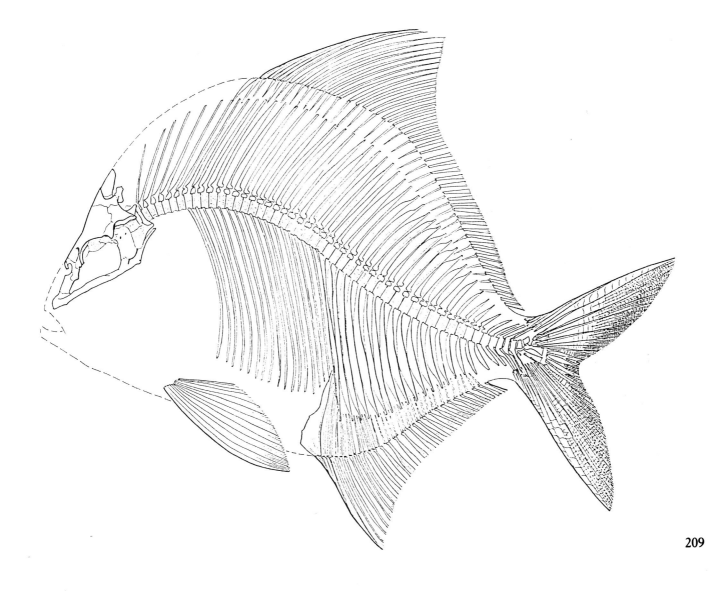

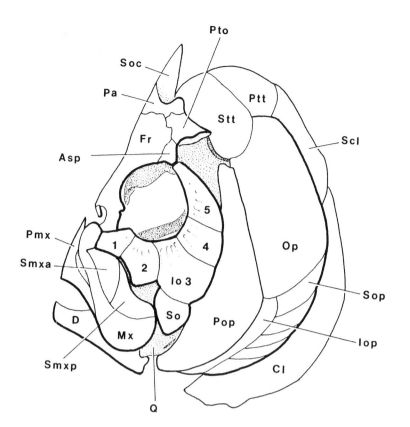

Araripichthys castilhoi. Outline reconstruction of head in lateral view.

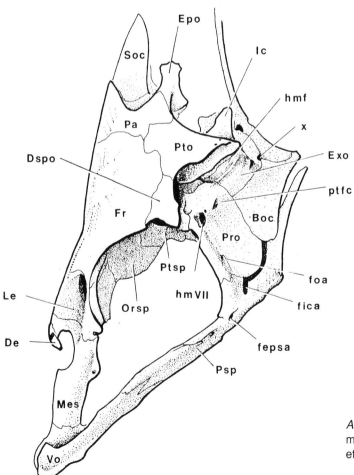

Araripichthys castilhoi. Skull in lateral view, mainly from AMNH 11948 but with parts of ethmoid region from AMNH 11944 and 12633.

relationship. Furthermore, in some lampridiform fishes the pelvic (ventral) fins are reduced or absent (e.g., the trachipterid *Regalecus*, lophotids, *Stylephorus*). Counter to any hypothesis of acanthopterygian relationship, however, the caudal fin endoskeleton in *Araripichthys* (according to its interpretation by Silva Santos, 1985c, pl. 3, fig. 3) is decidely primitive.

The largest specimen available to Silva Santos (1985c) had a standard length of approximately 28 cm. AMNH 11949 is considerably smaller (estimated standard length of 15 cm), while AMNH 12576 and 11973 are both around 28 cm standard length. The head is approximately one-third of the standard length and forms a deep equilateral triangle with a strongly inclined dorsal profile. The skull roof is quite short, with a posterior expansion produced by the frontals. The maxilla (like all the other mouthparts) is edentulous and is greatly elongated antero-dorsally. Its anterior extremity is enlarged into a condyle that articulates with the vomer, and its dorsal margin received two large supramaxillae (absent in most living acanthopterygians, but retained by beryciforms and fossils such as *Aipichthys*). The oral margin of the mouth is formed by the premaxilla, which has a very long ascending process with a shallow groove that receives the ascending part of the maxilla. The maxillary condyle appears to be analogous with

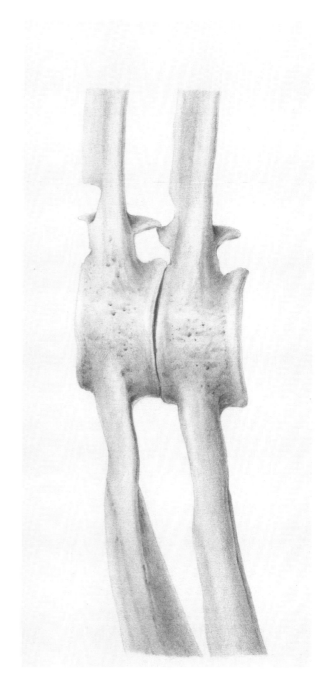

Above: *Araripichthys castilhoi*. Caudal vertebrae, from AMNH 11950.

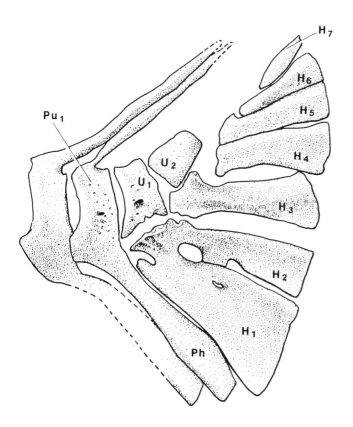

Left: *Araripichthys castilhoi*. Caudal endoskeleton, from AMNH 11944.

the "inner fork" of the maxilla in *Lates niloticus* (Gregory, 1959: fig. 115). The premaxillary component of the mouth probably was protrusible, but from the well-developed condylar articulation between the vomer and maxilla, protrusibility of the latter seems unlikely. In lampridiforms the maxilla and premaxilla both are highly mobile, and the maxilla may be protruded along with the premaxilla in some forms (Regan, 1907). In *Velifer* and *Trachypterus* the maxillae meet below the ascending process of the premaxilla and can slide along a median keel on the vomer or pre-ethmoid cartilage. In *Araripichthys*, however, the articular ends of the maxillae are separated by a thin lamina of bone arising dorsally from the vomer.

In the lower jaw of *Araripichthys* the retroarticular is well developed and clearly contributes to the joint surface for the quadrate (AMNH 12633). The angular and articular bones apparently are separate. Exclusion of the retroarticular from the joint surface and co-ossification of the angular and articular have been regarded as shared derived characters of all clupeocephalans (clupeomorphs plus euteleosteans) (Nelson, 1973; Patterson and Rosen, 1977). *Araripichthys* thus lacks these two important clupeocephalan characters.

The parasphenoid is narrow and edentulous, with short dorsally directed ascending processes, behind which the posterior part of the parasphenoid is angled sharply upward. There are large foramina, presumably for the efferent pseudobranchial artery, and a notch in the posterior margin of the ascending process, probably for the internal carotid artery.

The vomer is edentulous and has large paired lateral grooves postero-dorsally that carry the semicircular condyles of the maxillae. Articulation between these bones is very general, but the development of these condyles is extraordinary.

The frontals meet the lateral ethmoids in the anterior third of the orbit, with a broad sutural contact ventrally. The mesethmoid probably did not meet the frontals, although a thin bridge may have extended postero-dorsally toward the frontals. The lateral ethmoids are separated anteriorly by the mesethmoid and are penetrated by the olfactory canal (probably a plesiomorphic condition). A large part of the snout region thus is formed by the mesethmoid. There is a peculiar separate dermethmoid located between the "posterior" mesethmoid, with a dermal component (dermethmoid?), "anterior" mesethmoid (or pre-ethmoid?), and lateral

ethmoid, shaped like an inverted Y from above, anterior to the orbits. There appears to be a foramen in each arm of the dermal component, perhaps for an ethmoid commissure. Within the orbit, the lateral ethmoids extend posteriorly almost to the orbitosphenoid. According to Stiassny (1986: 449), in acanthomorph fishes (including acanthopterygians, "paracanthopterygians," and polymixines) the ethmoid cartilage is reduced and the lateral ethmoids extend close to the vomer, to which they even may be sutured. In *Araripichthys*, however, the lateral ethmoids are widely separated from the vomer by the two mesethmoids.

The pterosphenoid is well ossified, as in more generalized teleosts. In derived acanthopterygians this bone usually is absent, but one is primitively present in lampridiforms and most beryciforms.

There is a prominent round fenestra passing from the orbit to the deep dilatator fossa. This fenestra is defined laterally by the autosphenotic and mesially by the pterosphenoid. Its function is unclear. In AMNH 11948 there is a deep dilatator fossa that probably was floored with cartilage. It is roofed posteriorly by the pterotic and anteriorly by the autosphenotic. This specimen also shows the intercalar, lying behind the cartilaginous component of the pterotic. The intercalar spans the suture between the exoccipital and pterotic and is restricted to the posterior face of the skull.

The prootic is pierced by a vertically-oriented canal for the orbital artery. Farther dorsally, openings for the jugular canal and hyomandibular nerve are discernible.

Facing page: A complete specimen of *Araripichthys castilhoi* (top) with well-preserved scales and fins (below). Photos by E. Garvens.

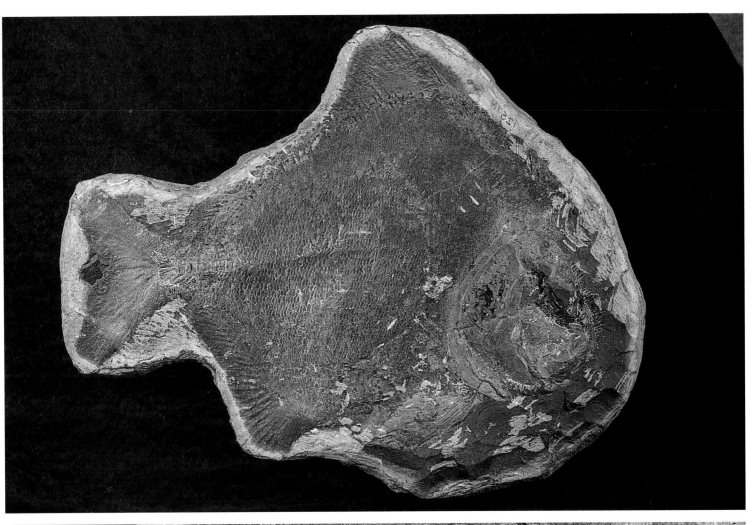

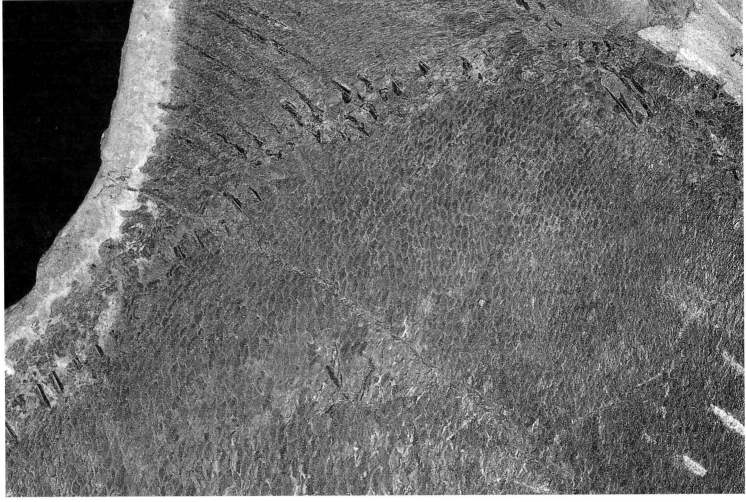

The epioccipital is V-shaped, with a dorsal arm sutured beneath the parietal and a ventral part extending mesially to meet the supraoccipital. The large post-temporal fossa is partly defined dorsally by the epioccipital and ventro-laterally by the pterotic; most of its inner surface was cartilaginous. Mesial to the epioccipital, and defined by that bone and the supraoccipital, there are large "sub-epiotic" fossae divided by a low ridge extending from the supraoccipital to the epioccipital. This ridge separates lower and upper parts of the "sub-epiotic" fossa.

The endochondral part of the supraoccipital does not extend any great distance ventrally between the epioccipitals. It lacks a spina occipitalis of the kind found in acanthomorph fishes. According to Stiassny (1986, fig. 27), this process (separating the paired epi- and exoccipitals and descending ventrally to the dorsal margin of the foramen magnum) is a defining character of acanthomorphs. Its absence in *Araripichthys*, which retains a more generalized teleostean occipital configuration, casts serious doubt upon a relationship with acanthopterygians.

According to Silva Santos (1985c: 135), the parietals are separated by the supraoccipital (a derived condition among teleosts), but this is not the case in AMNH 11948, an acid-prepared specimen in which the skull is well preserved. The parietals continue dorsally over the endochondral portion of the supraoccipital and thus conform to the primitive teleostean condition. Moreover, the supraoccipital crest is larger than Silva Santos (1985c) suggested, extending for a considerable distance behind the parietals and separating the supratemporals (= extrascapulars of Silva Santos) and post-temporals. There is no evidence in our material to suggest that the supratemporals overlap the parietals anteriorly. Dorsally the supratemporals and post-temporals are scale-covered.

The exoccipitals meet at the midline above the foramen magnum (a primitive character), but also articulate with small processes that extend anteriorly from the first neural arch. In AMNH 11947, a small individual, the first vertebral centrum is incorporated into the occipital region but is essentially unfused. Larger specimens display varying degrees of fusion between the vertebra and basioccipital, but the exoccipitals remain separated from the centrum in all examples seen. The neural arch and spine of this first vertebra are both complete.

There are 24 free abdominal vertebrae in AMNH 11947, and 23 in AMNH 11948.

According to Silva Santos (1985c: 237), there are 23 caudal vertebrae, but this has not been confirmed. The vertebral centra are strongly ossified, without any pronounced fossae or ridges. All neural and hemal arches are fused to their respective centra, as are the apophyses that support pleural ribs. The neural and hemal spines are expanded anteriorly into a broad lamina. Each neural arch additionally has a short pair of processes anteriorly and posteriorly. These are arranged so as to define an opening between adjacent neural arches, through which a spinal nerve could pass.

The dorsal fin is very extensive. It is supported by approximately 30-33 ossified pterygiophores, of which the first is greatly enlarged. Anteriorly to this there are approximately six supernumerary spines. As discussed earlier, the anteriormost fin-rays are spinous but paired rather than median. There are approximately six short supernumerary rays and over 45 principal rays. This discrepancy between pterygiophores and fin-ray number suggests that many of the former were unossified and therefore were not fossilized.

In the anal fin a similar situation exists. The first anal pterygiophore is large and bears two or three radial laminae suggesting a compound origin from several originally discrete elements. The proximal ends of this and the next four pterygiophores are crowded together anterior to the first hemal spine, and the last ribs are in turn crowded distally against the proximal part of the first pterygiophore. Crowding of the anteriormost anal pterygiphores is not unusual among acanthopterygians, particularly in deeper-bodied forms. There are four supernumerary and about 28 principal fin-rays.

The caudal fin was intepreted by Silva Santos (1985c, pl. 3, fig. 3) as having two separate ural centra, parhypural separate from hypurals 1 and 2, a total of six hypurals, two uroneurals, a "stegural," and three epurals. From his illustration it could not be determined whether there is a neural arch on the putative first preural centrum.

Based upon that interpretation, the caudal fin of *Araripichthys* lacks most of the specializations generally seen in acanthopterygians. Instead, it more closely resembles the generalized basal teleostean condition in which there are two free ural centra, three epurals, two lower hypurals, and five (or more) upper hypurals (Patterson, 1968: 84). A fully developed second preural neural arch, ostensibly present in *Araripichthys*, is found today in some elopomorphs (e.g., *Tarpon*) and in some primitive fossil teleosts (e.g., *Allothrissops*, *Ichthyodectes*), but it usually is somewhat reduced in length (e.g., *Elops*) or represented by only a low crest (e.g., berycoids, generalized percoids) or even absent.

According to Patterson (1968: 85), the primitive acanthopterygian (i.e., his "myctophoid-ctenothrissiform-beryciform assemblage") caudal fin may be characterized as including only six hypurals (instead of seven), two uroneurals (instead of three), fusion of the first ural and preural centra, and fusion of the first uroneural with the first ural and preural neural arches to produce a stegural. Such an arrangement is at variance with Silva Santos's (1985c) conclusion that *Araripichthys* is an acanthopterygian. His "stegural" (not fused to the neural arches in AMNH 11944, and regarded here as a first uroneural) could pertain to either of the centra he identified as PU_1 and U_1. It is doubtful whether *Araripichthys* possesses a typically euteleostean stegural.

The pectoral fins are attached low on the shoulder girdle and are elongate and rounded, reaching almost to the insertion of the anal fin. There are at least 12 pectoral fin-rays, possibly more. It is difficult to establish the exact number because the pectorals, like the median fins, are completely scale-coved. There are no traces of pelvic fins or girdle in any of the specimens examined by us or Silva Santos (1985c), and these structures probably were absent.

The entire body, including the fins and some parts of the head, is covered by small, rounded, deeply overlapping, thin cycloid scales. Their arrangement is beautifully displayed in AMNH 12576 and 11973. The largest scales (along the flanks of the body) are approximately 7 or 8 mm deep in these examples. Scale size diminishes greatly over the fins, immediately behind the shoulder girdle, and antero-dorsally just behind the head. The lateral line is well developed, with approximately 86 scales along its length. At the deepest part of the body there are up to 33 scales in a vertical series above the lateral line and 18-20 scales below it. The lateral line is fairly straight.

Araripichthys lacks three of four characters (the other cannot be compared) used by Stiassny (1986) to unite all acanthomorph fishes (spina occipitalis contributing to foramen magnum; reduction of ethmoid cartilage and close approximation or sutural contact between lateral ethmoids and vomer; upper limb of post-temporal firmly bound to exoccipital). It also is primitive in lacking fin spines and retaining an orbitosphenoid, two large supramaxillae, seven hypurals, autogenous hypurals 1 and 2, a second ural centrum, and a first uroneural not fused into a stegural. The scales presumably are primitive in being cycloid rather than ctenoid.

Similarities with lampridiforms (e.g., mobile, sliding premaxilla, modified maxillary-vomer articulation, absence of pelvics) offer tempting but not compelling support for a relationship. These taxa are further united by two primitive characters (ossified orbitosphenoid, lack of median spiny fin-rays), but this too is unconvincing. It long has been suggested that lampridiforms are derived from some early acanthopterygian stock prior to the major radiation of the group during later Cretaceous and Early Tertiary times (Tate Regan, 1907; Gregory, 1959; Lauder and Liem, 1983). The presence of a few lampridiform-like features in an Aptian fish such as *Araripichthys* is congruent with that view but does nothing to resolve the systematic position of the genus.

For want of more diagnostic evidence, the systematic position of *Araripichthys* must be regarded as unresolved above the elopocephalan level. It lacks or else is unknown in features used by Patterson and Rosen (1977: 130) to define clupeocephalans. The presence of only two uroneurals (Silva Santos, 1985c: 137) supports the inclusion of *Araripichthys* within the Elopocephala.

Assemblages: Jardim, Old Mission.

(J. G. Maisey, S. Blum)

Facing page: Representative specimens of *Araripich-thys castilhoi*. The braincase (top right) belongs to composite specimen at top left and displays elongate supraoccipital spine and deep sub-epiotic fossa. Specimen at bottom right, reproduced here close to life-size, is one of smallest examples known.

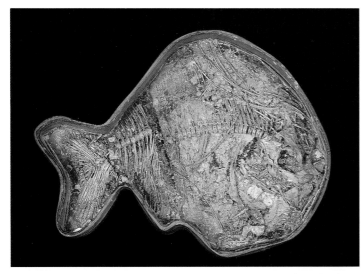

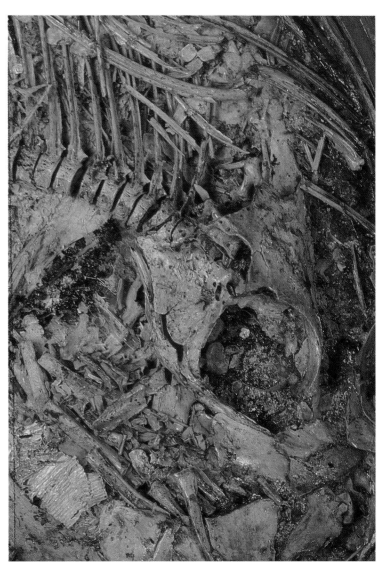

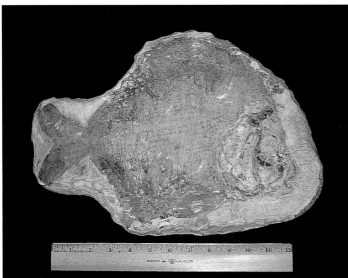

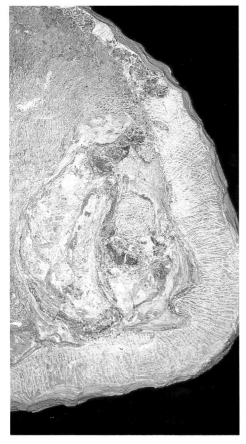

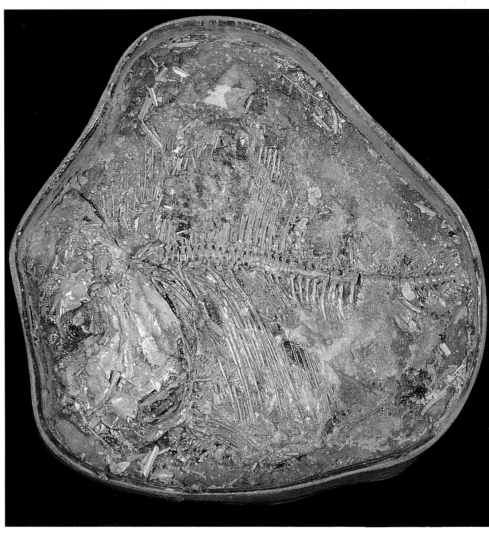

BRANNERION Jordan, 1919

Cohort ELOPOMORPHA
Order ANGUILLIFORMES
Suborder ALBULOIDEI
incerta sedis
*Genus **Brannerion*** Jordan, 1919
Emended diagnosis: Albuloid fishes with blunt snout; large eyes (eye diameter about 35 percent of neurocranium length); relatively deep body (maximum body depth 35 to 40 percent of SL); long anal fin base; elongated fourth dorsal and anal fin rays; cycloid scales of moderate size and with numerous horizontal radii; scales tightly imbricated such that exposed portion is approximately twice as high as long; rostral commissure contained in dermethmoid, flanked by at least four lateral rostral ossicles; sensory

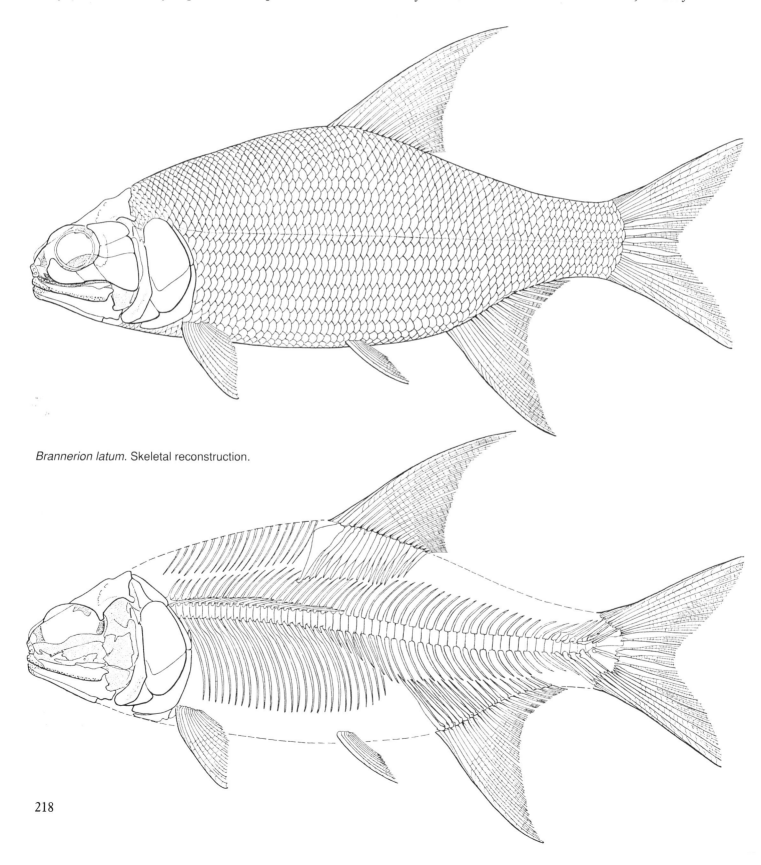

Brannerion latum. Skeletal reconstruction.

canal in dentary nearly open, pores more than three times longer than inter-pore distance; jaw teeth blunt, or conical and slightly recurved, toothed surface of dentary extending onto labial surface beyond the level of mandibular sensory canal near symphysis, but confined to normal position postero-laterally; parasphenoid toothplate broad, flat to concave ventrally, bearing many small molariform teeth; basibranchial and basihyal tooth plates present, strongly ossified in large individuals, bearing small molariform teeth; retroarticular fused to angular, angular contributes lateral portion of articulating facet; dentary and angular with reverse overlap dorsally; large median gular present; single supramaxilla; mesopterygoid strongly ossified, with well developed ventro-medially convex toothed surface, teeth as on parasphenoid; hyomandibula with well-developed laminar lateral apophysis projecting antero-dorsally at the level of the opercular ramus; D19; A20; caudal 10 upper, 9 lower; P at least 14; V at least 11 (AMNH 11931); vertebrae 51 to 62; caudal skeleton with two ural centra, 3 epurals, 3 uroneurals, 7 hypurals (all autogenous, but with H_1 and H_2 fused proximally at their articulation with U_1), ventralmost principal caudal fin rays supported by parhypurals from first and second preural centra.

Type species: *Calamopleurus vestitus* Jordan and Branner 1908, by original designation (Jordan, 1919: 209).

Brannerion vestitum Jordan and Branner
1908 *Calamopleurus vestitus* J & B: 19
1919 *Calamopleurus vestitus* J & B; Jordan: 209
1923 *Brannerion vestitum* (J & B); Jordan: 35
1968 *Brannerion vestitum* (J & B); Silva Santos and Valença: 348
1977 *Brannerion vestitum* (J & B); Forey: 142
1986 *Brannerion vestitus* (J & B); Mones: 34 [*sic*]

Holotype: Originally Rocha collection No. 11, Museu Rocha, Fortaleza; major part presumably now in Museo Nacional do Rio de Janeiro, specimen number unknown; counterpart Stanford University no. 58295, now in California Academy of Sciences, San Francisco; part of small individual; Santana formation, Chapada do Araripe (precise locality not known).

Diagnosis: (Abstracted after Jordan and Branner 1908.) Subopercle smaller than in *Notelops brama* (the literal reference is to *Calamopleurus cylindricus*, but the specimens Jordan and Branner referred to that species are actually *N. brama*; see earlier discussion of *Enneles* and *Calamopleurus*); head about 3½ in length (to base of caudal fin); distance from gill opening to dorsal a little more than greatest

Brannerion species A. Skeletal reconstruction.

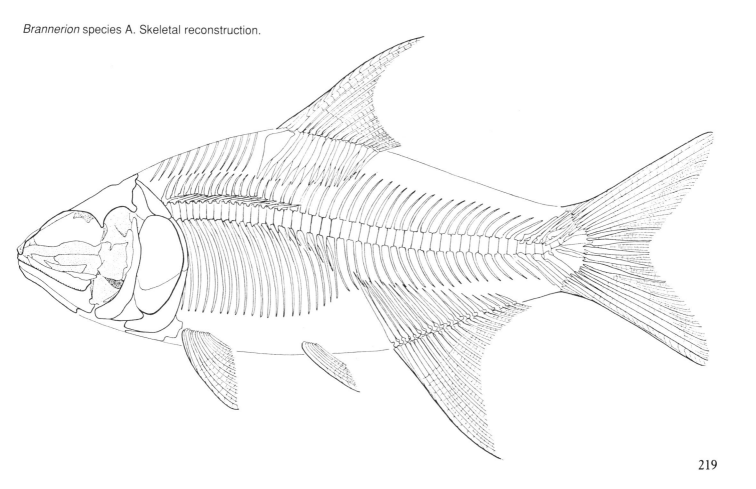

Facing page: Representative *Brannerion* specimens.
Top: A fine example in "Old Mission" matrix. Photo by J.
Maisey. **Center:** Two specimens in "Jardim" matrix.
Bottom: Two specimens in "Santana" matrix, showing
full extent of graceful fin rays.

Below: *Pterothrissus gissu*, a Recent deepsea bonefish.
Art by Tomita.

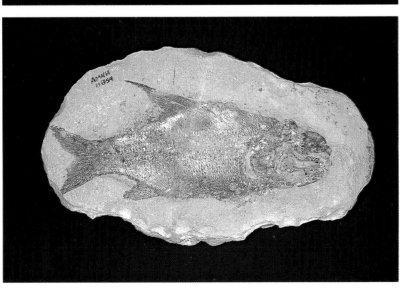

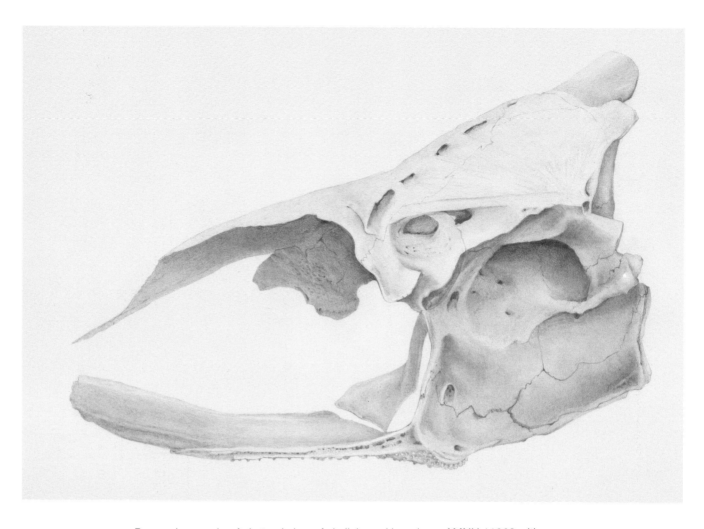

Brannerion species A. Lateral view of skull, based largely on AMNH 11863 with some information from AMNH 11856.

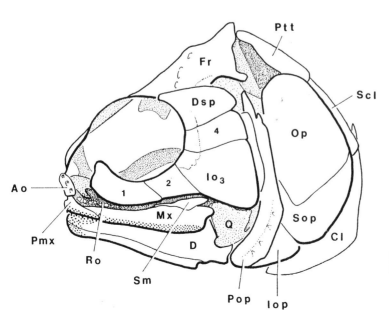

Brannerion latum. Outline reconstruction of head in lateral view.

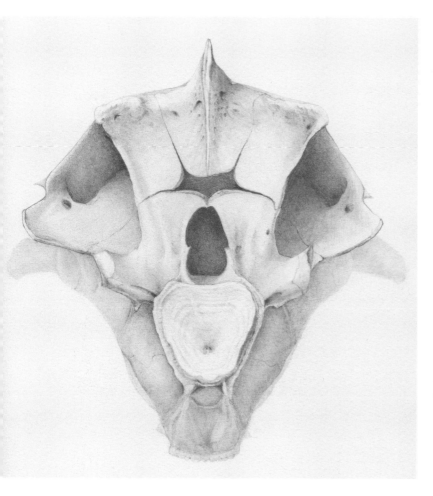

Brannerion species A. Posterior view of skull, based on AMNH 11863 and 11856.

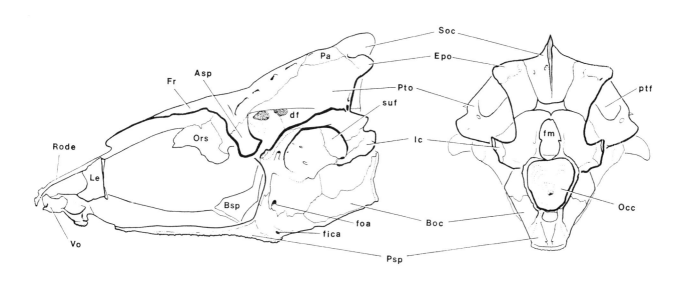

Brannerion species A. Annotated outline of skull.

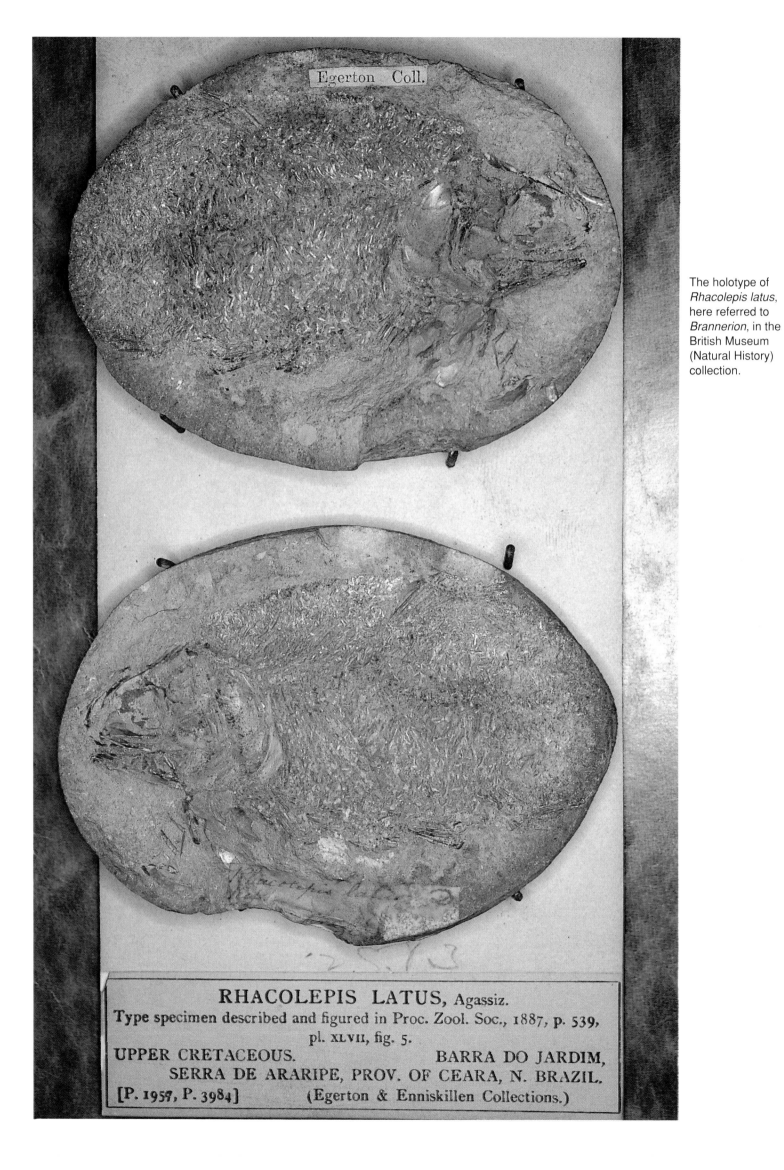

The holotype of
Rhacolepis latus,
here referred to
Brannerion, in the
British Museum
(Natural History)
collection.

RHACOLEPIS LATUS, Agassiz.
Type specimen described and figured in Proc. Zool. Soc., 1887, p. 539,
pl. XLVII, fig. 5.
UPPER CRETACEOUS.   BARRA DO JARDIM,
SERRA DE ARARIPE, PROV. OF CEARA, N. BRAZIL.
[P. 1957, P. 3984]   (Egerton & Enniskillen Collections.)

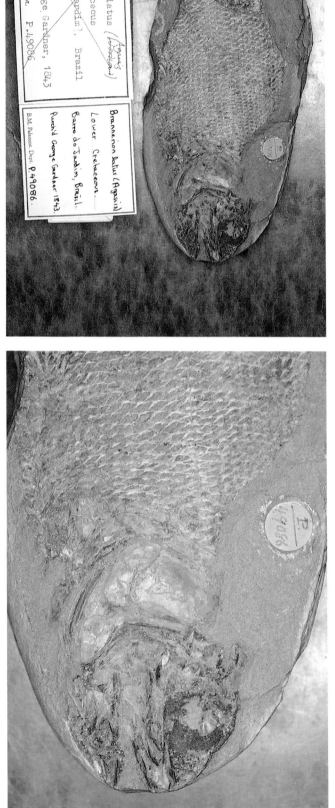

The holotype of "*Calamopleurus*" *vestitus* in the California Academy of Sciences, the type species of *Brannerion* (**top**), and a specimen in the British Museum (Natural History) referred to *B. latus* and originally owned by George Gardner (**bottom**).

depth; upright limb of preopercle inclined slightly to the anterior; opercle large, convex, with some black pigment within the bone, as long as deep; subopercle with concentric striae, its depth about 3½ times in depth of opercle; suture between opercle and subopercle very oblique (approximately 45° from horizontal) and somewhat curved; scales cycloid, deeper than long, much larger than in any other of the Cretaceous Elopidae from Brazil, about 28 along lateral line to front of dorsal; 8 in a vertical series from front of dorsal to lateral line; 10 to 12 between lateral line and ventrals; lateral line very distinct, nearly median, slightly decurved anteriorly; dorsal mostly obliterated and pectorals also; ventrals and anal wholly wanting, as is whole caudal fin; gular plate obliterated.

Discussion: The counterpart of the type specimen (formerly SU 58295) has been examined, and the preceeding description can be amended as follows. The counterpart bears a clear impression of the opercle, which is taller than long (height to length = 1.5). The impression of the subopercle also is clear, and its maximum depth is contained 5.45 times in the height of the opercle. The impression of the supracleithrum is clear dorsally but partially obscured by the cleithrum ventrally. The length of the supracleithrum approaches the height of the opercle. The origin of the dorsal fin is obscure, and all counts and measurements based on this landmark must be considered approximate. The rays of the dorsal fin are depressed, and it is clear that the longest ray originates anteriorly in the fin and extends posteriorly to the caudal peduncle. A marked depression indicates the path of the vertebral column through the caudal region. The lateral line diverges from it and is displaced ventrally about half a scale height along the last fifth of the body. The depression created by the vertebral column is inflected sharply (dorsally) just before the end of the concretion, indicating that the ural centra probably are contained in the major part (which was unavailable for study). The origins of a few pelvic fin rays are present in the counterpart and indicate that the origin of this fin is nearly opposite the origin of the dorsal. Fragments of anal fin rays or their impressions indicate that the anal fin contained at least 15 rays, although this fin is incomplete anteriorly.

Neither the description given by Jordan and Branner nor the characters observable in the counterpart of the holotype allow this nominal taxon to be associated positively with either of the two *Brannerion* species that are present in the fauna. It is possible, however, that preparation of the major part (previously Rocha collection No. 11, Rocha Museum, Fortaleza, but presumably transferred to the Museo Nacional do Rio de Janeiro; see Silva Santos and Valença 1968: 349) could reveal distinguishing characters, which would then enable the name-bearing type to be associated with one of the two species described below.

Brannerion latum (Agassiz)

1841 *Rhacolepis latus* Agassiz: 83
1844a *Rhacolepis latus* Agassiz: 1012
1887 *Rhacolepis latus;* Agassiz; Woodward: 539
1901 *Rhacolepis latus* Agassiz; Woodward: 32 (holotype designated)
1908 *Rhacolepis latus* Agassiz; Jordan & Branner: 22

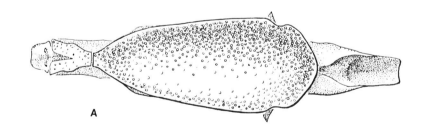

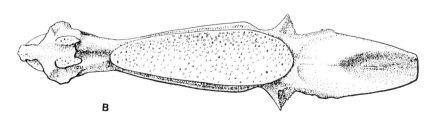

Palatal views of the parasphenoid in (A) *Brannerion latum,* from AMNH 11917, and (B) *B. species A,* from AMNH 11934.

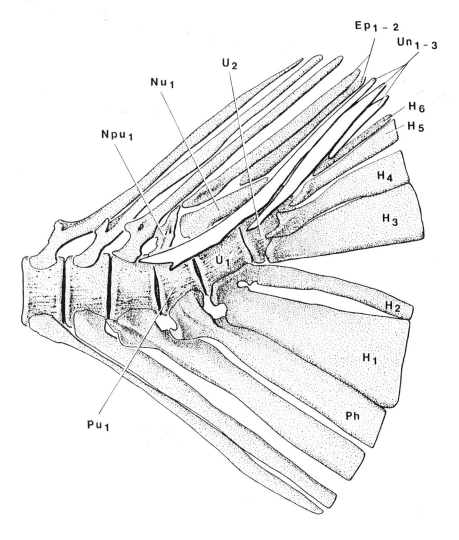

Brannerion latum. Caudal endoskeleton, from AMNH 11932.

1923 *Rhacolepis latus* Agassiz; Jordan: 67

1968 *Rhacolepis latus* Agassiz: Silva Santos & Valença: 348

1977 *Rhacolepis latus* Agassiz; Forey: 162

1986 *Rhacolepis latus* Agassiz; Mones: 44

Holotype: British Museum (Natural History), part BM(NH) P.3984 and counterpart BM(NH) 1959; complete fish to caudal peduncle (tail missing), concretion split sagittally but off-center, such that neither squamation nor vertebral column is revealed clearly; Santana formation, Chapado do Araripe (precise locality not known).

Emended diagnosis: Vertebrae 60 to 62; parasphenoidal toothplate wide and distinctly concave; anterior opening of posterior myodome wide; anterior lateral profile rounded (dermethmoid curved ventrally); toothed surface of dentary broad and horizontal along lateral margin of jaw; toothed surface of ectopterygoid wide and flat.

Brannerion sp. A

Referred specimens: American Museum of Natural History, AMNH 11856; nearly complete fish in part and counterpart, acid-prepared, vertebral column complete and sequentially articulated, except at occiput; Santana

formation, Jardim, Chapada do Araripe.

AMNH 11863, nearly complete fish in part (acid-prepared) and counterpart (unprepared).

Diagnosis: Vertebrae 53 to 55; parasphenoidal toothplate moderately wide and flat; anterior opening of posterior myodome narrow; anterior lateral profile angular (not rounded); toothed surface of dentary narrow and rounded along lateral margin of the jaw; toothed surface of ectopterygoid narrow.

Discussion: The diagnoses for *B. latum* and *B.* sp. A given above admittedly are terse, but the characteristics presented are the only ones that consistently and reliably differentiate the two species. We have considered the possibility that there is only a single species of *Brannerion*, particularly in light of recent studies on Central American cichlids that indicate that different feeding morphologies can be produced by different diets (see Meyer, 1988, and references contained therein). However, dietary differences do not plausibly account for the difference between modal vertebral counts (61 vs 54).

Additional support for the systematic significance of vertebral number and the shapes of tooth-bearing structures in albuloids is provided by the work of Shaklee and Tamaru

Representative specimens of *Brannerion*. The example at top right is associated with a specimen of *Tharrhias*.

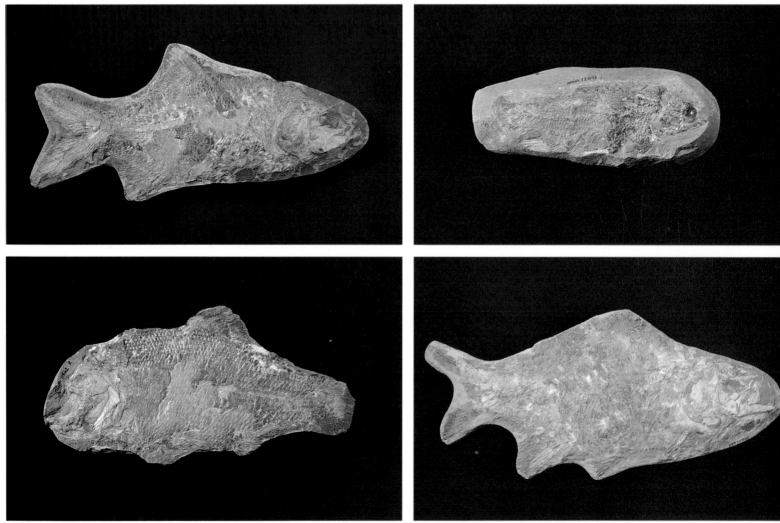

(1981). Their study on Recent central Pacific albulids revealed that two sympatric species, *Albula glossodonta* and *A. neoguinica*, are separated by a genetic distance (as estimated by allozyme electrophoresis) that usually is found between fishes of different genera. Shaklee and Tamaru also showed that while these species are nearly identical externally, they have non-overlapping differences in vertebral number and differently shaped parasphenoidal and basibranchial toothplates.

Albulids (bonefishes) occur in most tropical seas and comprise a single Recent genus, *Albula*. Before the work of Shaklee and Tamaru (1981), *Albula* was considered to contain two species, the circumtropically distributed *A. vulpes* Linnaeus, and *A.* (=*Dixonia*) *nemoptera* (Fowler) from the Atlantic and Pacific coasts of the Americas. However, these authors demonstrated that *A.* "*vulpes*" contains at least three biological species. The other family of Recent albuloids, the Pterothrissidae, also contains a single genus, *Pterothrissus*, with two species, one from tropical western Africa and the other from Japan.

Albula has a well-developed crushing dentition presumably adapted for feeding on bottom-dwelling invertebrates such as shrimps, crabs, and clams, although some fishes also are taken. Shoals of feeding *Albula* may work their way over the bottom, and in shallow water their tails frequently break the surface. The morphology and distribution of molariform teeth are similar in *Albula* and *Brannerion*, suggesting that their feeding habits were broadly comparable, although *Albula* has a smaller gape than *Brannerion* and thus may be more limited in the upper size limit of its prey.

Nomenclatural History and Issues: Agassiz (1841) described the first fossil fishes from the Santana formation in a short note without figures. He named five genera and seven species, four of which (*Rhacolepis buccalis, R. brama, R. latus,* and *Calamopleurus cylindricus*) are relevant to the nomenclature of *Brannerion*. The specimens examined by Agassiz subsequently were acquired by the British Museum (Natural History). In 1887, Woodward published a review of *Rhacolepis* and therein provided figures of the specimens that bore labels penned by Agassiz (a clear indication that these were the specimens upon which Agassiz based his names). Later, Woodward (1901) removed *R. brama* to a new genus, *Notelops*, designated the type specimens for the remaining two species of *Rhacolepis*, and designated *R. buccalis* as the type species for that genus.

Several years later additional material from the Santana formation was presented to Branner and described by Jordan and Branner (1908). These authors were aware of the taxa described by Agassiz and Woodward, but believed that one of their specimens represented a new species of *Calamopleurus*, which they named *C. vestitus*. Later, Jordan (1919) removed this species to a new genus, and the species has since been known as *Brannerion vestitum* (Jordan and Branner, 1908). In his most detailed review of fishes from the Santana formation, Jordan (1923: 67) stated that the type of *Rhacolepis latus* (which Jordan knew only from the figure in Woodward, 1887) was "obviously crushed and telescoped and the species is very likely a *Rhacolepis buccalis* or perhaps a *Notelops brama* pressed flat." Subsequent authors (e.g., d'Erasmo, 1938: 34; Forey, 1977: 162) have followed Jordan (1923) in doubting the validity of *Rhacolepis latus*. However, Forey (1977) noted a similarity between the type of *Rhacolepis latus* and specimens identified as *Brannerion vestitum*.

The Axelrod collection contains some 30 specimens that may be referred positively to the genus *Brannerion*, most of which have been acid-prepared. This material has revealed a number of osteological features that clearly place *Brannerion* among the Albuloidei (see below). The detailed study of *Rhacolepis buccalis* by Forey (1977) has shown that this species (the type of that genus) is a pachyrhizodontid and not an elopid as was once thought. Following an examination of the type specimen of *Rhacolepis latus* (part and counterpart), we concluded that it is not a pachyrhizodontid but rather exhibits several features that positively are diagnostic of *Brannerion*. These features include head and body shape, a curved dermethmoid showing a cross-section through the ethmoid commissure, opercular shape, and short pebble-like teeth on the dentary. Hence the oldest name for a *Brannerion* species is *B. latum* (=*Rhacolepis latus* Agassiz, 1841).

Discrete variation among the acid-prepared specimens of *Brannerion* shows that two species of *Brannerion* are present in the fauna. These species can be differentiated reliably by vertebral number, shape of the snout, and (in specimens larger than 250 mm SL) parasphenoid morphology and dentition (smaller specimens show an intermediate condition of the parasphenoid).

As two species of *Brannerion* exist in the fauna, and two specific names are available, it may be the case that the two type specimens were drawn from different species. We have examined the types of both *Rhacolepis latus* (part and counterpart) and *Brannerion vestitum* (counterpart only). Unfortunately, all of the features that diagnose the two species, except snout shape, usually are observable only in relatively complete, acid-prepared material, and none of the type material has been acid-prepared. Moreover, the Agassiz type represents a small fish (about 100 mm SL) and probably would not show most of the diagnostic qualitative features even if it were acid-prepared. Additionally, its tail is missing, and thus a complete vertebral count could not be an expected result of further preparation. Its snout, however, clearly is rounded. By this single feature the most common species (round snout, high vertebral count, and concave parasphenoid) is here associated with the type specimen of *Rhacolepis latus*.

The Jordan and Branner type represents a larger fish (approximately 285 mm SL), but the counterpart bears only the scales (medial surfaces exposed), some incomplete fin rays, and fragments and impressions of right lateral skull bones. The snout, lower jaw, and posterior caudal skeleton are missing. The counterpart of this type consequently is indeterminate at the species level and would remain so even after acid-preparation. It is possible, however, that the major part (previously Rocha collection No. 11) could reveal diagnostic features, particularly a complete vertebral count, if it were acid-prepared. It would therefore be inappropriate to recognize the nominal taxon *Brannerion* (= *Calamopleurus*) *vestitum* (Jordan and Branner) as a *nomen dubium*, even though the type specimen is presently indeterminate at the species level.

Workers concerned with the diversity of this fauna should exclude the species *Brannerion vestitum* from tabulations because its existence as a distinct biological entity cannot be demonstrated. We suspect that it eventually will fall into synonymy under *Brannerion latum*.

Description: Because this work represents the first major revision of *Brannerion*, a fairly detailed morphological description follows here, even though this information will be of interest only to specialists.

In the anterior neurocranium, the rostral commissure is contained in the dermethmoid, with large medial and lateral pores (a total of three, in addition to openings that receive the sensory canal laterally). The nasal is large and flat and does not enclose the sensory canal, but does bear foramina for neuromasts. There are at least four rostral ossicles. The adnasal is wrapped around but does not enclose the sensory canal. The mesethmoid presumably was not ossified. The ventral face of the vomer has two distinct postero-ventrally directed pedestals bearing teeth.

In the skull roof, the frontals are wide over the orbits, narrowing quickly over the rostrum. There is a marked depression in the skull roof between the supraorbital canals, running the entire length of the frontals and extending posteriorly almost to the supraoccipital. The section of the supraorbital canal over the orbits has three large, medially directed pores. A postero-medial branch of the canal overlying the neurocranium has four laterally directed pores, the last of which is borne on the parietal. The paired parietals are as wide as long. The medial suture between them is not interrupted by the supraoccipital. The dermal portion of the pterotic is broad posteriorly and is nearly as broad as long.

The premaxilla is without a sensory canal. There is a well-defined dorso-medial facet on the premaxilla for articulation with the dermethmoid. The premaxilla forms less than one-third of the gape. The maxilla is long, extending slightly beyong the posterior margin of the orbit, is flat posteriorly, and lacks a posterior spine. A single supramaxilla is present. This is rod-like anteriorly, compressed and taller posteriorly. The toothed surface of the dentary extends antero-ventrally well beyond the biting surface antero-medially, but teeth are confined to the dorso-lingual surface posteriorly. The retroarticular is fused to the angular, which contributes to the lateral portion of the articulating facet. The dentary and angular have a reverse overlap dorsally. A large median gular is present. Dermo- and auto-palatines are fused, and the palatine and ectopterygoid are tightly sutured, forming a continuous wide toothed surface. The ectopterygoid bears a large, flat, dorso-laterally directed flange. The mesopterygoid is strongly ossified, with a well-developed medially convex toothed surface. The metapterygoid is sutured to the hyomandibula and lacks any foramen for the deep section of the levator arcus palatini muscle. The anterior border of the quadrate is located under the posterior border of the mesopterygoid.

In the braincase an orbitosphenoid is present, with a single median foramen for the olfactory nerves, and does not form an ossified interorbital septum. The basisphenoid contacts the pterosphenoids and prootics dorso-laterally and the parasphenoid mid-ventrally. The parasphenoid toothplate is relatively narrow and lightly concave in small individuals, becoming either moderately wide and flat or else very wide and ventrally concave (in larger individuals), and bears numerous molariform teeth. A foramen for the internal carotid artery lies within the parasphenoid. The foramen for the orbital artery is located just behind the antero-lateral edge of the prootic. A posterior venous foramen is situated near the posterior margin of the prootic, being partially covered by the intercalar bridge. The foramen for the facial nerve is located just below the facet for the hyomandibular. Autosphenotic, prootic, and pterotic bones all contribute to the long, continuous, hyomandibular facet. The dilatator fossa is shallow, narrowly roofed by the pterotic, with the inner face of the fossa (autosphenotic and pterotic) often weakly ossified and frequently fenestrated (the number and shape of fenestrae are variable among individuals). There is a deep subtemporal fossa, with its walls formed by the prootic, pterotic, and exoccipital bones. The posterior myodome is deep, but capped posteriorly by the basioccipital. The intercalar contacts the exoccipital, pterotic, and prootic (by an anteriorly directed bridge), but not the epiotic. The post-temporal fossa also is deep, with its antero-lateral wall formed by the autosphenotic. The posterior face of the exoccipital is taller than wide. Paired exoccipitals meet under the foramen magnum and are excluded from the occipital condyle (the posterior end of the basioccipital may be formed by a fused hemicentrum).

There are five infraorbital bones, the third, fourth, and fifth reaching the preopercular posteriorly. The infraorbital canal is open postero-ventrally. No evidence of a supraorbital or an antorbital has been found, and they presumably are lacking. The preopercular is without a sharp angle. Its ventral ramus is short and does not curve completely to the horizontal. There are usually about nine pores in the preopercular sensory canal, but their size and exact number vary. The opercular is taller than long.

A basihyal and three separate basibranchial ossifications are present. There is a single toothplate over the basibranchials. This toothplate is wide and dorsally convex, strongly ossified in larger individuals (where a swirling pattern of striations is apparent ventrally), and bears numerous molariform teeth. A separate basihyal toothplate is present. Dorsal and ventral hypohyals are present, tightly articulated with the anterior ceratohyal. The dorsal hypohyal bears a dorso-medial protuberance. The hyoid artery entered the ventral hypohyal postero-medially, turned dorsally into the dorsal hypohyal and exited antero-laterally, then proceeded in a deep groove along the dorso-lateral edge of the anterior ceratohyal. At least eight branchiostegal rays are present, with the more posterior ones greatly expanded.

In the pectoral girdle, the dorsal arm of the post-temporal is laminar and the ventral arm strut-like. The length of the supracleithrum is nearly equal to the height of the operculum. A mesocoracoid is present. The exact number of postcleithra is indeterminate, but at least a single long and splint-like one is present.

Relationships of *Brannerion*: In their original description of *Brannerion* (=*Calamopleurus*) *vestitum*, Jordan and Branner (1908) aligned this species with other elopids for its possession of a gular plate, cycloid scales, large circumorbitals extending posteriorly to the preopercle, and ventral fins originating beneath the last rays of the dorsal. All of these are unfortunately primitive teleostean features. Although the diagnosis of elopomorph fishes has more recently come to incorporate derived features (e.g., Greenwood et al., 1966; Forey, 1973a and b; Greenwoood, 1977; Patterson and Rosen, 1977), none of these revisionary works has addressed the relationships of *Brannerion*, and the genus has remained poorly known. After Jordan (1923), most workers who discussed or mentioned *Brannerion* continued to include it among the Elopidae (e.g., d'Erasmo, 1938; Santos and Valença, 1968). The material examined here provides the first opportunity to evaluate the phylogentic position of this genus more critically.

Patterson and Rosen (1977, p. 126) summarized the evidence for the monophyly of elopomorph fishes (Taeniopaedia of Greenwood, 1977) as follows: "elopocephalans in which there is a leptocephalous larva, angular and retroarticular bones fused, rostral and prenasal ossicles present and a compound neural arch formed in cartilage over PUI and UI." The larval form in *Brannerion* is not known, but the other three features clearly are present, indicating that this genus is a member of the Elopomorpha. It also is relevant that *Brannerion* lacks all of the features these authors used to diagnose the Clupeocephala (sister group of the Elopomorpha).

It is generally held that the Elopomorpha comprises four major groups: the elopids (ten-pounders), megalopids (tarpons), albuloids (osmeroidids, albulids, pterothrissids,

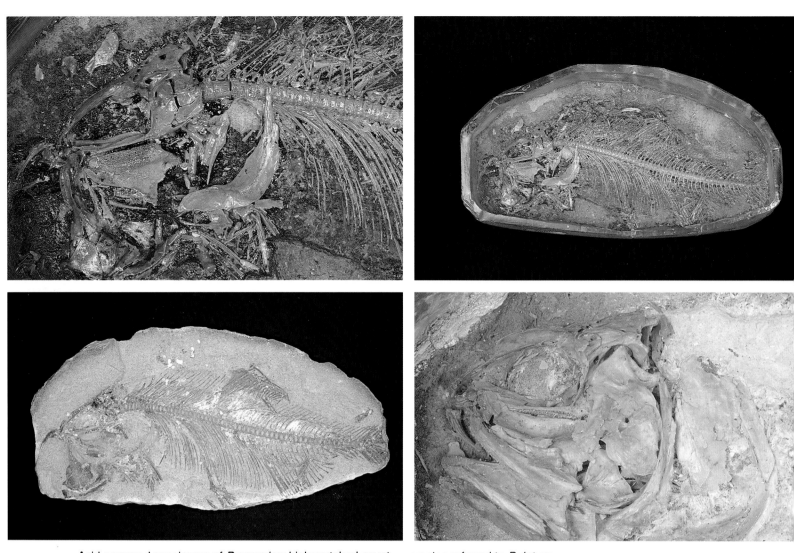

Acid-prepared specimens of *Brannerion*; high vertebral count examples referred to *B. latum*.

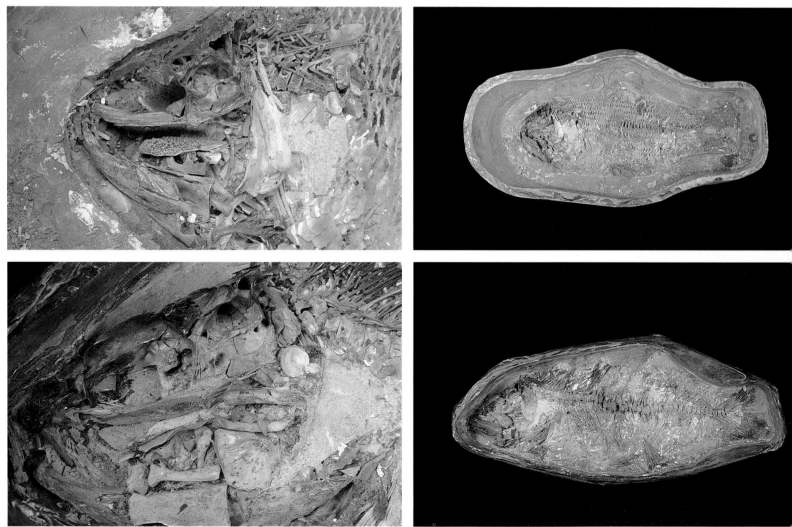

Caudal fins of two specimens referred to *Brannerion latum*.

notocanthids, and halosaurids), and anguilloids (eels). Each of these groups (except perhaps the elopids), is demonstrably monophyletic, but the relationships among these groups are less clear. Nelson (1973: 347) proposed a relationship between the albuloids and anguilloids based on Marshall's (1962) review of swim-bladder morphology and associated vasculature. Marshall was impressed by the similarities in the retia mirabilia of representative anguilloids, notacanthids, and halosaurids. He interpreted these similarities as strongly indicating descent from a common ancestor. When queried by Nelson about the condition present in *Albula*, Marshall replied that this genus also shows the specialized condition. Thus, Marshall's unpublished results constitute the only evidence for a closer relationship among two of the four basal taxa in the Elopomorpha. In a subsequent examination of elopomorph fishes, Greenwood (1977: 100) concluded that "None of the characters dealt with in this paper weakens this hypothesis, and consequently Nelson's recognition of the Anguilliformes and Albuliformes as sister groups is accepted." This situation is particularly frustrating for paleontologists as the evidence for this relationship pertains to soft anatomy and therefore is unavailable in fossils.

Several of the features that diagnose albuloids (including halosauroids) are nevertheless osteological and allow a comparison with *Brannerion*. Greenwood (1977), based on his own work and that of Nelson (1973), Forey (1973b), and McDowell (1973), cited the following characters as evidence for the monophyly of albuloid fishes: 1) mandibular sensory canal lying in a open groove in both the dentary and angular bones (Nelson, 1973: 346); 2) probably the way in which the ligamentum primordium is either absent or not associated with any part of the adductor mandibulae; 3) a specialized ethmoid commissure (in Recent albuloids it is medially incomplete and carried in more than two rostral ossicles or within the premaxilla); and 4) a reduced intercalar (without a bridge to the prootic). In *Brannerion*, the mandibular canal is enclosed along its short passage through the angular, but in the dentary the "pores" in the canal become so large that the canal is nearly open. The ligamentum primordium is not observable. The ethmoid commissure is complete through the dermethmoid (the primitive teleostean condition), but there are four to five lateral rostral ossicles (not found in the more plesiomorphic elopids and megalopids) that are similar to those found in "halosaurids"

and reminiscent of the inter-pore bridges or struts present on the premaxilla of *Albula* and *Pterothrissus*. In *Brannerion*, the intercalar is not as reduced as it is in other "albuloids," and the intercalar bridge to the prootic persists as it does in *Elops*.

Thus, of the four albuloid synapomorphies listed above, *Brannerion* has two conditions that are consistent with albuloid relationship (1 and 3), one that is unobservable (2), and one primitive condition (4). The nearly open mandibular canal and the number and character of the lateral rostral ossicles indicate that *Brannerion* is more closely related to "albuloids" than to any other group of elopomorphs. Although the ethmoid commissure is complete in *Brannerion*, Forey (1973b) showed that it also is complete in *Osmeroides lewesiensis*, an early fossil albuloid. The medial interruption of the commissure seen in Recent albuloids thus has a more restricted distribution within "albuloids", and the medially complete condition of *Brannerion* does not exclude it from the larger group.

Within the "albuloids," however, the situation again becomes muddled. A clearly apomorphic group, the halosauroids, may be diagnosed by their common possession of a posterior spine on the maxilla, extreme reduction of the caudal fin skeleton, pelvic fins connected basally by a membrane, pectoral fins set high on the body, and the presence of a large and characteristically shaped fibrous (sometimes cartilaginous) nodule between the maxillary head and the palatine (Greenwood, 1977). However, relationships among the remaining "albuloid" taxa are less clear. Greenwood's (1977, fig. 23) cladogram showed the remaining albuloids, the Osmeroididae, Pterothrissidae, and Albulidae, as forming a monophyletic group, but in the text (ibid.: 99) he characterized this lineage as plesiomorphic relative to the halosauroids. Greenwood offered a list of synapomorphies, compiled by Forey (1973b), to link the families Pterothrissidae and Albulidae, and stated that these features are not present in halosaurids. Only one of those features, a reduced intercalar, is clearly present in the species of *Osmeroides*, and according to McDowell's (1973) fig. 5, the intercalar is not merely reduced but is absent in *Halosaurus guentheri*. Thus, while it is probable that the pterothrissids and albulids form a monophyletic group (these are the only albuloids in which the ethmoid commissure is carried within the premaxilla), there are no characters to indicate that osmeroidids are more closely related to Recent albuloids than are halosauroids (i.e., the Albuoidei of Greenwood, 1977, is paraphyletic).

It is relevant to note that by 1977 Greenwood had begun to recognize only monophyletic groups in his classifications, whereas Forey (1973a and b) intentionally retained several paraphyletic groups in his classification of the Elopiformes. In particular, Forey (1973b: 202) contended that the three species of his Osmeroididae "are a link between the Elopidae on the one hand and the Albulidae and Pterothrissidae on the other." He remarked later (p. 208) that "*Osmeroides lewesiensis* appears to be the most primitive species . . . [whereas] *O. latifrons* appears closest to the ancestry of both the Albulidae and Pterothrissidae."

In addition to the features listed by Greenwood (1977; see above), Forey (1973b) characterized albuloids as having the anterior portion of the supraorbital canal set in grooves on the frontals. These grooves are well developed in pterothrissids, albulids, and halosauroids (McDowell, 1973: 10, and figs. 1, 5). By contrast, *Osmeroides lewesiensis* lacks these grooves, and in *O. latifrons* the grooves are only incipient (Forey, 1973b). There consequently is at least some evidence (supraorbital canals carried in grooves anteriorly, and ethmoid commissure incomplete medially) to support the hypothesis that halosauroids are more closely related to pterothrissids and albulids than are any of the osmeroidid species.

Regardless of the eventual position of the osmeroidids relative to each other and the halosauroids, *Brannerion* appears to be the most primitive albuloid known to date, both cladistically and morphologically. All other albuloids (except *Paraelops*) have a reduced gape (maxilla does not reach the posterior margin of the orbit). All other albuloids (including *Paraelops*) have a reduced intercalar (without a bridge to the prootic). *Brannerion* also is one of the two oldest known albuloids, predating *O. lewesiensis* (upper Albian; Gault Clay at Folkestone, Kent) by some 10-20 million years (the other is *Paraelops*; see below). *Brannerion* does, however, have a number of peculiar features (e.g., elongate fourth dorsal and anal fin rays and a long anal fin base) and cannot be considered directly ancestral to the remaining albuloids.

Relationships among the more primitive albuloids are confounded by parallelisms or reversals in several characters. For example, in *Brannerion, Osmeroides lewesiensis, O. latifrons,* and *Albula*, the parasphenoidal toothplate is relatively broad and bears hemispherical, pebble-like teeth. In elopids, megalopids, *Paraelops, O. levis, Pterothrissus,* and halosauroids, the parasphenoidal toothplate is narrow and bears unspecialized conical teeth. In *Brannerion* and *O. levis* (fig. 54, Forey, 1973b) the posterior branch of the supraorbital canal extends posteriorly onto the parietals, whereas in primitive elopomorphs and all other albuloids it terminates on the frontals. In *O. lewesiensis* and *Albula*, the orbitosphenoid forms an ossified interorbital septum, extends ventrally to contact the parasphenoid, and bears two foramina for the olfactory nerves (a similar, but less developed condition occurs in *Pterothrissus*). In primitive elopomorphs, *Brannerion,* and most other albuloids the orbitosphenoid does not form an interorbital septum and bears a single median foramen for the olfactory nerves. *Brannerion* and *Paraelops* share a peculiar jaw morphology in which the tooth-bearing surface extends onto the labial portion of the jaw, but the two genera may not be each other's closest relatives, as *Paraelops* shares the reduced intercalar that unites all other albuloids. At present, the relationships within the Albuloidei, both fossil and Recent, must be considered poorly known and in need of further study.

(S. Blum)

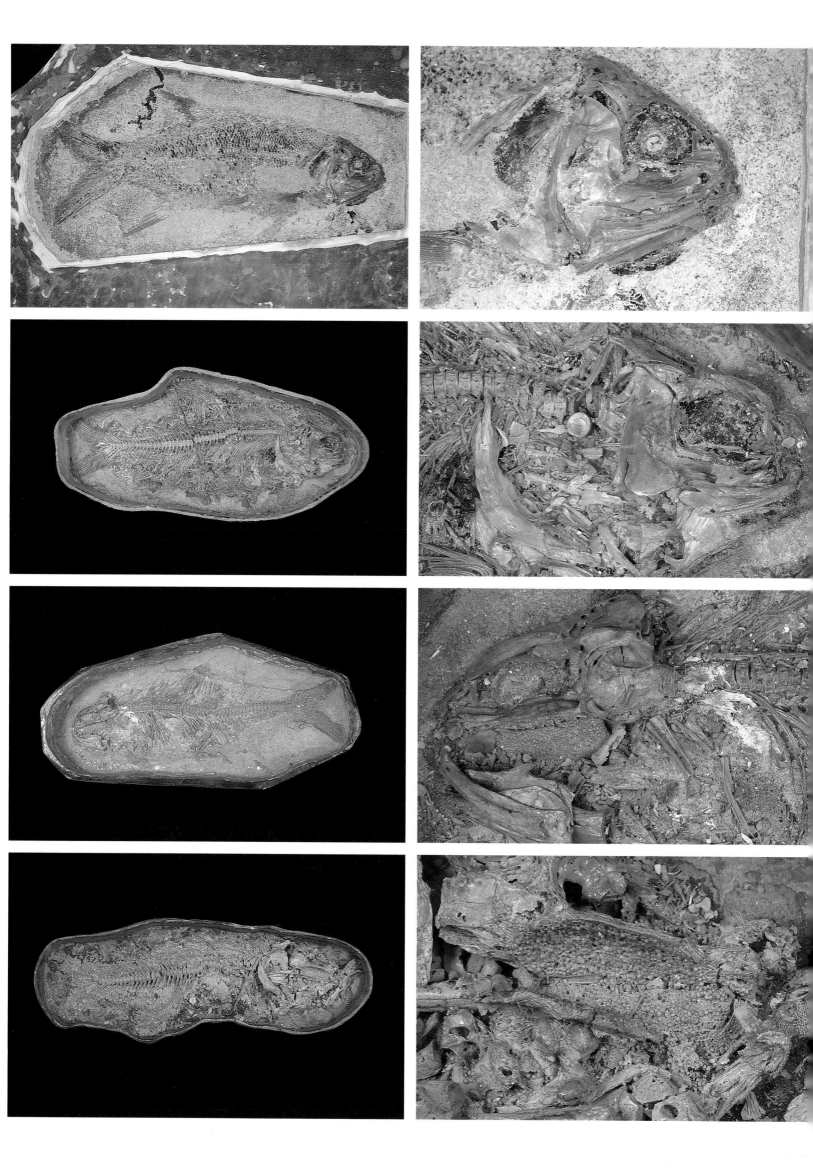

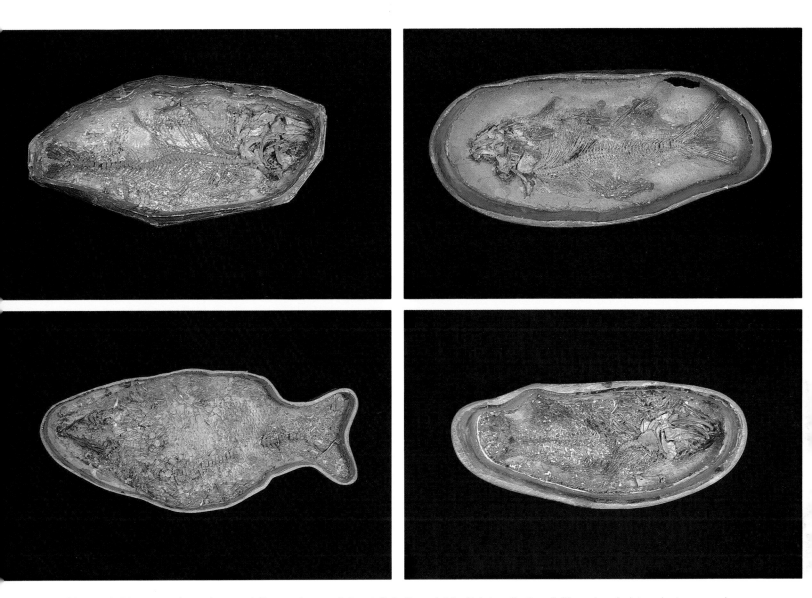

Above: Acid-prepared specimens of *Brannerion* sp. A (top left, bottom right), *B. latum* (bottom left), and an indeterminate example (top right).

Facing page: *Brannerion latum* (top four views); other views are of *B.* sp. A.

PARAELOPS Silva Santos, 1971

Suborder ALBULOIDEI
incertae sedis
Genus **Paraelops** Silva Santos, 1971
  1968 *Paraelops* Silva Santos and Valença: 349 (nomen nudum)
  1971 *Paraelops* Silva Santos: 439

Emended diagnosis: Albuloid with short, upturned snout, large eyes, body moderately deep (approx. 25 percent of SL at deepest point, anterior to dorsal fin); parietals about three times longer than wide, incompletely separated by supraoccipital; pterotics large, L-shaped; three infraorbitals; ossicle-like antorbital; nasals broad, curved antero-laterally over snout; dilatator fossa roofed by pterotic; extremely deep subtemporal fossa, floored by cartilage, without intercalar-prootic bridge; deep sub-epiotic fossa mesial to post-temporal fossa; large, well-ossified rostral ossicles present, not completely enclosing sensory canal; numerous jaw-teeth, small and conical, attached to inflated bony pads extending laterally onto labial surfaces of maxilla, premaxilla, and dentary; large median gular present; operculum somewhat triangular, with inclined upper posterior margin; supracleithrum strongly inclined; moderately long anal fin base, no fin-rays particularly elongated; elongate cycloid scales of moderate size, with notched anterior and posterior margins; median fins scale-covered; P19; V12; D29; A10-11; caudal fin lacks median notch; approximately 65 preural vertebrae, of which 18 are caudal.

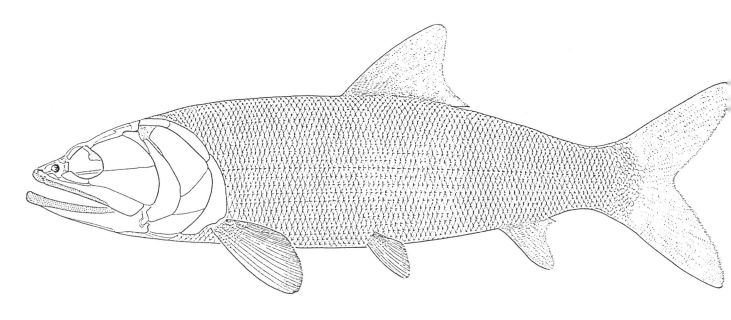

Paraelops cearensis. Skeletal reconstruction.

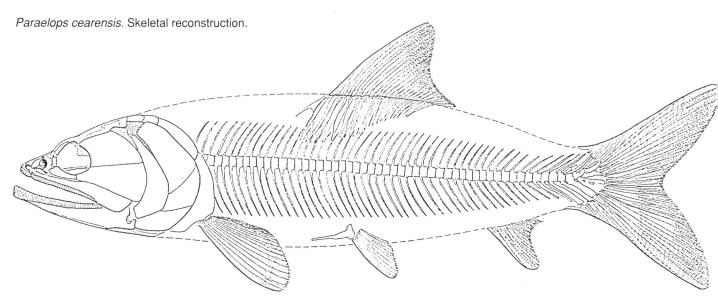

Type species: *Paraelops cearensis* Silva Santos, 1971.

Paraelops cearensis Silva Santos

1968 *Paraelops cearensis* Silva Santos and Valença: 349 (nomen nudum)

1971 *Paraelops cearensis* Silva Santos; Silva Santos: 439

1973 *Paraelops cearensis* Silva Santos; Mabesoone & Tinoco: 105

1986 *Paraelops cearensis* Silva Santos; Mones: 37

Diagnosis: As for genus.

Holotype: Divisão de Geologia e Mineralogia, Departamento Nacional da Produção Mineral, Rio de Janiero DGM-DNPM 971-P; head; Santana formation, Lagòa de Dentro, Chapado do Araripe, Pernambuco.

This large fish was first described formally on the basis of ten incomplete specimens, all consisting of only the head region. By virtue of their size, these specimens all were considered to represent adults (Silva Santos, 1971). The postcranial skeleton was at that time unknown.

Silva Santos (1971) suggested that *Paraelops* and *Notelops* differ in parietal morphology, infraorbital arrangement, and dentition. The parietals in *Paraelops* certainly are longer than in *Notelops brama*, but are not appreciably different from those in *N.* sp. A. Specimens of *Paraelops* in the AMNH collection (particularly 12792, which has been acid-prepared) have three separate infraorbitals, as in *Notelops*. In parietal and infraorbital arrangement, therefore, *Paraelops* and *Notelops* are similar. These taxa certainly differ in their dentition, however, and also can be distinguished by their overall shape (*Paraelops* is less streamlined than *Notelops*, with a deeper body and thicker caudal peduncle, more lobate fin outlines, and no median notch in the caudal fin). Scale morphology also is different in *Paraelops*, with a distinct notch in the posterior margin of each scale, and the unpaired fins are almost completely covered by small scales. In spite of these differences, it sometimes is difficult to distinguish specimens of *Notelops* and *Paraelops* without careful inspection, as there is a superficial resemblance and both taxa can attain lengths of over 3 ft (80 cm).

The braincase in *Paraelops* is relatively broad in comparison with *Notelops* and *Rhacolepis*, becoming gradually wider from front to back. The skull roofing bones are ridged, particularly the frontals, and there are distinctly raised areas above the orbits.

The dermethmoid is roughly triangular, with paired posteriorly directed processes that overlap the frontal much as in *Notelops*. There are paired ventro-lateral projections directed posteriorly toward each lateral ethmoid. There is no evidence of a dermethmoid commissure (present in *Notelops* but not in *Rhacolepis*; Forey, 1977).

The frontals meet for much of their length along a median suture, except anteriorly where they presumably were separated by cartilage. Their suture has a complex zig-zag in the epiphyseal region, as in *Rhacolepis* and unlike in *Notelops* (where the suture merely undulates). The frontal has a prominent thickening above the orbit. There appears to be a medial opening for the supraorbital sensory canal in the epiphyseal region, as in *Rhacolepis*, as well as openings above the orbit. Farther anteriorly the supraorbital canal lay in a shallow groove (as in *Albula*, but less pronounced). The lateral margin of the frontal has a short excavation above the autosphenotic. A similar (but longer) excavation occurs in *Rhacolepis* and *Pachyrhizodus*, but in *Notelops* the frontal margin is entire.

The pterotic forms a larger proportion of the skull roof than in either *Rhacolepis* or *Notelops*. It is distinctly L-shaped in dorsal aspect, with an elongate antero-lateral component flanking the posterior third of the frontal. Among Recent elopomorphs, the pterotic is strongly L-shaped in *Albula vulpes* (and in the extinct *A. oweni*; Forey, 1973, figs. 75, 85). As in *Notelops* and albuloids, the supratemporal sensory canal turns away from the lateral margin of the pterotic, leaving a roof of bone overlying the dilatator fossa.

The parietals are elongate, slightly waisted at their mid-point, and in contact with each other for most of their length (Silva Santos, 1971, figs. 1, 4, confirmed in AMNH 12792), except where the supraoccipital is wedged between them posteriorly. The parietals also are elongate in *Notelops* sp. A (see this volume), but in *N. brama* the parietals are almost square in outline. *Rhacolepis* differs from both *Notelops* and *Paraelops* in having its parietals separated by the supraoccipital.

The supraoccipital bears a well-developed median spine, to either side of which is a foramen. The epioccipital has a process to receive the dorsal limb of the post-temporal. An extremely deep sub-epiotic fossa is present, formed by the supraoccipital and epioccipital as in *Albula*, *Pterothrissus*, and various fossil albuloids. Unlike in *Albula vulpes*, the pterotic is not exposed in the floor of the sub-epiotic fossa in *Paraelops*. Since this does not occur in

Pterothrissus or the extinct *Albula oweni*, however, it may represent an autapomorphy of *A. vulpes*.

There is a deep post-temporal fossa in *Paraelops*, separated from the sub-epiotic fossa as in *Albula vulpes* by a thin wall formed by the epioccipital and exoccipital. The intercalar is small and is confined to the posterior face of the neurocranium, where it floors the post-temporal fossa. It is sutured to the exoccipital, pterotic, and epioccipital as in living albuloids. This pattern also occurs in *Notelops*, *Rhacolepis*, *Pachyrhizodus*, and *Osmeroides lewesensis*, as well as in Recent *Arapaima*, *Esox*, *Salmo*, *Chanos*, *Amia*, and fossils such as "Callovian *Pholidophorus* sp." (Patterson, 1975a, fig. 50), *Leptolepis*, caturids, *Oshunia* (see this volume) and *Macrepistius*. The intercalar and epioccipital are separated by the pterotic in *Pholidophorus bechei*, *P. germanicus*, *Cladocyclus*, *Luisichthys*, *Protarpon*, *Promegalops*, *Elops*, *Megalops*, *Brannerion*, *Osmeroides latifrons*, and many Recent teleosts.

The exoccipitals meet above the foramen magnum in *Paraelops*, but it is not known whether they also meet below it as in *Notelops*.

There is an extremely deep subtemporal fossa formed by the exoccipital, pterotic, and prootic. The jugular canal emerges near the center of the prootic. In AMNH 12792 the autosphenotic evidently had only a cartilaginous connection with the prootic, although these two bones fit closely together. There is no indication of a large unossified fenestra between them as Forey (1977: 133) found in *Notelops*. The hyomandibular facet is mostly formed by the pterotic and autosphenotic, with little contribution by the prootic.

The pterosphenoid, orbitosphenoid, and basisphenoid are largely unknown in *Paraelops*. The parasphenoid of AMNH 12792 is badly preserved but still has traces of a toothpatch that probably was quite extensive.

The lateral ethmoid is largely perichondral, with some spongy endochondral bone. In lateral view it closely resembles that of *Megalops* (e.g., Forey, 1973, fig. 30). As in that form the lateral ethmoid extends beneath the olfactory recess and probably meets the postero-lateral process of the dermethmoid. This similarity in morphology of the snout region almost certainly represents a generalized condition in comparison with the greatly elongate snout of modern albuloids. The vomer has a large, diamond-shaped tooth-bearing surface (seen in AMNH 12792). Little else can be determined in this specimen except that the vomer apparently is

Megalops atlanticus, the Recent Atlantic tarpon. Dr. H. R. Axelrod photo.

fused to the ventral ethmoid, as in most teleosts, and that it probably meets the dermethmoid dorsally. A similar diamond-shaped vomerine toothpatch is present in modern *Megalops*. In *Albula* there is only a small, transversely-oriented toothpatch, and in *Pterothrissus* the vomer is edentulous. The arrangement of vomerine teeth in *Paraelops* may represent a primitive elopomorph condition, retained by *Megalops* and divergently specialized in albuloids on one hand and *Elops* on the other (in the latter the vomerine toothpatch is bilobed). The vomer, dermethmoid, and lateral ethmoid surround the nasal pit, in which the olfactory capsule was situated.

Facing page: *Paraelops cearensis*, anterior half of large flattened specimen showing jaws, branchiostegal rays, and paired fins.

There are two pairs of curious, well-ossified dermal ossicles in the snout region of *Paraelops*. These ossicles are elongate and clearly were canal-bearing, although it appears that the sensory canal lay in a groove rather than in a closed tube. The presence of rostral ossicles in *Paraelops* is an important similarity with modern elopomorph fishes, although the arrangement in *Paraelops* seems to be unique. In both the part and counterpart of AMNH 12792 the ossicles originally were positioned nearly vertical with respect to the body axis. A posterior pair lies across the olfactory recess and an anterior pair flanks the dermethmoid. Assuming that the ossicles are undisturbed, the anterior pair may have carried the ethmoid commissural canal, which either terminated on either side of the dermethmoid (as in *Albula*) or else passed from side to side external to that bone. The posterior pair of ossicles is even less straightforward to interpret. As preserved they could have borne an additional vertical sensory canal, which would have no Recent homolog. Alternatively, these ossicles may represent the antorbital, which in *Albula*, *Pterothrissus*, and fossil albuloids such as *Istieus* is cylindrical or tube-like. In AMNH 12792, 12797, and 11887 the first infraorbital (in which the sensory canal follows an upward curve, as in *Megalops*) lies close to the posterior (antorbital?) ossicle. This is the preferred interpretation of the posterior ossicles in *Paraelops*, and it is concluded that this fish represents a morphologically intermediate condition between *Megalops* and *Albula* in its rostral sensory canal arrangement. It appears that "reduction" of the antorbital to an ossicle-like element may have phylogenetically preceded many of the other specializations found in the sensory canal system in the snout of *Albula*. Furthermore, the condition in *Megalops*, where the antorbital is small and splint-like, more closely resembles that in *Paraelops* (and, by inference, primitive albuloids in general) than does *Elops* (where the antorbital is larger and more closely resembles a "typical" circumorbital bone).

There is an elongate supraorbital that extends from the mid-orbital region anteriorly toward the "antorbital" ossicle. The supraorbital is present in only one AMNH specimen (11887), where it apparently is *in situ*. The supraorbital is shown displaced within the orbit of a specimen figured by Silva Santos (1971, fig. 5). A large supraorbital of this type is unusual in teleosts but occurs in *Tharrhias*, *Chanos*, characins, and catfishes, as well as in *Notelops*, *Rhacolepis*, and *Pachyrhizodus*. Although Forey (1977: 186)

declined to draw any phylogenetic inferences, it may be significant that the large supraorbital occurs only in pachyrhizodontoids and *Paraelops* among non-euteleosts.

Silva Santos (1971) reported only a single large infraorbital in *Paraelops*, but this cannot be confirmed. In AMNH 12569, 12792, 12797, and 11887 there is evidence for three infraorbitals plus a large dermosphenotic, arranged much as in *Notelops*. The first infraorbital extends beneath the orbit and broadens anteriorly. The second is by far the largest and is even bigger than in *Notelops*. The third is as long as the second, but much narrower. The circumorbital series is completed by a large dermosphenotic.

Forey (1977: 186) considered "fusion between the second and third infraorbitals and the large size of the dermosphenotic and posterior infraorbitals" represented a unique attribute of pachyrhizodontoid fishes. The presence of an identical arrangement in *Paraelops* therefore is of considerable interest and has implications for the phylogenetic position of pachyrhizodontoids (discussed below).

The hyopalatine series includes an extensive toothed ectopterygoid that extends from the quadrate to about half-way along the gape, where it has a broad contact with the palatine toothplate. The autopalatine is a separate ossification and has only a single articular surface for the ethmoid region (in *Albula* this articulation is double). The endopterygoid is covered by teeth, although these are smaller than those of the ectopterygoid and palatine. The hyomandibula resembles that of *Notelops* but has a more recurved lower limb and a somewhat deeper dorsal part containing a large, ovoid fenestra. The metapterygoid is poorly known but apparently also was toothed.

The upper jaw is slender and reaches behind the orbit. The premaxillary and maxillary dentition is well developed and consists of hundreds of minute enamel-capped conical teeth attached to broad and specialized bony surfaces ("une superficie gonflee"; Silva Santos, 1971: 440). These surfaces wrap around the biting surfaces and extend onto the outer (labial) parts of the jaws. The premaxilla is short and has a narrow anterior extremity. It is less strongly attached to the ethmoid region than in *Albula* and apparently is not canal-bearing (modern albuloids are peculiar in having part of the infraorbital sensory canal located within the premaxilla). The maxilla is long and slender, with a double condylar surface forming a strong ethmoidal articulation. There is a single elongate supramaxilla.

The lower jaw also is slender. The long dentary encloses the mandibular sensory canal (e.g., AMNH 11865) and has a broad tooth-bearing pad that covers about half of its outer surface as well as the occlusal area. The coronoid process is stronger than in *Notelops*, with a longer postero-dorsal margin formed by the angular. It is not known whether the angular and dentary have a "reverse overlap" as in *Notelops*. There is a well-developed postarticular process on the angular, which apparently is fused to the retroarticular in characteristic elopomorph fashion (Nelson, 1973; Patterson and Rosen, 1977). The floor of the glenoid fossa is formed by the angular, and its anterior surface is formed by the separate articular. The latter is a large ossification resting on a ledge of the angular. As in *Elops* and *Megalops*, the posterior opening for the mandibular sensory canal is on the medial (rather than the lateral or posterior) surface of the angular. This is also the condition in *Notelops* and *Rhacolepis*. Paleontological evidence refutes Nelson's (1973: 346) contention that the mesial position of the opening in the angular unites living elopids and megalopids, and instead primitively characterizes teleosts (Patterson and Rosen, 1977: 101). The mandibular sensory canal in modern albuloids is largely external to the dentary and angular, although it passes through the posterior part of the angular in *Albula* (Nelson, 1973). The arrangement in *Brannerion* approaches the albuloid condition, but the canal is partly bridged by bone. The condition in *Paraelops* apparently is even more primitive.

The ceratohyal is ossified in two sections. Neither section is fenestrated, although there is a large ovoid depression in the lateral surface of the posterior ceratohyal. The dorsal and ventral hypohyals are composed of spongy endochondral bone with a thin perichondral sheath. As in *Notelops*, the canal for the afferent hyoidean artery enters the ventral hypohyal and leaves the dorsal hypohyal mesially.

In AMNH 12797 the head is exposed in ventral view, displaying the entire operculogular series. In this individual there are 13 branchiostegals attached to the posterior ceratohyal. All but the last two are slender and elongate, particularly those of the anterior ceratohyal. Anteriorly the left branchiostegal series overlies the right, and most of the anterior branchiostegals are covered by a large, triangular median gular.

The gill-arches have not been reconstructed. Parts of the elongate ceratobranchials and epibranchials are preserved in the acid-prepared

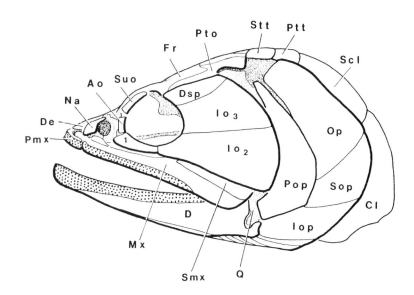

Paraelops cearensis. Outline reconstruction of head in lateral view.

specimen AMNH 12792. Small compound tooth-plates are associated with the epibranchials and ceratobranchials.

The opercular series resembles that of *Notelops brama* more than *N.* sp. A in general arrangement, except that the opercular is more triangular in *Paraelops*, with its antero-dorsal margin sloping obliquely forward more as in *N.* sp. A. The operculum is heavily ornamented with radial ridges and grooves in *Paraelops* and is somewhat less curved in the transverse vertical plane than that of *Notelops*.

The supratemporal is large and carries the supratemporal commissure (e.g., AMNH 12569). The post-temporal resembles that of *Notelops*, with a stout dorsal (epioccipital, canal-bearing) and slender ventral (intercalar) limb. It is uncertain whether the supracleithrum is thickened anteriorly where it meets the post-temporal, as in *Notelops*. The cleithrum, scapula, coracoid, and mesocoracoid (seen in AMNH 12792) closely resemble those of *N. brama* (Forey, 1977, fig. 7). There are four proximal radials, three articulating with the scapula and one with the coracoid. There is at least one postcleithrum, which in *Paraelops* resembles the ventral one in *N. brama*.

The pectoral fin has about 19 rays (e.g., AMNH 12797), although the last five or six are extremely fine and are easily overlooked. The longest (outermost) ray articulates directly with the scapula (e.g., AMNH 12792), as in *N. brama*.

243

Megalops cyprinoides, the Recent oxeye tarpon. Dr. S. Shen.

The pelvic fin originates beneath the posterior half of the dorsal fin. The pelvic bone is elongate and slender, with a shaft-like anterior region, but more blade-like and finally inflated posteriorly. It is pierced by foramina on its outer ("iliac") margin, and there is a medially-directed "ischiadic" process that is separated from the opposite one by only a very narrow gap. To some extent the pelvic bone in *Paraelops* resembles that of *Rhacolepis*, but it lacks an anterior bifurcation like that noted in *Rhacolepis* by Forey (1977, fig. 27). In AMNH 12792 there is evidence of one small and one much larger proximal radial, the latter forming a spinous process and apparently articulating with the last four or five fin-rays. There are approximately 12 pelvic fin-rays in all. The first four or five articulate directly with the pelvic bone.

The dorsal fin originates approximately mid-way along the body. There are approximately 28 fin-rays, of which the first four or five are unbranched. The first several pterygiophores have membranous expansions anteriorly and posteriorly, and the first pterygiophore is greatly expanded anteriorly. As in *Notelops brama*, the fifth fin-ray is longest. The tip of the dorsal is rounded, rather than pointed as in *Notelops*.

The anal fin is slightly closer to the caudal peduncle than to the pelvic fins. There are 10-11 fin-rays, of which the third is the longest and is the first branched ray of the series. The pterygiophores are unknown.

The caudal fin lacks a notch of the kind seen in *Notelops*, and the tips of the tail are gently rounded, although the tail is strongly forked. There are two ural centra, the first of which supports a low neural arch consisting mainly of perichondral bone. The first preural centrum has a similar neural arch, and together the arches of U_1 and PU_1 are arranged as in other elopomorphs (Patterson and Rosen, 1977: 137).

There are three uroneurals, only two of which extend forward beyond U_2. The first extends beyond PU_1 and terminates against the side of PU_2. The neural spine of the latter is shorter and thinner than the one preceding it.

All the hypurals are autogenous. The first ural centrum is associated with hypurals 1 and 2, which are separate distally but fused proximally. At least two hypurals are associated with the second ural centrum. These hypurals have expanded bases that cup the centrum, as in *Elops*, *Megalops*, and *Albula*. In *Notelops*, *Rhacolepis*, and *Brannerion* the second ural centrum also is cupped by the hypurals. This feature has not been observed in other teleosts and is tentatively proposed as a synapomorphy uniting pachyrhizodontoids with elopomorphs.

The parhypural is fused to the first preural centrum. Forey (1977: 186) regarded the morphology of the caudal skeleton (parhypural fused to PU_1, H_1 and H_2 fused to each other and to U_1) to be a unique morphotype among teleosts, because although such fusions are common in various euteleosts, Forey knew "of no instance in which this has taken place without prior fusion between the first ural centrum and the first pre-ural centrum." Fusion between PU_1 and the parhypural is rare but occurs in some osteoglossomorphs and clupeomorphs. Its occurrence in an albuloid elopomorph affects Forey's assessment of caudal fin morphology (discussed further below).

There are ten dorsal principal rays in the caudal fin, of which the first is unbranched. Additionally there are several fringing fulcra preceded by ten unsegmented procurrent spines plus a large caudal scute. Fringing fulcra are primitively present in elopoids (e.g., *Megalops*, *Sedenhorstia*, *Anaethalion*, *Davichthys*) and also occur in the fossil albuloid *Lebonichthys* (Forey, 1973: 199). *Paraelops* resembles *Megalops* and

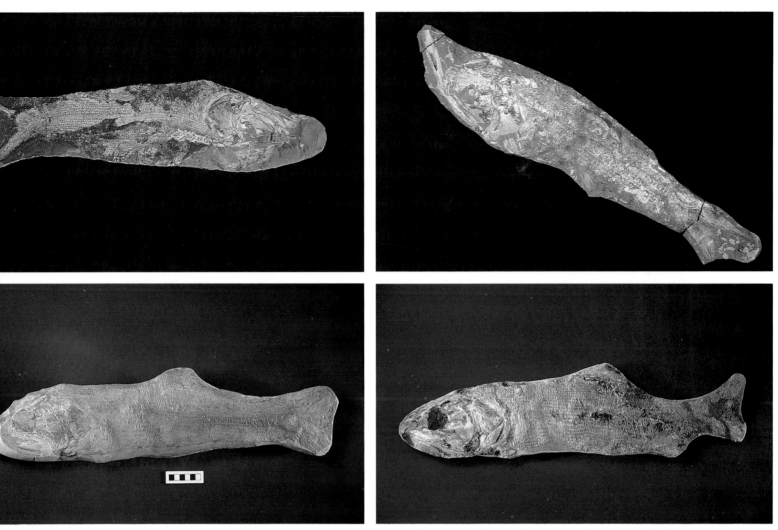

Representative specimens of *Paraelops cearensis* in "Old Mission" (top) and "Jardim" matrix (all other views). Specimen at bottom is acid-prepared and provided much of the data on which the present description is based.

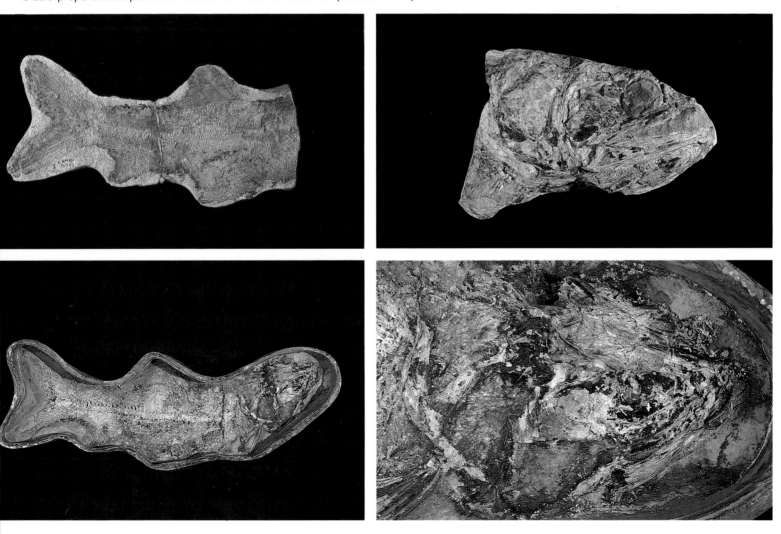

Sedenhorstia in having a series of several fringing fulcra instead of only one or two. Fringing fulcra are not developed in *Brannerion* and are otherwise absent in teleosts except in fossils including some "leptolepids" and "pholidophorids."

There are eight ventral principal rays, of which the first is unbranched. Fringing fulcra are absent, but there are eight or nine segmented procurrent rays and a large caudal scute.

A precise vertebral count is not available. There are approximately 18 caudal vertebrae in AMNH 12793, and 30-31 abdominal vertebrae up to the point where they become obscured behind the bones of the head. Assuming that the hidden vertebrae are of similar proportions, a total of 44-45 abdominal vertebrae is estimated. This assumption is justifiable on the grounds that in AMNH 11875 and 12569 some of the more anterior vertebrae are clearly of comparable shape and size to those farther posteriorly. The neural and hemal arches are all fused to their respective centra. The ossification pattern of the vertebral centra is similar in *Paraelops* and *Notelops*. Epineurals are associated with the anteriormost abdominal centra, but their number and arrangement have not been determined. It is not known whether supraneurals are present.

Cycloid scales cover the entire body and extend onto much of the caudal, dorsal, and anal fins. The scales are thin and rounded, with a shallow indentation anteriorly and a deeper notch posteriorly. Scales situated close to the dorsal midline are strongly bilobed. The indentations are paralleled by circuli (growth lines). Because of this, each horizontal scale row appears to have a median stripe. *Paraelops* is readily distinguished from *Notelops* and *Rhacolepis* by this feature. The scales in *Paraelops* are relatively larger than in *Notelops* and *Rhacolepis*. At the deepest part of the body there are about 30 horizontal scale rows, of which 11 or 12 are above the lateral line. There are over 100 scales along the lateral line series. An enlarged scute occurs at the base of the dorsal and ventral lobes of the caudal fin.

Silva Santos (1971) placed *Paraelops* within the family Elopidae and suggested that it represented a lineage directly ancestral to *Elops*. It is clear from that work that his concept of the Elopidae was somewhat broad and roughly equivalent (if fossils are excluded) to the suborder Elopoidei of Forey (1973). Silva Santos (1971: 441) recognized three "elopid" groups, one characterized by having a dentition of numerous minute teeth covering the superficial surfaces of the mouth (including *Elops*, *Megalops*, *Holcolepis*, and *Paraelops*), a second comprising taxa with straight pointed and spaced teeth (including *Protelops*, *Notelops*, *Elopopsis*, and *Eoprotelops*), and a third group with coarse, globose teeth (*Brannerion*).

Forey (1973) separated *Elops* and *Megalops* at the family level. The Elopidae was restricted to *Elops* plus two extinct taxa (*Davichthys*, *Anaethalion*). *Megalops*, *Tarpon* (now usually synonymized with *Megalops*), and several extinct genera including *Protarpon*, *Promegalops*, *Elopoides*, *Sedenhorstia*, and *Pachythrissops* were grouped in the Megalopidae (*Pachythrissops* subsequently was removed; Forey, 1977). *Paraelops* unfortunately was not discussed in either of Forey's works. Forey (1973) recognized three albuloid families: the extinct Osmeroididae (including *Osmeroides* and *Dinelops*), the Pterothrissidae (*Pterothrissus*, *Istieus*, *Hajulia*), and the Albulidae (*Albula*, *Lebonichthys*). The phylogenetic relationships among elopomorph fishes is reviewed elsewhere (see this volume: *Brannerion*, *Notelops*, *Rhacolepis*). It is clear that *Paraelops* possesses several elopomorph characters (paired post-temporal foramina in supraoccipital; rostral ossicles; fused angular-retroarticular; specialized compound neural arch formed above PU$_1$ and U$_1$, extending posteriorly beneath epurals) as well as an elopocephalan synapomorphy (only two uroneurals extending forward beyond U$_2$).

Albuloids have been defined on the following characters (Forey, 1973; Greenwood, 1977): mandibular sensory canal lying in an open groove on the dentary and angular; arrangement of *ligamentum primordium*; medially incomplete ethmoid commissure, carried by more than two rostral ossicles or within the premaxilla; reduced intercalar (without prootic bridge); and supraorbital canal lying in grooves on the frontal. Additional albuloid characters may include sutural contact between the intercalar and epioccipital and the presence of a deep sub-epiotic fossa.

Of these characters, *Paraelops* is known to possess four (reduced intercalar meeting the epioccipital, deep sub-epiotic fossa, supraorbital canal in grooves on frontal) but is unknown with respect to the other features. There are at least two ossicle-like bones on each side of the snout, one of which may represent the antorbital as in *Albula*. The ethmoid commissure did not pass through the dermethmoid, but whether it was merely located outside that bone or was actually interrupted as in modern albuloids is unknown.

246

As an albuloid, *Paraelops* is phylogenetically advanced over *Brannerion* in lacking an intercalar-prootic bridge and an ethmoid commissure contained within the dermethmoid, and in possessing a sutural contact between the intercalar and epioccipital, an ossicle-like antorbital, the supraorbital canal lying partly in a groove on the frontal, and an *Albula*-like sub-epiotic fossa. *Brannerion* nevertheless is more like *Albula* in its pebble-like parasphenoid dentition, delicate rostral ossicle morphology, and lack of fringing fulcra. Together, *Paraelops* and *Brannerion* are more primitive than other albuloids (including fossils such as *Osmeroides*, *Istieus*, *Hajulia*, and *Lebonichthys*) in having an elongate gape with the mandibular joint located behind the orbit. Forey (1973: 123) noted that in *Dinelops* the joint also is located posteriorly, beneath the occiput, but the relationships of this genus are in doubt.

Paraelops and *Brannerion* share the presence of specialized tooth-bearing areas extending laterally onto the labial surfaces of the mouthparts. This similarity may represent a synapomorphy of these taxa, but the distribution of other albuloid characters suggests instead that this feature is either a primitive albuloid condition lost in more derived members of the group, or a convergent similarity of the two Santana albuloids. It is concluded that *Paraelops* is morphologically closer to Recent albuloids than is *Brannerion*, but otherwise the phylogenetic relationships of these taxa to each other and to other fossils included in the Albuloidei by Forey (1973) remain unresolved. Neither *Brannerion* nor *Paraelops* sheds much light on the phylogenetic relationship of albuloids to halosauroids or anguilloids, except to suggest that all these higher taxa probably were represented by the Lower Cretaceous.

Two morphological aspects of *Paraelops* potentially have impact upon the conclusions reached by Forey (1977) concerning the monophyletic status and phylogenetic position of pachyrhizodontoid fishes. The circumorbital and caudal endoskeletal patterns found in *Paraelops* conform to those seen in pachyrhizodontoids, especially *Notelops*. Forey regarded these patterns as unique characters by which pachyrhizodontoids could be defined as a monophyletic group. On that basis, *Paraelops* would be a pachyrhizodontoid, but we regard this alignment of *Paraelops* as untenable because the pachyrhizodontoids have only two osteological characters that may represent elopomorph synapomorphies (hypurals cupping second ural centrum; paired foramina entering

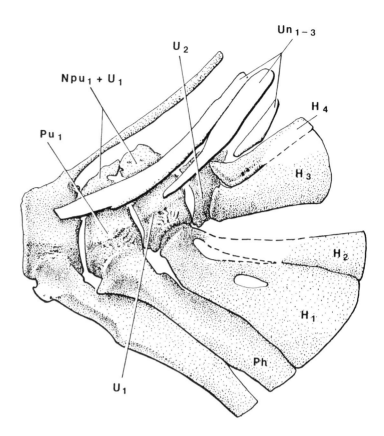

Paraelops cearensis. Caudal endoskeleton, from AMNH 12792.

post-temporal fossa via supraoccipital), and have none of the anguilliform and albuloid synapomorphies. The two pachyrhizodontoid-elopomorph similarities mentioned above, however, seem sufficient evidence to resurrect the notion that pachyrhizodontoids are primitive elopomorphs rather than mere elopocephalan orphans. The pachyrhizodontoid circumorbital and caudal endoskeletal patterns are here regarded as primitive characters, although their level of generality within elopomorphs is unresolved.

Assemblages: Jardim, Old Mission. According to Silva Santos (1971: 439), *Paraelops* heads have been recovered from Brejo Santo, on the northern side of the Chapada do Araripe, and from Lagòa de Dentro, south of Araripina in Pernambuco State. Two specimens were noted from other sites, one (designated the paratype) from Piau (collected in 1946 by Dr. L. I. Price), and one from Ouricuri, Pernambuco (collected in 1950 by H. O. Leonardos). The holotype is from Lagòa de Dentro.

(J. G. Maisey, S. Blum)

RHACOLEPIS Agassiz, 1841

Cohort ELOPOMORPHA
incertae sedis
Family PACHYRHIZODONTIDAE
Genus **Rhacolepis** Agassiz 1841
1841 *Phacolepis* Agassiz: 83 (typographical error)

Emended diagnosis: Pachyrhizodontid fishes in which the skull roof is without a marked depression at the level of the autosphenotics, dermethmoid with lateral projections, dilatator fossa without a complete roof, pterotic reduced to a short spine; exoccipitals meeting above but not below foramen magnum, endochondral elements of otic region united by interdigitating sutures, no fenestra between autosphenotic and pterotic, lateral face of prootic with well-developed ridge running from posterior opening of jugular canal to orbital artery foramen; vomer with two recurved teeth; ectopterygoid with short dorsal process and single row of pointed teeth; anterior ceratohyal fenestrated; posterior infraorbitals overlying preoperculum; preoperculum with truncated vertical limb and produced to spine-like process antero-ventrally; operculum with oblique ventral margin, interoperculum longer than deep; posterior margin of cleithrum excavated opposite fin insertion; body recessed to house pectoral fins; caudal fin-rays not crossing hypurals at steep angle; scales small, ovoid, marked by circuli in dorsal, and ventral fields, posterior field with fine radiating ridges, focus central; scales extending over base of caudal, dorsal, and anal fins, cloaca surrounded by approximately 16 modified scales; 9-10 enlarged scales along dorsal midline of caudal peduncle.

Type species: *Rhacolepis buccalis* Agassiz.
Rhacolepis buccalis Agassiz
1841 *Phacolepis buccalis* Agassiz: 83 (sic)
1844b *Rhacolepis buccalis* Agassiz: 1011
1887 *Rhacolepis buccalis* Agassiz; Woodward: 539
1901 *Rhacolepis buccalis* Agassiz; Woodward: 30
1908 *Rhacolepis buccalis* Agassiz; Jordan and Branner: 21
1923 *Rhacolepis buccalis* Agassiz; Jordan: 62

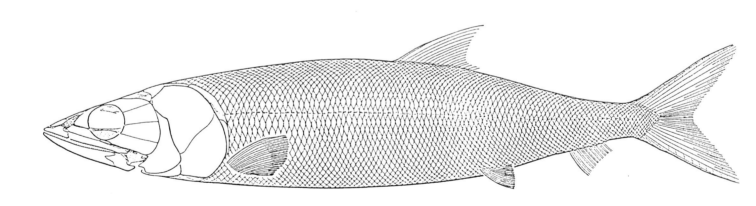

Rhacolepis buccalis. Skeletal reconstruction.

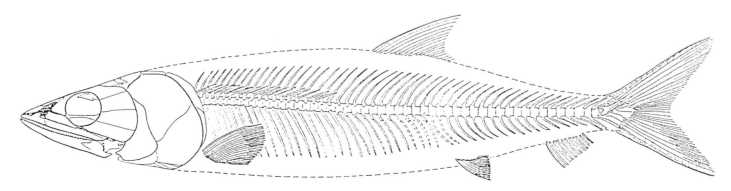

Rhacolepis buccalis specimens. An almost undistorted three-dimensional body removed entirely from the rock by mechanical preparation (**top**); only the fins (which remained embedded in rock) are missing; photo of AMNH 13106 by J. Maisey. Acid-prepared skull roof in a different specimen (**bottom**) illustrates arrangement of frontals, dermosphenotics, and supratemporals; slight telescoping has occurred, obscuring parietals and supraoccipital.

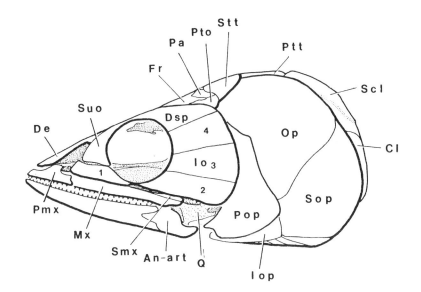

Rhacolepis buccalis. Outline reconstruction of head in lateral view.

1938 *Rhacolepis buccalis* Agassiz; d'Erasmo: 29

1968 *Rhacolepis buccalis* Agassiz; Silva Santos and Valença: 348

1977 *Rhacolepis buccalis* Agassiz; Forey: 143

1986 *Rhacolepis buccalis* Agassiz; Mones: 44

Emended diagnosis: *Rhacolepis* reaching 250 mm total length; head length equal to 22 percent of standard length, maximum trunk depth equal to 25-26 percent of standard length; fin-ray counts: P17-19; V11-13; D17; A10; approximately 57-58 preural vertebrae, of which 20 are caudal; paired fins short, pelvic fin originating behind level of dorsal fin, anal fin closer to caudal than to pelvics, immediately behind ring of modified cloacal scales; posterior infraorbitals twice as broad as deep; diameter of orbit equal to about 20 percent of head length; premaxilla equal to 21 percent of upper jaw length, with about 10 marginal teeth; maxilla with about 35 teeth; dentary with about 35 teeth; preopercular sensory canal with 9-10 ventral branches; about 90 lateral line scales, approximately 33 scales in transverse series anterior to dorsal fin; scales deeper than long, deeply overlapping.

Holotype: British Museum (Natural History), BM(NH) P. 4313a; crushed head; Santana formation, Chapada do Araripe, Jardim, Ceará.

Rhacolepis defiorei d'Erasmo

1938 *Rhacolepis defiorei* d'Erasmo: 31

1968 *Rhacolepis defiorei* d'Erasmo; Silva Santos and Valença: 348

1977 *Rhacolepis defiorei* d'Erasmo; Forey: 162

1986 *Rhacolepis defiorei* d'Erasmo; Mones: 44

Revised diagnosis: *Rhacolepis* said to differ from *R. buccalis* in having a deeper body and proportionally shorter trunk, and in having the ventral fins a little in advance of the dorsal.

Holotype: Uncataloged (?) specimen in the Instituto di Geologia e Paleontologia, Universidade Federal do Sao Paulo, Brazil; see d'Erasmo, 1938, pl. 6, fig. 1.

Rhacolepis buccalis is the only one of three species originally assigned to *Rhacolepis* by Agassiz (1841) that is today retained within the genus. *Rhacolepis brama* (=*R. olfersii* of Agassiz, 1844) was removed to *Notelops* by Woodward (1901), and *Rhacolepis latus* is here referred to *Brannerion*. Another species, *Rhacolepis defiorei*, was erected by d'Erasmo (1938). Although it was recognized by Silva Santos and Valença (1968) and mentioned by Forey (1977), *R. defiorei* never has been reinvestigated.

According to Woodward (1901: 30), the earliest illustration of a fossil fish from the Santana formation is of a *Rhacolepis buccalis* specimen figured by Spix and Martius (1831, *Atlas*, pl. 22, fig. 5, and reproduced in this book). Unfortunately this specimen (along with other fossils obtained with it) are now lost (P. Wellnhofer, pers. comm.), so its identification cannot be corroborated.

Rhacolepis is perhaps the most abundant fossil fish occurring in "Jardim" calcareous concretions of the Santana Formation, and it also is found in the "Old Mission" lithology. Preservation of *Rhacolepis* is often superficially excellent, with many specimens still "in-the-round." Study of such specimens has provided valuable information concerning the taphonomy and preservation of Santana formation fossils (see earlier section).

The distribution of *Rhacolepis* is correlated strongly with differences in concretion matrix. The absence of *Rhacolepis* from "Santana" concretions most likely reflects some aspect of paleoecology within the Araripe basin. Curiously, despite its apparent local endemism only within parts of this particular basin, *Rhacolepis* has been reported from Lower Cretaceous sediments in other Brazilian basins, and according to Professor Rubens da Silva Santos (pers. comm.), *Rhacolepis* also occurs in deposits of the same age from Colombia (specimens were illustrated, but not identified or described, in two papers dealing with the origins of calcareous concretions; Weeks, 1953, 1957). This wider distribution perhaps is not surprising, because the closely related Cretaceous genus *Pachyrhizodus* has an impressive pandemic occurrence. The restriction of *Rhacolepis* to only certain kinds of concretions within the Santana formation therefore presents a paradox that clearly merits further investigation.

According to Forey (1977), *Rhacolepis* belongs to a now extinct primitive teleostean group called pachyrhizodontids. *Pachyrhizodus* itself is known from several species, many of which have been assigned to other genera, and all of which are of slightly younger geologic age than *Rhacolepis*. The earliest described *Pachyrhizodus* are from the Albian (late Lower Cretaceous) of Queensland, Australia (*P. marathonensis*; Etheridge, 1905; Bardack, 1962; Bartholamai, 1969; Forey, 1977) and England (*P. salmoneus*; Gunther, 1872; Woodward, 1901; Forey, 1977). Other English species are of Cenomanian age, while North American species are younger still (Upper Cretaceous; Turonian to Campanian). Pachyrhizodontids thus seem to represent a purely Cretaceous group, and *Rhacolepis* is its earliest known member. The group achieved greater success than the notelopids, both in terms of distribution and longevity, but apparently left no descendants at the close of the Mesozoic era. Pachyrhizodontids and notelopids have been treated as sister-groups and were collectively placed in the order Pachyrhizodontiformes by Forey (1977). These fishes were regarded as *incertae sedis* within the Teleostei by Forey (1977) but are clearly elopocephalans (*sensu* Patterson and Rosen, 1977). There is some evidence supporting an elopomorph relationship (see this volume: *Paraelops, Notelops*), although many of the

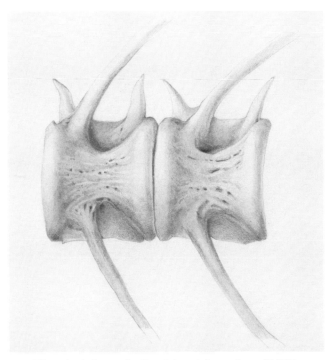

Rhacolepis buccalis. Caudal vertebrae, from AMNH 11987.

characters used to support that hypothesis in the past were shown to be primitive by Forey (1977).

The skeletal anatomy of *Rhacolepis* has been thoroughly described by Forey (1977). Only those features having some bearing on the identification and systematic position of *Rhacolepis* will be discussed here, as no significant departures from Forey's account have been discovered. From that account it is clear that *Rhacolepis* shares several specialized features with *Pachyrhizodus* (particularly *P. megalops*, the best known species), and that a number of other characters unite these genera with *Notelops*. Unfortunately, the principal characters used by Forey (1977) to establish pachyrhizodontoid monophyly also occur in *Paraelops*, an early albuloid (see this volume), and it is no longer clear that pachyrhizodontoids form a monophyletic group. Notelopids and pachyrhizodontids therefore are treated as *incertae sedis* elopomorphs in this work. Generic level identification of *Rhacolepis* and *Notelops* is facilitated by a few characters, but separation of *Rhacolepis* from *Pachyrhizodus* is less straightforward.

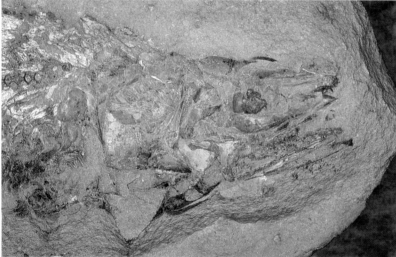

Above: Three views of the holotype of *Rhacolepis buccalis* in the British Museum (Natural History) collection. Photos by J. Maisey.

Right: Representative specimens of *Rhacolepis*.

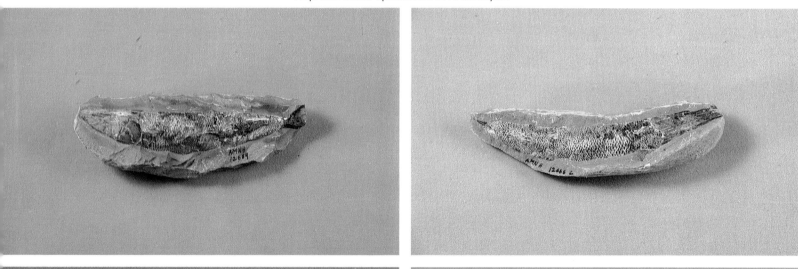

Representative specimens of *Rhacolepis*.

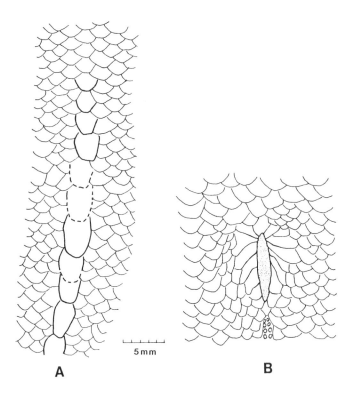

Rhacolepis buccalis. A: Enlarged dorsal caudal scales, from AMNH 13106. B: Modified cloacal scales, from AMNH 12619.

In the braincase, the parietals are small and are completely separated by the supraoccipital. A similar arrangement occurs in *Pachyrhizodus* and *Elopopsis*, whereas in *Notelops* and *Paraelops* the parietals meet at a median suture. The parietals are relatively smaller in *Pachyrhizodus megalops* than in *Rhacolepis buccalis* (Forey, 1977: figs. 12, 25). The supraoccipital crest is well developed in *Rhacolepis*. On either side of the crest there are paired foramina (e.g., AMNH 11978, 11982, 12782, 12783, 12785).

The lateral margins of the frontals are excavated above the autosphenotic in *Rhacolepis*, producing a characteristic indentation in the frontal outline posteriorly. Similar frontal excavation occurs in *Pachyrhizodus* (at least from England; Forey, 1977), but not in *Elopopsis* and notelopids. The pterotics are sutured to the posterior part of the frontals in *Rhacolepis*, lacking a pronounced L-shaped extension along the frontal margin as seen in *Paraelops*. There is a pronounced pterotic spine in *Rhacolepis*, an apparent difference from *Pachyrhizodus*.

Rhacolepis and *Pachyrhizodus* lack a subtemporal fossa (depression for hyoid adductor muscles), which Forey (1977) regarded as a shared derived character relating to increased curvature and broadening of the area of attachment for this musculature. Its absence in pachyrhizodontids is not unique among teleosts, as the condition appears in several other groups. Perhaps coupled with the absence of a subtemporal fossa, a bony intercalar-prootic bridge also is lacking in *Rhacolepis* and *Pachyrhizodus* (these features are discussed in greater detail in the section on *Notelops*).

Other apparently derived features in the head of *Rhacolepis* include the location of the trigeminal nerve foramen (opening directly to the orbit, instead of the pars jugularis); myodome open instead of closed posteriorly; a deep posterior part of the parasphenoid beneath the otic region; a mandibular joint consisting only of a fused angulo-articular and a retroarticular (instead of three separate bones, as in *Notelops*); and the absence of a ventral gular plate.

Rhacolepis and *Pachyrhizodus* have a single row of dentary teeth, a toothed ectopterygoid, and a short palatine bone. All these are probably primitive attributes but help to distinguish these taxa from *Notelops*, which has several rows of dentary teeth, an edentulous ectopterygoid, and elongate palatine.

The circumorbital bone pattern offers a seemingly reliable means of distinguishing between *Rhacolepis* and *Notelops* specimens in Santana formation concretions. In *Rhacolepis* (and *Pachyrhizodus*) there is a large dermosphenotic plus four infraorbitals and a supraorbital. The orbit is thus ringed by six dermal bones, whereas in *Notelops* this number is lower, possibly a result of fusion. A single supramaxilla is present in *Rhacolepis*, instead of the usual two as in other teleosts.

The restoration of *Rhacolepis* offered here differs from that presented by Forey (1977, fig. 23) in the positions of the dorsal, pelvic, and anal fins. All of these are more posteriorly situated than previously supposed. Additionally, the pelvic fins are located entirely behind the level of the dorsal fin, not under its posterior margin. The anal fin, situated close to the caudal, lies behind a ring of specialized cloacal scales. In *Elopopsis microdon* (considered to be closely related to pachyrhizodontids by Taverne, 1976) there is single specialized scale that surrounds the anus anteriorly and laterally, like the cloacal scale complex in *Rhacolepis*. The caudal fin is forked but lacks a median notch

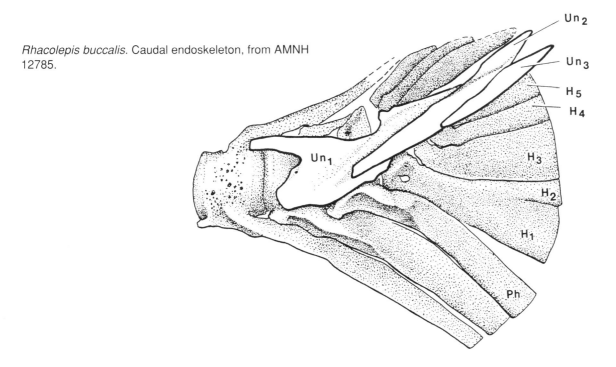

Rhacolepis buccalis. Caudal endoskeleton, from AMNH 12785.

like that of *Notelops*. The first preural centrum is separate, instead of being fused to the first ural centrum as in most other euteleosts, but in *Rhacolepis* the first ural centrum may be partly unossified (in *Notelops* the separate first ural and preural centra are both well-ossified). The first and second hypurals are fused to the ossified part of the first ural centrum, and are also fused proximally to each other. At least two further hypurals (separate from the ural centra) are present in some specimens. The first preural centrum is fused to the parhypural. There are two uroneurals, of which the first is forked so as to partly overlie the first preural centrum.

A few details may be added to enhance the description of *Rhacolepis buccalis*, especially regarding its shape and scale arrangement. These details are visible on three-dimensional specimens in which the body, although perhaps bloated, has apparently retained many in-life nuances. There are shallow depressions running posteriorly from the pectoral insertion, perhaps to house the retracted pectoral fins during brief intervals of high-speed swimming. The caudal region is rounded but is flatter dorsally than ventrally, and there is a rounded lateral keel in the caudal peduncle. Behind the dorsal fin, the scales along the dorsal midline are progressively enlarged posteriorly. Those immediately behind the dorsal fin are equal in size to the flanking scales, but farther caudally each dorsal scale may extend across two or even three lateral scale rows, forming a series of ridge scales. Similar dorsal ridge scales primitively occur in many early "paleoniscoid" fishes and also are present in semionotids. A series of dorsal ridge scales does not occur in the caudal region of any living teleost, although they may be present in some fossil "pholidophorids." A caudal scute is present in various "leptolepids," *Pachythrissops*, *Diplomystus*, *Paraelops*, *Brannerion*, and primitive extant teleosts (e.g., *Elops*, *Albula*).

Assemblages: Jardim (abundant), Old Mission (common). See remarks earlier in section. *Rhacolepis* is also reported from a new locality in bituminous shales at Pedra Blanca, near Olinda (Viana, Brito & Silva-Telles, MS)

(J. G. Maisey)

Above and below:
Representative specimens of *Rhacolepis*.

Above and below:
Acid-prepared specimens of *Rhacolepis*.

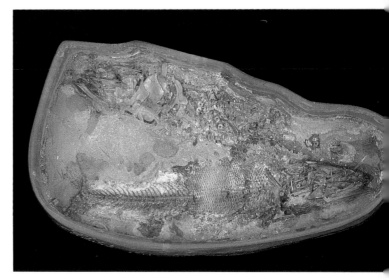

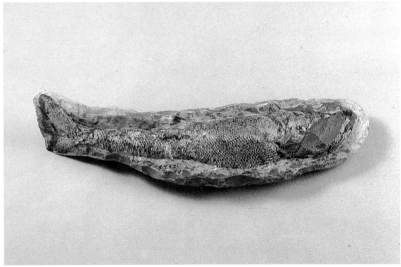

Representative specimens of *Rhacolepis*.

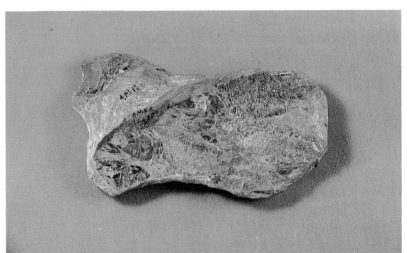

NOTELOPS Woodward, 1901

Cohort ELOPOMORPHA
incertae sedis
Family NOTELOPIDAE Forey 1977
Genus **Notelops** Woodward 1901
  1901 *Notelops* Woodward: 27
Emended diagnosis: Notelopid fish in which the dermethmoid bears lateral projections, dilatator fossa with roof, pterotic without posterior spine, exoccipitals meeting above and below foramen magnum, large fenestra between autosphenotic and pterotic, lateral face of prootic without a crest above the orbitonasal foramen; parietals not separated by supraoccipital; palatine long and dentigerous, ectopterygoid edentulous; anterior ceratohyal fenestrated; fourth and fifth infraorbitals fused together, posterior infraorbitals just reaching preoperculum; preoperculum relatively small; operculum with oblique ventral margin, interoperculum short and deep; cleithrum expanded over fin insertion; origin of pelvic fin below posterior end of dorsal fin, pelvic splint-bone present; upper principal caudal fin-rays crossing hypural supports at steep angle; short central branching caudal fin-rays defining notch in tail.

Type species: *Rhacolepis brama* Agassiz.
Notelops brama (Agassiz)
  1833 *Amblypterus olfersii* Agassiz, 2: 40 (nomen nudum)

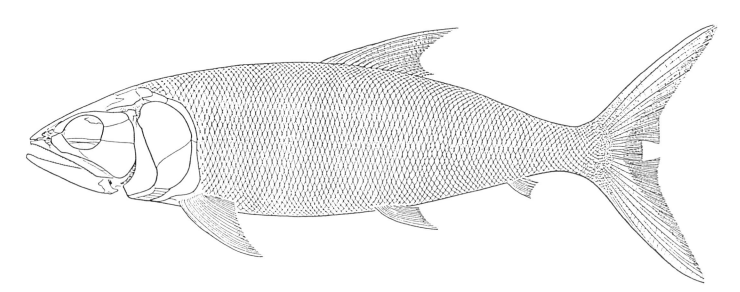

Notelops brama. Skeletal reconstruction.

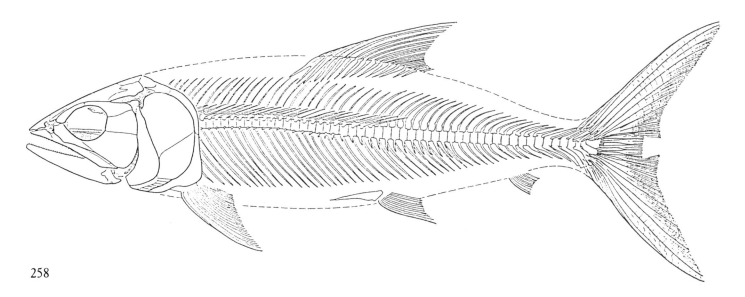

1841 *Phacolepis brama* Agassiz: 83 (*sic*)
1844a *Rhacolepis olfersii* Agassiz; Agassiz, 4: 293
1844b *Rhacolepis olfersii* Agassiz; Agassiz: 1012
1887 *Rhacolepis brama* Agassiz; Woodward: 539
1901 *Notelops brama* (Agassiz); Woodward: 27 (holotype designated)
1907 *Calamopleurus cylindricus* Agassiz; Jordan: 139
1908 *Calamopleurus cylindricus* Agassiz; Jordan & Branner: 16
1908 *Notelops brama* (Agassiz): Jordan & Branner: 20
1923 *Calamopleurus brama* (Agassiz); Jordan: 46
1938 *Notelops brama* (Agassiz); d'Erasmo: 27
1940 *Notelops brama* (Agassiz); Dunkle: 157
1968 *Notelops brama* (Agassiz); Santos and Valença: 348
1974 *Notelops brama* (Agassiz); Taverne: 78
1976 *Notelops brama* (Agassiz); Taverne: 304
1977 *Notelops brama* (Agassiz); Forey: 130
1986 *Notelops brama* (Agassiz); Mones: 44

Revised diagnosis: *Notelops* reaching 600 mm total length; proportions (as percentage of standard length): head length 20, maximum depth of trunk 25, predorsal 48-51, prepectoral 27, prepelvic 62, preanal 83; fin-ray counts D17-18; A9-10; P17-20; V10-12; caudal notch formed by four short central fin-rays (two dorsal, two ventral); approximately 55 preural vertebrae, of which 18-19 are caudal; premaxilla equal to 22 percent of upper jaw length, with about 18 marginal teeth; maxilla with about 50 teeth; dentary with three or four rows of teeth, each row with approximately 60 teeth; preopercular sensory canal with three to five ventral branches; diameter of orbit equal to 30 percent of head length; approximately 82-85 lateral line scales, 30-31 scales in transverse series anterior to dorsal fin; large axillary scale above pectoral fin; central part of shoulder girdle and posterior margin of opercular and subopercular nearly vertical; parietals as wide as long.

Holotype: British Museum (Natural History), BM(NH) 15490; head plus cleithrum; Santana formation, Chapada do Araripe, Ceará (precise locality not known).

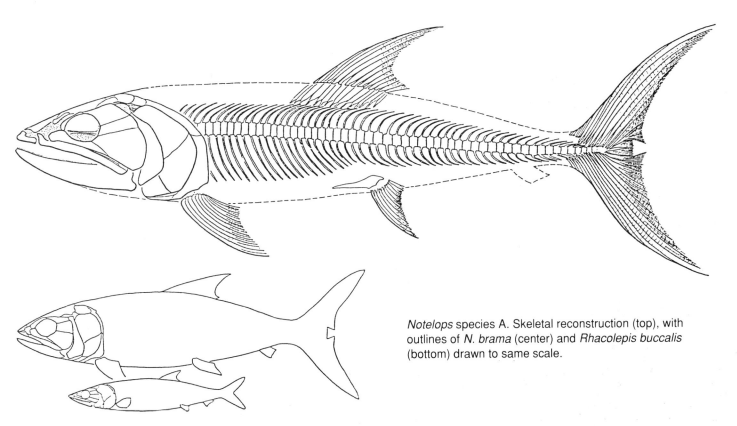

Notelops species A. Skeletal reconstruction (top), with outlines of *N. brama* (center) and *Rhacolepis buccalis* (bottom) drawn to same scale.

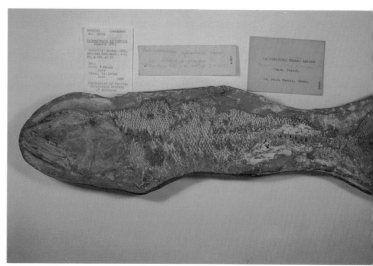

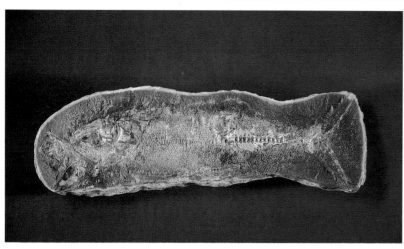

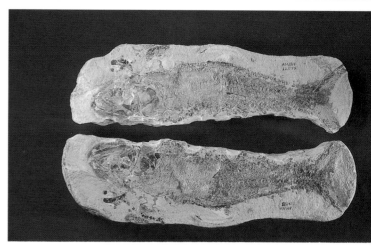

Notelops brama. The holotype (**top**), in the British Museum (Natural History) collection, was not examined by Jordan, who errone-ously referred a more complete specimen to *Calamopleurus* (upper center, California Academy of Sciences). Large specimens of *Notelops* (lower four views) are easily confused with *Paraelops*. Top three photos by J. Maisey.

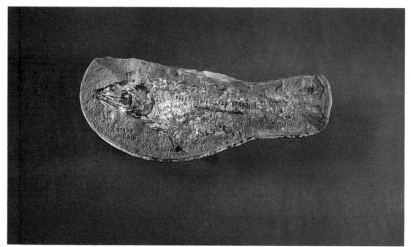

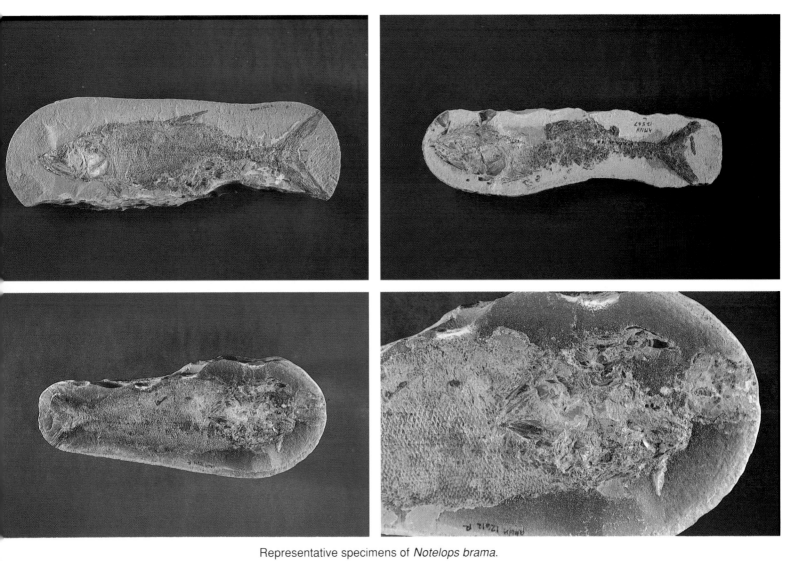

Representative specimens of *Notelops brama*.

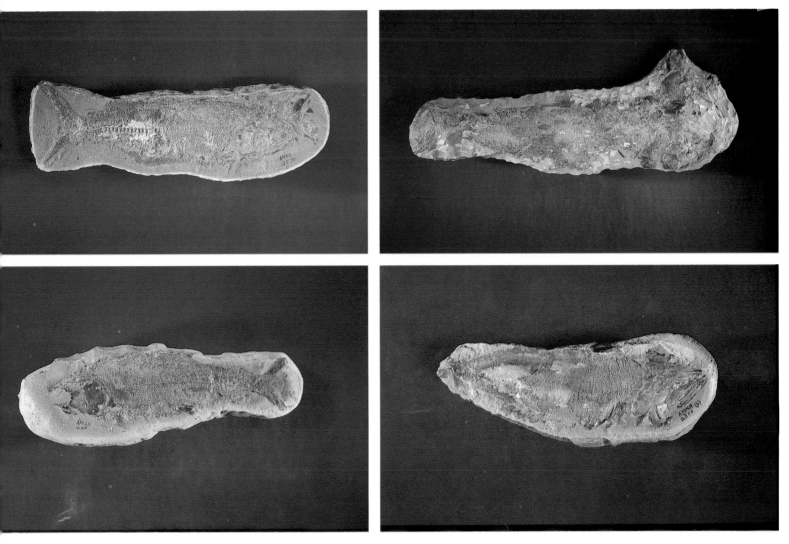

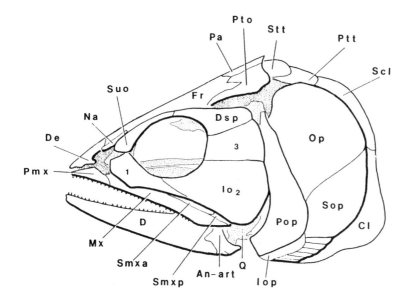

Left: *Notelops brama*. Outline of head in lateral view.

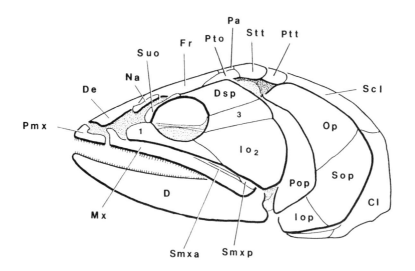

Left: *Notelops* species A. Outline of head in lateral view.

Below: Dorsal views of skull roof in (A) *Paraelops cearensis* (after Silva Santos); (B) *Notelops brama* (after Forey); and (C) *Rhacelepis buccalis* (after Forey).

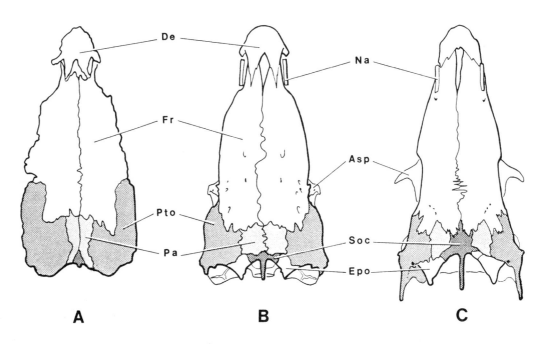

Notelops sp. A

Diagnosis: *Notelops* reaching over 1000 mm total length; proportions (as percentage of standard length): head length 25, maximum depth of trunk 20, predorsal 52-53, prepectoral 30, prepelvic 62, preanal uncertain, at least 85; fin ray counts: D15; A unknown; P11-14; V10; caudal notch formed by two short central fin-rays; vertebrae approximately 62, of which 32-34 are caudal; premaxilla equal to 17-18 percent of upper jaw length, with about 15 marginal teeth; maxilla with about 55 teeth; dentary with several rows of teeth, numerous teeth per row; diameter of orbit equal to 25 percent of head length; scales small, cycloid; number of lateral line scales and scale rows unknown; central part of shoulder girdle and posterior margin of opercular and subopercular strongly inclined; parietals about three times longer than wide.

Referred specimen: AMNH 11991; complete specimen in part and counterpart; Santana formation, Chapada do Araripe, Barro do Jardim, Ceará.

Rhacolepis brama was one of the seven original species of fossil fishes from the Santana formation to be named by Agassiz (1841 as *Phacolepis*, apparently a typographical error; 1844b as *Rhacolepis olfersii*). Of the three species Agassiz originally assigned to *Rhacolepis*, only *R. buccalis* is retained there (see elsewhere, this volume). Woodward (1901) erected the genus *Notelops* for *R. brama*, and the third species (*R. latus*) is here referred to *Brannerion* (see earlier).

Louis Agassiz and Sir Arthur Smith Woodward both recognized that "*Rhacolepis*" *brama* was taxonomically distinct from another fossil fish from the same locality and named *Calamopleurus cylindricus* by Agassiz (1841). David Starr Jordan, working with some newly acquired material from the Santana formation, erroneously regarded *Calamopleurus cylindricus* and *Notelops brama* as identical (Jordan, 1907, 1923; Jordan and Branner, 1908). From then on, *Calamopleurus cylindricus* has been treated as a synonym of *Notelops brama* (e.g., d'Erasmo, 1938; Forey, 1977; Mones, 1986). Elsewhere in the present volume it has been determined that *Calamopleurus cylindricus* is a distinct, valid taxon of amiid fish, and that this name in fact has priority over *Enneles audax*. *Calamopleurus cylindricus* is not a synonym of *Notelops brama*.

Early views on the relationships of "*Rhacolepis*" are clouded by the failure to recognize that the included species belonged to different genera, families, and even suborders. Woodward (1887: 540) was the first to suggest "elopine" or "chanine" affinity and was impressed by similarities to *Megalops* (tarpon) and *Elops* (ten-pounders). Woodward (1901) subsequently placed *Notelops* and *Rhacolepis* within his family Elopidae, uniting *Notelops* with *Elops*, *Megalops*, and the fossils *Elopopsis* and *Osmeroides* within an unnamed group on the basis that in all five genera the parietal bones meet in the midline. *Rhacolepis* was placed in another unnamed group containing only fossils and characterized by having the parietals separate.

For some time it remained customary to associate *Notelops* and *Rhacolepis* with elopoids (Elopiformes), but Forey (1977: 188) concluded that these fossil genera have little in common with elopoids except for primitive teleostean characters and moreover lack critical elopoid characters such as rostral or prenasal ossicles and fusion between the angular and retroarticular bones. Taverne (1974b) suggested that *Notelops* should be placed in the Salmoniformes, in a phylogenetic position intermediate between elopomorphs and euteleosts. Elsewhere Taverne (1976, fig. 6) made a more specific proposal that pachyrhizodontids (including *Elopopsis*), tselfatiids, and bananogmiids are collectively an extinct sister-group to *Albula*. Forey (1977: 196) presented a brief but compelling argument against Taverne's views, concluding instead (ibid.: 195) that *Notelops* and *Rhacolepis*, together with some other fossils including *Pachyrhizodus*, belong to a monophyletic group (Pachyrhizodontoidei) of uncertain phylogenetic position within the Teleostei. Unfortunately, Forey's (1977) characterization of pachyrhizodontoids is no longer substantiated (see sections on *Rhacolepis* and *Paraelops*, this volume).

Forey proposed that *Notelops* and *Rhacolepis* have no specific recognizable living teleostean relatives. There are two features that may nevertheless unite *Notelops*, *Rhacolepis*, and *Pachyrhizodus* with the Elopomorpha among teleost fishes. One character is the presence of a pair of small foramina near the top of the supraoccipital crest, leading from the posterior face of the braincase into the post-temporal fossa. These foramina were reported in *Pachyrhizodus megalops* by Forey (1977: 165, fig. 27), who also mentioned their occurrence in *Rhacolepis* and *Notelops*. They are confirmed in AMNH 11907, 11918 (*Notelops*) and 11978, 11982, 12782, 12783 and 12785 (*Rhacolepis*). A similar pair of foramina also occurs in *Paraelops* and *Brannerion* (primitive albuloids), as well as in Recent *Elops* and *Megalops*. In *Albula* there is

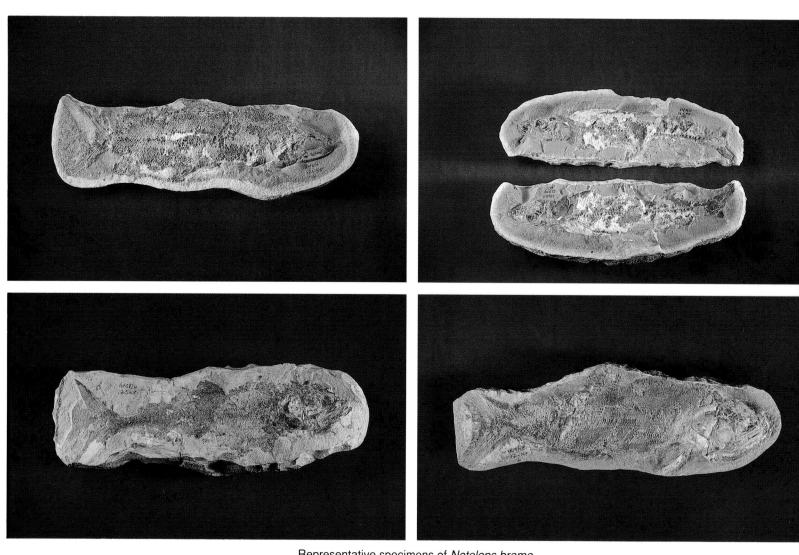

Representative specimens of *Notelops brama*.

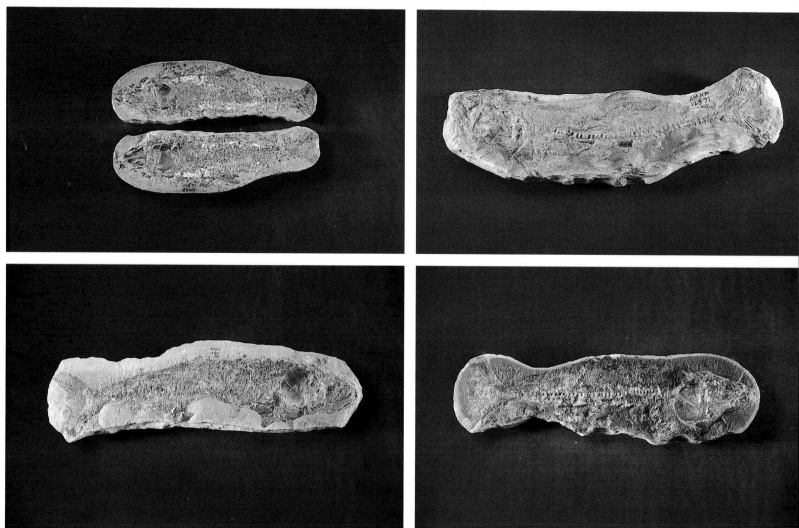

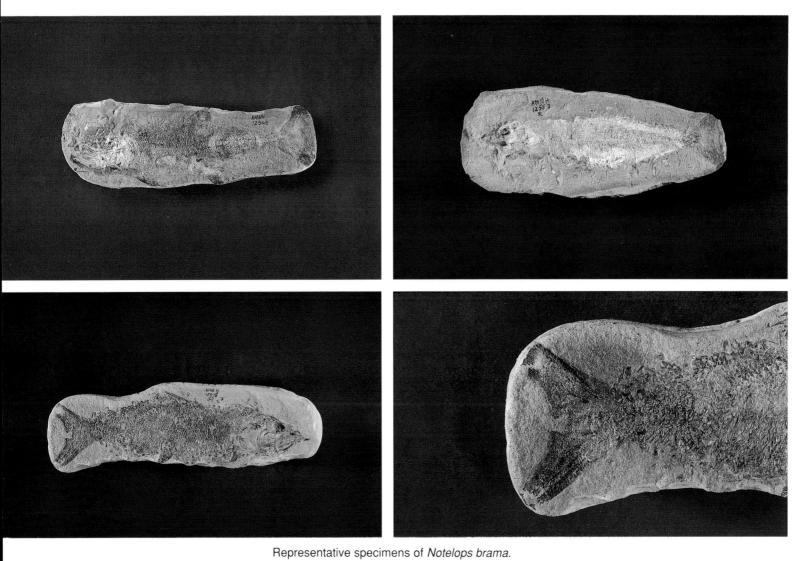

Representative specimens of *Notelops brama*.

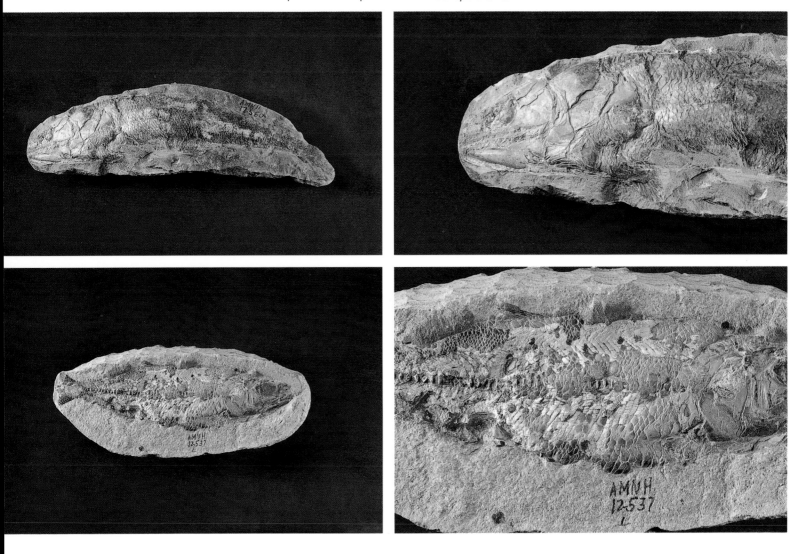

Notelops brama. Caudal vertebrae, from AMNH 11918.

a communication between the sub-epiotic fossa and post-temporal fossa via a foramen located partly in the supraoccipital and partly in the epioccipital, although its homology with the supraoccipital foramina of other elopomorphs is uncertain.

Significantly, these supraoccipital foramina have not been reported in primitive (leptolepid, pholidophorid) teleosts. They are absent in *Cladocyclus* and Recent *Coregonus* (a salmoniform), *Osteoglossum, Pantodon, Papyrocranus, Arapaima, Heterotis,* and *Mormyrops* (osteoglossomorphs), and all clupeomorphs examined (e.g., *Pterengraulis, Engraulis, Dorosoma, Odoxathrissa, Alosa, Brevoortia, Clupea*). Supraoccipital foramina are lacking in anguilloids (where the post-temporal fossa also is absent). Although the value of this character (presence of paired supraoccipital foramina) requires further appraisal, it is tentatively regarded here as a synapomorphy uniting notelopid and pachyrhizodontid fishes with other elopomorphs. The second character uniting pachyrhizodontids and elopomorphs is the arrangement of hypurals associated with the second ural centrum, which is cupped by them (discussed further below).

Although *Notelops* primitively resembles modern tarpons and ten-pounders, these similarities may be of functional rather than phylogenetic significance. From its broad gape, powerfully built trunk region, and forked, notched tail, we may infer that *Notelops* was a fast, efficient predator. Shoals of adult ten-pounders frequently are found in surf, where they presumably are feeding on smaller fishes and crustaceans. The strength and agility of ten-pounders and tarpons make them a popular challenge for sportsmen. The young of both these fishes are often found in mangrove swamps, sheltered bays, and salt marshes, where even low oxygen levels can be tolerated. A similar environment could have existed as the Santana formation was being deposited, although its ecological setting has not yet been clarified (see earlier in the present work).

The osteological structure of the head in *Notelops brama* has been thoroughly investigated by Dunkle (1940) from serial sections and by Forey (1977) from acid-prepared specimens. Their findings are merely summarized here. The morphology of *N*. sp. A is known in less detail, and most of the following remarks refer to *N. brama*.

In the braincase, the medially united parietals are small and with irregular margins. A different pattern is seen in *Rhacolepis buccalis*, where the small parietals are completely separated by the supraoccipital. According to Silva Santos (1971), *Paraelops cearensis* differs from *Notelops brama* in having parietals that are nearly three times as long as wide, with their posterior extremities separated by the supraoccipital. The latter feature is somewhat variable in different specimens referred to *Notelops brama*, but the relative proportions of the parietals seem to provide a means of distinguishing *N. brama* and *N.* sp. A. Separation of the parietals in *Rhacolepis* and *Pachyrhizodus* probably represents a derived character (Forey, 1977).

The lateral margin of the frontals in *Notelops* have been described as "entire," in contrast to those of *Rhacolepis* and *Pachyrhizodus*, which are excavated above the autosphenotic. The frontal margin also is entire in primitive teleosts including modern elopiform fishes. The pterotic spine is primitively weakly developed in *Pachyrhizodus* and *Notelops*, but is pronounced in *Rhacolepis*.

The supraoccipital crest is well developed in *Notelops* as well as in *Rhacolepis* and apparently in *Pachyrhizodus*. Taverne (1974b) has remarked on this similarity with salmoniform fishes, but Forey (1977) has disputed its phylogenetic significance.

A subtemporal fossa is well developed below the hyomandibular facet in *Notelops* to accommodate the adductor hyomandibulae muscle. The fossa also is prominent in living elopiform fishes and in *Brannerion*, but is absent in *Rhacolepis* and *Pachyrhizodus*. Forey (1977: 194) has argued that the absence of a subtemporal fossa in *Rhacolepis* and *Pachyrhizodus* is secondary, related to broadening and increased convexity of the otic region, which in turn provides greater space for the adductor hyomandibulae muscle. Among Recent teleosts a subtemporal fossa occurs only in osteoglossids, elopids and albuloids, some characins, and cyprinoids; among fossil teleosts it occurs in ichthyodectoids, "leptolepids," and "pholidophorids" (Patterson, 1975). From this distribution it seems that the subtemporal fossa has been independently lost in a number of higher teleost lineages, and its presence in *Notelops* is simply primitive.

A bridge of bone extends between the intercalar and prootic ossifications of the braincase in *Notelops*, crossing the subtemporal fossa. A similar bridge occurs in "leptolepid" and "pholidophorid" teleosts, *Brannerion*, ichthyodectoids, and in Recent *Elops*, *Osteoglossum*, and *Scleropages* (Patterson, 1975: 396). In all cases the bridge arises as an outgrowth from the membranous wall of the jugular canal. Its function in *Elops* is to provide

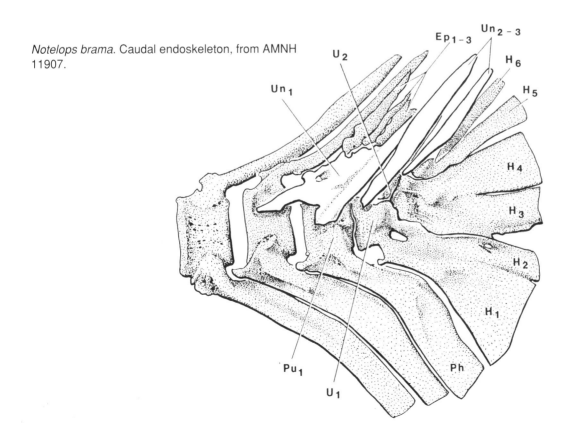

Notelops brama. Caudal endoskeleton, from AMNH 11907.

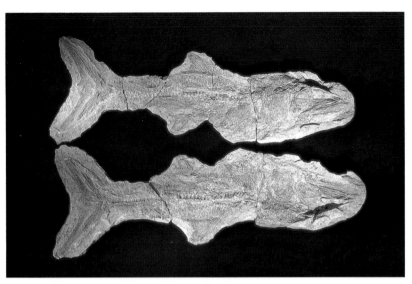

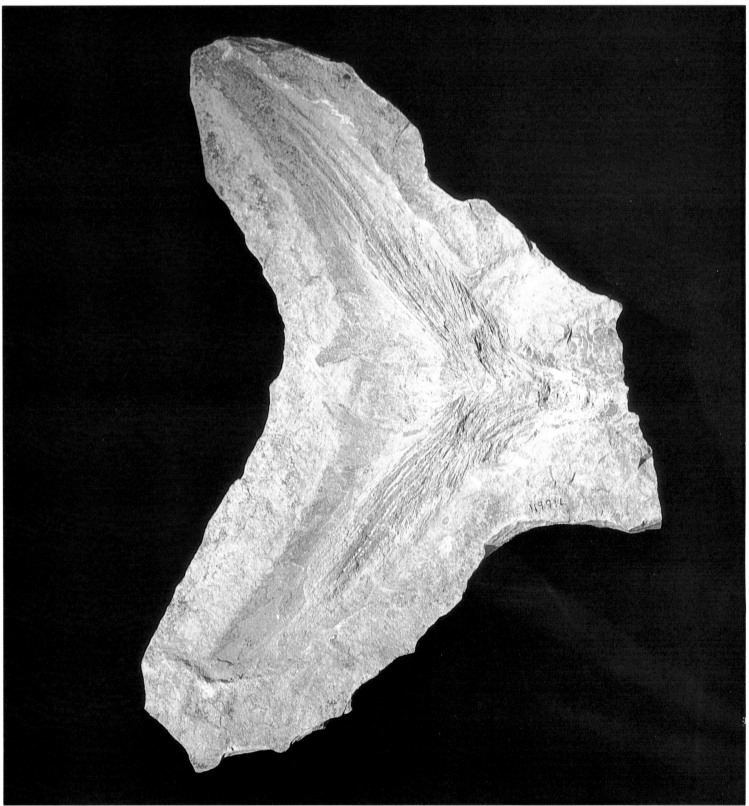

Notelops sp. A, AMNH 11991: complete fish in part and counterpart (top left); detail of head (top right); detail of caudal fin (bottom).

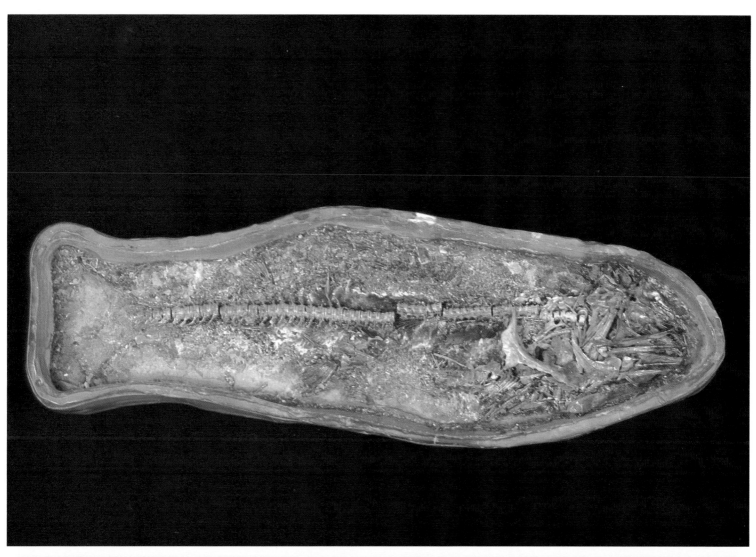

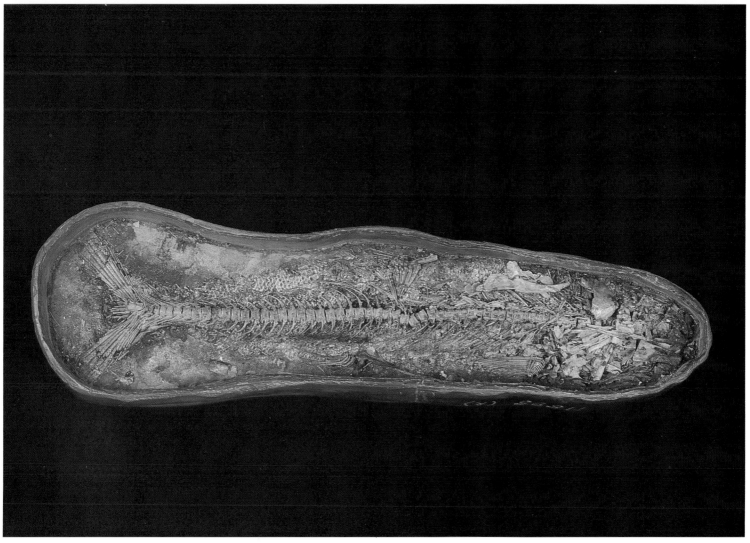

Notelops brama. Two acid-prepared specimens.

the origin for levator muscles of the branchial arches. The intercalar-prootic bridge is absent in *Rhacolepis* and *Pachyrhizodus* (Forey, 1977), as well as in *Paraelops* and Recent albuloids.

There is a large fenestra (opening) between the autosphenotic and pterotic in *Notelops*, within the wall of the dilatator fossa (area of origin for the opercular dilatator muscle). Having the fossa extend onto the pterotic is a teleostean feature found in "leptolepids" but not "pholidophorids" (where it is confined to the autosphenotic). The fenestra within the dilatator fossa of *Notelops* may have been open, leaving a direct communication with the post-temporal fossa, although its function is unknown (Forey, 1977: 133). The autosphenotic and pterotic are firmly sutured in other pachyrhizodontiforms, the more usual teleostean condition.

Some other features of the head skeleton in *Notelops* also are considered primitive by Forey (1977:193), including the condition of the trigeminal foramen (opening into the pars jugularis in *Notelops*, directly to the orbit in *Rhacolepis* and *Pachyrhizodus*), myodome closed posteriorly (open in *Rhacolepis* and *Pachyrhizodus*), parasphenoid shallow beneath the otic region (deep in *Rhacolepis* and *Pachyrhizodus*), and presence of a gular plate (absent in *Rhacolepis* and *Pachyrhizodus*, present in *Paraelops*).

In the palate of *Notelops*, the palatine bone is long, functionally replacing the ectopterygoid as part of the biting surface. By contrast, in *Rhacolepis* and *Pachyrhizodus* the palatine is short and the ectopterygoid is toothed. The condition in *Notelops* it is probably derived. According to Taverne (1974b), *Notelops* lacks teeth upon the endopterygoid, but Forey (1977) has contested this. Endopterygoid teeth are present in AMNH 11898 and in a very large acid-prepared specimen (AMNH 11913).

The circumorbital series of *Notelops* displays several features that Forey (1977: 195) regarded as synapomorphies uniting pachyrhizodontids and notelopids. These features include lack of a separate antorbital and fusion of its fourth and fifth infraorbitals. Thus in *Notelops* there are only five separate bones surrounding the eye (dermosphenotic, supraorbital, and three infraorbitals) instead of the six found in *Rhacolepis* and *Pachyrhizodus* (dermosphenotic, supraorbital, and four infraorbitals). Nevertheless, an identical pattern occurs in the albuloid *Paraelops*, indicating a wider distribution of the pattern among primitive elopomorph fishes.

The parasphenoid in *Notelops* is toothless. According to Taverne (1974b) there are two supramaxillae in *Notelops*, but several other authors reported only one (Woodward, 1901; Jordan and Branner, 1908; Dunkle, 1940; Forey, 1977). In some specimens of *Notelops* there is only an elongate, splint-like supramaxilla (e.g., AMNH 11906), but in other specimens there is also a much smaller dermal bone posteriorly (e.g., AMNH 11920), suggesting that a second supramaxilla is variably developed in this genus.

The caudal fin skeleton of *Notelops* resembles that of pachyrhizodontids in having separate first ural and preural centra (a primitive condition among teleosts, found also in *Paraelops*, *Araripichthys*, elopomorphs, salmonids, esocoids, and alepocephaloids). The parhypural is fused to the first preural centrum and both the first and second hypural are fused to their supporting centrum in *Notelops* and pachyrhizodontids, as well as in *Paraelops* and probably *Araripichthys*. Fusion of the parhypural and ural centrum also occurs in a few osteoglossomorphs and clupeomorphs. Fusion of the second hypural with its centrum occurs in clupeomorphs and ostariophysans, but the first hypural is autogenous and there are some other associated features of the preural and ural centra not found in notelopids or pachyrhizodontids. Remaining hypurals are autogenous and have a greatly expanded proximal region that cups the second ural centrum as in *Elops*, *Megalops*, *Albula*, and *Paraelops*. In *Notelops* there are at least two, possibly three uroneurals (e.g., AMNH 11907). As Forey (1977: 141) noted, the first is expanded and covers much of the lateral face of the first uroneural onto the second preural centrum, which has a small depression to receive it (e.g., AMNH 11898, 11907, 11918). This arrangement also is found in *Rhacolepis* and *Pachyrhizodus*, where it may be more extreme. For example, the process of the first uroneural reaches the third preural centrum in *Pachyrhizodus caninus* (Forey, 1977, fig. 36), and the fifth preural centrum in an indeterminate *Pachyrhizodus* from the Cretaceous of northern Italy (Taverne, 1987, fig. 4). In the living *Elops* the first uroneural also overlies the first preural centrum and sends a process anteriorly to reach the second. The first uroneural similarly flanks the first two preural centra in the fossil elopiform fishes *Anaethalion* and *Istieus* although it is unbranched (Forey, 1973b). In other fossil and Recent elopiforms the first uroneural typically is unbranched and does not extend beyond the first preural centrum.

The notched shape of the caudal fin characterizes *Notelops*, but has not been reported previously. Four central branched fin-rays (two dorsal, two ventral) are about half as long as the neighboring ones in *Notelops brama*. In *N.* sp. A only one dorsal and ventral fin-ray appear to be shortened, but they branch to cover as broad an area as in *N. brama*. A caudal notch is unusual among teleostean fishes, although it occurs in some caturids and many scombroids. This feature tentatively is regarded as a notelopid autapomorphy, as it apparently does not occur in other pachyrhizodontiforms.

Assemblages: Jardim, Old Mission.

(J. G. Maisey)

Elops machnata, a Recent ladyfish. Art by Tomita.

"LEPTOLEPIS"

Cohort CLUPEOCEPHALA
Subcohort EUTELEOSTEI
incertae sedis
"Leptolepis" diasii Silva Santos
 1958 *Leptolepis diasii* Silva Santos: 3
 1968 *Leptolepis diasii* Silva Santos; Silva Santos and Valença: 349
 1970 *Leptolepis diasii* Silva Santos; Patterson: 289

Emended diagnosis: Small fish, standard length approx. 45 mm; body length 3.3 times head length; head height 0.6 of length; gape of mouth not very inclined; mandibular articulation under extreme anterior of orbit; dentary apparently toothless, with high and broad coronoid process; orbital diameter less than preorbital distance, contained 4.5 times head length; sclerotic ring ossified; operculum trapezoidal, with some striae on inferior border; preoperculum large, semilunar; preopercular canal posteriorly sends off striated postero-inferior border; maximum body height 0.2 of total length; origin of dorsal fin just behind pelvics; anal fin located posteriorly, near base of caudal fin; homocercal caudal fin with four or five vertebrae; ten caudal vertebrae; relatively large, cycloid scales; P14; V9; D10-11; A7-8.

Holotype: Divisão de Geologia e Mineralogia, Departamento Nacional de Produção Mineral, Rio de Janeiro, DGM-DNPM 647P; complete fish; Santana formation, Chapada do Araripe, Pernambuco (precise locality not unknown).

The type species of *Leptolepis* Agassiz, 1832 is *L. coryphaenoides* (Bronn, 1830) from the Lower Jurassic (Toarcian Stage, Upper Lias) of Europe. A great many other species also have been erected, usually for stratigraphic or geographical reasons rather than on morphological grounds. Species sometimes have been referred to *Leptolepis* simply because of stratophenetic resemblances such as small size, ossified vertebrae, thin scales, and Mesozoic age. It is important to realize that these species

collectively do not constitute a monophyletic group. For example, Patterson and Rosen (1977) have restricted *Leptolepis* to the type species and have referred other species either to other genera (e.g., *Proleptolepis*, *Tharsis*, *Leptolepides*) or else to *"Leptolepis"* (indicating that, in their view, such species should not be referred to *Leptolepis* but were not sufficiently well-known to assign them to existing or new genera). The species from the Santana formation certainly falls into this category and is here referred to as *"Leptolepis" diasii*.

"Leptolepid" fishes are all superficially rather similar, but only in a number of extremely generalized teleostean characters. Collectively, these fishes perhaps are best regarded as an assemblage of primitive teleosts that includes some basal members of the Teleostei, plus slightly more advanced forms that may be more closely related to major groups within the teleosts. For example, according to Patterson and Rosen (1977) some "leptolepids" are primitively related to a group comprising ichthyodectiforms plus all living teleosts (e.g., *Proleptolepis*, *Leptolepis*); others fall between ichthyodectids and living teleosts (e.g., *Tharsis*); and yet others may be related to some, but not all living teleosts (e.g., *"Leptolepis" sprattiformis*).

There are relatively few records of other "leptolepids" from South America, although they have been reported from the Cretaceous of Argentina (Cabrera, 1927; De Saez, 1939, 1949) and from the Neocomian (Lower Cretaceous) of Bahia, Brazil (Schaeffer, 1947). At least one of these fishes (*Haplospondylus clupeoides* Cabrera) seems to resemble *Tharrhias*, which was itself regarded as a "leptolepid" until a relationship to *Dastilbe* and Recent *Chanos* was proposed (Silva Santos and Valença, 1968). *"Leptolepis" australis* and *"L." leanzai* from Argentina are not known in detail (De Saez, 1939, 1949), and since the material has not been re-examined these taxa cannot be included in the present study. Limited comparison of *"Leptolepis" diasii* with *"L." bahiaensis* and *Scombroclupeoides scutata* is possible, although the paucity of material has limited the investigation and little can be added to what has already been discussed (Schaeffer,

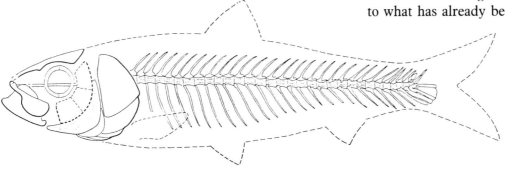

"Leptolepis" diasii. Skeletal reconstruction, based on information obtained from incomplete specimen AMNH 12780 and isolated bones. This reconstruction should be regarded as rather speculative.

1947; Patterson and Rosen, 1977).

Woodward (1908) described what was thought to be a clupeoid from the Ilhas series of Bahia, naming it *Scombroclupea scutata*. Patterson (1970b) referred this species to *Scombroclupeoides*, but found no evidence that it is a clupeoid. Schaeffer (1947) described *"Leptolepis" bahiaensis* from the same stratigraphic sequence. Patterson (1970b) regarded these as distinct taxa, but according to Patterson and Rosen (1977) the two probably are synonymous. They regarded *"Leptolepis" bahiaensis* (? = *Scombroclupeoides*) as an *incertae sedis* species of clupeocephalan (i.e., it could be a primitive clupeomorph, a primitive euteleost, or a sister-taxon to both these, like *"Leptolepis" sprattiformis*).

"Leptolepis" diasii was described originally on the basis of three individuals (two complete, plus one lacking head and tail; Silva Santos, 1958). The specimens were found in fragments of nodules and reportedly were associated with *Tharrhias* and *Brannerion*. Our material is mostly fragmentary, consisting of elements recovered during acid preparation of larger fishes (mainly *Brannerion*, and only in "Santana"-type concretions). It appears that *"L." diasii* is rare, perhaps occurring only in the "Santana" assemblage, and usually occurs only in association with larger fishes, not inside its own nodules. The remains may be recovered at various levels within nodules, not necessarily on the same bedding planes as larger fishes, and recovery of the tiny "leptolepids" is largely serendipitous. One partial skeleton lacking fins and some skeletal elements was recovered intact after it emerged from acid-prepared matrix. Because of these sampling limitations, this description is incomplete, and the restoration must be treated as rather speculative in many respects.

Despite these shortcomings, it has been possible to examine much of the caudal skeleton in our partial skeleton and to determine that this fish differs significantly from *"L." bahiaensis*, according to the reconstruction of the caudal fin given by Patterson and Rosen (1977, fig. 47). They found that *"L." bahiaensis* resembles living teleosts in having a low hypural number (six in this case), caudal axis upturned at the first preural centrum, hypural and fin-ray alignment (no fin-ray base overlies more than one hypural), only two uroneurals, and perhaps an anteriorly directed membranous outgrowth of the first uroneural and a reduced neural arch over the first ural centrum.

In *"L." diasii* the hypural number apparently is low, although in our specimen only hypurals

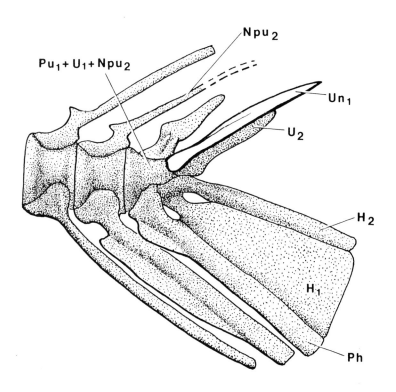

"Leptolepis" diasii. Caudal endoskeleton as preserved in AMNH 12780; additional hypurals probably were present originally, but were lost during acid preparation.

1 and 2 are preserved. The caudal axis is upturned at the first preural centrum rather than beginning to curve farther anteriorly. Few fin-ray bases are preserved, and it cannot be determined whether they are *in situ*. There apparently are only two uroneurals, the first of which bears a membranous anterior flange, and the neural arch of the first ural centrum apparently is absent.

If our specimens are correctly referred to *"Leptolepis" diasii*, it is a more advanced species than *"L." bahiaensis* in having the first preural and ural centra fused, with the parhypural and first two hypurals all attached to it. This arrangement is reminiscent of that found in *Gaudryella* and *Humbertia*, two "salmoniform" genera from the Middle Cenomanian (Upper Cretaceous) of Lebanon (Patterson, 1970b). In particular, the first preural neural arch seems to be fused to the first uroneural to produce a stegural. This structure today characterizes a group comprising salmonoids, esocoids (pike), osmeroids (smelts), stomiatoids (various deep-water, luminescent fishes), and the "neoteleosts" of Rosen and Patterson (1969). In other words, *"L." diasii* is more closely related to living euteleosteans than to other clupeocephalans.

Assemblage: Apparently restricted to "Santana" concretions.

(J. G. Maisey)

DASTILBE Jordan, 1910

Subcohort EUTELEOSTEI
Superorder OSTARIOPHYSI
Order GONORYNCHIFORMES
incertae sedis
Genus *Dastilbe* Jordan, 1910
  1910 *Dastilbe* Jordan: 30
Diagnosis: Primitive gonorynchiform fishes up to 200 mm; 36 to 38 vertebrae; jaws toothless, short, not extending beyond anterior margin of the orbit; horizontal and vertical limbs of preopercle nearly equal in length (horizontal limb slightly shorter), angle between limbs nearly 90 degrees and relatively sharp (not broadly rounded); hyomandibula wide antero-posteriorly; first pleural rib slightly enlarged; neural arches above first four vertebrae enlarged; D13 (the first pterygiophore bears three unbranched and unsegmented supernumerary rays, the first two of which are easily overlooked); A8–10; P10-13; V9; pelvic fin originates under middle of the dorsal fin base, pelvic splint present; anal fin originates more posteriorly than half way between pelvic and caudal fins; caudal fin composed of 19 principal rays (17 branched); caudal skeleton composed of two ural centra, six hypurals (all autogenous), two epurals, two uroneurals, and two parhypurals (a third parhypural supports only procurrent rays). Approximately 13 procurrent rays precede dorsal caudal fin rays and nine precede ventral ones.

  Type species: *Dastilbe crandalli* Jordan, 1910.
Dastilbe crandalli Jordan
  1910 *Dastilbe crandalli* Jordan: 30
  1935 *Dastilbe crandalli* Jordan; Arambourg: 2111
    1947 *Dastilbe crandalli* Jordan; Schaeffer: 16
    1947 *Dastilbe crandalli* Jordan; Silva Santos: 1
    1981a *Dastilbe crandalli* Jordan; Taverne: 973
  Emended diagnosis: *Dastilbe* up to 60 mm; pectoral fin with 10 rays.

Holotype: Carnegie Museum of Natural History, Pittsburgh, CMNH 5247/91; complete specimen; Muribeca formation (L. Cretaceous; Aptian), Riacho Doce, Maceió Municipality, Alagoas.
Dastilbe elongatus Silva Santos
  1947 *Dastilbe elongatus* Silva Santos: 1
  1968 *Dastilbe elongatus* Silva Santos; Silva Santos & Valença: 349
  1984 *Dastilbe elongatus* Silva Santos; Wenz: 277.

  Emended diagnosis: *Dastilbe* up to 200 mm; pectoral fin with 13 rays.
  Lectotype: Divisão de Geologia e Mineralogia, Departamento Nacional de Produção Mineral, Rio de Janeiro, DGM-DNPM 176-P; complete specimen; Crato member, Romualdo locality, Crato, Ceará.

Dastilbe crandalli Jordan (1910) was described from specimens obtained from Riacho Doce, Alagoas, Brazil. *Dastilbe elongatus* Silva Santos (1947) was described from specimens found in the Crato member of the Santana formation. Silva Santos (1947) did not identify any morphological features that distinguish *D. crandalli* from *D. elongatus*, and apparently distinguished the second species by its different locality, preservational environment, and larger maximum size. The Riacho Doce material is preserved in a black shale and attains a maximum size of about 70 mm SL. Specimens from the Crato member are preserved in bedded limestone, and while most specimens are smaller than 70 mm SL, some are as large as 170 mm SL.

Silva Santos (1947) apparently believed that the Crato member specimens comprise a single species. This was not stated explicitly, but is supported by the fact that only *D. elongatus* was subsequently listed in his published card catalog (Silva Santos, 1966) and in the review of fishes

Dastilbe elongatus. Skeletal reconstruction, mostly from AMNH 12721.

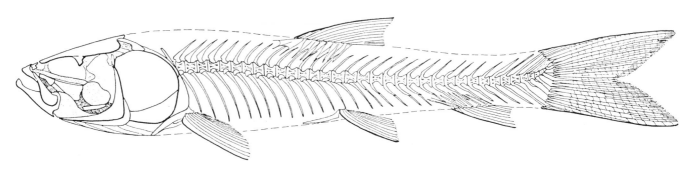

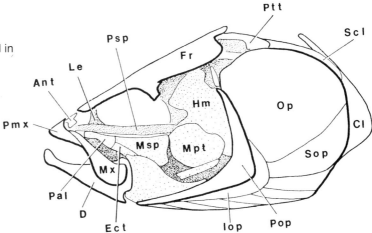

Dastilbe elongatus. Outline reconstruction of head in lateral view.

from the Araripe series published by Silva Santos and Valença (1968). The Crato member specimens are, however, heterogeneous with respect to one character, the number of pectoral fin rays. Among specimens in which pectoral fin rays can be counted, all smaller individuals have 10 rays, and all larger indivduals have 13. No specimens have been found to have 11 or 12 pectoral rays.

Fin-ray numbers typically remain constant as an individual becomes larger. Existing fin-rays simply become longer and more robust. Growth does not satisfactorily account for the pectoral variation in *Dastilbe*. The pattern of variation also is atypical for modern species in which the number of fin-rays is variable. Meristic variation usually is strongly unimodal (i.e., there are no gaps within the range). Jordan (1910) did not provide pectoral ray counts for *D. crandalli*, but other specimens from the type locality (AMNH 10021, 10023, 10027) show 10 pectoral rays. *Dastilbe elongatus*, on the other hand, has 13 pectoral rays (Silva Santos, 1947). Pectoral fin ray counts thus provide evidence for the existence of two *Dastilbe* species in the Crato member.

Jordan (1910) interpreted the morphology of *Dastilbe* to be diagnostic of a clupeid, but did not state which features prompted that interpretation. The currently accepted placement of *Dastilbe* within the Gonorynchiformes resulted from a circuitous series of associations. Weiler (1922) described several new fossil fishes from a bituminous shale in Gabon and Spanish Guinea, western Africa. Weiler believed that one of the new species was very similar to fossil *Leptosomus* species he knew from Westphalia (Germany) and Syria, and consequently named that species *Leptosomus aethiopicus.*

In 1935, Arambourg and Schneegans removed Weiler's species from *Leptosomus* and made it the type species of a new genus, *Parachanos*. More importantly, they aligned it and two other fossil genera, *Prochanos* and *Dastilbe*, to the Recent genus *Chanos* (which at that time was considered to be a clupeiform fish). The only difference between *Dastilbe* and *Parachanos* cited by Arambourg and Schneegans was the persistence of a notochordal canal in the vertebral centra of *Dastilbe*.

Silva Santos (1947) agreed with Arambourg and Schneegans (1935) that *Dastilbe* is closely related to *Chanos*, but differed from those authors in suggesting that *Parachanos* might be regarded as a synonym of *Dastilbe*. He regarded the supposed differences between *Dastilbe* and *Parachanos* (vertebral number and the persistence of a notochordal canal in *Dastilbe*) to be of the same taxonomic significance as those between species of *Dastilbe*.

Taverne (1981a) went further than Silva Santos (1947) in suggesting that the species of *Dastilbe*, plus *Parachanos aethiopicus*, might represent separate populations of a single species. The sympatry of 10- and 13-rayed individuals (in the Crato member), however, does not support this interpretation. At least *D. crandalli* and *D. elongatus* should be regarded as valid species. The validity of *P. aethiopicus* remains to be tested by further morphological study.

Relationships among fossil and Recent gonorynchiforms: Gonorynchiforms are represented today by the commercially important milkfish, *Chanos chanos* (tropical Indo-Pacific nearshore marine and estuarine habitats) and the lesser known species of the Gonorynchidae (Indo-Pacific coral reefs) and Kneriidae and Phractoleamidae (both in African freshwaters). The members of this assemblage

Representative specimens of *Dastilbe* sp. Top photo by J. Maisey.

Two examples of *Dastilbe* sp. from the Crato member, both greatly enlarged. **Top:** An unprepared example. **Bottom:** A specimen cleaned by the Waller method to remove iron oxides. Top photo by J. Maisey.

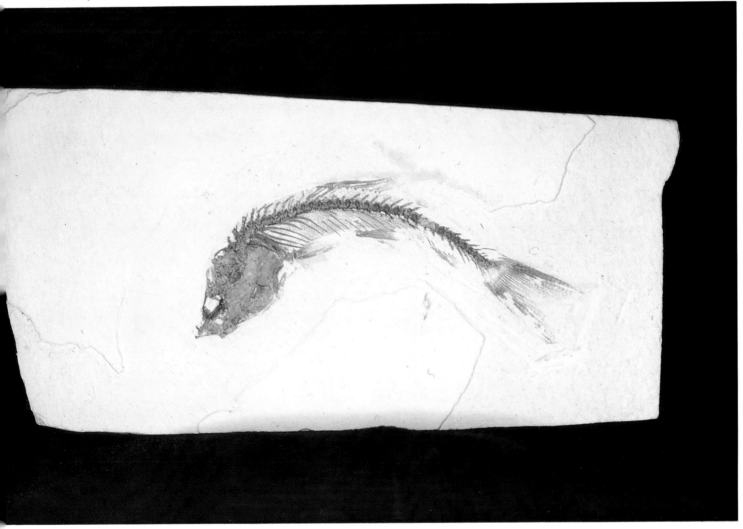

are morphologically heterogeneous, and a relationship among them was not proposed until Gosline (1960) recognized the suborder Gonorynchoidei as "isospondylous" fishes with: a small and toothless mouth; gill membranes attached to the isthmus and gill openings restricted; maxillaries running forward and nearly touching medially behind the premaxillaries; the absence of supramaxillaries; long lower limb of the preopercular; a suprapreopercular; and parietals narrow and nearly restricted to the posterior border of the skull roof.

Greenwood, et al. (1966) elevated Gosline's Gonorynchoidei to ordinal status and proposed that the Gonorynchiformes is the sister-group of all other ostariophysan fishes (the Otophysi: carps, minnows, tetras, catfishes, knifefishes, etc.). All otophysan fishes have a Weberian apparatus, a series of bones that conduct vibrations (sound) from the gas-bladder to the skull. The gonorynchiform-otophysan relationship proposed by Greenwood, et al. (1966) was based on their interpretation of the double-chambered gas-bladder and expanded anterior ribs in gonorynchiforms as a primitive, or incipient, Weberian apparatus. Rosen and Greenwood (1970) studied the ontogeny of the weberian apparatus in *Brycon* (Characidae) and concluded that the elements of the weberian apparatus are modified ribs, neural arches, and supraneurals. They also found that the gonorynchiform-otophysan relationship presented by Greenwood et al. (1966) could be supported by several other characters, including contact between the exoccipitals across the floor of the foramen magnum; position and orientation of the inner ear; the presence of fright cells, fright substance, and nuptial tubercles; and fusion of the two ural centra, first preural centrum, and first uroneural.

The conclusions of Rosen and Greenwood (1970) later were challenged by Roberts (1973) and Gosline (1980). Neither of these authors provided a specific alternative hypothesis, let alone one with better support from the available data. A stronger challenge was presented by Taverne (1981a), who noted that fossil gonorynchiforms (e.g., *Aethalionopsis*, *Tharrhias*, and *Dastilbe*) have very primitive caudal skeletons. The similarities between the caudal skeletons of Recent gonorynchiforms and otophysans thus appear to have resulted from parallel evolution, rather than direct inheritance from a common ancestor. While that observation effectively refutes homology of the gonorynchiform and otophysan caudal fusions,

the sister-group relationship between these fishes still is indicated by a host of other characters. In their comprehensive review of ostariophysan anatomy, Fink and Fink (1981) summarized the evidence for a gonorynchiform-otophysan relationship as: 1) basisphenoid absent; 2) sacculus and lagena (the more ventral two of the three otoliths in the teleostean inner ear) situated posteriorly and toward the midline; 3) dermopalatine absent; 4) gas-bladder divided into a small anterior and large posterior chambers, covered by silvery peritoneal tunic; 5) supraneural in front of first neural arch absent; 6) dorso-medial parts of first four neural arches expanded and abutting against one another, roofing the neural canal; 7) expanded part of first neural arch abutts against exoccipital; 8) alarm substance; 9) free neural arch between occiput and first neural arch absent; 10) hemal spines anterior to PU$_2$ fused to centra. Fink and Fink (1981) also found that the monophyly of Recent gonorynchiforms is indicated by the following characters: 11) orbitosphenoid absent, pterosphenoids reduced and widely separated; 12) parietals very small, little more than canal-bearing ossicles; 13) exocciptials with prominent postero-dorsal cartilaginous margin; 14) quadrate condyle far forward, result of elongated quadratojugal process of quadrate, symplectic, interopercle, and lower limb of preopercle; 15) premaxilla thin and flat; 16) no teeth on fifth ceratobranchial; 17) anterior neural arch especially large, with tight joint to exoccipitals; 18) no teeth in jaws; 19) no teeth on phyarygobranchials; 20) epibranchial organ behind fourth epibranchial; 21) no postcleithra; 22) one or two epurals; 23) no adipose fin.

After Arambourg and Schneegans (1935) recognized the similarity between *Dastilbe* and *Chanos*, most workers have placed *Dastilbe* and other Cretaceous gonorynchiforms (e.g., *Aethalionopsis*, *Tharrhias*, *Rubeisichthys*) within the Chanidae (Silva Santos and Valença, 1968; Oliveira, 1978; Taverne, 1981a; Wenz, 1984). Only Patterson (1984: 136) recognized that these genera do not share any derived characters exclusively with *Chanos*, and that they consequently should be regarded as "stem-group gonorynchiforms, unassignable to a Recent subgroup."

Because of the excellent preservation of fossils in the Santana formation, *Tharrhias* is the best known of all fossil gonorhynchiforms (see elsewhere in this volume). Acid-prepared specimens of *Tharrhias* were first described by Patterson (1975b). Later, Patterson (1984)

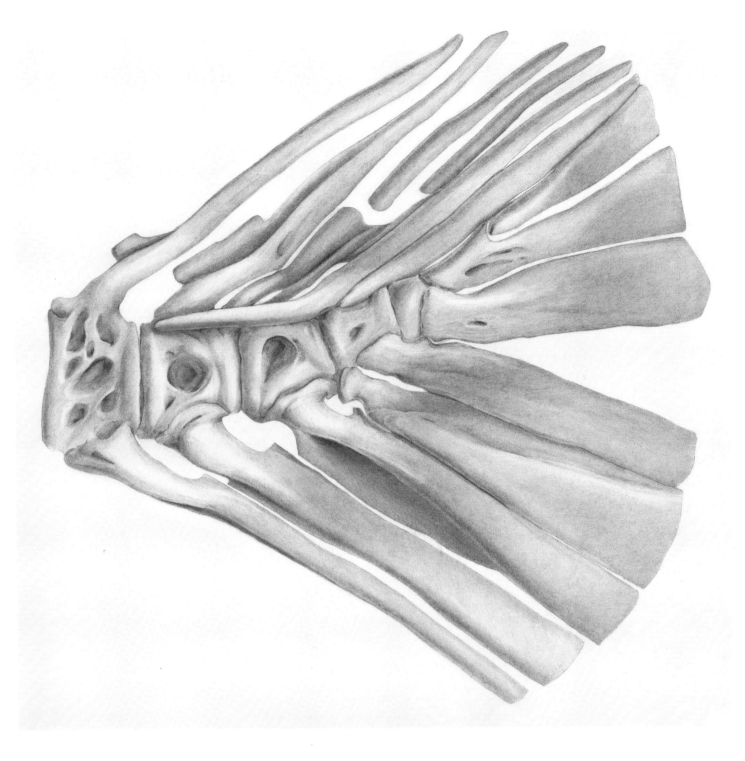

Dastilbe elongatus. Caudal endoskeleton, from AMNH
12734.

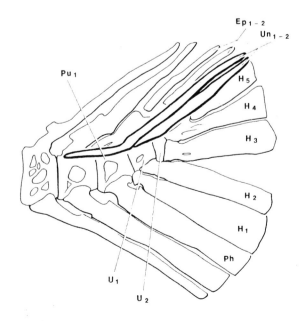

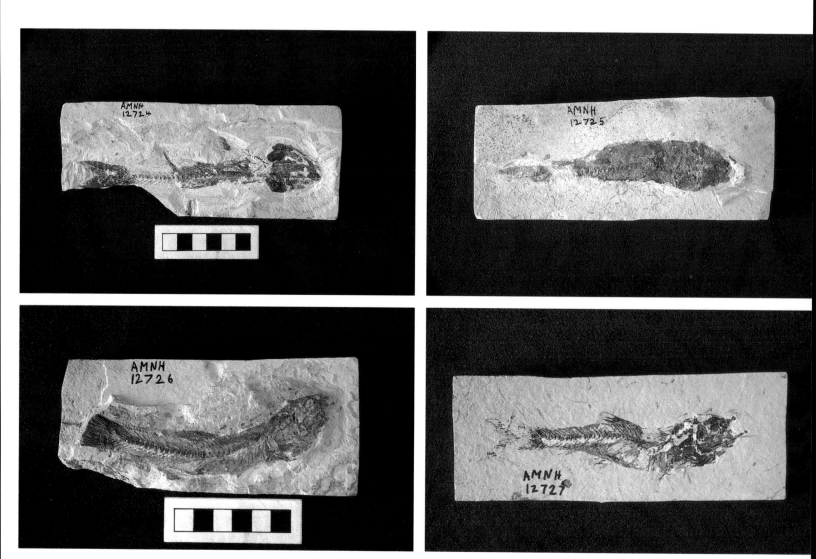

Representative specimens of *Dastilbe* sp.

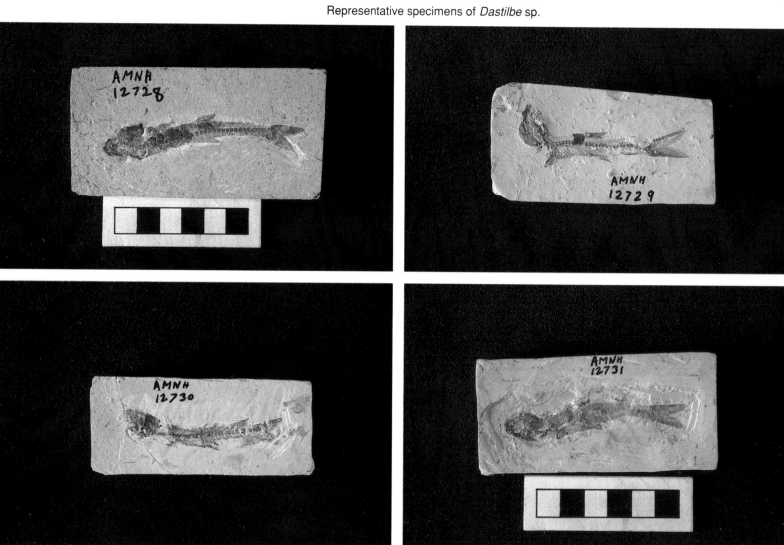

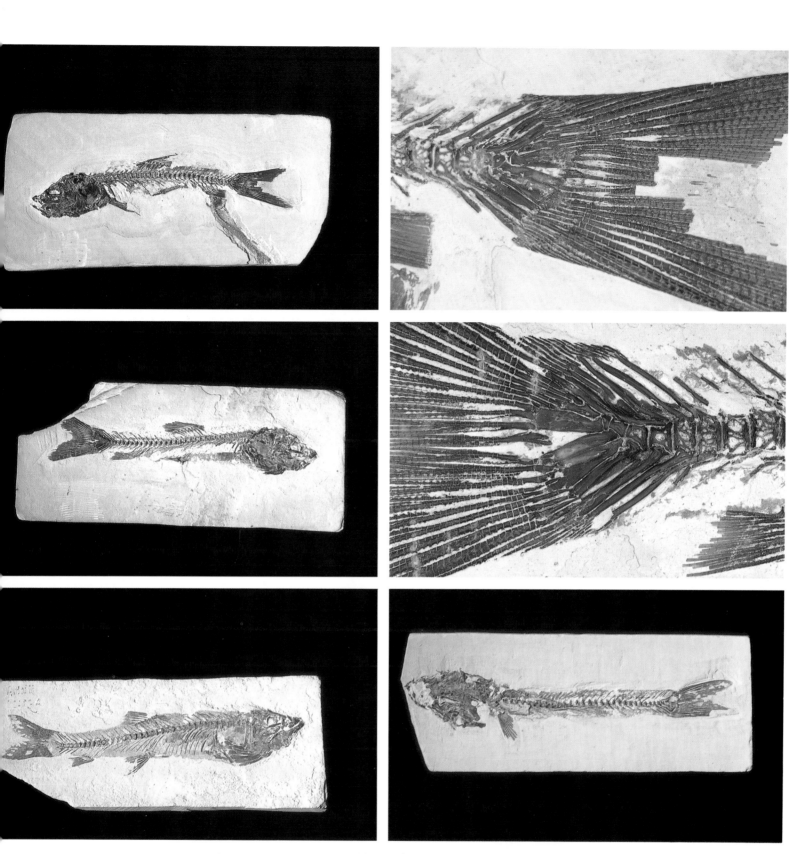

Am. Mus. Nat. Hist. Vert. Palæont

Acc.#704

No.

Parachanos aethiopicus (Weiler)

(See Arambourg & Schneegans, Ann. Paléo., vol. 24, 1935)

Up. Cret. ? Period.   Format: Bituminous Sh. Beds

Loc. N. bank, mouth Rio San Benito, nr. Ibando, Spanish Guinea, W. Africa.

Top four views: Two specimens of *Dastilbe* sp. after treatment with the Waller method; fine details of the caudal fin are easily examined in the close-up views. Two other examples are also shown (**lower center**). *Parachanos* (**bottom**) from the Lower Cretaceous of Africa may be identical to *Dastilbe*.

281

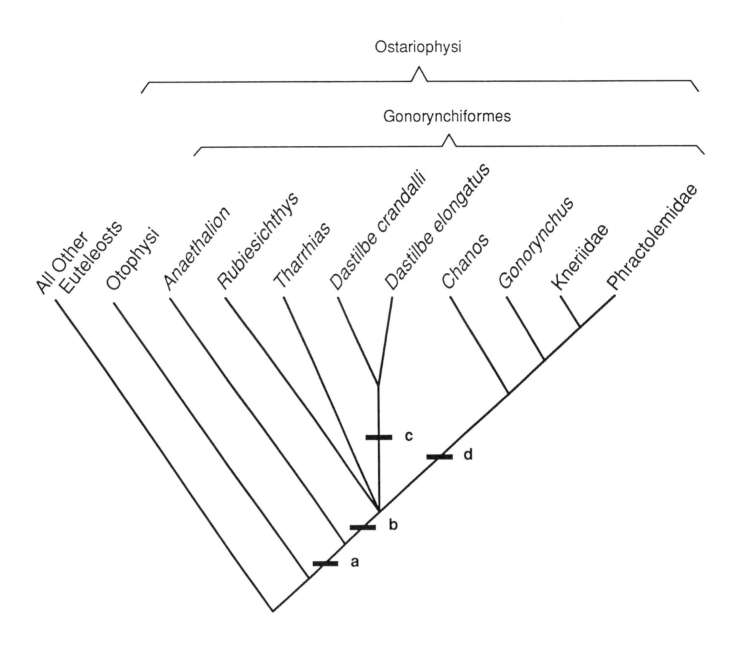

Hypothesis of relationships among gonorynchiform fishes, based on the following characters: (**a**) orbitosphenoid absent, pterosphenoids small and widely separated, parietals reduced to canal-bearing ossicles, quadrate condyle far forward, with elongation of quadratojugal process of quadrate, symplectic, interopercular and lower limb of preopercular, premaxilla thin and flat, no teeth on fifth ceratobranchial, no teeth in jaws, pharyngobranchials or basihyal, epibranchial organ behind fourth epibranchial; (**b**) fourth infraorbital absent, third epural absent; (**c**) see diagnosis; (**d**) postcleithra absent, occipital joint. For other data, see Fink and Fink (1981) and Patterson (1984).

reevaluated his conclusions in light of the work by Fink and Fink (1984). Patterson (1984) observed that *Tharrhias* shares characters 11, 12, 14, 15, 16, 18, 19, and 22 (above) with Recent gonorynchiforms, but has more primitive states in characters 17 and 21 (characters 20 and 23 are unobservable in fossils). The tight joint between the first neural arch and exoccipitals (17) and the absence of postcleithra (21) thus indicate that *Chanos* is the sister-group of all other Recent gonorynchiforms.

Additional support for the monophyly of Recent gonorynchiforms is provided by the reinterpretation of caudal fusions, further reduction in parietals, a junction in the parietal between the supraorbital sensory canal and supratemporal commissure, and the more anterior position of the mandibular joint (the quadratojugal process of quadrate, lower limb of preopercle, symplectic, and interopercle all more elongate in Recent gonorynchiforms).

In addition to *Tharrhias* and the species of *Dastilbe*, other Cretaceous gonorynchiforms include *Aethalionopsis robustus* (lower Wealden of Bernissart, Belgium; Taverne 1981a), *Parachanos aethiopicus* (Aptian?, Gabon, West Africa), and *Rubeisichthys* (Berriassian-Valanginian, Lerida, Spain; Wenz, 1984). *Tharrhias*, *Rubeisichthys*, *Parachanos*, and *Dastilbe* are shown to be more closely related to *Chanos* and more derived gonorynchiforms by loss of the fourth infraorbital (or fusion with the third; the infraorbitals are unknown in *Rubeisichthys*) and the presence of only two epurals (as opposed to three) in the caudal skeleton. *Aethalionopsis* has the more primitive conditions, five infraorbitals and three epurals.

The addition of fossils to the analysis of ostariophysan relationships does not change the topology of the cladogram proposed by Fink and Fink (1981), but does alter the interpretation of one character. Fink and Fink interpreted the loss of teeth in *Chanos* and the African freshwater gonorynchiforms as having occurred independently (basibranchial and mesopterygoid teeth are present in *Gonorynchus*). The cladistically more distant relationships of *Aethalionopsis* and the other Cretaceous gonorynchiforms, indicate that the absence of teeth is the primitive condition for the Gonorynchiformes. The presence of teeth should be considered apomorphic in *Gonorynchus*, and the absence of teeth plesiomorphic in African freshwater gonorynchiforms.

Assemblage: Crato member; reported from the concretionary limestones of the Romualdo member, but no specimens have ever been described, nor have we seen any. *Dastilbe* may be present at a new locality at Pedra Blanca, near Nova Olinda, within bituminous shales, in association with *Rhacolepis*, *Vinctifer*, and *Cladocyclus* (Viana, Brito & Silva-Telles, MS).

(S. Blum)

Above: *Tharrhias araripis*: A fine example in "Santana" matrix reveals many areas inside the skeleton where no sediment or secondary calcite has ever penetrated, particularly in the braincase (bottom left) and between the vertebrae (lower right). Photos by J. Maisey.

Below: *Chanos chanos*, the Recent milkfish. Art by Tomita.

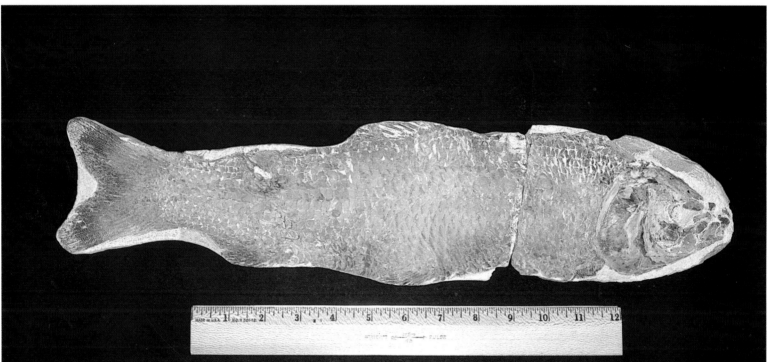

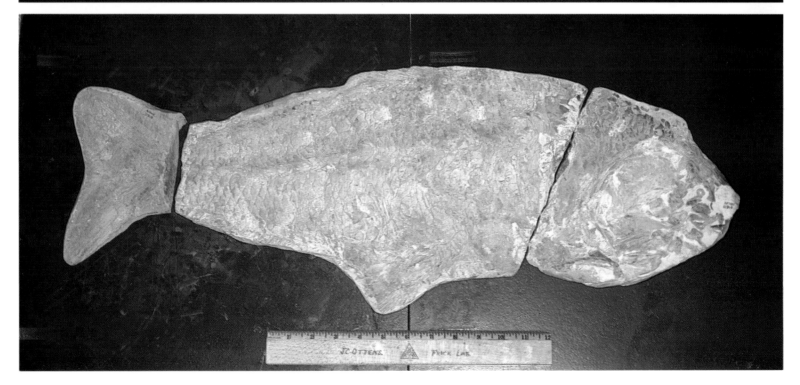

Holotypes of *Tharrhias araripis* (top right) and *Cearana rochae* (top left) in the California Academy of Sciences collection. Two extremely large *Tharrhias* specimens are also shown (center, bottom), both in "Jardim" matrix.

THARRHIAS Jordan and Branner, 1908

Subcohort EUTELEOSTI
Superorder OSTARIOPHYSI
Order GONORYNCHIFORMES
incerta sedis
Genus ***Tharrhias*** Jordan and Branner 1908
  1908 *Tharrias* Jordan and Branner: 13
  1908 *Cearana* Jordan and Branner: 27
Emended diagnosis: Gonorynchiform fishes up to 700 mm (usually less than 300 mm); first two pleural ribs enlarged; a terminal mouth; no teeth on jaws, palate, and hyobranchial apparatus; dermethmoid without rostral commissure; jaws short, not extending past anterior margin of the orbit; articular facet of mandible faces posteriorly, formed entirely by co-ossified articuloangular; retroarticular separate; condyle of quadrate projects anteriorly; supramaxilla absent; quadratojugal process of quadrate produced posteriorly, with its basal length twice height of anterior margin; dermal portion of palatine absent; parasphenoid wider under ethmoid region than under basioccipital, forked anteriorly and posteriorly, with lateral basipterygoid process (as flat spine) just behind orbit; lateral ethmoid with posterior strut descending laterally to the parasphenoid; ventral arm of preopercular longer than dorsal; separate suprapreopercular present as thin tube (thin posterior lamina not readily preserved); opercular taller than long (length 1.35 into height); orbitosphenoid and basisphenoid absent; lateral extrascapular (=supratemporal) present; median extrascapular lost or fused into parietal; supratemporal commissure in parietal, without anterior ramus connecting to supraorbital canal; parietals not so narrow antero-posteriorly as in *Chanos*; vertebrae 47 to 52; first four neural arches expanded anteriorly; neural arches autogenous before origin of dorsal fin origin, remainder fused to centra; caudal

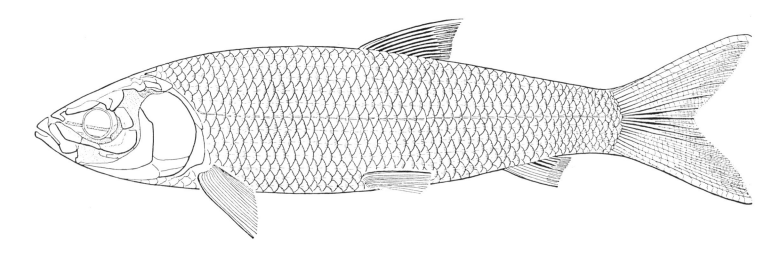

Tharrhias araripis. Skeletal reconstruction.

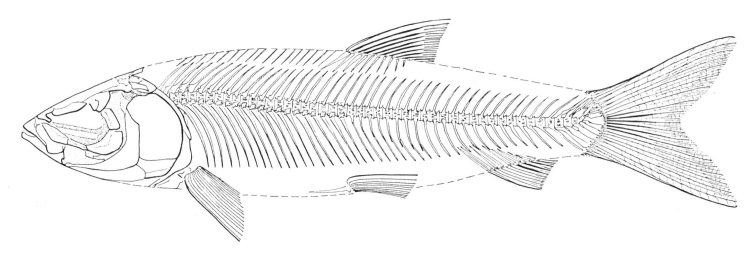

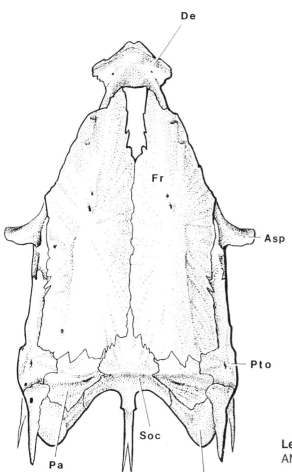

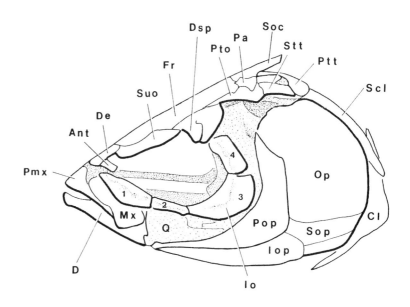

Above: *Tharrhias araripis.* Outline reconstruction of head.

Left: *Tharrhias araripis.* Dorsal view of skull roof, from AMNH 11908.

skeleton with two ural centra, two epurals, three uroneurals, six hypurals (all autogenous). Lateral line scales 48-50, scales from origin of dorsal to lateral line 6, scales from origin of pelvic fin to lateral line 6; dorsal fin with 13 rays, first 3 unbranched and supernumerary, anal 12 (first 3 as in dorsal), pectoral 13-15, ventral 10, caudal 19 (9 lower, 10 upper).

Type species: *Tharrhias araripis* Jordan & Branner, 1908:14.

Tharrhias araripis Jordan & Branner

1908 *Tharrhias araripis* Jordan & Branner: 14
1923 *Tharrhias araripis* J & B; Jordan: 20
1923 *Cearana rochae* J & B; Jordan: 28
1938 *Tharrhias araripis* J & B; D'Erasmo: 17
1938 *Tharrhias rochai* (J & B); D'Erasmo: 19 [*sic*]
1968 *Tharrhias araripis* J & B; Silva Santos & Valença: 348
1968 *Tharrhias rochae* (J & B); Silva Santos & Valença: 348
1974 *Tharrhias araripis* J & B; Taverne: 56
1974 *Tharrhias araripis* J & B; Taverne: 686

1975 *Tharrhias araripis* J & B; Patterson: 167
1975 *Cearana rochae* (J & B); Taverne: 15
1978 *Tharrhias araripis* J & B; Oliveira: 539
1978 *Tharrhias rochae* (J & B); Oliveira: 544
1981 *Tharrhias araripis* J & B; Taverne: 973
1984 *Tharrhias araripis* J & B; Patterson: 135
1984 *Tharrhias araripis* J & B; Wenz: 277
1984 *Tharrhias rochae* (J & B); Wenz: 282

Diagnosis: As for genus.

Holotype of *Tharrhias araripis*: Museu Rocha collection No. 4, present location of major part unknown; counterpart California Academy of Sciences (*ex* Stanford University Department of Geology), CAS 58318; Santana formation, Romualdo member, Chapada do Araripe, Ceará.

Holotype of *Cearana rochae*: Museu Rocha collection no. 5; present location unknown; counterpart CAS 58297 (*ex* Stanford University Department of Geology).

The two nominal species of *Tharrhias* from the Santana formation originally were described as distinct genera from different families (Jordan and Branner, 1908). *Tharrhias araripis* was

287

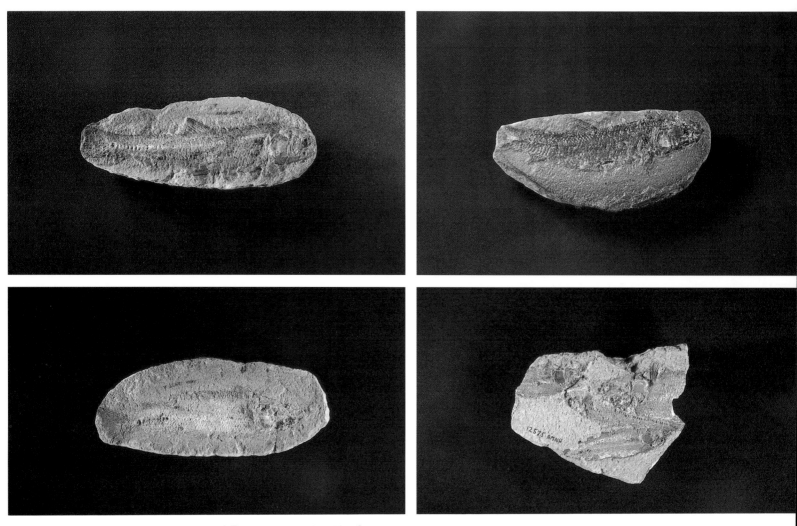

Representative specimens of *Tharrhias araripis*, all in "Santana" matrix. Multiple occurrences of specimens in single concretions suggest a schooling habit. Rarely, other taxa are associated with *Tharrhias* in the same concretion (e.g., see illustrations of *Araripelepidotes* and *Brannerion*).

Representative specimens of *Tharrhias araripis*, all in "Santana" matrix.

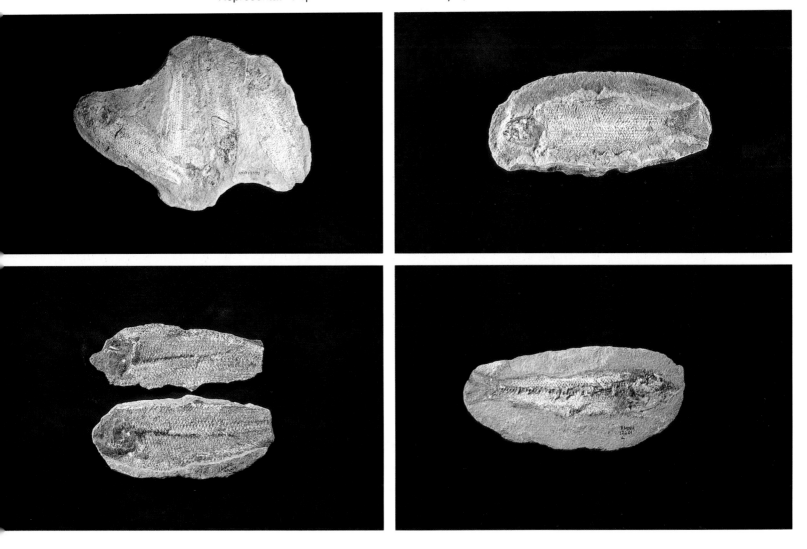

referred to the Leptolepidae and *Cearana rochae* to the Osteoglossidae (for its supposed lack of a subopercle). Later, Jordan (1923) treated *Cearana* as a synonym of *Tharrhias*, believing that the lack of a subopercle in *Cearana* was a preservational artifact. He maintained, however, that *T. araripis* and *T. rochae* were distinct species because the two type specimens have different body shapes. Jordan was impressed by the greater distance between the head and dorsal fin, and by the larger and more rounded opercle in *T. rochae*. These features are not reliably diagnostic when additional material is considered, however, and thus the validity of the second species, *T. rochae*, has been questioned. Taverne (1975, fig. 2) found traces of a subopercle in the holotype of *Cearana rochae*.

D'Erasmo (1938), in his review of the Santana fossil fishes, provided separate descriptions for the two *Tharrhias* species, but did so only for the sake of stability. D'Erasmo believed that the differences between the two species could be explained by preservational variation in a single species.

The validity of *T. rochae* was first addressed directly by Oliveira (1978). He identified six features that supposedly differentiate the two nominal species:

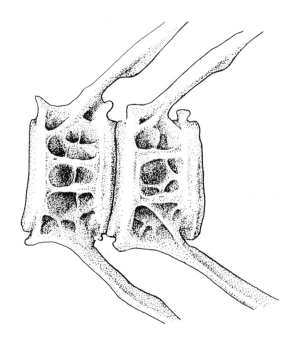

Tharrhias araripis. Caudal vertebrae, from AMNH 11909.

	Tharrhias araripis	Tharrhias rochae
1	body fusiform	body elongate
2	head length into body length 3⅔ times	head length into body length 4 times
3	dorsal and ventral body outlines slightly convex after dorsal fin	dorsal and ventral body outlines straight after dorsal fin
4	head length about equal to maximum body depth	head length clearly greater than maximum body depth
5	vertebral centra longer than tall	vertebral centra taller than long
6	scales as long as tall	scales longer than tall

Oliveira concluded that these features provide evidence for the existence of two species. The evidence, however, is more problematic than implied by this list of features. Most importantly, characters 1, 3, and 4 are, in essence, the same feature, a measure of body depth relative to body length. This aspect of body shape is variable in *Tharrhias*; some specimens are rotund, while others are slender. Variation of this magnitude is rarely encountered within a single Recent species and leads one to suspect that the fossils were in fact derived from two species. The variation in body shape appears to be nearly continuous between the two extremes, however, and by this feature alone some individuals cannot be identified as

one species or the other.

The other features Oliveira considered distinctive are more problematic. The shape of whole scales (character 6) cannot be seen in most specimens. Individuals are almost always preserved with their scales overlapping as in life. Although it is possible to measure the height of a scale, it is impossible to measure its length (the anterior margin is hidden beneath the preceeding scale) or determine the ratio of scale height to length. Even if the ratio of scale dimensions was absolutely diagnostic, it would not be applicable to most specimens.

Vertebral height and length (character 5) can be measured if the specimen has been acid-prepared or was split midsagittally when the

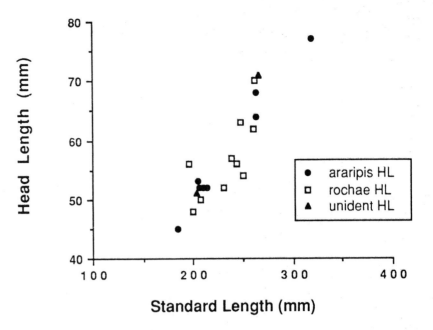

Top right: A scatterplot of head length against standard length in *Tharrhias*. Closed circles represent individuals provisionally identified as *T. araripis*, open squares *T. rochae*, and closed triangles specimens that were unidentified. No separation is apparent between the two putative species.

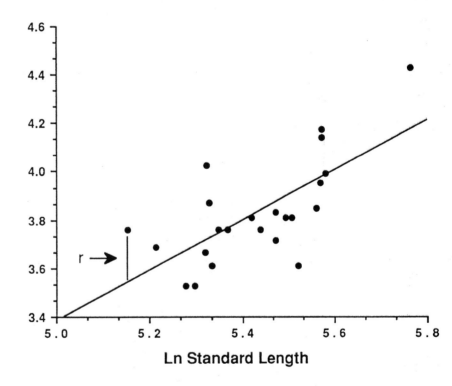

Bottom right: A scatterplot of body depth against standard length in *Tharrhias*. The line was determined by model I least squares regression. The difference between the observed and predicted body depth (residual) for one individual is indicated by "r".

concretion was opened. The height to length ratio of vertebral centra was compared in two acid-prepared specimens provisionally identified as *T. araripis* and *T. rochae* by their oppositely extreme ratios of body depth to length. Because the dimensions of vertebral centra change with their position along the vertebral column (centra near the occiput and caudal fin are shorter than intervening centra), height and length measures were taken from the 34th and 35th vertebrae in both specimens. All height to length ratios were between 1.06 and 1.09, and the two extreme values were taken from consecutive vertebrae in the same individual. This indicates that shape of the vertebral centra does not separate specimens having different body shape.

Character 2 (head length relative to body length) is similarly ineffective as a discriminator between the two putative species. Head length (tip of snout to posterior margin of opercle) and standard length (tip of snout to end of hypurals) have been measured in 21 specimens, and the two measurements plotted against each other (this graphical test for a species difference avoids the assumption implicit in using ratios that the line describing the relationship between the two metric variables passes through the origin). If the two species have different head lengths for a given body length, then two distinct linear arrays of points should be apparent in such a plot, one above the other. No separation is apparent, however, and specimens tentatively

Representative specimens of *Tharrhias araripis*, all in "Santana" matrix.

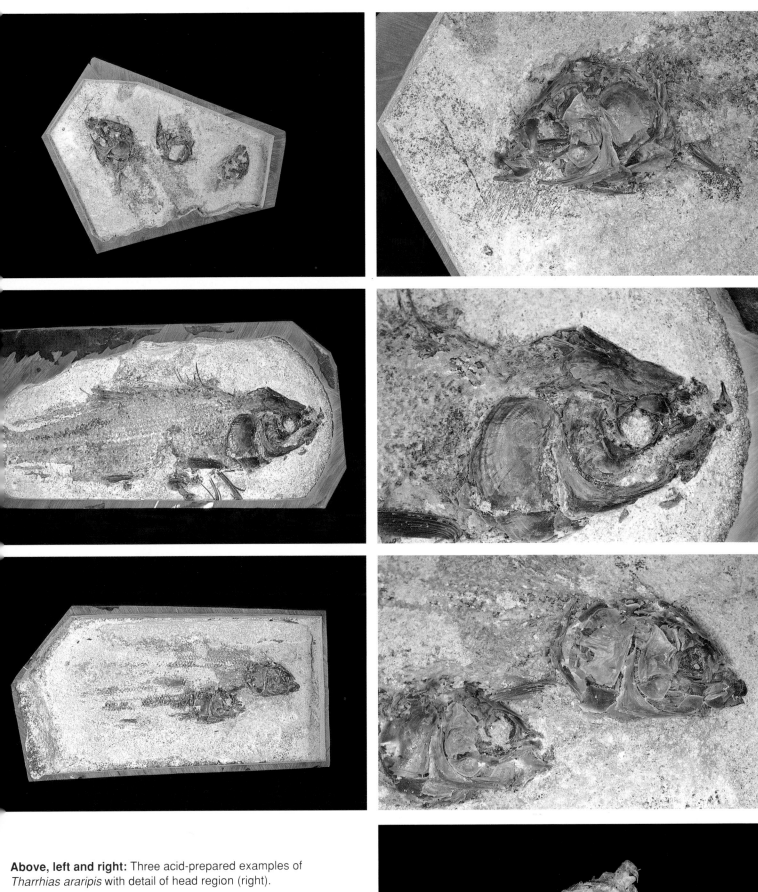

Above, left and right: Three acid-prepared examples of *Tharrhias araripis* with detail of head region (right).

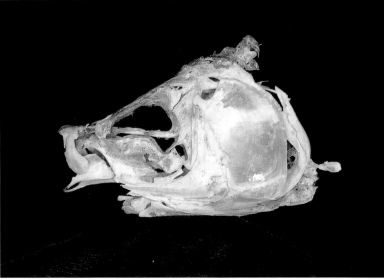

Right: The skull, jaws, and other bones of the head in the modern milkfish, *Chanos*.

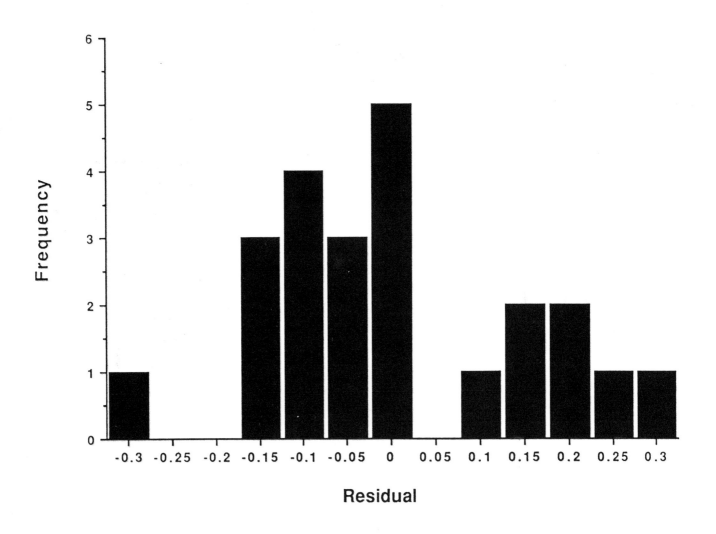

A histogram showing the distribution of residuals from the regression of body depth on standard length in *Tharrhias*. Although two groups are suggested by a lack of individuals in the 0.05 class, this sample does not depart significantly from normality.

identified as *T. araripis* and *T. rochae* (by body depth to length proportions) overlap extensively. Contrary to Oliveira's assertion, therefore, specimens assigned to the two putative species do not differ in their relative head lengths.

Among the supposedly distinctive characters, only the comparison of body depth to body length remains to test the hypothesis that a single species of *Tharrhias* exists in the fauna. Body depth (distance between origins of the dorsal and pelvic fins) and standard length have been measured in 23 specimens. Again, a bivariate plot was used to assess the variation among individuals. In this comparison, the measurements were transformed by their natural logarithms to reduce any non-linearity that might result from an allometric relationship between the two variables. Unlike the plot of head length against standard length, the plot of body depth against standard length shows substantially greater scatter (as would be expected from a heterogeneous sample). Two discrete linear arrays are still not clearly evident, however.

Under the single species "null" hypothesis, one would predict a unimodal type of variation around an average body shape. This null hypothesis was tested by regressing body depth on standard length and examining the distribution of residuals (the deviations of individuals from the regression line, which describes the average proportional change in body depth with increasing standard length). If the sample (23 individuals) is drawn from a single population, the distribution of residuals from regression should be approximately normal. There is a hint of bimodality in the distribution of residuals, but a Kolmogorov-Smirnov test (Sokal and Rohlf, 1981) for lack of fit to an intrisic hypothesis of normality (where the mean and variance are measured from the data) is not significant. The variation in body shape shown by this sample, despite the hint of bimodality, is well within the bounds of expectation for a single population. The evidence for heterogeneity or bimodality is not strong enough to reject the null hypothesis that only a single species of *Tharrhias* exists in the assemblage.

A larger sample might show that the suggested bimodality is real. However, this would not necessarily indicate that the two modes represent species. It is possibile that the variation in body depth represents sexual dimorphism within a single species. For example, deeper-bodied individuals might have been gravid females. Unless additional features are found to covary with body depth (ones that do not correspond to male-female differences commonly encountered in fishes), the sexual dimorphism hypothesis cannot be rejected. *Tharrhias rochae* therefore should be regarded as a junior synonym of *T. araripis*.

Tharrhias is considered to be closely related to another fossil gonorynchiform (*Dastilbe*) that is known from the slightly older Crato member of the Santana formation. To avoid repetition, a discussion of important morphological features and the phylogenetic relationships of both taxa is appended to the section on *Dastilbe*.

Assemblages: Santana (abundant); Jardim (rare, and only exceptionally large individuals).

(S. Blum)

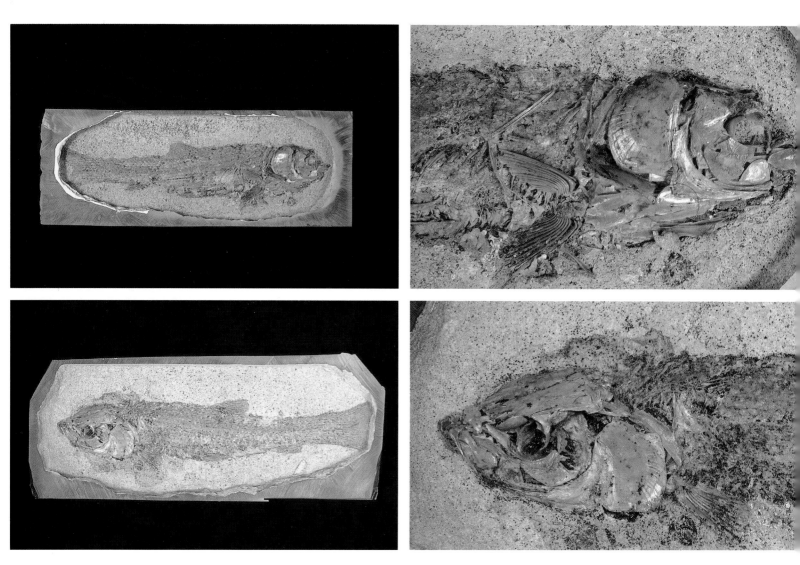

A particularly fine specimen of *Tharrhias araripis* in which both halves have been prepared in acid. The skeletal anatomy of the head is exposed in exquisite detail.

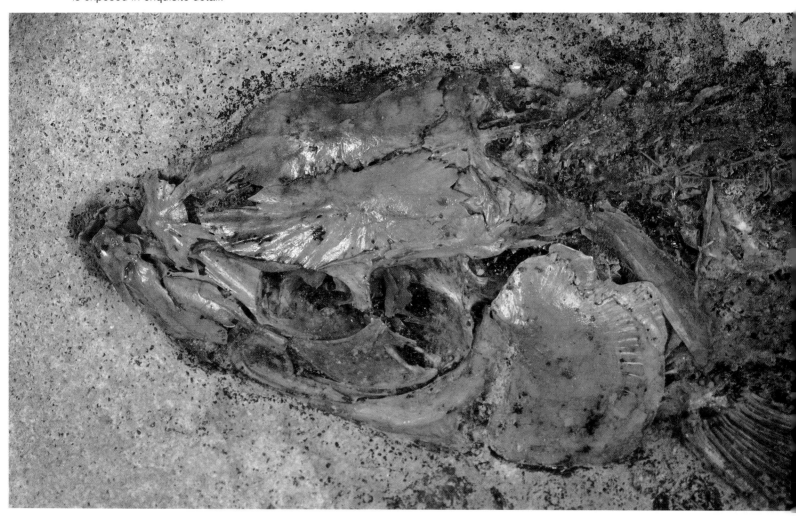

UNDETERMINED SANTANA CLUPEIFORM

Cohort CLUPEOCEPHALA
Subcohort CLUPEOMORPHA
Order CLUPEIFORMES
incertae sedis

Undetermined Clupeiform Genus A

Diagnosis: Clupeomorph fish with smooth cranial bones, parietals separated by supraoccipital, supratemporal canal passing through parietals and supraoccipital, roofed post-temporal fossa, dilatator fossa unroofed, pre-epiotic fossa absent or rudimentary, temporal foramen exposed, no frontal fontanelle, recessus lateralis present, pterotic bulla present; parasphenoid edentulous; premaxilla, maxilla, and dentary toothed, jaw elements elongate and slender; preoperculum with short horizontal limb, operculum large; suboperculum small; hyomandibular head angled slightly forward; coracoids meeting ventrally; caudal skeleton with large first uroneural apparently fused with first pre-ural centrum, first ural centrum not reduced, parhypural and first hypural apparently separate from first ural centrum; lateral line scales apparently absent, eight or nine keeled ventral scutes immediately anterior to pelvic fins, nine or ten behind them; one or two small dorsal scutes perhaps present; scales cycloid, marked by concentric circuli. Reaching about 45 mm standard length, 55 mm overall length; proportions (as percent of standard length): head length 22, maximum trunk depth 33, predorsal 45-47, prepelvic 51-53, preanal 75; D14; A11; P12; V8-9, C19 (10 upper, 9 lower); approximately 38 preural vertebrae, of which probably 23 are abdominal, 2 free ural centra; no lateral line scales; approximately 10-12 scales in transverse series anterior to dorsal fin.

Referred specimens: AMNH 12790; complete specimen; acid-prepared; Santana formation, Chapada do Araripe, Santana, Ceará. AMNH 12789, associated with AMNH 12790 in single concretion, also acid-prepared.

The single concretion containing both referred

Undetermined clupeomorph. Skeletal reconstruction.

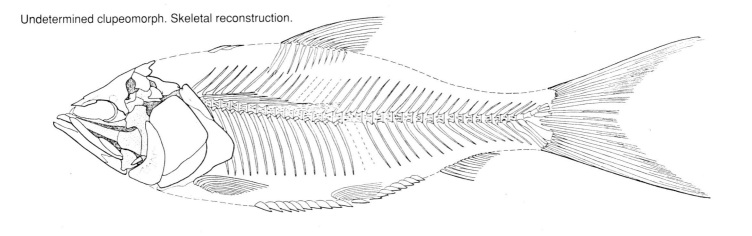

Undetermined clupeomorph, AMNH 12790.

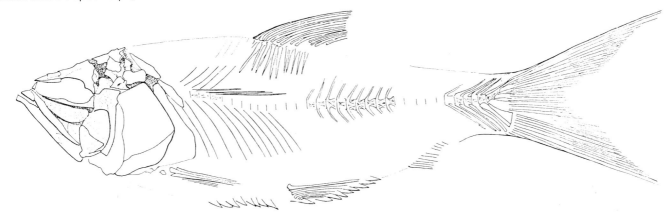

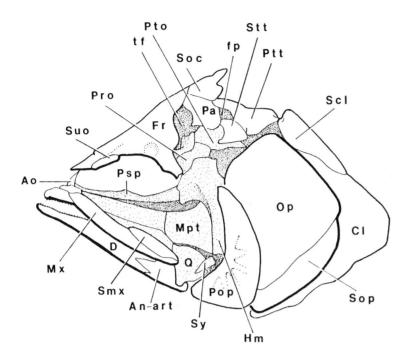

Undetermined clupeomorph. Outline reconstruction of head.

specimens was acid-prepared using the transfer technique. The ostracod-rich "Santana" matrix lithology and the presence of numerous disarticulated bones of a large *Tharrhias* (cataloged as AMNH 12791), recovered during acid preparation, suggest that the provenance of this specimen may have been near Santana do Cariri.

The Clupeomorpha (herrings and herring-like fishes) form a diverse and successful group containing more than 300 living and 150 fossil species (Grande, 1985). They occur in marine, brackish, and freshwater habitats, and certain species inhabit more than one of these environments during their lifetimes. About one-third of the annual global commercial fishing catch consists of these fishes. All living clupeomorphs are grouped within the order Clupeiformes, and all but one of these (*Denticeps clupeoides*, from a freshwater stream on the Dahomey-Nigerian border) are placed within the suborder Clupeoidei. The principal living groups of clupeoid fishes are the chirocentrids (wolf-herring), engraulids (anchovies), dussumierines (round herrings), clupeines (true herrings, pilchards, sprats, and sardines), alosines (shads, menhadens, alewives), dorosomatines (gizzard shads), and three groups (pellonulines, pristigasterines, and congothrissines) having no common name.

Until fairly recently the phylogenetic relationships of clupeomorphs had received little attention. Most investigators were satisfied merely to document features of the external morphology and to produce annotated keys for species identification. Moreover, despite the fact that there is almost one fossil clupeomorph species for every two living ones, the majority of ichthyologists who have studied living clupeomorphs have not compared them with fossils, and paleontological studies have

Undetermined clupeomorph, AMNH 12789.

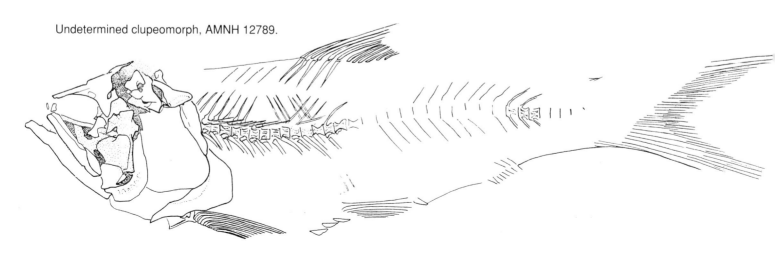

generally compared the fossils with relatively few Recent species. This unfortunate situation has changed dramatically with the publication of important reviews by Grande (1982, 1985). For the first time, an array of shared derived characters to support a phylogenetic hypothesis of clupeomorph relationships was presented, serving as a basis for future investigations. The analysis presented here is based largely on Grande's (1985) character analysis, and the following discussion will be restricted essentially to certain critical features (not all of which have been satisfactorily determined in the Santana herring).

According to Grande (1982, 1985), various extinct clupeomorphs cannot be included within either the Clupeidae or Clupeiformes, but instead represent primitive sister-groups. Initially, Grande (1982) considered the early Upper Cretaceous *Ornategulum* from Lebanon to be the most primitive known clupeomorph. Previously *Ornategulum* had been regarded as Clupeomorpha *incertae sedis* (Forey, 1973c). However, in his subsequent monograph Grande (1985) effectively removed *Ornategulum* from the Clupeomorpha, leaving its relationships with other clupeocephalans (euteleosts plus clupeomorphs) uncertain. Instead, the Lower Cretaceous (Albian) *Erichalcis* from Canada (Forey, 1975) was treated as the most primitive known clupeomorph. *Erichalcis* and an Albian form (*Spratticeps*, from the Gault Clay of England; Patterson, 1970a) have until now been among the earliest clupeomorphs known in any detail. Thus the presence of a clupeomorph in the even older (Aptian) Santana formation assemblage is a significant discovery. Unfortunately, only a single half-concretion containing two small and imperfectly preserved individuals was available for this study following acid preparation. Many characters thought to be of critical phylogenetic significance remain unknown, and the degree of confidence with which certain other features can be determined is low.

According to Grande (1985), the Clupeomorpha are characterized by three features, all of which are present in the available material. These include the presence of unpaired abdominal scutes along the ventral midline; expanded, ossified bullae in the prootic (associated with the development of an otophysic connection with the swim-bladder); and the arrangement of the supratemporal commissural sensory canal passing through the parietals and the supraoccipital. In most Recent clupeomorphs there are ossified bullae in the

pterotic as well as the prootic, but this cannot be determined in available specimens of the Santana clupeomorph. Grande (1985: 253) speculated that at least prootic bullae are present in *Erichalcis*, based on the external appearance of the bone. According to Forey (1973c: 1308), the prootic in *Ornategulum* "is very thin and slightly inflated, suggesting a rudimentary prootic bulla." Thus the prootic bulla in the Santana clupeomorph appears to be better developed than in other Cretaceous examples. The supratemporal commissural canal clearly passes through the posterior region of the parietal, a derived condition according to Patterson and Rosen (1977: 126) that may have arisen from fusion of extrascapular bones to the parietals (Patterson, 1970a: 177). This feature is present in *Erichalcis* and *Ornategulum* but was included only tentatively as a clupeomorph synapomorphy by Grande (1985) because it also occurs in characoids and osteoglossomorphs.

Within clupeomorphs, Grande (1985) recognized a large group ("Clupeomorpha Division 2") comprising all clupeomorphs apart from *Erichalcis* and defined on the basis of three characters. These are: fusion of hypural 2 with the first ural centrum and a free (autogenous) first hypural; a well-defined pre-epiotic fossa; and dorsal scutes.

The first of these characters occurs in *Ornategulum*. In the Santana clupeomorph the first hypural is autogenous but the second is too poorly preserved to be certain of its condition with respect to the first ural centrum. In *Erichalcis* the second hypural is unfused like the first. A small pit at the junction of the epiotic, parietal, and pterotic in *Ornategulum* may represent a rudimentary pre-epiotic fossa, although Forey (1973c: 1306) was cautious over such an interpretation. The fossa may be absent in *Erichalcis* and it cannot have been well developed in the Santana clupeomorph. A small pre-epiotic fossa is present in *Spratticeps* (Patterson, 1970a). Dorsal scutes apparently are absent in *Erichalcis* and *Ornategulum*. They certainly are not prominent in the Santana form, but upon careful examination some thin, keeled scale-like dorsal scutes were inferred to be present from faint impressions in the embedding plastic of the specimen. Nevertheless, none of the characters said by Grande (1985) to unite his "Clupeomorpha Division 2" has been convincingly demonstrated in the Santana form, inviting the conclusion that this form is an extremely primitive clupeomorph.

That interpretation is not entirely consistent with certain other observations, however, and

Above: Undetermined clupeomorph, the only known examples. Large brown object in lower center is part of disarticulated *Tharrhias* skull included within concretion.

Engraulis mordax, a Recent anchovy. Dr. G. R. Allen photo.

Spratelloides robustus, a Recent clupeid. Dr. G. R. Allen photo.

Diplomystus, an Eocene clupeid. A. Kerstitch photo.

this form could conceivably occupy a more derived phylogenetic position within the Clupeomorpha. The degree to which prootic bullae are developed is suggestive of more advanced taxa than *Erichalcis* and *Ornategulum*, and the bullae are certainly as well developed as in *Spratticeps*. Furthermore, the Santana clupeomorph apparently possesses at least two of the three clupeiform characters discussed by Grande (1985), specifically the presence of a recessus lateralis (an intracranial space into which the supraorbital, infraorbital, preopercular, and temporal sensory canals open, bounded by the pterotic and sphenotic, and partly roofed by the frontal) and separation of the parietals by the supraoccipital (the third character, "beryciform foramen" absent in the anterior ceratohyal, cannot be determined in the material available). The supraoccipital separates the parietals in *Spratticeps*, but in that form a recessus lateralis is absent and the sensory canal arrangement is generalized in several respects (Patterson, 1970a). As in *Spratticeps*, the supraoccipital portion of the supratemporal commissural canal in the Santana clupeomorph is enclosed by bone, unlike in living clupeomorphs where the canal is superficial to the supraoccipital.

Within the Clupeiformes, Grande (1985) defined the Clupeoidei on the basis of four characters: fusion of the first uroneural with the first preural centrum; reduction in size of the first ural centrum; separation of the parhypural from the first ural centrum; and loss of most or all lateral line scales. The first uroneural and parhypural are visible in are visible in the Santana clupeomorph, but preservational factors do not permit a determination as to whether they are fused to or separate from their respective centra. The first ural centrum certainly is not "reduced" in size, particularly when compared to the situation in Recent clupeomorphs. Scales are present in both individuals of the Santana form. Although the scales are not well preserved, the mid-trunk region is fairly intact in both individuals, but no specialized lateral line scales are discernible. Thus of Grande's (1985) clupeid characters, one is probably present, another is definitely absent, and two others are equivocal. Placement of the Santana clupeomorph within the Clupeidae may seem far-fetched but nevertheless remains a possibility.

With the Clupeidae, Grande (1985) recognized three groups of superfamily rank, the Engrauloidea, Pristigasteroidea, and Clupeoidea. Characters used by him to establish pristigasteroid and clupeoid monophyly are either absent or cannot be determined here. Of the two engrauloid characters (see also Grande and Nelson, 1985), one (mesethmoid projecting in advance of vomer, snout pig-like) cannot be determined, but the other one (suspensorium inclined obliquely backward) is suggested by a slight forward inclination of the hyomandibular head. The gape is long, somewhat as in anchovies, but the mandibular joint lies below rather than behind the orbit and the articular head of the quadrate is oriented posteriorly rather than anteriorly. Because the evidence is so weak and certain critical characters cannot be determined from the specimens available, the Santana clupeomorph is here left as Clupeiformes *incertae sedis*.

To summarize, there is compelling evidence that the Santana clupeomorph displays certain more derived attributes than *Erichalcis* and *Ornategulum*. The new form resembles *Spratticeps*, *Erichalcis*, and *Ornategulum* in having a recessus lateralis, but is more primitive than modern clupeomorphs in retaining an enclosed supraoccipital commissural canal. Possibly this was primitively retained by primitive clupeids. The Santana form thus may represent the most primitive known clupeid, with which it is tentatively united because it appears to lack lateral line scales (at least in the mid-trunk). The three extant clupeid superfamilies still may be united by four characters (fusion of uroneural and first preural centrum; autogenous parhypural; first ural centrum reduced; superficial supratemporal commissure above supraoccipital), although the caudal fin characters have yet to be properly investigated in the Santana form.

Assemblage: Santana.

(J. G. Maisey)

AXELRODICHTHYS Maisey, 1986

Class OSTEICHTHYES
Subclass SARCOPTERYGII
Order ACTINISTIA
Family COELACANTHIDAE Agassiz, 1844
Genus *Axelrodichthys* Maisey, 1986
1986 *Axelrodichthys* Maisey: 13

Diagnosis: Coelacanths reaching lengths of 1-2 m; first dorsal fin with 10-11 rays, second dorsal with 9-10, caudal with 17-18 in upper lobe, 15-16 in lower lobe, pectoral fin with 12-15 rays, pelvic with 17-18, anal fin probably 9-10; bones of skull roof ornamented with rugosities, especially supraorbital and tectal bones; anterior (ethmosphenoid) part of skull two to five times longer than posterior (otico-occipital) part and at least three times as long as broad; posterior skull roof comprising paired parietals, supratemporals, and postparietals, plus a unique median postparietal; no free extrascapulars; dermosphenotic bone behind eye extends in front of intracranial joint; supraorbital sensory canal confined to snout; antotic process of basisphenoid short and robust; foramina for facial nerve and jugular vein extremely small.

Type species: *A. araripensis* Maisey, 1986.
Axelrodichthys araripensis Maisey
1986 *Axelrodichthys araripensis* Maisey: 13
Diagnosis: As for genus.

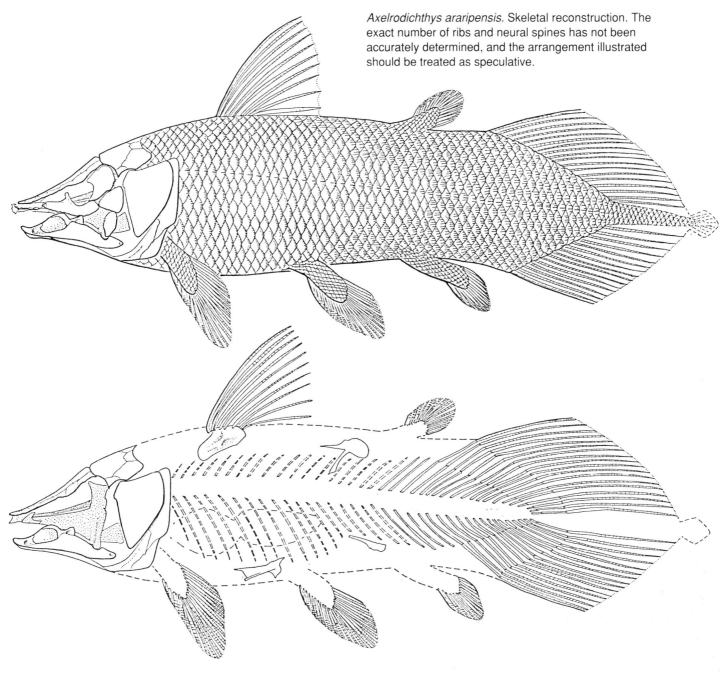

Axelrodichthys araripensis. Skeletal reconstruction. The exact number of ribs and neural spines has not been accurately determined, and the arrangement illustrated should be treated as speculative.

Axelrodichthys araripensis. Holotype (**top**) before preparation, and its head (**center, bottom left**) after limited mechanical preparation. Braincase of another much larger specimen is shown after acid preparation (**bottom right**). Photos by J. Maisey.

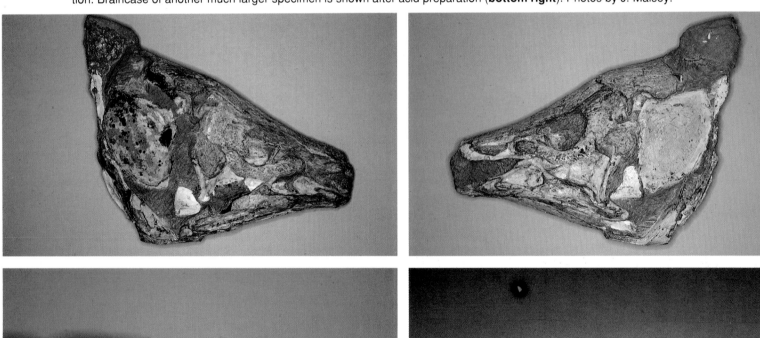

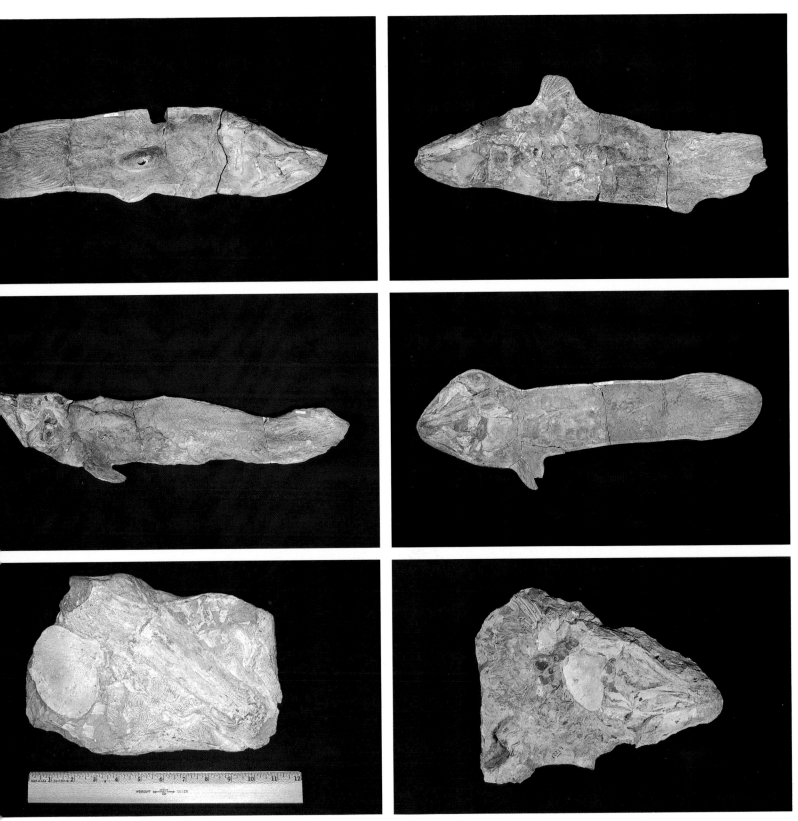

Representative specimens of *Axelrodichthys araripensis*.

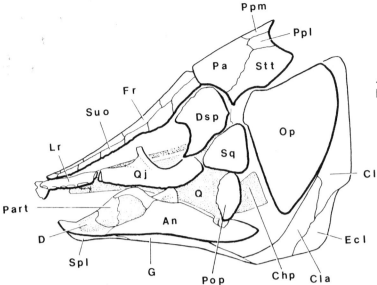

Axelrodichthys araripensis. Outline reconstruction of head.

Holotype: American Museum of Natural History, New York, AMNH 1759; complete fish; Santana formation, Romualdo member Chapada do Araripe, Barro do Jardim, Ceará.

Axelrodichthys araripensis is one of only two species of coelacanth fish recorded to date from the Santana formation. At present this is its only known occurrence. However, a skull roof recently collected from Ingall (Niger) is said to be very similar to that of *Axelrodichthys* (Gee, 1988).

Axelrodichthys is a unique coelacanth in possessing a median postparietal bone in the skull roof. In most coelacanths, the posterior skull roof consists of just two pairs of bones (commonly identified as parietals and supratemporals). Behind these bones there usually is an extrascapular series containing the transverse commissural sensory canal. The number and arrangement of extrascapulars is variable and may be of systematic importance.

Forey (1981) united *Latimeria* and *Macropoma* partly on the basis that each has a series of seven extrascapulars, but this number also occurs in *Diplurus newarki* (Schaeffer, 1952, fig. 4).

Maisey (1986) noted that free extrascapulars are lacking in both *Mawsonia* and *Axelrodichthys*. Instead, there are additional bones ("postparietals" of authors) sutured into the posterior margin of the skull roof. Since these bones contain the transverse commissure in *Mawsonia* and *Axelrodichthys*, they were considered the topographic homologs of extrascapulars. It was concluded that sutural inclusion of these elements into the skull roof represented a synapomorphy of these two genera.

Interestingly, the skull roof of the Triassic coelacanth *Chinlea sorenseni* also includes a postparietal series (Schaeffer, 1967, fig. 14). Their sutural incorporation into the the skull roof in this form has not been noted previously, although it is clearly evident from illustrations of a new specimen of *Chinlea sorenseni* (Elliott, 1987, figs. 1-3) and can be confirmed in the holotype (AMNH 5652). According to the phylogenetic hypothesis advanced by Forey (1981, 1984) and modified by Maisey (1986), incorporation of extrascapulars into the skull roof would have a remarkably disjunct distribution among cladistically derived coelacanths. In view of the paucity of characters supporting various aspects of the original hypothesis, however, alternative models are distinctly possible, including one in which sutured "postparietals" help to define a monophyletic group containing *Mawsonia*, *Axelrodichthys*, and *Chinlea*.

The jugal sensory canal of *Latimeria* passes within the squamosal bone, close to its ventral margin, before turning ventrally to pass through the posterior part of the preoperculum (Millot and Anthony, 1958, pl. 32). The jugal canal similarly is located within the ventral margin of the squamosal in *Holophagus* (Gardiner, 1960, fig. 55) and apparently in *Macropoma* (Forey, 1981, 1984). According to Maisey (1986: 28), the jugal canal in *Mawsonia* and *Axelrodichthys* lies toward the ventral margin of the squamosal. Although some branches of the jugal canal emerge as pores low down on the squamosal, the main canal itself passes deeper inside this bone (e.g., *Mawsonia* cf. *gigas*; Maisey, 1986, fig. 7). Although this canal was not illustrated in

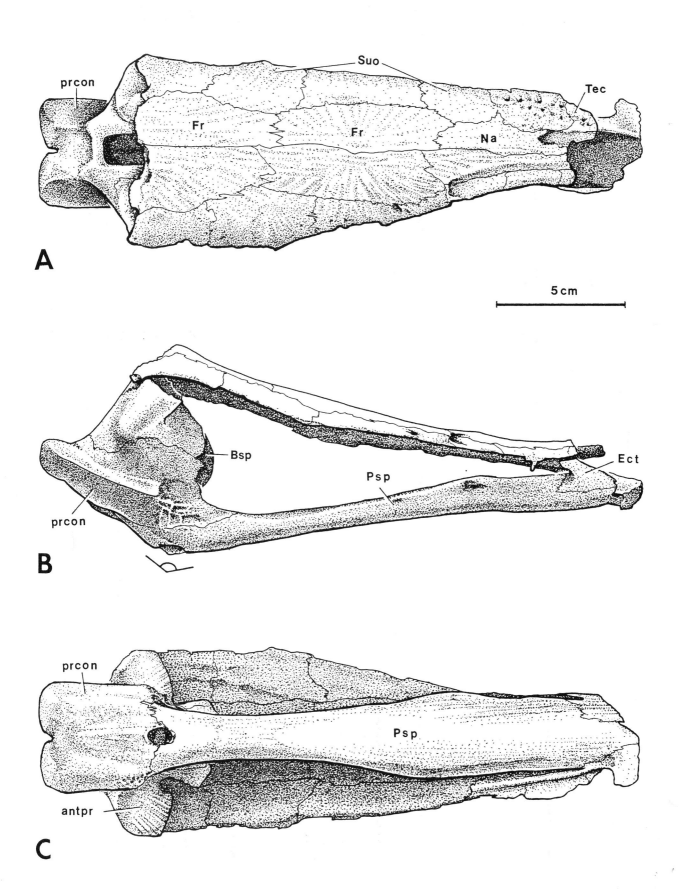

Axelrodichthys araripensis. Anterior part of acid-prepared braincase, AMNH 11760, seen in (A) dorsal, (B) lateral, and (C) ventral aspects (from Maisey, 1986).

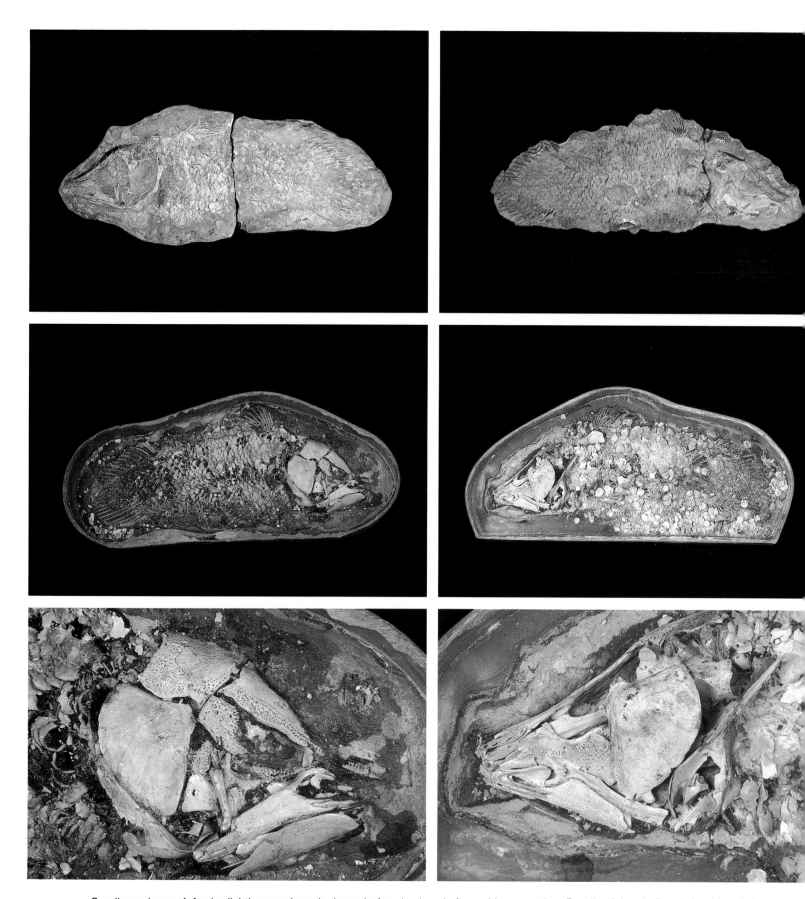

Small specimen of *Axelrodichthys araripensis* shown before (top) and after acid preparation. Details of the skull and shoulder girdle are clearly visible (bottom).

Above: Model of *Latimeria chalumnae*, the living coelacanth. K. Lucas photo, Steinhart.

Axelrodichthys, inspection of acid-prepared material now suggests that it lay farther centrally within the squamosal as in *Mawsonia*; i.e., in a cladistically primitive location according to Forey's (1981, 1984) characterization. The ventral position of the jugal canal within the squamosal thus continues to unite only *Latimeria*, *Macropoma*, and *Holophagus*, as Forey suggested.

The posterior part of the coelacanth braincase is made up principally from paired prootics. In some coelacanths there is a prootic ascending process that is in sutural contact with a descending process of the parietal. Maisey (1986) used the presence of this process in part to define a monophyletic group including *Latimeria*, *Macropoma*, *Mawsonia*, and *Axelrodichthys*. Unfortunately the prootic is badly preserved in many other fossil actinistians. Consequently, the level of generality represented by the ascending process cannot be regarded as accurately determined.

In many fossil coelacanths the dermosphenotic lies essentially behind the level of the dermal intracranial joint, in the angle formed between the postotic and infraorbital sensory canals. With this configuration, the posterior margin of the orbit is effectively on a level with the dermal intracranial joint (e.g., *Rhabdoderma*, *Laugia*,

Above: *Latimeria* crudely mounted for sale to tourists in the Comores. Dr. E. Balon photo.

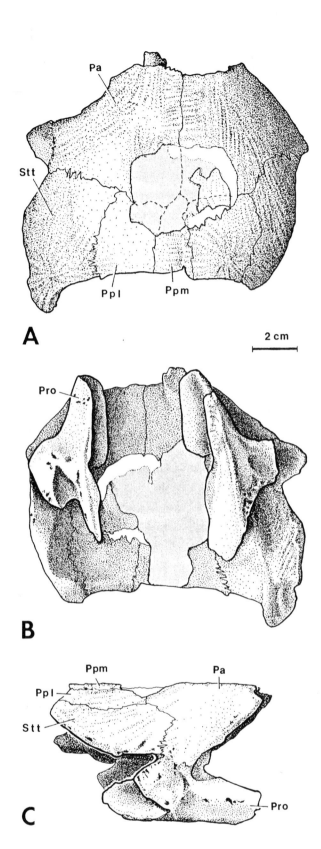

Pa

Stt

Ppl   Ppm

A   2 cm

Pro

B

Ppm   Pa
Ppl
Stt
                              Pro
C

Axelrodichthys araripensis. Posterior part of acid-prepared braincase, AMNH 11760, seen in (A) dorsal, (B) ventral, and (C) lateral aspects (from Maisey, 1986).

Nesides, Whiteia, Caridosuctor, Hadronector, Polyosteorhynchus, Allenypterus, Lochmocercus, Macropoma, Latimeria, Diplurus).

In *Chinlea sorenseni*, the dermosphenotic extends in front of the level of the dermal intracranial joint. Although this is not apparent from the original restoration of *C. sorenseni* (Schaeffer, 1967, fig. 14), it is unmistakable in the new specimen described by Elliott (1987) and can with hindsight be observed in other specimens including the holotype (e.g., Schaeffer, 1967, pl. 28).

This unusual configuration also has been reported in *Axelrodichthys* and *Mawsonia* (Maisey, 1986). In *Axelrodichthys* the dermosphenotic is located in virtually the same position as in *Chinlea*, although this bone is slightly more elongated in the latter (compare Maisey, 1986, fig. 26, with Elliott, 1987, figs. 2, 3). The dermosphenotic of *Mawsonia* cf. *gigas* is aligned below the dermal intracranial joint but sends an elongate splint anteriorly parallel to the posterior end of the lachrymojugal (Maisey, 1986, fig. 7). Wenz (1975, fig. 1 and pl. 1) illustrated a similar pattern in *M. tegamensis*. In that species, the dermosphenotic (= "postorbital") lies slightly farther anteriorly to the dermal intracranial joint than shown by Maisey (1986) for *M.* cf. *gigas*.

To summarize, the dermosphenotic extends for a considerable distance anterior to the dermal intracranial joint in *Chinlea*, *Mawsonia*, and *Axelrodichthys*, unlike in other actinistians in which the bone is confined farther posteriorly. It is worth noting that in *Mawsonia* and apparently in *Axelrodichthys* the infraorbital canal is located within the dermosphenotic some distance from anterior margin, unlike in *Rhabdoderma*, *Whiteia*, or *Latimeria*. The position of this canal within the dermosphenotic in *Chinlea* has yet to be verified, but also seems to be located away from the leading edge.

In *Mawsonia* there is no descending process on the supratemporal (Wenz, 1975; Maisey, 1986), and in *Axelrodichthys* there is only a very weak ridge (Maisey, 1986). Schaeffer (1952: 41) commented that it also is absent in *Diplurus*. It has not been possible to determine the character state in *Chinlea*.

According to Schaeffer (1952: 41), in *Diplurus* there is a strong ventral ridge antero-medially on the parietal (= intertemporal). Schaeffer (ibid.) speculated that the prootic has an anterior dorsal process which met this ridge, as Moy-Thomas (1937, fig. 3) suggested in the case of *Rhabdoderma*. A parietal descending process occurs in *Mawsonia* and *Axelrodichthys* (Maisey,

1986). The ventral surface of the parietal previously has not been documented in *Chinlea*, but there is evidence of a descending lamina in AMNH 5654, beneath the broken roof of the left parietal.

Forey (1981, 1984) has claimed that the presence of dorsal laminae at the anterior end of the parasphenoid is a derived character of *Latimeria*, *Macropoma*, and *Holophagus*. In *Latimeria* these thin laminae are prominent (e.g., in transverse sections through the head illustrated by Millot and Anthony, 1958, pls. 11 and 12), although in fossils their delicate nature may preclude their preservation except under extraordinary circumstances. In *Latimeria*, expansion of the dorsal laminae apparently is greatest immediately posterior to the paired ectethmoids, and the laminae are confluent with the dorsal process of the ectethmoids. A comparable arrangement is seen in *Mawsonia lavocati* (Wenz, 1981, fig. 1) and *Axelrodichthys araripensis* (Maisey, 1986, fig. 18B).

Unfortunately, the dorsal surface of the parasphenoid is unknown in a number of fossil actinistians, and the systematic value of Forey's character consequently is limited. The parasphenoid of *Diplurus newarki* also has well-developed dorsal laminae anteriorly (Schaeffer, 1952, fig. 1). As in *Latimeria*, *Mawsonia*, and *Axelrodichthys*, the dorsal laminae apparently are confluent with the posterior margins of the ectethmoid dorsal process. According to Moy-Thomas (1935), the anterior part of the parasphenoid in *Whiteia woodwardi* also may possess dorsal laminae.

To summarize, the presence of dorsal laminae on the actinistian parasphenoid seems to characterize a larger group than Forey (1981, 1984) postulated, one which includes *Latimeria*, *Mawsonia*, *Axelrodichthys*, *Diplurus*, and *Whiteia*, although its actual level of generality among actinistians is incompletely known.

In *Diplurus newarki* there are about 28 or 30 pairs of elongate, well-ossified pleural ribs (Schaeffer, 1948, 1952). Pleural ribs of this type are atypical of actinistians generally, although there may be short ventral arcualia in the precaudal region.

Chinlea sorenseni became the second actinistian known to possess elongate pleural ribs (Schaeffer, 1967). This similarity between *Chinlea* and *Diplurus* has become accepted as a shared derived character (Schaeffer, 1967; Forey, 1981; Elliott, 1987).

De Carvalho (1982) has described elongate, ossified pleural ribs in specimens of *Mawsonia gigas* from the Neocomian of Bahia and commented on the similarity with *Chinlea* and *Diplurus*. The postcranial skeleton has not yet been described in other *Mawsonia* spp. Following additional preparation, the presence of elongate pleural ribs now has been established in three specimens of *Axelrodichthys* from Araripe (AMNH 12211, 12212, 12220). A well-ossified pleural rib-cage therefore is known in four extinct actinistian genera. Much shorter ossified ventral arcualia also are known in *Coelacanthus* and perhaps *Laugia* (Moy-Thomas and Westoll, 1935; Stensiö, 1932).

The coelacanth upper jaw comprises several ossifications, including a metapterygoid that articulates with the skull; a quadrate with an articulation for the lower jaw; an autopalatine (a small bone at the anterior end of the upper jaw); and a broad pterygoid sheathing most of the upper jaw. Differences are found in the shape of the metapterygoid and pterygoid of *Mawsonia* and *Axelrodichthys*, relating to the obliquity of the jaw suspension (which is more upright in *Axelrodichthys* than in *Mawsonia*).

Related to this difference in jaw suspension, the large basisphenoid ossification of the braincase has pronounced lateral "wings" in *Mawsonia*, aligned almost horizontally, whereas in *Axelrodichthys* the wings are comparatively small and are angled obliquely upward.

A detailed phylogenetic analysis of these and other morphological characters in coelacanths has been made, but the details are omitted here for brevity. This analysis nevertheless suggests that the Lower Cretaceous coelacanth genera *Mawsonia* and *Axelrodichthys* are more closely related to the Late Triassic *Chinlea* than to any other actinistians, and that *Mawsonia*, *Axelrodichthys*, *Chinlea*, and *Diplurus* collectively represent a monophyletic group. The hypothesis of Maisey (1986) that *Mawsonia* and *Axelrodichthys* are more closely allied to *Latimeria* and *Macropoma* is no longer tenable in the light of the data presented here.

Forey (1981) declined to erect a classification to reflect every aspect of his branching diagram, but did formally separate the Family Coelacanthidae (containing *Whiteia*, *Diplurus*, *Chinlea*, *Holophagus*, *Macropoma* and *Latimeria*) from cladistically primitive actinistians. His phylogeny nevertheless included two subgroups within the Coelacanthidae, even though one of them (*Chinlea* + *Diplurus*) was not characterized by synapomorphies. A fundamental dichotomy of the Coelacanthidae is retained here, and can be formally expressed as follows:

Above: *Holophagus*, close relative of *Latimeria*. Dr. E. Balon photo.

Suborder **Coelacanthoidei** Vorobyeva and Obruchev, 1967
Plesion **Laugiidae** Berg, 1940
　Laugia
Plesion **Whiteiidae**
　Whiteia
Family **Coelacanthidae** Agassiz, 1844
Plesion **Diplurinae**
　Diplurus, Chinlea, Mawsonia, Axelrodichthys
Subfamily **Coelacanthinae**
　Holophagus, Macropoma, Latimeria

According to the present hypothesis, the Coelacanthoidei are characterized by the presence of a medial branch of the otic sensory canal (Forey, 1981, 1984), the Coelacanthidae by the presence of parasphenoid dorsal laminae and having the lachrymojugal meeting the tectals (a separate antorbital is absent), the Coelacanthinae by the ventral position of the jugal canal in the squamosal, and the Diplurinae by the presence of elongate, ossified pleural ribs and absence of a supratemporal descending process. To avoid generating a plethora of new higher categories, *Whiteia* and *Laugia* are treated as plesion sister-groups of the Coelacanthidae.

Below: *Lepidosiren paradoxa*, a Recent lungfish. E. C. Taylor photo.

Above: Underwater photo of *Latimeria*, the Recent coelacanth. Dr. H. Fricke photo.

Above: Mounted holotype of *Latimeria chalumnae* in the East London Museum, South Africa. Dr. E. Balon photo.

The end of the coelacanth fossil record coincides with the end of the Cretaceous period, some 65-70 million years ago. Yet the group lingered on to the present day, confined to parts of the Indian Ocean. So profound is the absence of fossil remains that scientists had long assumed that coelacanths were extinct. That misconception was exploded in December of 1938, when a five-foot, 127-pound specimen of a strange, evil-smelling oily fish was caught by a trawler in some 40 fathoms of ocean off Chalumna, about 20 miles southwest of East London, South Africa. It was brought to the attention of Miss M. Courtenay-Latimer, a young curator at the East London Museum. She immediately contacted Dr. J. L. B. Smith of Grahamstown University, who was recuperating from an illness in Knysna, 350 miles from East London.

The details of this saga are now famous, and a full account can be found in J. L. B. Smith's book, *Old Fourlegs*, published in 1956 by Longmans, Green and Co. (London). Dr. Smith, realizing the scientific importance of Miss Latimer's report, rushed to preserve what was left of the specimen. Overcoming the incredulity of his colleagues that such a fish might still exist, Smith finally published an account and photograph of the coelacanth fish in *Nature*, on March 18th, 1939, naming it *Latimeria chalumnae*. After WWII, the hunt for more coelacanths was resumed, and additional specimens were successfully collected from the Comores, particularly by French scientific expeditions. Since that time volumes have been written and international conferences have been convened dealing purely with *Latimeria* and its fossil relatives, so important was this discovery to science.

More recently the daring exploits of Dr. Hans Fricke (Max Planck Institute for Animal Behavior) and his colleagues have revealed to the world some aspects of coelacanth behavior in its natural habitat, filmed from a tiny two-person submersible (Fricke, et al., 1987; Fricke, 1988). Even from the brief glimpses provided by those observations it is evident that the behavior and locomotion of *Latimeria* are unique and bizarre. One spectacular habit of *Latimeria* is to perform a curious head-stand lasting for up to two minutes. Individuals also have been observed holding their body steady in a variety of positions, such as belly-up, and others were observed swimming laterally and even backward. When drifting or in contact with the substrate, *Latimeria* can flex the accessory terminal lobe of its caudal fin up to 90° laterally to the body axis. The paired fins, as well as the anal and second dorsal fins, are highly mobile and can be rotated and sculled to permit movement in virtually any direction and with different stroke frequencies. Despite an evident ability to move the paired fins alternately (as in tetrapods and some bottom-living fishes, including lungfishes), there is as yet no evidence that *Latimeria* uses its paired fins to walk or support itself on the substrate. Preliminary investigations by Dr. Fricke and his colleagues suggest that *Latimeria* is electroperceptive, perhaps using its rostral organ to detect weak electrical fields in the surrounding water.

What happened to coelacanths during that 70-million-year interim we call the Cenozoic era? They have left no fossil record, and once seemed to have disappeared as abruptly as the dinosaurs. Survival of the coelacanths has clearly been minimal, yet survive they did. But, as film taken by Dr. Fricke and his colleagues amply reveals, they exist today in an environment that is not conducive to fossilization. It may be that the direct ancestors of *Latimeria* inhabited similar environments and that their remains consequently were not preserved. *Mawsonia* and *Axelrodichthys* lived either in a shallow epicontinental sea or even perhaps in non-marine habitats (as did a great many more ancient coelacanths). One other fossil, *Macropoma*, seems even closer to *Latimeria*, but it also lived in shallow seas. Nevertheless, the morphological evidence gleaned from the fossil record suggests that the lineage directly ancestral to *Latimeria* had appeared by Upper Cretaceous times and perhaps by then had already occupied its paleontologically inhospitable environment. We are unlikely ever to know; younger (Cenozoic) oceanic sediments have yielded no clues, and older sediments have perhaps been lost during subduction of oceanic floors beneath the drifting continental plates. The Cretaceous coelacanths of Brazil and elsewhere reveal that the group was occupying various shallow-water niches just as successfully as in the previous 250 million years, but that they then almost followed the dinosaurs into oblivion. Only one ecological specialist, the enigmatic *Latimeria chalumnae*, has survived.

Assemblages: Santana, Jardim. Only one small individual has been observed in a "Santana" concretion.

(J. G. Maisey)

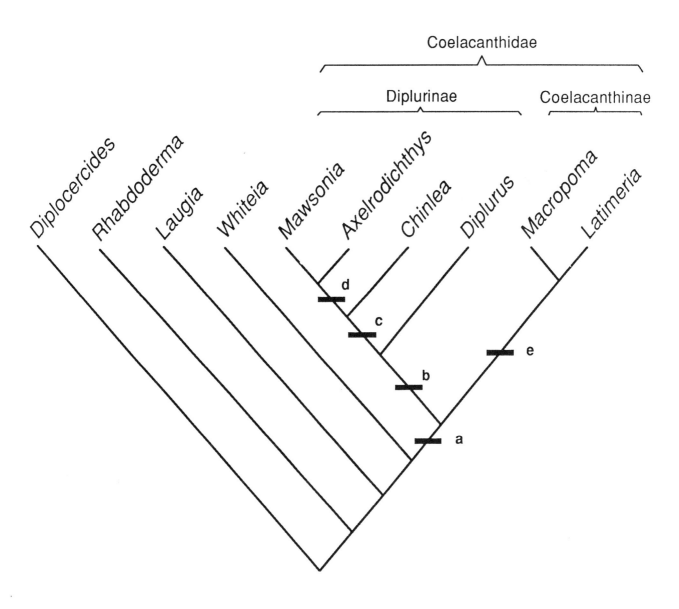

Hypothesis of relationships among selected actinistian fishes, based on the following characters: (**a**) parasphenoid dorsal laminae, lachrymojugal contacts tectal series; (**b**) elongate ossified pleural ribs, supratemporal descending process absent; (**c**) extrascapulars incorporated into skull roof, dermosphenotic extending anteriorly; (**d**) single pair of extrascapulars, slender pterygoid, ectopterygoid not ossified; (**e**) ventral position of jugal canal in squamosal. For additional data, see Forey (1981, 1984) and Maisey (1986).

Impressively large acid-prepared basisphenoid of *Mawsonia*, a giant Lower Cretaceous coelacanth also known from Africa. *Mawsonia* is the largest fish in the Santana formation, yet its existence went unnoticed until recently.

316

MAWSONIA Woodward, 1907

Class OSTEICHTHYES
Sublass SARCOPTERYGII
Order ACTINISTIA
Family COELACANTHIDAE Agassiz, 1844
Genus *Mawsonia* Woodward, 1907
1907 *Mawsonia* Woodward (*in* Mawson and Woodward): 134

Emended diagnosis: Coelacanths of large size (estimated body lengths up to 3 + m); skull roofing bones and angular bone ornamented by heavy rugosities; operculum and gular ornamented by fine radiating striae; anterior part of skull roof one and a half to two times as long as posterior part and from two to two and a half times as long as broad; posterior skull roof with three paired bones (parietals, supratemporals, and postparietals); no free extrascapulars; dermosphenotic has a splint-like anterior projection, with infraorbital canal located away from the anterior margin; lachrymojugal elongate, the posterior two-thirds almost straight, anteriorly extending to the tectal series.

Type species: *M. gigas* Woodward, 1907.
Mawsonia gigas Woodward
1907 *Mawsonia gigas* Woodward (*in* Mawson and Woodward): 134
1908 *Mawsonia minor* Woodward: 358
1982 *Mawsonia gigas* Woodward; de Carvalho: 522
1986 *Mawsonia gigas* Woodward; Mones: 45

Holotype: British Museum (Natural History), BM(NH) P10355; large incomplete head; Bahia supergroup, Ilhas group (Lower Cretaceous, Neocomian), Almeida Brandao, Salvador, state of Bahia.

Paratypes: BM(NH) P10356, P10357; same locality as holotype.
Mawsonia cf. *gigas*
1986 *Mawsonia* cf. *gigas* Maisey: 3

Mawsonia gigas, the type species of this genus, was first described on the basis of an incomplete skull from the Cretaceous deposits of Bahia (Mawson and Woodward, 1907). The species, as its name implies, grew to great size.

Mawsonia is an uncommon find in the Santana formation and seems to be considerably rarer than the other coelacanth from these deposits, *Axelrodichthys* (see earlier). To date, only fragmentary specimens of *Mawsonia* have been retrieved, mostly partial skulls, although their preservation (particularly after acid preparation) is excellent. Nevertheless, even these fragmentary examples show that *Mawsonia* attained a greater size than *Axelrodichthys* (overall length estimates given above are extrapolated from comparative measurements of skull bones in both genera). A maximum snout-to-tail length in excess of 3 meters seems possible, making *Mawsonia* perhaps the largest coelacanth to have existed (living *Latimeria* apparently reaches just over half this length).

Several other species of *Mawsonia* have been described, although apparently none attained the proportions of *M. gigas*. Interestingly, all of the published reports of *Mawsonia* are either from Brazil or from northern and western Africa (see below), and its distribution therefore is of considerable interest to scientists investigating the distributions of extinct species and wandering continents.

Coelacanth fishes (also termed actinistians) are represented today by a single species, *Latimeria chalumnae*, which lives only around the Comoro Islands of the Indian Ocean. The oldest known coelacanths occur in rocks of Middle Devonian age, and we therefore can trace the ancestry of this ancient group back some 360 million years to a time when the vertebrates had not yet ventured onto land. Cretaceous examples, from the Santana formation and elsewhere, are among the last-known fossil coelacanths.

Coelacanths are members of a large group of bony fishes called the Sarcopterygii or "lobe-fins." This group underwent great evolutionary diversity during the latter part of the Paleozoic era, producing several distinct lineages, many of which long have been extinct. Three surviving lineages are now recognized: the coelacanths (considered by some scientists to be the most primitive extant sarcopterygians); the lungfishes (represented by the African *Protopterus*, the South American *Lepidosiren*, and the Australian *Neoceratodus*); and the tetrapods or limbed vertebrates (it may seem strange to some readers to consider themselves as bony fishes, but a tetrapod is fundamentally an air-breathing fish whose paired fins have become adapted to load-bearing). We see a kind of morphological precursor of our own limbs in the peculiar fleshy fins of the coelacanth.

The coelacanth skull is peculiar among living vertebrates in consisting of separate anterior and posterior parts that articulate at a mobile intracranial joint. This joint also is found in various ancient fossil sarcopterygians that may

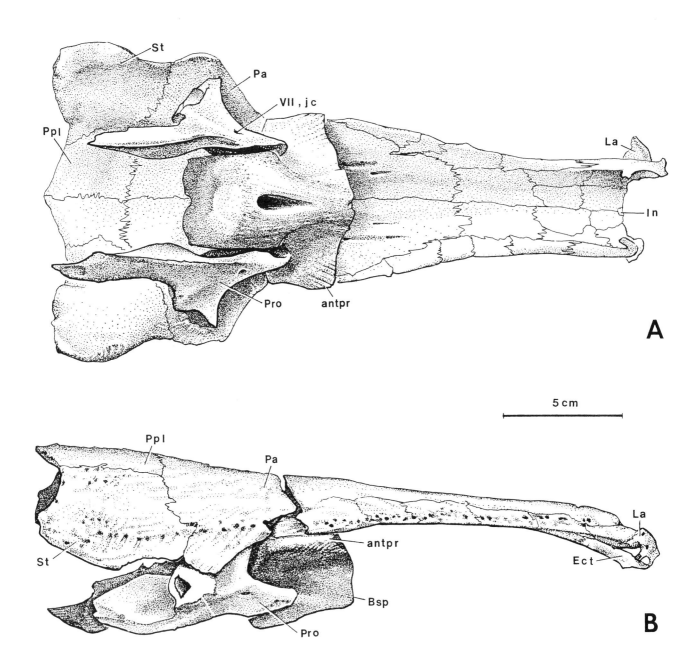

5 cm

Mawsonia cf. *gigas*. Acid-prepared skull, lacking the parasphenoid and part of the snout, AMNH 11758. From Maisey (1986).

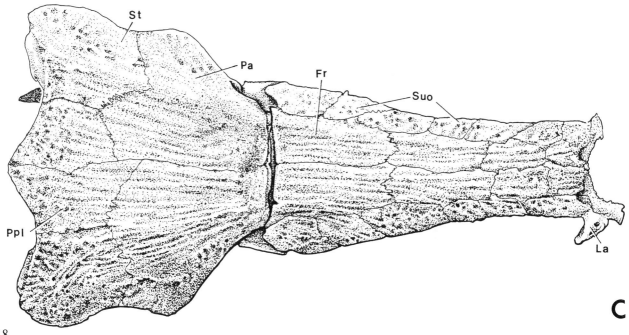

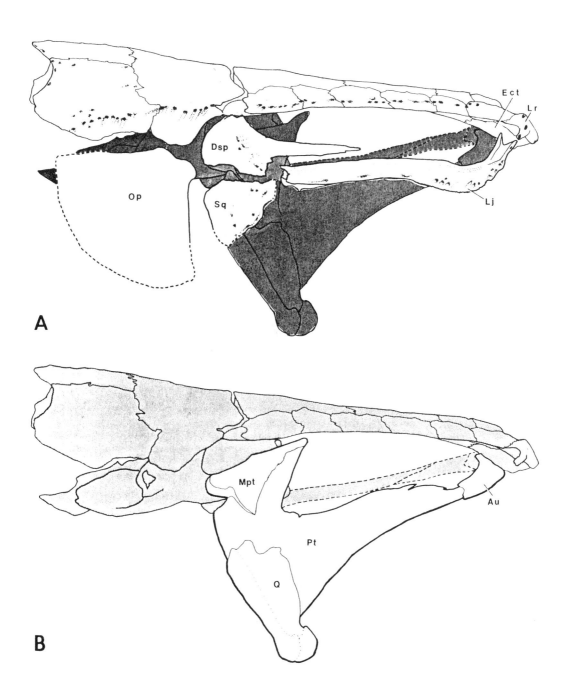

A

B

Above: *Mawsonia* cf. *gigas*. Partial reconstruction of
head, showing (A) dermal bones and sensory canals
(light shading), also parts of palate, basisphenoid,
parasphenoid (dashed), and prootic (all shaded darker).
From Maisey (1986).

Right: *Mawsonia* cf. *gigas*. Ventral view of posterior part
of skull roof with prootics removed to reveal parietal
descending lamina, AMNH 11758. From Maisey (1986).

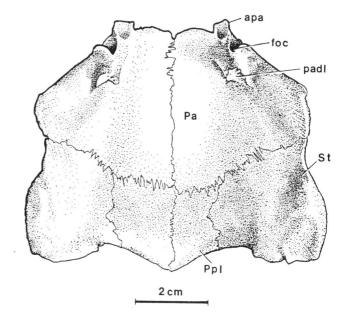

2 cm

319

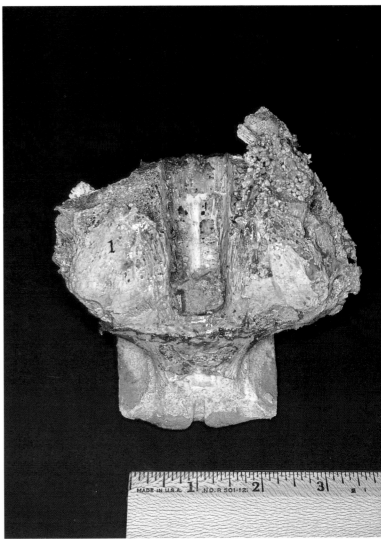

Mawsonia basisphenoid (**top left**) shown in previous color plate, and another slightly smaller example (**top right**), both acid-prepared. Partial skull roof of yet another *Mawsonia* specimen (**bottom**) has suffered from erosion, revealing sensory canals usually covered by bone. Photos by J. Maisey.

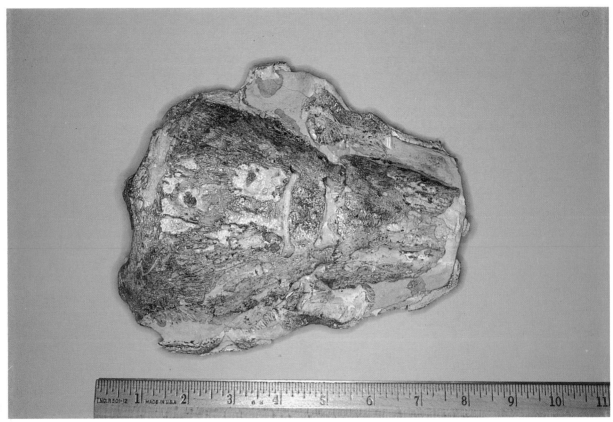

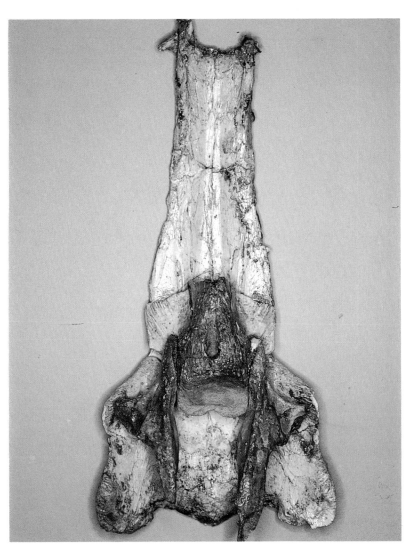

Small and incomplete acid-prepared *Mawsonia* skull roof (top) in dorsal (left) and ventral (right) views. Associated right upper jaw and cheek bones (bottom) in mesial (left) and lateral (right) views. Photos by J. Maisey.

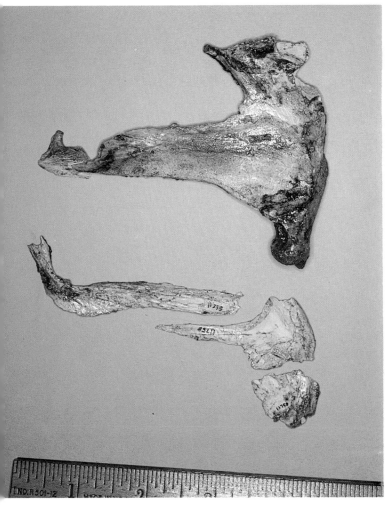
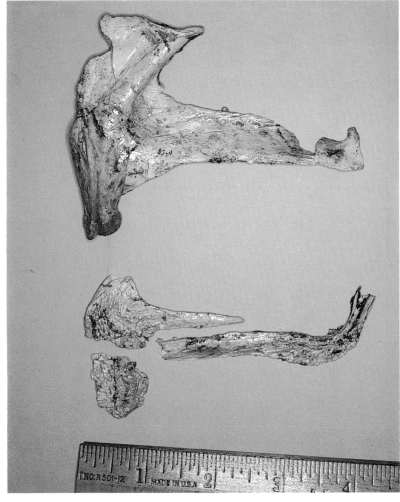

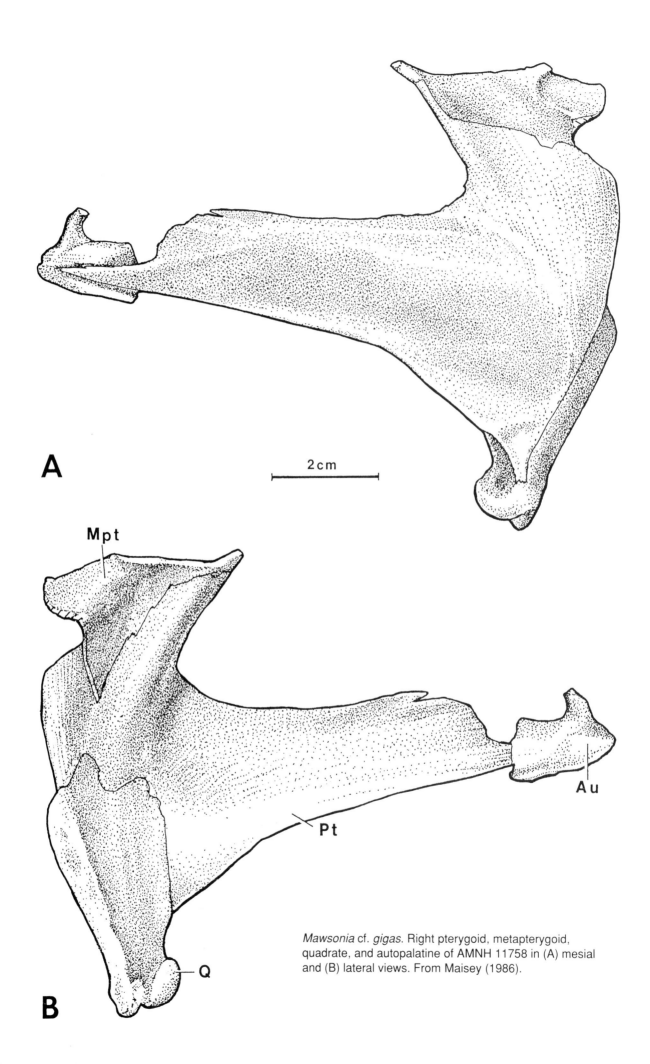

A

2 cm

Mpt

Au

Pt

Q

B

Mawsonia cf. *gigas*. Right pterygoid, metapterygoid, quadrate, and autopalatine of AMNH 11758 in (A) mesial and (B) lateral views. From Maisey (1986).

have been ancestral to lungfishes and tetrapods, and it therefore is possible that this coelacanth curiosity really is an ancient attribute of our fishy ancestors.

In *Mawsonia* the posterior part of the skull roof consists of three paired bones. This is extremely unusual, as in most other coelacanths only two pairs are present. The extra pair in *Mawsonia* occurs at the hind margin, and these bones possibly represent extrascapulars (bones above the shoulder girdle) that have secondarily become incorporated into the skull roof. Curiously, in the other genus of coelacanth from the Santana formation (*Axelrodichthys*; see earlier), this extra pair of bones is also present plus an extra median bone, and separate extrascapulars again are absent. *Mawsonia* and *Axelrodichthys* from the Santana formation also are distinguishable on several other anatomical criteria that are reviewed in the section on *Axelrodichthys*.

The known occurrence of *Mawsonia* is very restricted geographically and in geological time. All the species described to date are of Lower Cretaceous age. The geologically oldest species are *M. gigas* (including *M. minor*) from the Ilhas group of Bahia, Brazil (Mawson and Woodward, 1907; Woodward, 1908; de Carvalho, 1982) and *M. ubangiana* from the Bokungu series of Zaire, Africa (Casier, 1961), both of which are dated as Neocomian (i.e., lowermost Cretaceous). Slightly younger records (from the Aptian) include *M.* cf. *gigas* from the Santana formation (Maisey, 1986) and *M. tegamensis* from Niger (Wenz, 1975). The genus also is recorded from Albian sediments of northern Africa (e.g., *M. libyca* from Egypt, *M. lavocati* from Morocco; Weiler, 1935, Tabaste, 1963), but is so far unrecorded in rocks of that age from South America. *Mawsonia* is also reported from the Albian of Algeria, and an isolated bone was found in Albian deposits in Niger (Wenz, 1980).

Placing this admittedly patchy distributional data on a paleogeographic map of Africa and South America during the Lower Cretaceous, we get the distinct impression that *Mawsonia* was strongly endemic and until the Albian did not range outside an area extending more than a few hundred miles in any direction. It appears to have been restricted to shallow epicontinental basins and probably was non-marine. Very crudely, the data suggest a slightly more southerly distribution in the Neocomian (e.g., Bahia, Zaire) and a progressively more northward distribution during the Aptian (Araripe, Niger) and Albian (Morocco, Algeria, and Egypt). It is tempting to correlate this apparent shift with another event that seemingly occurred from south to north during this time, namely the separation of Africa and South America and development of a seaway that ultimately was to connect the more northerly Tethyan realm with the embryonic South Atlantic. There is ample paleontological evidence from Brazil and Africa that a continuous seaway had developed by the end of the Albian stage, effectively bisecting *Mawsonia*'s earlier area of endemism. Present evidence suggests that *Mawsonia* briefly survived this event in northern Africa, but possibly not in South America. Geologically slightly younger coelacanths are known from the Cenomanian (early Upper Cretaceous) of Syria and Lebanon (e.g., *Macropomoides*), from the European Chalk (e.g., *Macropoma*), and more recently from the Upper Cretaceous of Alabama. It may be significant that the living coelacanth genus *Latimeria* occurs today off the coast of eastern Africa. If the distribution of all post-Jurassic coelacanths is plotted paleogeographically, it reveals a distinct concentration within the northwestern part of Gondwanaland (i.e., Africa and South America). It seems that coelacanths survived the Jurassic-Cretaceous transition only in this region, although they formerly had enjoyed a much more cosmopolitan distribution (e.g., in the Jurassic of eastern North America, central Africa, Europe, and India, and in the Triassic of North America, Greenland, Spitzbergen, Europe, South Africa, Madagascar, and Asia). Throughout the entire Mesozoic era, however, it is noteworthy that the region represented today by Africa may have been continuously occupied by coelacanths, as it has produced Triassic, Jurassic, Cretaceous, and Recent representatives. Europe (including Britain) has the next best "continuous" Mesozoic record but lacks any known Recent representative. In other parts of the world, by contrast, the Mesozoic coelacanth record has even less longevity, and except during the Triassic it is extremely sparse.

Assemblages: As far as can be determined, the Santana formation *Mawsonia* sp. forms part of the Jardim assemblage only.

(J. G. Maisey)

UNDETERMINED SANTANA FROG

Class AMPHIBIA
Subclass LISSAMPHIBIA
Order ANURA
incertae sedis
Genus and sp. indet.

The discovery of a fossil frog within the Crato member of the Santana formation was reported in a short note by Kellner and Campos (1988). No description or illustration yet has been published. The specimen represents parts of the skull, jaws, pelvic girdle, and hind limbs of an individual approximately 20 mm long. According to the extent of ossification, it was in the final stages of development and approaching adulthood when it died.

This important discovery reinforces the already well-established hypothesis that the Crato member is of lacustrine origin. The prolific insect fauna of that time (discussed elsewhere in this volume) probably provided a rich food source for frogs and other small vertebrates living among vegetation close to the lake margins.

Records of Mesozoic frogs are exceptionally rare, and any new discovery such as this is therefore important to an understanding of anuran evolutionary history and biogeography. Two extant lineages, the Ascaphidae and Discoglossidae, are known from Jurassic examples. The early Jurassic ascaphid *Vieraella* from Argentina is the oldest so far discovered and is considered by Estes and Reig (1973) to be morphologically "a good structural ancestor" (i.e., the plesiomorphic sister-group) of both discoglossids and ascaphids. The later Jurassic *Notobatrachus*, also from Argentina, was placed by Estes and Reig within the Ascaphidae, albeit as its most primitive member. Upper Jurassic or Lower Cretaceous deposits at Lérida, in Spain, have produced well-preserved discoglossids (*Eodiscoglossus*; Vergnaud-Grazzini and Wenz, 1975). Another frog from that locality, *Montsechobatrachus gaudryi*, is known only from the poorly preserved type specimen; it may be a discoglossid or else a paleobatrachid (otherwise known only from the Eocene to Pliocene of Europe). Other fossil discoglossids are known from the Upper Cretaceous of North America and the Tertiary of Europe. The discoglossid fossil record therefore is restricted to the Northern Hemisphere, with no Gondwanan records.

Fossil pipids are known from the Early Cretaceous of Israel (e.g., *Cordicephalus gracilis*; Nevo, 1968; Estes and Reig, 1973) and from the Paleocene of Brazil, Argentina, and South Africa (for references see Estes, 1982). Other fossil pipids are known from the Late Cretaceous (Senonian) of Niger (de Broin, et al., 1974). Pipids are interpreted by Estes (1982) as a Gondwanan group that never had a distribution in the northern hemisphere.

Pelobatids are definitely known from the Eocene and possibly the Upper Cretaceous of North America. Previous Cretaceous records of leptodactylids and a ranid are considered erroneous by Estes and Reig (1973). No other living anuran groups have a fossil record extending back into the Mesozoic. The only groups known to have a Gondwanan Mesozoic history are the Ascaphidae and Pipidae. The fossil record is consistent with a widely held view that anurans are of Gondwanan origin, although the record is too incomplete to identify the area of origin.

Assemblage: Crato member of the Santana formation.

(J. G. Maisey).

Undetermined frog, Crato member. Photo courtesy A. Kellner.

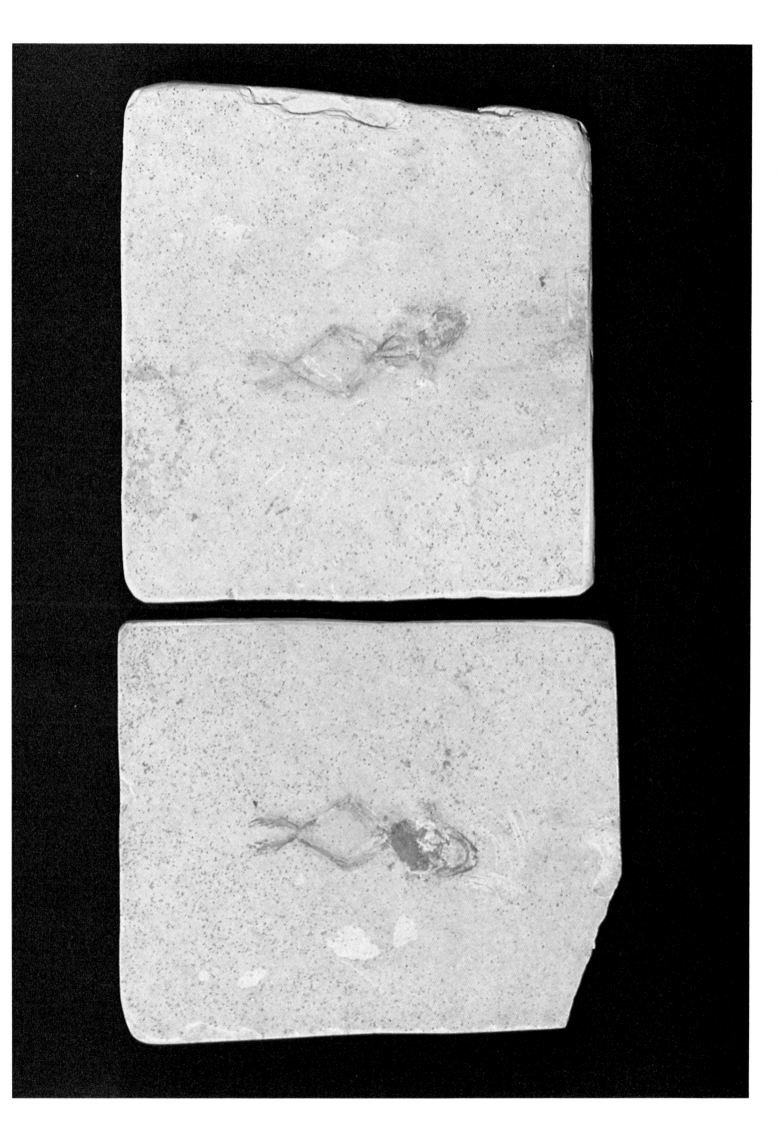

ARARIPEMYS Price, 1973

Order TESTUDINES
Infraorder PLEURODIRA
Family PELOMEDUSIDAE Cope, 1868
Genus *Araripemys* Price, 1973
1973 *Araripemys* Price: 86
Diagnosis: Turtles recognizable as pleurodires by presence of laterally folding cervical vertebrae, pelvis sutured to carapace and plastron, internal carotid entering prootic, lateral process of pterygoid modified into trochlear mechanism; resembling other Eupleurodira in lacking supramarginals or mesoplastra that are wider than long; resembling other Pelomedusidae in possessing deep temporal emargination, cheek emargination limited by quadratojugal-jugal contact; opisthotic extending posteriorly well beyond squamosal, nasal and splenial bones absent, precolumellar fossa deep; a)l((2))3))4))5))6))7))8) cervical series, and no nuchal scute; differs from all other described pelomedusids in long neck, no mesoplastra, and open incisura columella auris; differs from all other pleurodires in having very flat, sculptured shell in which first costal bones reach margin of shell between nuchal and first peripherals, and reduced plastron that includes an inverted V-shaped entoplastron and J-shaped epiplastron, as well as large midplastral fontenelles.

Type species: *Araripemys barretoi* Price, 1973
Araripemys barretoi Price
1973 *Araripemys barretoi* Price: 87
1988 *Araripemys barretoi* Price; Mones: 49
Diagnosis: As for genus.
Holotype: Divisão de Geologia e Mineralogia, Departamento Nacional de Produção Mineral, Rio de Janeiro, DGM-DNPM 756-R; shell and plastron; Santana formation, Romualdo member, from gypsum mine approx. 2 km northeast of Santana do Cariri, Ceará.

Two species of turtle are known from the Santana formation. Only one of them has been formally described, as *Araripemys barretoi* by Llewellyn Price in 1973. Price recognized *Araripemys* as a primitive turtle and placed it in its own family, the Araripemydidae, which he allocated to the superfamily Pleurosternoidea and the suborder Amphichelydia. The Amphichelydia is an assemblage of turtles that lacks any distinguishing features. Gaffney (1975)

Araripemys barretoi. Skeletal reconstruction in dorsal (left) and ventral (right) aspects.

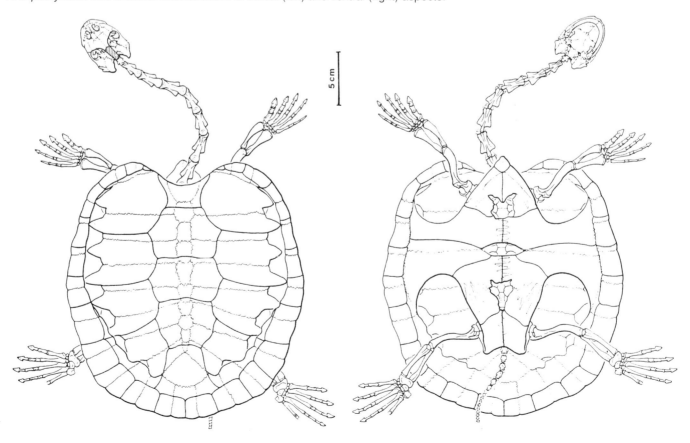

5 cm

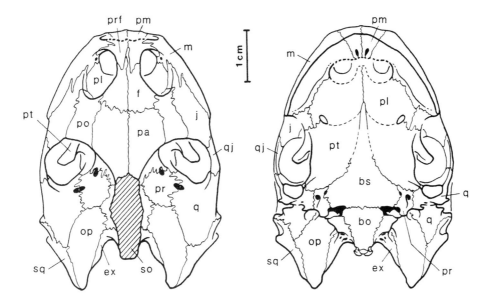

Araripemys barretoi. Skull reconstruction, mostly based on AMNH 24454 with additional data from AMNH 24452 and 24453; dorsal view to left (hatched area represents incomplete supraoccipital, not complete in any specimens available), palatal view to right.

disbanded this paraphyletic group and placed all of its members, including the Pleurosternoidea, in the monophyletic suborder Cryptodira. Thus *Araripemys* was, by inference, placed among the Cryptodira. However, de Broin (1980) suggested that *Araripemys* was not a cryptodire but a member of the pleurodire family Chelidae. Preparation of additional specimens has confirmed the assignment of *Araripemys* to the Pleurodira but suggests that it is a member of the family Pelomedusidae rather than the Chelidae.

All living turtles belong to one of two groups, the Pleurodira (side-necked turtles) or Cryptodira (hidden-necked turtles). All fossil turtles can be assigned to one of these groups with a single exception, *Proganochelys*, which currently is regarded as the sister-group of all other turtles (Gaffney, 1975, 1984).

Pleurodires differ from cryptodires not only in the way they fold their necks but also in skull and pelvis morphology. The articulations between the cervical vertebrae of pleurodiran turtles are vertical. This restricts the mobility of the neck largely to lateral motion. When it assumes a defensive posture, a pleurodiran turtle folds its head to the side and tucks it under the edge of the shell. Cryptodires have horizontal articulations in the cervical vertebrae that allow greater mobility in a dorso-ventral plane. Cryptodires can curl their neck in a vertical S and pull the neck and head into the shell between the forelimbs. The neck, and sometimes the head, can disappear between the forelimbs, hence the name Cryptodira (or hidden-neck).

The skulls of cryptodires and pleurodires differ in two important respects. First, in cryptodires the musculature that closes the lower jaw operates over the otic capsule (ear region), using it like a pulley to redirect the force that the adductor muscles generate. In pleurodires these muscles operate over a lateral process of the pterygoid bone that is not part of the ear but part of the palate. Second, in cryptodires the otic capsule is stabilized against the braincase by the pterygoid, while in pleurodires the otic region is braced by the quadrate, which produces its own buttress to the braincase. In addition to these differences in the neck and skull, these two groups also differ in the relationship of the pelvis to the shell. The pelvis of pleurodires always is sutured into the shell, while that of cryptodires is free.

The numerous specimens of *Araripemys* now known are, like many of the other fossils from the Santana formation, preserved in limestone concretions. Therefore, they can be prepared by dissolving the matrix away. This reveals the fossils in exquisite detail.

Neck vertebrae have been recovered from five *Araripemys* specimens. They are elongate and have articulations that restrict dorso-ventral motion and suggest lateral folding. In fact, the postzygapophyses of the most posterior cervicals are joined. These button-like postzygapophyses lie over the flat prezygapophyses of the next vertebra, minimizing the possibility for dorso-ventral rotation.

Skulls are now known from several *Araripemys* specimens. These show skeletal features characterizing the derived jaw adductor

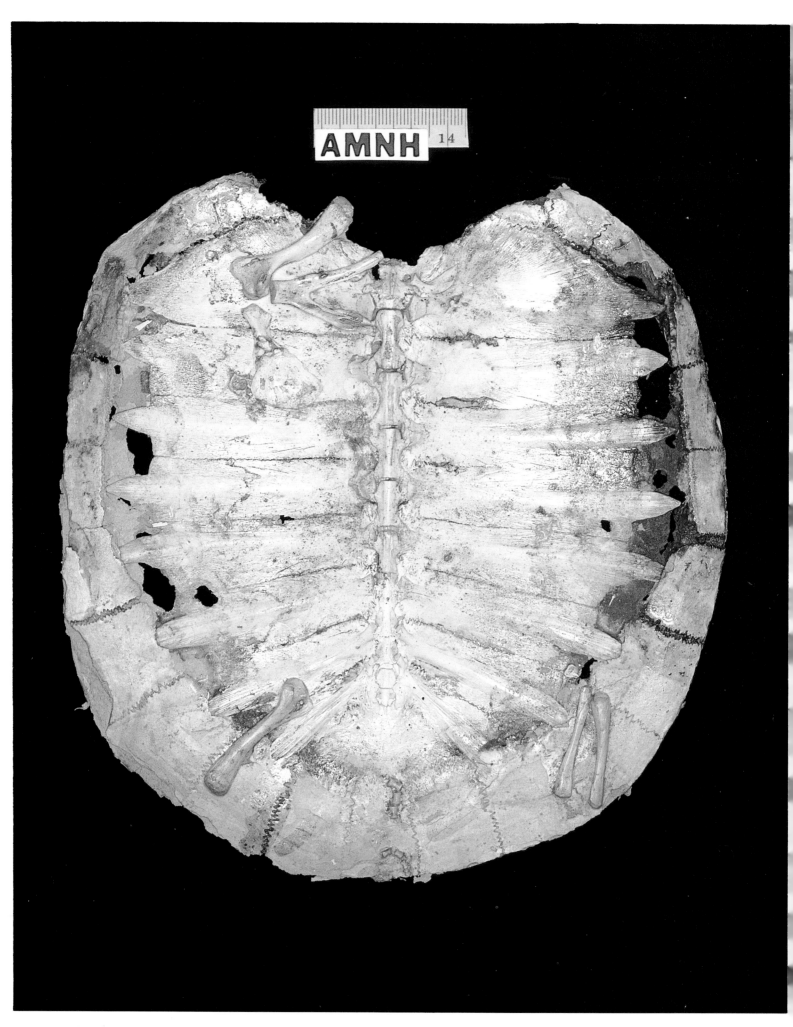

Araripemys barretoi; ventral view of complete carapace after acid preparation. Photo by E. Gaffney.

Pelusios castaneus, a Recent pelomedusid. Photo by Dr. P. C. H. Pritchard.

Araripemys barretoi; the holotype, DGM 7-56-R. Photo courtesy A. Kellner.

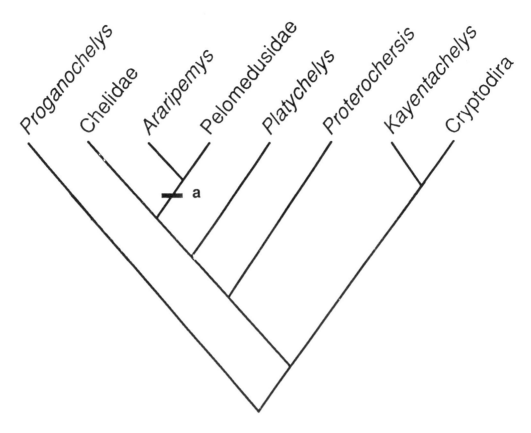

Hypothesis of relationships for *Araripemys*; characters shared with pelomedusids (A) prefrontals meet in midline, nasals absent, splenial absent, cervical scute absent.

mechanism typical of pleurodires. The otic capsule is not produced into a trochlear process as in cryptodires, but instead the pterygoid has a lateral process that is modified to redirect the action of the adductor musculature.

In *Araripemys*, the pelvis is sutured to the carapace and plastron, although not strongly. The three elements that make up the pelvis (ilium, ischium, and pubis) have greatly expanded sutural areas that contact the carapace (ilium) or plastron (pubis, ischium) as in other pleurodires. With this evidence in hand there can be little doubt that *Araripemys* is a pleurodire.

The identification of *Araripemys* as a pleurodire is important. Its Early Cretaceous age makes it one of the oldest pleurodires known, and it is the oldest known side-necked turtle in the world for which skeletal data are complete. Its osteology, which is of primary importance in classification, could become as well known as that of any living turtle species.

All known pleurodires belong to one of four groups: *Proterochersus*, *Platychelys* (two extinct Mesozoic genera), Chelidae, or Pelomedusidae (two families with living and extinct members). Determining the relationships of *Araripemys* to these four known groups of pleurodires has been a challenge.

Araripemys clearly is more advanced than *Proterochersus* and *Platychelys*, as it has lost the primitive supramarginals that are still present in these genera. Thus the relationship of *Araripemys* can best be discussed in terms of three alternative possibilities: 1) that *Araripemys* is more closely related to chelids than to pelomedusids; 2) that *Araripemys* is more closely related to pelomedusids than to chelids; or 3) that chelids and pelomedusids are more closely related to each other than either is to *Araripemys*.

With these alternatives in mind the most important aspects of the morphology of *Araripemys* are discussed below under two headings: characters of *Araripemys* that suggest affinities to the Pelomedusidae, and characters of *Araripemys* that suggest affinities to the Chelidae.

Characters of *Araripemys* and the Pelomedusidae: The skulls of pelomedusids and chelids are quite different in dorsal view due to the type of skull emargination present. Chelids have well-developed cheek emargination, while pelomedusids have well-developed temporal emargination. *Araripemys* is like pelomedusids in having very well developed temporal emargination that exposes all of the otic region and the posterior part of the pterygoid. It is possible, however, that well-developed temporal emargination is primitive for pleurodires, in which case it could not be used as evidence that *Araripemys* is a pelomedusid.

In all chelids except *Chelus* there are nasal bones between the orbits and the external nares. In all pelomedusids these bones are absent. They also appear to be absent from the skull of *Araripemys*, suggesting that this turtle is a pelomedusid.

A splenial is present in the lower jaw of chelids but absent in pelomedusids. Although it would be useful to have better material, it seems fairly certain that the splenial is absent from the lower jaw of *Araripemys*. This too would be evidence that *Araripemys* is a pelomedusid.

A well-developed quadratojugal is present in pelomedusids, but this element is absent from chelids. In *Araripemys* a small quadratojugal is present. This cannot be used as evidence that *Araripemys* is a pelomedusid, but it certainly suggests that it is not a chelid.

In most turtles the squamosal is the most postero-lateral element of the skull table. It projects postero-laterally from the quadrate beyond all other elements. This is the case in all chelids. In pelomedusids and in *Araripemys* the opisthotic extends posteriorly beyond the squamosal such that it is the most postero-lateral part of the skull. This may be evidence that *Araripemys* is a pelomedusid. However, this condition also occurs in the sister-group to all other turtles, *Proganochelys* (Gaffney and Meeker, 1983), which suggests that it might be primitive for pleurodires.

All turtles except for *Proganochelys* and a few primitive cryptodires have ball and socket articulations between all of the cervical vertebrae. These joints vary along the neck from group to group. All pelomedusids have a biconvex second vertebra with cervical vertebrae three through eight procoelous (concave anteriorly, convex posteriorly). The first vertebra, a somewhat elongate atlas, is biconcave. In *Araripemys* cervicals three through eight are procoelous and in one specimen the complete second cervical is biconvex, as in pelomedusids. Chelids have cervicals five and eight biconvex. Unless it is shown by future fossil finds that the condition found in *Araripemys* and pelomedusids is primitive for pleurodires, this is important evidence of shared ancestry in these two taxa.

One additional character might suggest that *Araripemys* is a pelomedusid, but this character has not been surveyed among all side-necked

turtles. This is the presence of a depression called the precolumellar fossa (Williams, 1954), which is located in the quadrate just anterior to the opening for the stapes (the incisura columella auris). With one exception (*Platemys*) the chelids studied so far have no evidence of a precolumellar fossa. The only turtles with this strucure as well developed as it is in *Araripemys* are some of the Pelomedusidae. Further research on this character may reveal whether its presence is primitive for pleurodires or it is a unique condition of *Araripemys* and pelomedusids.

There is a total of seven features that suggest that *Araripemys* is a pelomedusid. However, there are also five characters that suggest that it may be closely related to chelids, as suggested by de Broin (1980), and these deserve review.

Characters of *Araripemys* and the Chelidae: The most obvious of the chelid-like characters of *Araripemys* is the absence of mesoplastra. These paired elements are present primitively in the plastron of turtles. Among the Pleurodira they are absent only in chelids and in *Araripemys*.

One of the interesting discoveries made by acid preparation is that *Araripemys* has a very long neck. The combined length of the cervical series is at least as long as the carapace. This feature is unknown among the Pelomedusidae, but some chelids have a similarly long neck. This feature might be used to place *Araripemys* among the long-necked Chelidae.

These long-necked chelids and several other chelid genera have the dentaries sutured together rather than fused as in most turtles. This also occurs in *Araripemys*. The rarity of this feature has been used to suggest that it is derived within the Chelidae (Gaffney, 1977). However, Bour (1986) has recently pointed out that *Pelomedusa* (a living pelomedusid) has sutured dentaries, and studies at the AMNH indicate that the other (undescribed) pelomedusid from the Santana formation treated elsewhere in this volume also does. The distribution of this feature suggests that sutured dentaries are actually primitive for all pleurodires. Sutured dentaries therefore do not support a close relationship between chelids and *Araripemys*.

Primitively, all turtles had scales covering the top of the head. In several different lineages these scales have been lost. Among pleurodires they are lost in all chelids but are present in all pelomedusids. Although this needs to be verified with additional fossil skulls, it seems that *Araripemys* resembles members of the

Juvenile *Trionyx spinifera*. There is a strong superficial similarity in the surface ornamentation of the carapace in trionychids and *Araripemys*, suggesting paralell evolution of this feature. Photo by William B. Allen, Jr.

Chelodina longicollis, a long-necked chelid. Photo by Dr. P. C. H. Pritchard.

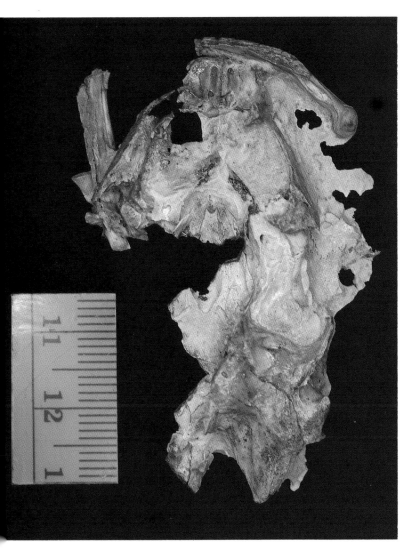

Araripemys barretoi; three skulls and a partly-prepared carapace (top right). Photos by E. Gaffney.

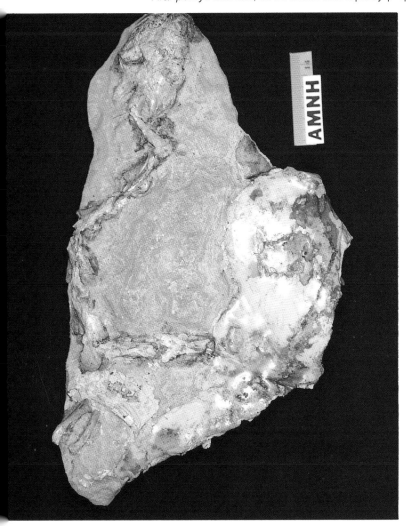

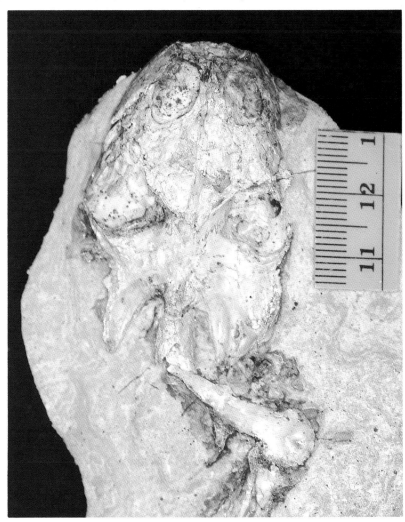

Chelidae in having no head scales.

Finally, the condition of the opening for the stapes (the incisura columella auris) in *Araripemys* is more like that of certain chelids than pelomedusids. Primitively this opening is not enclosed by the quadrate. In certain turtles, however (including the majority of pelomedusids), the quadrate completely surrounds the incisura. The open condition occurs in some chelids, including the long-necked forms, as well as *Araripemys*. The distribution of this character would be explained more easily if it were a chelid than if *Araripemys* were placed within the pelomedusids. Alternatively, however, the recent discovery that in the other, as-yet-undescribed turtle from the Santana formation there also is an open incisura columellae auris indicates that this may be the primitive condition for the Eupleurodira.

Although five characters are found in *Araripemys* and some or all Chelidae, two of these are likely to be primitive features and do not support placement of *Araripemys* among the Chelidae. In addition to these conflicting character sets there are some unique features of *Araripemys* that further complicate the resolution of its relationships.

Features of *Araripemys* unique among the Pleurodira: If only the shell of *Araripemys* had been preserved and we knew nothing of the girdles, limbs, neck, and skull, we would probably associate this genus with the soft-shelled turtles (family Trionychidae), which are cryptodires. The shell of *Araripemys* is quite like that of soft-shelled turtles. The two show many of the same deviations from the normal sort of turtle shell.

Where most turtles have a fairly smooth shell, *Araripemys* is like soft-shells in having a finely textured surface to all shell bones. Soft-shelled turtles lack the scales that cover the shell of most turtles. *Araripemys* still has scales, but judging from the depth of the scute sulci they must have been very weakly developed. The overall form of the shell of *Araripemys* is low and flat like soft-shells, and there are large fontanelles in the carapace and plastron.

In detail, the rib attachments of *Araripemys* are much like those of trionychids. They are very broad and are strongly sutured to the vertebral centra. Most turtles have weak connections between the rib heads and thoracic centra.

The plastron of *Araripemys* is remarkable in the degree to which it resembles that of soft-shells. In both, the hyo- and hypoplastra are quite reduced at the bridge but have large medial and lateral portions. The longest suture in both taxa is that between the hyo- and hypoplastron. This is due to the presence of large midline openings, or fontanelles. The anterior lobe of the plastron in *Araripemys* and trionychids is unlike that of any other turtles. The entoplastron is an inverted V covered by a dermal callosity, and the epiplastra are J-shaped with the longer part lying along the entoplastron.

Because *Araripemys* shows so many features of the Pleurodira we can be certain that its similarity to soft-shelled turtles is due to parallelism. It is an extremely modified side-necked turtle. Its similarity to soft-shells suggests only that, like soft-shells, it was a highly aquatic form. *Araripemys* nevertheless demonstrates that soft-shelled ornamentation is not restricted to trionychids, and some previous trionychid fossil records based only on shell fragments therefore may be incorrect.

Summary and Conclusions: A decision about the relationships of *Araripemys* based on the data discussed above can best be reached by parsimony analysis. A computer program has been used to determine the hypothesis of relationship for *Araripemys* and other pleurodires that most efficiently explains the distribution of skeletal characters among these turtles. This analysis suggests that *Araripemys* is a pelomedusid. It also reveals that there are no features to indicate a special relationship between *Araripemys* and either living pelomedusid subfamily, the Pelomedusinae or Podocneminae; rather it suggests that these two subfamilies are more closely related to one another than either is to *Araripemys*.

Assemblages: Jardim, Santana.

(P. Meylan, E. Gaffney)

PRIMITIVE PELOMEDUSID TURTLE

Order TESTUDINES
Infraorder PLEURODIRA
Family PELOMEDUSIDAE Cope, 1868
Genus and sp. undescribed
Diagnosis: A pelomedusid with the following pelomedusid synapomorphies: nasals absent, prefrontals meeting in midline, splenial absent, cervical scute absent; differs from all other pelomedusids in having an open incisura columellae auris; well-developed cheek emargination as in *Podocnemis;* parietal-quadratojugal contact present but not as extensive as in *Podocnemis*, temporal emargination more extensive than in podocnemines but not as extensive as in living pelomedusines; medial process of quadrate nearly reaches basioccipital; foramen posterior canalis carotici interni formed by pterygoid, basisphenoid, and prootic; triturating surface moderately expanded as in *Podocnemis* but differs from that genus in being broader anteriorly rather than posteriorly; condylus occipitalis formed by both exoccipitals and basioccipital.

Two taxa of turtles are known from the Santana formation. Both turtles are pleurodires, or side-necked turtles, a group that is common in South America today. One of the turtles, *Araripemys*, is a bizarre, long-necked form that is quite different from any known pleurodire. Its relationships are unclear although it is interpreted in this volume as an aberrant pelomedusid. The other turtle, as yet unnamed, is much more primitive morphologically and similar to what might be expected in a primitive member of the family Pelomedusidae. *Araripemys* is known from a number of skeletons, but the unnamed turtle is based on

Undetermined pelomedusid turtle. Skeletal reconstruction in dorsal (left) and ventral (right) aspect.

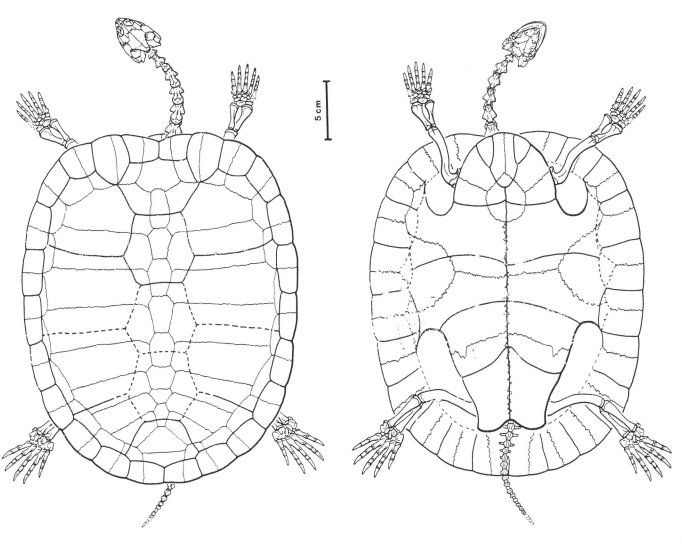

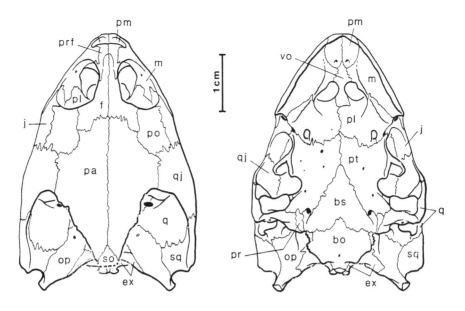

Undetermined pelomedusid turtle. Skull reconstruction, based on specimen loaned by Senckenberg Museum, Frankfurt; dorsal view to left, palatal view to right.

one skeleton owned by the Senckenberg Museum in Frankfurt, West Germany. For a discussion of the main groups of turtles the reader is referred to Gaffney and Meylan (1988). For further information about pleurodire systematics and morphology the reader is referred to Gaffney (1979).

Morphology: The skull of the Senckenberg specimen is damaged in the interorbital region, but it is unlikely that nasal bones are present. The prefrontals meet in the midline above the nasal opening, but for most of their length they are separated by anterior projections of the frontals. In all previously described pelomedusids the prefrontals have a transverse suture with the frontals. This condition could be primitive or derived for all pelomedusids. Each prefrontal in the Senckenberg turtle is relatively narrow and extends posteriorly to enter the dorsal margin of the orbit. The absence of nasals and the medial meeting of the prefrontals are derived characters for pelomedusids.

The frontal bone is a relatively large, triangular element forming most of the dorsal rim of the orbit, as in other pelomedusids, and has a very narrow interorbital region. This feature, however, is variable in pelomedusids (e.g., *Erymnochelys*, *Podocnemis*) and probably is not of significant systematic value above the generic level in pelomedusids. It is best interpreted as an autapomorphy for the Brazilian genus.

The parietal is most similar to that bone in *Podocnemis* because a moderate amount of temporal emargination is present. In other podocnemines, such as *Erymnochelys*, the parietal is more extensive posteriorly, while in living pelomedusines (unnamed taxon B7 of Gaffney and Meylan, 1988) there is a much more extensive emargination and a smaller parietal. Moderate emargination may be the primitive pelomedusid condition, but this is not demonstrable at present. The contacts of the parietal with the postorbital and quadratojugal are, nevertheless, what would be expected in a generalized pelomedusid.

The jugal and quadratojugal form the dorsal margin of a well-developed cheek emargination. Among living pelomedusids, *Podocnemis* has the best developed cheek emargination, similar in extent to that found in the Senckenberg specimen. However, in most other pelomedusids the jugal is much larger than in the Senckenberg turtle. Presumably correlated with this condition is its relatively limited jugal-quadratojugal contact; in all living pelomedusids this contact is more extensive. The quadratojugal in the Senckenberg turtle has a moderately extensive contact medially with the parietal, similar in extent to that seen in *Podocnemis*, but less than in *Erymnochelys*.

The postorbital is similar in its size and sutural contacts to that of most living pelomedusids. However, it differs distinctly from the very small postorbital seen in *Podocnemis*. In living pelomedusines the postorbital is reached by the temporal emargination, while in the Senckenberg turtle there is a well-developed parietal-quadratojugal contact separating the postorbital from the

Podocnemis unifilis. Photo by Dr. P. C. H. Pritchard.

emargination. The squamosal is similar to that bone in other pelomedusids. It contacts the quadratojugal above the ear opening and is tightly sutured to the quadrate.

The premaxilla and maxilla form the triturating surfaces that bear the horny beak of turtles. These bones in the Senckenberg turtle are generally similar to such living pelomedusids as *Podocnemis expansa* that have a moderately expanded triturating surface. In *Pelomedusa* the triturating surface is relatively narrow, and this usually has been interpreted as the primitive pelomedusid condition. Some extinct pelomedusids developed secondary palates (unnamed taxon B9 of Gaffney and Meylan, 1988) and bizarre pits (*Bothremys*), but there is no indication of these in the Senckenberg specimen. The triturating surface in this specimen has a low accessory ridge similar to that in some species of *Podocnemis*. In those podocnemines with triturating surfaces most similar to the Senckenberg turtle, the posterior part of the surface is wider than the anterior part, whereas in the Senckenberg specimen the anterior region is distinctly wider than the posterior area. This is interpreted as an autapomorphy of the Brazilian genus.

The reduction and absence of the vomer is an important feature of pelomedusids and has been used to differentiate more advanced forms from more generalized ones. The vomer is present in only one species of living pelomedusid, where it is a small, variably developed element. A well-developed vomer is present in *Bothremys* and a Cretaceous form from Africa. The Senckenberg turtle also has a "normal" chelonian vomer extending from the premaxillae anteriorly, separating both maxillae and contacting the palatines posteriorly. The vomer separates the two internal choanae.

The palatine also is similar to that bone in *Podocnemis* and is what might be expected in a generalized pelomedusid. The entire palatal morphology is consistent with a primitive morphotype for pelomedusids; only the somewhat broad triturating surface might be considered an advanced feature at some level, and even this is ambiguous.

The quadrate is of typical pleurodiran shape, with a well-developed medial process and no otic trochlea. The tympanic cavity, or cavum tympani, generally is similar to that in *Podocnemis*, but it differs from *Podocnemis* and all other described pelomedusids except

Araripemys in having an open incisura columellae auris; that is, the notch containing the stapes is not entirely surrounded by bone. The open condition clearly is primitive for pleurodires and is presumed to be primitive for pelomedusids as well. The antrum postoticum is moderately well developed and there is no precolumellar fossa.

The foramen stapedio-temporale, which contains the stapedial artery, is formed in the suture between the quadrate and prootic as in most other pleurodires. It is in the anterior part of this suture but still clearly seen in dorsal view. On the ventral surface, the quadrate has a medial process that contacts the prootic. In nearly all pelomedusids the prootic exposure is relatively small and there is a basisphenoid-quadrate contact, but in the Senckenberg turtle the prootic exposure is more extensive and there is no quadrate-basisphenoid contact in ventral view. This latter condition appears to be primitive for pelomedusids because it is the most common (and primitive) condition within the Chelidae, the sister-group of the Pelomedusidae.

The pterygoid has the pleurodiran process that bears the "pulley" for the jaw musculature, the processus trochlearis pterygoidei. In *Podocnemis* and some other pelomedusids, this process usually extends directly laterally while in chelids it usually is nearly parallel to the midline. In the Senckenberg specimen, as in many pelomedusids, the process extends postero-laterally. The processus trochlearis pterygoidei is continuous with a thin flange that lies postero-laterally. This flange has a unique shape, although it is clearly homologous to similar flanges in other pelomedusids.

The supraoccipital in the Senckenberg specimen is broken off, but it does not appear to have been as long as that in *Podocnemis*. The supraoccipital probably was no more extensive than it is in *Pelomedusa*. The occipital condyle is made up of equal parts of three bones (both exoccipitals and the basioccipital) rather than just the exoccipitals, a derived condition diagnostic of the subfamily Pelomedusinae of Gaffney and Meylan (1988).

The formation of the opening for the internal carotid artery also provides useful systematic information. The Podocneminae of Gaffney and Meylan (1988) is characterized by a very large canalis caroticus internus that contains not only the internal carotid artery but also a branch of the pterygoideus muscle. The Senckenberg turtle lacks this condition and has a "normal"-sized carotid opening. This opening (the

foramen posterius canalis carotici interni) is formed by the pterygoid, prootic, and basisphenoid in the Senckenberg skull. In pelomedusids this foramen apparently is formed primarily by the prootic, with a small contribution by the basisphenoid. The addition of the pterygoid in the Senckenberg turtle may be autapomorphic for that genus, but the bones around the foramen tend to be variable in Recent pelomedusids.

The medial process of the quadrate extends postero-medially to contact the prootic ventral to the processus interfenestralis of the opisthotic, thereby covering the process in ventral view. In chelids and living pelomedusines, the processus is not covered ventrally; this is interpreted as the primitive condition for pelomedusids. Nevertheless, the ventral covering of the processus interfenestralis appears to consist of two different conditions. One condition, found in *Bothremys* and closely related forms, involves a number of ear modifications, while the other condition occurs in the podocnemine group. The Senckenberg specimen has the podocnemine condition. In most podocnemines, however, the quadrate extends posteriorly to reach the basioccipital. This is not the case in the Senckenberg turtle. Although the quadrate comes very close to the basioccipital, it does not contact it.

The basisphenoid is triangular and is bordered by the pterygoid antero-laterally, the prootic postero-laterally, and the basioccipital posteriorly. The basisphenoid separates the pterygoids for more than half of their length, a condition that varies in pelomedusids but that is more characteristic of pelomedusines than podocnemines.

Much of the shell is preserved in the Senckenberg specimen, even though the quality of preservation for the carapace is poor. The carapace does show the absence of a cervical scute, a diagnostic synapomorphy for the Pelomedusidae. The number of neural bones also is of systematic interest. The Senckenberg shell has eight neurals, a primitive condition for pelomedusids that also occurs in *Araripemys*. In all other pelomedusids there are fewer than eight neurals and the eighth costals meet at the midline. In *Araripemys* the eighth costals are partly or wholly separated by a suprapygal located behind the eighth neural. The plastron of the Senckenberg shell has paired mesoplastra, longer than they are wide (an autapomorphic condition). The shell is consistent with what would be expected in a generalized pelomedusid. The cervical series shows the same central articulation pattern as *Araripemys* and all other pelomedusids. The Senckenberg specimen also has the postzygapophyses fused for nearly all the cervicals, again as in *Araripemys* but in contrast to all other pelomedusids.

Relationships: In sharp contrast to the apomorphies of *Araripemys*, the Senckenberg specimen is very close to a generalized morphotype for the Pelomedusidae. Rather than having a surfeit of contradictory derived features, the Senckenberg specimen retains the primitive condition for most of the important characters in pelomedusid systematics.

The Senckenberg specimen is clearly a pleurodire because it has the following derived characters:
1. Processus trochlearis pterygoidei for the jaw muscle trochlea.
2. Medial process of quadrate.
3. Foramen posterius canalis carotici interni formed by prootic at least in part.
4. Pelvis sutured to carapace and plastron.
5. Foramen palatinum posterius behind orbit.
6. Epipterygoid absent.

The Senckenberg specimen is also clearly identifiable as a member of the Pelomedusidae on these characters:
1. Nasal bones absent.
2. Prefrontals meet in midline.
3. Splenial absent.
4. Cervical scute absent.

Within the Pelomedusidae, the Senckenberg specimen occupies a relatively primitive position but its more precise relationships are unclear. There are two reasons for this. First of all, the pelomedusids have not been subjected to a detailed character analysis (Gaffney, 1988). Secondly, the presence of a number of relatively well-preserved but undescribed fossil pelomedusids makes it difficult to analyze the known taxa comprehensively.

The Senckenberg specimen nevertheless provides an important example of a genus very close to the primitive morphotype for pelomedusids.

Assemblages: Jardim, ?Santana.

(E. Gaffney, P. Meylan)

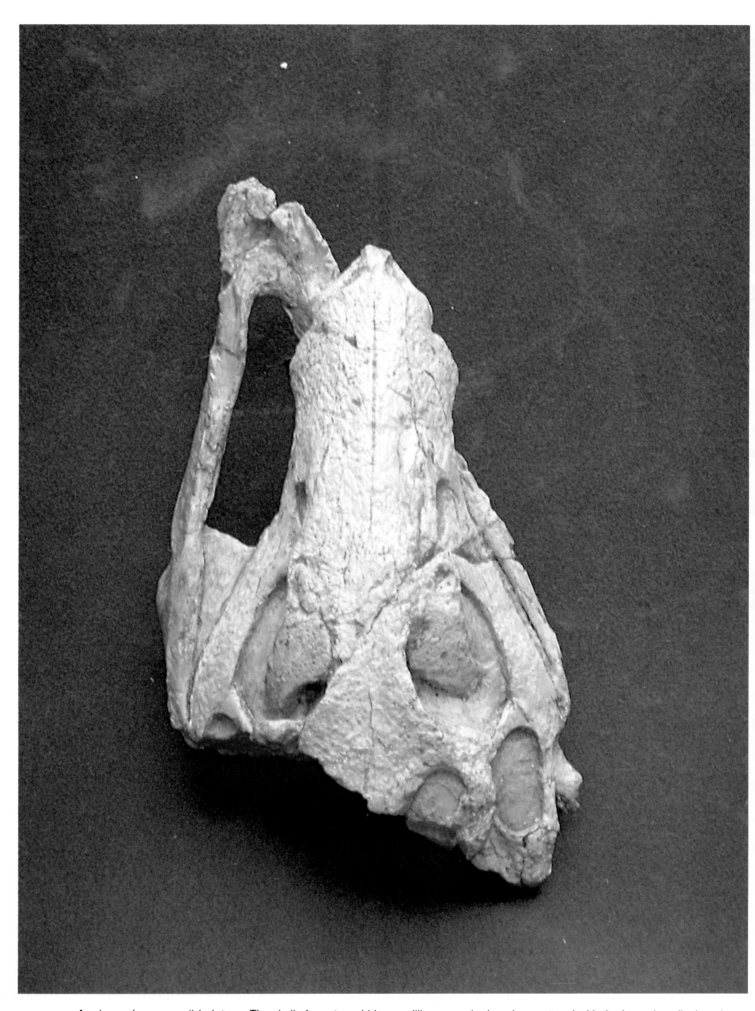

Araripesuchus gomesii; holotype. The skull of a notosuchid crocodilian, seen in dorsal aspect and with the lower jaw displaced to the left. Photo courtesy A. Kellner.

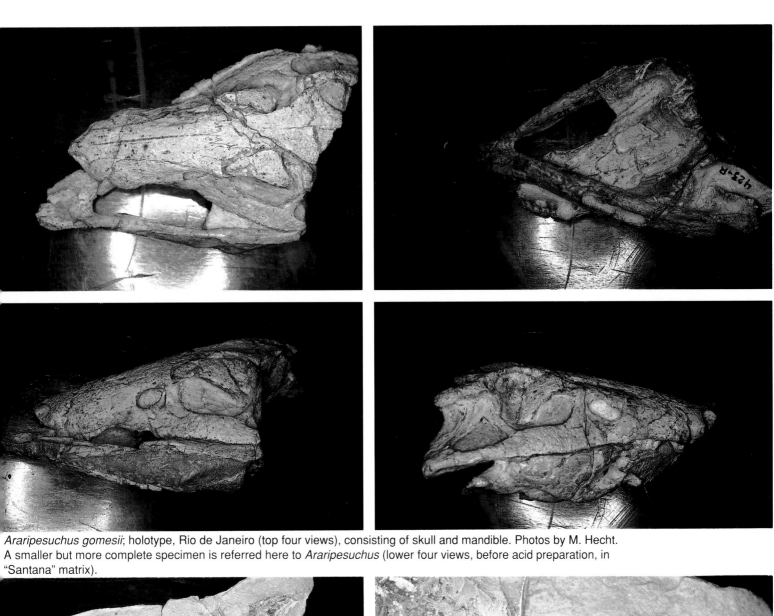

Araripesuchus gomesii; holotype, Rio de Janeiro (top four views), consisting of skull and mandible. Photos by M. Hecht. A smaller but more complete specimen is referred here to *Araripesuchus* (lower four views, before acid preparation, in "Santana" matrix).

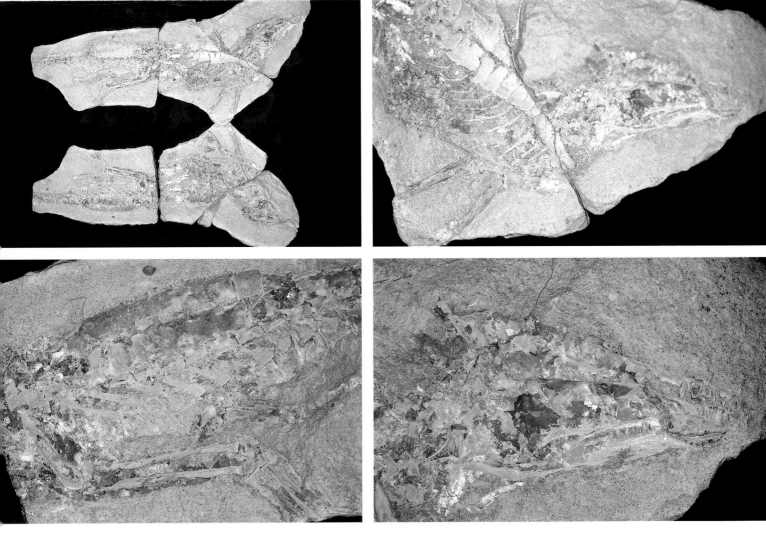

ARARIPESUCHUS Price, 1959

Order CROCODYLIA
Suborder MESOSUCHIA
Family NOTOSUCHIDAE
Genus *Araripesuchus* Price, 1959
   1959 *Araripesuchus* Price: 14
Emended diagnosis: Short-snouted crocodilian with advanced mesosuchian palate (nares not enclosed entirely within pterygoid bone) and high cranium with large antorbital fenestra; dermal armor composed of two rows of slightly overlapping thin, flattened, mid-dorsal osteoderms extending from neck region to end of tail; mid-ventral secondary row of reduced thin, non-overlapping osteoderms present on tail; forelimbs much shorter than hind limbs.
Type species: *Araripesuchus gomesii* Price, 1959.
Araripesuchus gomesii Price
   1959 *Araripesuchus gomesii* Price: 15
Diagnosis: As for genus.

Holotype: Divisão de Geologia e Mineralogia, Departamento Nacional de Produção Mineral, Rio de Janeiro, DGM-DNPM 423-R; skull; Santana formation, Romualdo member, Chapada do Araripe.

The genus *Araripesuchus* is known from three specimens, two from Brazil and one from Africa. The type of *Araripesuchus gomesii* (from the Santana formation) consists of only a skull and lower jaw, whereas the second specimen from the same formation (AMNH 24450) is an almost complete skeleton. A second species of this genus, *A. wegeneri*, has been found in a synchronous fauna from the Niger Republic in West Africa (Buffetaut, 1981).

Of the Brazilian specimens, the skull of the type is about 20% larger than the skull of the second, more complete, specimen. The maximum estimated length of the type skull is about 118 mm and its interorbital width is about

Araripesuchus gomesii. Skeletal reconstruction, from AMNH 24450 (extremity of tail unknown). The stance illustrated is based on information generously provided by Dr. S. Gatesy (Dept. of Anatomy and Cell Biology, Emory University, Atlanta), from his studies of locomotory patterns in modern alligators. The limbs of *Araripesuchus* are longer than in any living crocodilian, suggesting that this form was capable of relatively rapid movement. Only the left row of dorsal scutes is shown for clarity.

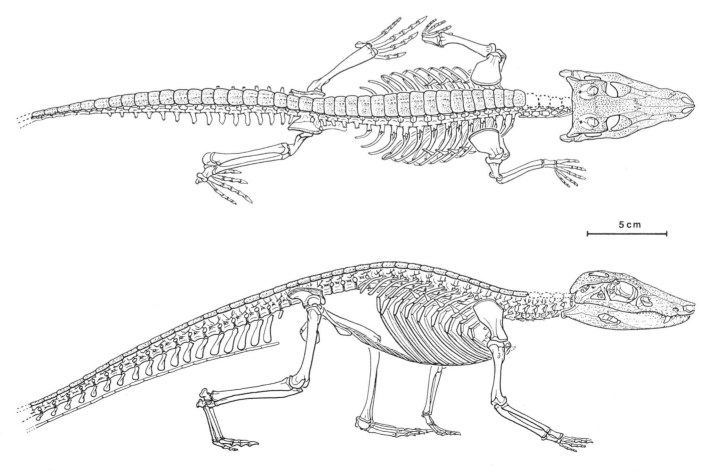

5 cm

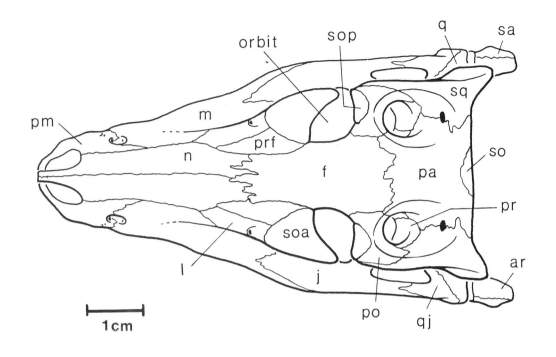

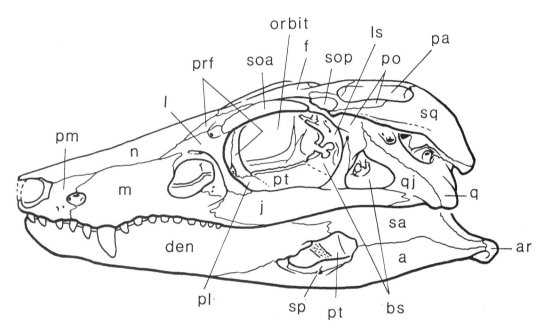

Araripesuchus gomesii. Skull reconstruction in dorsal (above) and lateral views, from AMNH 24450.

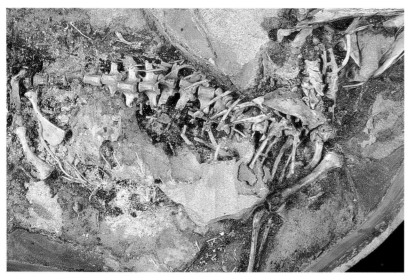

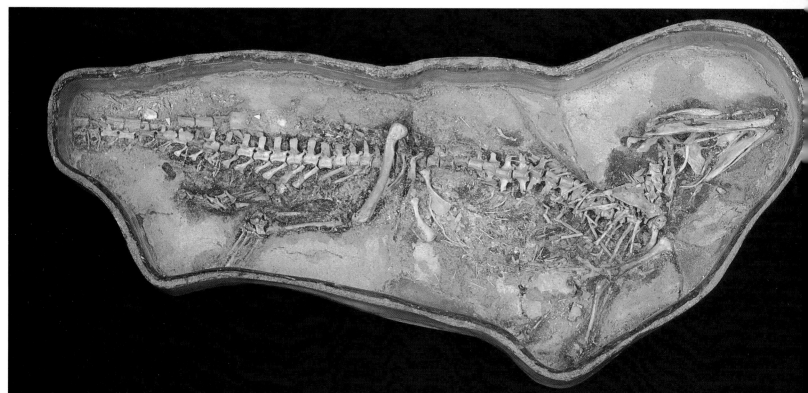
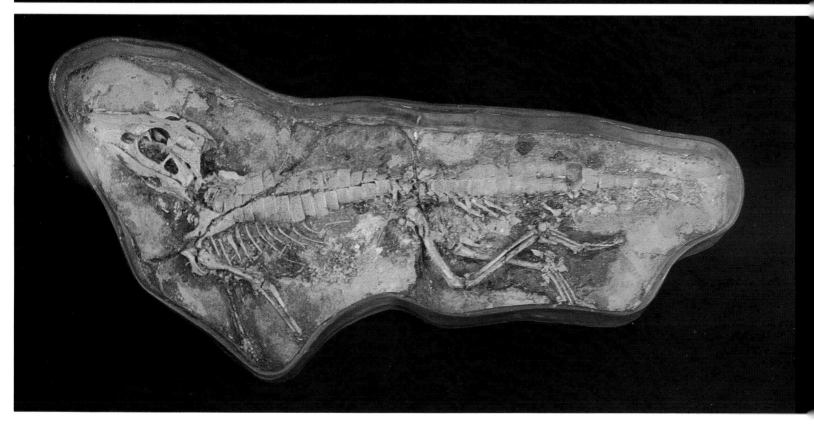

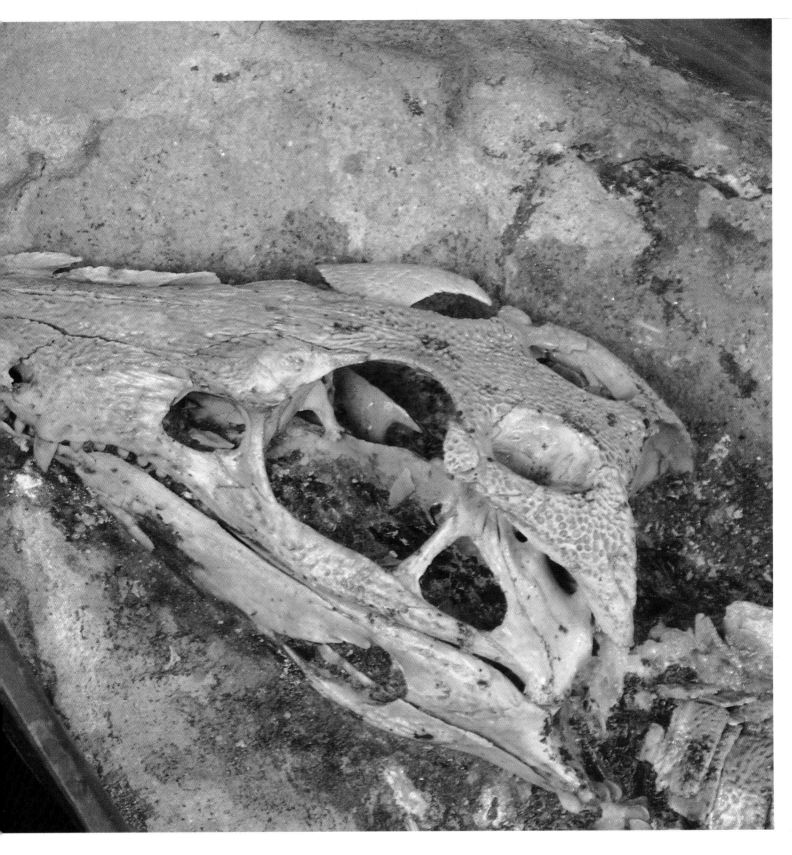

Above: Close-up view of small acid-prepared *Araripesuchus* reveals details of sculptured bony skull ornament, teeth, two pairs of supraorbitals, antorbital fenestra, and many other features including bony scutes.

Facing page: Nearly complete acid-prepared skeleton of *Araripesuchus*. Partially-prepared state (top left) reveals original position of gastralia (which were subsequently detached). Detail of palate shown at upper right.

13 mm. The smaller skull has a length of about 83 mm and minimum interorbital width of 11.5 mm. From the two specimens it can be determined that there are three teeth on the premaxilla and about 12 teeth on the maxilla. The third tooth on the maxilla is enlarged and the teeth posterior to it are reduced in size. The external nares are terminal and surrounded by the premaxilla and nasal bones. The premaxilla and maxilla join broadly and form a clear opening or foramen in the suture zone. The maxilla is high and almost vertical, contacting the nasals and bordering on the antorbital fenestra. The lachrymals lie above the antorbital fenestra and contact the prefrontal, which bears an articulating surface for the anterior palpebral. A single unpaired frontal forms the upper boundary of the orbit and bears a small ornamented posterior palpebral bone at the posterior dorsal edge of the orbit. The frontal extends onto the cranial table where it abuts against the smaller parietal. The parietal surrounds about half of the supratemporal fenestra, which is bordered externally by the postorbital and squamosal. The walls of the supratemporal fenestra are vertical except for a small shelf on the posterior lateral walls. The parietal reaches the posterior border of the cranial table, where it abuts against the supraoccipital bone in the middle of the posterior border, and it also abuts against the squamosal, which lies at each corner of the cranial table.

In lateral view the orbit is large and almost circular. By looking deeply into the orbit, the prefrontal pillar can be seen contacting the palatine, behind which the pterygoid extends posteriorly. The posterior wall of the orbit is incompletely closed by the laterosphenoids, leaving a wide gap between them. A large jugal extends from the anterior corner along the bottom of the orbit and infratemporal fenestra until it contacts the quadratojugal. The jugal contributes to the base of the postorbital bar (or pillar), which is columnar in form. The contact with the quadratojugal is extensive. The quadratojugal rises at a sharp angle toward the cranial roof where it abuts against the postorbital part of the pillar. This contact is unlike that found in the living crocodilians (Eusuchia), where the quadratojugal only marginally contacts the postorbital bar. The quadrate rises at almost a 45° angle to the cranial roof and makes contact with the squamosal. At its upper end the quadrate is pierced by large fenestrae such as the external auditory meatus which is partitioned into two canals by a double bar of bone. A secondary foramen at the level of the auditory meatus, enters into the core or cavity of the quadrate. This may indicate the presence of a siphoneal system although no foramina aereum are visible on the quadrate or elsewhere (probably because of incomplete exposure of the proper surfaces). The condylar surfaces of the quadrate are complex and incompletely exposed.

The palatine bones make up the anterior margin of the internal nares, which also are bordered by the pterygoid posteriorly. The internal nares have an advanced mesosuchian condition, with slightly angulated pterygoids that are firmly braced against the ectopterygoids. The rostrum and presphenoid lie between the two arms of the pterygoid. The pterygoid wings are partially vertical at less than an angle of 45° and apparently bear a thin torus transiliens. The basicranium is not as vertical as in modern adult crocodilians (Eusuchia), although the basioccipital appears to be horizontal, with a small indentation on its anterior border that may indicate the presence of the single eustachian tube. In the palatal view horns of the hyoid are visible.

The mandible is robust, and the dentary makes up more than half the lower jaw. There is a long mandibular symphysis that incorporates the anterior end of the long, large splenial. Posteriorly there is a well-developed angular, surangular, and articular. The retroarticular process of the articular is expanded as a thin triangular sheet. There is no evidence as to the presence or absence of foramen aereum. The left mandible is at least 94 mm long in AMNH 24450.

The vertebral column is made of at least five regions. There are about seven cervicals, 13 thoracics, four lumbar, two sacrals, and at least 21 caudals. The typical crocodilian atlas and axis are followed by the remaining cervical vertebrae and enlarged overlapping ribs that limit the movement of the neck. The vertebrae are weakly amphicoelous and bear erect neural spines with rounded tops. A small peg is present on many vertebrae that abut against the overlying osteoderm. The sacral vertebrae are strongly attached to the pelvis and are followed by characteristic caudal vertebrae with strong hemal spines becoming smaller posteriorly.

The dorsal osteoderms, which lie above the neural spines of the vertebrae, begin in the postcervical region and vary in size. They become wider in the midbody, then narrower in the sacral region, and expanded again in the anterior caudal region. The osteoderms are slightly overlapping and beveled anteriorly so as to make a complete armored chain down the back. There are only a few osteoderms in the cervical region, but they are round and not associated with particular vertebrae. In the caudal region the hemal arches are associated with reduced ventral osteoderms. These osteoderms have irregular borders and may not have completed their development. As compared to the dorsal osteoderms, they appear incomplete and probably lie in the ventral median position below the hemal arches. The osteoderms are ornamented with pits and a longitudinal ridge located on the outer third of the osteoderm running down its length. The pitting pattern is most distinct anteriorly, becoming reduced posteriorly as the ridge becomes more distinct.

A complete scapula bone is present and is about 24 mm high in AMNH 24450, with an expanded curved dorsal surface of about 30 mm. It makes contact with a well-preserved horizontal coracoid, and both contribute to the glenoid fossa. The coracoid contacts the interclavicle, which is associated with sternal elements and many fragments of the gastralia.

The front limb is about a third shorter than the hind limb. In AMNH 24450, the head of the humerus lies in the glenoid fossa and is about 44 mm long. Distally the humerus contacts the radius and ulna, which are complete and 42 mm long. Distal to these are the two enlarged crocodilian proximal carpals and the pisiform element. Distal to these bones are fragments of presumably five digits.

The pelvic girdle is quite typically crocodilian, with the ilium extended slightly posteriorly, well developed acetabulum and acetabular foramen, and a typical crocodilian pubis. The femur in AMNH 24450 is in close proximity to the acetabulum and is about 63 mm long. Distal to the femur lie a complete fibula and tibia; the latter is about 58 mm long. Articulating with the tibia and fibula are the astragalus and calcaneum, which were capable of interlocking. The calcaneal tuber is large, with a deep groove on its posterior surface. The well-developed articulating surfaces of these two bones suggest a more erect position for the hind limbs. At least two other distal tarsals are indicated, plus four large metatarsals and a short flattened fifth metatarsal. Four complete digits are present, with two phalanges on the first digit, three phalanges on the second digit, four phalanges on the third digit, and four phalanges on the fourth digit.

The morphology of *Araripesuchus* indicates that this fossil crocodilian is a member of a Mesozoic lineage of terrestrial habit. This interpretation is supported by the high short skull, subterminal external nares, biserial osteodermal armor, articulation of the proximal tarsal elements, and large calcaneal tuber. *Araripesuchus* probably occupied a different habitat from the much larger trematochampsid crocodilian from the Santana formation, which appears to have been more dedicated to an aquatic mode of life.

The array of "mesosuchian" characters seen in *Araripesuchus* represents a mixture of primitive and advanced states, and the genus lies between the early terrestrial crocodilians and the modern Crocodilia. "Mesosuchians" in all probability represent a paraphyletic assemblage of crocodilians, within which *Araripesuchus* may be viewed as a phylogenetically advanced taxon, perhaps more closely related to modern (eusuchian) crocodilians than are some other "mesosuchians." It is difficult to place the genus in the systematic hierarchy based on the conflicting phylogenetic views of modern systematists such as Benton and Clark (1988) and Buffetaut (1984).

The presence of *Araripesuchus* in both West Africa and Brazil testifies to the presence of a close geographic relationship of Africa and South America (Buffetaut, 1984) and probably to an origin of the lineage prior to the separation of the continents by the developing Atlantic Ocean. A similar evolutionary scenario has been advanced for the trematochampsid crocodilian from the Santana formation.

Assemblages: Santana, ?Jardim.

(M. K. Hecht)

ITASUCHUS Price, 1955

Order CROCODYLIA
Suborder MESOSUCHIA
Family TREMATOCHAMPSIDAE
Genus *Itasuchus* Price, 1955
    1955 *Itasuchus* Price: 492
    1987 *Caririsuchus* Kellner: 222

Emended diagnosis: Trematochampsid crocodilian with a relatively deep, narrow, and slender snout and a pair of preorbital swellings formed by the nasals and prefrontals.

    Type species: *Itasuchus jesuinoi* Price, 1955.
Itasuchus camposi (Kellner)
    1987 *Caririsuchus camposi* Kellner: 222

Emended diagnosis: *Itasuchus* with five teeth in the premaxilla, 18 teeth in the maxilla, fourth and tenth maxillary teeth the largest; extensive dermal armor covering entire tail and parts of limbs.

    Holotype: CD-R-O41 Desirée Collection/Divisão de Geologia e Mineralogia, Departamento Nacional da Produção Mineral, Rio de Janeiro, DGM-DNPM 1468-R; part of maxillary ramus, fragments of dermal scutes and ribs belonging to an entire skeleton that is now in private hands; Santana formation, Romualdo member, Chapada do Araripe (precise locality not known).

The type specimen of this species was described as *Caririsuchus camposi* by Kellner (1987) on the basis of photographs of a nearly complete skeleton plus jaw and scute fragments detached from it. The skeleton was exported from Brazil and brought to Europe, where the author (E. Buffetaut) was allowed to study it (unaware of Kellner's work) before it was sold to an unknown purchaser. The present whereabouts of the specimen are unknown, and, regrettably, all that are left of this type specimen in a public collection are small fragments.

To judge from its fairly deep, strongly festooned snout, its bulbous and ornamented posterior teeth, and its forward-facing nasal opening, this crocodilian is undoubtedly a trematochampsid. It closely resembles *Itasuchus jesuinoi*, described by L. I. Price (1955) from the Late Cretaceous Bauru group of Brazil, in the shape of its skull table and jaws, the appearance of its teeth, and the presence of preorbital swellings formed by the nasals and prefrontals. There seems to be no reason to separate the Santana crocodilian from the genus *Itasuchus*, and it therefore is referred to as *Itasuchus camposi* (Kellner), *Caririsuchus* being considered as a junior synonym of *Itasuchus*. Differences in

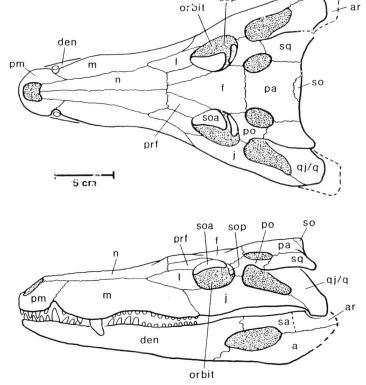

Itasuchus jesuinoi. Outline reconstruction of skull, based on photographs and published illustrations of the holotype. Many features of this reconstruction need to be verified from actual specimens before it can be regarded as reliable.

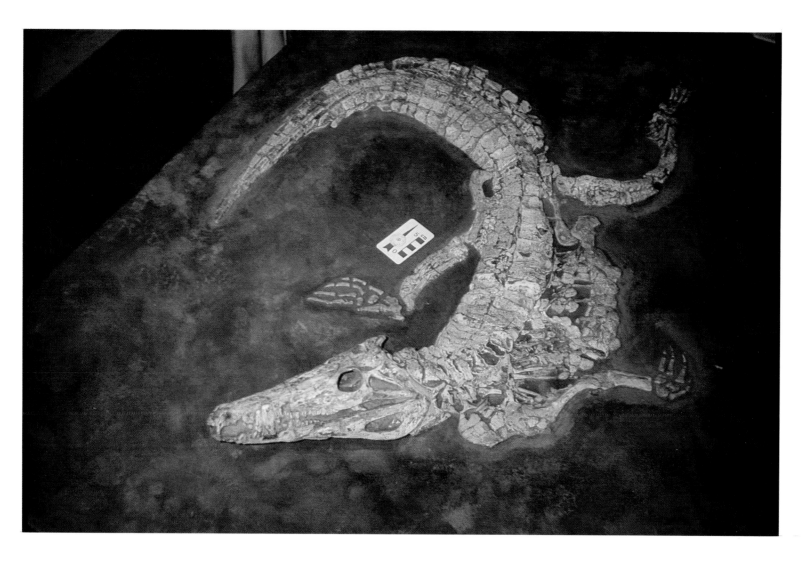

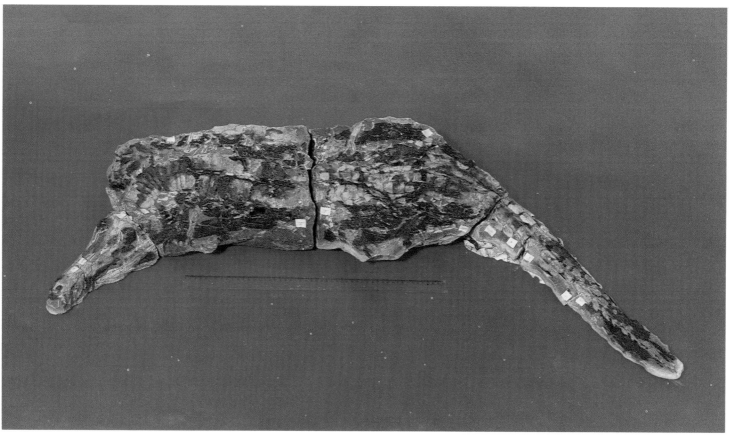

Itasuchus camposi, a large crocodilian. The holotype (top) is a complete specimen, of which only fragments are currently deposited in a museum (in Rio de Janeiro). This specimen symbolizes the difficulty of saving scientifically valuable specimens from commercial exploitation. The second specimen (below) reportedly also is for sale. No scientific institution currently has a complete specimen of this spectacular and important species. Top photo by E. Buffetaut.

Trematochampsid species from the Cretaceous of Africa, Madagascar, and South America.

Taxon	Age	Locality
Amargasuchus minor	Hauterivian	Patagonia
Itasuchus camposi	Aptian	Brazil
Trematochampsa taqueti	Early Senonian	Niger
Trematochampsa oblita	Campanian	Madagascar
Itasuchus jesuinoi	Maestrichtian (?)	Brazil

the number and relative sizes of the teeth justify a separation at the specific level.

The occurrence of a trematochampsid in the Early Cretaceous Santana formation of Brazil has interesting paleobiogeographical consequences, since it shows that this family of freshwater and terrestrial mesosuchian crocodiles was already present in Gondwana before the complete separation of Africa and South America by the proto-Atlantic toward the end of the Early Cretaceous. The presence of the family in the Lower Cretaceous of South America is suggested by an incomplete maxilla from the La Amarga formation of Argentina recently described as *Amargasuchus minor* by L. M. Chiappe (1989). The Late Cretaceous African (*Trematochampsa taqueti*) and South American (*Itasuchus jesuinoi*, *I. camposi*) representatives of the Trematochampsidae thus can be considered as offspring of an earlier trematochampsid stock that inhabited Gondwana before the break-up of that supercontinent. After the separation of Africa and South America, trematochampsids evolved separately along divergent lines on both sides of the proto-Atlantic. There also is some evidence that trematochampsids entered Europe sometime in the Cretaceous and gave rise to ziphodont ("dinosaur-toothed") forms on that continent during the early Tertiary.

The African and Madagascan trematochampsid genus *Trematochampsa* differs from *Itasuchus* in having much more robust jaws and teeth. The newly described *Amargasuchus* from Argentina, to the contrary, has a more slender and more elongated snout with a straighter maxilla.

An interesting anatomical feature of this crocodilian is its very well developed dermal armor, which covers not only the back and the belly but also extends all the way to the tip of the tail and protects parts of the limbs. *Itasuchus camposi* is one of the most heavily armored of all known crocodilians.

Assemblage: Not known with certainty, but the lithology of associated matrix suggests Jardim or perhaps Old Mission.

(E. Buffetaut)

THE SANTANA FORMATION PTEROSAURS

Editorial Note: Pterosaur fossils from the Santana formation are currently being studied by several investigators. The information included here comes from two sources. Dr. Peter Wellnhofer provided a systematic review of all taxa that were described up to 1988. Mr. Alexander Kellner (Federal University, Rio de Janeiro) has supplemented this with a recently reported discovery of what promises to be a significant new group of bizarre pterosaurs. Slightly different systematic arrangements were used by these contributors. Since it would be premature to adopt one arrangement in preference to the other at this time, both contributions are included essentially as they were received.

(J.G.M.)

Introduction

During recent years, fossil localities of the Chapada do Araripe in the provinces of Ceará and Pernambuco have produced an increasing number of skeletal remains of flying reptiles, the pterosaurs. Since Llewellyn Price (1971) described the first pterosaur from the Santana formation (*Araripesaurus castilhoi*), several more genera including more than a dozen different species have been established. Less than half of these are known by skull material, however, and two more are based on lower jaws. Only in three species is cranial material associated with postcranial bones, whereas the remaining species are based on postcranial elements, mostly wing bones and vertebrae.

In the present state of knowledge we do not know whether the isolated pterosaur skulls and mandibles from the Santana formation can be correlated with some of the postcranial remains hitherto assigned to different taxa (Unwin, 1988). It may well be that the discovery of more complete material will result in a reduction of taxonomic units. It is obvious that the solution of this problem depends on specimens of individuals with the skull *and* postcranial material preserved.

Fortunately, there have been finds of this kind. The most complete pterosaur skeleton from the Santana formation was in fact part of the Axelrod Collection of the American Museum of Natural History, New York. In one composite nodule were included: skull, vertebral column, shoulder girdles, pelvis, and parts of the wings and hind legs. The skeleton comes from one individual with a wing span of 4.5 meters. One result of the study of this specimen was that pterosaurs could not have been bipedal on the ground, but must have walked quadrupedally (Wellnhofer, 1988).

New material presently being studied by several investigators suggests even more new forms of pterosaurian life, indicating a high degree of diversity in the Araripe region during Early Cretaceous times.

With regard to the excellent quality of fossil preservation and to the increasing number of pterosaur fossils being collected, the Santana formation of the Chapada do Araripe has become one of the most important pterosaur localities in the world. The fragile, hollow, thin-walled bones of pterosaurs enclosed in concretions usually are preserved uncrushed and hardly compressed. If thorough and skillful preparation is applied most bones can be prepared out of the matrix completely. This provides a unique opportunity to manipulate the bones as if they were from extant vertebrates, in order to study their function and implications for the life habits of pterosaurs in general.

Conventionally, pterosaurs are regarded as an order of the subclass Archosauria (Wellnhofer, 1978). Recently, their relationship has been hypothesized as being a sister-group of the dinosaurs. Their suggested origin from Triassic thecodontian archosaurs cannot be proven on the basis of the fossil record, however. Study of the oldest known pterosaurs from the Upper Triassic of Italy suggests that pterosaurs could be derived from Permian diapsid reptiles, the Eosuchia. The earliest pterosaurs known have already developed typical pterosaurian characters. They are characterized by a large skull with correspondingly large fenestrae, a strongly developed and elongated neck, relatively short trunk, large bird-like shoulder girdles, and a broad ossified sternal plate with a prominent cristospina (bony crest extending anteriorly from the breast bone). The wing skeleton is the most remarkable evolutionary adaptation in the structure of the pterosaurs. It is greatly enlarged, with a relatively stout humerus with a well-developed lateral crest and an extremely elongated fourth finger that has become a long, slender wing spar supporting a tough wing membrane. Unlike the wing

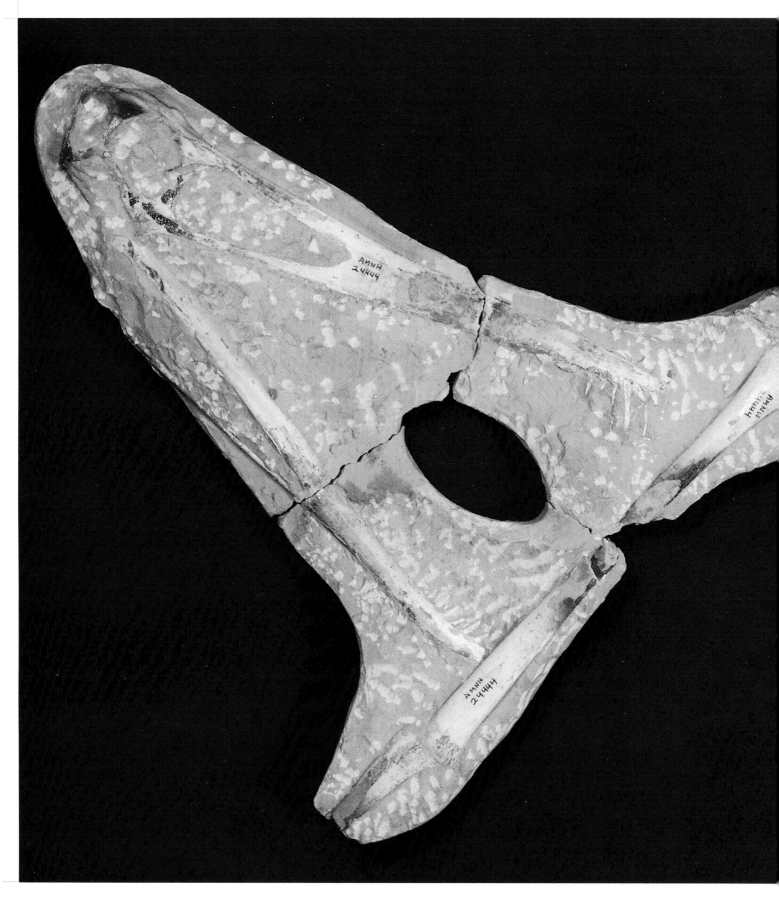

Skull, mandible, and wing bones of a large pterosaur from the Santana formation. Specimens like this are of considerable scientific importance because parts of the skeleton are associated in a single concretion. Many of the nominal species described have been founded upon isolated fragments, which later may lead to nomenclatural difficulties.

Facing page: *Santanadactylus*. **Top left:** Holotype (proximal part of right humerus) and paratype (two articulated neck vertebrae, probably not from same taxon as holotype) of *S. brasiliensis*. **Top right:** Acid-prepared notarium of *S.* cf. *brasiliensis* from P. Gigase collection, Antwerp, Belgium. **Upper center:** Holotype of *S. araripensis* before preparation (left); skull after preparation, lateral view (right). **Lower center:** *S. araripensis* holotype; skull in palatal view (left) and lower jaw in dorsal view (right). **Bottom:** *S. pricei*, paratype (left humerus, left) and holotype (wrist with radius, ulna, carpus, metacarpus and pteroid bone). Photos by P. Wellnhofer

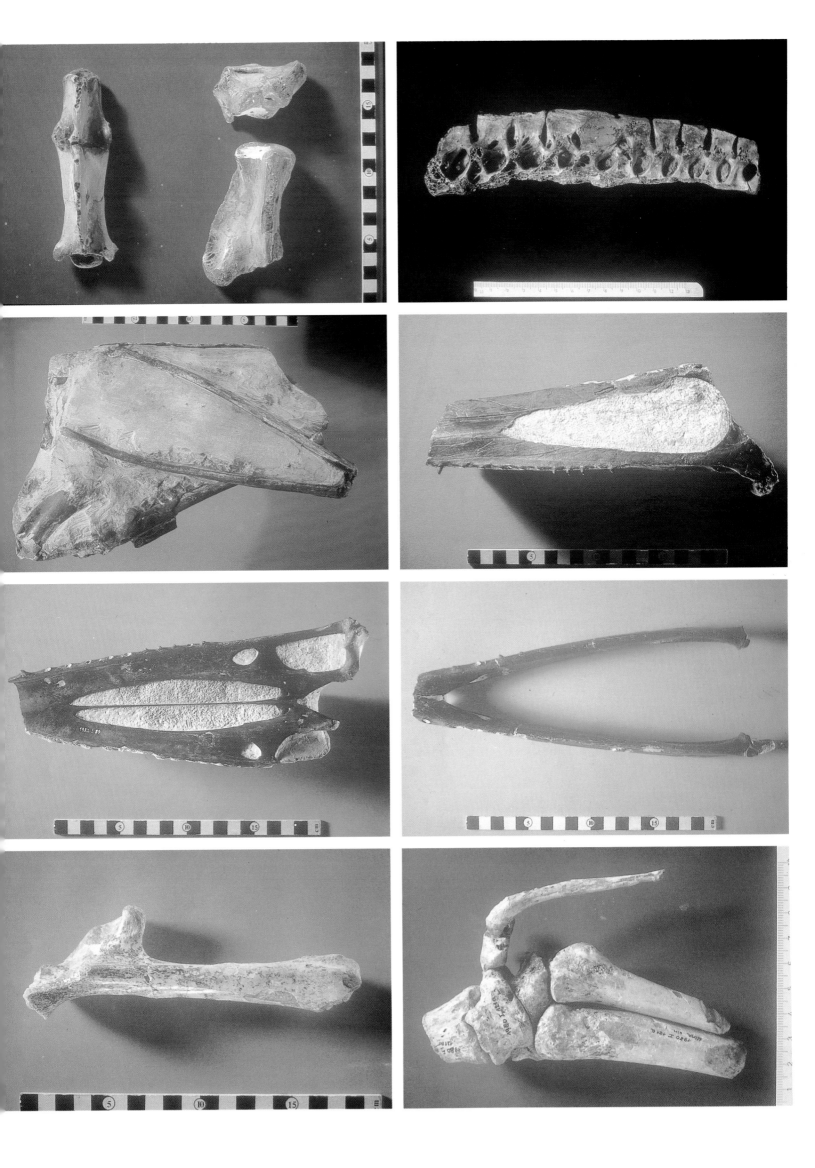

membrane of bats, the pterosaurian wing membrane was stiffened by a dense series of parallel strengthening fibers, termed actinofibrillae. These fibers have been discovered in wing impressions of Santana pterosaurs (Campos, et al., 1984).

Compared with the wings, the hind legs were disproportionately weak. The adaptations to flight are so dominant that walking on the ground must have been difficult for pterosaurs.

The more primitive pterosaurs, the Rhamphorhynchoidea, have among other features a long vertebral tail, shorter neck, short metacarpal, and other distinctive characters. Stratigraphically, they range from the Upper Triassic to the Upper Jurassic. A more advanced group, the Pterodactyloidea, is characterized by a short tail, longer neck, long metacarpal, and other distinctive characters and ranges from the Upper Jurassic to the end of the Cretaceous. Among the Pterodactyloidea were the largest flying animals of all times, the giant *Quetzalcoatlus* from the Maestrichtian of Texas, with a wing span of 11 to 12.2 meters.

The Santana pterosaurs were all pterodactyloids. Most of them were large, with wing spans of several meters, and they had teeth. Toothless genera are also represented by recently described material (Kellner and Campos, 1989).

Systematics and Taxonomy

It has always been difficult to assign the Santana pterosaurs to established families. Price (1971) assigned his *Araripesaurus* material to the Ornithocheiridae, a family known mainly from the Cretaceous of England but based on very fragmentary remains. The genera *Santanadactylus* and *Brasileodactylus* also have been classified as ornithocheirids. For *Tropeognathus* a possible assignment to the family Criorhynchidae has been suggested. This is another family known only by fragmentary jaws and postcranial bones from the Cretaceous of England. A new family Anhangueridae has been proposed for the genus *Anhanguera*, and the genera *Araripedactylus* and *Cearadactylus* were placed in indeterminate families.

In general, there are similarities between the Santana pterosaurs from northeastern Brazil and

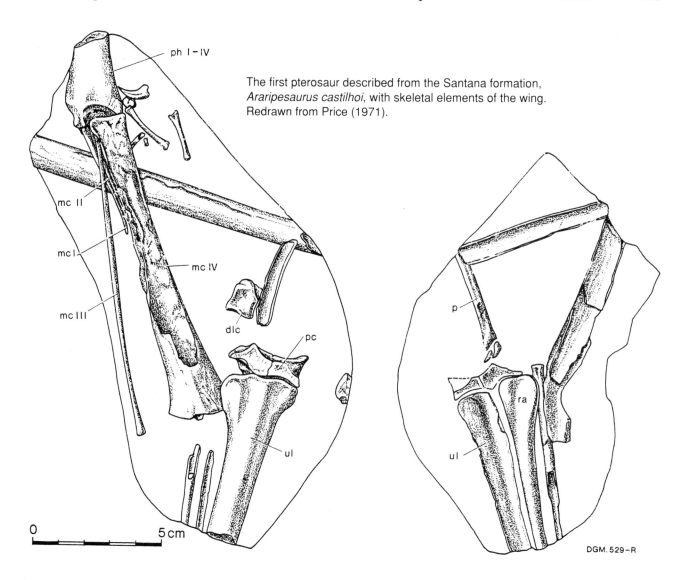

The first pterosaur described from the Santana formation, *Araripesaurus castilhoi*, with skeletal elements of the wing. Redrawn from Price (1971).

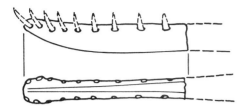

Brasileodactylus
araripensis

Brasileodactylus araripensis. Front end of lower jaw in lateral and dorsal aspects. From Wellnhofer (1987).

the English pterosaurs, especially from the Cambridge Greensand. This is not surprising, however, when we take into account that in late Lower Cretaceous and Early Upper Cretaceous times the paleogeographic positions of both Europe and South America were much closer than today, and that large pterosaurs, so perfectly adapted to sustained flight as the Santana pterosaurs, could have spread easily along the paleo-coastlines over wide distances.

Order PTEROSAURIA Kaup, 1834
Suborder PTERODACTYLOIDEA Plieninger, 1901
Family ?ORNITHOCHEIRIDAE Seeley, 1870
This family is diagnosed by a dentition that extends to the tip of the snout and by a medial keel on the palate corresponding to a groove on the mandibular symphysis.

Araripesaurus Price, 1971
Diagnosis: Ornithocheirid pterosaurs with proximal series of the carpus composed of two carpals; metacarpals I and II proximally reduced, not extending to the carpus.
Type species: *Araripesaurus castilhoi* Price, 1971.
Araripesaurus castilhoi Price, 1971
Holotype: Distal parts of ulna and radius, proximal carpals, a distal lateral carpal, a pteroid bone, the metacarpals, the proximal end of the first wing phalanx, several phalanges of the small fingers, a claw, part of the shaft of the presumed second wing phalanx, and a few sesamoid bones. All this material is part of the right wing of one individual, from a single concretion. Divisão de Geologia e Mineralogia, Departamento Nacional da Produção Mineral, Rio de Janeiro, DGM-DNPM 529-R; Santana formation, Chapada do Araripe.

Diagnosis: As for genus.
Size: The only complete bone is the fourth metacarpal. It is 118 millimeters long, indicating an approximate wing span of 2.2 meters.

Brasileodactylus Kellner, 1984
Diagnosis: Mandibular symphysis slightly bent upward, triangular in cross-section, and with a spoon-shaped expansion anteriorly; longitudinal medial groove present dorsally; nine rounded and elliptical tooth alveoli on each side, increasingly wider spaced from the tip of the jaw in posterior direction.
Type species: *Brasileoactylus araripensis* Kellner, 1984.
Brasileodactylus araripensis Kellner, 1984
Holotype: Mandibular symphysis, front end; Divisão de Geologia e Mineralogia, Departamento da Produção Mineral, Rio de Janeiro, CD-R-002.
Diagnosis: As for genus.
Size: Length of preserved portion of mandible 11.2 cm, maximal width across anterior expansion 1.9 cm.

It seems likely that more complete material will reveal the synonymy of *Brasileodactylus araripensis* and *Araripesaurus santanae*. At present, however, this speculation cannot be based on positive evidence.

Santanadactylus de Buisonjé, 1980
Diagnosis: Relatively large ornithocheirid pterosaurs with complete fusion of pterygoid, quadrate, and basipterygoid process of basisphenoid; notarium present with articulation for scapulae; scapula and coracoid co-ossified in a single scapulocoracoid; fused carpus with three carpals, one proximal, one distal, and one lateral distal carpal bone.
Type species: *Santanadactylus brasilensis* de Buisonjé, 1980.
Originally, the type species was established on the basis of skeletal elements from two different concretions and therefore probably of two different individuals (de Buisonjé, 1980, 1981). One specimen includes the proximal portion of a humerus with the glenoid portion of the scapulocoracoid, and the other comprises two articulating cervical vertebrae.
Santanadactylus brasilensis de Buisonjé, 1980
Holotype: Geological Institute, University of Amsterdam, M4894; proximal part of the right humerus and glenoid section of the right scapulocoracoid from one individual. **Paratype:** M4895; two articulated cervical vertebrae from a different nodule from the holotype.

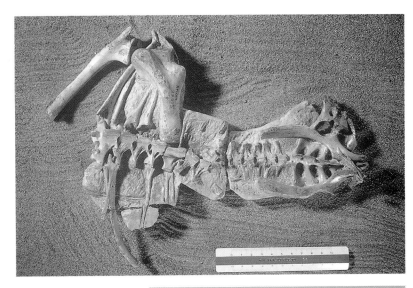

Facing page: *Anhanguera santanae*. **Top:** Holotype in Munich collection shown before preparation (left), and skull after preparation (right). **Upper center:** Part of vertebral column and shoulder girdle of holotype (see p. 362). **Lower center:** AMNH 22555, the most complete pterosaur skeleton hitherto discovered in the Santana formation, with skull, vertebral column, shoulder girdle, fragments of humeri, both wrist sections, pelvis, and both femur heads (left); skull shown separately (right). **Bottom:** Neck vertebrae of AMNH 22555 in lateral (left) and dorsal (right) views. Photos by P. Wellnhofer.

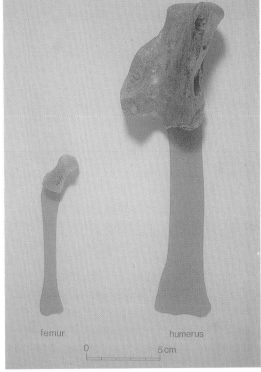

femur   humerus

0   5 cm

Right: Top: *Anhanguera santanae*, AMNH 22555, dorsal vertebral column in articulation with ribs, the right shoulder girdle, the sacrum, and pelvis, in dorsal view. **Upper center:** AMNH 22555, femur and humerus, both restored to their original lengths, demonstrating the great disproportion between wing skeleton and hind legs. **Lower center:** Holotype of *Tropeognathus mesembrinus* in Munich collection, skull and mandible, skull length 63 cm. **Bottom:** Holotype of *Araripedactylus dehmi* in Munich collection, first phalanx of wing finger, 55 cm long. Photos by P. Wellnhofer.

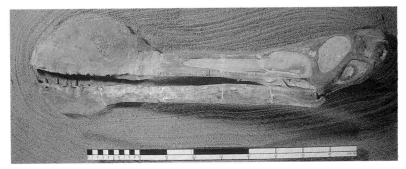

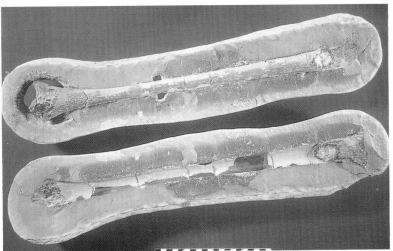

It is doubtful whether the neck vertebrae can be assigned to the same species or even genus, since they represent a long-necked form with low neural spines, quite distinct from the ornithocheirid-like short cervicals with tall spines.

Diagnosis: Humerus with steeply descending deltopectoral crest whose upper edge shows no bend.

Size: Proximal part of humerus as preserved 9.0 cm, total length calculated 29 cm. Estimated wing span approximately 5.7 meters.

Santanadactylus **cf.** *brasilensis* de Buisonjé, 1980

Material: A section of the vertebral column consisting of the last cervical, the first five dorsals fused to a notarium, and the following four dorsals in natural articulation. This specimen was tentatively referred to *S. brasilensis* by Wellnhofer, Buffetaut and Gigase (1983). Its vertebral column has been pepared out of the matrix by using acetic acid. The vertebrae are uncrushed and not compressed, although the ventral parts of the centra have been eroded away. The neural spines of the third, fourth, and fifth dorsals are fused, forming a thickened bony plate with oval lateral facets for the articulation with the scapulae.

Housed in the collection of Dr. Paul Gigase, Antwerpen, Belgium, No. V-201.

Size: Total length of the vertebral column from the last cervical to the ninth dorsal 20.5 cm. Length of the notarium 11 cm.

Santanadactylus araripensis Wellnhofer, 1985

Type material: Bavarian State Collection of Paleontology and Historical Geology, Munich, No. BSP 1982 I 89; skeletal elements from one large concretion including skull and mandible without the front ends, five isolated teeth, two hyoid bones, humerus, ulna, radius, carpals, proximal parts of metacarpals, and two sesamoids of the right wing.

Santanadactylus araripensis. Partial restoration of the skull, based on type specimen. From Wellnhofer (1987).

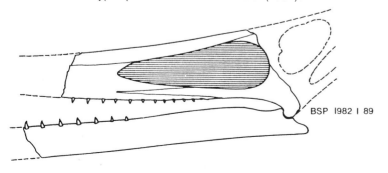

BSP 1982 I 89

Diagnosis: Large species of *Santanadactylus*; no nasal process protruding into the nasopreorbital opening; sharp upper edge of premaxilla in front of nasopreorbital fenestra; margins of jaws are slightly bent laterally in ventral aspect; upper edge of deltapectoral crest of humerus has a bend.

Size: Skull length as preserved 24.3 cm, as restored approximately 60 cm. Humerus length 24 cm. Calculated wing span approximately 4.7 meters.

Santanadactylus **cf.** *araripensis* Wellnhofer, 1985

Material: Left humerus, distal part of the right humerus, proximal parts of an ulna and a radius, all from one concretion and probably one individual. Due to differences in the morphology of the proximal and distal articulations of the humerus, Wellnhofer (1985) suggested only comparative assignment of this specimen to *S. araripensis*.

Deposited in the Bavarian State Collection of Paleontology and Historical Geology, Munich, No. BSP 1982 I 92.

Size: Length of humerus 27 cm. Estimated wing span 5.3 meters.

Santanadactylus pricei Wellnhofer, 1985

Holotype: Bavarian State Collection of Paleontology and Historical Geology, Munich, No. BSP 1980 I 122; skeletal elements of the left wing of one individual, including ulna, radius, proximal and distal carpals, fourth metacarpal, fragments of other metacarpals, a pteroid bone, a digit claw, and the shaft of the first wing phalanx. **Paratype material:** BSP 1980 I 43; left isolated humerus, 17 cm long, articular surface of the head damaged. BSP 1980 I 120; skeletal elements of the left wing, including distal ends of radius and ulna, proximal part of the fourth metacarpal, and a fragment of the proximal carpal. Institute and Museum of Paleontology of the University of Zürich, Switzerland, No. A/III 522; first and second phalanges of the left wing finger of one individual, with restored lengths of 40 and 32.5 cm, suggesting an estimated wing span of 3.5 meters.

Referred specimen: American Museum of Natural History, New York, AMNH 22552; almost complete right wing skeleton preserved in a large concretion, including humerus (17 cm), radius (24 cm), ulna (24.3 cm), three carpals, first and second metacarpal (reduced proximally), third metacarpal (not reduced), fourth metacarpal, the wing metacarpal (17.2 cm), the pteroid bone, several phalanges of the digits I, II, and III, three phalanges of the wing finger (37.2; 32.4; 25.2 cm), and the proximal fragment of the fourth wing finger phalanx. The wing span of this pterosaur can be reconstructed with high reliability as 3.27 meters.

Diagnosis: Smaller species of *Santanadactylus*; upper edge of the deltopectoral crest of humerus with a bend; radius considerably more slender than ulna; distal articular surface of distal carpal with deep sulcus; metacarpals I and II reduced; phalanges of wing finger bent ventrally.

Size: Length of ulna 21.5 cm. Estimated wing span 2.9 meters (holotype).

Santanadactylus spixi Wellnhofer, 1985

Holotype: Bavarian State Collection of Paleontology and Historical Geology, Munich, No. BSP 1980 I 121; skeletal elements of both wings of one individual, including distal parts of radius and ulna, the carpals, a pteroid bone, a proximal end of the fourth metacarpal, and a few sesamoids.

Diagnosis: Smaller species of *Santanadactylus*; radius more robust than in *S. pricei*; proximal carpal rounded quadrangular in outline; distal articular surface of distal carpal with sharply offset dorsal area.

Size: Length of ulna as restored 26 cm, suggesting an estimated wing span of 3.5 meters.

cf. *Santanadactylus*

Material: Leonardi and Borgomanero (1987) published a preliminary description of a pair of wings that they assigned tentatively to the genus *Santanadactylus*. The wing bones are enclosed in a single, very large L-shaped nodule. Measurements have been given of the humerus (19 cm), ulna (27.5 cm), fourth metacarpal (18.5 cm), the first wing phalanx (35.5 cm), the second wing phalanx (33.5 cm), and the third wing phalanx (20 cm). The fourth wing phalanges are missing. The wing span of this individual can be calculated as being approximately 3.5 meters.

Family ANHANGUERIDAE Campos and Kellner, 1985b

Anhanguera Campos and Kellner, 1985b

Diagnosis: Large pterosaurs with long, slender skull bearing low sagittal crest on top of premaxilla in front of nasopreorbital opening, except at tip of snout; a similar crest may have been developed ventrally on the mandibular symphysis.

Type species: *Anhanguera blittersdorffi* Campos and Kellner, 1985b.

Anhanguera blittersdorffi Campos and Kellner, 1985b

Holotype: Complete skull without mandible. Housed in the Collection Desirée of Mr. Rainer Alexander von Blittersdorff, Rio de Janeiro, Brazil.

Diagnosis: As for genus.

Size: Skull length 50 cm, maximal width between the quadrates approximately 8 cm, maximal height at the sagittal crest 6 cm.

The skull shows similarities with the Munich specimen of *Anhanguera santanae* (No. BSP 1982 I 90). The nasopreorbital fenestra is larger in *Anhanguera blittersdorffi*. The quadrate is steeper in *A. santanae* so that the skull appears to be higher posteriorly.

Anhanguera santanae (Wellnhofer, 1985)

1985 *Araripesaurus santanae* Wellnhofer: 148

Holotype: Skeletal elements from one large individual including skull and mandible without the front ends, right ulna and radius, two proximal and three distal carpals, proximal part of the fourth metacarpal, and the wing metacarpal. All bones originate from one concretion. Bavarian State Collection of Paleontology and Historical Geology in Munich, No. BSP 1982 I 90.

Diagnosis: Skull long and slender, front ends of the jaws slightly bent upward; margins of jaws straight in ventral aspect; pointed, recurved teeth decreasing in size antero-

Anhanguera blittersdorffi. Restoration of the skull with premaxillary crest. From Wellnhofer (1987).

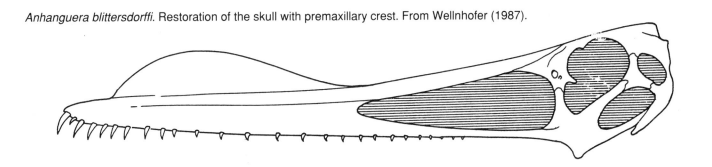

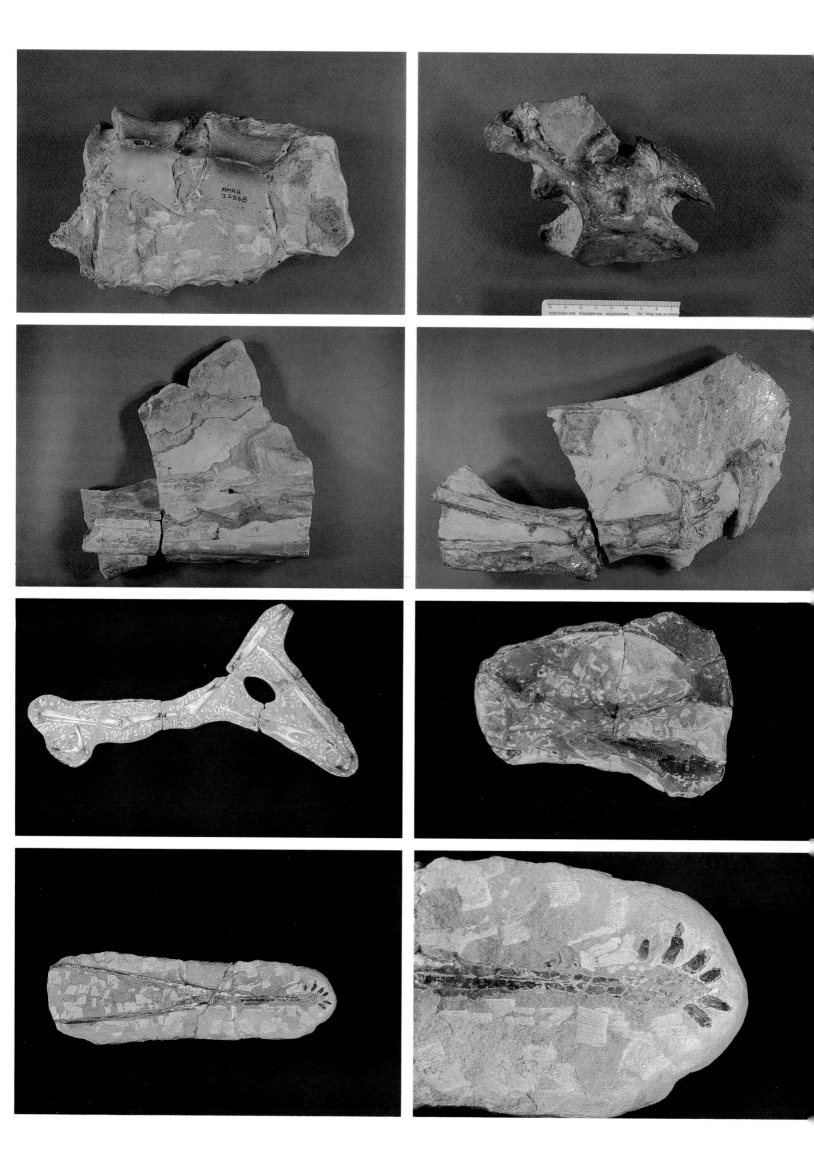

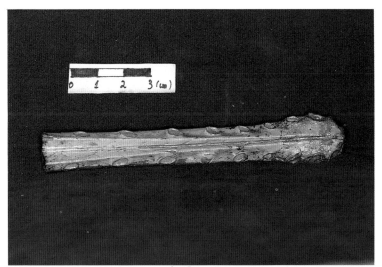

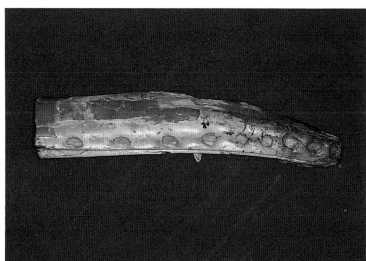

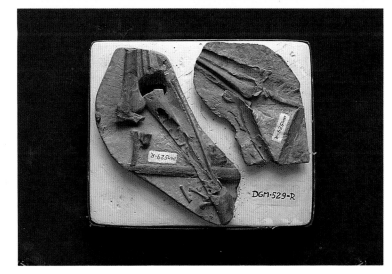

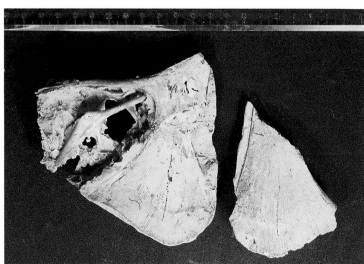

Above: Top: *Brasileodactylus araripensis*, two views of the holotype, CD-R-00. Bottom left: *Araripesaurus castilhoi*, the holotype. Bottom right: *Tapejara wellnhoferi*, a crested pterosaur allied to *Tupuxuara*; holotype, partial skull, CD-R-080. Photos courtesy A. Kellner.

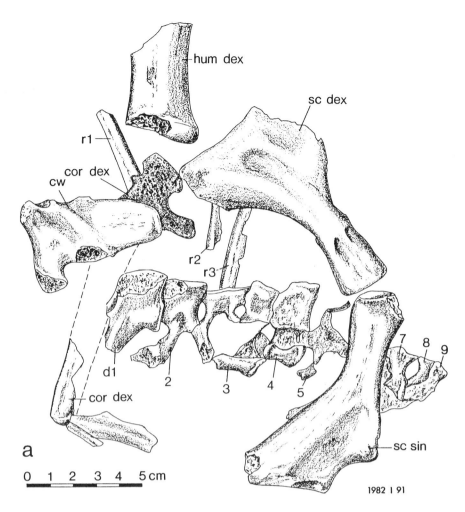

a

0 1 2 3 4 5 cm

1982 I 91

Anhanguera santanae. Part of vertebral column and shoulder girdle in dorsal (A) and ventral (B) views. From Wellnhofer (1985).

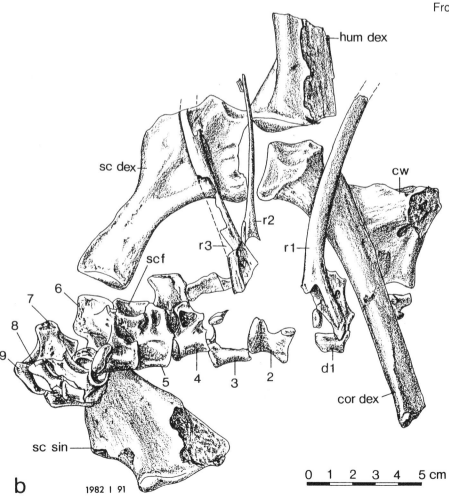

b

1982 I 91

0 1 2 3 4 5 cm

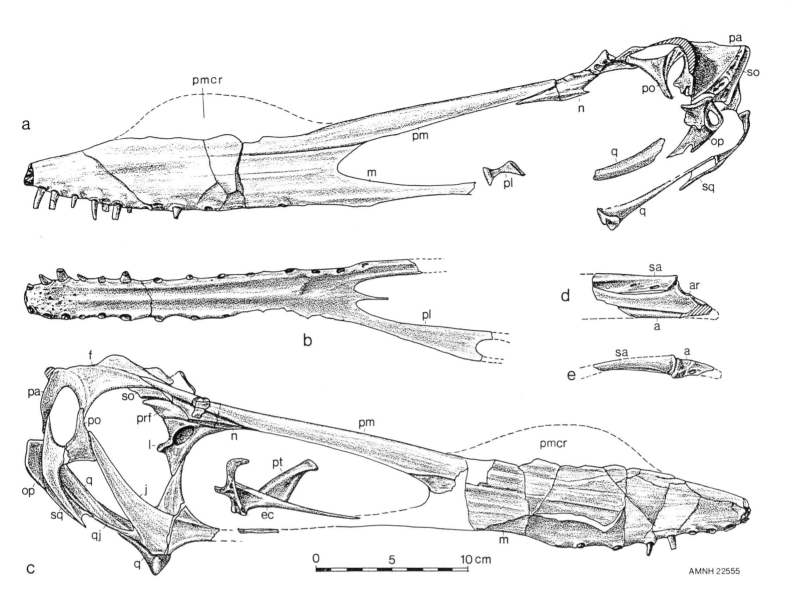

Anhanguera santanae. Skull, AMNH 22555, as preserved in left lateral view (A), in palatal view (B), in right lateral view (C); articular portion of the right mandible in medial (D) and in dorsal (E) views.

posteriorly; processus nasalis protruding into nasopreorbital opening; pterygoid, basipterygoid process of basisphenoid, and quadrate not fused, but separated by sharp sutures; dorsal edge of premaxilla in front of the nasopreorbital opening, developing into a carina or crest anteriorly.

Size: Skull length, restored, approximately 52 cm. Ulna length, restored, 35 cm. Estimated wing span approximately 4.7 meters.

Additional skeletal remains in the Bavarian State Collection of Paleontology and Historical Geology, originally assigned to *Araripesaurus* (Wellnhofer, 1985: 164-171), are now referred to *Anhanguera santanae.*

Specimen No. BSP 1982 I 91: The last cervical vertebra, a series of nine dorsal vertebrae (not fused to form a notarium as in *Santanadactylus*), three dorsal ribs, both

scapulae and the right coracoid (not fused) and a proximal fragment of the right humerus. The neural spine of the fifth dorsal has shallow lateral facets for articulation with the scapulae. Size: Scapula length 10 cm, coracoid length 12.6 cm.

Specimen No. BSP 1982 I 93: Distal parts of both humeri, proximal parts of both radii and ulnae from one individual. The distal articulation of the humerus shows two epiphyses with separate centers of ossification that make up the articular condyles. The assignment of this specimen is uncertain. Size: Distal width of humerus 4.15 cm, diameter of humerus shaft 1.3 cm.

Specimen No. AMNH 22555: The most complete Santana pterosaur found until now is in a large composite concretion from Jardim, Ceará (Axelrod Collection, American Museum

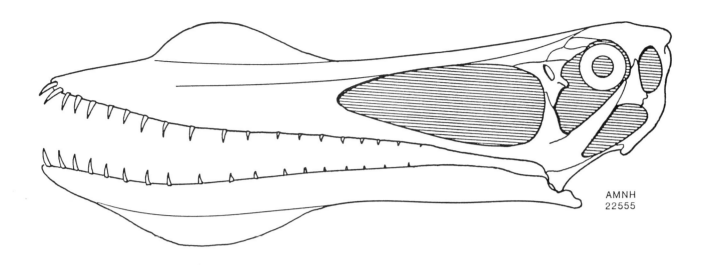

Anhanguera santanae. Restoration of the skull and mandible based on AMNH 22555.

of Natural History, New York). The bones could be prepared out of the limestone matrix completely. The specimen is assigned to *Anhanguera santanae* because the skull shows indications for a premaxillary crest.

The material includes the skull, the articular end of the right mandible, the complete vertebral series including the sacrals but without the caudals, several ribs, both scapulae and coracoids (not fused), the proximal parts of both humeri, both carpal regions with fragments of radius, ulna, and metacarpals. The pelvis is almost complete and preserved three-dimensionally along with the proximal ends of both femora and a few phalanges of the foot. This is the first time that so many postcranial elements of an individual of this size have been found preserved together with the skull.

Size: Length of the skull 46.5 cm, length of the precaudal vertebral series 50 cm, humerus length (restored) 19.2 cm, estimated wing span 4.55 meters.

A sagittal crest on the front end of the head would certainly have served as a display structure, perhaps for males. On the other hand, an aerodynamic function during flight or a hydrodynamic function during skimming the water may have played a minor role.

On the basis of the well-preserved pelvis of this individual, Wellnhofer (1988) concluded that *Anhanguera* could not have walked on the ground bipedally in a bird-like manner. The anatomical construction of the hip socket and of the head of the femur suggest rather a quadrupedal semierect stance and gait that probably was the case in all pterosaurs.

Family ?CRIORHYNCHIDAE Hooley, 1914

This family was established on the basis of fragmentary skull material of *Criorhynchus simus* (Owen) from the Cenomanian Cambridge Greensand of England. The front end of the premaxilla is rather high, suggesting a high sagittal crest at the anterior extremity of the skull. For this reason also the Santana genus *Tropeognathus* is tentatively assigned to this family.

Tropeognathus Wellnhofer, 1987
Diagnosis: Large pterodactyloid pterosaurs with premaxillary and mandibular sagittal crests at the front ends of skull and mandible; strong, curved teeth from tip of jaws backward for at least half length of jaws, decreasing in size.

The advantage of these large and high crests on the front ends of the skull and jaw could have been that they functioned like the keel of a boat, stabilizing the jaws in the water. We can suppose that these large pterosaurs were fish-eaters. When catching prey the tips of the jaws were submerged, skimming the water at high speed. Due to the keel-like V shape of the crests, flow resistance was reduced and the long head remained stable in this action. The terminal crests of *Tropeognathus* could thus be viewed as hydrodynamic rather than aerodynamic stabilizers.

Type species: *Tropeognathus mesembrinus* Wellnhofer, 1987
Tropeognathus mesembrinus Wellnhofer, 1987
Holotype: Bavarian State Collection of

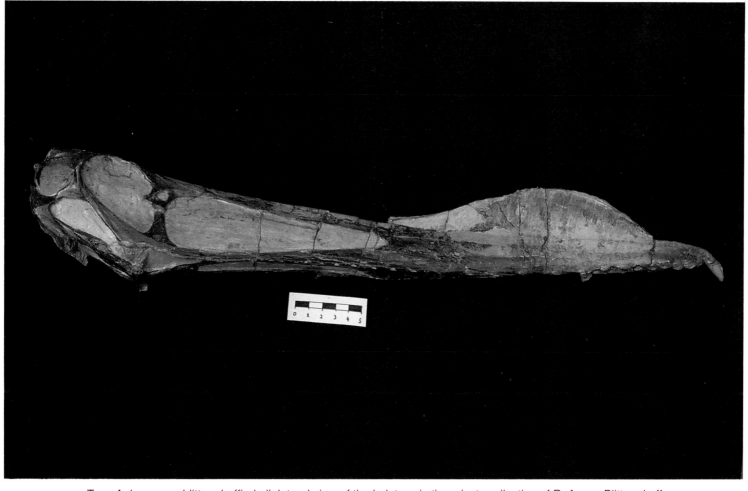

Top: *Anhanguera blittersdorffi*, skull, lateral view of the holotype in the private collection of R. A. von Blittersdorff.
Bottom: *Tupuxuara longicristatus*, partial skull with sagittal crest, the holotype, in the private collection of R. A. von Blittersdorff. Photos courtesy of A. Kellner.

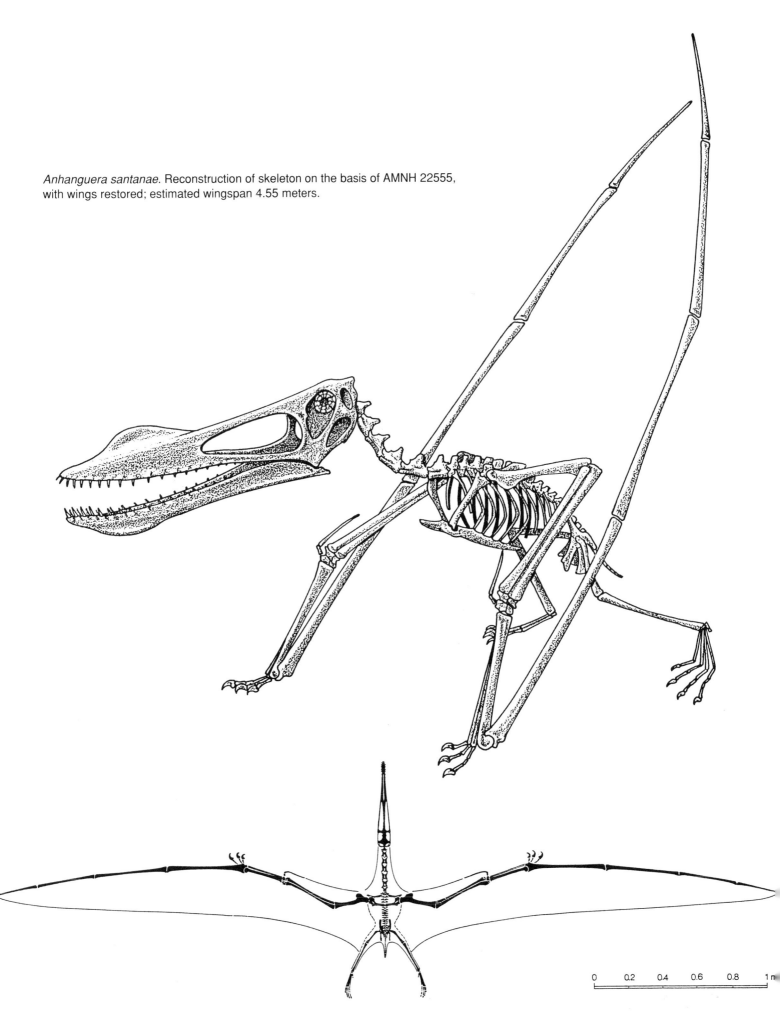

Anhanguera santanae. Reconstruction of skeleton on the basis of AMNH 22555, with wings restored; estimated wingspan 4.55 meters.

0   0.2   0.4   0.6   0.8   1 m

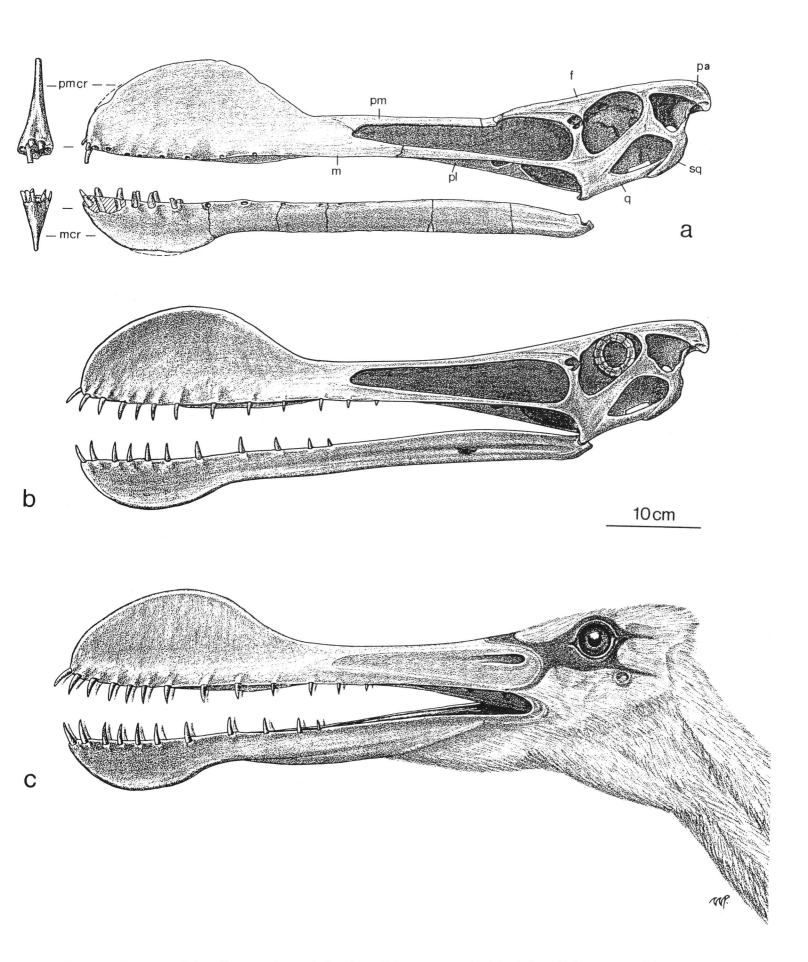

Tropeognathus mesembrinus. Type specimen, skull and mandible as preserved in lateral view with front aspect of the crested jaws (A); skull length 63 cm, Munich Collection. Restoration of the skull and mandible (B); life restoration of the head (C).

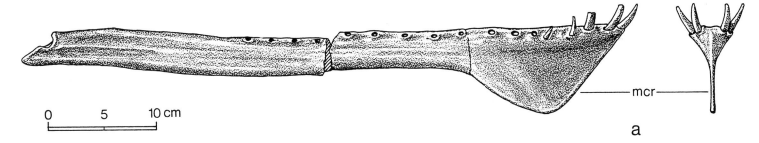

Tropeognathus robustus. Type specimen, lower jaw in lateral view with front aspect (A) and in dorsal view (B), Munich Collection. Length of mandible 56 cm, estimated wing span 6.2 meters, and thus probably the largest Santana pterosaur so far discovered. From Wellnhofer (1987).

BSP 1987 I 47

Paleontology and Historical Geology, Munich, No. BSP 1987 I 46; complete skull and mandible from one large concretion.

Diagnosis: *Tropeognathus* with high, rounded sagittal crest on top of premaxilla and similar but smaller mandibular crest on the symphysis; short and blunt parietal crest overhanging occiput; high medial ridge on the palate corresponding to a deep medial groove on mandibular symphysis; upper and lower jaws not expanded anteriorly; dentition with 13 premaxillary and maxillary teeth and 11 mandibular teeth each side.

Size: Total length of skull 63 cm, width over the quadrates 13.7 cm, maximum height of premaxillary crest 10.5 cm, length of mandible 52 cm. The size of the skull indicates a wing span for this individual of approximately 6 meters.

Tropeognathus robustus Wellnhofer, 1987

Holotype: Bavarian State Collection of Paleontology and Historical Geology, Munich, No. BSP 1987 I 47; lower jaw, complete but still partly enclosed in the concretion.

Diagnosis: *Tropeognathus* with deep mandibular crest; front margin straight, forming an angle of about 50° with upper edge of lower jaw; spatulate expanded anterior end of jaw; in dorsal view strong and long teeth visible, especially anteriorly, 17 in each side, widely spaced, over 65% length of the mandible.

Size: Total length of lower jaw 56 cm, depth of mandibular crest 7.6 cm, length of mandibular crest 14.5 cm. Based on the size of the lower jaw, the skull length of this individual can be calculated as 67 cm, and its wing span as approximately 6.2 meters. This makes *Tropeognathus robustus* the largest pterosaur from the Santana formation so far discovered.

Family indet.

Araripedactylus Wellnhofer, 1977

Diagnosis: Large pterodactyloid pterosaur with robust and straight first wing phalanx; relatively thick bone wall and short proximal process for extensor tendon.

Type species: *Araripedactylus dehmi* Wellnhofer, 1977.

Araripedactylus dehmi Wellnhofer, 1977

Holotype: Bavarian State Collection of Paleontology and Historical Geology, Munich, No. BSP 1975 I 166; first phalanx of a right wing finger, imbedded in a split concretion.

Diagnosis: As for genus.

Size: Length of the phalanx 55 cm, proximal width 6.5 cm, distal width 5 cm, minimal diameter of the shaft 2.2 cm, thickness of the bone wall in the middle part of the shaft 3 mm. Estimated wing span 4.8 meters.

More complete material, still to be discovered, possibly could clear the assignment of this single wing phalanx to one of the taxa based only on large skulls, i.e., *Cearadactylus* or *Tropeognathus*.

Cearadactylus Leonardi and Borgomanero, 1985

Diagnosis: Large pterodactyloid pterosaurs with long and low skull; expanded, spatulate front ends of jaws; premaxillary teeth and front teeth of the mandible much longer and stronger than posterior ones; no occlusion of the jaws possible, leaving a gap, but posterior parts of the jaws are closed, and maxillary dentition occludes with mandibular teeth; maxillary teeth spaced, short, and conical; no sagittal crest in the anterior part of the skull; postero-ventral corner of long nasopreorbital fenestra forms a right angle.

Life restoration of *Tropeognathus* catching fish. Redrawn and changed after a drawing by Peter Schouten.

Type species: *Cearadactylus atrox* Leonardi and Borgomanero, 1985.

Cearadactylus atrox Leonardi and Borgomanero, 1985

Holotype: Collection of Mr. Guido Borgomanero, Curitiba, PR, Brazil, No. F-PV-93; large skull with mandible enclosed in a limestone concretion. Posterior part of skull with skull roof, braincase, and occiput missing.

Diagnosis: As for genus.

Size: Length of the skull as preserved 54 cm, as restored 57 cm. Length of the mandible 48.2 cm. The skull length indicates a wing span of approximately 5.5 meters.

Undetermined material

Campos, Ligabue, and Taquet (1984) published a preliminary description of a remarkable pterosaur specimen from the Santana formation. It was one nodule containing a portion of a right femur, the tibia, fibula, metatarsals, and phalanges of the right foot, and the folded wing with the radius, ulna, carpals, pteroid, the metacarpal IV, and the phalanges of the wing finger. The bones are still connected and well preserved. In addition, the imprint of the wing membrane is perfectly preserved around the bones of the wing.

Although wing impressions have been known

Cearadactylus atrox. Restoration of skull and mandible based on the type specimen. Skull length 57 cm. From Wellnhofer (1987).

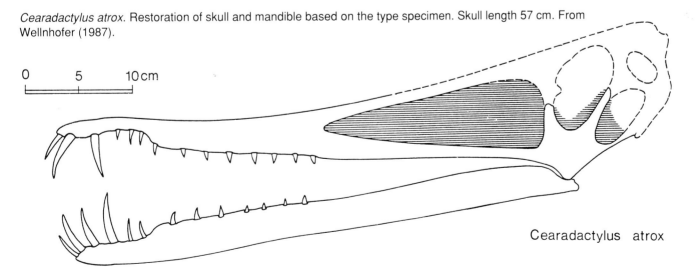

0   5   10 cm

Cearadactylus atrox

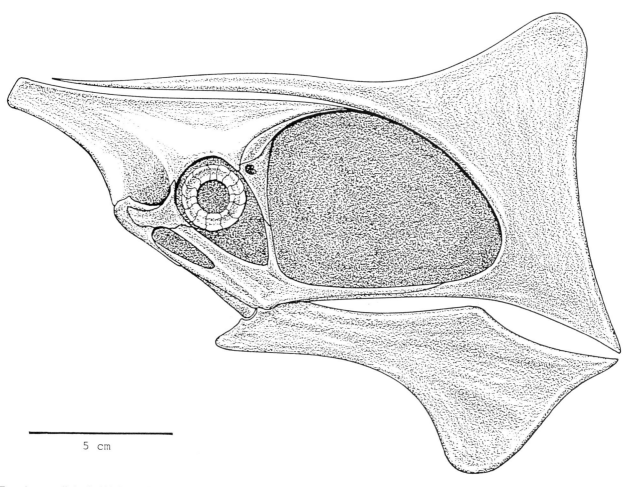

Tapejara wellnhoferi Kellner. Reconstruction of skull in lateral view, based on the holotype and specimen AMNH 24440 (see photos on pages 360-361), showing the greatly enlarged antorbital fenestra and spectacular crests on the skull and mandible. Illustration courtesy of P. Wellnhofer.

from many Upper Jurassic Sölnhofen pterosaurs, this was the first time that the wing membrane on skeletal elements has been observed on a South American pterosaur. In several places on the black and brown impressions of the wing area, parallel striations could be recognized. This is another evidence for the presence of strengthening fibers, the actinofibrillae, embedded in the membrane of the pterosaur wing, providing stability and toughness without diminishing flexibility and elasticity.

(P. Wellnhofer)

Supplementary Notes and Comments

The first pterosaur from the Santana formation (Aptian-Albian) was found about two decades ago. The material consists of wing bones that were studied by Llewellyn Ivor Price (1971) and named *Araripesaurus castilhoi*. Since that time many additional specimens of pterosaurian remains have been recovered from those sediments, including skulls. Many different species have been described, but some of these were based on very incomplete material (see Wellnhofer's contribution in this volume), so several eventually may be relegated to synonymy with others.

Some researchers believe that the pterosaurs from the Santana formation are related closely to those of the Cambridge Greensand (Cenomanian) and have classified some of the Brazilian species in two pterosaur families found in those sediments from England: Ornithocheiridae (Price, 1971; Wellnhofer, 1985) and Criorhynchidae (Buisonjé, 1980; Wellnhofer, 1987).

Other paleontologists have suggested that a new group of pterosaurs is present in the Santana formation. This group is represented by

Anhanguera blittersdorffi, which is placed in a new family Anhangueridae by Campos and Kellner (1985a, 1985b). The main characteristic of those pterosaurs is the presence of two sagittal crests, one at the anterior part of the premaxillae and a second one at the ventral part of the mandibular symphysis.

Other interesting pterosaurs described recently from the Santana formation represent the first toothless examples from South America. One is *Tupuxuara longicristatus* Kellner and Campos, 1988, with a low sagittal crest beginning at the anterior part of the premaxillae and extending to the back of the skull. Another is *Tapejara wellnhoferi* Kellner, 1989, with a much higher sagittal crest. Togther, *Tapejara* and *Tupuxuara* are believed to form a monophyletic group of specialized toothless pterosaurs and are placed in a new family (Tapejaridae Kellner, 1989). These genera are very different from other toothless pterosaurs such as *Pteranodon* and *Nyctosaurus* from the Niobrara formation (Santonian) of the USA. The present stage of investigations therefore suggests that there are at least two very distinctive groups of pterosaurs in the Santana formation; one is represented by the Anhangueridae, and the other is a new family characterized by an enormous crest, a very large nasopreorbital fenestra, and the lack of teeth. At present both families are known only from the Araripe basin. It is worthwhile to point out that for the morphological study of pterosaurs, the sediments of the Santana Formation are surely one of the most important in the world, because the preservation of the material is the best ever reported.

Suborder PTERODACTYLOIDEA
incertae sedis
Family Tapejaridae Kellner, 1989

Tapejara Kellner, 1989
Emended diagnosis: Large and very high sagittal crest on anterior part of skull, extended backward; rostrum very inclined downward; palate lacks a mesial ridge; orbit situated below level of upper margin of nasopreorbital fenestra.

Type species: *Tapejara wellnhoferi* Kellner, 1989.
Tapejara wellnhoferi Kellner, 1989
Diagnosis: As for genus.
Holotype: CD-R-080, Desiree collection of Rainer Alexander von Blittersdorff, Rio de Janeiro; incomplete skull with the anterior part of both sides as far as the lower margin of the orbit and the lower temporal fenestra, the left

lacrimal, and some unidentified bones.
Tapejara? sp.
Material: AMNH 24440; fairly complete toothless pterosaur skull and mandible approx. 20 cm total preserved length; strongly compressed from side to side, with crest extending from snout along entirety of premaxilla and to back of skull; mandible also with deep ventral crest anteriorly.

Comments: The presence of a mandibular as well as a prefrontal crest in this specimen is an interesting feature. The observable features of this specimen indicate affinity with *Tapejara*, but this can be confirmed only after careful preparation.

Tupuxuara Kellner and Campos, 1988
Emended diagnosis: Low sagittal crest on the anterior part of the skull, extended backward; rostrum horizontal; mesial ridge on palate; first wing phalanx and metacarpal IV long and slender; first wing phalanx with two pneumatic foramina, one situated at superior part of articulation with metacarpal IV.

Type species: *Tupuxuara longicristatus* Kellner and Campos, 1988.
Tupuxuara longicristatus Kellner and Campos, 1988
Diagnosis: As for genus.
Holotype: CD-R-003, Desirée Collection of Rainer Alexander von Blittersdorf, Rio de Janeiro; anterior part of skull with sagittal crest, distal part of right metacarpals I to IV, proximal part of both first wing phalanges, distal part of left metacarpal IV, and one ungual, all belonging to the same individual; Santana formation, Chapada do Araripe.

Comments: The Tapejaridae comprise the toothless pterosaurs of the Santana formation. The most important derived character of this group is the unusual position of the orbit, which in lateral view is situated below the upper level of the nasopreorbital fenestra. Another outstanding feature of these pterosaurs is the sagittal crest, which begins on the anterior part of the skull and extends backward, apparently reaching the back of the head. The dimensions of the nasopreorbital fenestra are also remarkable for their great size (relative to the rest of the skull, they are larger than in any other known pterosaurs).

(A. W. A. Kellner)

Assemblages: The provenance of many pterosaurs from the Santana formation is poorly documented, but discussions with local collectors suggest that Jardim is the principal area, with Santana a close second.

DINOSAURS OF THE SANTANA FORMATION
with Comments on Other Brazilian Occurrences

Introduction

Dinosaur remains have been found in a number of Brazilian sedimentary basins. These are mostly Cretaceous in age, except those from the Santa Maria formation (Triassic of the State of Rio Grande do Sul). This contribution gives a complete listing of dinosaur localities known from Brazil. Some results of current studies on unpublished dinosaur material from the Araripe basin also are presented.

The first announcement of dinosaurs in South America was made in 1859 and refers to a centrum of a dorsal vertebra found in the Cretaceous sediments of the Reconcavo basin in the State of Bahia (Allport, 1859; Price, 1961). This vertebra is, however, referable to the crocodilian *Sarcosuchus hartti* (P. Taquet, personal communication).

Dinosaurs from the Araripe basin

In recent years some very interesting dinosaur material has been recovered from the Santana formation (Romualdo member). The first to be noticed was reported by Leonardi and Borgomanero (1981). They described a possible ischium fragment (Borgomanero Collection CB-CV-F-089), referred with doubt to an ornithischian of undeterminable family. Although this material probably is dinosaurian, its skeletal position is questionable and its classification difficult. More complete preparation is required.

The second record of dinosaurs in the rocks of the Araripe basin was presented by Campos (1985). It is the centrum of a procoelous vertebra, probably a cervical one, collected in the vicinity of Sobradinho, Ceará. The absence of diagnostic anatomical features makes it difficult to assign to either of the two orders of dinosaurs. This vertebra (DGM 1474-R) is deposited in the paleontological collection of the Departamento Nacional da Produção Mineral, Rio de Janeiro.

Other evidence of Araripean dinosaurs is provided by an almost complete manus with five fingers and some bones of the carpus. At present, the study of this fossil hand is being carried out and preliminary findings spur comparison with African theropods. The

original piece belongs to the Josa Collection, and a cast of it has been donated by the Museum national d'Histoire Naturelle in Paris to the DNPM, Rio de Janeiro (DGM 1470-R).

At the present time, the most outstanding dinosaur remains from the area are two calcareous nodules with a complete pelvic girdle, parts of the hind limbs (one toe has a large sickle claw), and a series of articulated caudal vertebrae, deposited in the Desiree Collection (CD-R-011) in Rio de Janeiro. Following preliminary studies, these remains are tentatively compared to a specialized predatory dinosaur of the megalosaurian type. In the same collection is another piece from an Araripean dinosaur, including three sacral and six caudal vertebrae (CD-R-064), now being prepared.

Dinosaurs from other Brazilian localities

Santa Maria formation (Rio Grande do Sul) The skeletons of the oldest dinosaurs from Brazil come from the Santa Maria formation (Late Triassic) in the southernmost part of the Paraná basin. There are two different saurischian taxa described, the prosauropod *Spondylosoma absconditum* Huene, 1942, and the primitive theropod *Staurikosaurus pricei* Colbert, 1970. These dinosaurs were associated with rhynchocephalians, dicynodonts, cynodonts, and thecodonts.

Northern Brazil Inside São Marcos Bay, in the state of Maranhão, the remains of Cretaceous dinosaurs were reported by Price (1947).

In the state of Amazonas, a dinosaur tooth was retrieved from the core sample of an oil drilling operation at Nova Olinda do Norte, extending the known distribution of these reptiles in the Cretaceous to the Amazon region (Price, 1961).

Rio do Peixe basin, Paraíba (northeastern Brazil) Ever since Luciano J. de Moraes discovered two dinosaur tracks in 1924, hundreds of others have been discovered in Cretaceous rocks of the Rio do Peixe basin, in the state of Paraíba. Almost all these have been uncovered by Guiseppe Leonardi, according to whom both saurischian and ornithischian

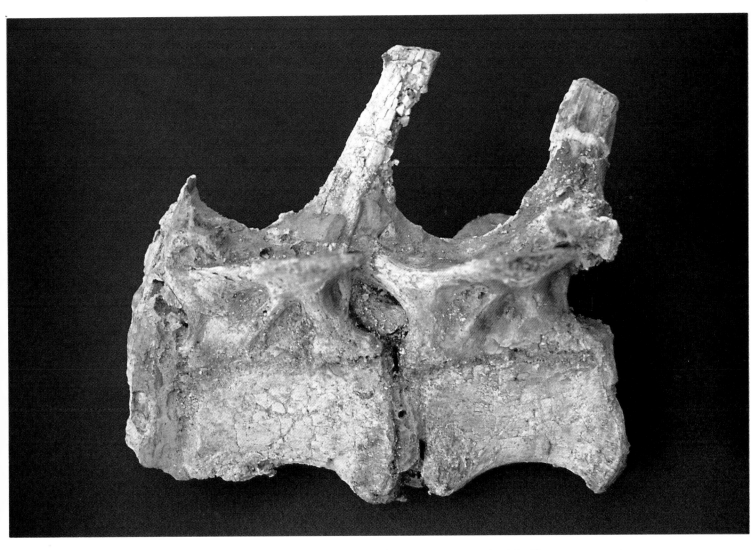

Top: Undetermined dinosaur, caudal vertebrae. Bottom: Undetermined dinosaur, part of pelvis. Photos courtesy A. Kellner.

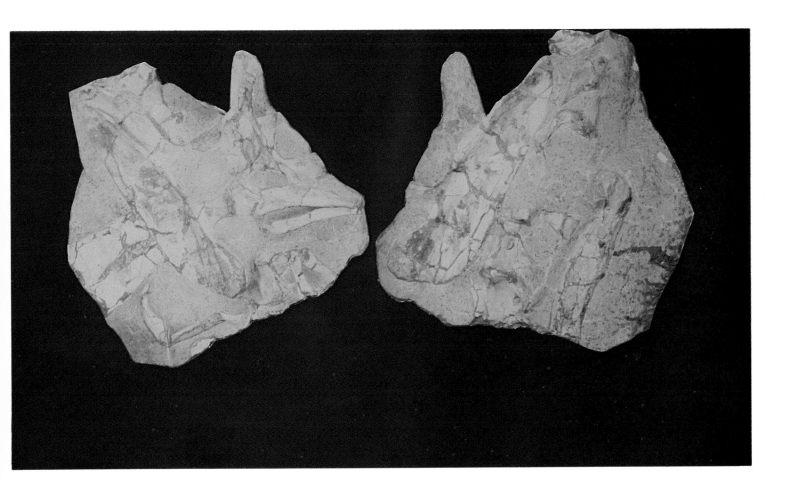

Map showing all Brazilian dinosaur localities: RIO GRANDE DO SUL: 1. Santa Maria; SÃO PAULO: 2. Presidente Bernardes; 3. Adamantina; 4. Pacaembu Paulista; 5. Guararapes; 6. São José do Rio Preto; 7. ibirá; 8. Colina; 9. Monte Alto; MINAS GERAIS: 10. Uberaba; MATO GROSSO: 11. Cambambe Hill; CEARÁ: 12. Sobradinho; 13. Chapada do Araripe; PARAÍBA: 14. Rio do Peixe; MARANHÃO: 15. São Marcos Bay; AMAZONAS: 16. Nova Olinda do Norte.

dinosaurs are represented by the trackways (Price, 1976; Leonardi, 1984).

Bauru formation (São Paulo, Mato Grosso, Minas Gerais) The Late Cretaceous Bauru formation of the Paraná basin has produced some interesting dinosaur remains. The most important localities are situated in the states of São Paulo, Mato Grosso, and Minas Gerais. Skeletal remains were first noted from Cambambe Hill, northeastern Cuiabá, in Mato Grosso (Price, 1961). The earliest evidence for these reptiles in the state of São Paulo dates from 1909, when sauropod bones and teeth were reported from São José do Rio Preto (Ihering, 1911; Price, 1961), including a tooth that was attributed to a species of *Thecodontosaurus* (Woodward, 1910: 483; Roxo, 1929; Huene, 1931: 190; Moraes Rego, 1935). A femur and teeth collected in the vicinity of the Colina Station near Barretos were doubtfully attributed to *Megalosaurus* by Pacheco (1913).

References to the genera *Ceratosaurus* and *Laelaps* among the material from Colina, made respectively by Roxo (1929: 39) and Moraes Rego (1935), are considered erroneous. Moraes Rego has also reported *Ceratosaurus* from a locality at Monte Alto. Huene (1931) referred to carnosaur teeth from Guarucaia (today Presidente Bernardes; Mezzalira, 1966: 92). More carnosaur teeth were found in Adamantina (Mezzalira, 1949, 1966).

Parts of the left femur, a right humerus, and a dorsal vertebra, found in the municipality of São José do Rio Preto, São Paulo, have been referred to a titanosaurid (atlantosaurid), *Antarctosaurus brasiliensis*, by Arid and Vizotto (1971). Seventeen tooth fragments attributed to carnosaurs were found in the municipality of Ibira (Arid and Vizotto, 1963: 181). Sauropod teeth were found along a railway in the municipality of Pacaemba Paulista (Mezzalira, 1966: 93). Skeletal remains of titanosaurids occur in the Bauru formation in the region of Guararapes, São Paulo. The finds include a diaphysis with a distal epiphysis of a left femur and part of the proximal epiphysis of a left humerus, belonging to different individuals (Leonardi and Duszczac, 1977).

In the state of Minas Gerais, the most important work on Brazilian dinosaurs was performed by L. I. Price in the locality of Periopolis, municipality of Uberaba, in the Triãngulo Mineiro region. The Bauru formation here has produced a considerable number of bones and teeth, especially of sauropods referred to the family Titanosauridae (Price, 1961). Dinosaur eggs also have been reported; one of these was attributed by Price (1951) to Saurischia (Titanosauridae), and others have been referred to Ornithischia (Ceratopsida).

(D. de A. Campos, A. W. A. Kellner)

UNDETERMINED FEATHER

Class AVES
incertae sedis

The first (and so far the only) evidence for a Brazilian Mesozoic bird recently was described by Martins-Neto and Kellner (1988). A single well-preserved feather was recovered from the lacustrine laminated limestone sequence of the Crato member. The specimen (now deposited in the Instituto de Geociências of the University of São Paulo, catalog no. GP/2T-136) is probably from the municipality of Santana do Cariri, Ceará, and likely as not comes from one of the sites around Crato or Nova Olinda, but unfortunately there is no precise locality information.

The feather is well-preserved and measures approximately 64 mm in length and 8 mm in maximum breadth. Preservation is sufficiently good to permit recognition of barb impressions in the asymmetrical calamus and rhachis (parts of the vane), although finer structures such as barbules hooking individual barbs together have not been described. The unbarbed quill is approximately 12 mm long.

Mesozoic bird remains are exceptionally rare, and the discovery of this feather is of considerable scientific interest. Furthermore, it is from a locality that already is known to produce small, well-preserved vertebrate fossils including fishes (*Dastilbe, Cladocyclus*) and a frog, raising the prospects for future discoveries of more complete bird fossils. These limestones therefore offer considerable potential as a source of Mesozoic avian skeletons. Other fossils (insects, plant seeds) from these deposits indicate that an abundant and varied food source for birds certainly existed. According to Dr. G. Barrowclough, an ornithologist at the American Museum of Natural History, the solitary feather recovered from this limestone may represent either one of the trailing primaries or else a secondary flight feather. If we assume that it came from a volant bird with essentially modern flight characteristics, Dr. Barrowclough suggests the bird was approximately the size of a brush finch, with a body weight of perhaps 35-40 g. Of course this should not be taken to imply anything concerning the actual relationships of this fossil.

The scanty Mesozoic avian fossil record includes several Upper Jurassic skeletons of *Archaeopteryx* from Sölnhofen, West Germany (reviewed in Wellnhofer, 1988) and a feather from the Karatau lake deposits of the USSR (Rautian, 1978). A few other Lower Cretaceous localities around the world have produced avian fossils, including Montsech (Spain), Jezzini (Lebanon; Schlee, 1973), Khurilt-Ulan-Bulak (Mongolia; Kuroshkin, 1982), and Victoria and Queensland, Australia (Waldman, 1970; Elzanowski, 1983; Molnar, 1986). Upper Cretaceous bird fossils are known from the Niobrara Chalk of North America (Williston, 1896; Marsh, 1897; Cracraft, 1986).

Assemblage: Crato limestone.

(A. W. A. Kellner,
R. G. Martins-Neto, J. G. Maisey)

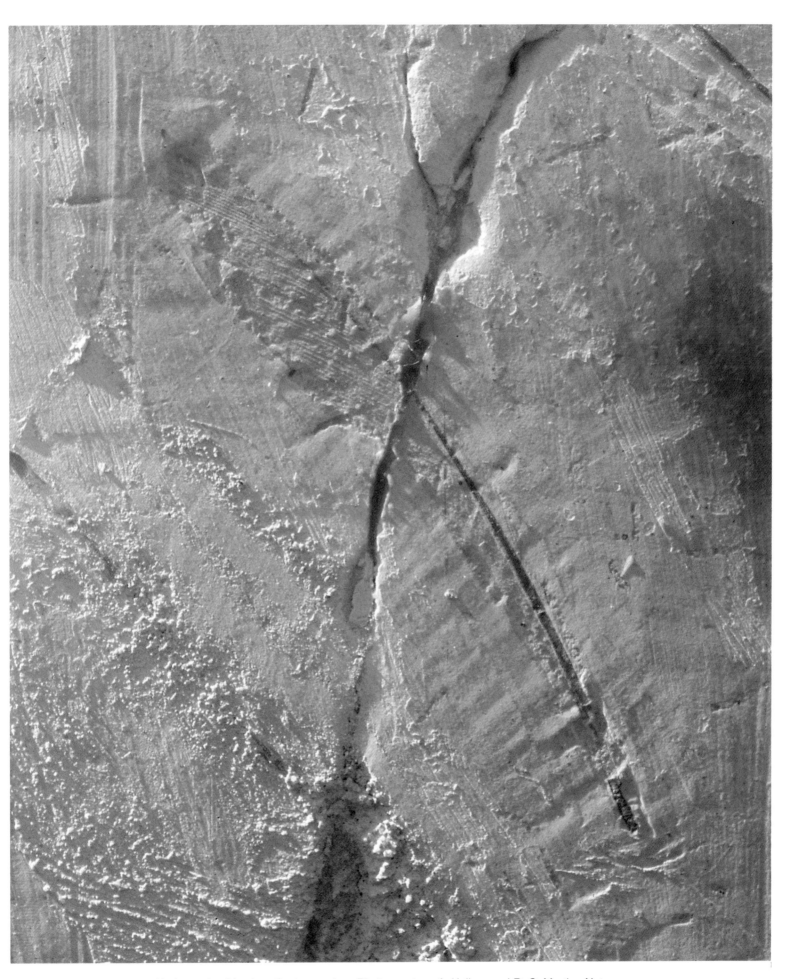

Undetermined feather, Crato member. Photo courtesy A. Kellner and R. G. Martins-Neto.

ECHINODERMATA

Class ECHINOIDEA
  Order CASSIDULOIDA
  Family CLYPEIDAE Lambert, 1839
Genus *Pygurus* Lambert, 1839
Pygurus tinocoi Beurlen, 1966
  1966 *Pygurus (Echinopygus) tinocoi* Beurlen:
458
  1973 *Pygurus (Echinopygus) tinocoi* Beurlen;
Mabesoone and Tinoco: 104
  1979 *Pygurus (Echinopygurus) tinocoi* Beurlen;
Lima: 548
  1981 *Pygurus tinocoi* Beurlen: Brito: 517
  Holotype: No. 997, Instituto de Geociências
da Universidade Federal de Pernambuco.
  Localities: Santana formation, near
Rancharia and Lagoa de Dentro, in the extreme
west of the Chapada do Araripe, close to the
borders of Ceará and Piauí.
  Remarks: Brito (1981) noted similarities with
Pygurus jagueyanus from the Albian of Colombia
and with *P. africanus* from the Albian of
Angola. He suggested (ibid., p. 526) that
further investigation might result in transferring
P. tinocoi to the genus *Astrolampas*.

  Family FAUJASIDAE Lambert, 1905
Genus *Pygidiolampas* Clark, 1923
Pygidiolampas araripensis (Beurlen, 1966)
  1966 *Faujasia araripensis* Beurlen: 456
  1973 *Faujasia araripensis* Beurlen; Mabesoone
& Tinoco: 104
  1977 *Faujasia araripensis* Beurlen; Lima: 548
  1981 *Pygidiolampas araripensis* (Beurlen);
Brito: 524
  Holotype: No. 999, Instituto de Geociências
da Universidade Federal de Pernambuco.
  Paratype: No. 998, IGUFP.
  Localities: Santana formation, near
Rancharia and Lagoa de Dentro, Chapada do
Araripe, Ceará.
  Remarks: This species occurs at the same
localities and stratigraphic level as *Pygurus
tinocoi*.

Echinoids are exclusively marine organisms
today and according to the fossil record always
have been so. The presence of these echinoids
within the Santana formation therefore has
paleoecological and stratigraphic significance,
but only with certain qualifications. Firstly,
these fossils are uncommon, suggesting that
echinoids were not well established in the
Araripe basin at the time. Secondly, the
occurrence is entirely restricted to a
stratigraphic level that is considerably above the
concretion-bearing horizons in which the fossil
fishes occur (Beurlen, 1966; Mabesoone and
Tinoco, 1973; Brito, 1981). The presence of
these echinoids thus provides no information
concerning the habitats of the fossil fishes from
the Santana formation. Thirdly, the species are
known only from the western part of the
Araripe basin and are thus of little correlative
value, although the genera broadly suggest a
Late Aptian to Albian age.

A marine incursion (perhaps of limited
duration) is indicated toward the end of the
period during which the Santana formation was
accumulated. Beurlen (1966) suggested that this
transgressive episode was linked with formation
of the South Atlantic. According to recent
studies, the final separation of northeastern
Brazil from Africa occurred immediately to the
east at about that time (Reyment and Dingle,
1987; Petri, 1987; Szatmari, et al., 1987; Popoff,
1988). It is tempting to correlate this stage in
rifting with the late transgression witnessed in
the Santana formation, but such a correlation
cannot be documented with any accuracy.
Echinoids have been recorded from the Lower
Cretaceous Riachuelo formation of the Sergipe-
Alagoas basin and Jandaíra formation of the
Potiguar basin (Lima, 1977).

(J. G. Maisey)

THE SANTANA FORMATION INSECTS

Introduction

In terms of sheer numbers of individuals, biomass, numbers of species, and their existence over geological time, insects have been and continue to be the most successful terrestrial organisms. Present estimates place the number of named species at nearly 900,000, but, based on the rates of descriptions for new species, it is quite likely that between 2 and 2.5 million species actually exist.

The fossil record for insects is nearly 370 million years long and much remains to be learned about their paleontology. The important Lower Cretaceous insect assemblage from the Chapada do Araripe is the best testimony as to how ignorant we are about fossil insects, particularly those from the Cretaceous period.

The oldest known insects are Collembola and Archaeognatha from Lower Devonian deposits in England and Quebec. Insects with wings—considered one of the pivotal morphological innovations of insects (and they fossilize more readily than most other portions of the body)—appeared first in the Carboniferous period and are represented by primitive forms allied to extant Ephemeroptera and Odonata (including huge forms in the Protodonata). Numerous orders occurred from the Carboniferous to the Permian, when many of them became extinct, such as the Palaeodictyoptera, Megasecoptera, Diaphanopterodea, Miomoptera, Protelytroptera, Caloneurodea, and Protorthoptera. It is really from the Permian and later that orders of insects with representatives most closely related to living forms first appeared, such as Coleoptera, Dermaptera, Phasmatodea, Psocoptera, Megaloptera, Raphidioptera, Neuroptera, and Mecoptera. A few groups are extremely conservative, such as the mayflies (Ephemeroptera, mentioned above), the dragonflies (Odonata), cockroaches (Blattodea), and the Orthoptera, which have records extending from the Pennsylvanian. Virtually none of the living orders have family-level records extending back beyond the Lower Cretaceous. There has always been great uncertainty as to whether this observation is a result of a fossil record highly biased in lieu of Cretaceous representatives or in fact represents reality. The fossil insects discussed in this volume are thus of relevance to this question.

A detailed account of most of the major localities and deposits of Cretaceous insects is given in Hennig (1981). Several deposits have been discovered since then, including ones in Australia, China, Botswana, Mongolia, and Spain. There are only three Gondwanan Cretaceous insect localities, and the Chapada do Araripe has yielded by far the largest and most diverse assemblage; it may in fact be the largest Cretaceous assemblage in the world.

Cretaceous insects have actually been known from the Chapada do Araripe for nearly 40 years, the earliest report being that of da Costa Lima (1950), who described two mayfly nymphs. Other papers subsequently appeared by Pinto and Ornellas (1974), for several true bugs (Heteroptera); Brito (1984b), on the general aspects of a collection of 56 specimens; Pinto and Purper (1986) on a cockroach; Martins-Neto (1987) on an acridoid (grasshopper-like insect); and Wighton (1987) on a genus of dragonfly (Odonata).

At least 15 orders of insects (all living) are represented in the assemblage (Ephemeroptera, Odonata, Dermaptera, Isoptera, Homoptera, Hymenoptera, Raphidioptera, Diptera, Trichoptera, Blattodea, Coleoptera, Orthoptera, Neuroptera, Phasmatodea [based on a fragment and not treated further], and Heteroptera). Living orders not yet known to occur in the assemblage include Archaeognatha, Thysanura, Mantodea, Grylloblattodea, Plecoptera, Megaloptera, Lepidoptera, and (not unexpectedly) orders of tiny and/or highly specialized (e.g., parasitic) forms such as Zoraptera, Embioptera, Psocoptera, Phthiraptera, Thysanoptera, Strepsiptera, and Siphonaptera. These insect fossils occur in laminated limestones from the Crato member of the Santana formation, a lacustrine sequence containing numerous specimens of the small gonorynchiform fish *Dastilbe*. No insect remains have been found yet in the fossiliferous concretions of the overlying Romualdo member.

Specimens can be prepared by physically removing large amounts of matrix around the body of the specimen and allowing a 1-2% solution of acetic acid to dissolve the calcium carbonate lying over the fragile wings and around the antennae and legs. Scanning electron microscopy has revealed that the impressions of ommatidia (eye facets), hair fringes, setae, and

Top row: Adult mayflies (Ephemeroptera). Upper center: Mayfly nymph (left), dragonfly nymph (right). Lower center: Adult dragonflies. Bottom: Dragonfly wing (left) and adult damselfly (right). Photos by D. Grimaldi.

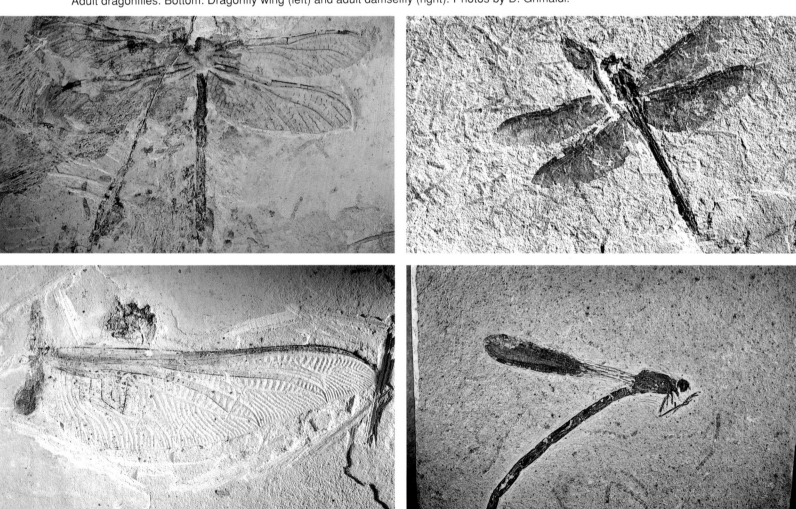

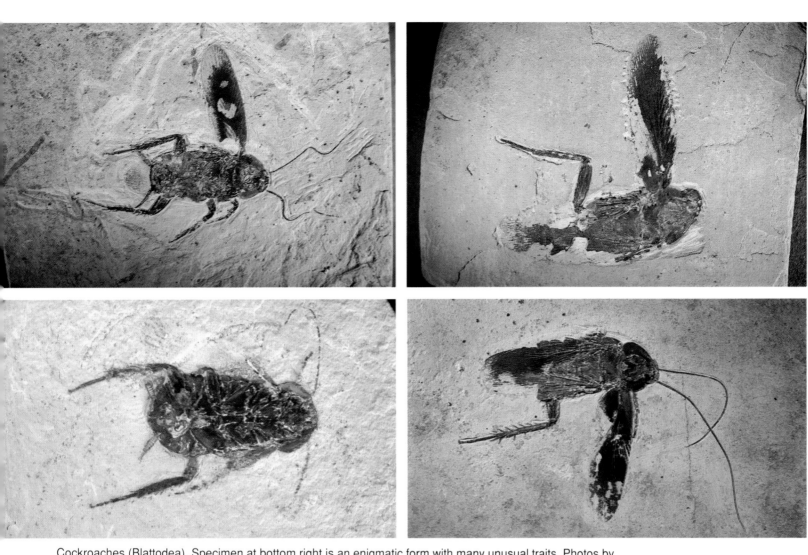

Cockroaches (Blattodea). Specimen at bottom right is an enigmatic form with many unusual traits. Photos by D. Grimaldi.

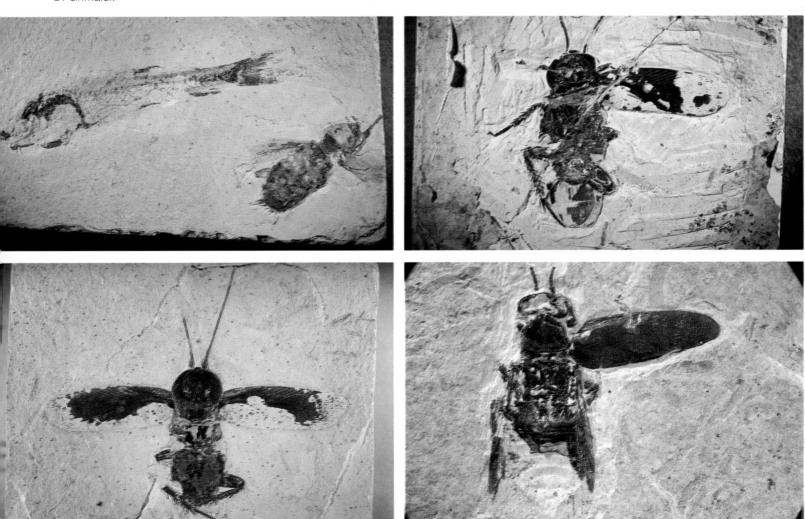

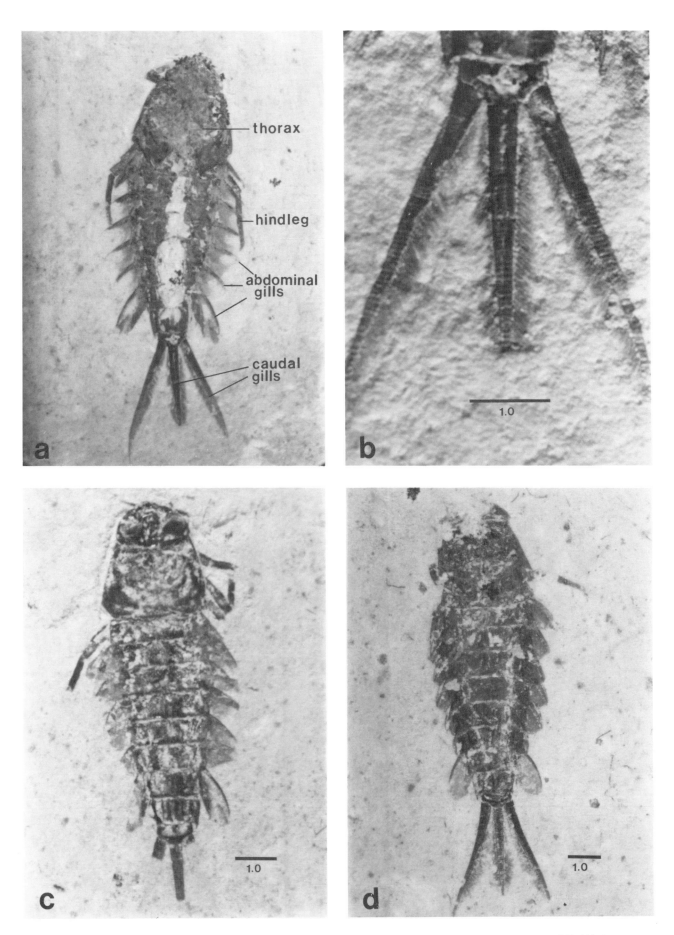

Ephemeroptera (mayfly) nymphs, showing details of caudal gills and gill filaments in (B). Scale bars in all B&W photos are in mm.

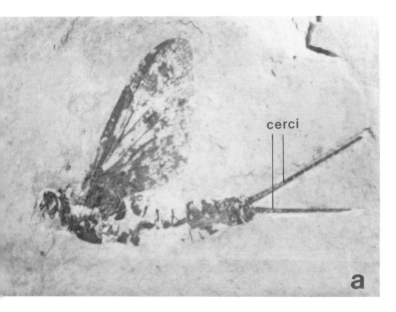

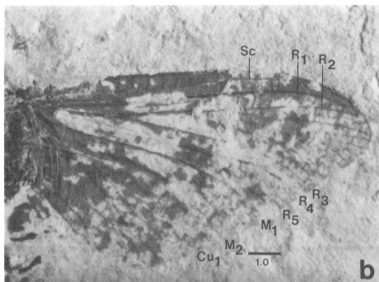

Adult Ephemeroptera (mayflies), showing details of forewing venation in (B).

the fine hairs and punctures on the cuticle of most specimens are preserved in considerable relief. Automated X-ray diffraction indicates that the specimens are composed of almost pure goethite (iron oxide hydroxide); in fact, despite the natural appearance of some of the specimens, no original carbon or cuticle is at all present.

The following is an order-by-order account of the major insect groups represented in the assemblage. Because the Santana insects have been treated in detail in Grimaldi (1990), this chapter only attempts to present an overview of the group. A listing of known species will be found on page 434.

Ephemeroptera

This order, the mayflies, consists of soft-bodied, frail insects whose immature stages live in fresh water. Since these insects are unique for being able to molt as adults one or more times, the winged stage is usually termed "alate." Alates are characterized by a complex network of wing veins, particularly many cross veins; reduced antennae; wings that are held vertically over the abdomen when at rest; and long, trailing caudal (tail) filaments. The nymphs can be extremely abundant on the bottoms of streams and ponds, where some forms actively filter feed or burrow and are even predaceous. Nymphs characteristically have gills along the sides of the abdomen.

Among the mayflies in the assemblage (first reported by Costa Lima, 1950), both alates and nymphs are well represented. The following families have been tentatively identified: Siphlonuridae (nymphs and alates), Oligoneuriidae (nymphs and alates),

Ephemeridae (alates), Euthyplociidae (alates), Hexagenitidae, Potamanthidae (?) (alates), and Leptophlebiidae (?) (nymphs). These represent the first fossil representatives for the families Oligoneuriidae and Euthyplociidae, and possibly for the Potamanthidae as well. The Potamanthidae, interestingly, are presently Holarctic and Oriental in distribution. Some

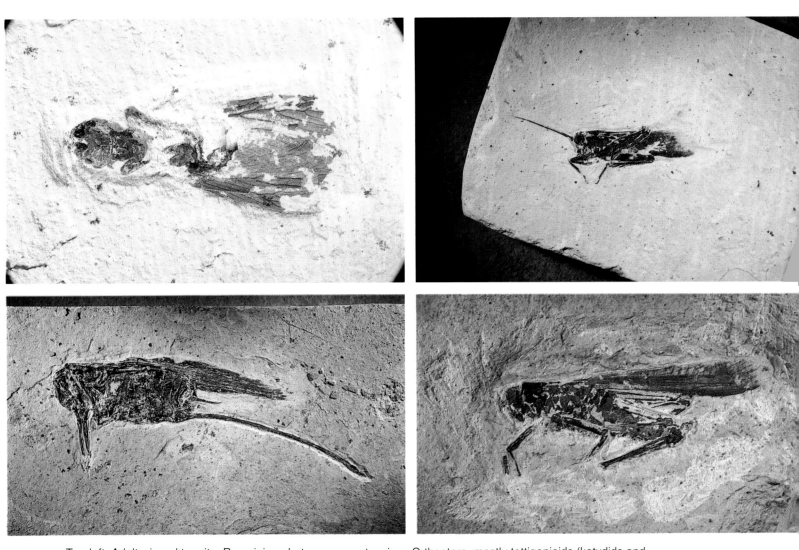

Top left: Adult winged termite. Remaining photos represent various Orthoptera, mostly tettigonioids (katydids and relatives) except bottom row, which shows tridactylid pygmy mole crickets. Photos by D. Grimaldi.

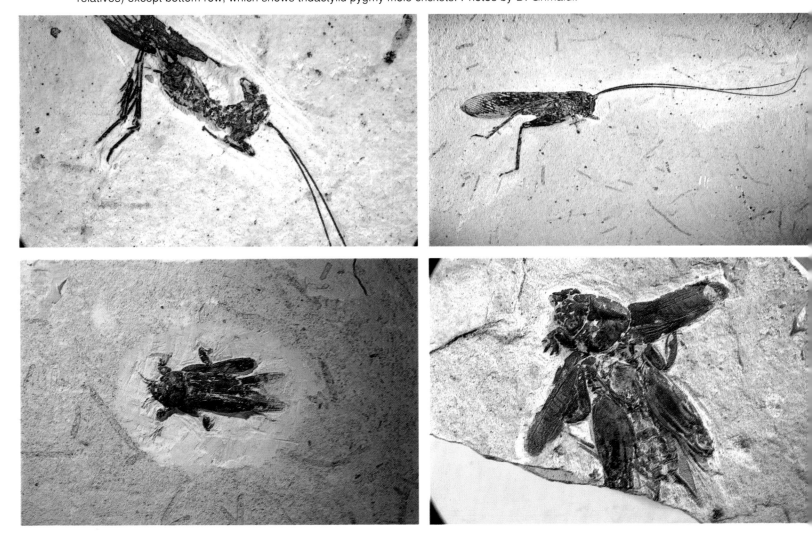

Ground crickets, family Gryllidae, subfamily Gryllinae. Photos by D. Grimaldi.

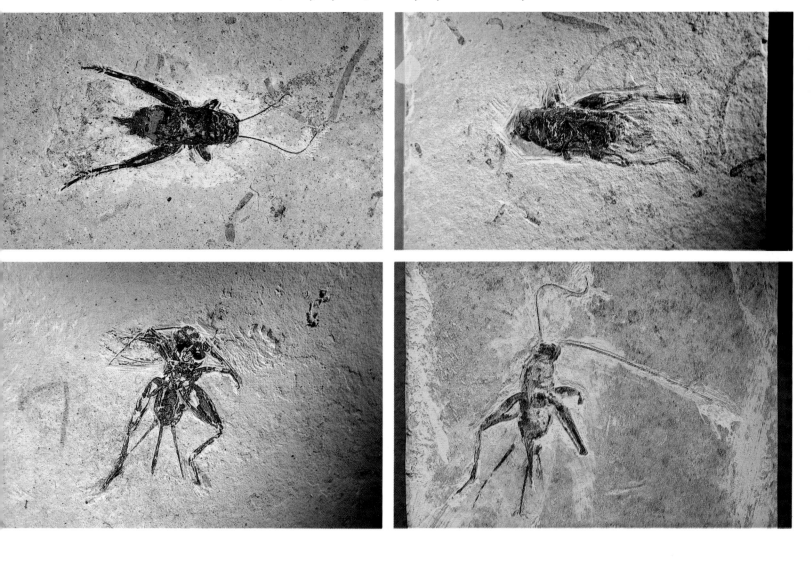

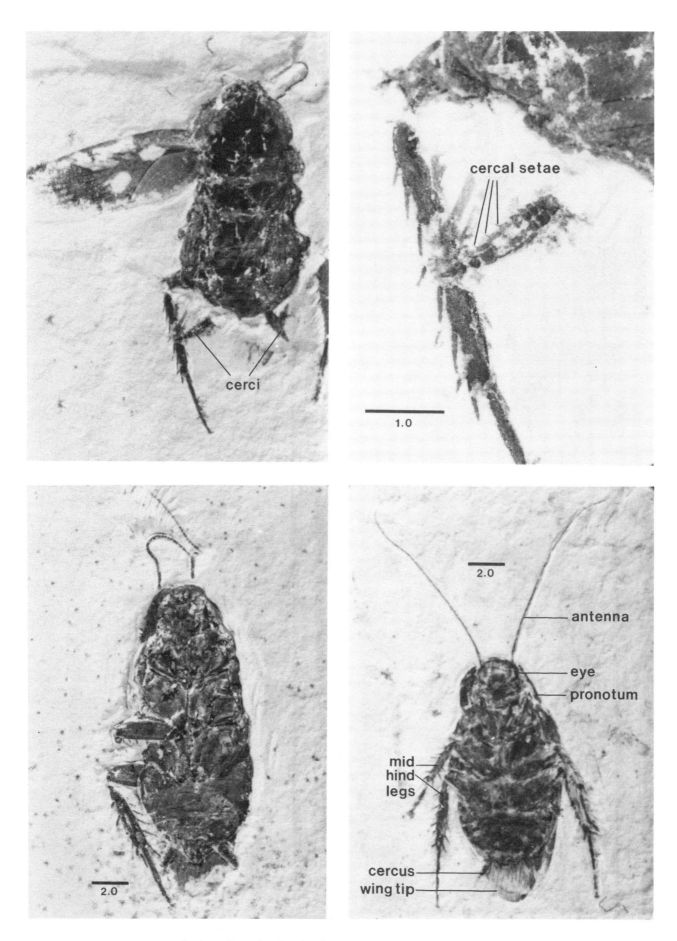

Cockroaches, showing detail on cercus and spination of hind leg.

geographical extinction of mayfly families is demonstrated by the presence of specimens of Siphlonuridae in the deposit, which are presently Austral and Holarctic. The family Ephemeridae is actually quite speciose but is very poorly known from the present-day tropics. The extinct Mesozoic family Hexagenitidae, which was previously known only from Laurasia, also is apparently represented in the deposit. Many of the nymphs have a morphology strongly indicative of being inhabitants of running water.

Odonata

Dragonflies and damselflies form a cosmopolitan order composed of species that have predaceous adults and nymphs. The nymphs inhabit all sorts of freshwater bodies, including such unusual habitats as water-filled bromeliads and the splash zones of streams and waterfalls, but generally are found in quiet or slow-moving water. Nymphs have a specialized labial mask, armed with spines, that is rapidly slung out to seize prey. The adults are active, flying predators with a series of distinctive features in wing venation, with an archedictyon (primitive arrangement of many veins in a complex network). They have large spherical eyes, small bristle-like antennae, and spiny legs that are used for seining midges and other frail insects in flight. The great majority of species fall into two suborders, the Zygoptera (damselflies) and Anisoptera (dragonflies).

Represented in the assemblage are several Zygoptera, one of which appears to represent a new subfamily of the family Pseudostigmatidae. There are also specimens belonging to the superfamily Coenagrioidea, although their family position is uncertain. These specimens nevertheless represent the first known Early Cretaceous coenagrioids and are the first fossil members of the superfamily from South America. In the Anisoptera, there are two species of Gomphidae that probably belong in a new subfamily (Wighton, 1987). Other gomphids also have been recognized, one from a wing (which is extremely well preserved, including the "fluting" that is generally present between wing veins), another from a larva, and a third individual, perhaps representing a new genus. A significant finding is a mature or near mature nymph belonging to the Macromiidae, distinctive for its very long antennae and a few other features. This family has not been recorded previously from South America, living or extinct. The macromiid apparently resembles a species from East Africa.

Blattodea

The cockroaches are flat, cursorial (running) insects with coriaceous (leathery) forewings. They have spiny legs, long antennae, cerci (caudal appendages) that are well developed, a complete wing venation (composed almost entirely of parallel longitudinal veins), and generally a large pronotum that conceals the head in dorsal view. There are many new species yet being discovered from tropical regions around the world, where they are by far the most speciose. Taxonomic features that are most important at generic and higher levels are spination on the legs, wing venation, and genitalic morphology. The rich fossil history of the roaches extends from the Carboniferous period. Cockroach paleontology has existed for at least a century, and nearly 1000 generic fossil names have been given to specimens (in some cases just wing fragments). No doubt many synonyms exist, so comprehensive revisionary work is needed to bring order to the study of fossil roaches. The specimens in the assemblage (first reported by Pinto and Purper, 1986) are very likely to elicit strong interest from some future researcher on fossil roaches, for they have probably the most complete detail and relief of any fossil roaches. In some entire specimens, all the details of the spination on the legs, wing venation, and even the fine hairs on the cerci are observable.

At least three families are represented in the assemblage, and it remains for a roach specialist to determine the subfamilies, genera, and gross morphospecies. At least one taxon of roaches in the assemblage is enigmatic. It was at first believed to belong to the extinct Permian order Protelytroptera, which are thought to be the closest relatives of the earwigs (order Dermaptera). This hypothesis was based on the following features in the fossils: head is broad, with large, round eyes that are distantly separated; pronotum is well developed, rectangular, but not concealing the head; antennae are filiform; forewings are elytrous (like that of a beetle) with even, fine punctation over the surface and a simple, dichotomous branching pattern to the wing veins; the hind wings are expansive and have an unusual system of crossveins unlike any blattoid, and even possess a costal stigma (dark, sclerotized spot on leading edge); and they have segmented cerci with readily observable setae or hairs. The venation does not exactly match that of the Protelytroptera, but virtually all of the above features do not match the roaches, either! A new higher taxon for this group of roaches seems necessary.

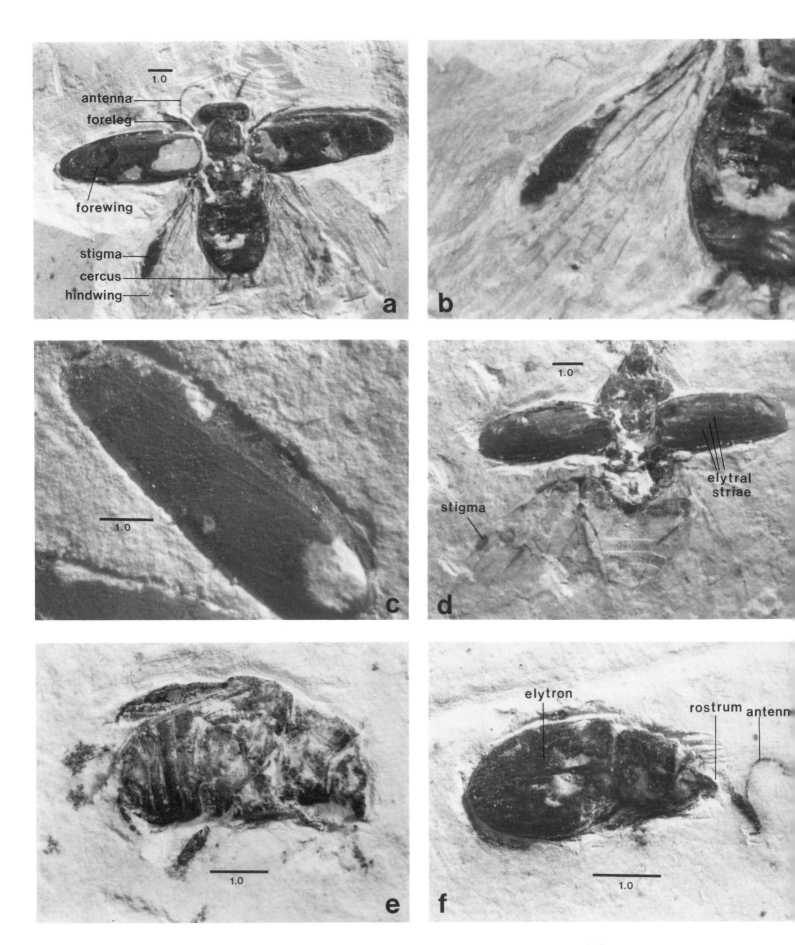

(A-C) Enigmatic cockroach, showing detail of unusual hind wing (B) and forewing (C) venation; (D-F) Coleoptera.

Homoptera (leaf hoppers and plant hoppers). Photos by K. G. A. Hamilton.

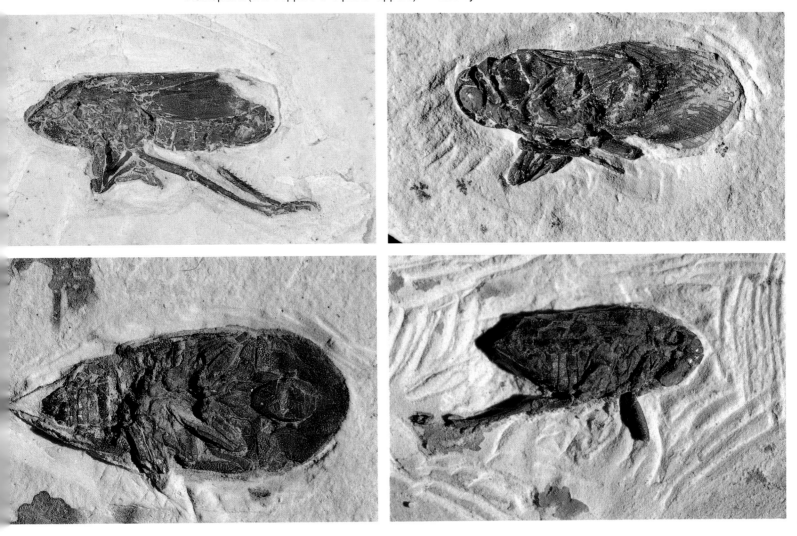

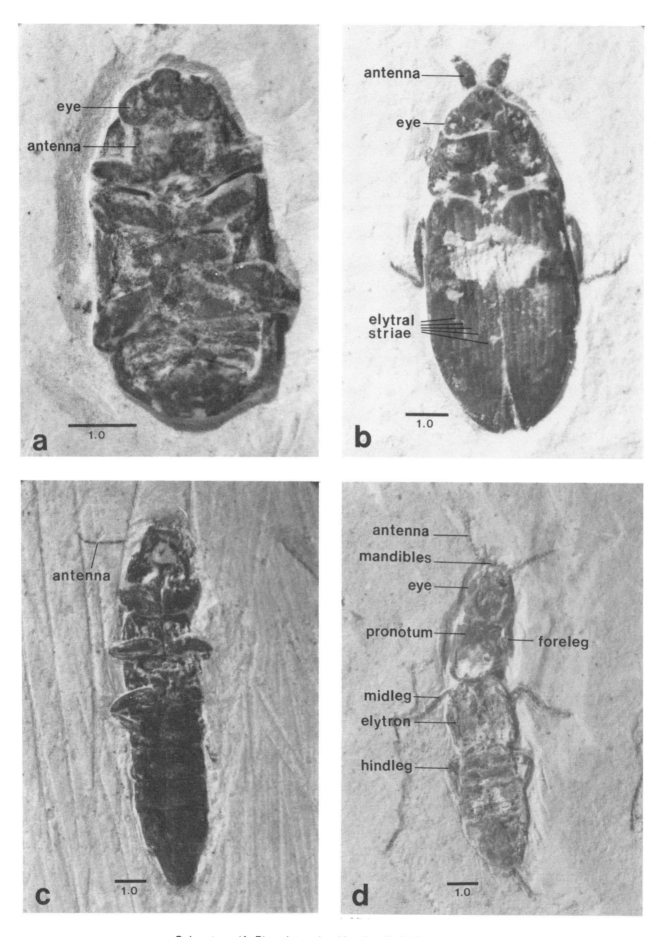

Coleoptera: (A, B) undetermined family; (C, D) Staphylinidae.

Isoptera

The Isoptera, or termites, are essentially highly modified social cockroaches. They are morphologically very specialized and reduced, with very little sclerotization of the chitinous body parts, possessing (usually) small eyes, filiform antennae, tiny cerci, rudimentary genitalia (no doubt a feature of the caste system), and wings that are possessed only by reproductives (they are shed immediately upon descent to the ground after the nuptial, swarming flights). The wings are characteristically very lightly sclerotized (even the veins) and diaphanous. Moreover, termites are almost all eusocial, with division of labor and morphological specialization among several castes (workers, soldiers, queen). The colonies of some tropical species apparently are the largest aggregations of any social insect. It is mostly a tropical order, containing just over 2000 species. The relationship of the termites to the cockroaches would not be obvious were it not for our understanding of several taxa intermediate between the two orders. The Australian termite *Mastotermes darwiniensis*, the most primitive living termite, retains several primitive features of the cockroaches; the genus is known from the lower Cretaceous to the Tertiary, from Europe, North America, and even in amber of Central America and the Dominican Republic. All termites have intestinal symbionts that aid them in metabolizing cellulose.

Previously there were just three known Cretaceous taxa of termites. The assemblage from the Chapada do Araripe presents us with a fourth, and the only Gondwanan taxon known. It apparently belongs to the family Hodotermitidae (subfamily Hodotermitinae), which makes this record the first fossil species of the family from the tropics. There are six living species in the family Hodotermitidae that occur in the tropics.

Orthoptera

The order Orthoptera, in the strict sense, includes grasshoppers (and locusts) and the crickets and their relatives. Most orthopterans are distinguished by enlarged hind femora containing large muscles used in jumping; hind coxae (basal segments of the legs) that are small and separated; and a large pronotum that covers most of the dorsum and sides of the thorax. The forewings usually are coriaceous and reduced, the hind wings usually are fan-like, expanding upon flight and with a complete system of longitudinal and cross veins. Their habits vary more than most people realize, but in general they are phytophagous (feeding on monocots, dicots, and even gymnosperms); some are predaceous. Many of them "sing," using a system of stridulation that varies with the group. Because they are heavily sclerotized, orthopterans are well preserved in fossil deposits.

This is another well-represented group in the assemblage that has yet to studied in detail by a specialist. In some cases, specimens are preserved simply as the coriaceous wings or as legs, but always with a great amount of detail intact (such as complete venation and spination). Preserved detail on the incomplete specimens should allow association of the fragments with complete, better understood specimens. In the case of some Ensifera ("long horned" grasshoppers, named for the length of the antennae), complete specimens lie on one side. In the case of many Grylloidea (crickets and allies) and the Tridactylidae (pygmy mole crickets), the bodies of complete specimens lie ventral or dorsal side down. Apparently all of the grasshoppers present in the assemblage are ensiferans, belonging to the Tettigoniidae and perhaps to the Haglidae and Prophalangopsidae. The Grylloidea is especially speciose in the assemblage, with representatives of both the true ground crickets (Gryllinae) and the tree crickets (Oecanthinae) present. Gryllines feed on living and decaying plant matter, and the oecanthines live on exposed foliage and lay their eggs in plant stems. For some of the crickets, entire wings are preserved that fully display the stridulatory portions (e.g., the mirror [which is like a drum and amplifies the sound], the cordal area, harp, and basal area). Stridulatory structures are important in taxonomy of the group. Ovipositors are also very well preserved.

Perhaps the most exquisite among the Orthoptera from the assemblage are specimens of Tridactylidae, pygmy mole crickets. Tridactylids dig burrows in loose, sandy substrate near streams, ponds, and lakes, and they apparently are capable of swimming on and beneath the surface of water. Fossils of this family are extremely rare.

Dermaptera

The order of earwigs, the Dermaptera, is an enigmatic one. Some evidence suggests that their closest relatives may be the Permian order Protelytroptera (see discussion of cockroaches, above); other evidence, based on morphology of living forms, strongly suggests that they are most closely related to the Grylloblattodea (an

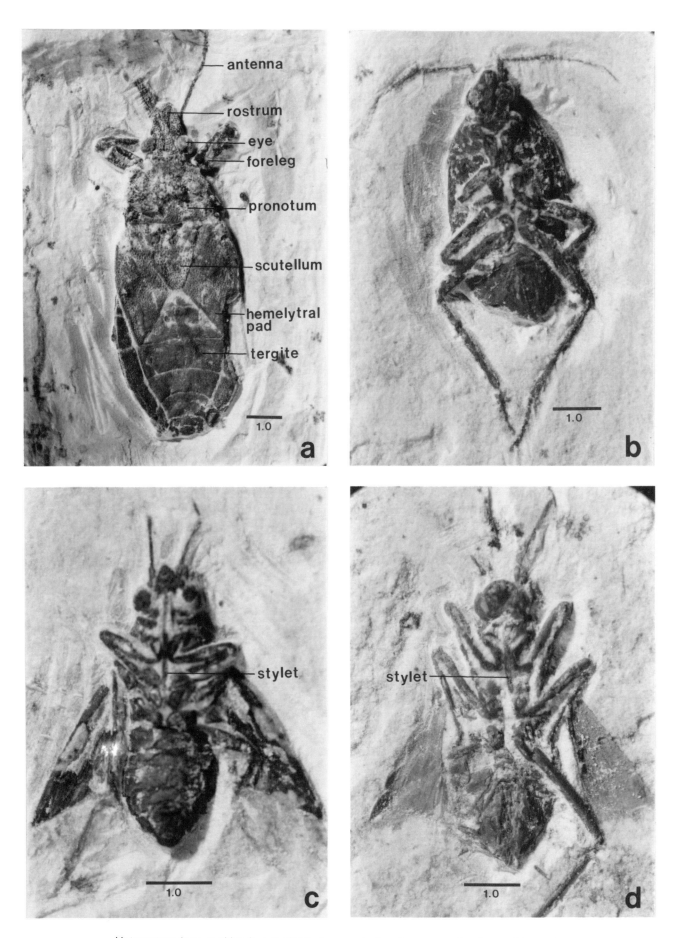

Heteroptera (true sucking bugs); (B-D) show ventral surface, exposing the sucking stylet.

Various Hemiptera. Top: Large heteropterans. Upper center: Heteropteran (left) and a large aquatic predaceous sucking bug (right). Others are all homopterans. Photos by D. Grimaldi.

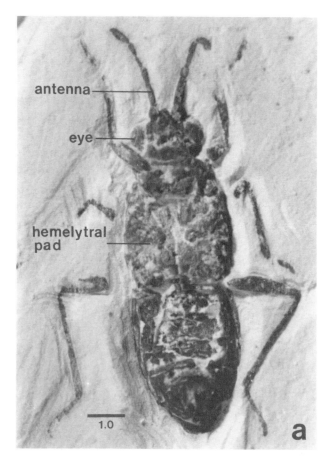

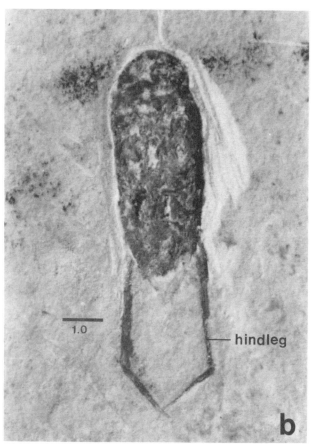

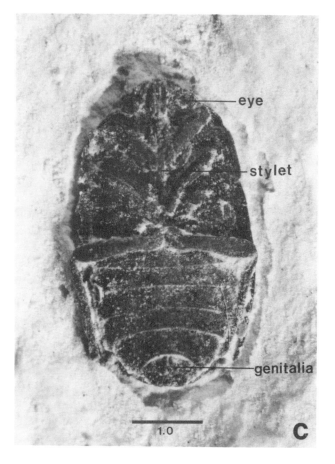

Heteroptera: (A) undetermined family; (B) family
Corixidae?; (C) family Cydnidae?

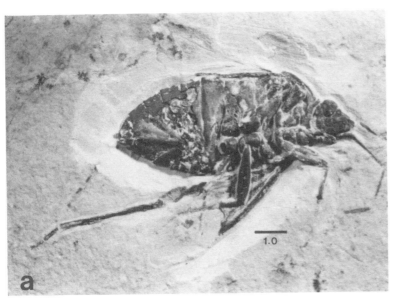

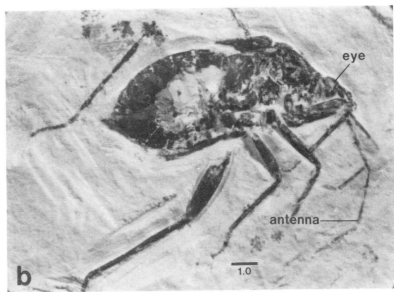

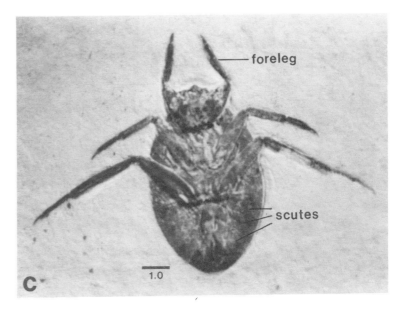

Heteroptera: (A, B) Pentatomoidea? (stink bugs and allies); (C) predaceous aquatic bug (family Naucoridae).

order containing 12 species of rare, primitive wingless insects with a disjuct distribution in western North America, Siberia, and Japan). The Dermaptera are monophyletic, being a natural group with obviously a single origin and with an array of distinctive features. These include the large cerci that are modified into sclerotized forceps, a thorax with many free sclerites (probably serving to aid in movement among interstitial spaces, since earwings live among soil, leaf litter, under bark, and in other concealed spaces), the forewings are shortened and elytrous, and the hind wings are fan-like, capable of being considerably expanded when unfolded. The distinctive fan-like hind wings have a peculiar radial arrangement of many anal veins.

Dermaptera are apparently quite rare as fossils (only about 40 total are known). Dermapteran specimens from the Chapada do Araripe apparently are referable to the family Labiidae, subfamily Labiinae. Given the present-day distribution of the subfamilies of the Labiidae, plus what is known about continental drift, these fossils lend support to the hypothesis that the labiid earwigs were widespread in Gondwana prior to its fragmentation.

Homoptera

The Homoptera, or planthoppers, leafhoppers, scale insects, and aphids, are placed with the Heteroptera, the true sucking bugs, into a superorder Hemiptera. This is based on the shared feature of a stylet (sucking proboscis) used for feeding either on plant liquids (all Homoptera, some Heteroptera) or for attacking prey (some Heteroptera). Besides the proboscis, other features of the Homoptera include a relatively complete wing venation (but reduced in some forms, like aphids, and wings entirely lost in some groups, such as certain sexes of many scale insects), the antenna ending in a stylus (hair-like segment), and some other morphological features.

Top left: Cricket-hunting wasp. Top right: Sawfly. Lower left: Parasitic wasp. Lower right: Cranefly. Photos by D. Grimaldi.

Homopterans are extremely diverse and well preserved in this assemblage, representing the families Cicadellidae (leafhoppers), Boreoscytidae (?), Achilidae, a possible Cixiidae, two families that are apparently new, and the two extinct (Mesozoic) families Jascopidae and Cicadoprosobolidae. The most abundant homopterans are cicadellids. One of the new families apparently contains numerous new species and genera. The other families are much less speciose but include a number of undescribed species and genera. The Cicadellidae are the oldest now known and belong to very primitive groups among the living subfamilies.

Heteroptera

This order contains the true bugs, sucking insects with a stylet-like proboscis that is used for ingesting fluids. The forewings have an anterior triangular portion that is heavily

sclerotized or coriaceous (known as the hemelytra). There is a tremendous diversity of habits, habitats, hosts, and feeding modes in this order. They include such insects as the aquatic, predaceous Belostomatidae (true water bugs), Corixidae (waterboatmen), and Notonectidae (backswimmers); the semi-aquatic bugs belonging to the Gerridae (water striders) and their relatives; small, primitive forms that dwell under bark (e.g., the Enicocephalidae); predaceous terrestrial families such as the Reduviidae (assassin bugs) and their relatives; and the myriad of terrestrial plant and seed-feeding families. Aquatic, terrestrial, phytophagous, and predaceous taxa are represented in the assemblage and, like the Homoptera, are extremely diverse. Unfortunately, it remains for a heteropterist to examine and study the specimens at length.

Tentative determinations (not representative of the total Heteroptera in the assemblage), reveal

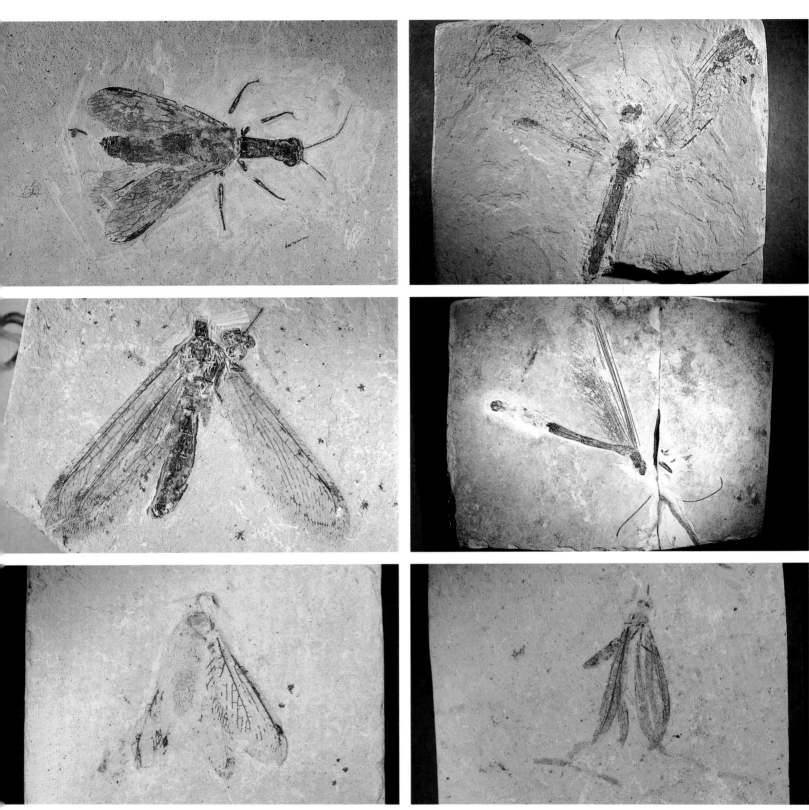

Various Neuropterodea (lacewings and allies), including a snakefly (top left), an ant lion (upper center left), and owl flies (top right, upper center right). Photos by D. Grimaldi.

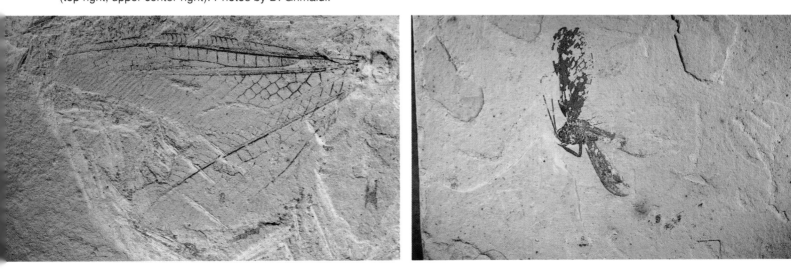

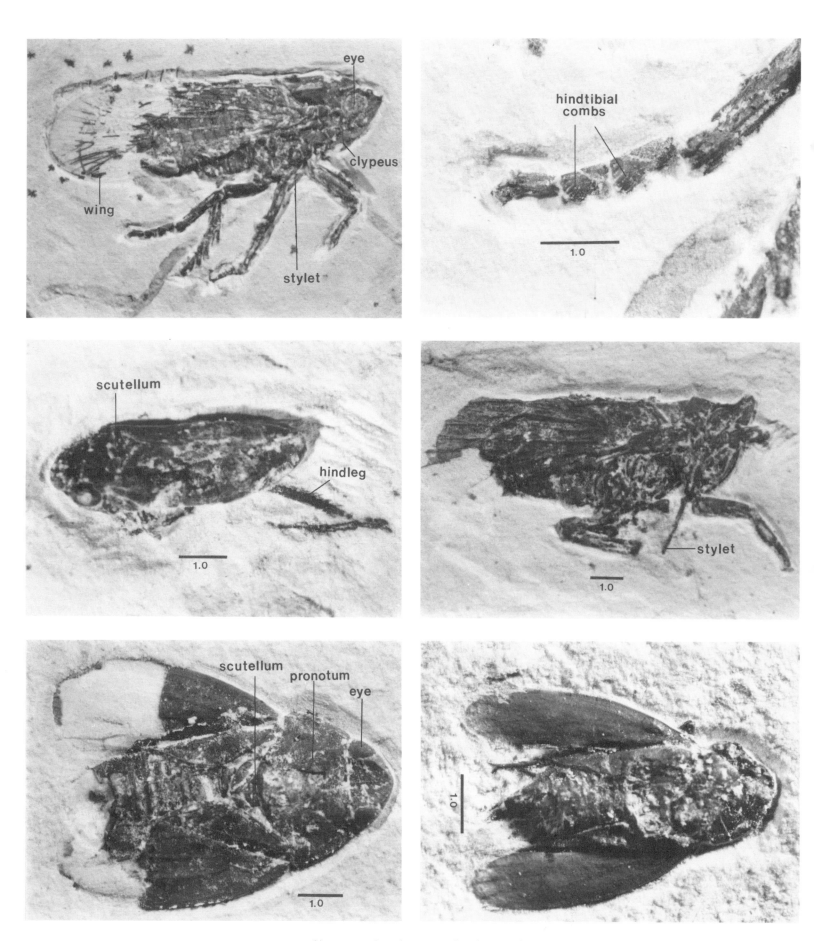

Homoptera (tree hoppers, plant hoppers).

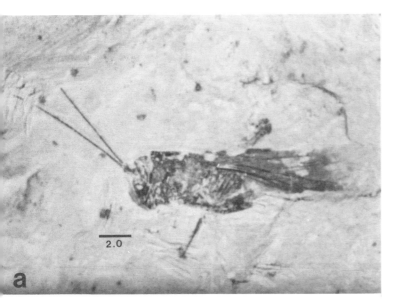

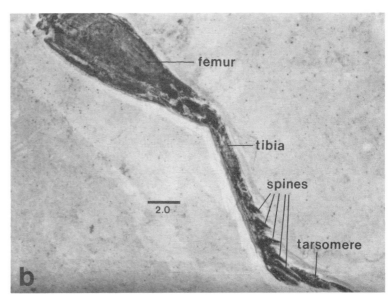

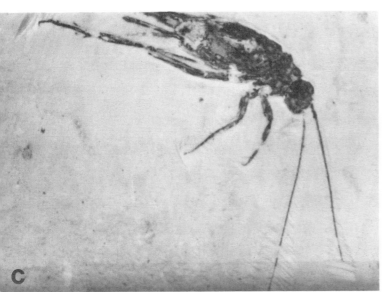

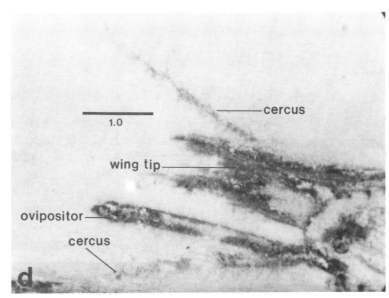

(A, B) Grasshoppers, with detail of saltatorial leg (different specimens); (C, D) tree crickets (Oecanthinae, Gryllidae), with detail of posterior end.

the presence of several groups. There are specimens of Naucoridae, which are flat, round, aquatic predaceous bugs with small raptorial forelegs that are used to capture prey, usually other aquatic insects. These specimens superficially resemble nymphal Belostomatidae (a closely related family with a similar mode of life) from the same assemblage. Unplaced Nepomorpha are represented by a massive species (by far the largest heteropteran in the assemblage). Other Heteroptera include a possible saldid (shore bug), a possible reduviid (assassin bug), specimens in the Cimicomorpha and in the superfamily Lygaeoidea (includes modern Lygaeidae, Pyrrhocoridae, and some other families, some of which feed on seeds), as well as specimens in the Pentatomorpha (including the extant family of stink bugs, the Pentatomidae, and allied families). Other heteropterans in the assemblage are as yet unplaced at family or subfamily level.

Hymenoptera

This order contains the sawflies, ants, bees, and wasps. By far the most diverse type of living species in the order are the parasitic wasps, which generally are small and very unlikely to be preserved (or preserved well) as compression fossils. The bias in this fossil assemblage is for large, heavily sclerotized Hymenoptera to be preserved. This order is extremely heterogeneous today in morphology and habits, including such disparate groups as the phytophagous sawflies, parasitic wasps (endoparasitic as larvae in other insects), flower-foraging bees, and the ants. Hamuli, which are tiny hooks aligned in a row on the costal edge of the hind wing that serve to keep the fore and hind wings coupled, are one of the diagnostic features of this diverse group. Others include the presence of a marked constriction between the first and second segments of the abdomen (the "abdomen" in Hymenoptera thus being

399

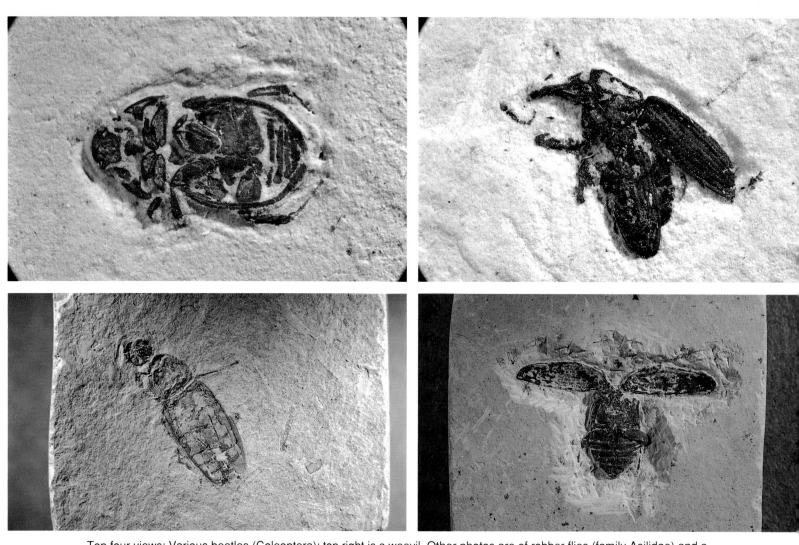

Top four views: Various beetles (Coleoptera); top right is a weevil. Other photos are of robber flies (family Asilidae) and a large spider. Photos by D. Grimaldi, except for spider by J. Maisey.

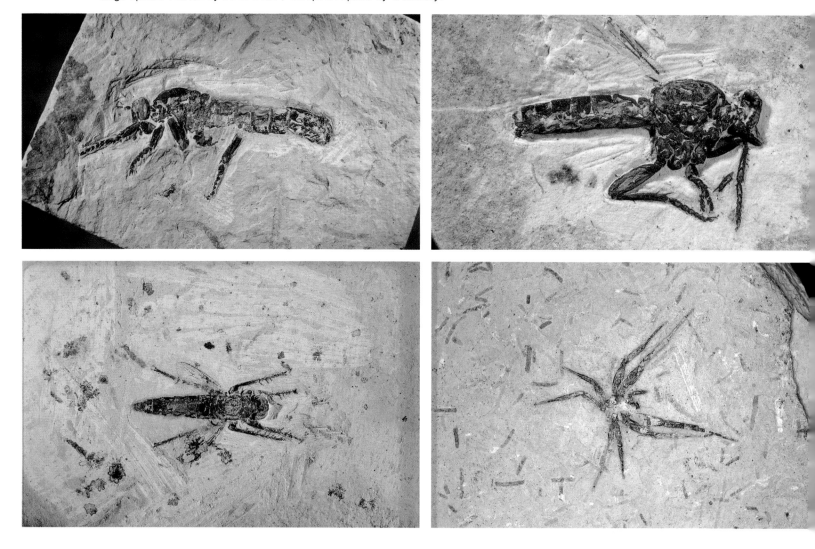

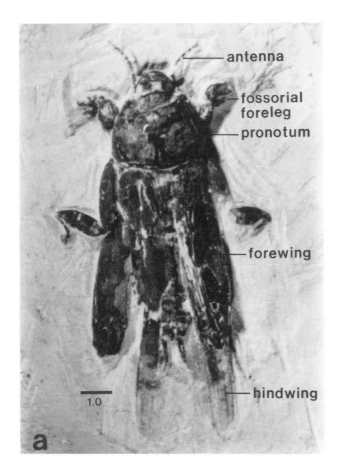

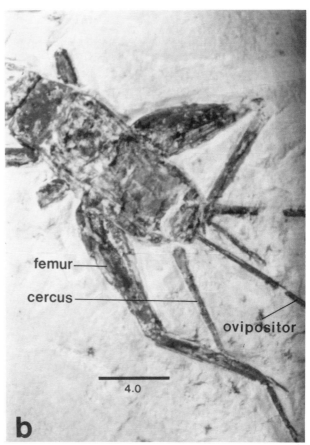

Crickets (Grylloidea): (A) beautifully preserved pygmy mole cricket (Tridactylidae); (B, C) female ground crickets (Gryllinae).

called the gaster), which is found in the more derived taxa (exclusive of the sawflies). One of the most intriguing aspects of the Hymenoptera is the evolution of eusociality, which apparently has independently evolved at least a dozen times in various stinging wasps, the bees, and the ants.

The Hymenoptera from the fossil assemblage apparently include the first fossil representative of the subfamily Syntexinae (family Anaxyelidae), which is a group of sawflies presently represented by one species living in the Nearctic region. An ephialtitid (family of parasitic wasps) now extends the distribution of this family from the Jurassic to the Cretaceous. In the Aculeata (stinging wasps), the oldest known Tiphiidae occurs in the assemblage (extending the range from the Oligocene). There is also the first known fossil representative of the family Rhopalosomatidae. These large wasps are superficially similar to the Pompilidae, the spider wasps, and are parasites of crickets. This is an interesting fossil association, since grylline and oecanthine crickets are common in this fossil assemblage. There are also species apparently referable to the fossil genus *Cretosphex*, and another species also placed probably in the superfamily Apoidea. These apoids are controversial for the possible positions they may occupy with regard to the families Sphecidae and Apidae (both in the broad sense). Sphecids are the most closely related group to the bees (comprising about 20,000 species). However, a Lower Cretaceous sphecid or apid is startling to some entomologists. Since most bees forage on the pollen and nectar of angiosperm flowers, and the known angiosperm fossil record is extremely poor in the lower Cretaceous, the inference has always been that bees did not appear until the Middle to Late Cretaceous. Other evidence shows this to be an unreasonable assumption, and hopefully even better preserved *Cretosphex* and "Apoidea sp." specimens eventually will be found in the Crato member to clarify the situation in the Lower Cretaceous.

Neuroptera

The lacewings, ant lions, mantispids, etc., are regarded as close allies based on larval features, which include a diet of usually quite small, sessile insects eaten by employing a distinctive pair of long, sucking mandibles. Various adult and larval features are taxonomically distinctive at several levels, such as the wing venation. There are 17 families included in this small order, and it is one of the most archaic of living orders. Families represented in the assemblage apparently include the Myrmeleontidae and Chrysopidae.

Raphidioptera

Closely related to the Neuroptera is the small order of snakeflies. This order contains about 170 living species in two families, the Raphidiidae and Inocelliidae (the latter with only about 20 species). Members of the group are distinguished by an elongate pronotum, bulging eyes, wing venation, and the well-developed, heavily sclerotized ovipositor. Snakeflies are represented in the assemblage and are the first ones known from the Southern Hemisphere; all other living and fossil ones are Holarctic.

Coleoptera

The beetles are the most successful group of insects in terms of number of species (presently about 250,000 in slightly over 200 families). They are rather uniform in adult morphology (there is rarely a question as to whether a newly discovered species is a beetle at all), and the ground plan of the beetles includes their most obvious feature: the hardened forewings or elytra. The diversity of habits and habitat is staggering: today there are leafminers, wood borers, fungal feeders, predators, and even a group that is ectoparasitic on beavers. Elytral imprints, presumably of beetles, are known from the Permian, but many modern families made their debut during the Mesozoic era.

Despite the present diversity and abundance of beetles, they seem to be uncommon in the assemblage. There are some aquatic beetles, probably in the family Dytiscidae. These are predaceous diving beetles commonly found in the littoral zone of still freshwater bodies such as ponds and lakes, and with a habit and habitat preference similar to the Naucoridae and Belostomatidae (Heteroptera) mentioned above. There also are some Staphylinidae, or rove beetles. This is a huge modern group of about 20,000 species; some have very specialized habits (e.g., inquilines in nests of social insects, etc.), but the vast majority are predatory inhabitants of leaf litter and soil. There is a probable carabid (predaceous ground beetles). Carabids also form a very speciose group today, with habits similar to staphylinids. There also are possible members of the Scarabaeidae, Passalidae, and Nitidulidae. The most common groups are Curculionoidea (the superfamily of weevils, possibly in the family Oxycorynidae) and Scarabaeidae, probably in the subfamily

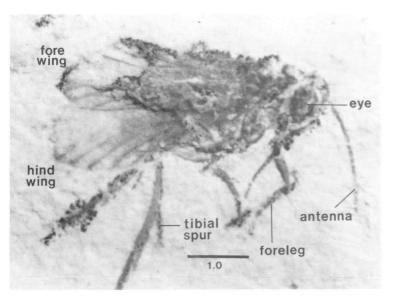

fore wing

hind wing

eye

tibial spur

foreleg

antenna

palp

tibial spur

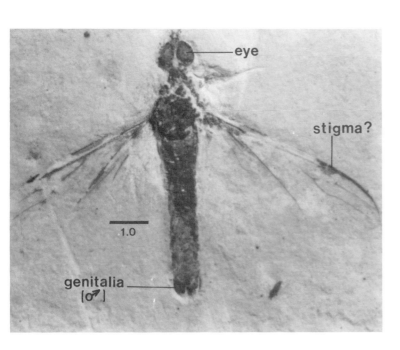

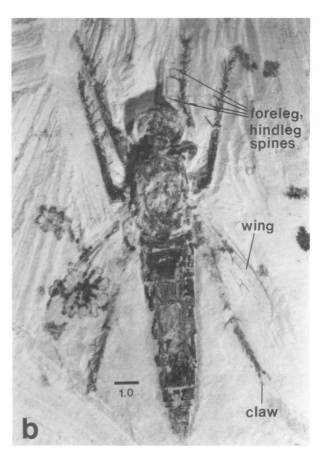

eye

stigma?

genitalia [♂]

foreleg, hindleg spines

wing

claw

Upper four views: Adult caddisflies (Trichoptera), undetermined to family. Bottom row: Tipuloid cranefly (left); robber fly (right).

b

403

(A) Tipuloidea; (B-F) Hymenoptera, including parasitic wasps (B, C) showing ovipositors, and a sphecoid wasp (E, F).

Aphodiinae. Both the oxycorynids and aphodiines are rather small but very well preserved. Weevils are easily recognized by the elongate rostrum, at the end of which is a pair of small, heavily chitinized mandibles. The antennae and their position of attachment along the rostrum are apparent in some specimens, as is the elytral microsculpture.

Trichoptera

The Trichoptera, or caddisflies, is the most closely related group to the Lepidoptera (moths and butterflies). Virtually all caddisflies have larvae that are aquatic, living in any sort of fresh water from highly eutrophic shallow ponds to swift, cold mountain streams. Some build distinctive, even elaborate, tubular cases, varying with the family or genus; others are web-builders that use the web to snare food particles carried down the current. Unfortunately, trichopterans in the assemblage all seem to be rather small and obscure in the details of their preservation. Features that are important in classification are the position and number of large leg spines, the palps of the mouthparts, and the venation. The families Hydroptilidae, Psychomyiidae, Baissoferidae, and Philopotamidae are recognized tentatively among the caddisflies in this assemblage.

Diptera

The true flies constitute a very large order of nearly 100,000 living species. They are probably the most diverse group of insects morphologically and ecologically, living such lifestyles as leafminers, blood-suckers, insect predators, and endoparasites. They are a clearly monophyletic group distinguished by just one pair of real wings (the hind pair is modified into a pair of knob-like gyroscopic organs, the halteres). The group is known from the Triassic, when it is represented by primitive forms allied most closely to extant Tipuloidea (craneflies and their relatives). Most of the modern family diversity, however, is not known before the Cretaceous.

In the Cretaceous assemblage of the Crato member there are specimens of Tipulidae or a close relative thereof, and a midge or gnat apparently in or closely related to the family Chironomidae. The Chironomidae have a rich amber fossil record, and the family is represented in Lower Cretaceous (Aptian) amber from Lebanon. Chironomid larvae are aquatic or semi-aquatic and most commonly found in still freshwater bodies. There apparently is a march fly (family Bibionidae), which if verified would make this the earliest record of a bibionid. There are examples of the small, dark fungus gnats, the Sciaridae, and at least one member of a closely related family, the Mycetophilidae. Undoubtedly the most exciting fossil Diptera present are species of robber flies (family Asilidae). These provide the oldest definitive record of the Asilidae. Members of this large family are entirely predaceous as larvae and adults. Today they are most speciose and abundant in open, and especially dry, scrub-like areas, but also are quite speciose in tropical regions as well.

Conclusions

One of the most obvious features of this fossil insect assemblage is that it is essentially modern in its representation of families. However, below the level of family for most of the orders, and certainly for almost all of the genera (most of which are undescribed), the modern aspect of the assemblage is unapparent. Virtually all the genera are extinct, and this holds true for many of the subfamilies. In several instances, such as in the Homoptera, several new families probably are represented. In only a few cases, such as in the Raphidioptera, can the fossil species be tentatively assigned to extant genera. There also are a number of important records of the oldest specimens of several families, including the Asilidae and perhaps the Bibionidae (Diptera), Cicadellidae (Homoptera), Rhopalosomatidae and Tiphiidae (Hymenoptera), Macromiidae (Odonata, Anisoptera), the Oligoneuriidae, Potamanthidae, and Euthyplociidae (Ephemeroptera), and the Labiidae (Dermaptera).

Another substantial finding (with implications as to how we view the evolution of South American faunas) is that several groups of insects were present in South America that are no longer found there. In most cases the extant relatives of the groups in the from the assemblage from the Crato member now live only in the Northern Hemisphere, especially the Nearctic region.

Study of the fossil insects from this occurrence offers some potential for understanding the taphonomy of the original fossil site. Specifically, a reconstruction of the area, at least at some time in its history, would include a freshwater body, probably quite eutrophic and rather shallow, in which only small fish (e.g., *Dastilbe*) could swim. There was almost certainly an abundance of thick, emergent vegetation, either at the margins or throughout the pond or lake. This is based on the presence of an incredible diversity of aquatic, semi-aquatic, and terrestrial groups of insects; the terrestrial taxa, in addition, are most diverse for the phytophagous groups.

Assemblage: Crato member laminated limestones.

(D. A. Grimaldi)

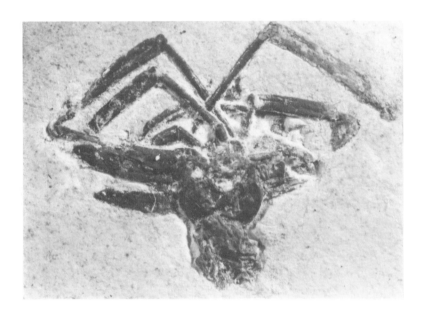

Spider of undetermined family.

ARACHNIDS

Spiders
  Class ARACHNIDA
  Order ARANEAE
  MYGALOMORPHA
  incertae sedis
Genus and sp. indet.
  A fairly large (40 mm) mygalomorph spider (tarantula) is reported here from the lacustrine laminated limestones of the Crato member. Only a single example is known. No further information is available pending its study and eventual description.

  A few other smaller and poorly preserved spiders have been identified from the same deposits. It has not been possible to determine their relationships.

  Assemblage: Crato member.

Scorpions
  Order SCORPIONIDA
  Incertae sedis
Araripescorpius Campos, 1986
  1986 *Araripescorpius* Campos: 135
  Diagnosis: "Carapace trapezoidal; only the 2nd pair of appendages known; preabdomen with seven tergites, and postabdomen with five segments, and the telson incomplete."
  Type species: *Araripescorpius ligabuei* Campos, 1986.
Araripescorpius ligabuei Campos, 1986
  1986 *Araripescorpius ligabuei* Campos: 135.
  Diagnosis: As for genus.
  Holotype: Divisão de Geologia e Mineralogia, Departamento Nacional da Produção Mineral, Rio de Janiero, DGM-DNPM 6.216-I; individual showing body and pedipalps; Lower Cretaceous (Aptian), Santana formation, Crato member, Tatajuba, Santana do Cariri, Ceará.

  Although Campos (1986) erected a new genus and species, no distinguishing characters (other than some shared by scorpions in general) were given. The holotype is approximately 27 mm long.

  Scorpions today prefer tropical, subtropical, and dry climates, although some species occur in temperate regions. They are all terrestrial, generally living at ground level. By day they hide beneath rocks or in crevices, coming out by night to feed. Some species have adapted to arid environments, but others can tolerate high humidity. Most scorpions prey on large insects and other terrestrial arthropods, capturing prey in their massive pedipalps and sometimes subduing it by stinging. A pair of poison glands secrete a powerful neurotoxin that can kill the scorpion's usual prey immediately. It seems likely that *Araripescorpius* was a capable and efficient predator, and it clearly had an abundant insect fauna on which to prey.

  The fossil record of scorpions extends back more than 400 million years, to the Silurian period. A "mere" 110 million years ago these animals evidently resembled their modern counterparts very closely. Mesozoic and Tertiary scorpions are nevertheless extremely rare, and *Araripescorpius* therefore is important. The phylogenetic relationship of *Araripescorpius* to Recent scorpions is unknown.

  Assemblage: Crato member laminated limestones, where it may be considered exotic like the other terrestrial arthropods.

(J. G. Maisey)

CRUSTACEANS

Ostracods
  Class CRUSTACEA
  Subclass OSTRACODA
  Order PODOCOPIDA
  Family CYPRIDIDAE
  Subfamily CYPRIDINAE
Genus **Pattersoncypris** Bate, 1972
  1972 *Pattersoncypris* Bate: 380A
  Diagnosis: Cypridinae having oval carapace with acute antero-dorsal hump.
  Type species: *Pattersoncypris micropapillosa* Bate, 1972.
Pattersoncypris micropapillosa Bate
  1972 *Pattersoncypris micropapillosa* Bate: 381
  Diagnosis: *Pattersoncypris* in which small papillae cover the shell.
  Holotype: British Museum (Natural History), BM(NH) Io 4680; adult instar; Santana formation, Romualdo member, Chapada do Araripe, Ceará.

Ostracods are abundant small crustaceans, mostly under 1 mm long but sometimes attaining a length of over 10 mm. Some 2000 recent species are known, of which about two-thirds are marine. Ostracods possess a bivalved carapace enclosing a small, highly specialized body, lacking external segmentation. Some ostracods are powerful swimmers, but many prefer to live close to or within the substrate. Most are filter-feeders, but a few are carnivorous and some others are parasitic.

Four ostracod orders are commonly recognized, only one of which (the Podocopida) includes freshwater as well as marine species. This also is the largest order in number of species. Members of this order are characterized by a second antenna having either no exopodite or else only a minute one, and by endopodites ending in claws. Clearly any systematic classification based on appendage characters such as these is of limited use where fossils are concerned, because the carapace usually is the only part preserved.

In the course of preparing some fossil fishes in concretions from the Santana formation, Dr. Colin Patterson of the British Museum (Natural History) recovered more than 250 phosphatized ostracods from the residues (Bate, 1971). Normally the ostracods are preserved in calcium carbonate and are destroyed during acid preparation of fossil vertebrates. These phosphatized examples provided a unique opportunity to examine a large sample of well-preserved ostracod fossils and represent the best-preserved fossil ostracod material ever found. Besides the carapace, the internal morphology is preserved largely intact, revealing details of appendages including antennules, antennae, mandibles, maxillae, and thoracic appendages, as well as furcae, sensory bristles, and testes. A detailed description of these features was provided by Bate (1972).

From the sample recovered by Dr. Patterson, 138 were complete carapaces, of which 103 retain appendages. The remainder seem to represent empty valves of molted instars (Bate, 1972, fig. 1). The sample revealed a linear increase in size of instars, ranging from a height/length of approximately 0.2/0.3 mm to just above 0.7/1.0 mm.

Pattersoncypris is a typical cypridid ostracod, differing from *Cypris* in the form and arrangement of the dorsal hump and from *Brasacypris* in the less angular posterior cardinal angle and more equivalve appearance.

Bate (1972) contended that *Pattersoncypris* was a strong swimmer. The antennules almost certainly bore long swimming setae and are very long. The antennae are also long, bearing swimming setae on their inner surface. The segments (podomeres) of the antennae also could have been used in walking over the substrate. The mandibles are toothed and probably were capable of scraping algae or scavenging from decaying plant and animal remains. The maxillae are modified so as to be capable of pushing food forward into the mouth, and also bear a flattened branchial plate, used to generate water flow through the carapace. The first thoracic appendages are modified to help in feeding rather than locomotion, as in other cypridids. The second thoracic appendages are true walking limbs terminating in a claw, and the third thoracic appendages are adapted to grasping and also for cleaning the inside of the carapace.

Bate (1972: 392) theorized that these ostracods had been scavenging the specimens of *Cladocyclus* with which they were associated, suggesting that they may have been suddenly overwhelmed by sediment and asphyxiated, and then replaced by phosphate that permeated from the decaying fish. Although this is an attractive scenario, it is not supported by sedimentological data suggesting slow sediment accumulation, and it is now clear that phosphatization is an erratic and localized phenomenon within Santana formation concretions. Bate (1972) further noted that the proportion of juvenile to adult instars apparently is abnormal in his sample and suggested that this was because juvenile instars lived largely elsewhere, perhaps among aquatic vegetation, and mostly adult instars were involved in scavenging. Alternatively, he suggested that a seasonal fluctuation of instars may have been responsible for a largely adult population.

There is disagreement in the literature over the taxic diversity of ostracods in the Santana formation. According to Bate (1972), it is extremely low; he observed only the single species *Pattersoncypris micropapillosa* and suggested that *Hourequia angulata salitrensis* described by Krommelbein and Weber (1972) from the Santana formation of Pernambuco might be referable to *Pattersoncypris*. Bate (1972: 392) took this apparently low taxic diversity to indicate a non-marine habitat for the Santana formation concretions.

Lima (1979b) published a list of ostracods reported by other authors from the Santana formation, as follows:

Family BAIRDIDAE
Bithocypris sp.
Family CYPRIDIDAE
Pattersoncypris micropapillosa
Paracypridea obovata obovata
Heterocypris sp.
Cypridea araripensis
Cypridea sp.
Family EUCANDONIDAE
Candonopsis sp.
Family DARWINULIDAE
Darwinula martinsi
Darwinula sp.
Family CYTHERIDEIDAE
Ovocytheridea sp.
Dolocytheridea sp.
Family PROGNOCYTHERIDAE
Paraschuleridea micropunctata
Paraschuleridea sp.
Family LYMNOCYTHERIDAE
Bisulcocypris silvai
B. nunizi
B. quadrinodosa
B. sp.
INCERTAE SEDIS
Hourequia sp.

As Lima pointed out, all the ostracods in this list are either smooth or else little-ornamented and consequently are difficult to distinguish. The possibility that all the ostracods reported actually belong to just one or two species, as Bate (1972) contended, requires careful investigation.

Assemblages: Jardim, Old Mission, Santana, although Bate's (1972) sample apparently is from the Jardim assemblage. Ostracods are particularly abundant in "Santana" concretions, although they unfortunately are calcareous and do not survive acid preparation. In these concretions a large part of the biogenic sediment consists of ostracod tests.

(J. G. Maisey)

Copepods

Subclass COPEPODA
Order SIPHONOSTOMATA
Family DICHELESTHIIDAE
Genus **Kabatarina** Cressey and Boxshall, 1989
1989 *Kabatarina* Cressey and Boxshall: 151

Diagnosis: Dichelesthiid copepod with elytra on third and fourth pedigerous somites, non-retractile antennae, four pairs of legs, and a terminal maxillary claw; shares with other dichelesthiids a medial groove delimiting distal part of maxillary claw.

Type species: *Kabatarina pattersoni* Cressey and Boxshall, 1989

Kabatarina pattersoni Cressey and Boxshall
1989 *Kabatarina pattersoni* Cressey and Boxshall: 151

Diagnosis: As for genus; total body length approx. 1 mm; parasite of *Cladocyclus gardneri* gill region; both sexes apparently parasitic.

Holotype: British Museum (Natural History), BM(NH) IN. 63466; cephalothorax with mouthparts, oral cone, first and second legs of presumed female; Santana formation, Romualdo member, Chapada do Araripe, Ceará. Other referred material: seven specimens, BM(NH) 63467-70 and 62625-7, plus five others now destroyed.

Copepods are abundant and successful small crustaceans in marine and freshwater habitats, and many are parasitic on invertebrates and aquatic vertebrates. The free-living forms are an important link in aquatic food chains, as they feed on microscopic organisms. Many modern species are known, but virtually nothing is known of their ancient history.

Many parasitic copepods are known to occur on the body surface or gills of marine and freshwater fishes. In less specialized forms the parasite is not permanently attached to the host but can move about using legs and their flexible body. In more extreme examples there is a free-swimming reproductive phase followed by permanent attachment of the female, which bores into the host and loses body flexibility. In even more extreme cases the female is greatly modified and the dwarfed male is permanently attached to the female; here both sexes become rigid and immobile.

The discovery of fossil parasitic copepods among the gill arches of specimens of the extinct ichthyodectid fish *Cladocyclus gardneri* is of considerable scientific importance for a number of reasons. Firstly, this particular record (first reported by Cressey and Patterson, 1973) pushes back the known fossil record of copepods from the Miocene (Palmer, 1960) to the Lower Cretaceous (more than seven times older). Secondly, these particular copepods are clearly well adapted to a parasitic mode of life and possess numerous anatomical features that are peculiar to these epiparasites, indicating that these peculiar attributes were fully evolved at least 110 million years ago. These fossils therefore provide a glimpse at an ancient host-parasite relationship having close modern parallels and offer compelling evidence for complex ecological relationships that must have existed then as now.

The phylogenetic implications of this discovery are considerable, for it has become increasingly evident in recent years that the systematic hierarchy of host and parasite species may display strong parallels. The most plausible scenario for such a link is that the host organism and its obligate parasites have evolved in tandem. By studying the phylogenetic relationships and distribution of host-specific parasitic species, systematists may be able to gain further insight into the relationships of host species (and vice-versa, at least theoretically). In theory, the presence of a primitive dichelesthiid parasite in *Cladocyclus* may provide supplementary data concerning the host's phylogenetic position among teleosts. In this particular case the information content is low, because *Cladocyclus* is in many respects a generalized teleost and *Kabatarina* apparently is a generalized dichelesthiid; nevertheless, the phylogenetic data from the fossil host is at least consistent with that obtained from the parasite.

The first specimens of *Kabatarina* were discovered by Dr. Colin Patterson, a

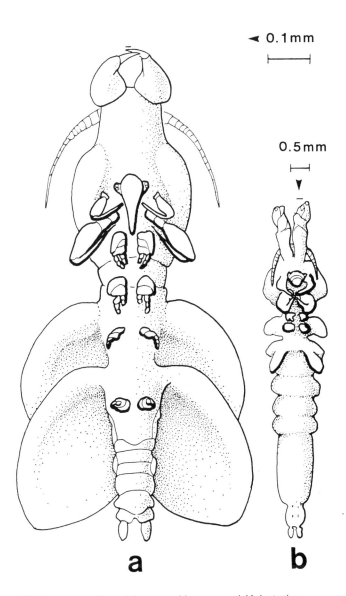

(A) Reconstruction of the parasitic copepod *Kabatarina pattersoni*, ventral aspect of presumed female showing the oral cone, mouthparts and first legs on the cephalothorax, and large paired dorsal elytra on the third and fourth pedigerous segments (scale bar = 0.1 mm). (B) Ventral aspect of a female *Dichelesthium oblongum*, an extant parasitic copepod (scale bar = 0.5 mm). After an original illustration by Carolyn Gast.

paleontologist at the British Museum (Natural History), while he was preparing some specimens of *Cladocyclus gardneri* in acetic acid. One skull yielded parts of three copepods, and another provided parts of several more, one of which differed significantly in size and shape from the others. Although the single specimen could represent another species, Cressey and Boxshall (1989) instead concluded that it represents a male. Modern parasitic copepods typically display strong sexual dimorphism, and *Kabatarina* may have been similar. Usually the female is larger and more highly modified, and the smaller male often is attached to the female instead of the host.

Based on the fragments at their disposal, Cressey and Boxshall (1989) were able to reconstruct their ancient parasite. The presumed female has a body length of about 1 mm and has a cephalothorax comprising five cephalic somites plus two thoracic somites. The cephalothorax has an extensive shield ornamented with a dense coat of fine spinules. There apparently are five abdominal somites, lacking appendages. The male was approximately 0.7 mm long, with finer antennae. Mouthparts in the fossils closely resemble those of modern siphonostomatoid copepods, which are adapted for an ectoparasitic mode of life. The second antennae are provided with a strong terminal claw, which may have assisted in anchoring the parasite to its host. The maxillipeds apparently were adapted for holding the cephalothorax in the correct position for feeding, with the oral cone of the mouthparts erected perpendicular to the long axis of the parasite.

The abdominal somites of the larger, presumably female, individuals bear dorsal plates (elytra). Cressey and Boxshall (1989) speculated that these plates may have functioned to protect egg-strings. They are absent from the smaller (presumably male) individuals.

Kabatarina displays several characters that are considered to be phylogenetically primitive, including a high number of segments in the first antennae, separate praecoxa not fused to the coxa in the maxillae and maxillipeds, distal three segments of the maxillipeds not fused, and segments of leg exopods not fused. Two of these features (many-segmented first antenna, segmented maxilliped claw) today characterize siphonostomatoids that parasitize invertebrate hosts, whereas those having a fish as host possess fewer antennal segments and have a fused maxilliped claw. In these features *Kabatarina* is less specialized than its modern counterparts, although it shares some features with modern families that are parasitic on fishes, such as loss of an exopod on the second antenna.

Cressey and Boxshall (1989) tentatively assigned *Kabatarina* to the Recent family Dichelesthiidae on the basis of a single shared derived character, the presence of a groove on the maxillary claw. *Kabatarina* lacks several characters uniting all other dichelesthiids (elytra present on second pedigerous segment; retractile antennae; 3 pairs of legs; maxilla with "prehensile" apex).

To conclude, *Kabatarina* appears to be a very primitive dichelesthiid that has retained certain presumably plesiomorphic characters occurring today only in those copepods parasitic on invertebrates. Since nothing more is known of Mesozoic copepods, and their earlier history has yet to be recorded, further speculation would be premature.

Assemblage: Uncertain; recorded examples may be from Jardim assemblage, but distribution could be much wider.

(J. G. Maisey)

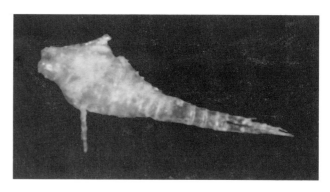

Anostracan (fairy shrimp). Incomplete adult individual retrieved from acid-prepared residue of a *Brannerion* specimen, showing the carapace, a thoracic appendage, and the two branches of the telson; specimen now unfortunately is lost.

Fairy Shrimp
Subclass BRANCHIOPODA
Order ANOSTRACA
Incertae sedis

A single incomplete specimen of a presumed anostracan (fairy shrimp) was recovered from the residue during acid preparation of a "Santana" lithology concretion containing a *Brannerion* specimen (AMNH 11931). This represents the first anostracan recorded from the Santana formation.

Today the majority of branchiopods occupy freshwater habitats (except for a few marine cladocerans). Anostracans generally cannot tolerate high temperatures and usually disappear during late spring or summer. They are easy prey for carnivorous fishes and insects, usually occurring in habitats lacking such predators. A wide range of pH and salinity can be tolerated, however, as evidenced by the living brine shrimp (*Artemia*).

The presence of any anostracan in a fossil assemblage teeming with predaceous fishes is clearly peculiar. It may indicate that this crustacean was accidentally introduced (perhaps after death). Alternatively, there may have been a major invasion of a normally predator-free freshwater environment by the larger fishes.

Assemblage: Santana.

(J. G. Maisey)

Clam Shrimp
Order DIPLOSTRACA
Suborder CONCHOSTRACA
Incertae sedis

Fossil conchostracans (clam shrimps) have been recorded by Oliveira and Leonardos (1943), Paes Laeme (1943) and Beurlen (1963) from bituminous shales, especially from the region of Casa de Pedra (Municipality of Ipubi), Rancharia (Municipality of Araripe), and Romualdo (Municipality of Crato). Although the stratigraphic data are sparse, these records suggest that the conchostracans occur in the Araripina formation, underneath the Santana formation. Descriptions of the material are inadequate, partly for preservational reasons. Specimens have been referred to *Estheria* and *Bairdestheria*, but these identifications must be treated with some reservations.

Assemblages: Araripina formation? (bituminous shales).

(J.G. Maisey)

Undetermined palaemonid shrimp from the Crato member. Photo by R. G. Martins-Neto.

Shrimp
Subclass MALACOSTRACA
Order DECAPODA
Suborder NATANTIA
Family PALAEMONIDAE?

Fragments of shrimp-like crustacean cuticles are often recovered during acid preparation of numerous fossil fishes using acetic or formic acid. These fragments evidently are better phosphatized than many of the other crustacean remains, suggesting that there may have been more phosphate present originally (not unusual among decapods). Identification of similar remains as coming from palaemonids (a group including most freshwater shrimp as well as some brackish and marine forms such as glass shrimp) was first made by Beurlen (1963: 25).

Shrimp are known in both the upper and lowest units of the Santana formation. Palaemonid shrimp are found in concentrations at the nuclei of calcareous concretions and around fishes such as *Rhacolepis* or even as stomach contents of these fishes. The state of preservation of such material is very fragmentary. In the Crato member, however, whole well-preserved palaemonid shrimp are known from completely articulated specimens representing a new genus (Martins-Neto, in press).

Assemblages: Old Mission (uncommon), Jardim (rare) concretions of the Romualdo member, and in laminated limestones of the Crato member (rare).

Crab
Suborder BRACHYURA
Superfamily PORTUNOIDEA?
incertae sedis

Araripecarcinus Martins-Neto, 1987

Emended diagnosis: Small crab approximately 10 mm long as well as wide, carapace convex with surface granulated, outline ovoid, lateral and postero-lateral outlines not well delimited, without lateral spines; branchial lobes well developed; last pair of legs reduced, with natatory adaptation; long merus in ambulatory legs.

Type Species: *Araripecarcinus ferreirai* Martins-Neto, 1987

Araripecarcinus ferreirai Martins-Neto, 1987

Diagnosis: As for genus.

Holotype: Almost complete individual on outer surface of calcareous concretion from upper unit of Romualdo member, Santana formation, near Porteiras, Ceará USP (GP/1 T 1477). See photo, page 432.

This peculiar species of crab recently was described from the upper unit of the Santana formation. It is a small crab and tentatively is assigned to the superfamily Portunoidea (a pelagic family that today includes some of the most agile and powerful of swimmers of all crustaceans) because of its peculiar adaptation to fast swimming by means of a transformation of the fifth pair of legs. Reduction in size of these appendages may be a primitive condition, however, found also in the Torynomidae.

Araripecarcinus is clearly related to the torynomid genus. *Mythracites* from the Aptian of England, although the fast swimming ability is not verified in this form. This ability therefore may have been attained independently in portunoids and *Ararpiecarcinus*. Alternatively, it is possible that torynomids do not constitute a monophyletic group unless portunoids are included.

(R. G. Martins-Neto)

Undetermined gastropods: small specimen partly dissolved by acid (below right); another example retrieved from acid-prepared residue and photographed in the scanning electron microscope (left).

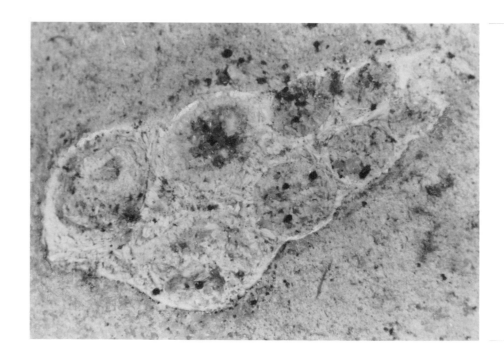

MOLLUSCS

The molluscan fauna of the Santana formation has received less attention than it perhaps deserves. It is remarkably biased in as much as there are no "typical" benthic marine molluscs (ammonites, belemnites, nautiloids) that one might expect were there to have been an open connection with the ocean, nor are there any scaphopods. Only gastropods (snails) and bivalved lamellibranchs (clams) have been reported. The most extensive taxonomic lists are those of Mabesoone and Tinoco (1973) and Lima (1979b), from which the following list was extracted.

This list is impressively long for the Santana formation as a whole, but it does not reflect the relatively depauperate molluscan fauna found in the fish-bearing concretions. A few small turritellid gastropods and corbulid-like pelecypods have been found in some concretions, usually in distinct layers that do not correspond to the bedding planes on which the fossil fishes occur. The presence of these molluscs within the concretions thus is accidental, and it cannot be assumed that the local paleoenvironment was the same when the molluscs and fishes were alive.

(J. G. Maisey)

Class GASTROPODA
  Family TURRITELLIDAE
  Craginia araripensis
  Gymnentone romualdoi
  Turritella lucianoi
  Turritella sp.
  Mesalia sp.
  Glauconia sp.
  Family NATICIDAE
  Natica sp.
  Polinices sp.
  Lunatia *sp.*
  Ampullina sp.
  Family EPITONIIDAE
  Epitonium smalli
  Family SCALIDAE
  Turriscala sp.
  Scala sp.
  Family CERITHIIDAE
  Cerithium sp. cf. *C. austinense*
  Hemicerithium? sp.
  Family APORRHAIDAE
  Aporrhais sp.
  Family NERITIDAE
  Neritoma sp.

Class PELECYPODA
  Family PTERIIDAE
  Eupteria sp. cf. *E. flicki*
  Pteria sp. A
  Pteria sp. B
  Family ISOGNOMONIDAE
  Aguileria sp.
  Family ANOMIIDAE
  Anomia sp.
  Family MYTILIDAE
  Brachidontes sp.
  Family CRASSATELLIDAE
  Crassatella sp.
  Family OSTREIDAE
  Ostraea sp.
  Family CORBULIDAE
  Corbula sp. A
  Corbula sp. B
  Family VENERIDAE
  Venus sp.
  Family UNIONIDAE
  indet.
  Family CYRENIDAE
  indet.

FOSSIL PLANTS

Insights into the plants and vegetation in the vicinity of the Araripe basin during the mid-Cretaceous are provided by macroscopic plant organs (e.g., leaves, seeds) as well as microscopic fossils (e.g., pollen, spores). Pollen/spore assemblages (palynofloras) from the Santana formation and the overlying Exu formation have been treated in several papers (Mabesoone and Tinoco, 1973; Lima 1978a, b, c, 1979a, b, 1980), but a comprehensive account has not yet been published. These palynofloras are broadly similar to those from other mid-Cretaceous low paleolatitude areas (Northern Gondwana, Brenner, 1976), and when compared with data from eastern South America and West Africa they also provide some information on the age of the associated fauna. Plant macrofossils occur in both the Crato and Romualdo members of the Santana formation, although current collections suggest that the "flora" from the Crato member is more diverse. Macrofloras from Cretaceous low paleolatitude areas are sparse, and although the Araripe flora has not been collected extensively or studied in detail, it provides useful insights complementary to palynological information.

Paleobotanical data document that the mid-Cretaceous was a critical interval in the evolution of terrestrial vegetation, characterized by the first appearance, and apparent extinction, of many taxa in several plant groups. Most significantly, between the Barremian and Cenomanian stages, angiosperms (flowering plants) undergo their first major systematic diversification, and other taxa show equally dramatic changes in abundance and diversity. Although these changes are manifested on a global scale, and perhaps were associated with marked environmental changes that also occurred during the mid-Cretaceous, palynological data indicate that they probably were initiated at low paleolatitudes (Brenner, 1976; Hickey and Doyle, 1977). The Araripe plant fossils therefore are of particular significance because of the information they provide on mid-Cretaceous vegetation in these low latitude areas.

Palynostratigraphy

Plant macrofossils recovered so far from the Araripe basin contribute little stratigraphically useful information, but pollen/spore assemblages provide a basis for more accurate age determinations. The list of palynomorphs published by Mabesoone and Tinoco (1973) from the Romualdo member as part of a paleoecological study contains diverse pteridophyte spores and ephedroid pollen, with less diverse angiosperm and conifer components. According to Professor G. Brenner (State University College, New Paltz, N. Y.; pers. comm.) this list does not contain certain significant Middle or Late Albian palynomorphs and suggests a Late Aptian to Early Albian age. Based on the data of Lima (1978a, 1979b, 1980), Doyle, et al. (1982, p. 68) have listed the characteristic palynomorphs of the Santana formation that include *Cicatricosisporites nuni*, *C. avnimelechi*, *Ischyosporites granulosus*, and *Chomotriletes almegrensis*, as well as a diversity of ephedroid forms including "*Galeacornea causea* form B," *Sergipea naviformis*, and numerous polyplicates (e.g., *Singhia reyrei*, *Gnetaceaepollenites uesuguii*, *G. rectangularis*, and *?Gnetaceaepollenites* sp.). The Santana palynoflora is considered by Doyle, et al. (1982, p. 68) to show many similarities to those of the oldest marine sediments of the Ivory Coast described by Jardiné and Magloire (1965) and Zone IA of the Brazilian sequences studied by Herngreen (1975). Comparable palynofloras from the Ivory Coast occur in undifferentiated Aptian-Albian marine sediments (Doyle, et al., 1982, p. 71). The age of Zone IA (Herngreen, 1975) in the northeastern Barreirinhas (Maranhao) basin is not well constrained but its upper limit is thought to be Early-Middle Albian (Herngreen, 1975). According to Doyle, et al. (1982), if the determination of *Sergipea naviformis* from the Santana formation is correct (Lima, 1979b), then this also supports correlation with palynozones C-IX to C-XI in Gabon that are thought to be of Upper Aptian to Lower Albian age. The angiosperm component of a Santana formation sample examined by Doyle, et al. (1982, p. 68) contained forms "characteristic of zone C-IX of Gabon, including small gemmate and striate tricolpates (*Tricolpites* sp. 1 and *Striatopollis* sp. 1) and *Clavatipollenites* sp. 1 (Doyle et al., 1977), *Retimonocolpites* cf. *dividuus*, *R.* cf. *peroreticulatus*, *Stellatopollis barghoorni* (described by Lima as *Crotonipollis*), as well as *Afropollis* aff. *jardinus*." Zone C-IX is thought to be of Upper Aptian age.

The Santana formation is unconformably overlain by massive cross-bedded fluviatile sandstones of the Exu formation thought to be of Middle Albian age based on palynological data (Lima, 1978b). Although this is consistent with age determinations for the Santana formation, certain palynomorphs in Lima's (1978b) list from the Exu formation (e.g., *Equisetosporites concinnus*, *E. albertensis*, *E. dudarensis*, and *E. elongatus*) suggest a maximum age of Late Albian (Brenner, pers. comm.), and further analyses are needed to clarify the extent of the depositional hiatus between the two formations. Taken together, published and unpublished data (Professors G. Brenner and J. Doyle, pers. comm.) suggest that the Santana formation is probably of late Upper Aptian or possibly Early Albian age. In the Sergipe-Algoas basin, fossil fish reported from stratigraphic levels below Upper Aptian ammonites (Brito, 1984) are similar to those from the Santana formation. While this may suggest a slightly earlier age for the Santana formation than that indicated by the pollen data, more detailed studies are necessary to test the utility of the "*Vinctifer* biozone" established by Brito (1984; see earlier discussion in this volume). Unfortunately, in the Araripe basin the age of the (supposedly Jurassic) Missao Velha formation that underlies the Santana formation is not well constrained, although there is now some (largely unpublished) paleontological evidence that these sediments are of Lower Cretaceous age.

Comparison of Palynoflora and Macroflora

In terms of abundance, conifers are one of the most conspicuous elements in palynofloras from the Santana formation. *Classopollis* pollen is known to have been produced by the Cheirolepidiaceae, a family of diverse and distinctive Mesozoic conifers (Watson, 1988), while pollen of *Araucariacites* probably was produced by conifers resembling extant Araucariaceae (Norfolk Island pine and related taxa). Both the Araucariaceae and the Cheirolepidiaceae are common components of mid-Cretaceous palynofloras from low paleolatitudes (Vakhrameev, 1970) and both also appear to be represented as macrofossils in the Santana formation.

In the limestone concretions from the Romualdo member the most common macrofossils are probable cheirolepidiaceous branch systems with lateral shoots that usually are narrow at their point of attachment but broader distally. The shoots bear many small, helically arranged leaves that are seen as numerous distinctive diamond-shaped scars on the stem. Although relatively uncompressed, most specimens appear to be poorly preserved, with the cavity left by the original plant material filled to various extents by coarse calcite crystals. More detailed studies are needed to determine whether useful anatomical details are preserved as impressions in the limestone matrix. The only other macrofossils recorded from the concretions are more or less spherical masses consisting of numerous, pale-colored, ovoid seeds embedded in a dark carbonaceous matrix. These structures may be cheirolepidiaceous ovulate cones produced by the same species as the shoot systems described above. Details of individual cone scales do not seem to be preserved, but seeds and associated tissues are at least partially mineralized, and further studies may help to clarify current uncertainties in the interpretation of cheirolepidiaceous seed-bearing structures (Watson, 1988).

Plant macrofossils from the Crato member are mainly preserved as impressions although anatomical details are visible in a few specimens either as detailed imprints in the fine limestone matrix or as permineralizations resulting from partial replacement of plant tissues by iron minerals. Probable cheirolepidiaceous leafy shoots have much larger leaves than those in the Romualdo member concretions and also show stomata arranged in longitudinal rows. Parts of these shoots have a distinct longitudinal groove that marks the position of a relatively small central core of woody tissue. The thicker outer parts of the stem evidently were composed of softer, possibly succulent tissues. The only other conifer remains known from the Crato member are dispersed cone scales resembling those of extant Araucariaceae.

Among the most characteristic palynomorphs from the Araripe basin are ephedroid pollen grains (e.g., *Galeacornea*, *Gnetaceaepollenites*) with a folded-striate wall that sometimes is extended into horn-like or elongated projections. Comparisons with the distinctive polyplicate pollen of the extant "gymnosperms" *Ephedra* and *Welwitschia* suggest that these mid-Cretaceous grains were produced by plants similar to extant Gnetales (Crane, 1988). This is supported further by detailed comparison of pollen wall structure in fossil and extant grains (Trevisan, 1980) and also by associations, outside Northern Gondwana, between fossil ephedroid pollen and macrofossils of Gnetales (Crane and Upchurch, 1987, Krassilov, 1986).

Although diverse ephedroid pollen is one of the most distinctive features of mid-Cretaceous low latitude palynofloras, there has until now been no direct macrofossil evidence of other parts of these plants. One of the most intriguing aspects of the macroflora from the Crato member is the possibility that some of these extinct Gnetales may be present. A characteristic feature of extant gnetales, also seen in some of the fossils from the Crato member, is the occurrence of opposite leaf arrangement and branching patterns. Several macrofossils consist of slender axes that have distinct opposite branching, but more detailed anatomical studies are needed to determine whether these specimens can be assigned to the Gnetales. One specimen also shows several small seeds attached at the point of branching. These seeds have several apical spines, and comparison with other mid-Cretaceous taxa from mid-paleolatitude areas suggests that these may be apical extensions of the bracts or bracteoles that virtually enclose the seed body. Spiny seeds also occur dispersed in the matrix from the Crato member.

In addition to conifers and ephedroids, other gymnosperms are represented in the Araripe Cretaceous by the presence of *Monosulcites* pollen. Unfortunately, the generalized structure of these grains precludes a more detailed assessment of their relationships. Two different kinds of macroscopic vegetative remains in the Crato member may also have been produced by non-conifer, non-ephedroid gymnosperms. One of these consists of several simple, entire margined, broadly elliptical leaves attached to a slender stem. The venation consists of numerous fine, occasionally anastomosing, veins that diverge from the leaf base. The leaf texture is thick and in places the leaf tissue appears to have been replaced by iron minerals. Similar early Cretaceous leaves have been interpreted as *Sagenopteris* leaflets (e.g., Barale, 1982), but in the Crato member example the leaves are simple rather than compound. The second leaf type is a frond fragment that may have been produced by either a fern or some kind of seed plant ("seed fern"). The leaf has three pinnately divided lobes and is covered by a dense covering of numerous long, simple hairs.

The only unequivocal pteridophyte remains recovered from the Santana formation are a variety of monolete and trilete spores, most of which probably were produced by ferns. Based on comparisons of *Gleicheniidites* and *Cicatricosisporites* spores to those from extant taxa, both Gleicheniaceae and Schizaeaceae are probably represented, but the systematic relationships of most other dispersed spore genera are uncertain.

Angiosperms are represented in the Santana formation by a variety of angiosperm pollen types (Mabesoone and Tinoco, 1973; Doyle, et al., 1982), including several tricolpate forms (e.g., *Striatopollis*, *Tricolpites*) that are diagnostic of nonmagnoliid dicotyledons (subclasses Asteridae, Caryophyllidae, Dilleniidae, Hamamelidae, Rosidae). Tricolpate pollen is first recorded at around the Barremian-Aptian boundary, and thus the grains from the Araripe basin provide some of the earliest evidence of this group. In contrast, angiosperm pollen with a single distal germinal aperture (monosulcate or derivative types) is first recorded from the Hauterivian, and the presence of such forms as *Afropollis*, *Clavatipollenites*, *Retimonocolpites*, and *Stellatopollis* in this sequence indicates the presence of monocotyledons or dicotyledons at the magnoliid grade. As in most pre-Albian palynofloras, the relative diversity of angiosperm pollen is typically low, and with the exception of the distinctive genus *Afropollis* (Doyle et al., 1982; Penny, 1989), angiosperm pollen rarely is abundant. The macrofossil flora from the Santana formation concretions so far includes no unequivocal angiosperm fossils. Conceivably some of the thick, reed-like leaf macrofossils with parallel venation preserved in the Crato member could represent monocotyledons or other plants that produced monosulcate pollen, but there is no evidence of laminar, reticulate-veined leaves resembling those of extant dicotyledons.

Paleobotanical Evidence on Paleoecology

The palynomorph associations recovered from the Araripe Cretaceous sequence are typical of many Northern Gondwana floras of this age that are broadly characterized by high abundances of *Classopollis*, the presence of angiosperm pollen, and a diverse, abundant group of striate-polyplicate ephedroid grains. In general the relative diversity of spores is less than in Northern and Southern Laurasia. This distinctive palynological assemblage has been used to define the mid-Cretaceous WASA Province (West Africa-South America Province; Herngreen and Chlonova, 1981), but it now is clear that a similar palynological assemblage was much more widespread in an equatorial belt extending from Ecuador in the west to southern China (Yu Jingxian, 1981) and Papua New Guinea in the east. Although there is much local variation in the nature of floras and sediments in Northern Gondwana, evidence from both paleobotany and sedimentology broadly indicates that most of the area was subject to at

Small fernlike frond, Crato member, approx. 3 cm across, with dense indumentum of numerous simple hairs.

least seasonally arid or semiarid conditions. In general, as noted by Doyle, et al. (1982: 69), palynological resemblances to the more northerly floras of Maranhão, Ivory Coast and Senegal, and Zone C-IX floras of the South Atlantic salt basins suggest broadly similar climatic conditions.

The most detailed consideration of the plant paleoecology in the mid-Cretaceous WASA province is provided by Doyle, et al. (1982) based predominantly on palynofloras from West Africa. One of the most distinctive ecological patterns in these sequences is the inverse relationship between the abundance of fern spores and the abundance of *Classopollis*. This broadly supports the view that cheirolepidiaceous conifers were relatively common, and perhaps best adapted to more arid environments (Doyle, et al., 1982), whereas ferns were more common in less arid situations. However, the Cheirolepidiaceae evidently occupied a broad range of environments probably ranging from salt marshes to better drained uplands (Upchurch and Doyle, 1981; Doyle, et al., 1982; Watson, 1988), and it is also clear that many of the characteristic ferns from these areas (e.g., *Weichselia*) also exhibit strongly xeromorphic characteristics (Alvin, 1974).

Patterns in the abundance and diversity of ephedroid and angiosperm pollen with respect to *Classopollis* and spores are complex, but in general pollen of both groups is negatively correlated with high levels of *Classopollis*, although changes in their abundance do not always parallel changes in the abundance of fern spores (Doyle, et al., 1982). These patterns suggest that ephedroids were probably not important in the driest habitats and that traditional interpretations of this group as indicators of aridity, based on simple extrapolation of the ecology of extant *Ephedra* and *Welwitschia*, may be misleading. Angiosperm pollen exhibits broadly similar patterns to the ephedroids, and the general association with aridity supports the idea (Stebbins, 1974) that this may have been an important ecological factor in angiosperm origins. However, as pointed out by Doyle, et al. (1982), angiosperms also appear equally early in areas that are thought to have been more equable.

The macroflora contributes direct evidence of the morphology of plants from the Santana formation and also provides some indication of possible climatic conditions. The Cheirolepidiaceae have "reduced" leaves and

rather broad (possibly succulent?) stems. In addition, the occurrence of regularly deciduous branches is suggested by the constricted branch attachments in the material from the Crato member. The "*Sagenopteris*" leaves and some of the reed-like remains have a thick fibrous texture, and the "seed fern" leaf has a heavily developed covering of hairs. All of these features are broadly consistent with other botanical and geological indications of aridity.

Evolutionary Significance of the Araripe Plants

The evolutionary significance of the Araripe flora centers on its potential to clarify aspects of early angiosperm evolution and the insights it provides into interactions between evolutionary and environmental effects in mid-Cretaceous vegetational change at low paleolatitudes. Recent phylogenetic analyses suggest that angiosperms are most closely related to Gnetales and Bennettitales, and this has been used to infer that angiosperms may have separated from related "gymnosperm" groups by the Late Triassic (Crane, 1985; Doyle and Donoghue, 1986). However, the earliest unequivocal angiosperm pollen so far recorded is from the Hauterivian of Israel and southern England (Brenner, 1984; Hughes and McDougall, 1986), and there is strong evidence that angiosperms first underwent their major phylogenetic and ecological diversification between the Aptian and Cenomanian. Palynological data indicate that the mid-Cretaceous radiation was dominated by an increase in the abundance and diversity of nonmagnoliid dicotyledons, and the distinctive tricolpate or tricolpate-derived pollen diagnostic of this group shows a marked latitudinally diachronous pattern of first appearance. At low paleolatitudes triaperturate grains are first recorded, and become important, at around the Barremian-Aptian boundary (Brenner, 1976; Doyle and Hickey, 1976; Crane and Lidgard, 1989), while at higher paleolatitudes in both hemispheres they are not recorded until the Early Albian. The Araripe flora therefore is critically positioned, both stratigraphically and geographically, to contribute important insights into early angiosperm evolution.

With the exception of palynological data, almost nothing is known of early angiosperms from mid-Cretaceous low paleolatitudes. However, given the early focus of flowering plant diversification in this area, there is a strong possibility that much of the extinct diversity critical to resolving relationships among major clades of monocotyledons and of magnoliid and nonmagnoliid dicotyledons may not be recoverable from more intensively studied mid-high paleolatitude floras. Phylogenetically, current hypotheses of nonmagnollid dicot evolution suggest that the earliest producers of triaperturate pollen may have included taxa closely related to extant basal hamamelids such as Trochodendraceae, Tetracentraceae, and Cercidiphyllaceae. Exine ornamentation of some early tricolpate pollen from other low latitude areas (e.g., Egypt, Penny, 1988) is consistent with this hypothesis, but increased knowledge of macrofossils from the Araripe basin and elsewhere will be necessary to test these hypotheses. Similarly, detailed studies of *Clavatipollenites* pollen and associated reproductive structures from mid-latitude areas strongly suggest a close relationship to the extant family Chloranthaceae (Walker and Walker, 1984; Pedersen, et al., MS), but comparable studies have not been published on pollen from low latitudes assigned to this genus.

The Araripe plant macrofossils and comparable floras also are important for the information they can potentially provide on extinct Gnetales. Increased knowledge of diversity in this group could have important implications for resolving seed plant phylogeny (Crane, 1985, 1988) and also would clarify the extent of inferred structural, biological, and ecological similarities between mid-Cretaceous Gnetales and angiosperms (Doyle, et al., 1982; Crane and Lidgard, 1989). Such data will be critical for correctly interpreting the remarkably similar low latitude pattern of increasing mid-Cretaceous palynological diversity shown by both groups (Crane and Lidgard, 1989).

Ecologically, documentation of Gnetales and angiosperms in the Araripe basin and other inland locations provides clear evidence of the importance of both groups in a variety of locations rather than solely in lowland coastal habitats as implied by some hypotheses of early angiosperm evolution (Retallack and Dilcher, 1981). Increased information on Gnetales and angiosperms also will provide an opportunity to assess the early phases in the evolution of insect pollination, occur in both these groups. The Araripe biota provides an important opportunity to gauge simultaneously the level of differentiation in potential insect pollinators and putatively insect-pollinated plants.

Paleobotanical studies at mid-paleolatitudes provide important information on the structure, biology, and relationships of early angiosperms and help to clarify some aspects of mid-Cretaceous vegetational change. However, it is clear that a more comprehensive understanding of early angiosperm evolution will require comparable data from low paleolatitude areas. Some progress will be possible with extensive palynological sampling in Northern Gondwana, but the current paucity of macroflora data indicates a critical need for extensive collections of mid-Cretaceous macrofossil plants from the Araripe Basin and similar areas. Integration of macrofossil and palynological studies in these regions offers particular promise for clarifying the early history of angiosperms and associated vegetational changes.

(P. R. Crane, J. G. Maisey)

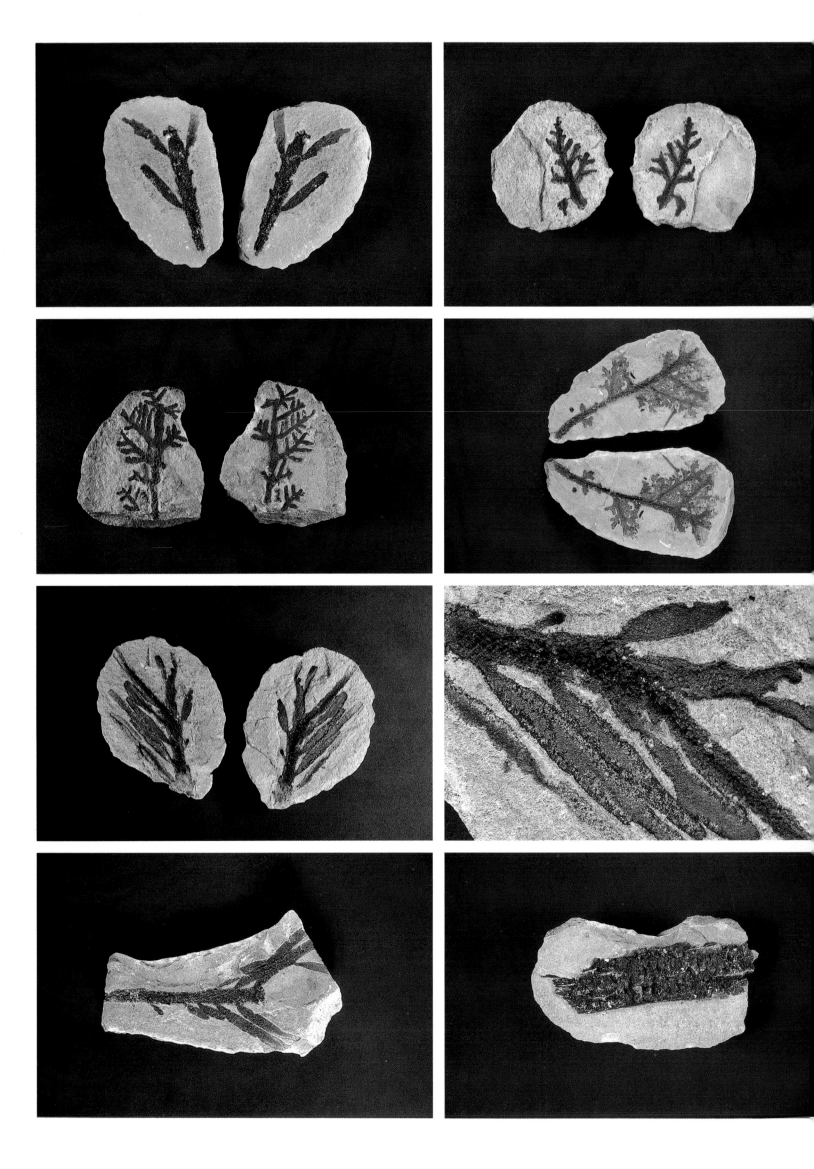

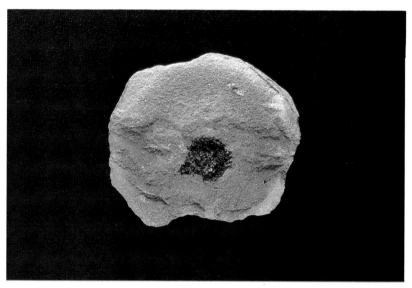

Above: Cones preserved in "Santana" matrix as carbonized masses with carbonate seeds. These cones probably come from the same species of cheirolepidiaceous conifer as the leafy fronds (opposite).

Facing page: Cheirolepidiaceous conifer fragments in "Santana" matrix, mostly leafy fronds except (bottom right) for a piece of carbonized wood.

421

14: Concluding Remarks

The Araripe basin contains what is probably the world's most important Lower Cretaceous Gondwanan fossil assemblages, not only in terms of taxic diversity and abundance, but also because of its paleogeographic and temporal setting. It is located close to the final area of disconnection between South America and Africa, and its sedimentary sequences were laid down contemporaneously with momentous tectonic events related to this final separation.

One of the goals of producing this volume was to synthesize as much of the data as possible in order to produce an overview of this classic area and its geological history. Whether this work has done anything to solve problems is doubtful; at best, it may have focused upon some critical problems for future investigation and debate.

It seems appropriate to summarize some aspects of what has been described and discussed in the preceding pages, especially the paleontological, paleoecological, and biogeographical data, in order to separate fact from controversy (fully realizing that what is the fact of today may be the controversy of tomorrow!).

Paleontology

Taken together, the Crato and Romualdo members of the Santana formation are documented here as having produced 29 nominal taxa of fossil fishes referable to 21 genera and 14 families (Rhinobatidae, Hybodontidae, Semionotidae, Macromesodontidae, Gyrodontidae, Amiidae, Ionoscopidae, Ophiopsidae, Aspidorhynchidae, Cladocyclidae, Araripichthyidae, Pachyrhizodontidae, Notelopidae, and Coelacanthidae), plus *incertae sedis* members of the Albuloidei, Gonorynchiformes, Clupeiformes, and Euteleostei. This represents a flat increase of 11 nominal taxa (some undescribed) and three families over the list provided by Silva Santos and Valença, although for taxonomic reasons the lists are not strictly comparable. The number of higher taxa (at family level or above) is now 18, or ten more than listed by Silva Santos and Valença. Perhaps the most profound addition is that of the giant coelacanths *Mawsonia* and *Axelrodichthys*.

The lists of fossil fishes from the Santana formation and other localities compared by Silva Santos and Valença have grown since 1973. They listed eight "families" out of 11 common to both the Santana formation and the

Benevento assemblage from Italy, seven out of 12 from the English Wealden and Purbeckian, and seven out of 11 from the Kimmeridgian of Cerin, France. It has not been possible to provide a comprehensive revision of their analysis at this time, but a few general remarks are appropriate. By expanding the Santana assemblage to reflect current knowledge, while retaining the informal spirit of their comparison, it could now be argued that all 11 "families" listed for Benevento are shared by the Santana formation, with eight out of 12 for the English Wealden and Purbeckian, and ten out of 11 for the Kimmeridgian of Cerin. As it stands, unfortunately, this comparison is not particularly useful because some of the "families" recognized by Silva Santos and Valença are of questionable validity, and also because the diversity of higher taxa is now apparently even higher in the Santana formation than in some of the assemblages that were being compared. The comparison nevertheless verifies (and even seems to strengthen) the view that the fossil fish assemblage of the Santana formation is characteristic for the Aptian-Albian despite its strong endemism at generic level. It is now clearer than ever that there are important differences from later Cretaceous assemblages such as those from Lebanon and elsewhere.

Besides fishes, these Brazilian formations have now produced a frog, two distinct genera of pelomedusid turtles, two crocodilians (a notosuchid and a trematochampsid), several genera with numerous species of pterosaurs, dinosaur bones, and a bird feather. Usually the skeletal remains of these tetrapods and fishes are complete and undistorted by diagenetic processes, providing a wealth of anatomical detail about the animals represented. In many (perhaps all) cases, the fossils are the finest examples of their kind in existence. The vertebrates include the oldest known albuloids and pelomedusids and some of the oldest gonorynchiforms, pachyrhizodontids, and clupeiformes (perhaps the world's earliest anchovy?). An undescribed gar-like fish is also known.

The Crato member has produced the most diverse and speciose Gondwanan Cretaceous insect assemblage, including numerous undescribed species representing 14 or 15 orders and many more families. According to Grimaldi's report this assemblage includes the oldest known examples of oligoneuriid, euthyplociid, and potamanthid mayflies, coenagrioid and macromiid odonates, cicadellid leafhoppers, anaxyelid sawflies, tiphiid and rhopalosomatid wasps, apoid bees, bibionid march flies, and asilid robber flies. In addition, many of the taxa represent new records for a Gondwanan locality. At family level the assemblage is essentially modern. Besides insects, the assemblage also includes scorpions and spiders, including an early mygalomorph.

An important but still little-investigated floral assemblage also is present in the Crato member, including the remains of cheirolepidiaceous conifers; possible gnetales; a non-coniferous, non-ephedroid gymnosperm; a fern-like plant; and a puzzling reed-like leaf with parallel venation that could be an angiosperm. Rarely, concretions from the Romualdo member contain fronds, cones, and carbonized wood, possibly from large cheirolepidiaceous conifers.

The invertebrates of the Santana formation include definite marine components (e.g., echinoids, certain pelecypods and gastropods), but stratigraphic data for these taxa are not well documented. It is known, however, that the echinoid occurrence is considerably higher in the Romualdo member than the fossiliferous concretions. Characteristic marine molluscs such as belemnites, ammonites, and scaphopods are notably absent, as are corals, crinoids, and brachiopods. Ostracods associated with some fossil fishes are uniquely preserved with appendages intact, making them the most complete fossil examples known. The geological range of copepods is extended back almost 100 million years, with the discovery of specialized epiparasitic examples among the gills of *Cladocyclus* specimens.

Paleoecology and Paleoenvironment

The Araripe basin is essentially a half-graben similar to those of the Recôncavo-Tucano-Jatobà basinal complex farther south, with its downthrown side to the south of the Patos lineament. Sedimentological data suggest that the Crato member is lacustrine but are ambiguous regarding the Romualdo member, perhaps because of environmental fluctuations ranging from lacustrine through lagoonal to marine. Even when non-marine conditions existed, salinity levels may have been elevated at certain times during the deposition of both the formations.

The Crato member comprises black shales, laminated limestones (sometimes ripple-marked) and dolostones, algal-laminated shales, and evaporites (especially gypsum and anhydrite).

These beds are truncated by an erosion surface, with a caliche-like calcrete surface to the north and east and (according to Silva, 1986a) a paleokarst topography with deep solution cavities infilled by muds and conglomerates of the Romualdo member to the south and west. Most fossils in the Crato member, including terrestrial and aquatic arthropods, plants, and the small gonorynchiform fish *Dastilbe*, occur in algal-laminated carbonates that are interpreted as a marginal lacustrine facies. The presence of halite pseudomorphs on some bedding planes in the laminated carbonates indicates at least periodic episodes of elevated salinity that may have caused the deaths of *Dastilbe* and many of the aquatic insects; alternatively, *Dastilbe* (and other, much rarer fishes including *Cladocyclus*) may have invaded the lake during periods of high salinity.

The Romualdo member includes basal conglomeratic muds, alternating layered concretionary calcareous shales, limestones, and sandstones. It rests unconformably on older rocks, locally overlapping onto the Paleozoic and Pre-Cambrian basement. Echinoderms indicate marine conditions late in its depositional history.

The Exu formation consists largely of current-bedded fluviatile sandstones deposited by a northerly-draining river system. It lies unconformbly on older sediments and has produced few fossils apart from wood fragments and an important palynoflora suggesting an Albian date for its deposition.

Paleogeographically, the Araripe basin probably lay close to a watershed during the Early Cretaceous, because sedimentological data suggest that the Parnaiba basin to its north had a northerly drainage ultimately connecting it to the North Atlantic, whereas drainage of the Recôncavo limb in the basinal complex to its south was controlled by southerly rift-related events. Prior to activation of the Pernambuco lineament, similar sedimentary sequences were accumulated in both the Recôncavo and Araripe basins, hinting at a southerly drainage pattern. Drainage within the Araripe basin conceivably changed from south to north prior to the Albian. This area lay on the principal axis of rotation between South America and Africa during the Neocomian, but this axis was abruptly shifted 1900 km (1200 miles) farther to the northwest during the Aptian and Albian.

There is evidence (chiefly from offshore borehole data) for a "great drying" of the northerly parts of the South Atlantic toward the end of the Neocomian. Many marginal basins

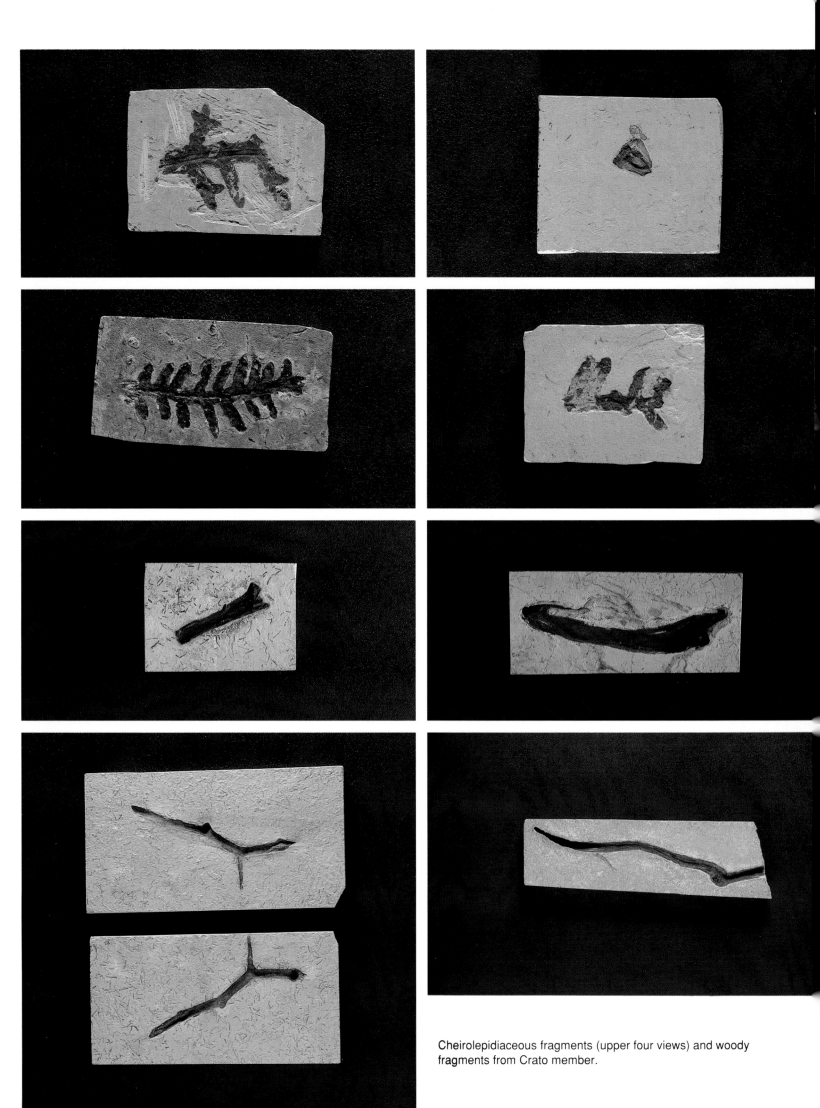

Cheirolepidiaceous fragments (upper four views) and woody fragments from Crato member.

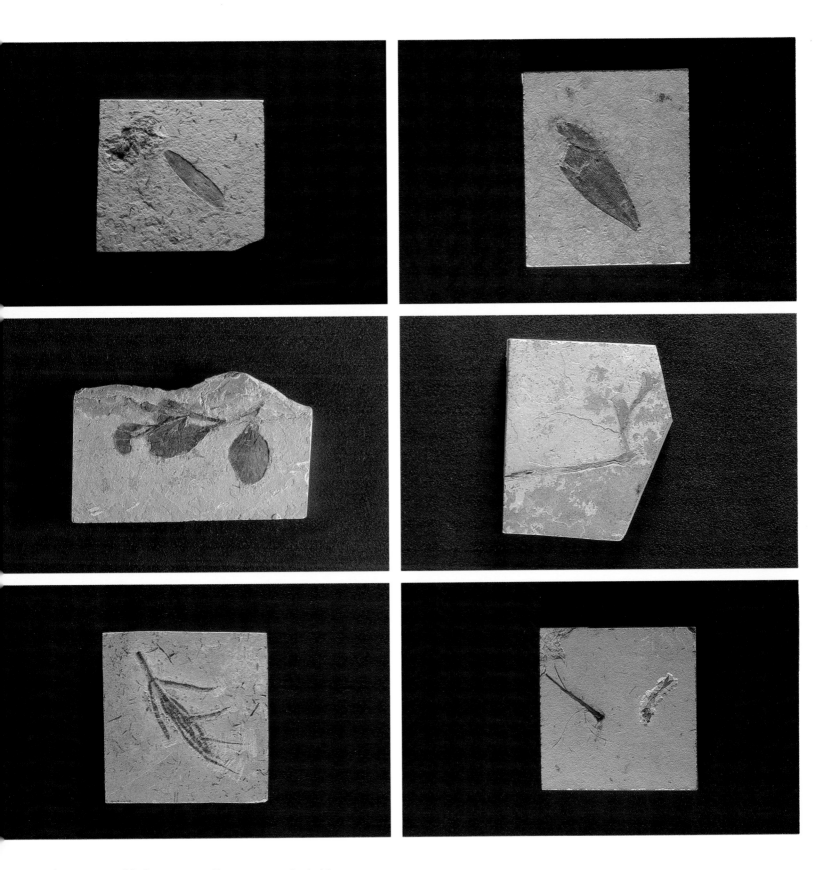

Leaves, possibly from non-coniferous, non-ephedroid gymnosperm.

show signs of aridity, and this undoubtedly was the climatic situation farther inland. The Crato member evidently represents an increasingly dry climatic situation, with terrestrial plants and arthropods from groups capable of tolerating high aridity and ultimately terminating in a sabkha-like environment.

The Romualdo member begins with high-energy conglomeratic sediments, but its subsequent history is mostly represented by low-energy regimes. Episodic (storm?) events may be represented by thin shell banks with graded detrital sediments. The bottom environment was generally anoxic except perhaps for the "Santana" assemblage, which is characterized by clean, ostracod-rich carbonates.

Local environmental variations may be reflected by the lithological and faunal composition of Romualdo member concretions from different parts of the Araripe basin. Three fossil fish assemblages are recognizable, here named after important collecting sites (Santana, Jardim, Old Mission). These assemblages are broadly contemporaneous, with many shared taxa, and all have a marine to mixihaline aspect. But important differences are noted in the relative abundance of particular taxa, their distribution, and to some extent the size of individuals. The distributional data can be summarized as follows (for convenience, data for the Crato member are also included):

A. Taxa apparently restricted to a single assemblage.

1. Crato member: *Dastilbe crandalli*, *D. elongatus*.

2. Santana: *"Leptolepis" diasii*, Santana clupeid.

3. Jardim: *Mawsonia* cf. *gigas*, ?*Oshunia brevis*, ?*O.* sp. form A.

4. Old Mission: ?*Oshunia* sp. form B, *Notelops* sp. A.

B. Taxa shared only by Jardim and Santana assemblages.

"Rhinobatos" beurleni, *Araripelepidotus temnurus*, *Tharrhias araripis*, *Axelrodichthys araripensis*.

C. Taxa shared only by Jardim and Old Mission assemblages.

Neoproscinetes penalvai, *Araripichthys castilhoi*, *Paraelops cearaensis*, *Rhacolepis buccalis*, ?*R. defiorei*.

D. Taxa shared only by Santana and Old Mission assemblages.

None.

E. Taxa shared by all Romualdo member assemblages.

Calamopleurus cylindricus, *Vinctifer comptoni*, *Cladocyclus gardneri*, *Brannerion vestitum*, *B.* sp. A, *Notelops brama*.

F. Taxa shared by Romualdo and Crato members.

Cladocyclus sp. (?*ferus*).

G. Taxa of undetermined distribution within Romualdo member.

Tribodus limae, *Iemanja palma*, *Ophiopsis cretaceus*, *Cladocyclus ferus*, *Brannerion latum*.

Terrestrial elements (viewed as exotic and serendipitous discoveries in the assemblages) such as plants and tetrapods are more common in the Santana assemblage, less so in the Jardim assemblage, and virtually absent from the Old Mission assemblage.

Sedimentologically, "Santana," "Jardim," and "Old Mission" concretions are evocative of progressively deeper and/or muddier and increasingly anoxic bottom environments. Some paleontological support for this view comes from the distribution of *"Rhinobatos"* (today rhinobatids prefer shallow sandy marginal areas of marine to brackish water) and the generally larger sizes of fishes in the Jardim and Old Mission assemblages, especially fast-swimming forms such as *Notelops*, fanged predators such as *Cladocyclus* and *Calamopleurus*, and coelacanths. Although several species are shared by all three assemblages, it is noteworthy that none is found only in the presumably shallowest (Santana) and deepest (Old Mission) ones, although both may share taxa with only the Jardim assemblage.

These differences between assemblages may reflect local biological compartmentalization of the Araripe basin, suggesting that the fishes belonged to established resident populations. A more random distribution of taxa and sizes would be expected were they carried in by some catastrophic event such as a storm surge (as proposed at Sölnhofen, for example). Even though the fishes may have been resident within the basin, however, several aspects of the assemblages are peculiar and deserve particular note.

First, there is a remarkable discrepancy in taxic diversity between the Crato and Romualdo members of the Santana formation. Moreover, the most abundant Crato member fishes (*Dastilbe* spp.) seem to be absent from the Romualdo member, which nevertheless shares at least one taxon (*Cladocyclus*). Interestingly, *Dastilbe* is now reported at a new locality (Pedra Branca) from bituminous shales also containing *Vinctifer*, *Rhacolepis*, and *Cladocyclus* (Viana, Brito and Silva Telles, MS).

Second, the Santana formation assemblages from concretions are characterized by very high numbers of individuals of many taxa, and taxic diversity at family level or higher is also high.

Third, the Romualdo member assemblages are dominated by large predators, giving the impression of ecological imbalance. Assuming that a large percentage of individuals comprising these original populations has been preserved as fossils, this imbalance may have been a real feature of the communities represented. Benthic dwellers are rare but taxonomically diverse; according to Brito and Ferreira (1989) these include *Tribodus*, "*Rhinobatos*," semionotids, pycnodontids, and coelacanths.

Fourth, although some specimens display evidence of direct predation, there is very little sign of scavenging. This seems a strong indication of sudden mortality, especially in view of the sedimentological evidence for slow burial.

Collectively, these observations suggest that the Araripe basin offered only temporary refuge for a large and taxonomically diverse marine or mixihaline fish fauna and ultimately proved to be a death trap. In spite of this, some ecological compartmentalization apparently was achieved by the fishes, chiefly in relation to water depth and possibly distance from shore.

Although the Crato member culminates in an evaporitic and calcrete facies, the presence of a frog, mayflies, dragonflies, damselflies, caddisflies, aquatic bugs, and aquatic beetles offers compelling evidence of low salinity during an earlier stage in its depositional history. We may visualize an open, quiet body of fresh water surrounded by an arid and perhaps inhospitable hinterland supporting a flora of cheirolepidiaceous conifers, ephedroids, and some other gymnosperms, plus large reed-like plants of uncertain phylogenetic position; presumably most or all these plants grew at or adjacent to the shoreline. The flora helped support a rich insect fauna as well as some predaceous spiders, scorpions, frogs, and birds. There is no evidence of larger terrestrial predators, although this may partly be a consequence of preservational bias.

The marginal terrestrial environment during Romualdo member times probably was similar, with large cheirolepidiaceous conifers dotting the landscape. No insects and no other plants have yet been documented, but there evidently were small terrestrial crocodilians (e.g., *Araripesuchus*) as well as a much larger aquatic trematochampsid, dinosaurs, and two pelomedusid turtles. The skies evidently were filled with pterosaurs, some of which were probably specialized as fish-feeders. Freshwater conditions are hinted at by the rare presence of an anostracan. Many of the fishes present in the Romualdo member belong to genera or families that are known from freshwater as well as marine deposits. Some belong to groups that are more convincingly marine, such as rhinobatids, pycnodontiforms, and ionoscopids. Environmental data provided by the fishes are not straightforward and have been used to defend both marine and non-marine hypotheses. Periodic inundation by oceanic waters is a possibility, although a considerable body of geological and paleogeographic data has been put forward in opposition of a marine environment except at the end of Romualdo member times. Future investigations, particularly of microfossils and isotopes, hopefully will clarify the paleoenvironmental picture.

Biogeography

The physical location of the Araripe basin, combined with the stratigraphic age of its sedimentary sequence, makes this a critical area in which to investigate Early Cretaceous Gondwanan biogeography. The basin lies adjacent to the last continental connection between South America and Africa and is one of precious few inland Mesozoic basins with the potential for preserving truly continental aspects of early Cretaceous floras and faunas.

Aquatic vertebrates, especially fishes, indicate that periodic connections existed between adjacent basins within what is now northeastern Brazil and equatorial West Africa. Continued investigation of this and other Brazilian basins has revealed the presence of common faunal elements during some stages of their histories and has even inspired some attempts at correlation (e.g., the "*Vinctifer* biozone"). Whether such correlations are particularly useful is doubtful, as the stratigraphic ranges of the taxa being pressed into service are not fully documented. It is nevertheless clear, as Professor Silva Santos points out in this book, that the Araripe region was not an isolated intracontinental basin.

The distribution of the small gonorynchiform fish *Dastilbe* is of some biogeographical interest. It occurs in the Neocomian of both northeastern Brazil and West Africa, probably within different parts of a central rift-controlled lake system. West African *Dastilbe* probably occupied the same drainage basin, possibly even the same lake, as those from the Alagoas and

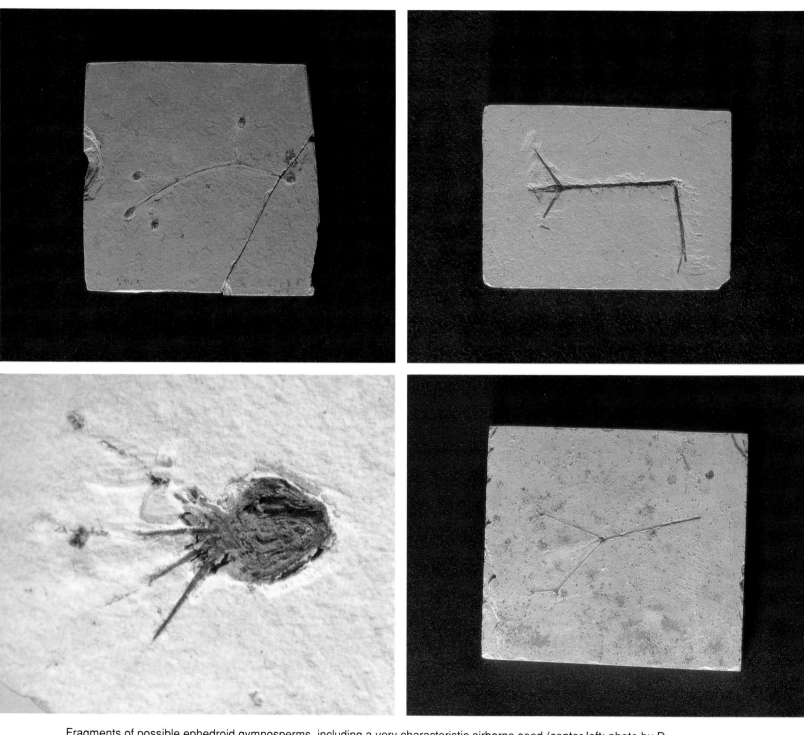

Fragments of possible ephedroid gymnosperms, including a very characteristic airborne seed (center left; photo by D. Grimaldi).

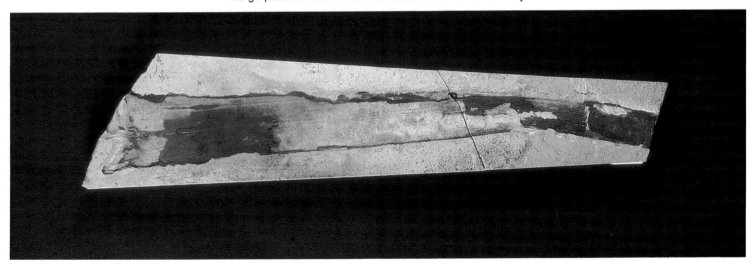

Large parallel-veined reed-like leaves of uncertain affinity.

Recôncavo basins of Brazil. All these sites are tectonically related to rifting of the South Atlantic, whereas *Dastilbe* from more northerly basins (e.g., Parnaiba) may have occupied a system of rivers and lakes that ultimately connected with the North Atlantic. The Araripe basin seems to be a crucial link between these two Lower Cretaceous catchment areas. This connection may have been severed following elevation of the Araripe region at the end of Crato member times, possibly at about the time that the rotation axis of South America became shifted from this region to the northwest. That tectonic event, marking the end of the connection with western Cameroon and Niger, had enormous impact on the geological and presumably the biogeographical history of these two continents. It may be viewed as the last stage of a vicariant event that had its beginnings far to the south some 10-15 million years earlier. Several taxa endemic to this part of Gondwanaland were immediately affected, including *Araripesuchus* (which apparently became extinct on both continents), trematochampsids (which continued to survive on both continents into the Upper Cretaceous), *Mawsonia* (which apparently died out in South America but briefly continued through the Albian of Africa), and *Dastilbe* (which disappeared on both continents). As additional data from Africa become available, the fate of many other taxa presently known only from the Cretaceous of South America hopefully will become available.

Most of the Cretaceous fishes from the Araripe basin are endemic to Gondwanaland at the generic level, although most belong to families with much wider distributions that certainly extend into the Northern Hemisphere. The apparent exceptions to this Gondwanan generic-level endemism are taxa of doubtful attribution (e.g., *"Rhinobatos" beurleni*, *Ophiopsis cretaceus*, *"Leptolepis" diasii*) or else have non-Gondwanan records that are founded upon dubious material (e.g., *Cladocyclus*). It is possible that the fossil fishes of the Santana formation are entirely endemic to Gondwanaland at generic level. Their history on both sides of the South Atlantic before, during, and after their vicariant dispersal is an exciting area for future investigation.

Elsewhere in this volume, Grimaldi noted several new and important biogeographical records among the fossil insects from the Crato member, including taxa otherwise known (either as fossils or from living species) only from non-Gondwanan localities. These include:

Potamanthidae (presently Holarctic and Oriental), Hexagenitidae (Laurasian fossils only), Siphloneuridae (presently Austral and Holarctic), Syntexinae (presently only one species, Nearctic), and Rhaphidioptera (Holarctic). Other significant records include the first fossil coenagrioid and first macromiid (living or fossil) from South America, and the first Cretaceous Gondwanan termite. These data represent profound range extensions for some higher taxa of insects. At generic level many of the insect fossils probably will remain known only from this locality but likely as not are Gondwanan endemics.

The Araripe basin also is a source of potentially informative plant macrofossils to supplement palynological records from this region. Great significance may be attached to this place and time regarding the origins and early evolution of flowering plants. It would be premature to discuss the biogeographical implications of the material from the Santana formation beyond reiterating the remarks of Doyle, et al. (1982) that there are many similarities with Aptian-Albian palynofloras of the Ivory Coast, and that Crane (this volume) has confirmed the importance of ephedroids ("one of the most distinctive features of mid-Cretaceous low-latitude palynofloras") from macrofossils.

Conservation

The Araripe basin clearly represents a major resource to paleontologists and biogeographers concerned with Aptian-Albian faunas and floras and the break-up of Gondwanaland. Continued studies of the rich fossil record from this and other Gondwanan Cretaceous localities may provide insights into one of the last great vicariant events in evolutionary history. Only now are the faunal and floral assemblages of the Araripe Cretaceous being adequately sampled. New species and genera are being discovered at a remarkable rate that is unprecedented in its 160+ years of documentation. There clearly is a need for further alpha-level systematic work, especially in previously neglected but important areas such as fossil insects and plants, but also among the diverse fossil vertebrates. Further investigation of stratigraphic sections is required in order to provide more accurate correlations both within the Araripe basin and between it and other basins of northeastern Brazil and western Africa.

In order to continue these important researches, it must be hoped that further conservation measures will be taken to preserve the classic collecting areas as sites of scientific interest, open to scholarly study by established Brazilian and international scientists.

The protection of important paleontological sites around the world is of increasing concern to professional scientists, especially in view of greater commercial exploitation of fossils as collectable objects. Most museums and universities lack the financial means to compete with wealthy private collectors for important fossil specimens. Only rarely can an institution benefit from the far-sighted support of philanthropic individuals with an interest in saving some of this material for scientific and scholarly study.

Various regulatory processes have been introduced by certain nations or states, but most have met with only limited success. It is one thing to mandate the regulation of collecting or sale of fossils, but quite another to provide assurances that collectors will comply, or that such legislation will achieve its fundamental goal, which is to ensure that important fossil specimens ultimately are deposited in a recognized scientific collection.

There are some who would say that all collecting (even though it is conducted largely on privately owned land) and sale of Araripe fossils should be prohibited, a view strongly criticized by others who argue that this would simply drive the practices underground, thereby even further denying legitimate scientists access to important material. I am reminded of a passage by that great 19th-century Scottish writer and geologist, Hugh Miller, concerning the possibility of such prohibition on paleontological collecting at a classic site in Scotland. With characteristic humor, he wrote:

"I was tickled with the idea of a fossil preserve, which coupled itself in my mind, through the trick of the associative faculty, with the idea of a great fossil act for the British empire, framed on the principles of the gamelaws; and, just wondering what sort of disreputable vagabonds geological poachers would become under its deteriorating influence, I laid hold of the pickaxe . . . .

"I trust, should the case ever come to a serious bearing, the members of the London Geological Society will generously subscribe half-a-crown apiece to assist me in feeing counsel. There are more interests than mine at stake in the affair. If I be case and committed—I, who have poached over only a few miserable districts in Scotland—pray, what will become of some of them—the Lyells, Bucklands, Murchisons and Sedgwicks—who have poached over whole continents?"

(H. Miller, *The Cruise of the Betsey*, 1858, p. 52)

At the opposite extreme, some have advocated a free-for-all open approach to collecting Araripe fossils, on the ground that it would be a self-regulated activity, controlled by normal economic factors of supply and demand. Non-regulation, it has been suggested, would potentially enhance the availability of material for scholarly study. Given the dramatic increases in prices of many fossil specimens (not only those from Brazil) being offered by commercial collectors and dealers in Europe, Japan, and the U.S. over the past few years, however, it seems likely that declaring "open season" on Araripe fossils might put scientifically important material beyond the reach of all but the world's wealthiest institutions.

In the U.S., the Society of Vertebrate Paleontology has opposed a proposal to allow commercial collection of fossil vertebrates on Federal lands. If permitted, such collecting would almost certainly have a severe adverse impact upon long-range field investigations conducted by paleontologists and other scientists in these areas, besides creating even greater economic pressures for available material.

Fossil collecting on state-controlled lands in the U.S. is regulated in the vast majority of states, although existing legislation varies in scope (West, 1989). Most states claim public ownership of all paleontological, archaeological, and geological materials collected on public lands and require that these materials be placed in a public repository. Some states make allowances for certain materials to move into private ownership, usually with the proviso that they are for personal, non-commercial use.

Virtually anyone can collect on privately owned lands in the U.S., provided they have the owner's consent. Few states have attempted to control collecting on private land. According to West (1989), private landowners in New Mexico do not need permits to excavate on their own land, but other persons must demonstrate that they have the landowner's permission and must obtain permits from the State Historic Preservation Ofice to conduct mechanical excavation.

The Kansas legislature has been trying to pass a bill requiring commercial fossil hunters to

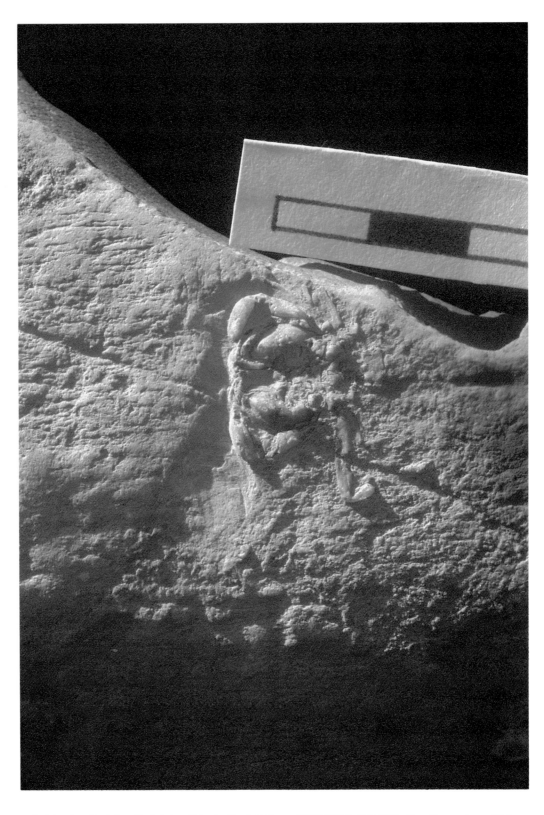

Araripecarcinus ferreirai, a small crab; the holotype, USP (GP/1-T-1477). For discussion of this species, see page 411. Photo by R. G. Martins-Neto.

obtain written permission from landowners to excavate on private lands, to notify the landowner of the nature and value of fossils collected, and to obtain written authorization for their removal. Such a bill would undoubtedly provide assurances that the landowners would be compensated for any specimens collected commerically on their property, but seems to offer little benefit to the scientific community.

In Florida, all vertebrate fossils on state lands are protected by law. Additionally, a mechanism exists whereby private land can be designated as a "State vertebrate paleontological site" with the written consent of the owner. Vertebrate fossils found on such controlled lands are afforded the same protection as if they were collected on state lands and cannot be purchased or sold.

A model example of successful regulation is offered by the State of Baden-Württemburg (West Germany), where strict rules control the sale of fossil vertebrates and certain other fossils found there (chiefly in the classic Holzmaden area), even on private land. No "protected" specimen can be sold without a permit granted by the State Museum, ensuring that the legal sale of these specimens can take place only after they have been examinied by a competent authority. More importantly, the State Museum is endowed with funds (generated by a State lottery that helps support a number of cultural institutions) to compensate owners should their specimens be required for the State collection. In this way, commercial collectors have little reason to avoid compliance with the regulatory process, and the State Museum in its turn has reaped enormous benefits from its continued healthy relationship with these individuals.

Whether such an approach is feasible or appropriate in the case of other important sites, such as the Araripe Plateau, can of course only be determined following careful examination of the pertinent economic, sociological, and scientific factors. It may be unrealistic to expect a procedure that has proven successful in a part of West Germany to be workable in a part of northeastern Brazil. Whatever the case, however, some form of balanced regulation tempered by incentive to encourage collectors to come forward with scientifically important material may be desirable.

(J. G. Maisey)

Appendix One:

Fossil Insects from the Santana Formation (Crato Member)

EPHEMEROPTERA
indet. 1
indet. 2

  Hexagenitidae
    Protoligoneuria limai
  Siphloneuridae
    Siphgondwanus occidentalis
    indet. 1
    indet. 2
    indet. 3
  Oligoneuriidae
    Colocrus indivicum
  Ephemeridae
    Australiphemera revelata
    Microphemera neotropica
  Euthyplociidae
    Pristiplocia rupestris
  Potamanthidae
    indet.
  Leptophlebiidae
    indet. 1
    indet. 2
    indet. 3

  indet. ephemeroid 1
  indet. ephemeroid 2

ODONATA
ZYGOPTERA
  Pseudostigmatidae
    Euarchistigma atrophium
  Protoneuridae
    Eoprotoneura hyperstigma
ANISOPTERA
  Gomphidae
    Cordulagomphus tuberculatus
    C. fenstratus
    C. santanensis
    Gomphaeschnaoides obliqua
  Aeschnidiidae
    Wightonia araripina
  Pseudomacromiidae †
    Pseudomacromia sensibilis

DERMAPTERA
  Cretolabia cearae

PHASMATODEA
  Cretophasmatidae †
    Cretophasma araripensis

ISOPTERA
  Hododermitidae
    Meiatermes araripina

HOMOPTERA
  Jascopidae
    Paracarsonus aphrodoides
    Platyjassites inflatifrons
    Platyjassites sp.
  Cicadellidae
    Proerrhomus rugosus
    Proerrhomus sp. A
    Proerrhomus sp. B
    Ovojassus concavifer

    O. minor
    Hallex xestocephalus
    H. gongrogony
    H. brevipes
    H. laticeps
    H. gracilior
    H. sp.
Cicadoidea
  Cicadoprosbolidae
    Architettix compacta
Cercopoidea
  Cercopionidae
    Cercopion reticulata
Aleyrodoidea
  Boreoscytidae ?
    Megaleurodes megocellata
Fulgoroidea
  Achilidae
    Acixiites immodesta
    A. costalis
    Fennahia cretacea
  Cixiidae ?
    indet.
  Lalacidae
    Protodelphax miles
    P. macroceps
    P. rhinion
    P. chamus
    P. sp.
    Ancorale flaccidum
    A. aschemon
    A. sp.
    Kinnarocixius quassus
    K. sp.
    Lalax mutabilis
    Lalax sp.
    Patulopes setosa
    P. myndoides
    P. sp.
    Carpopodus difficilis
    C. sp. A
    C. sp. B
    Psestocixius fuscus
    P. delphax
    Vulcanoia membranosa
    V. apicalis
    V. acuceps
    V. sp.

HETEROPTERA
  Belostomatidae
    indet.
  Pentatomorpha
    indet.
  Gerromorpha (?)
    indet.
  Naucoridae
    indet.
  Corixidae
    indet.
  Peloridiomorpha
    indet.
  Saldidae
    indet.

  Reduviidae
    indet.
  Cimicomorpha
    indct.

BLATTODEA
  indet.

ORTHOPTERA
  indet.
CAELIFERA
  indet.
ENSIFERA
  Gryllidae
    (Gryllinae, Oecanthinae)
    several spp.
    Araripegryllus camposi
  Tridactylidae
    indet.
TETTIGONIOIDEA
  indet.
ACRIDOIDEA
  Archaeopneumoridae †
    Archaeopneumoridae cretacea, ms
  Bouretidae
    Bouretia elegans, ms

NEUROPTERA
  Chrysopidae
    Limaia conspicua
    Araripechrysa magnifica
    Caririchrysa criptovenata
    C. confusa
  Myrmeleontidae
    Caldasia cretacea
    Blittersdorffia pleoneura
    B. volkheimeri
    Araripeneura regia
    A. gracilis
    Pseudomyphes araripensis
    Caririneura microcephala
  Ascalaphidae
    Cratopteryx robertosantosi
  Nymphidae
    Babinskaia pulchra
    B. formosa
    Nelia maculata
    Alloneura acuminata
  Nemopteridae
    Roesleria exotica
    Megalopteryx audax
    M.? robusta

RHAPHIDIOPTERA
  Baissopteridae
    Baissoptera brasiliensis

COLEOPTERA
  Pyrochroidae
    Cretaceimelittommoides cearensis
  Dytiscidae indet.
  Staphylinidae indet.
  Passalidae indet.
  Nitidulidae ? indet.

  Curculionoidea indet.
  Carabidae indet.
  Scarabaeidae indet.

DIPTERA
  Tipuloidea
    indet. **Tipulidae**
  Bibionoidea
    indet. **Bibionidae**
  Sciaroidea
    indet.
  Mycetophilidae
    indet. Macrocerinae
  Chironomoidea
    indet. **Mesotendipedidae**
  Asiloidea
  Asilidae
    Araripogon axelrodi

HYMENOPTERA
SYMPHYTA
  Anaxyelidae
    Prosyntexis gouleti
APOCRITA
  Ephialtitidae †
    Karataus kourios
  Proctotrupidae
    Proctoprocto asodes
  Mesoserphidae †
    indet.
ACULEATA
  Tiphiidae
    Architiphia rasnitsyni
  Rhopalosomatidae
    Mesorhopalosoma cearae
  Sphecidae
    Cretosphex parvus
    C. magnus
    indet. sphecid
    indet. Aculeata
  Formicidae
    Cariridris bipetiolata, ms

LEPIDOPTERA
  Micropterygidae
    Parasabatinica caldasae
  indet.
    Undopterix caririensis
    Gracilepterix pulchra

TRICHOPTERA
  indet.

Also reported:
MECOPTERA

PLECOPTERA

PSOCOPTERA

Total named taxa: **97**
Total taxon estimate: **148** (number of spp. probably *much* higher, because higher taxa known to contain various undescribed forms)

Glossary

acrozone (range zone): A stratum defined by the time-span of a species.

actinopterygians: Bony fishes in which the fins are supported only by fin rays; the "ray-finned fishes" (cf. sarcopterygians).

adipocere: Whitish waxy material consisting of saturated fatty acids, usually produced during decay of organic matter.

albian: Stratigraphic stage name, originally for the base of the British Lower Cretaceous.

amniote: Vertebrate in which the developing embryo is protected by a fluid-filled amniotic sac (includes mammals, birds).

anaerobic: Without free oxygen.

anamestic: Dermal bones in the skull that do not contain a sensory canal.

angiosperms: Vascular plants with seeds in ovaries—the flowering plants.

anoxic: Without free oxgen.

Aptian: Stratigraphic stage name, originally for the base of the British Lower Cretaceous.

assemblage: The fossils found within a particular stratum, representing organisms that may or may not have coexisted in one or more original faunas and floras.

assemblage zone: Series of strata characterized by a faunal assemblage. Note that some species may occur above or below an assemblage zone.

authigenic: Formed in place during or after deposition of sediment.

autogenous: Term referring to neural and hemal arches that are not fused to a vertebral centrum.

Barremian: Stratigraphic stage name, originally for the European mid-Lower Cretaceous.

Bennettitales: Non-angiosperm seed plants with pinnate or simple cycad-like leaves and flower-like reproduction structures.

benthos; epibenthos; endobenthos: Those organisms that live on, just above, or within (respectively) the sediments of the sea floor.

biostratinomy: Study of post-mortem disturbance of organic remains.

biota: The total flora and fauna of an area.

biozone: Rocks deposited during the total time range of a species.

boreal realm: A "northern" or "Arctic" region.

breccia; brecciated: Sediments consisting of angular fragments indicating minimum transport, generally poorly sorted and derived from a restricted source.

caatinga: Term for parts of NE Brazil characterized by tropical steppes (short grass, few shrubs) to tropical savanna (tall grass, tree growth near water), mostly used for livestock ranching and plantation farming.

calcrete: Superficial gravels cemented by a calcareous deposit (tufa).

caliche: Hard, cement-like surface layer produced in arid sabkha environments by evaporite minerals.

Campanian: Stratigraphic stage name, originally for part of the European Upper Cretaceous.

Cenomanian: Stratigraphic stage name, originally for the basal European Upper Cretaceous.

Cenozoic: The last of three geological eras, beginning after the Cretaceous period; sometimes loosely called "The Age of Mammals."

cheirolepidiaceous: Leaf arrangement of many small, helically arranged leaves covering stems and shoots, characteristic of a group of conifers including Norfolk Island pines and the "monkey puzzlers."

chronostratigraphy: See **stratigraphy.**

cladistics: A procedure whereby organisms are grouped together on the basis of shared derived characteristics (synapomorphies), which are considered to be the most reliable indicators of phylogenetic or evolutionary relationships.

cladogram: A branching diagram or map of character distributions among different organisms, as distinct from an evolutionary tree that intimates at lines of ancestry and descent. Several (sometimes many) alternative evolutionary trees can be advocated using the character distributions given by just a single cladogram.

coloite: The fossilized contents of the intestinal tract.

compressional margin: the contact between two crustal plates that are moving toward each other.

conglomerate: Sediments consisting of rounded or sub-rounded fragments, implying greater transport and erosion than breccias.

Coniacian: Stratigraphic stage name, originally for part of the European Upper Cretaceous.

coprolite: Fossilized fecal pellet of vertebrates, usually from fishes.

correlation: The practice of determining whether rock strata in different places are of equivalent age.

Cretaceous: The last geological period of the Mesozoic era, named by d'Halloy in 1822, beginning some 135 million years ago and ending about 65 million years ago.

ctenoid: Type of fish scale with one edge toothed like a comb; found chiefly in spiny-rayed fishes (acanthopterygians).

cycloid: Type of fish scale with rounded or elliptical shape, such as those of salmon.

diagenesis: Process affecting sediments at or near to the Earth's surface, at low temperatures and pressures (excluding processes of weathering), leading to formation of solid rock from loose sediment.

dinoflagellates: Green, yellow, or brown protozoans protected by cellulose plates and having two flagella at right-angles to each other.

diplospondylous: Condition in which there are two vertebral centra per body segment, instead of the more usual one (monospondylous condition).

dolostone: Rock consisting entirely of the mineral dolomite (magnesium carbonate).

drusy: Layer or coating of minute crystals.

endemic: Being restricted in geographical distribution to a particular continent or region.

endobenthos: See **benthos.**

eolian: Formed in a terrestrial, non-aquatic environment.

epicontinental sea: A shallow sea covering part of the continental shelf and lacking a basaltic ocean floor.

ephedroids: A group of pollen grains with morphology comparable to pollen of extant *Ephedra* and *Welwitschia* (Gnetales), characterized by a distinctive, longitudinally folded pollen wall.

epibenthos: See **benthos.**

epural: Modified neural spine in the caudal fin of ray-finned fishes.

erosion: Lowering of the land surface by weathering, corrosion, and transportation under the influence of gravity, wind, and running water.

Eurasia: A hypothetical part of the Laurasian supercontinent, roughly the part left after the separation of North America.

eustatic changes: Absolute worldwide changes in sea level, as against local fluctuations caused by movements of land or sea floor.

evaporite: Crystalline sediments resulting from evaporation of saline water, usually in shallow lakes and enclosed epicontinental seas.

extensional margin: The contact between two crustal plates that are moving away from each other; new (usually basaltic) crust is added here, and the margin often forms a mid-oceanic ridge.

facies: Sum total of features of a sedimentary rock type, including mineralogy, sedimentary structures, fossil content. Facies characterized by a particular rock type are called lithofacies; facies characterized by particular fossils are called biofacies.

family: Group of organisms consisting of closely related genera.

fault: Fracture in the Earth's crust, along which the rocks on one side have been displaced relative to those of the other.

fin ray; marginal, principal: Bony supports of the fins. In ray-finned fishes, these include unbranched marginal rays (not reaching the full height of the fin) and principal rays, which may be branched or unbranched.

fluviatile: Pertaining to a river system.

formation: Sedimentary rock sequence that can be mapped. Several formations collectively may constitute a group. One formation may consist of several members.

fossa bridgei: Pair of hollow depressions just above the auditory (otic) capsules, usually roofed over by dermal bones of the skull, and receiving anterior slips of the trunk muscles.

fracture zone: Region of the Earth's crust in the process of breaking up into smaller plates.

fulcral scale: fish scale at the base or leading edge of a fin (friging fulcra), often found in primitive ray-finned fishes.

ganoid: Type of fish scale with a hard, shiny outer layer of enamel-like ganoin, found in living gars and many fossil ray-finned fishes.

gemmate: Pollen surface sculpture consisting of minute bud-like processes.

gnetales: Group of gymnosperms with resemblances to angiosperms, especially in the presence of true vessels and absence on some of archegonia (part of female sex organ) in the ovule. Often adapted to arid environments. Three extant genera (*Ephedra, Gnetum, Welwitschia*).

Gondwanaland: Southern supercontinent consisting at its maximum extent (during the late Paleozoic and early Mesozoic) of South America, Africa, Madagascar, India, Arabia, Malaya and the East Indies New Guinea, Australia, and Antarctica.

graben: A rift valley, where the crust is locally dropped down between fault-bounded upland areas.

group: Name given to a succession of sedimentary formations.

gymnosperms: Vascular plants with ovules not enclosed in ovaries: includes the conifers.

halecostomes: Group of neopterygian fishes including teleosts and bowfins, but excluding gars.

halocline: Layer of water separating waters of high and low salinity, which because of their differing salt content have different densities.

hamamelids: Subclass of flowering plants, forming a heterogeneous group close to the base of the non-magnolid dictyledons

Hauterivian: Stratigraphic stage name, originally for the European mid-Lower Cretaceous.

heterodont: Having teeth of different shapes or sizes around the jaw.

homodont: having similar teeth throughout the mouth.

homoplasy: Presence of a primitive character, either through its being primitively retained or from phylogenetic "reversal," so that the previously suppressed genotypic trait is once again manifested.

horizon: Particular level in a stratigraphical sequence.

hyoid arch: Series of bones between the jaws and gill region, adapted to help brace the jaws against the skull.

hypolimnion: The bottom layer of waters in a stratified lake, generally low in oxygen, high in carbon dioxide, colder and with a more uniform temperature and higher hydrogen ion concentration (i.e., lower pH) than overlying waters (epilimnion), from which it is separated by a thermocline (layer of water whose temperature declines rapidly with depth)

hypural: Enlarged hemal arch supporting the ventral lobe of the tail fin in ray-finned fishes.

induration: See **permineralization.**

karst: Landscape of denuded limestone or dolostone, produced by solution of percolating ground waters and underground streams.

lacustrine: Pertaining to a lake system.

lagerstätten: Loosely translated, a rich deposit. The term was originally applied to ore-bodies and borrowed by German paleontologists for fossiliferous deposits.

Laurasia: Northern supercontinent consisting at its maximum extent of North America, Europe, and Asia north of the Himalayas.

lineament: A major fault line crossing part of a continent and forming the landward end of an oceanic transform fault.

lithostratigraphy: See **stratigraphy.**

Maestrichtian (Maastrichtian): Stratigraphic stage name, originally for the top of the European Upper Cretaceous.

marl: Calcareous clay.

member: Sedimentary rock sequence forming part of a formation.

Mesozoic: An era spanning some 160 million years, including the Triassic, Jurassic, and Cretaceous periods, recognized originally by fossils of "Middle Life," i.e., some organisms different from those of today, plus some more familiar ones.

Messinian event: Period during the Miocene period (approximately 7–10 million years ago) marked by the drying out of the Mediterranean Sea.

monospondylous: The normal condition of having one vertebral centrum per body segment.

monosulcate pollen: Type of pollen associated with many flowering plants, having a single distal germinal aperture.

necrolytic: Features associated with the death of an organism, including immediate post-mortem changes.

Neocomian: Stratigraphic stage name, originally for a large part of the British Lower Cretaceous.

neopterygian: Group of ray-finned fishes including the gars, bowfins, and teleosts, plus their immediate fossil relative.

non-magnoliid dicotyledons: A group of angiosperms defined by the presence of tricolpate pollen (or derivative forms); includes all dicotyledons except those assigned to the subclass Magnoliidae (e.g., magnolia, laurel, water-lilies, and their allies).

paleogeography: Study of ancient geographic positions of land and sea.

paelokarst: Ancient remains of former karst environment.

paleomagnetism: Residual magnetic field within rocks, representing a record of the Earth's magnetic field at the time the rocks were formed.

paleontology: The study of ancient life from fossil remains that are compared with living organisms.

Paleozoic: The first of three eras, recognized orginally by fossils of "Ancient Life," i.e., very different-looking organisms from those of today.

palynoflora: Fossil assemblage of pollen and spores.

palynology: The study of pollen and spores, living and fossil.

Pangaea: Hypothetical supercontinent believed to have once existed in the Paleozoic, including both Gondwanaland and Laurasia.

parhypural: First hemal arch in front of the hypurals, supported by the first preural centrum.

peduncle: The constriction between the body and tail of a fish.

pelagic: Term for organisms that live in the open sea but not at its surface nor on the sea floor.

permineralization. The process whereby minerals are deposited within and around porous materials such as bones, shells, wood, and soft sediments.

phylogeny: The study of evolutionary

relationships.

plate tectonics: Process of crustal mobility, involving movement of large pieces of the Earth's crust against each other; the cause of continental drift.

polyplicate pollen: Pollen grains with a distinctive folded-striate pollen wall characteristic of ephedroids.

preural centrum: Vertebral centrum in front of the ural centra in the tail fin of ray-finned fishes. The first preural supports the parhypural.

pteridophytes: Heterogeneous group of land plants characterized by specialized water-conducting cells and free-sporing (non-seed plant-reproduction; ferns, horsetails, clubmosses.

pterygiophore: Splint-like internal support for the dorsal and anal fins.

pyrite: "Fool's gold;" sulfide of iron, produced in a variety of geological circumstances but especially within sediments lacking free oxygen.

Quaternary: The latest period of geological time, extending back some two million years and including glacial (Pleistocene) and postglacial (Holocene) deposits; usually regarded as that period of time that mankind has existed on Earth.

ridge axis: The line along a mid-oceanic ridge where new ocean floor is forming; effectively the axis marks an extensional margin between plates of oceanic crust.

sabkha: Salt-encrusted supra-tidal surfaces bordering lagoonal or inner shelf areas in arid coastal or lacustrine regions that are characterized by high evaporation rates and formation of evaporite deposits.

sarcopterygians: Bony fishes in which the fins are supported by internal skeletal elements as well as fin rays: the "lobe-finned fishes."

sedimentology: The study of sediments and how they accumulated.

Senonian: Stratigraphic stage name, originally for part of the European Upper Cretaceous.

siderite: Mineral consisting of carbonate of iron, often formed in shallow bottom environments and within soft sediments.

stage: An implied period of absolute geological time, often regarded as the equivalent of a biostratigraphic unit as defined by zone fossils.

stomata: Pores and associated cells (guard cells) in the surface of plant tissues that regulate the gaseous exchange with the environment.

stratigraphy: lithostratigraphy; chronostratigraphy: Study of stratified rocks, including rock sequence (lithostratigraphy) and time sequence (chronostratigraphy).

Because any particular sediment can form in different places at different times, lithostratigraphic units do not necessarily represent actual periods of time.

striate: Pollen surface sculpture consisting of numerous ridges, frequently with more or less parallel alignment.

symplectic: Cartilage bone forming part of the hoid arch in bony fishes, located immediately beneath the hyomandibula and next to the quadrate bone, that articulates with the lower jaw.

synapomorphy: Term for a shared, derived feature found in two or more different species.

synarcual: Part of the internal skeleton in some fishes, attached to the back of the skull and formed around several vertebrae.

taphonomy: Study of changes occurring to organic remains after death and up to the time of burial.

tectonic domain: Large regions of crustal activity involving the formation of an oceanic basin. In the case of the South Atlantic, three such domains have been identified; the more southerly Austral domain was the earliest to develop, followed successively by the Tropical and Equatorial domains.

teleosts: Large group of extant ray-finned fishes, including elopomorphs, osteoglossomorphs, gonorynchiforms, clupeomorphs, salmon-like fishes, and acanthopterygians.

Tethys; Tethyan: Mesozoic ocean developed between Laurasia and Gondwanaland, covering southern Europe, the Mediterranean, North Africa, Iran, and the Himalayas.

transform fault: Generally very long faults crossing the ocean floors, characterized by horizontal movement of adjacent slices of the ocean floor past each other.

tricolpates: A group of pollen grains with three longitudinally elongate germinal apertures equally arranged around the equator of the grain; tricolopate or tricolpate-derived pollen is diagnostic of non-magnoliid dicotyledons.

Turonian: A stratigraphic stage name, originally for the European mid-Upper Cretaceous.

type specimen: An individual organism chosen by scientists to represent any given species. As such, every type specimen is unique and valuable scientific resource deserving of the utmost care. Most type specimens are preseved in the great museums and universities of the world.

unconformity; unconformable: A break in the sedimentary sequence, resulting from any number of causes, including non-deposition of sediments or uplift and erosion. A simple analogy is a book with pages missing originally or torn out subsequently.

ural centrum: Vertebral centrum in the tail fin of ray-finned fishes, supporting the hypurals.

urodermal: Specialized dermal element in the dorsal part of the tail fin of certain ray-finned fishes.

vicariant event: Hypothetical splitting of an originally unique species into two (or more) new ones, following the geographical isolation of its populations (e.g., by geological processes).

Wealden: Stratigraphic stage name, originally for a large part of the British Lower Cretaceous.

xeromorphic; xerophytic: Having structural characteristics typically associated with dry habitats (e.g., thick leaf texture, thick leaf cuticles).

zone: Any rock stratum that can be precisely defined in terms of paleontological features. See **biozone.**

zone fossil: A particular fossil species selected (either singly or with others) to represent a particular interval of geological time.

Bibliography

Agassiz, L. 1841. On the fossil fishes found by Mr. Gardner in the Province of Ceará, in the north of Brazil. *Edin. New Phil. J.*, 30: 82-84.

————. 1833-1844a. *Recherches sur les Poissons fossiles.* 5 vols., 1420 pp., with supplement. Neuchatel.

————. 1844b. Sur quelques poissons fossiles du Brésil. *Compt. Rendus Acad. Sci. Paris*, 18: 1007-1015.

Allis, E. 1897. The cranial muscles and cranial and first spinal nerves in *Amia calva. J. Morph.*, 12(3): 487-808.

Allport, S. 1859. On the discovery of some fossil remains near Bahia in South America. *Quart. Jour. geol. Soc.*, London, 16: 263–268.

Alvin, K. L. 1974. Leaf anatomy of *Weichselia* based on fusainized material. *Palaeontology*, 17: 587-598.

Ames, L. L., Jr. 1959. The genesis of carbonate apatites. *Economic Geology*, 54: 829-841.

Andrews, S. M., B. G. Gardiner, R. S. Miles, and C. Patterson. 1967. Pisces: 637-683, *in* Harland, W. B., et al. (eds.), *The Fossil Record.* Geol. Soc. London.

Anjos, N. F. R. dos. 1963. Novos elementos sôbre a Hidrogeologica do Alto Jaquaribe, Ceará. *Superintendência do Desenvolvimento do Nordeste (SUDENE), Ser. Hidrogeologica*, 1: 1-19.

Arai, M. and J.C. Coimbra (in press). Análise paleoecológica do registro das primeiras ingressões marinhas na Formação Santana (Cretáceo Inferior da Chapada do Araripe). I Sympósio sobre a Bacia do Araripe e bacias interiores do nordeste, 1990.

Arambourg, C. 1935. Observations sur quelques poissons fossiles de l'ordre des halécostomes et sur l'origine des clupéidés. *Compt. Rendus Acad. Sci. Paris*, 200(25): 2110-2112.

————and L. Bertin. 1958. Super-Ordres des holostéens et des halécostomes (Holostei et Halecostomi), *in* Grassé, P-P. (ed.), *Traité de Zoologie*, 13(3): 2173-2203. Massson et Cie, Paris.

————and D. Schneegans. 1935. Poissons fossiles du bassin sédimentaire du Gabon. *Ann. Paléont. Paris*, 24: 139-160.

Arid, F. M. and L. D. Vizotto. 1963. Sôbre vertebrados fosseis no município de Ibirá, São Paulo. *Ci. Cult.*, 15 (3): 181-182.

————and L. D. Vizotto. 1971. *Antarctosaurus brasiliensis*, um novo saurópode do Cretáceo Superior do Sul do Brasil. *Anais XXV Congr. brasil. Geol., São Paulo 1971*, 2: 297–305.

————et al. 1962. A ocorrência de um jazigo fossilífero nos arredores de São José do Rio Preto. *Ci. Cult.*, 14 (3): 172.

Asmus, H. E. 1975. Controle estructural da deposição mesozóica nas bacias da margem continental brasileira. *Rev. Bras. Geoc., São Paulo,* 5(3): 160-175.

———and D. A. Campos. 1983. Stratigraphic division of the Brazilian continental margin and its paleogeographic significance. *Zitteliana,* 10: 265-276.

———and W. Guazelli. 1981. Descrição sumária das estrutas da margem continental brasileira e das áreas oceânicas e continentais adjacentes, *in* Petrobras, *Estruturas e tectonismo da margem continental brasileira, e suas implicações nos processos sedimentares e na avaliação do potencial de recursos minerais. Rio de Janeiro, Cenpes/Dintep:* 187-269 (Projeto Remac 9).

———and F. C. Ponte. 1973. The Brazilian marginal basins, *in* Nairn, A. E. M. and F. G. Stehli (eds.), *The ocean basins and margins. Vol. 1. The South Atlantic:* 87-133. New York, Plenum.

Assmann, P. 1906. Über *Aspidorhynchus. Arch. Biont.,* 1: 49-79.

Axelrod, D. I. 1952. A theory of angiosperm evolution. *Evolution,* 6: 29-60.

———. 1970. Mesozoic paleogeography and early angiosperm history. *Bot. Rev.,* 36: 277-319.

Baird, G. C., S. D. Sroka, C. W. Shabica, and G. J. Kuecher. 1986. Taphonomy of Middle Pennsylvanian Mazon Creek Area fossil localities, northeast Illinois: Significance of exceptional fossil preservation in syngenetic concretions. *Palaios,* 1(3): 271-285.

Barale, G. 1982. Les genres *Sagenopteris* Presl. et *Ginkgo* Linné dans la flore des calcaires lithographiques du Crétacé Inferiéur du Montsec (Provice de Lérida, Espagne). *La Revista Ilerda,* 43: 335-355.

Bardack, D. 1962. Taxonomic status and geologic position of the Cretaceous fish *Ichthyodectes marathonensis. Australian J. Sci.,* 24(9): 387.

———. 1965. Anatomy and evolution of chirocentrid fishes. *Univ. Kansas Paleont. Contrib., Vertebrata,* Art. 10: 1-88.

———and G. Sprinkle. 1969. Morphology and relationships of saurocephalid fishes. *Field. Geol., Chicago,* 16(11).

Barthel, K. W. 1978. *Fossilien aus Sölnhofen. Ein Blick in die Erdgeschichte.* Ott, Thun. 393 pp.

Bartholomai, A. 1969. The Lower Cretaceous Elopoid fish *Pachyrhizodus marathonensis* (Etheridge, Jnr.), *in* Campbell, K. S. W. (ed.), Stratigraphy and Palaeontology, *Essays in Honor of Dorothy Hill.* A. N. U. Press, Canberra.

Bartram, A. 1975. The holostean fish genus *Ophiopsis* Agassiz. *Zool. J. Linn. Soc.,* 56(3): 183-205.

———. 1977. The Macrosemiidae, a Mesozoic family of holostean fishes. *Bull. Brit. Mus. (Nat. Hist.), Geol.,* 29(2): 137-234.

Bate, R. H. 1971. Phosphatized ostracods from the Cretaceous of Brazil. *Nature,* 230: 397-398.

———. 1972. Phosphatized ostracods with appendages from the Lower Cretaceous of Brazil. *Palaeontology,* 15(3): 379-393.

Beltan, L. 1968. *La faune ichthyologique de l'Eotrias du N.W. de Madagascar: le neurocrâne.* 135 pp., 55 pls. Centre national de la Recherche Scientifique, Paris.

Bengtson, P. 1979. A bioestratigrafia esquecida—avaliação dos métodos bioestratigráficos no Cretáceo Médio do Brasil. *An. Acad. brasil. Ciênc.,* 51: 535-544.

———. 1983. The Cenomanian—Coniacian of the Sergipe Basin, Brazil. *Fossils and Strata,* No. 12. 78 pp. Universitetsforlaget., Oslo.

Bennett, S. C. 1989. A pteranodontid pterosaur from the early Cretaceous of Peru, with comments on the relationships of Cretaceous pterosaurs. *J. Paleont,* 63 (5): 669–677.

Benton, M. J. and J. M. Clark. 1988. Archosaur phylogeny and the relationships of the Crocodylia. *Syst. Assoc., Spec. Vol.,* 35A: 295-338.

Berg, L. S. 1940. Classification of fishes, both Recent and fossil. *Trudy zool. Inst. Leningr.,* 5: 87-517. Various reprints in book form available.

Berner, R. A. 1968. Calcium carbonate concretions formed by the decomposition of organic matter. *Science, N.Y.,* 159: 195-197.

Bertini, R. J. and D. A. Campos. 1987. Restos de um grande saurópodo em Monte Alto, estado de São Paulo. *Resumos das communicacdes do 10 Congresso Brasileiro de Paleontologia (Rio de Janeiro 1987):* 10.

Beurlen, K. 1961. Die Kreide im Küstenbereich von Sergipe bis Paraiba do Norte (Brasilien). *Zeit. Deutsh. Geol. Ges.,* 112(3): 378-384.

———. 1962. A geologia da Chapada do Araripe. *An. Acad. brasil. Ciênc.*, 34(3): 365-370.

———. 1963. Geologia e Estratigrafia da Chapada do Araripe. *XVII Congr. brasil. Geol. Publ. SUDENE*: 1-47.

———. 1966. Novos equinóides no Cretáceo do Nordeste do Brasil. *An. Acad. brasil. Ciênc.*, 38(3/4): 455-464.

———. 1970. *Geologie van Brasilien.* Gebrüder Borntraeger, Berlin. viii—444 pp.

———. 1971a. As condições ecológicas e faciológicas da formação Santana na Chapada do Araripe (Nordeste do Brasil). *An. Acad. brasil. Ciênc.*, 43: 411-415 (suplemento).

———. 1971b. Contributions to the paleography of the Cretaceous in North-east Brazil. *Neues Jahrbuch Geol. Polarcontrol Abhandl.*, 139: 1-28.

———and J. M. Mabesoone, 1969. Bacias Cretaceas Intracontinentais do Nordeste do Brasil. *Not. Geomorfol., Campinas*, 9(18): 19-34.

Blainville, H. M. D. 1818. *Sur les ichthyolites ou les poissons fossiles.* Paris.

Blot, J. 1987. *L'Ordre des Pycnodontiformes.* Studi e Richerche sui Giacimenti Terziari di Bolca. V. 212 pp. Museo Civico di Storia Nat. Verona, Italie.

Blum, S. D., J. G. Maisey, and I. S. Rutzky. 1989. A method for chemical reduction and removal of ferric iron applied to vertebrate fossils. *J. Vert. Paleo.*, 9(1): 119.

Bonaparte, C. 1837 (1832-1841). *Iconografia della fauna italica per le quattro classi delgi animali vertebrati.* 3 vol. Tip. Salviucci, Rome.

Bour, R. 1986. Note sur *Pelusios adansonii* (Schweigger, 1812) et sur une nouvelle espece affine du Kenya (Chelonii, Pelomedusidae). *Stud. Palaeochel.*, 2(2): 23-54.

Braun, O. P. G. 1966. Estratigrafia dos sedimentos da parte interior da regiao Nordeste do Brasil (Bacias de Tucano—Jatoba, Mirandiba e Araripe). *D. N. P. M./ Div. Geol. Miner., Bol.*, No. 236: 1-15.

Brenner, G. J. 1976. Middle Cretaceous floral provinces and early migrations of angiosperms: 23-47, *in* Beck, C. B. (ed.), *Origin and early evolution of angiosperms.* Columbia Univ. Press, New York.

———. 1981. Pre-tricolpate pollen from the late Hauterivian of Israel and its paleoclimatic implications. *Amer. Assoc. Strat. Palynol., 14th ann. Mtg., Program and Abstracts:* 13.

———. 1984. Late Hauterivian angiosperm pollen from the Helez Formation, Israel. *6th Int. Palyn. Conf., Calgary, 1984, Abstracts:* 15.

Brito, I. M. 1981. Os equinóides fósseis do Brasil. II–Holectipóides e Cassidulóides. *An. Acad. brasil. Ciênc.*, 53(3): 513-527.

———. 1984a. The Upper Lower Cretaceous in Brazil, its divisions and boundaries. *An. Acad. brasil. Ciênc.*, 56: 287-293.

———. 1984b. Nota preliminar sobre os insetos da formação Santana, Cretáceo inferior da Chapada do Araripe. *Anais XXXIII Congr. brasil. Geol., Rio de Janeiro:* 530-535.

———and D. A. Campos. 1982. O Cretáceo no Brasil. *An. Acad. brasil. Ciênc.*, 54: 197-218.

———and ———. 1983. The Brazilian Cretaceous. *Zitteliana*, 10: 277-283.

Brito Neves, B. B. de. 1983. *O mapa geologico do Nordeste oriental do Brasil, escala 1/1000000.* Tese, University São Paulo, Brasil. 375 pp.

Brito, P. M. 1988. La structure du suspensorium de *Vinctifer*, poisson actinoptérygien mésozöique: remarques sur les implications phylogénétiques. *Geobios*, 21(6): 819-823.

Brito, P. M. and P. L. N. Ferreira. 1989. The first hybodont shark, *Tribodus limae* n.g., n.sp., from the Lower Cretaceous of Chapada do Araripe (North-East Brazil). *An. Acad. brasil Cienc.*, 61(1): 53–57.

Broin, F. de. 1980. Les tortues de Gadou fauna (Aptien de Niger); aperçu su la paléobiogéographie des Pelomedusidae (Pleurodira). *Mém. Soc. Géol. Fr., N.S., 1980*, No. 139: 39-46.

———, E. Buffetaut, J. Koeniguer, J. Rage, D. Russell, P. Taquet, C. Vergnaud-Grazzini, and S. Wenz. 1974. La faune de vertébrés continentaux du gisement d'In Beceten (Sénonien du Niger). *Compt. Rendus Acad. Sci. Paris*, 279: 469-472.

Brown, W. H. 1900. Dates of publication of "Recherches sur les Poissons fossiles"... par L. Agassiz, pp. xxv-xxix, *In* Woodward, A. S. and C. D. Sherborn, *A Catalogue of British fossil vertebrata.* London, Dulau and Co., xxxv—396 pp.

Bryant, L. J. 1987. A new genus and species of Amiidae (Holostei: Osteichthyes) from the Late Cretaceous of North America, with comments on the phylogeny of the Amiidae. *J. Vert. Paleo.*, 7(4): 349-361.

Buch, L. de. 1839. *Petrifications recueielles en Amerique, par Mr. Alexandre du Humboldt et Mr. Charles Degenhardt; decriptes par Leopold de Buch.* Folio, pp. 1-22. Berlin.

Buffetaut, E. and P. Taquet. 1979. An early Cretaceous terrestrial crocodilian and the opening of the South Atlantic. *Nature,* 280: 486-487.

———. 1981. Die biogeographische Geschichte der Krokodilier, mit beschreibung einer neuer art, *Araripesuchus wegeneri. Geol. Rund.,* 70(2): 611-624.

———. 1982. Radiation evolutive, paleoécologie et biogéographie des crocodiliens mesosuchiens. *Mém. Soc. Geol. Fr.,* 142: 1-88.

Buisonjé, P. H. De. 1980. *Santanadactylus brasiliensis* nov. gen., nov. sp., a longnecked large pterosaur from the Aptian of Brasil. *Proc. Koninkl. nederl. Akad. Wetensch.,* (B), 83(2): 145-172.

———. 1981. *Santanadactylus brasiliensis:* skeletreconstructie van een vliegend reptiel met zes meter vlucht. *Gea,* 14(2): 37-49.

Cabrera, A. 1927. Sobre un pez fósil. *Rev. Museo de La Plata,* 30: 317-319.

Campos, D. A. 1985. Ocorrência de um novo arcossauro na Chapada do Araripe. *An. Acad. brasil. Ciênc.,* 57 (1): 140–141.

———and R. J. Bertini. 1985. Ovos de dinossauro da formação Uberaba, Cretáceo Superior do estado de Minas Gerais. *Resumos das comunicacões do 9 Congresso Brasileiro de Paleontologia (Fortaleza 1985): (Fortaleza 1985):* 19. Fortaleza. p. 19.

———. and A. W. A. Kellner. 1985a. Panorama of the flying reptiles study in Brazil and South America. *An. Acad. brasil. Ciênc.,* 57: 453-466.

———and A. W. A. Kellner, 1985b. Um novo exemplar de *Anhanguera blittersdorffi* (Reptilia, Pterosauria) da formaçao Santana, Cretáceo Inferior do Nordeste do Brasil. *In: Congresso Brasilieiro de Paleontologia,* ge, Rio de Janeiro. *Resumos. Rio di Janeiro, Sociedade Brasileira de Paleontologia,* 1985: 13.

———,G. Ligabue, and P. Taquet. 1984. Wing membrane and wing supporting fibers of a flying reptile from the Lower Cretaceous of the Chapada do Araripe (Aptian, Ceará State, Brazil). *Third Symp. Mesoz. Terrestr. Ecosystems, Short Papers:* 37-39. Tübingen, Attempto.

———and S. Wenz. 1982. Première découverte de coelacanthes dans le Crétacé inférieur de la Chapada do Araripe (Brésil). *Compt. Rendus Acad. Sci. Paris,* II, 294: 1151-1154.

Campos, D. R. B. 1986. Primeiro registro fóssil de Scorpionoidea na Chapada do Araripe (Cretáceo Inferior), Brasil. *An. Acad. brasil. Ciênc.,* 58(1): 135-137.

Cappetta, H. 1980. Les sélaciens du Crétace supérieur du Liban. II. Batoides. *Palaeontographica,* Abt. A, 168: 149-229.

———. 1987. Chondrichthyes II. Mesozoic and Cenozoic Elasmobranchii, *in* Schultz, H. P. (ed.), *Handbook of Paleoicthyology,* 3B. Gustav Fischer Verlag, Stuttgart and New York.

Carlquist, S. 1975. *Ecological strategies of xylem evolution.* Univ. Calif. Press, Berkeley and Los Angeles. 259 pp.

Carvalho, M. S. S. de. 1982. Ó gênero *Mawsonia* na ictiofáunula do Cretáceo do Estado da Bahia. *An. Acad. brasil. Ciênc.,* 54(3): 519-539.

Casier, E. 1961. Materiaux pour la fauna ichthyologique Eocretacique du Congo. *Ann. Mus. Roy. Afr. Centr., Tervuren,* ser. 8, Sci., géol., 39: 1-96.

Chalifa, Y. and E. Tchernov. 1982. *Pachyamia latimaxillaris,* new genus and species (Actinopterygii: Amiidae), from the Cenomanian of Jerusalem. *J. Vert. Paleo.,* 2(3): 269-285.

Colbert, E. H. 1970. A saurischian dinosaur from the Triassic of Brazil. *Amer. Mus. Novitates,* 2405: 1–39.

Compagno, L. J. V. 1973. Interrelationships of living elasmobranchs, *in* Greenwood,P. H., R. S. Miles, and C. Patterson (eds.), *Interrelationships of Fishes, Zool. J. Linn. Soc.,* 53 (Suppl. 1): 15-61.

Conway, M. S. 1985. Cambrian Lagerstätten: their distribution and significance. *Phil. Trans. Roy. Soc. London,* B 311: 49-65.

Cope, E. D. 1868. On the origin of genera. *Proc. Acad. Nat. Sci., Phila.,* 20: 242-300.

———. 1871. On two extinct forms of physostomi of the neotropical region. *Proc. Amer. Phil. Soc., Phila.,* 12(86): 53-55.

———. 1885. A contribution to the vertebrate

paleontology of Brazil. *Proc. Amer. Phil. Soc., Phila.*, 23: 1-21.

Costa Lima, A. da. 1950. Ninfa de efemerido fossil do Ceará. *An. Acad. brasil. Ciênc.*, 22(4): 419-420.

Cracraft, J. 1986. The origin and early diversification of birds. *Paleobiology*, 12(4): 383-395.

Crane, P. R. 1985. Phylogenetic analysis of seed plants and the origin of angiosperms. *Ann. Missouri Bot. Garden*, 72: 716-793.

————. 1988. Major clades and relationships in the "higher" gymnosperms: 218-272, *in* Beck, C. B. (ed.), *Origin and evolution of gymnosperms*. Columbia Univ. Press, New York.

————and S. Lidgard. 1989. Angiosperm diversification and paleolatitudinal gradients in Cretaceous floristic diversity. *Science*, 246: 675–678.

————and G. R. Upchurch. 1987. *Drewcia potomacensis* gen. et sp. nov., an early Cretaceous member of the Gnetales from the Potomac Group of Virginia. *Amer. J. Botany*, 74: 1722-1736.

Cressey, R. and G. Boxshall. 1989. *Kabatarina pattersoni*, a fossil parasitic copepod (Dichelesthiidae) from a Lower Cretaceous fish. *Micropalaeontology*, 35(2): 150-167.

————and C. Patterson. 1973. Fossil parasitic copepods from a Lower Cretaceous fish. *Science, N.Y.*, 180: 1283-1285.

Davis, J. W. 1887. The fossil fishes of the Chalk of Mount Lebanon in Syria. *Trans. Roy. Dublin Soc.*, (2) II: 457-636.

Dickinson, W. R. 1974. Plate tectonics and sedimentation. *Tectonics and Sedimentation. Soc. Econ. Paléont. Miner., Spec. Publ.*, No. 22: 1-27.

Doyle, J. A., P. Biers, A. Doerenkamp, and S. Jardiné. 1977. Angiosperm pollen from the pre-Albian Lower Cretaceous of Equatorial Africa. *Bull. Centres Rech. Explor.-Prod. Elf-Aquitaine*, 1(2): 451-473.

————and M. J. Donoghue. 1986. Seed plant phylogeny and the origin of angiosperms: an experimental cladistic approach. *Botanical Rev.*, 43: 3-104.

————and L. J. Hickey. 1976. Pollen and leaves from the mid-Cretaceous Potomac Group and their bearing on early angiosperm evolution, *in* C. B. Beck (ed.), *Origin and Early Evolution of Angiosperms*: 139–206. New York: Columbia University Press.

————, S. Jardiné, and A. Doernenkamp. 1982. *Afropollis*, a new genus of early angiosperm pollen, with notes on the Cretaceous

palynostratigraphy and paleoenvironments of northern Gondwana. *Bull. Centres Rech. Explor.-Prod. Elf-Aquitaine*, 6(1): 39-117.

Duarte, L. 1969. Paleoflórula da Formação Santana. *Soc. Brasil. Geol. nucl. Bahia, Spec. Bull.*, 1: 59 (summary).

————. 1985a. Vegetais fósseis da Chapada do Araripe. *VIII Congr. brasil. Paleont., 1983, MME-DNPM, Serv. Geol., Rio de Janeiro, 27 Paleont. Estrat.*, 2: 557-563.

————. 1985b. Vegetais fósseis da Formação Areado, Mun. Presidente Olegário. *IX Congr. brasil. Paleont., 1985, MME-DNPM, Serv. Geol., Rio de Janeiro*.

————. 1989. Remains of the lower Cretaceous plants from NE of Brazil.

Dunkle, D. H. 1940. The cranial osteology of *Notelops brama* (Agassiz), an elopid fish from the Cretaceous of Brazil. *Lloydia*, 3: 157-190.

Elliot, D. K. 1987. A new specimen of *Chinlea sorenseni* from the Chinle formation, Dolores River, Colorado. *J. Arizona—Nevada Acad. Sci.*, 22: 47-52.

Elzanowski, A. 1983. Birds in Cretaceous ecosystems. *Acta Paleont. Pol.*, 28(1/2): 75-92.

D'Erasmo, G. 1915. La faune e l'età dei calcarei a ittioliti di Pietraroia (Prov. di Benevento). *Paleontogr. ital.*, 21: 1-53.

————. 1938. Ittioliti Cretacei del Brasile. *Atti Acad. Sci. fis. mat., Napoli*, (3)1 (3): 1–44.

Estes, R. D. 1982. Systematics and palaeogeography of some fossil salamanders and frogs. *Nat. Geogr. Soc. Res. Reports*, 14: 191-210.

————and O. A. Reig. 1973. The early fossil record of frogs: a review of the evidence: 11-63, *in* Vial, J. L. (ed.), *Evolutionary Biology of the Anurans*. Univ. Missouri Press, Columbia, Missouri.

Etheridge, R., Jnr. 1905. Description of a mutilated cranium of a large fish from the Lower Cretaceous of Queensland. *Rec. Australian Mus.*, 6: 5-8.

Falvey, D. A. 1974. The development of continental margin in plate tectonic theory. *Petrol. Explor. Assoc. J.*: 95-106.

Fell, H. B. and D. L. Pawson. 1966. Echinodermata, Echinacea: 367-695, *in* Moore, R. C. (ed.), *Treatise on Invertebrate Paleontology*. Part U, 3, vol. 2.

Felix, J. 1890. Beitraege zur Kenntniss der Gattung *Protosphyraena* Leidy. *Dtsch. Geol. Ges., Z.*, 42: 278-302.

Figueiredo, F. J. and R. da Silva Santos. 1986. Sobre o *Microdon penalvai* Silva Santos, do Cretáceo Inferior da Formação Santana. Nordeste do Brasil. *IX Congr. brasil. Pa-*

leont., *Fortaleza. Resumos das Commun.*: 13 (abstract).

————and R. da Silva Santos. 1987. Considerações taxinômicas dos picnodontidos da Formação Gramame (camada de Fosfato), Pe. *Anais X Congr. brasil. Paleont., Rio de Janeiro*: 21-35.

Fink, S. V. and W. L. Fink. 1981. Interrelationships of the ostariophysan fishes (Teleostei). *Zool. J. Linn. Soc.*, 72(4): 297-353.

Forey, P. L. 1973a. Relationships of elopomorphs, *in* Greenwood, P.H., R. S. Miles, and C. Patterson (eds.), *Interrelationships of Fishes. Zool. J. Linn. Soc.*, 53 (Suppl. 1): 351-368.

————. 1973b. A revision of the elopiform fishes, fossil and recent. *Bull. Brit. Mus. (Nat. Hist.)*, Geol., Suppl. 10: 1-222.

————. 1973c. A primitive clupeomorph fish from the Middle Cenomanian of Hakel, Lebanon. *Canadian J. Earth Sci.*, 10(8): 1302-1318.

————. 1975. A fossil clupeomorph fish from the Albian of the Northwest Territories of Canada, with notes on cladistic relationships of clupeomorphs. *J. Zool., London*, 175: 151-177.

————. 1977. The osteology of *Notelops* Woodward, *Rhacolepis* Agassiz, and *Pachyrhizodus* Dixon (Pisces: Teleostei). *Bull. Brit. Mus. (Nat. Hist.)*, Geol., 28(2): 125-204.

————. 1981. The coelacanth *Rhabdoderma* in the Carboniferous of the British Isles. *Paleo.*, 24(1): 203-229.

————. 1984. The coelacanth as a living fossil, *in* Eldredge, N. and S. M. Stanley (eds.), *Living Fossils.* Springer-Verlag, New York.

Fowler, H. W. 1941. The fishes of the groups Elasmobranchii, Holocephali, Isospondyli and Ostariophysi obtained by the United States Bureau of Fisheries Steamer "Albatross" in 1907 to 1910, chiefly in the Philippine Islands and adjacent seas. *U. S. Nat. Mus. Bull.*, 100(13): 1-879.

Franzen, J. L. 1985. Exceptional preservation of Eocene vertebrates in the lake deposits of Grube Messel (West Germany). *Phil. Trans. Roy. Soc. London.*, B 311: 181-186.

Fricke, H. 1988. Coelacanths: the fish that time forgot. *National Geographic*, 173(6): 824-838.

————, O. Reinicke, H. Hofer, and W. Nachtigall. 1987. Locomotion of the coelacanth *Latimeria chalumnae* in its natural environment. *Nature*, 329: 331-333.

Gaffney, E. S. 1975. A phylogeny and classification of the higher categories of turtles.

Bull. Amer. Mus. Nat. Hist., 155: 387-436.

————. 1977. The side-necked turtle family Chelidae: a theory of relationships using shared derived characters. *Amer. Mus. Novitates*, No. 2620: 1-28.

————. 1979. Comparative cranial morphology of recent and fossil turtles. *Bull. Amer. Mus. Nat. Hist.*, 164: 65-375.

————. 1984. Historical analysis of theories of chelonian relationships. *Syst. Zool.*, 33: 283-301.

————. 1988. A cladogram of the pleurodiran turtles. *Acta Zool. Cracov.*, 31(15): 487-492.

————and P. A. Meylan. 1988. A phylogeny of turtles: 157-219, *in* Benton, M. J. (ed.), *The Phylogeny and Classification of the Tetrapods. Vol. 1: Amphibians, Reptiles, Birds. Syst. Assoc. Spec. Vol.*, 35A. Oxford, Clarendon.

Gardiner, B. G. 1960. A revision of certain actinopterygian and coelacanth fishes, chiefly from the Lower Lias. *Bull. Brit. Mus. (Nat. Hist.)*, Geol., 4: 239-384.

Gardner, G. 1841. Geological notes made during a journey from the coast into the interior of the Province of Ceará, in the North of Brazil. *Edin. New Phil. J.*, 30: 75-82.

————. 1849. *Travels in the Interior of Brazil, principally through the Northern Provinces.* Reeve, Benham and Reeve, London. 428 pp.

Gee, H. 1988. Cretaceous unity and diversity. *Nature*, 332: 487.

Gistl, J. 1848. *Naturgeschichte des Thierreichs für höhere Schulen.* Hoffman'sche Verlags-Buchhandlung, Stuttgart. xvi—216 pp.

Gosline, W. A. 1960. Contributions toward a classification of modern isospondylous fishes. *Bull. Brit. Mus. (Nat. Hist.)*, Zoology, 6(6): 325-365.

————. 1980. The evolution of some structural systems with reference to the interrelationships of modern lower teleostean fish groups. *Japanese J. Ichthy.*, 27(1): 1-28.

Grande, L. 1982. A revision of the fossil genus *Diplomystus* with comments on the interrelationships of clupeomorph fishes. *Amer. Mus. Novitates*, No. 2738: 1-34.

————. 1985. Recent and fossil clupeomorph fishes with materials for revision of the subgroups of clupeoids. *Bull. Amer. Mus. Nat. Hist.*, 181(2): 231-372.

————and G. Nelson. 1985. Interrelationships of fossil and Recent anchovies (Teleostei: Engrauloidea) and description of a new species from the Miocene of Cyprus. *Amer. Mus. Novitates*, No. 2826: 1-16.

Greenwood, P. H. 1977. Notes on the anatomy

and classification of elopomorph fishes. *Bull. Brit. Mus. (Nat. Hist.)*, Zoology, 32(4): 65-102.

———, D. E. Rosen, S. H. Weitzman, and G. S. Myers. 1966. Phyletic studies of teleostean fishes with a provisional classification of living forms. *Bull. Amer. Mus. Nat. Hist.*, 131: 339-455.

Gregory, W. K. 1959. *Fish Skulls*. Lundberg, Laurel, Florida. vii, 75-481. Reprint of: Gregory, W. K. 1933. Fish Skulls: a study of the evolution of natural mechanisms. *Amer. Philos. Soc.*, 23 (2): 75–481.

Grekoff, N. and K. Krömmelbein. 1967. Etude comparee des ostracodes Mesozoiques continentaux des bassins Atlantiques: Serie de Cocobeach, Gabon et Serie de Bahia, Bresil. *Rev. Inst. Pétrol, Paris*, 22: 1307-1353.

Grimaldi, D. A. (ed.). 1990. Insects from the Santana formation, Lower Cretaceous, of Brazil. *Bull. Amer. Mus. Nat. Hist.*, 195: 1-191.

Günther, A. 1872. Description of *Thrissopater salmones*, n. sp., *in: Great Britain and Ireland Geological Survey. Figures and descriptions illustrative of British organic remains.* Decade xiii. London.

Hartt, C. F. 1870. *Geology and physical geography of Brazil.* Fields Osgood, Boston. 620 pp.

Hecht, F. 1933. Der Verblieb der organischen Substanz der Tiere bei meerischen Einbettung. *Senckenberg. Naturf. Ges.*, 15(3/4): 165-249.

Heckel, J. J. 1856. Beiträge zur Kenntniss der fossilen fische Österreichs. *Denkschr. K. Akad. Wissensch. mathem. naturw. Cl.*, 11: 187.

Hennig, W. 1981. *Insect Phylogeny*. Winchester, Wiley. 514 pp.

Herngreen, G. F. W. 1975. Palynology of Middle and Upper Cretaceous strata in Brazil. *Meded. Rijks. Geol. Dienst.*, n. s., 26: 39-91.

———and H. F. Chlonova. 1981. Cretaceous microfloral provinces. *Pollen et Spores*, 23: 441-555.

Hickey, L. J. and J. A. Doyle. 1977. Early Cretaceous fossil evidence for angiosperm evolution. *Botanical Rev.*, 43: 3-104.

Hooley, R. W. 1914. On the ornithosaurian genus *Ornithocheirus* with a review of the specimens from Cambridge Greensand in the Sedgwick Museum, Cambridge. *Ann. Mag. Nat. Hist.*, 8(13): 529-557.

Huene, F. 1931. Verschiedene mesozoische Wirbeltierreste aus Südamerika. *Neues Jahrb.*

F. Min. Geol. Paleont., 66 B: 181–196.

———. 1942. *Die fossilen Reptilien des südamerikanischen Gondwanalandes.* C. H. Beck'sche Verlagsbuchhandlung. Munich. viii + 332 pp., 1935–1942.

Hughes, N. F. and A. B. McDougall. 1986. Records of angiospermid pollen entry into the English Early Cretaceous succession. *Rev. Palaeobotany Palynology*, 50: 255-272.

Hyatt, A. 1875. The Jurassic and Cretaceous ammonites collected in South America by Prof. James Orton, with an appendix upon the Cretaceous ammonites of Prof. Hartt's collection. *Proc. Boston Soc. Nat. Hist.*, 17: 365-378.

Ihering, R. 1911. Fósseis de São José do Rio Preto. *Rev. Mus. Paulista*, 8: 141–146.

Jaekel, O. 1909. Beiträge zur Geologie von Kamerun. X. Fischreste aus der Mamfe Schiefern. *K. Preuss Geol. Landesanst., Abhandl.*, n. s., 62: 392-398.

Jain, S. L. 1983. A review of the genus *Lepidotes* (Actinopterygii: Semionotiformes) with special reference to the species from Kota Formation (Lower Jurassic), India. *J. Palaeont. Soc. India*, 28: 7-42.

———. 1985. Variability of dermal bones and other parameters in the skull of *Amia calva*. *Zool. J. Linn. Soc.*, 84: 385-395.

Janot, C. 1967. A propos des Amiidae Actuels et Fossiles. *Colloq Internat. C.N.R.S., Probl. Actu. Paléont.-Evol. Vert. 163:* 139-153 (June 6-11, 1966 meeting).

Jardiné, S. and L. Magloire. 1965. Palynologie et stratigraphie du Crétacé des bassins du Sénegal et de Côte-d'Ivoire. *Memoires du Bureau de Recherches Géologiques et Miniès:* 187–245.

Jordan, D. S. 1907. The fossil fishes of California, with supplementary notes on other species of extinct fishes. *Univ. Calif. Publ., Bull. Dept. Geol.*, 5(7): 95-144.

———. 1910. Description of a collection of fossil fishes from the bituminous shales of Riacho Doce, State of Alagôas, Brazil. *Ann. Carnegie Mus.*, 7(1): 22-34.

———. 1919. New genera of fossil fishes from Brazil. *Proc. Acad. Nat. Sci., Phila.*, 71: 208-210.

———. 1921(1923). Peixes cretaceos do Ceará e Piauhy. *Monogr. Serv. geol. min. Brasil, Rio de Janeiro*, 3: 1-97.

———and J. C. Branner. 1908. The Cretaceous fishes of Ceará, Brazil. *Smithsonian Misc. Coll.*, issue 5, 52: 1-29.

Kaup, J. 1834. *Isis*, p. 315. Jena.

Kellner, A. W. A. 1984. Ocorrência de uma

mandibula de Pterosauria (*Brasileodactylus araripensis*, nov. gen.; nov. sp.) na Formação Santana, Cretáceo da Chapada do Araripe, Ceará—Brasil. *Anais XXXIII Congr. brasil. Geol.*, 1984: 578-590. Rio de Janeiro.

———. 1987. Ocorrência de um Novo Crocodiliano no Cretáceo Inferior da Bacia do Araripe, Nordeste do Brasil. *An. Acad. brasil. Ciênc.*, 59(3): 219-232.

———.1989. A new edentate pterosaur of the Lower Cretaceous from the Araripe Basin, northeast Brazil. *An. Acad. brasil. Ciênc., 61(4): 439-446.*

———and D. A. Campos. 1986. *Primerio registro de amphibia (Anura) no Cretáceo Inferior da bacia do Araripe, nordeste do brasil. An. Acad. brasil. Ciênc.,* 58(4): 610.

———and D. A. Campos. 1988. Sobre um Novo Pterossauro com Crista Sagital da Bacia do Araripe, Cretáceo Inferior do Nordeste do Brasil. *An. Acad. brasil. Ciênc.*, 60(4): 459–469.

Kennedy, W. J. and W. A. Cobban. 1976. Aspects of ammonite biology, biogeography and biostratigraphy. *Spec. Pap. Palaeont.*, 17: 1-94.

Keupp, H. 1977. Der Sölnhofener Plattenkalk—Ein Blau-grün algen-Laminit. *Paläont. Z.*, 51: 102-116.

King, R. J. 1982. The care of minerals. *J. Russell Soc.*, 1(1): 42-54.

———. 1983. The care of minerals. *J. Russell Soc.*, 1(2): 54-77.

Knoll, A. H. 1985. Exceptional preservation of photosynthetic organisms in silicified carbonates and silicified peats. *Phil. Trans. Roy. Soc. London*, B 311: 111-122.

Krassilov, V. A. 1986. New floral structure from the Lower Cretaceous of Lake Baikal area. *Rev. Palaeobotany and Palynology*, 36: 279-295.

Krömmelbein, K. 1965a. Neue, für Vergleiche mit West. Afrika wichtige, Ostracoden-Arten der brasilianischen Bahia-Series (Ober-Jura?/Unter-Kreide in Wealden-Fazies). *Senk. Leth.*, 46a: 177-213.

———. 1965b. Ostracoden aus der nicht-marinen Unter-Kreide (Westafrikanischer Wealden) des Congo-Küstenbeckens. *Meyniana*, 15: 59-74.

———and R. Wenger. 1966. Sur quelques analogies remarquables dans les microfaunes crétacées du Gabon et du Brésil Oriental (Bahia et Sergipe), *in* Reyre, D. (ed.), *Sedimentary Basins of the African Coasts: First Part, Atlantic Coast.* Assoc. Afr. Geol. Surv., Paris.

Kuroshkin, Y. N. 1982. New order of birds from the Lower Cretaceous in Mongolia. *Dok. Akad. Nauk. URSS*, 262(2): 215-218.

Lambers, P. 1988. *Orthocormus teyleri* nov. spec., the first pachycormid (Pisces, Actinopterygii) from the Kimmeridge lithographic limestone at Cerin (Ain), France; with remarks on the genus *Orthocormus* Weitzel. *Proc. Koninkl. Ned. Akad. Wetens.*, ser. B, 91(4): 369-391.

Lange, S. 1968. Zur Morphologie und Taxonomie der Fischgattung *Urocles* aus Jura und Kreide Europas. *Paleontographica, Stuttgart*, 139(1/4): 78 pp.

Lea, I. 1840. Notice of the Oolitic formation in America, with descriptions of some of its organic remains. *Trans. Amer. Philos. Soc.*, (n. s.), 7: 251-257.

Lehman, J. P. 1952. Etudes complémentaire des poissons de l'Eotrias de Madagascar. *K. Svenska Vetensk. Akad. Handl.*, 4(2): 1-201.

———. 1966. Actinopterygii, *in* Piveteau, J. (ed.), *Traité de Paléontologie*, 4(3): 1-242. Paris, Masson et Cie.

Leonardi, G. 1984. Le impronte fossili di dinosauri, *in* Bonaparte, F., et al. (eds.), *Sulle orme dei dinosauri.* Erizzo, Venezia. pp. 165–186.

———and G. Borgomanero. 1981. Sobre uma possível occorência de Ornitischia na formação Santana, Chapada do Araripe (Ceará). *Rev. bras. Geoci.*, 11: 1–4.

——— and ———. 1983. *Cearadactylus atrox* nov. gen., nov. sp.: novo pterosauria (Pterodactyloidea) da Chapada do Araripe, Ceará, Brasil. *VIII Congr. brasil. Paleont., Resumos dos commun.:* 17. Rio de Janeiro.

———and ———. 1985. *Cearadactylus atrox* nov. gen., sp.: Novo Pterosauria (Pterodactyloidea) da Chapada do Araripe, Ceará, Brasil, *in: Brasil, DNPM, Coletanea de trabalhos Paleontologicos, Seria Geologica,* 27: 75-80. Brasilia.

———and ———. 1987. The skeleton of a pair of wings of a pterosaur (Pterodactyloidea, ?Ornithocheiridae, cf. *Santanadactylus*) from the Santana Formation of the Araripe Plateau, Ceará, Brasil. *Anais X Congr. brasil. Paleont., Rio de Janeiro.*

———and S. C. Duszczak. 1977. Ocorrência de Titanosaurinae (Sauropoda, Atlantosauridae) na formação Bauru (Cretáceo Superior) em Guararapes, São Paulo. *Atas do 1 Simpósio de Geologia Regional (São Paulo 1977).* São Paulo. p. 396–403.

Lima, H. R. de. 1979. Considerações sobre a subdivisão estratigráfica da Formação Santana, Cretáceo do Nordesto do Brasil. *Rev. brasil. Geoc.*, 9(2): 116-121.

Lima, M. R. de. 1978a. Palinologia da Formação Santana (Cretáceo do Nordeste do Brasil). I. Introdução geológica e descrição sistemática dos esporos da Subturma Azonotriletes. *Ameghiniana*, 15: 333-365.

———. 1978b. Microfósseis da Formação Exu, Cretáceo do Nordeste do Brasil. *Anais XXX Congr. brasil. Geol., Recife*, 2: 965-969.

———. 1978c. O Paleoambiente deposicional da formação Santana (Grupo Araripe). Segundo evidencias palinológicas. *Anais XXX Congr. brasil. Geol., Recife*, 2.

———. 1979a. Palinologia da Formação Exu, Cretáceo do Nordeste Brasil. *Ameghiniana*, 16: 27–63.

———. 1979b. Paleontologia da Formação Santana (Cretáceo do Nordeste do Brasil): Estagio Actual de Conhecimentos. *An. Acad. brasil. Ciênc.*, 51: 3.

———. 1980. Palinologia da Formação Santana (Cretáceo do Nordeste do Brasil). III. Descrição sistemática dos esporos da Turma Plicates (Subturma Costates). *Ameghiniana*, 17: 15-47.

Link, H. F. 1790. Versuch einer Eintheilung der Fische nach den Zähnen. *Mag. Physik Naturgesch.*, 6(3): 28.

Linnaeus, C. 1758. *Systema Naturae*. Ed. 10.

Liu, T.-S., H.-T. Liu, and T.-T. Su. 1963. The discovery of *Sinamia zdanskyi* from the Ordos region and its stratigraphic significance. *Vertebr. PalAsiat.*, 7(1): 1-30.

McCune, A. R. 1986. A revision of *Semionotus* (Pisces: Semionotidae) from the Triassic and Jurassic of Europe. *Paleontology*, 29(2): 213-233.

McDowell, S. B. 1973. Order Heteromi, *in: Fishes of the Western North Atlantic. Mem. Sears Found. Mar. Res.*, 1(6): 1-228.

Mabesoone, J. M. and I. M. Tinoco. 1973. Paleoecology of the Aptian Santana Formation (Northeastern Brazil). *Paleogeogr., Paleoclimat., Paleoecol.*, 14(2).

Magnavita, L. P. and J. A. Cupertino. 1988. A new approach to the geological configuration of the Lower Cretaceous Tucano and Jatoba basins, northeastern Brazil. *Rev. brasil. Geoc.*, 18(2): 222-230.

Mainwaring, A. J. 1978. *Anatomical and systematic revision of the Pachycormidae, a family of Mesozoic fossil fishes*. Unpubl. Ph. D. thesis, Westfield College, London. 127 pp.

Maisey, J. G. 1984. Higher elasmobranch phylogeny and biostratigraphy. *Zool. J. Linn.*

Soc., 82: 33-54.

———. 1986. Coelacanths from the Lower Cretaceous of Brazil. *Amer. Mus. Novitates*, No. 2866: 1-30.

———. 1988. Diagenetic features and the origin of calcareous concretions from the Santana Formation (N. E. Brazil). *J. Vert. Paleo.*, 8 (Suppl. to 3): 21A.

Marsh, O. C. 1897. The affinities of *Hesperornis*. *Amer. J. Sci.*, 4(3): 347-348.

Marshall, N. B. 1962. Observations on the Heteromi, an order of teleost fishes. *Bull. Brit. Mus. (Nat. Hist.)*, Zool., 9: 249-270.

Martill, D. M. 1985. The preservation of marine vertebrates in the Lower Oxford Clay (Jurassic) of central England. *Phil. Trans. Roy. Soc. London*, B 311: 155-165.

———. 1988. Preservation of fish in the Cretaceous Santana Formation of Brazil. *Palaeontology*, 31(1): 1-18.

———. 1989. The Medusa Effect: instantaneous fossilization. *Geology Today*, Nov–Dec, 1989: 201–205.

———. 1990. Macromolecular resolution of fossilized muscle tissue from an elopomorph fish. *Nature*, 346: 171-172.

Martins-Neto, R. G. 1987. Descrição de três novos gêneros e três novas espécies de Orthoptera (Insecta, Acridoidea) da formação Santana, Bacia do Araripe (Cretáceo Inférior), Nordeste do Brasil, representando três famílias, sendo que duas novas: Archaeopneumonidae nov. fam. e Bouretidae nov. fam. *An. Acad. brasil. Ciênc.*, 59(4): 444.

———and A. W. A. Kellner. 1988. Premeiro registro de pena na Formação Santana (Cretáceo Inférior), Bacia do Araripe, Nordeste do Brasil. *An. Acad. brasil. Ciênc.*, 60(1): 61-67.

Maury, C. J. 1934. Fossil invertebrata from northeastern Brazil. *Bull. Amer. Mus. Nat. Hist.*, 67: 123-179.

———. 1936. O Cretáceo de Sergipe. *Monogr. Serv. Geol. Minerol. Brasil*, 11: 283 pp.

Mawson, J. and A. S. Woodward. 1907. On the Cretaceous Formation of Bahia (Brazil), and on vertebrate fossils collected therein. *Quart. J. Geol. Soc., London*, 63: 128-139.

Meyer, A. 1987. Phenotypic plasticity and heterochrony in *Cichlasoma managuense* (Pisces, Cichlidae) and their implications for speciation in cichlid fishes. *Evolution*, 41(6): 1357-1369.

Mezzalira, S. 1949. Ocorrência de vertebrados fósseis em Adamantina, S.P. *Min. e Met.*, 14(82): 11.

———. 1966. Os fósseis do estado de São Paulo. *Bol. Inst. Geogr. Geol.*, 45: 132, 10 est, mapa.

Miller, H. 1858. *The Cruise of the Betsey*. Gould & Lincoln, Boston. 251 pp.

Millot, J. and J. Anthony. 1958. *Anatomie de Latimeria chalumnae 1. Squelette, muscles et formations de soutier*. C.N.R.S., Paris. 118 pp.

Molnar, R. E. 1986. An enantiornithine bird from the Lower Cretaceous of Queensland, Australia. *Nature*, 322: 736-738.

Mones, A. 1986. Palaeovertebrata Sudamericana. Catálogo Sistemático de los Vertebrados fósiles de America del Sur. Parte I. Lista Preliminar y Bibliografia. *Cour. Forsch.–Inst. Senckenberg*, 82: 1–625.

Moraes, J.F.S. de 1976. *Relatório final da Etapa I Projeto Santana. Comp. Pesq. Rec. Min.:* 1-261.

———, C. Scheid, and J. da S. A. Santos. 1975. *Projeto Santana. Relatório Preliminar da Etapa I, Recife*. D.N.P.M./C.P.R.M., p. 104.

———, J. da Silva Santos, and J. de C. Masarenhas. 1976. *Projeto Santana. Relatório Final da Etapa I, vol. I.* C.P.R.M./ D.N.P.M. 269 pp.

Moraes, L.J. 1928. Estudos geológicos no Estado de Pernambuco, Brasil. *Serv. Geol. Minerol. brasil.*, 32: 1-100.

———, F. C. Barros, and E. Ramos. 1963. *Reconhecimento Fotogeológico da Região Nordeste do Brasil*. Div. Fom. Prod. Mineral., D.N.P.M. Fôlha Crato SB240, Esc. 1:250,000. Rio de Janeiro.

Moraes Rego, L. F. 1935. Camadas cretaceas do sul do Brasil. *Ann. Esc. Polytech.*, 4 (2): 231–274, 1 mapa.

Moy-Thomas, J. A. 1935. The coelacanth fishes of Madagascar. *Geol. Mag.*, 72(851): 213-227.

———. 1937. The Carboniferous coelacanth fishes of Great Britain and Ireland. *Proc. Zool. Soc. London*, 107(B): 383-415.

———and T. S. Westoll. 1935. On the Permian coelacanth, *Coelacanthus granulatus*, Agaz. *Geol. Mag.*, 72: 385-415.

Müller, J. and F. G. J. Henle. 1838-1841. *Systematische Beschreibung der Plagiostomen*. Berlin. xxii–200 pp.

Nelson, G. J. 1973. Relationships of clupeomorphs, with remarks on the structure of the lower jaw in fishes, *in* Greenwood, P. H., R. S. Miles, and C. Patterson (eds.), *Interrelationships of Fishes. Zool. J. Linn. Soc.*, 53 (Suppl. 1): 333-349.

Nevo, E. 1968. Pipid frogs from the early Cretaceous of Israel and pipid evolution. *Bull. Mus. Comp. Zool., Harvard Univ.*, 136(8): 255-318.

Nicholson, H. A. and R. Lydekker. 1889. *A Manual of Palaeontology for the Use of Students*. 2 vol. Edinburgh and London.

Nybelin, O. 1966. On certain Triassic and Liassic representatives of the family Pholidophoridae s. str. *Bull. Brit. Mus. (Nat. Hist.)*, Geol., 11: 351-432.

Obruchev, D. V. 1967. *Fundamentals of Paleontology. Vol. XI. Agnatha, Pisces*. Isracl Prog. Sci. Transl., U. S. Dept. Comm. x— 825 pp.

Oliveira, A. F. de. 1978. O genero *Tharrhias* no Cretáceo da Chapada do Araripe. *An. Acad. brasil. Ciênc.*, 50(4): 537-552.

Oliveria, A. A. de, A. de L. F. Brito, M. E. C. M. Santos, and M. S. S. Carvalho. 1979. *Projeto Chapada do Araripe. Relatório Final. Recife*. D. N. P. M./C. P. R. M. Vol. I, 123 pp.

Oliveira, A. I. and O. H. Leonardos. 1943. *Geologia do Brasil*. Inf. Agric. Ser. Did., 2: 1-813.

Olsen, P. E. 1984. The skull and pectoral girdle of the parasemionotid fish *Watsonulus eugnathoides* from the early Triassic Sakamena group of Madagascar, with comments on the relationships of the holostean fishes. *J. Vert. Paleo.*, 4(3): 481-499.

Pacheco, J. A. A. 1913. Notas sobre a geologia do valle do rio Grande a partir da Fóz do rio Pardo até a sua confiuência com o rio Paranahyba, *in:* SÃO PAULO. *Exploração do rio Grande e de seus afluentes. S. José dos Dourados*. Commissão Geographica e Geologica, São Paulo, pp. 33–38. geol. map.

Paes Laeme, A. B. 1943. *História Física da Terra*. F. Briquiet and Cia. 1020 pp.

Palmer, A. R. 1960. Miocene copepods from the Mojave Desert, California. *J. Palaeo.*, 34(3): 447-452.

Patterson, C. 1968. The caudal skeleton in Mesozoic acanthopterygian fishes. *Bull. Brit. Mus. (Nat. Hist.)*, Geol., 17(2): 1-102.

———. 1970a. A clupeomorph fish from the Gault (Lower Cretaceous). *Zool. J. Linn. Soc.*, 49(3): 161-182.

———. 1970b. Two Upper Cretaceous salmoniform fishes from the Lebanon. *Bull. Brit. Mus. (Nat. Hist.)*, Geol., 19(5): 205-296.

———. 1973. Interrelationships of holosteans, *in* Greenwood, P. H., R. S. Miles, and C. Patterson (eds.), *Interrelationships of Fishes. Zool. J. Linn. Soc.*, 53 (Suppl. 1): 233-305.

_____. 1975a. The braincase of pholidophorid and leptolepid fishes, with a review of the actinopterygian braincase. *Phil. Trans. Roy. Soc. London*, 269(899): 275-579.

_____. 1975b. The distribution of Mesozic freshwater fishes. *Mém. Mus. national Hist. naturelle*, ser. A, Zool., 88:156-174.

_____. 1982. Morphology and interrelationships of primitive actinopterygian fishes. *Amer. Zool.*, 22: 241-259.

_____. 1984. Family Chanidae and other teleostean fishes as living fossils, *in* Eldredge, N. and S. M. Stanley (eds.), *Living Fossils*. Springer Verlag, New York. 291 pp.

_____ and A. Longbottom. In Press. An Eocene amiid fish from Mali, West Africa. *Proc. Linn. Soc. London*.

_____ and D. E. Rosen. 1977. Review of ichthyodectiform and other Mesozoic teleost fishes and the theory and practice of classifying fossils. *Bull. Amer. Mus. Nat. Hist.*, 158(2): 81-172.

Pedersen, K. R., Crane, P. R., Drinnan, A. N. and Friis, E. M. (MS.) Fruits from the mid-Cretaceous of North America with pollen grains of the *Clavatipollenites* type. *Grana*.

Penny, J. H. J. 1988. Early Cretaceous striate tricolpate pollen from the Borehole Mersa Matruh 1, North West Desert, Egypt. *Journal of Micropalaeontology*, 7 : 201–215.

_____. 1989. New Early Cretaceous forms of the angiosperm pollen genus *Afropollis* from England and Egypt. *Review of Palaeobotany and Palynology*, 58: 289–299.

Petri, S. 1987. Cretaceous paleogeographic maps of Brazil. *Paleogeography, Paleoclimatology, Paleoecology*, 59: 117-168.

_____ and L. P. Ornellas. 1974. New Cretaceous *Hemiptera* from *An XXVIII Cong. Bras. Geol.*, 2:289–304.

Pinto, I. R. and I. Purper. 1986. A new blattoid from the Cretaceous of Brazil. *Pesquisas, Porto Alegre*, 18:5–10.

Pinto, I. D. and Y. T. Sanguinetti. 1958. *Bisulcocypris*, a new Mesozoic genus and preliminary note about its relation with *Metacypris*. *Bol. Soc. bras. Geol.*, 7(1): 75-90.

Plieninger, F. 1901. Beiträge zur Kenntnis der Flugsaurier. *Palaeontographica, Stuttgart*, 48: 65-90.

Ponte, F. C. and H. E. Asmus. 1976. The Brazilian marginal basins: current state of knowledge. *An. Acad. brasil. Ciênc.*, 48 (Suppl.): 215-239.

_____ and _____. 1978. Geological framework of the Brazilian continental margin.

Geol. Rund., 67(1): 201-235.

Popoff, M. 1988. Du Gondwana à l'Atlantique sud: les connexions du fossé de las Bénoué avec les bassins du Nord-Est brésilien jusqu'a l'overture du golfe de Guinée au Crétacé inférieur, *in* Sougy, J. and J. Rodgers (eds.), *The West African Connection. J. Afric. Earth Sci.*, spec. publ., 7(2): 409-431.

Price, L. I. 1947. Sedimentos mesozóicos na baía de São Marcos, estado do Maranhão. *Notas prelim. Est. Div. Geol. Mineral.*, 53: 7 pgs.

_____.1951. Um ovo de dinossaurio na formaço Baurú, do *Cretácico do estado de Minas Gerais. Notas prelim. Est. Div. Geol. Mineral.*, 53: 7pp.

_____. 1955. Novos crocodilideos dos arenitos da Série Bauru, Cretáceo do Estado de Minas Gerais. *An. Acad. brasil. Ciênc.*, 27(4): 487-498.

_____. 1959. Sôbre um crocodilídeo notosúquio do Cretácico Brasilèiro. *Bolm. Div. Geol. Mineral.*, 188: 1-155.

_____. 1961. Sôbre os dinossaurios do Brasil. *An. Acad. bras. Ciênc.*, 33 (3/4), xxviii-xxix.

_____. 1971. A presença de pterosauria no Cretáceo Inferior da Chapada do Araripe, Brasil. *An. Acad. brasil. Ciênc.*, 43 (Suppl.): 452-461.

_____. 1973. Quelônio Amphichelydia no Cretáceo Inferior do Nordeste do Brasil. *Rev. Bras. Geoc.*, 3: 84-96.

_____. 1976. Dinossauros no Brasil. *Resumos dos trabalhos do 29 Congresso Brasileiro de Geologia (Ouro Preto 1976)*. Ouro Preto, p. 380.

Pye, K. 1984. SEM analysis of siderite cements in intertidal marsh sediments, Norfolk, England. *Marine Geol.*, 56: 1-12.

Rautian, A. S. 1978. A unique bird feather from Jurassic lake deposits in the Karatan. *Paleont. J.*, 4: 520-528.

Rawson, P. F. 1980. Early Cretaceous ammonite biostratigraphy and biogeography, *in* House, M. R. and J. R. Senior (eds.), *The Ammonoidea. Syst. Assoc. Spec. Vol.*, 18: 499-529. Academic Press, New York.

Rayner, D. H. 1941. The structure and evolution of the holostean fishes. *Biol. Rev.*, 16: 218-237.

_____. 1948. The structure of certain Jurassic holostean fishes with special reference to their neurocrania. *Phil. Trans. Roy. Soc. London*, B 233: 287-345.

Regan, C. T. 1907. On the anatomy, classification and systematic position of the teleostean fishes of the sub-order Allotriognathi. *Proc. Zool. Soc. London*, 1907(2): 634-643.

Retallack, G. J. and D. L. Dilcher. 1981. A coastal hypothesis for the dispersal and rise to dominance of flowering plants, *in* Niklas, K. J. (ed.), *Evolution, Paleoecology and the Fossil Record*, 2: 27-77. Praeger, New York.

Reyment, R. A. and R. V. Dingle. 1987. Palaeography of Africa during the Cretaceous Period. *Paleogeography, Paleoclimatology, Paleoecology*, 59: 93-116.

Ridewood, W. G. 1904. On the cranial osteology of the fishes of the families Elopidae and Albulidae, with remarks on the skull in the lower teleostean fishes generally. *Proc. Zool. Soc. London*, 1904(2): 35-81.

Roberts, T. R. 1973. The interrelationships of ostariophysans, *in* Greenwood, P. H., R. S. Miles, and C. Patterson (eds.), *Interrelationships of Fishes. Zool. J. Linn. Soc.*, 53 (Suppl. 1): 373–395.

Romer, A. S. 1966. *Vertebrate Paleontology*. Univ. Chicago Press, Chicago. 486 pp.

Rosen, D. and P. H. Greenwood. 1970. Origin of the Weberian apparatus and the relationships of the ostariophysan and gonorynchiform fishes. *American Mus. Novitates*, No. 2428: 1-25.

————and C. Patterson. 1969. The structure and relationships of the paracanthopterygian fishes. *Bull. Amer. Mus. Nat. Hist.*, 141: 357-474.

Rosendahl, B. R., D. I. Reynolds, P. N. Lorber, C. F. Burgess, J. McGrill, D. Scott, J. J. Lambiase, and S. J. Derksen. 1986. *Structural expressions of rifting: Lessons from Lake Tanganyika, Africa*. Geol. Soc. London, Spec. Publ. 23.

Roxo, M.G.O. 1929. Geologia da região entre rio do Peixe e o Paranapanema. *Rel. Anu. Dir. Div. Geol. Min.*, 1927, pp. 35–39.

Saez, M. D. de. 1939. Noticias sobre peces fósiles Argentinos. *Notas Mus. La Plata*, IV, Paleont., 19: 423-432.

————. 1949. Noticias sobre peces fósiles Argentinos. *Notas Mus. La Plata*, Paleont., 96(14): 4.

Saint-Seine, P. 1949. Les poissons des calcaires lithographiques de Cerin (Ain). *Nouv. Arch. Mus. Hist. Nat. Lyon*, 2: 1-357.

Santos, M. E. C. M. 1982. Ambiente deposicional da Formação Santana—Chapada do Araripe. *Anais XXXIII Congr. Brasil. Geol.*, 4: 1413-1426.

Schaeffer, B. 1947. Cretaceous and Tertiary actinopterygian fishes from Brazil. *Bull. Amer.*

Mus. Nat. Hist., 89(1): 5-39.

————. 1948. A study of *Diplurus longicaudatus* with notes on the body form and locomotion of the Coelacanthini. *Amer. Mus. Novitates*, No. 1378: 1-32.

————. 1952. The Triassic coelacanth fish *Diplurus* with observations on the evolution of the Coelacanthini. *Bull. Amer. Mus. Nat. Hist.*, 99(2): 25-78.

————. 1967. Late Triassic fishes from the western United States. *Bull. Amer. Mus. Nat. Hist.*, 135(6): 287-342.

————. 1971. The braincase of the holostean fish *Macrepistius* with comments on neurocranial ossification in the Actinopterygii. *Amer. Mus. Novitates*, No. 2459: 1-34.

————and D. D. Dunkle. 1950. A semionotid fish from Chinle Formation, with consideration of its relationships. *Amer. Mus. Novitates*, No. 1457: 1–29.

Schaller, H. 1969. Revisão estratigráfica da Bacia de Sergipe—Alagoas. *Bol. Tecn. Petrobrás*, 12(1): 21-86.

Scheid, C., et al. 1978. *Projeto Santana. Relatório Final da Etapa II. Recife.* D.N.P.M./C.P.R.M., 131 pp.

Schlee, D. 1973. Harz Konservierte fossile vogelfedern aus der Unterstenkreide. *J. Orn.*, 114: 207-219.

Schultze, H.-P. 1966. Morphologische und histologische Untersuchungen an Schuppen Mesozoischer Actinopterygier (Übergang von Ganoid- zu Rundschuppen). *N. Jb. Geol. Paläont. Abh.*, 126(3): 232-314.

————. 1989. Three-dimensional muscle preservation in Jurassic fishes of Chile. *Rev. Geol. Chile.*, 16(2): 183–215.

————and G. Arratia. 1986. Reevaluation of the caudal skeleton of actinopterygian fishes: 1. *Lepisosteus* and *Amia. J. Morph.*, 190: 215-241.

————and E. O. Wiley. 1984. The Neopterygian *Amia* as a living fossil: 153-159, *in* Eldredge, N. and S. M. Stanley (eds.), *Living Fossils*. Springer Verlag, New York.

Seeley, H. G. 1870. *The Ornithosauria. An elementary study of the bones of Pterodactyles*. Cambridge. 130 pp.

Seilacher, A., W. E. Reif, and F. Westphal. 1985. Sedimentological, ecological and temporal patterns of fossil Lagerstätten. *Phil. Trans. Roy. Soc. London*, B 311: 5-23.

Selezneva, A. A. 1985. Intensification of respiration as a basis for evolutionary development of Actinopterygii. *J. Ichthyol.*, 25(1): 100-109.

Shaklee, J. B. and C. S. Tamaru. 1981. Biochemical and morphological evolution Hawaiian bonefishes (*Albula*). *Syst. Zool.*, 30(2): 125-145.

Silva, M.A.M. da. 1983. *The Araripe Basin, Northeastern Brazil: Regional Geology and Facies Analysis of a Lower Cretaceous Evaporitic Depositional Complex*. Ph.D. thesis, Columbia Univ., New York. 290 pp.

————. 1986a. Lower Cretaceous unconformity truncating evaporite-carbonate sequence, Araripe basin, Northeastern Brazil. *Revista Brazileira de Geociências*, 16(3): 301–310.

————. 1986b. Lower Cretaceous sedimentary sequences in the Araripe basin, Northeastern Brazil: A revision. *Revista Brazileira de Geociências*, 16(3): 311–319.

Silva Santos, R. da. 1945. Revalidação de *Aspidorhynchus comptoni* Agassiz, do Crétaceo do Ceará, Brasil. *D. G. M./D. N. P. M., Notas Prelim. Estudos*, 29: 1-13.

————. 1947. Uma rediscrição de *Dastilbe elongatus*, com algumas considerações sobre o genero *Dastilbe*. *D. G. M./D. N. P. M., Notas Prelim. Estudos*,42: 1-7.

————. 1949. Sobre alguns peixes fósseis do gênero *Chiromystus* da Ilha de Itaparica, Bahia. *D. G. M./D. N. P. M., Notas Prelim. Estudos*, 50: 1-12.

————. 1950. *Anaedopogon, Chiromystus* e *Ennelichthys*, como sinônimos de *Cladocyclus*, da família Chirocentridae. *An. Acad. brasil. Ciênc.*, 22(1): 123-134.

————. 1953. Lepidotídeos do Cretáceo da Ilha de Itaparica, Bahia. *Bol. D. G. M./D. N. P. M.*, 145: 1-29.

————. 1958. *Leptolepis diasii*, nôvo peixe fossil da Serra do Araripe, Brasil. *D. G. M./D. N. P. M., Notas Prelim. Estudos*, 108: 1-15.

————. 1960. A posição sistemática de *Enneles audax* Jordan e Branner da Chapada do Araripe, Brasil. *Monogr. D. G. M./D. N. P. M.*, 17: 1-25.

————. 1966. Catálogo de fósseis tipo. Parte 1. Paleovertebrado. *Soc. Brasil. Paleont., Rio de Janeiro*: boxed set of unnumbered 5x8 cards.

————. 1968. Paleoictiofauna da Formação Santana—Euselachii. *An. Acad. brasil. Ciênc.*, 40: 493-496.

————. 1970. A paleoictiofauna da Formação Santana—Holostei: Familia Girodontidae. *An. Acad. brasil. Ciênc.*, 42: 445-452.

————. 1971. Nouveau genre et espéce d'Elopidae du Bassin Sédimentaire de la Chapada do Araripe. *An. Acad. brasil. Ciênc.*, 43(2): 439-442.

————. 1972. *Peixes da Formação Marizal, Estado da Bahia*. Unpubl. Ph. D. thesis, University of São Paulo.

————. 1976. A paleoictiofáunula da Formação Muribeca (Resulta dos da Exc. Paleont. da Acad. bras. Ciênc., no NE brasil.). *An. Acad. brasil. Ciênc.*, 48(4): 788.

————. 1981. Sobre a occurência de uma fáunula de peixes na Formação Riachuelo, estado de Sergipe. *An. Acad. brasil. Ciênc.*, 53(1): 203 (summary).

————. 1983. *Araripichthys castilhoi* novo gênero e espécie de acantopterigio da Formação Santana, Chapada do Araripe, Brasil. *VIII Congr. brasil. Paleont., Rio de Janeiro, Resumos comm.*: 27.

————. 1985a. Sobre a presença do *Vinctifer* Jordan (Pisces, Aspidorhynchiformes) na Formação Mujribeca, Estado de Alagoas. *VIII Congr. brasil. Paleont., Rio de Janeiro, 1983, M.M.E.–D.N.P.M., Ser. Geol.*, No. 27, Paleont. Estrat., 2: 147-150.

————. 1985b. Nova caracterização do gênero *Vinctifer* Jordan, 1919. *VIII Congr. brasil. Paleont., Rio de Janeiro, 1983, M.M.E.–D.N.P.M., Ser. Geol.*, No. 27, Paleont. Estrat., 2: 151–154.

————. 1985c. *Araripichthys castilhoi* novo gênero e especie de teleostei da Formação Santana, Chapada do Araripe, Brasil. *Colet. trab. Paleont. brasil., D. N. P. M.*, 1985: 133-139.

————. 1985d. Paleoictiofáunula da Formação Codó, Bacia do Parnaiba, Nordeste do Brasil. *IX Congr. brasil. Paleont., Rio de Janeiro, 1985*.

————. 1985e. A ictiofauna de Formação Riachuelo, Estado de Sergipe. *VIII Congr. brasil. Paleont., Rio de Janeiro, 1983, Serv. Geol.*, No. 27, Paleont. Estrat.,2: 141-145.

————. 1985f. *Laeliichthys ancestralis*, novo gênero e especie de Osteoglossiformes do Aptiano da Formação Areado, Estado de Minas Gerais, Brasil. *VIII Congr. brasil. Paleont., Rio de Janeiro, 1983, Serv. Geol.*, No. 27, Paleont. Estrat., 2.

————. 1985g. Contribuição ao conhecimento da paleoictiofáunula do Cretáceo do Brasil. *VIII Congr. brasil. Paleont., Rio de Janeiro, 1983, M.M.E.–D.N.P.M., Serv. Geol.*, No. 27, Paleont. Estrat., 2: 169-174.

————. 1986. Posição taxinômica do *Cladocyclus woodwardi* (Silva Santos) do Cretáceo do Brasil. *An. Acad. brasil. Ciênc.*, 58(2): 229-231.

————and L. G. Valença. 1968. A Formação Santana e sua paleoictiofauna. *An. Acad. brasil. Ciênc.*, 40(3): 339-360; 40(4): 491- 497.

Simpson, E. S. W. 1977. Evolution of the South Atlantic. *Geol. Soc. South Africa, Alex L. du Toit Mem. Lect., Annex.*, 80(15): 1-15.

Small, H. 1913. Geologia e suprimento de água subterrânea no Ceará e parte do Piaui. *Insp. Obras Contra Secas., Ser. Geol.*, 25: 1-180.

Smith, J. L. B. 1956. *Old Fourlegs*. Longman, Green, London. 260 pp.

Sokal, R. R. and F. J. Rolf. 1981. *Biometry*. W. H. Freeman, New York. 859 pp.

Spix, J. B. and C. F. P. Martius. 1823-1831. *Reise im Brasilien*. 3 vols. and atlas. Munich.

Stebbins, G. L. 1974. *Flowering Plants: Evolution Above the Species Level*. Belknap Press, Harvard University Press, Cambridge, Mass. 399 pp.

Stensiö, E. 1932. Triassic fishes from East Greenland collected by the Danish expeditions in 1929-31. *Meddr. Om. Grønl.*, 38(3): 1-305.

————. 1935. *Sinamia zdanskyi*, a new amiid from the Lower Cretaceous of Shantung, China. *Paleont. Sinica.*, Ser. C, No. 3: 1-48.

Stiassny, M. 1986. The limits and relationships of the acanthomorph teleosts. *J. Zool., London*, (B), 1986(1): 411-460.

Suess, E. 1885. *Das Antlitz der Erde*. Vol. 1 (of 3). F. Tempsky, Wien. Translated as *The Face of the Earth*, parts I-V, Clarendon Press, Oxford. 1885–1901.

Swain, F. M. 1961. Contributions *in* Moore, R. C. (ed.), *Treatise on Invertebrate Paleontology*, Part Q, Arthropoda 3, Crustacea, Ostracoda. 442 pp.

Szatmari, P., J. B. L. Françolin, O. Zanotto, and S. Wolff. 1987. Evolução tectônica da margem equatorial Brasileira. *Rev. brasil. Geoc.*, 17(2): 180-188.

Tabaste, N. 1963. Etude de restes de Poissons du Crétacé Saharien. *Mem. IFAN*, 68: 437-485.

Taverne, L. 1969. Sur la présence d'un Aspidorhynchidae (Pisces Holostéens, ordre des Aspidorhynchiformes) dans les terrains éocrétaciques de las Guinée Equatoriale. *Rev. Zool. Bot. Afr.*, 79: 3-4.

————. 1974a. Sur le premier exemplaire complet d'*Enneles audax* Jordan, D. S. et Branner, J. C., 1908 (Pisces Holostei, Amiidae) du Crétacé Supérieur du Brésil. *Bull. Soc. belge Geol.*, 83(1): 61-71.

————. 1974b. L'ostéologie d'*Elops* Linné, C., 1766 (Pisces Elopiformes) et son interêt phylogénétique. *Mem. Acad. roy. belg. Cl. Sci. 80, Ser. II*, 41(2): 1-96.

————. 1975. A propos de trois téléostéens fossiles déterminés erronément comme ostéoglossides. *Ann. Soc. roy. Zool. belg.*, 105(1/2): 15-30.

————. 1976. A propos du poisson fossile *Notelops brama* (Agassiz, L., 1841) du Crétacé inférieur du Brésil et de sa position systématique au sein des téléostéens primitifs. *Biol. Jb. Dodonaea*, 44: 304-310.

————. 1981a. Ostéologie et position systématique d'*Aethalionopsis robustus* (Pisces, Teleostei) du Crétacé inférieur de Bernissart (Belgique) et considerations sur les affinities des Gonorhynchiformes. *Bull. Cl. Sci., Bruxelles, Pal. Acad., Ser. 5*, 67: 958-982.

————. 1981b. Les actinoptérygiens de l'Aptien Inférieur (Töck) d'Helgoland. *Mitt. Geol.-Paläont. Inst. Univ. Hamburg*, 51: 43-82.

————. 1986. Ostéologie et affinités systématiques de *Chirocentrites vexillifer* du Crétacé Supérieur de la Mésogée Eurafricaine. Considerations sur la phylogénie des Ichthyodectiformes, poissons téléostéens du Jurassique et du Crétacé. *Ann. roy. Soc. Zool. belg.*, 116(1): 33-54.

————. 1987. On the cranial and caudal osteology of the Cretaceous marine teleost *Pachyrhizodus* (Pachyrhizodontidae, Crossognathiformes). *Biol. Jb. Dodonaea*, 55(1): 136-145.

————and P. H. Ross. 1973. Fischreste aus dem Töck (Unter-Aptien) von Helgoland. *Meyniana*, 23: 99-111.

Tintori, A. 1981. Two new pycnodonts (Pisces, Actinopterygii) from the Upper Triassic of Lombardy (N. Italy). *Riv. It. Paleont. Strat.*, 86(1980): 795-824.

Toit, A. L. du. 1927. *A geological comparison of South America with South Africa*. Carnegie Inst. Wash., Publ. 381. 157 pp.

————. 1928. Some reflections upon a geological comparison of South Africa with South America. *Trans. Geol. Soc. S. Afr.*, 1928: 19-38.

————. 1937. *Our Wandering Continents*. Oliver and Boyd, Edinburgh.

Trask, P. D. 1937. Inferences about the origin of oil as indicated by the composition of the organic constituents of sediments. *U.S. Geol. Surv. Prof. Papers*, 186-H: 147-157.

Trevisan, L. 1980. Ultrastructural notes and considerations on *Ephedripites*, *Eucomiidites* and *Monosulcites* pollen grains from Lower Cretaceous sediments of southern Tuscany (Italy). *Pollen et Spores*, 22: 85-132.

Unwin, D. M. 1988. New pterosaurs from Brazil. *Nature*, 332: 398.

Upchurch, G. R. and J. A. Doyle. 1981. Paleoecology of the conifers *Frenelopsis* and *Pseudofrenelopsis* (Cheirolepidiaceae) from the Cretaceous Potomac Group of Maryland and Virginia: 167-202, *in* Romans, R. C. (ed.), *Geobotany II*. Plenum, New York.

Vakrameev. 1979a. Zakonomernosti rasprostraneniya i paleoekologiya mezozoyskikh khvoynykh Cheirolepidiaceae. *Paleontologicheskii Zhurnal*, 1970: 19–34.

Vergnaud-Grassini, C. and S. Wenz. 1975. Les discoglossidés du Jurassique Supérieur du Montsech (Province de Lérida, Espagne). *Ann. Paléontologie*, 61(1): 19-36.

Viana, C. F. 1966. Stratigraphic distribution of Ostracoda in the Bahia Supergroup (Brazil). *West African Micropal. Colloq., Ibadan, Proc.*, 2: 240-257.

Waldman, M. 1970. A third specimen of a Lower Cretaceous feather from Victoria, Australia. *Condor*, 72(1): 377.

Walker, J. W. and A. G. Walker. 1984. Ultrastructure of Lower Cretaceous angiosperm pollen and the origin and early evolution of flowering plants. *Ann. Missouri Bot. Garden*, 71: 464-521.

Waller, R. R. 1980. A rust removal method for mineral specimens. *Mineralogical Record*, 11: 109-110.

Watson, J. 1988. The Cheirolepidiaceae: 218-272, *in* Beek (ed.), *Origin and Evolution of Gymnosperms*. Columbia Univ. Press, New York.

Watts, N. L. 1978. Displacive calcite: Evidence from recent and ancient calcretes. *Geology*, 6: 699-703.

Weeks, L. G. 1953. Environment and mode of origin and facies relationships of carbonate concretions in shales. *J. Sediment. Petrology*, 23(3): 162-173.

———. 1957. Origin of carbonate concretions in shales, Magdalena Valley, Colombia. *Bull. Geol. Soc. Amer.*, 66: 95-102.

Wegener, A. 1929. *Die Entstehung der Kontinente und Ozeane*. Friedr. Vieweg. and Sohn, Braunschweig.

Weiler, W. 1922. Die Fischreste aus den bituminösen Schiefern von Ibando bei Bata (Spanische Guinea). *Paläont. Z.*, 5(2): 148-160.

———. 1935. Ergebnisse der Forschungsreisen Prof. E. Stromers in den Wüsten Agyptens. II. Wirbeltierreste der Batarije-Stufe, 16 Neue Untersuchungen an den Fischresten. *Abh. Bayer. Acad. Wissen. Math.-Nat. Abt., N. F.*, 32: 57.

Wellnhofer, P. 1977. *Araripedactylus dehmi* nom. gen., nov. sp., ein neuer Flugsaurier aus der Unterkreide von Brasilien. *Mitt. Bayer. Staatsslg. Paläont. hist. Geol.*, 17: 157-167.

———. 1985. Neue pterosaurier aus der Santanaformation (Apt.) der Chapada do Araripe, Brasilien. *Palaeontographia, Abt. A*, 187: 105-182.

———. 1987. New crested pterosaurs from the Lower Cretaceous of Brazil. *Mitt. Bayer. Staatsslg. Paläont. hist. Geol.*, 27: 175-186.

———. 1988. Terrestrial locomotion in pterosaurs. *Hist. Biol.*, 1: 3-16.

———, E. Buffetaut, and P. Gigase. 1983. A pterosaurian notarium from the Lower Cretaceous of Brazil. *Paläont. Z.*, 57: 147-157.

Wenz, S. 1968. *Compléments à l'étude des poissons actinoptérygiens du Jurassique française*. Centre nat. Rech. Scient., Paris. 276 pp.

———. 1971. Anatomie et position systématique de *Vidalamia*, poisson holostéen du Jurassique supérieur du Montsech (Province de Lérida, Espagne). *Ann. Paléont. (Vert.)*, 58(1): 43-62.

———. 1975. Un nouveau Coelacanthidé du Crétacé inférieur du Niger, remarques sur la fusion des os dermiques. *Colloq. Internat. C. N. R. S., Probl. Actu. Paléont.-Evol. Vert.*, 218 (for 1973): 175-190.

———. 1977. Le squelette axial et l'endosquelette caudal d'*Enneles audax*, poisson Amiidé du Crétacé de Ceara (Brésil). *Bull. Mus. national Hist. naturelle, Paris*, 3(490): 341-348.

———. 1979. Squelette axial et endosquelette caudal d'*Amiopsis dolloi*, Amiidé du Wealdien de Bernissart. *Bull. Mus. national Hist. naturelle, Ser. 4, Sect. C*, 1(4): 343-375.

———. 1980. A propos du genre *Mawsonia*, Coelacanthe géant du Crétacé inférieur d'Afrique et du Brésil. *Mem. Soc. geol. Fr., N. S.*, No. 139: 187-190.

———. 1981. Un coelacanthe géant, *Mawsonia lavocati* Tabaste, de l'Albien-Base du Cenomanien du Sud Marocain. *Ann. Paleo. (Vert.)*, 167(1): 1-20.

———. 1984. *Rubiesichthys gregalis* n. g., n. sp., Pisces Gonorhynchiformes, du Crétacé inférieur du Montsech (Province de Lérida, Espagne). *Bull. Mus. national Hist. naturelle, Ser. 4, Sect. C*, 6(3): 275-285.

———. 1989. *Iemanja palma* n. g., n. sp., gyrodontide nouveau (Pisces, Actinopterygii) du Crétacé inférieur de la Chapada do Araripe (N-E du Brésil). *Compt. Rendus Acad. Sci. Paris*, 308(2): 975-980.

———and A. W. A. Kellner. 1986. Découverte du premier Ionoscopidae (Pisces, Halecomorphi) sud-américain, *Oshunia brevis* n. g., n. sp., dans le Crétacé inférieur de la Chapada do Araripe (nord-est du Brésil). *Bull. Mus. national Hist. naturelle, Ser. 4, Sect. C,* 8(1): 77-88.

West, R.M. 1989. State regulation of geological, paleontological, and archaeological collecting. *Curator* (American Museum of Natural History), 32(4): 281–319.

Wetzel, R. G. 1975. *Limnology.* W. B. Saunders. 743 pp.

White, C. A. 1887. Contribuções á paleontologia do Brasil. *Arch. Mus. Nac. Rio de Janeiro,* 7: 273, v.

Wighton, D. C. 1987. *Gomphaeschna obliqua,* sp. nov., a new species of Gomphaeschninae from the lower Cretaceous of northeastern Brazil (Anisoptera: Aeshnidae). *Odontologica,* 16(3): 311-314.

Wilcox, D. A. and S. W. Effler. 1981. Formation of alewife concretions in polluted Onondaga Lake. *Envir. Pollution, Ser. B,* 2: 203-215.

Wiley, E. O. 1976. The phylogeny and biogeography of fossil and Recent gars (Actinopterygii: Lepisosteidae). *Misc. Publ. Univ. Kansas Mus. Nat. Hist.,* 64: 1-111.

Williams, E. E. 1954. A key and description of the living species of the genus *Podocnemis* (*sensu* Boulenger) (Testudines, Pelomedusidae). *Bull. Mus. Comp. Zool.,* 111(8): 279-295.

Williston, S. W. 1896. On the dermal covering of *Hesperornis. Kansas Univ. Quart.,* 5(1): 53-54.

Woodward, A. S. 1887. On the fossil teleostean genus *Rhacolepis* Agassiz. *Proc. Zool. Soc. London,* 1887:535-542.

———. 1888. Notes on some vertebrate fossils from the province of Bahia, Brazil, collected by Joseph Mawson, Esq. *Ann. Mag. Nat. Hist.,* (Ser. 2), 6: 133-136.

———. 1890. On some upper Cretaceous fishes of the family Aspidorhynchidae. *Proc. Zool. Soc. London,* 1890: 629-637.

———. 1895. *Catalogue of Fossil Fishes in the British Museum of Natural History.* Part 3: 534 pp. London.

———. 1901. *Catalogue of Fossil Fishes in the British Museum of Natural History.* Part 4: 617 pp. London.

———. 1908. Cretaceous fishes from Brazil. *Quart. J. Geol. Soc.,* 64: 358-362.

———. 1910. On a tooth of Triassic dinosaur from São Paulo, Brazil. *Report 7th Assoc. Adv. Sci.,* Winnipeg, 5: 483.

———. 1916-1919. The fossil fishes of the English Wealden and Purbeck formations. *Monogr. Palaeontogr. Soc.:* 1-148.

Yu Jingxian. 1981. Late Cretaceous sporo-pollen assemblages of Sache District, Xinjiang. *Acta Geologica Sinica,* 55: 93–102.

Index